*Historical
Social
Psychology*

Historical
Social
Psychology

Edited by
Kenneth J. Gergen and Mary M. Gergen
Swarthmore College

LEA LAWRENCE ERLBAUM ASSOCIATES, PUBLISHERS
1984 Hillsdale, New Jersey   London

Copyright © 1984 by Lawrence Erlbaum Associates, Inc.
All rights reserved. No part of this book may be reproduced in
any form, by photostat, microform, retrieval system, or any other
means, without the prior written permission of the publisher.

Lawrence Erlbaum Associates, Inc., Publishers
365 Broadway
Hillsdale, New Jersey 07642

Library of Congress Cataloging in Publication Data

Gergen, Kenneth J.
  Historical social psychology.

  Bibliography: p.
  Includes index.
  1. Social psychology—Philosophy—Addresses, essays,
lectures. 2. Social psychology—Methodology—Addresses,
essays, lectures. 3. Statics and dynamics (Social
sciences)—Addressess, essays, lectures. I. Gergen,
Mary M. II. Title.
HM251.G347   1984   302'.1   83-25475
ISBN 0-89859-349-2

Printed in the United States of America
10 9 8 7 6 5 4 3 2 1

Contents

Preface xi

I. METATHEORY, THEORY, AND METHOD IN HISTORICAL SOCIAL PSYCHOLOGY

1. An Introduction to Historical Social Psychology
Kenneth J. Gergen 3

The Emergence of Historical Social Psychology 14
Forms of Inquiry in Historical Social Psychology 20
Historical Social Psychology in Intellectual Context 24
Summary 29

2. Historiography as a Metatheoretical Text For Social Psychology
Jill G. Morawski 37

Quandaries in the Study of Masculine and Feminine 39
Pluralism in History 41
Historical Explanations 41
Models of Change 47
Skeptical Objectivity 51
Gender and History Revisited 53

3. **Theoretical Orientations in a Historical Psychology**
   Harry F. M. Peeters   **61**

   The Dialectic Frame   66
   The Structural Frame   70
   The Evolutionary Frame   76

4. **Modern Dialectics in Social Psychology**
   Marianthi Georgoudi   **83**

   Assumptions in Dialectic Theory   84
   The Problem of the Individual and Society   91
   The Dialectic Position in Current Controversy   94

5. **Dialectical Analysis and Psychosocial Epistemology**
   Leon Rappoport   **103**

   Structure and Dynamics of Dialectical Analysis   105
   Psychosocial Epistemology   108
   The Epistemological Instruction of Holocaust Interpretation   111
   Summary and Future Prospects   121

6. **Methodological Considerations in the Analysis of Temporal Data**
   David A. Kenny and Donald T. Campbell   **125**

   Time-reversed Analysis   126
   Temporal Invariance   129
   Stability   131
   Cross-lagged Correlations   134
   Summary   137

7. **Generational Time-Series Analysis: A Paradigm for Studying Sociocultural Influences**
   Dean Keith Simonton   **139**

   The Research Paradigm   140
   Methodology   143
   Conclusion   151

II. DIACHRONIC INQUIRY: FROM THE MICRO-SEQUENCE TO THE LIFE-SPAN

8. The Sense of Closure
Stuart Albert — **159**

Model I. Sequence Composite Analysis: Synchronous Termination as a Determinant of Closure   160
Model II. The Janus Sequence   163
Model III. The Embrace, A Model of Intensified Positive Affect (IPA) For the Object, Person, or Event that is Being Terminated   166
Model IV. A Model of Retrospective Closure   170

9. The Social Construction of Narrative Accounts
Mary M. Gergen and Kenneth J. Gergen — **173**

The Varieties of Narrative Form   174
Truth and Multiplicity in Narrative   182
The Social Negotiation of Narrative   184
Summary   189

10. Diverging Life Paths: Their Probabilistic and Causal Structure
William McKinley Runyan — **191**

Types of Life Courses and Their Distribution   195
Multistage Flow Tables   197
Comparison with a Path Analytic Approach   201
Comparison with Statistical Norms and Implicit Theories   202
Generalization and Applications   204
The Relationship of Conscious Agents to Studies of State Sequences   206
Conclusion   207

11. Homes and Social Change: A Case Study of the Impact of Resettlement
Mary Gauvain, Irwin Altman, and Hussein Fahim — **211**

Introduction   211
A Place-process Approach to Homes   212
Implications and Conclusions   231

12. **The Changing Character of Cultural Dispositions: A Social Indicators Approach**
   Joseph Veroff **237**

   Social History and Social Psychology:
      A Tale of Two Surveys   241
   Summary   254

III. HISTORICAL INQUIRY

13. **Love, Misogyny, and Feminism in Selected Historical Periods: A Social-Psychological Explanation**
   Paul F. Secord **259**

   Stages of the Sex Ratio Project   260
   Sex Ratio Effects in Selected Times
      and Places   262
   Explaining Sex Ratio Effects   269
   Conclusions   278

14. **Family Life and the Marketplace: Diversity and Change in the American Family**
   Jan E. Dizard and Howard Gadlin **281**

   Variations in the Contemporary Family   287
   Autonomy and the Market   296
   Family, Autonomy, and the Public Order   300

15. **Traditional, Present Oriented, and Futuristic Modes of Group-Environment Relations**
   Daniel Stokols and Maryann Jacobi **303**

   Psychological Perspectives on Time   305
   Implications of the Proposed Typology for
      Social Psychological Research   319
   Summary   322

16. **The Temporalization of the Self**
   Thom Verhave and Willem van Hoorn **325**

17. The Evolution of Aesthetic Taste
Colin Martindale — **347**

Aesthetic Evolution   347
Evolutionary Trends in British Art   356
Summary   366

18. History and the Study of Expressive Action
Peter Collett — **371**

Tracing the Origins of Social Practices   372
The Testimony of the Written Word   377
From Etiquette to Custom   381
Visual Images as Windows on the Past   385
Summary   394

Author Index   **397**

Subject Index   **407**

Preface

Alfred North Whitehead once wrote that the words of the hymn, "Abide with me/ Fast falls the eventide" captured the chief problem of metaphysical philosophy. Is the universe to be viewed as fundamentally enduring, with dependable elements upon which one can rest secure; or is all, like the eventide, disappearing from view into the maw of history? The Heraclitian dictum "All things flow" represented one of the first major commitments to a metaphysics of change. And, many thinkers over the ages have been equally impressed by the centrality of change in human experience. Within the past century, Hegel, Bergson, and Dewey have been among the most prominent exponents of this view. Yet, the dominant voice in Western thought has belonged to the proponents of permanence. Plato located permanence within pure forms; Aristotle subsumed permanence within his theory of identity. Within the present century, the philosophy of logical empiricism, with its attempt to legitimate the search for incorrigible truths, has captured the intellectual imagination.

Traditional social psychology has largely fallen heir to the advocates of permanence. It has been a field primarily devoted to the search for perduring principles of human behavior. Like the natural sciences, the chief hope has been to locate fundamental processes or mechanisms that would facilitate prediction (and control) of human conduct regardless of historic clime. Yet, as many have come to feel, in this attempt the discipline has largely obscured what may perhaps be the most prominent feature of human existence, its continuously changing character. As it is argued, it is movement or animation that serves as the essence of what we take to be human life. The sense of the permanent is not given directly through experience of self or others; rather, it must be achieved by abstracting from such experiences. As many have come to feel, in social psychology's search for the universal, human activity has been both conceptually and methodologically frozen. Theories focus on the inert moment, cut away from the passing of time, and the available methods (viz. experimentation) have been fashioned to sustain and support this view.

It is the prominence of change in human affairs that largely prompted an earlier critique (Gergen, 1973) of the logical empiricist view of knowledge as realized within social psychological research. This critique, "Social psychology as history," provoked broad controversy in the field (see Gergen, 1982, for a review). As this dialogue ensued, however, it also became apparent that there was developing in various research domains an increased sensitivity to cross-time transformations in social pattern. Theory and research were beginning to move beyond the static vision to explore new horizons of change. It was an awareness of this emerging pattern that struck the two of us during the winter of 1981 when driving through a perilous route in the Austrian Alps. Issues of permanence and change were much on our minds. As we began to discuss various names and works that focused on the problem of change, it became apparent that there was indeed a corpus of significant work at hand. Although the various investigations were largely isolated from each other, they were all united in their attempt to develop theories of cross time variation in a field where extant theorizing was largely of the static variety. Many were also concerned with fashioning research methods and statistical procedures relevant to such theorizing; others were confronting more directly the metatheoretical issues raised by a concern with change. The possibility of an edited volume that would bring together these various contributions was inviting. This was also a year in which we were located at the University of Heidelberg. Ever present was the spirit of Wilhelm Wundt, whose *Volkerpsychologie* represents a pioneering effort to understand the historical emergence of social pattern. It was also a year in which plans were being hatched with Carl Graumann of Heidelberg and Serge Moscovici of Paris for meetings of a continuing discussion group on historical issues in social psychology. The moment seemed an auspicious one for the demarcation of this particular form of social psychological study.

Within the next few months, we shared our vision with a score of scholars from the United States and Europe, individuals we felt to be central to the development of this orientation. The response was enthusiastic, and virtually all agreed to make a contribution to such a venture within the next 12 months. Later we also learned of others whose work was significant and germane, and they too joined the enterprise. A broad sense of a communal effort seemed to develop within the group. Most of these devoted scholars joined us for the final volume, and not one paper was submitted after the proposed deadline. In several cases authors were not satisfied with an initial draft and wrote wholly new manuscripts within the period. As editors we are deeply grateful to this group—not only for their enthusiasm and cooperative dispositions, but for their part in the creation of the vision.

The result of this collective effort is a volume divided into three major parts. The initial set of papers opens discussion on issues of metatheory and method. The first chapter (by KJG) contrasts the historical or diachronic orientation with traditional social psychology, traces the origins of the historical approach, and argues for closer linkages between social psychology and other disciplines concerned with human understanding. In the second chapter Jill Morawski elaborates on this latter theme in a discussion of historical analysis and its relevance for social psychology. Her treatment of contrasting models of change in historiographic work is of special pertinence. The Dutch historical psychologist, Harry Peeters, continues this exploration of explanatory theory in a pointed discussion of evolutionary, dialectic and structuralist positions. Although Peeters finds the evolutionary frame most compelling, many social psychologists have recently become interested in dialectic theory. The next two chapters, the one by Marianthi Georgoudi (Chapt. 4) and the other by Leon Rappaport (Chapt. 5), are representative of this investment. In the former case, Georgoudi sets out the bases of dialectic theory, demonstrates how the dialectic orientation may be applied to a long-standing problem in social psychology, and examines its metatheoretical implications. Rappaport's paper extends these latter concerns by adopting a critical theory stance toward contemporary understanding of the Holocaust. As he demonstrates, conventional research assumptions in the behavioral sciences not only bias our understanding, but such biases may indeed contribute to a context permitting such brutality.

The final two chapters in this section focus on methodological issues arising in the study of cross-time patterns. Dean Simonton's paper (Chapt. 6) outlines a method for examining change across generations. As Simonton argues, properly executed generational analysis may demonstrate systematic relationships between events occurring in widely diverging time periods. The following paper, by David Kenny and Donald Campbell (Chapt. 7) describes four statistical analyses especially useful for analyzing temporal data: Time-reversed analysis; temporal invariance; stability analysis; and, cross-lagged correlation. As this chapter indicates, as sensitivity to temporal change increases in social psychology, a new array of methods and statistics will be required for research.

In the second major section of the volume the focus shifts from general to substantive considerations. Each of the five chapters in the section represents a line of investigation into cross-time change. The span of time with which the chapters are concerned varies from brief sequences in social interchange to changes over a lifetime. Thus, Stuart Albert (Chapt. 8) takes as a point of departure the patterned sequence by which people close out social encounters. As he shows, four complementary models may be employed to account for these patterns. In Chapter 9 the two of us consider how people account for the ongoing patterns of their lives. After exploring the narrative forms taken by such accounts, we argue that such constructions are not the product of a single individual but of co-acting participants relating within a particular historical context. Mac Runyan (Chapter 10) continues this concern with life-accounts, but in this case shifts the focus to life-span theory. As he argues, certain life patterns may be favored within the culture and sensitive research can reveal their contours. The following chapter, by Gauvain, Altman, and Fahim shifts attention from the micro- to the macro-social order. They explore the ways in which a resettling culture modifies and is modified by the physical structures into which it moves. Again at the macro-social level, Joseph Veroff (Chapt. 12) employs survey indicators to trace the changes in American culture over a 20-year period. This latter chapter explicitly demonstrates the promise of linking various lines of social psychological inquiry with historical study more generally.

The final section of the volume opens fully the temporal scope of social psychological study. In the first of these contributions, Paul Secord compares cultural patterns within historical periods marked by their differential gender ratios. As Secord demonstrates, the character of heterosexual love, misogyny, and feminism may all shift in a culture as the ratio of men to women changes. The concern with heterosexual relations is extended in Dizard and Gadlin's analysis (Chapt. 14) of changing patterns of family life. Rather than gender-ratio, these investigators are specifically concerned with the social repercussions of changing economic structures. The chapter by Stokols and Jacobi (Chapt. 15) picks up the materialist concern of the preceding discussion in a theoretical analysis of group-environment relations over time. As maintained in this case, the symbolic value of the physical surrounds is vitally dependent upon the temporal orientation pervasive within the culture. The following chapter by Verhave and van Hoorn (Chapter. 16) rounds out the discussion of physical factors as they influence social pattern. Here the authors argue that the development and proliferation of the time clock, and later the technological revolution, have had profound effects on the dominant conception of self in Western culture.

The last two chapters of the book shift the focus from the material to the expressive. In Chapter 17, Colin Martindale summarizes his extensive research on the dynamics of aesthetic taste. As he proposes, regardless of artistic domain, a similar pattern of cross-time change in aesthetic expressiveness is discovered. In the final chapter, Peter Collett focuses on specific forms of non-verbal expression in various historical times. Here it is demonstrated how non-verbal expressions may be used to trace the dispersion and longevity of various sub-cultures.

In addition to these authors, many others have contributed significantly to the present endeavor. Carl Graumann, at Heidelberg University, furnished a working environment that was both supportive and stimulating. Alexandre Metraux, unhappily struck by an illness that prevented him from completing his contribution to the volume, was an especially invigorating member of this community, as was his office mate Horst Gundlach. Similarly, Gabi Gloger-Tippelt was most helpful in elucidating similarities between historical social and developmental psychological study. Paul Baltes, at the Max Planck Institüt für Bildungsforschung in Berlin, furnished an inspiring and exciting environment in which, for two months, we could pursue these parallels. Finally, Winnie Vaules at Swarthmore College played an invaluable role in turning the mad markings of scholarship-in-motion into ordered print. We thank you all.

Kenneth J. Gergen
Mary M. Gergen

*Historical
Social
Psychology*

METATHEORY, THEORY, AND METHOD IN HISTORICAL SOCIAL PSYCHOLOGY

1 An Introduction to Historical Social Psychology

Kenneth J. Gergen
Swarthmore College

For the better part of the present century social psychology inquiry has been dominated by three major romances, each of which has led to the birth of broad practices for generating knowledge. As time has passed, each of these romances has also proved deeply problematic, and much of the initial enthusiasm has waned. Yet, because viable alternatives have been unavailable, traditional scientific practices have continued relatively unabated. Historical social psychology attempts to furnish one such alternative, an alternative that may correct the deficits inherent in the earlier romances, and simultaneously create a new range of options. It attempts to extend substantially the range of research vistas, to open inquiry into fresh explanatory forms, to set the stage for important methodological advance, and to engender an enhanced level of self-consciousness regarding the scientific process. Such a cavalier promissory note demands explanatory collateral. After considering the rationale for such a venture, we may consider its origins, its various forms, and its relation to scholarly inquiry more generally.

From the Synchronic to the Diachronic

We may first consider the form of behavioral explanation that has pervaded traditional social psychology. The traditional preference has been to render human action intelligible through the positing of relatively stable, psychological structures or mechanisms. Constructs such as attitudes, concepts, perceptions, cognitions, schemata, and prejudices all fall within this preference range, as do psychological tendencies, dispositions, and traits of various kinds. This explanatory orientation has often been termed *mechanistic* (cf. Overton & Reese, 1973; Overton & Reese, 1970) as it is analogous to the means by which one might understand the industrial machine. The typical machine of the twentieth century is composed of stable or enduring units, and the functioning of these units is generally dependent on various exogenous inputs (e.g., electricity, gasoline, steam, etc.). In similar manner the social psychologist posits a stabilized structure or tendency that typically exists in a latent state until stimulated or triggered by environmental stimuli. The structure or tendency is then activated, and its activation is manifested in the subsequent activity of the individual. For example, attitudinal dispositions are generally viewed as relatively stable determinants of behavior subject to alteration by message inputs. Or, as it is ventured, the individual retains a state of cognitive balance until incoming information disrupts this state, thereby triggering an automatic tendency to regain the initial state.

The mechanistic form of explanation in social psychology hardly emerged as an intellectually isolated event (cf. Pieterson & van Hoorn, 1981). Such theorizing has been favored by a variety of circumstances. For example, one cannot avoid conjecturing on the effects of the technological revolution on the intellectual world; the metaphor of the machine is a choice favored by virtually all aspects of our daily ecology. And too, if the psychologist wishes ultimately to reduce psychological constructs to physiology, then the traditional image of the brain as an electronic circuit, an inert structure carrying environmentally induced impulses, strongly favors a mechanistic form of explanation at the psychological level. Yet, of more specific consequence to social psychology has been a set of prevailing beliefs about the nature of science and its subject matter. Social psychology as an institution has been largely committed to an empiricist world view in general, and vulnerable to the elaboration of this view by positivist-empiricist philosophers of the present century. From the empiricist standpoint human knowledge is principally a product of environmental inputs. As it is often proposed, the human mind is akin to a *tabula rasa* upon which the stimulus world inscribes its features. Human knowledge is thus built up from exposure to the environment.

Because of their grounding in an empiricist world view, social psychologists have typically conceived of the scientist as one who carefully and systematically attempts to chart the relationship among various observables in nature. If knowledge is to be obtained, it must derive from observation of events in nature. Further, the empiricist commitment has also encouraged the social psychologist to view not only the action of scientists, but human action more generally as based upon incoming stimuli. Human behavior, as it is generally envisioned, is fundamentally contingent upon environmental events. Thus, the human mind remains essentially unchanged, inert, or stable until environmental intervention occurs. As can readily be seen, the result of these conjoint views is first that the psychologist focuses research on relationships between observable stimulus events and "resulting" responses, with psychological terminology used to explain the linkage between the two. Second, and most important for present purposes, this psychological terminology also recapitulates the empiricist world view: within the individual lie inert, structured entities, mechanisms or potentials that remain dormant until the onset of environmental stimulation. By adopting an empiricist conception of the science, social psychologists have simultaneously committed themselves to a mechanistic form of behavioral explanation. In effect, metatheoretical commitment has preempted theoretical selection.

Yet, let us ask what account would be given from the mechanistic perspective of an individual's life over an extended period of time. How might ongoing life be characterized by existing theories of social psychology? Consider a possible description of an individual's typical day. It might be said of the person's waking moments that he first responded to an alarm clock with an unconditioned response. He was then confronted with a forced compliance situation in the form of his mate's urging to "get up" and subsequently, while reading the headlines of the morning paper, was exposed to a series of attitude change sequences. The latter were followed by a self-awareness experience while peering into the bathroom mirror, then a challenge to obese eating tendencies as breakfast was encountered, followed by an emotional labeling experience while rushing for the bus, replaced by an exercise in cooperative versus exploitative tendencies while maneuvering through the crowd, and so on.

As is evident, when the mechanistic form of understanding is applied to events across time, we find life composed of one disjointed micro-sequence after another—a concatenation of stimulus-organism-response combinations with neither direction nor temporal coherence. In a broad sense such an explanatory orientation appears peculiarly cut away from the fundamental character of social understanding itself. That is, the mere occurrence of segmented or temporally delineated events does not constitute comprehension; normal comprehension occurs when one is able to discern the connection among events across time, when one is able to place events within a temporally extended context. Thus, for example, the sudden appearance of a figure at the door who blurted, "Glad to see you are still among the living" would in itself be a matter of puzzlement. Random encounters with individuals who uttered such words would render life a chaos. However, when the utterance is located within a temporal context, such that the speaker can be identified as a friend with whom one attended an unusually indulgent party the previous night, the utterance is rendered fully intelligible. In effect, social intelligibility would typically seem to require the temporal contextualization of events.

To draw further illustration from the annals of psychology, it is not, as William James (1890) proposed, that the "booming, buzzing confusion" of the infant world is rendered intelligible by the process of conceptualization. To recognize a smile, a hand movement, a pleasant vocal sound, a flower, and other such events across time would not engender understanding. Rather, it would simply replace one form of confusion with another: An incoherent succession of stimuli would be replaced by an incoherent succession of labels. It is when conceptualized events are understood in their relationship to each other across time that the sense of comprehension emerges. It is when the child recognizes that the mother's smile is related to her hand pointing in the direction of the flower, and that the pleasant utterance is related to the remainder of the configuration in a functional way that comprehension begins to take place. Or to put it in Harry Stack Sullivan's (1953) terms, mature cognition begins as the child moves from the prototaxic to the syntaxic mode of thought, from a recognition of differentiated entities, to an understanding of the logical ordering of events. In these terms, mechanistic social psychology remains in a prototaxic stage of development.

Drawing from Saussure's distinction in linguistic study, social theorists such as Harré (1979), Riley & Nelson (1971) and Blank (1982) have distinguished between *synchronic theory,* which deals with the static state of a given entity, and *diachronic theory,* which treats states of an entity (or relations among entities) across temporal periods. As is clear from the present analysis it seems imperative that the synchronic form of understanding, embodied within the mechanistic model of traditional social psychology, be complemented (if not supplanted) by a diachronic orientation to social life. Required is an expanded emphasis on the direction of and relationship among social events across time. Or as Blank (1982) has put it, social psychology has thus far succeeded in furnishing only "snapshots" of decontextualized moments in social life. There is much to gain by expanding our perspective and replacing the snapshot by the moving picture.

Theories of the diachronic form have been elaborated over the years and applied to a variety of social phenomena. However, until recently these attempts have largely taken place outside the domain of social psychology. For example, a number of theorists have proposed what have variously been termed *teleological* (Rosnow, 1978), or *organismic* (Reese & Overton, 1970) theories of social development. Characteristic of such theories is their positing fixed stages of growth or development in the individual or the culture. Comte's (1853) "law of three stages" in the development of society, and Wundt's (1916) four stages of developing civilizations are illustrative. Such theories may be contrasted with *cyclical theories* (Rosnow, 1978) of social change in which progressive cycles of growth and decay are envisioned. Vico's (1744) early theory of the growth and decay of society along with the more recent historical accounts of Spengler (1926) and F. S. Chapin (1925) are exemplary. Both the organismic and cyclical change theories may be contrasted with *conflict theories* of change. In this case social change is traced to various interpsychic or intrapsychic elements in conflict. Such theorizing has been perhaps the most vital within the present century. Social Darwinism as developed by Spencer (1876–1897) and Sumner (1883) and various evolutionary theories of social development are among the most pervasive forms of conflict theory. Dialectic theory as initially developed by Hegel and later applied by Marx and many others (cf. Israel, 1979b, Wexler, 1983) to wide-ranging social phenomena must be viewed as a close contender. These three theoretical forms, and various combinations thereof, hardly exhaust the spectrum of possibilities. However, as will be evident from the chapters of this volume, they do form an invaluable intellectual resource for the development of historical social psychology.

From Temporal Truncation to Extended Pattern

The romance with mechanistic explanation has been accompanied by two others of no less constricting consequence. The second has taken the form of an almost exclusive concern with *temporally truncated sequences of events*. Since the inception of psychological research in late-nineteenth-century Germany, psychologists had been enamored with possible comparisons between their formulations and those of the natural sciences. The possibility of breaking down complex phenomena into sets of fundamental ingredients, as had proven so eminently successful in chemistry and physics, was optimistically endorsed by the mentalist psychologists of the period, and must surely be regarded as one of the formative or generic concepts within the discipline more generally. Early learning researchers argued convincingly that it was far too difficult to begin the task of understanding human behavior by focusing on the ongoing stream of daily events. Rather, it was essential at the outset to focus more systematically on the microscopic or more finely delineated elements. If the scientist were acutely sensitive, he or she might select elements foundational for understanding the more complex morass of daily life. In effect, then, the social psychologist was invited to view quotidian life as a complex array amenable to analysis through understanding its constituent elements. It was the simple elements that were worthy of scientific scrutiny, and not the synthetic by-products.

The result of this orientation in social psychology has been a host of studies on the impact of various situational variables on the immediate behavior of persons. For example, research has focused on the effects of various message and context variables on attitude change, personal attributes on social attraction, commands under varying contexts on obedience, group composition on conformity, and so on. Again, this prevailing tendency can hardly be understood apart from the historical context. As is clear, the focus on temporally truncated sequences is highly compatible with both the mechanistic form of explanation and the empiricist world view from which it was derived. If the scientist is to be concerned with the relationship between observable stimuli and responses, and persons are viewed as fundamentally dependent upon environmental inputs, then it is fully reasonable for the scientist to confine research to sequences of events that commence with a determining stimulus and terminate with the resulting response.

Yet, an additional influence must be earmarked in this case, one that plays a more immediate and concrete role in the daily life of the scientist. This is the influence of methodology, and more specifically, the controlled experiment. As it is said, the controlled experiment exceeds all other methodological forms in its capacity to trace the effects of selected factors, either singly or in combination, on a particular form of behavior. By manipulating variables in a systematic fashion, while holding all other factors constant, one may furnish clear, incorrigible support for theoretical propositions of the "if . . . then" variety. Most significant for present purposes, the greater the interval of time separating the exposure of persons to a stimulus condition and the subsequent measurement of their responses, the less confidence the scientist may have in drawing causal inferences from the results. As the temporal interval is increased, the experimental subject is potentially exposed to a wide range of contaminating variables over which the experimenter can scarcely gain control. Not only is it impossible on a practical level for the subject to be retained for long periods in a fully controlled environment, but so long as subjects have extended periods to consider and reconsider their situation, they may autonomously inject uncontrolled interpretations into the situation. The rigorous experiment is thus one that necessarily confines itself to temporally truncated phenomena.

In the same way that the mechanistic model of understanding is ill suited to the demands of understanding ongoing social activity, so the hegemony of the psychological experiment has been accompanied by a restricted consideration of the temporal boundaries of human interaction. Very few of the significant social processes would seem to approximate the reflex arc in their temporal duration. Rather, the vast share of significant social activity requires temporal duration, often of considerable magnitude. On the more restricted level, holding a conversation, playing games, teaching a lesson, having a fight, making love, and other familiar ingredients of daily life all require extended interchange. Or, to expand the temporal horizon, such activities as getting an education, developing friendships, carrying out a romance, raising a child, getting ahead occupationally, and so on, typically require extended periods of time. And, to broaden the scope still further, the evolution of a culture, the development of a social tradition, the achievement of harmonious relations among ethnic groups, and the building of governing institutions may require centuries. Each of the forms of interaction, from the delimited to the extended, is virtually excluded from study so long as the controlled experiment is presumed to be the hallmark of superior scholarship. To the extent that experimentation takes priority over subject matter, cross-time phenomena will be obscured from view.

One might wish to soften the impact of this argument by reasserting the traditional logic, to wit, temporally extended phenomena can be broken down into component parts. These more delimited segments may be studied more microscopically, and the experiment continues to be the most promising vehicle for such study. Such an argument does have a limited range of utility. However, it is essential to understand in what manner such applications can be made. A major error of traditional social psychology lay within the unarticulated premise that knowledge of the whole could be gradually constructed as isolated units were laid bare via experimental elucidation. The hope was then to build toward an understanding of the more complex manifold by mastering the constituent parts. Yet, from the perspective of a historical social psychology, this assumption of part-to-whole progress must be suspended.

Demanded in the present case is a commitment to the *definitional sanctity of the whole*. If, as we have reasoned, individual events derive their social meaning from their position within a more extended temporal sequence, then it is the more extended sequence that must take priority over constituents. As this view suggests, constituents only gain their identity as such by an understanding of the more extended process. One cannot build toward an understanding of the latter through an analysis of micro-segments as the micro-segments themselves are nonmeaningful ("non-sense"). For example, if one were to decompose a large painting into square millimeter fragments, and to learn everything there was to know about each of the separate fragments, one would know virtually nothing of the painting as a form of social communication. One would not be able to speak of the "pathos of Picasso's Guernica" or Hopper's depiction of the cavernous emptiness in daily life. This is because a painting as a whole constitutes the fundamental unit of understanding. The segments are only significant in this sense as they are understood within the context of the whole. In the same way one cannot isolate for study momentary fragments from an ongoing relationship, as the isolated fragments are important only as they appear within the more extended context.

As this analysis makes clear, the controlled experiment would have little place in historical psychology as an aid to induction. It would no longer function as a means of generating foundational elements. Rather, its function would principally be that of clarifying, demonstrating, illustrating, or vivifying aspects of one's understanding of temporally extended processes. To illustrate from the field of developmental psychology, Piaget's theory of cognitive development set the stage for wide-ranging experimentation on conservation, decalage, and sequence reversibility or regression. However, the theory of the extended process was a necessary prerequisite to such experimentation. The theory of the developmental process could never be derived from the results of such experimentation.

From Phenomenal Immutability to Temporal Contingency

The third prevailing but problematic romance in social psychology has been with what may be called *phenomenal immutability*. That is, the discipline has generally proceeded as if its subject matter stood outside of time, trans-historically perdurable or inherent in the natural order. Thus, it was believed, the science might discover the basic principles of attitude change, person perception, aggression, social attraction, intergroup hostility, and the like. The results of study at any given time period might be handed on to future scientists, who might themselves replicate or undertake to correct or elaborate through more detailed study. For example, Festinger's theory of social comparison was proposed in 1954, and has continued to stimulate researchers to carry out wider ranging investigations corroborating, attacking, or extending the basic propositions. Works edited by Latané in 1966 and Suls and Miller in 1977 furnished summaries of much of this work; and today additional researchers continue inquiry into this "basic" or "fundamental" process. As it is generally argued, research over time should enable the science to furnish well-corroborated and highly predictive principles of broad applicability. Science must adapt its theoretical templates so as to fit the basic contours of nature.

Again, there is much within the intellectual and ideological context that has sustained this generalized romance with phenomenal immutability. As Verhave and van Hoorn might propose (see Chapter 16 of this volume), the belief in a fundamental human nature represents a vestige of the early faith in the human soul—a basic essence beyond time and circumstance. It might also be ventured that the belief in the permanence of subject matter has had strong existential appeal. To believe one's research furnishes a brick in the edifice of ultimate truth is an effective redoubt against the ravaging possibility of a meaningless existence. However, perhaps the strongest impetus for the romance with phenomenal immutability was furnished by the attempt of the discipline to model itself (at least in North America) after the natural sciences. The natural sciences long assumed that the focus of their research was on the fundamental properties of the natural world. To be sure, what is considered "most basic" has undergone continuous transformation over time, with scientific progress over the past century generally pegged to increments in reductionism. However, as it is generally believed, the natural scientist is coming ever nearer to "carving nature at the joint." In part it is this natural science image that stimulated Wundt (1916) to develop the concept of "mental chemistry." It was also this image that encouraged psychologists to accept Pavlov's (1927) work as demonstrating fundamental principles of association learning. And, this image continues to flourish in the contemporary social psychologist's belief in basic principles of social cognition, attitude change, and the like.

Elsewhere I have attempted to open for question the assumption of phenomenal immutability (Gergen, 1973, 1976, 1982). This challenge has been based on two major lines of argument. The first is that most contemporary patterns of human interaction are subject to temporal decay or alteration. Many of today's patterns are the product of long-term development—sometimes of centuries duration. The quest for justice, investments in equality, beliefs in autonomy and individuality, and the various social institutions in which these various psychological dispositions are rooted have ancient origins and have undergone a slow and circuitous development. Other patterns have their origin within the present century. For example, concerns with democratic family life, existential despair and the search for life's meaning, and the sense of mass identification engendered by the media, have become focal within the lifetime of the discipline itself. Still other patterns have emerged within the past several decades. For example, concerns with occupational burnout, stress, androgyny, and their associated behavior patterns are of relatively recent vintage. Most important, however, when one takes into account the origins and alterations of interaction patterns and their psychological bases, it is clear that virtually all are expendable. That is, almost none seem demanded by the character of human nature itself. None seem genetically wired into the nervous system. Biology primarily seems to supply the limits of human action (one cannot run a two-minute mile or walk long distances on one's hands). However, within these limits there is potential for near infinite variation.

The second line of argument for challenging the belief in phenomenal immutability takes into account the embeddedness of science within cultural life. Traditionally psychologists have wished to see themselves as dispassionate observers of social life whose task it is to furnish objectively grounded accounts of human activity. Although the results of such work may be employed for passionate reasons, either by the scientist or others in the culture, the validity of the scientific account is not thereby impugned. Yet, upon closer examination such assumptions seem altogether misleading. Theories of social life are inherently no less potent than other cultural artifacts, including religious, economic, or political doctrines, in forming the basis for social change (or stasis). As the sciences make certain patterns of activity intelligible, determine in what manner they are reasonable, functional or adaptive, they thereby provide a form of cultural sanctification. And, as the sciences demonstrate how certain patterns of activity are abhorrent, unintelligent, irrational, self-defeating or socially disruptive, such activity becomes the target of shame. The sciences in this sense are arbiters of good and evil, making social judgments under the guise of neutrality. And, as evidenced in the broad-scale effects of Marxist and Freudian theories, such judgments may have enormous shaping potential. Social psychological work may thus be viewed as an active form of cultural participation, one that plays a role in altering or sustaining various patterns of social conduct.

To the extent that these theses are sustained, they add further gravity to the earlier exhortations for diachronic forms of understanding, and for broadening the scope of temporal concern. In the first instance, to the extent that contemporary patterns of activity are subject to alteration, fundamentally ephemeral, or inherently transient, the theorist's focus may appropriately shift from an understanding of the activity in itself, to an understanding of the context of its emergence and its potential longevity. It is insufficient to know, for example, that those persons in the present era whose freedom is being threatened will frequently respond by reasserting their autonomy (cf. Brehm, 1966; Wicklund, 1974). Rather, scientific inquiry would be expanded so as to take account of the historical conditions under which such a reaction evolved, its ramifications over time, the institutional or ideological supports that have emerged (or failed to emerge), and so on. Are such patterns in their zenith, or their nadir, and what does their cross-time trajectory tell us about the future? Such understanding would enable one to appreciate the possible longevity of various action patterns, and their potential for decay. For example, if such patterns are of a recent vintage and have acquired little institutional or ideological support, then a half-life of relatively brief duration might be anticipated. To gain such understanding, diachronic forms of theory are also required and one must expand the temporal scope within which contemporary patterns of conduct are viewed.

However, with this emphasis on the *temporal contingency* of action, historical social psychology acquires a new and crucial role within the discipline. We have spoken thus far about the value of historical social psychology in opening the way to new forms of explanation and to a consideration of new ranges of phenomena. However, as historical study brings transience into focus, the field begins to acquire a critically reflexive role within the discipline. The prevailing tendency within psychology has been toward unbridled temporal generalization: Theories and supporting evidence are generalized across the full range of human history. So long as there is no contravening account, the scientist is encouraged to assume the indefinite applicability of his or her knowledge. Thus far such tendencies have been freely and perhaps egregiously exercised in social psychology because there has been no critical voice. By exploring forms of human conduct in previous eras, the historical social psychologist throws the present into vivid relief. In the typical case one may come to see present patterns as historically contingent, rooted in a particular configuration or circumstance. In such cases the investigator may then be prompted to push beyond a mere concern with the pattern itself, and to inquire into the supporting context. How is it that the contemporary pattern came to be; on what does its continuance in social life depend? In some instances the historical study may reveal that today's patterns are indeed transhistorically general. In these cases inquiry may begin into both the possibility of genetic origin and of fundamental pragmatic or functional demands. In the former case, for example, one might wish to examine sociobiological means of explaining social pattern (cf. Campbell, 1978; Cunningham, 1981; Wilson, 1978). In the case of pragmatics, one may ask whether certain patterns of conduct are not essential for the existence of organized society (cf. Fox, 1971; Lonner, 1980). For example, any form of social order may have certain prerequisites; processes of communication and means of social sanctioning may be among them. By taking into account both biological and cultural necessity, the social psychologist can ultimately begin to differentiate between more and less ephemeral patterning.

In summary, we find that the long prevailing mechanistic forms of explanation furnish an incoherent account of social life across time. A form of social psychology seems required in which diachronic theory may flourish. And, in its near-exclusive concern with temporally truncated sequences of activity, traditional social psychology has remained largely oblivious of a potentially vast array of phenomena that extend over periods of time. A form of social psychology is required in which the principal concern is with temporally extended pattern. Finally, in its assumption of phenomenal immutability, the discipline has been systematically enticed into unwarranted transhistorical generalization. A form of psychology seems essential that will facilitate judgment of the potential sources and variability of contemporary patterns by viewing them against the backdrop of history. Historical social psychology represents a positive response to each of these demands.

THE EMERGENCE OF HISTORICAL SOCIAL PSYCHOLOGY

It may justly be said that historical social psychology has been practiced unselfconsciously since the emergence of historical narration itself. Some 400 years before Christ, Heroditus reported how a steward of a king, whose disobedience the king punished by serving the steward his son's flesh for dinner, later took revenge by leading the king's army to successful revolt. In this account Heroditus was essentially furnishing a diachronic explanation of a major social event: the overthrow of an empire. This form of explanation continues to thrive on both the informal and on the scholarly level. Perhaps the first to realize the potential of a scholarly discipline devoted to understanding human change was the philosopher Giambattista Vico (1668–1744). As Vico proposed in his *Scienza nuova (The new science)*, human activities are in a state of perpetual change. Certain changes are, however, recurring in character, and their recurrence can be ascertained through careful study. As it was ventured, every society traverses three ages, each dominated by certain forms of thought. There is first the age of gods, followed by the age of heroes and then by the age of men. In effect, a special form of science was viewed as essential for the study of the changing character of human patterning and its psychological basis.

The possibility for an independent science devoted to the history of humankind, and more specifically one that included "the mind" as a legitimate focus of study, emerged again in the following century. Hegelian philosophy was clearly a strong stimulus to such work. However, a more scientific program was first initiated by the German philosopher and physician, Herman Lotze (1817–1881) in his three-volume series *Mikrokosmus,* subtitled "an essay concerning man and his relation to the world." Lotze's concern with understanding the origins and evolution of the mind within culture was heavily linguistic in orientation. As such, it further inspired two Berlin intellectuals, Steinthal and Lazarus (see Woodward's 1982 account) to launch in 1850 a journal, *Zeitschrift fur Völkerpsychologie und Sprach Wissenschaft,* an empirically based discipline devoted to the "historical life of mankind." This discipline was to proceed primarily through an understanding of language, its physiological, social, and cultural roots. "Cultural minds" (Volksgeister) were to be a chief focus of study.

Within the emerging discipline of psychology it was Wilhelm Wundt who was most sensitized to such concerns. In his early work, such as *The Grundzüge der Physiologischen Psychologie,* Wundt attempted in large measure to isolate basic elements of experience through experimentation. However, during the last 20 years of his career Wundt expanded his concern to the realm of human interaction. As he reasoned (Wundt, 1916), although much about human consciousness could be derived from a reductionistically oriented mental chemistry, a great deal was left unanswered by this type of psychology. Specifically, there are many "mental products which are created by a community of human life and are, therefore, inexplicable in terms merely of individual consciousness, since they presuppose the reciprocal action of many" (p. 3). It is this range of phenomena that demands a different form of science—one more akin to history than chemistry or physics. For example, various patterns of religion, political, legal, and social thought cannot be derived from an understanding of the mental mechanisms alone. Rather, such patterns have their origins in social activity; they are artifacts of human interaction. As it was further proposed, an understanding of contemporary patterns must be achieved through diachronic analysis. The answer to why contemporary thought has the character it does is furnished by an account of its origins and development. Thus, borrowing from earlier work of Lotze, Steinthal, and Lazarus, Wundt employed the term *Völkerpsychologie* to title the ten-volume work in which he proceeded with the arduous task of documenting the origins of cultural institutions from prehistory to the present.

Wundt's work was both influenced by and congenial with Darwin's powerful theory of evolution (Farr, 1980a, 1980b). The contributions of Darwin and Wundt did not go unheeded within the early development of social psychology. Indeed, in Murchison's 1935 *Handbook of Social Psychology,* four chapters were devoted to issues in social history. In the same volume only two chapters featured the kind of situationally oriented social psychology that was later to become totemic within the discipline. Yet, from the 1930s until recent years, historical inquiry within psychology became virtually moribund. There were occasional exceptions: Vygotsky's (1934) discussion of the dependency of cognitive processes on existing cultural conditions; Fromm's (1941) account of the historical basis for fascism; McClelland's (1961) analysis of the dependency of achievement motivation on the configuration of historical conditions; Hovland & Weiss' (1951) study of the "sleeper effect"; and Berelson, Lazarsfeld, & McPhee's (1954) research on the phases of opinion formation are among the most prominent. However, in the main the historical enterprise entered a period of dormancy.

The major reasons for this latter turn should be evidenced from the preceding discussion of the prevailing romances. Each of these romances— with mechanistic explanation, events of brief duration, and immutable phenomena—were derived from a more general commitment to a particular view of science. This, the logical empiricist view, envisioned the scientist as chiefly concerned with ahistorical processes. Empirical observation was to be the cornerstone of such an enterprise, and the "if . . . then . . ." proposition was to serve as its theoretical counterpart. (Such historical sciences as geology and astronomy posed partial exceptions.

However, such sciences were not typically considered "fundamental," but rather, descriptive and ultimately derivative.) As the logical empiricist views were incorporated into psychology and came to form the basis for what many view as an era of self-conscious scientism (cf. Koch, 1959), diachronic theory became largely obsolete, concern with temporally extended phenomena became methodologically problematic, and historical change was virtually disregarded.

The fact that the historical orientation lost relevance during this period of scientism also furnishes insight into its more recent renaissance. Empiricist philosophy of science of the kind that promised truth through method and a unification of science during the 1930s–1940s now lies in disarray. Arguments over the indeterminacy of theoretical language, the inadequacy of induction, the empirical incommensurability of competing theories, the possibility of scientific progress, and the inapplicability of natural science metatheory and methods to problems of human action have all led to a loss in confidence (see Gergen's 1982 review). As it is commonly said, contemporary philosophy of science is in a "postempiricist" phase. It is a phase marked by heated disagreement over the grounds and possibility of empirically grounded, scientific knowledge. Because the orienting assumptions of traditional psychology were largely derived from the early logical empiricist program for science, the general deterioration in confidence at the philosophic level was inevitably to have repercussions within psychology. Within social psychology the extensive ferment over the past decade, often termed "the crisis in social psychology," must properly be viewed within this context. And, in cases where the criticisms of the traditional craft have been initiated on other than philosophical grounds, traditional logical empiricist answers have no longer been found sustaining. In effect, the science of psychology no longer rests on a firm metatheoretical base, and the future remains very much in the balance.

A second important influence on the reemergence of historical psychology must be traced to the impact of Marxist (1967) theory on social thought more generally. Two aspects of this development are particularly important, the one concerned with critique and the second with the theory of change. As argued by Marx in the former case, capitalist economic principles are typically treated as both temporally unbounded in their generality and as value neutral. Yet, closer inspection reveals that (1) capitalist economic principles rely for their predictive power on a historically contingent array of circumstances and (2) capitalist economic doctrine has typically served to legitimate and mystify an economic structure favoring the proponents of the doctrine. Such argumentation later became expanded and elaborated within what became the field of critical sociology (cf. Habermas, 1971; Horkheimer, 1972; Jay, 1973). As a result of such expansion, wide-ranging critical analysis has been directed toward various forms of seemingly general and value neutral theory. It is this critical stance toward seemingly objective theory that has insinuated itself importantly into social psychology. Although largely severed from its Marxist origins, critical analyses within social psychology have focused on the valuational investments or implications of conflict theory (Apfelbaum & Lubek, 1976), gender theory (Morawski, 1982a), cognitive psychology (Sampson, 1981), social attraction theory (Wexler, 1983), stimulus-response models (Hampden-Turner, 1970), moral development theory (Gilligan, 1982), dissonance theory (Israel, 1979a), and person-situation interactionism (Gadlin & Rubin, 1979) among others. Such work has served to enhance consciousness of the historical conditions giving rise to various psychological theories (cf. Buss, 1979), and of the ways in which theories themselves may alter social pattern. They have systematically and compellingly argued for historical-contextual basis of contemporary pattern and thus acted as potent stimulus to historical study of social phenomena more generally.

Marxist theory has not only stimulated the emergence of a critically oriented social psychology, but has also encouraged many to examine the relevance of dialectic theory to understanding social process. As pointed out by Rychlak (1976), Smith (1977), Altman (Altman & Gauvain, 1981) and others, while not committing the theorist to a Marxist economic view, dialectic theory can be a highly valuable instrument for understanding cross-time change at both the personal and interpersonal levels. The work of Buss (1979), Israel (1979), and Riegel (1979) has been most extensive in this respect. However, inquiries into dialectic thinking in cognitive development (Basseches, 1980), moral thinking (Hogan, 1974), applied social psychology (Janousek, 1972), mother-child interaction (Harris, 1975), learning and memory within sociohistorical circumstances (Kvale, 1977, Meacham, 1977), interpersonal attraction (Adams, 1977), the self-concept (Chandler, 1975), along with contributions by Georgoudi, Rappaport, and Gadlin to the present volume, are all indicative of the rich implications of the dialectic orientation for social psychology.

As this analysis indicates, the contemporary renaissance of historical social psychology can largely be traced to the general deterioration of confidence in the logical empiricist view of social psychology and its associated theories (mechanistic) and methods (experimentation). This argument is secured more tightly by considering the work that has bred new consciousness of the historical dimension in social psychology. Much of this work has been generated by those scholars actively engaged in critical reappraisal of the discipline. McGuire's (1973) "The Yin and Yang of progress in social psychology: Seven Koan" was considered a major defection from traditional social psychology. McGuire (1976) was also one of the first in contemporary times to turn his attentions to the systematic study of historical change. Harré's critique of mechanistic social psychology and the method of experimentation (Harré, 1980; Harré & Secord 1972) are widely known. In his more recent volume, *Social Being,* Harré also argues that structural models of action are best applied to short-term patterning. To account for cross-time change, he proposes both dialectic and evolutionary theories. Moscovici, whose critique of mainstream social psychology is widely cited (Moscovici, 1972), has been actively absorbed in historiographic work (Moscovici, 1968, 1981). Secord, who collaborated with Harré in the iconoclastic *Explanation of Social Behavior,* since embarked on the study of gender ratio in varying historical periods. Similarly, Rosnow's critique of traditional social psychology in *Paradigms in Transition* was followed by a proposal for a diachronic social psychology. The work of Blank (1982), Buss (1979), Gadlin (1978; with Ingle, 1975), Graumann (1979, 1982), Holzkamp (1976), Israel (1979a, 1979b), Jaynes (1976), Rappaport (1975), Riegel (1979), Morawski (1982b), Smith (1972; 1980), Wexler (1983), and the present author may all be characterized as well in terms of the dual concerns: critique coupled with concern for temporal transformation.

In the above instances misgivings about the tradition have acted as a direct stimulant to historically oriented work. However, such misgivings appear to have acted as a liberalizing agent in the field more generally. The atmosphere has increasingly been one in which social psychologists could more optimistically seek new avenues of departure. Several of these avenues have wended their way in the historical direction. Prominent among these is the increased concern with (1) rule-oriented research, (2) developmental processes and (3) historical reassessment of the discipline. As Schlenker (1977) has correctly pointed out, there is a close affinity between the view of social pattern as historically contingent and the rule-role approach in social psychology: both tend to see social patterns as dependent on historically situation products of social agreement. The rule-role orientation has undergone a virtual renaissance within recent social psychology. This proliferation is especially prominent in England where research into the sequential structure of personal action (Clarke, 1982), sequences of social interaction (Collett & Lamb, 1982; Kendon, Harris, & Key, 1975), contextual influences on interaction sequences (Argyle, 1981), rules of aggressive interchange (Marsh, 1978; Marsh, Rosser, & Harré, 1977), structured action (Brenner, 1980), and long-term relationships (Argyle, Clarke, & Collett, 1982), has demonstrated particular concern with cross-time patterning of activity. Similar trends may be located in the United States, especially in the work of Ginsburg and his colleagues (Bakeman & Ginsburg, in press; Ginsburg, 1979) on role playing and situated action, Sabini & Silver (1982) on the social construction of morality, and Kroger, (1982) on rules of address. Additionally relevant to these enterprises has been inquiry into social scripts

1. INTRODUCTION TO HISTORICAL SOCIAL PSYCHOLOGY   19

(Abelson, 1981), discourse analysis (Kreckel, 1980; Pearce & Cronen, 1980), processes of social construction (Coulter, 1979; Gauld & Shotter, 1977; Ossorio, 1978; Rommetveit, 1974) and ethnomethodology (Garfinkel, 1967; Kessler & McKenna, 1978; Psathas, 1979), each of which shares in the attempt to comprehend historically located, transtemporal patterns of interaction.

The renewed interest in cross-time change is even more pronounced in the emerging field of developmental social psychology. The developmental social domain has been a natural outcome of the cognitive turn in both social and developmental spheres, and much present work is concerned with social cognition (cf. Feldman & Bush, 1976; Flavell & Ross, 1981; Higgins, Ruble, & Hartup, in press; Brehm, Kussin, & Gibbons, 1981; Serafica, 1982). Many social psychologists and life span developmentalists (cf. Nesselroade & Baltes, 1974) have also begun to realize common research interests. The work of Suls & Mullen (1982) on social comparison processes over the life span, Ruble & Rholes (1981) and Blank (1982) on changes in attribution patterns, Ryff (1983) the phenomenology of aging, and Shaver & Klinnert (1982) on the development of affiliation and emotion, are all exemplary of this emerging affinity. Closely related is the renewed interest taken by social psychologists in biography and psychohistorical inquiry (Anderson, 1981; Runyan, 1982). Much of this latter work is concerned with single cases. However, as suggested by Elder's (1974, 1979) work on the life-span effects of growing up in the Great Depression, there is a broad and open vista for studying the cross-time trajectory of social groups as well as single individuals.

A third liberalizing influence is embodied in the concerted attempt to reassess the historical roots of present-day social psychology. In this case, it is maintained that existing historical accounts are largely presentist or self-justifying. As such, they furnish an implicit and unquestioning acceptance of contemporary scientific practices. Thus, investigators such as Samelson (1974; 1979), Morawski (1982a, 1982b), Lubek (1979), Finison (1976) and others have begun to demonstrate various biases and lacunae in earlier accounts and to carry out the kind of detailed historiographic work necessary for a sophisticated comprehension of the discipline's history. Such pursuits not only serve to legitimate historiographic research but also demonstrate the advantages of the diachronic orientation toward understanding social institutions.

Yet, the growing sensitivity to temporal issues in social psychology can hardly be credited, either directly or indirectly, to the generalized disenchantment with the traditional paths alone. There are many other wellsprings for such sensitivity. In Europe, where the positivist grip has been less firm, historically sensitive research had continued to enjoy a certain popularity (see Peeters' 1978 synthesis of European thought, van Hoorn's

1972 history of visual perception, and Porshnev's 1970 account of Russian thought). In the United States, one important source of interest in cross-time process has derived from the shift toward applied problems. Here social psychologists have been confronted with a variety of problems (e.g., program evaluation) which require multiple assessments across time. Such problems have also sensitized the field to statistical developments in stochastic modeling (Bartholomew, 1973; Cox & Miller, 1968) and other forms of time series analysis (Gottman, 1981; McCleary & Hay, 1980). Path or structural analysis, heavily used in sociology (Blalock, 1971), is becoming increasingly adopted by psychologists (cf. Bachman & O'Mally, 1977; Helmreich, Spence, Beane, Lucker, & Matthews, 1980; Reis, 1982). Over and above these pursuits, the work of Levinger and his colleagues (Levinger, 1980; Levinger & Huesmann, 1980; Levinger & Snoek, 1972) and Altman & Taylor (1973) on the development of intimacy grew in large measure from discontent with the exclusive focus of traditional attraction research on first encounters. The attempt to reconcile differential patterns of opinion survey results over an era led to a concern with diachronic process in attitude change in the case of Himmelweit, Humphreys, Jaeger, & Katz (1981). Similarly, Veroff and his colleagues (Veroff, Douvan, & Kulka, 1981; Veroff, Kulka, & Douvan, 1981) were moved to theories of social change upon comparing mental health surveys over an era. Festinger's (1983) recent work on the origins of social institutions is rooted in archeological interests. The sources of historical sensitivity are clearly variegated. And in the more liberalized context of present-day social psychology, one may hope to see the further burgeoning of such work.

FORMS OF INQUIRY IN HISTORICAL SOCIAL PSYCHOLOGY

As we see, diachronically oriented research in social psychology appears to be undergoing a brisk and multifaceted revitalization. Yet, within this broad expanse of research, one can discern a more limited number of prototypical forms. Three of these orientations are of special interest, first because each speaks in a different way to the future connection between historical social psychology and more traditional, synchronic pursuits. Further, each orientation carries with it a particular image of human functioning more generally, and therefore sets an implicit agenda for future research. Finally, each of these forms of understanding has differentiated implications for the definition of the behavioral sciences—how they are to be understood, and what function they are to play in society.

As it happens, the three major forms of inquiry in historical social psychology have their counterparts in the domain of human development

(Gergen, 1977, 1982). As a device for linking the social and developmental domains, it will prove useful to document these parallels as discussion proceeds. The first form of inquiry is based on the *assumption of stability*. The stability-oriented scholar is one who retains a commitment to the view of universal principles of human functioning, but is principally concerned with the varying manifestations of such principles within differing temporal contexts. As it is argued, the basic processes of social interaction endure, but the precise manner in which processes are realized may vary across time. This view is represented in developmental psychology by most learning theory accounts. As it is ventured, mechanisms of learning do not change; only the particular content is altered as the child develops. In social psychology, a convenient illustration of the stability orientation is furnished by the early work of McClelland on achievement motivation. McClelland (1961) attempted to demonstrate achievement needs, as indicated by economic spurts, systematically depend on the prevalence of achievement themes to which the generation has been exposed in their childhood stories. The stability orientation is also manifest in Richardson & Kroeber's (1940) attempt to demonstrate a cross-time relationship between women's dress styles and social conflict, the Fierabend & Fierabend (1966) analysis of cross-era correlates of political aggression, and Simonton's (1975) research on the historical context of creativity. The approach is represented in the present volume in Simonton's chapter on generational analysis (Chap. 7) and certain portions of Secord's (Chap. 13) account of gender ratio effects.

As is evident, this form of historical social psychology is in itself reasonably compatible with the more traditional, synchronically oriented social psychology. It retains certain important aspects of the three romances previously discussed. It shares the belief in a basic and unchanging human nature operating according to fixed principles. And accordingly, it implies that the scientist may properly set out to discover these principles through empirical means. The belief in the accumulation of scientific knowledge is also retained, as the scientist should presumably be able to sharpen his or her theoretical formulations as more is learned about history. Research in this domain is not in principle opposed to experimentation; such methods are merely precluded on practical grounds. Experimental data from widely disparate points in history are difficult to procure. Further, this form of historical social psychology does not fundamentally demand diachronic forms of theorizing. The investigator may be interested in differing historical periods, and much effort may be expended in collecting data regarding the precise aspects of a given historical context. However, the process by which transitions are made between one period of history and another is of peripheral concern. In effect, this form of investigation employs temporal slices (or snapshots) much as an experimentalist would compare differing cells of an experimental design. Each slice represents the results of a different configuration of determining or independent variables.

One discerns a significant contrast in assumptions when turning to a second significant orientation in historical social psychology, namely that of *ordered change*. In this case the commitment is retained to universal principles of human functioning, but these principles are viewed as diachronic in character. That is, the concern is not with the ways in which basic, stabilized processes manifest themselves in differing temporal periods, but in the orderly progression from one period to another. As it is generally assumed, such forms are reiterative, in the sense that they are subject to repetition—either within the life of a given person or culture, or in differing persons or cultures. To draw an analogy with botany, the stability-oriented botanist might be concerned with the effects of various environmental inputs on the process of photosynthesis; in contrast, the ordered-change orientation might emphasize the normal pattern of growth for a given species.

The ordered-change orientation is partially exemplified in the previously cited works of Vico and of Wundt. In both cases the theorists suggested that societies or cultural institutions progress through a series of fixed stages. Marxist theory of social change is similar in that it posits the inevitable emergence of a classless society. In developmental psychology, Freud's theory of psychosexual development and the ontogenetic theories of Piaget and Kohlberg are representative. In the social domain, Tesser's (1978) research on self-generated attitude change, and Davies' (1962) theory of the effects of rising and declining satisfaction on revolution, along with Crosby's (1976) extension, nicely illustrate the orientation. In the present volume, Martindale's (Chap. 17) account of evolution of aesthetic taste and, in certain respects, Albert's (Chap. 8) analysis of the ending phases of social encounters are illustrative.

As is clear, the ordered-change orientation does require a significant shift from a synchronic to a diachronic theoretical perspective. Further, it requires a reorientation in basic assumptions of human functioning. As indicated earlier, there is a close affinity between empiricist metatheory and mechanistic theory. Both assume organismic stasis; alterations in the state of organism (including increments in knowledge) are generally viewed as the result of environmental inputs. Yet, if organisms are endowed with inherent tendencies toward orderly change, the environment ceases to play a central role as the source of action or knowledge. In effect, as one shifts from a stability to an ordered-change orientation, one must be prepared to endow the organism with inherent tendencies and to reduce the emphasis placed upon environmental (situational) effects.

Although the ordered-change orientation would, if extended, demand a new form of scientific metatheory, such extensions have not yet been made. Most psychologists have thus found means of reconciling their work with the traditional empiricist conception of the science. Just as the child psychologist may hope to furnish accurate theoretical accounts of developmental trajectories, so may the social psychologist set out to discover patterned progressions in human interchange. And, given the recurring character of these progressions, the science should be able to correct various theoretical templates through continued observation. To be sure, the experimental method might play only a peripheral role in the endeavor, but the hope of accumulated knowledge is retained.

A third form of historical social psychology may also be isolated, one that is at radical variance with the preceding accounts. This, the *aleatory orientation,* is undergirded by the belief that most cross-time processes are not predetermined or fundamentally reiterative. Rather, it is assumed that cross-time processes may vary, sometimes dramatically, from either one person or era to another; most patterns of change are subject to substantial alteration. In effect, each cross-time process must be understood within a particularized confluence of historically situated circumstances.

As outlined elsewhere (Gergen, 1982) the aleatory perspective has gained a steadily increasing band of adherents within life span developmental psychology. This trend may be traced in part to the growing study of generational effects (cf. Buss, 1979; Elder, 1974) and the methodological breakthrough represented by cohort analysis. As the latter analyses consistently demonstrate, the life span trajectory of most behavioral tendencies tends to be specific to particular age cohorts (Baltes & Labouvie, 1973; Baltes & Schaie, 1973; Birren & Woodruff, 1973). Within historical social psychology the aleatory orientation figures in three distinct ways. First, historical inquiry in the aleatory mold is employed for *valuational* purposes. That is, the investigator typically harbors a moral or ideological concern with some aspect of contemporary society. By contrasting such patterns with earlier historical periods, he or she is able to bring the present into critical perspective, to demonstrate its shortcomings by comparison, and simultaneously to show how it might be otherwise. For example, Gadlin's (1978) research on the changing character of child discipline in the family nicely depicts the transformation of significant social patterns over several hundred years. However, the analysis also demonstrates what Gadlin feels are certain important shortcomings in contemporary family life—ways in which the quality of relationships in families has been negatively affected by the economic structure. The implicit message is thus that family structure can be altered, and that historical enlightenment will facilitate such alteration in a positive direction.

A second use of the aleatory orientation is to generate *reflexive scrutiny* within the discipline itself. This possibility was outlined in the earlier discussion of historicity in social psychology. However, a working example is represented in Eagly's (1978) study of the changing pattern of research findings related to sex differences in influencability. As her analysis indicates, earlier results showing women to be more susceptible to social influence than men have dropped away over time. Such an analysis cautions the discipline against assuming temporal generality in this domain and challenges it to correct its account of female behavior patterns. Again, the assumption underlying such work is that the patterns in question are historically contingent. Finally, the aleatory perspective is often assumed by those who are merely fascinated by earlier periods of history, and wish to render them intelligible by social psychological means. Moscovici's *L'Age des Foules* is a proximal example. Here the exploration is conducted into the sociopolitical circumstances responsible for certain conceptions of "the group" in French social thought.

Unlike the investigators using the stability and ordered-change perspectives, investigators in the aleatory mold are more inclined to accept an image of the human as a voluntary agent. For both the preceding perspectives, either environmental circumstance or inherent tendencies are typically viewed as constraining or determining patterns of behavior across time. However, when one abandons the assumption of enduring patterns, there is often a reduction of interest in "determinants," and an openness to the possibility of voluntary action. Although the voluntarist view is seldom articulated, it frequency becomes transparent when investigators use their work for either valuational or reflexive purposes. In both instances the assumption is made that once enlightened by knowledge of the past, one is free to abandon patterns or positions previously held.

The aleatory orientation also poses the most severe threat to the traditional empiricist view of science. To the extent that patterns of change are essentially nonrecurring, each born on the peculiar confluence of contemporaneous circumstances, then science can no longer be viewed as cumulative. The belief in scientific progress in the usual sense is no longer tenable. And, to the extent that the aleatory perspective is conflated with voluntarist views, the traditional attempt to use science for increasing prediction and control ceases to be other than a localized and transient goal. That is not to say that the aleatory orientation is devoid of a positive research program. The possibilities for such a program are outlined elsewhere (Gergen, 1982). However, it does invite serious exploration of alternative conceptions of behavioral science (see Gergen & Morawski, 1980).

HISTORICAL SOCIAL PSYCHOLOGY IN INTELLECTUAL CONTEXT

Having assayed the rationale, origins, and forms of historical social psychology, we may finally turn to its place within the field of scholarship more generally. What is the relationship of historical social psychology to other disciplinary pursuits? From what domains is intellectual companion-

1. INTRODUCTION TO HISTORICAL SOCIAL PSYCHOLOGY

ship likely to be obtained? How are the problems and methods of study to be envisioned? All are matters of continuing concern, and the future of the enterprise will largely rest on how such issues are resolved. Perhaps the most fruitful means of opening discussion of such matters is to retrace our steps to the seminal work of Vico (1744). Vico proposed that the understanding of cultural progression must proceed on different grounds from that employed in the case of various natural phenomena. Specifically, he argued that one can only understand an object or event if one penetrates how it came about or what made it as it is. Human institutions are creations of humans in relationship to each other. Thus, they may be known only by persons engaged in them. In what has come to be known as the *verum-factum* thesis, Vico laid the basis for a social science that would differ in its form of understanding from sciences of the natural order. Although the grounds proposed by Vico for separating the understanding of natural from social events remain controversial (cf. Berlin, 1976; Lana, 1980; Shotter, 1981) the intuition that the domains are somehow different and that such differences are more than trivial, has since been shared and elaborated by a wide number of scholars.

At the turn of the last century, a virtual phalanx of German scholars argued for a fundamental separation between the *Naturwissenschaften* and the *Geisteswissenschaften,* or the studies of the natural world from that of human action. As Dilthey contended, along with Windelband, Rickert, Weber and other participants in the German historical movement (see Iggers, 1968, account), the understanding of human action cannot be derived from the observation of bodily movements through space and time. Rather, such understanding must depend on one's comprehending underlying psychological disposition of the actor; it must thus proceed on different grounds than the understanding of physical events. For Dilthey (1977), this special process of *Verstehen* was cut away from abstract reasoning and included both contemplation of the person's individuality and intuition. A similar argument later became the basis for Collingwood's (1946) widely cited contention that historical accounts do not primarily represent recordings of spatiotemporal events, but reflect the thoughts of the actors. "When an historian asks, 'Why did Brutus stab Caesar' he means, 'What did Brutus think which made him decide to stab Caesar?' The cause of the event, for him means the thought in the mind of the person by whose agency the event came about" (Collingwood, 1946, p. 106). And, such arguments have come to be expanded and elaborated further by Peter Winch (1946/1958), Charles Taylor (1964, 1971) and a host of contemporary social thinkers.

As is clear, there is a long and well-articulated tradition encouraging those disciplines whose chief concerns are the intentional or meaningful actions of human beings (as opposed to mere bodily movements) to coordinate interests, to seek a common rationale of study, to share in methodologies, and ultimately to join in the process of generating understanding. To an emerging discipline such as historical social psychology these urgings are of no small moment. The general science of psychology, and in large measure social psychology, has allied itself with the natural sciences. The relationship between mind and brain is assumed to be a close one; physiological measures of psychological processes are often preferred above others; it is typically presumed that one's professional training includes biology, physiology, mathematics, and possibly physics, whereas the study of history, literature and philosophy would be viewed as largely irrelevant. However, as the present review suggests, it is an auspicious moment for critical scrutiny of this union. As the development of historical social psychology proceeds, it would seem far more fruitful to turn attention outward—to the social sciences and humanities—rather than in the reductionist direction. More is to be gained at this juncture by an immersion in the struggle toward understanding the processes of human signification than processes of neurotransmission.

Let us consider first several fruits of historical study. Within this realm there are two forms of inquiry that may specially benefit the historical social psychologist. First, much is to be gained through sensitization to metatheories and methods of history. Since at least the early 1700s, active inquiry has taken place regarding the character of historical knowledge, its grounds and its potential. Vico and Collingwood are but two of the scores of contributors to this colloquy. Within the past several decades historians and philosophers have carried out extended dialogue on preferred forms of explanation and their scientific merits. During the watershed years of logical empiricism Hempel (1959) along with Nagel (1959) and others proposed that historiography could, and often does, proceed according to the methods of the natural sciences. Ultimately, history should become integrated into the unified science movement. Although such views have been considerably modified through the careful analytic work of Morton White (1965), W. B. Gallie (1964) and others, there remains a strong commitment to what is termed "analytic history" (Danto, 1965), a form of historiography that retains a strong affinity with the lawlike forms of explanation and evidential grounds common within the behavioral and natural sciences. At the same time, many historians remain skeptical of the analytic approach in history (cf. Dray, 1959; Mink, 1968). A degree of creative preference is granted the historian in the development of the historical narrative. This narrative orientation is typically viewed as in contention with the analytic approach. Social psychologists concerned with change must ultimately make choices with respect to these positions, and informed choices would seem prescribed.

Regarding historical methods, numerous treatises have been devoted to the special pitfalls attending the recovery of past events. Developmental psychologists have also acquired an acute sensitivity to certain of these problems. However, it is also important to note the lively interest historians have taken within recent decades in behavioral science methods. What is frequently termed "the New History" (Stone, 1982) refers in large part to the attempt of historians to enhance the analytic and mensurational precision of historical study. Many of the emphases of the New History, including an increased reliance on the computer (Thernstrom, 1968), and the quantification of variables (Rowney & Graham, 1969; Swierenga, 1970) would be highly congenial to the social psychologist.

However, it is not only thinking about historiographic study from which historical social psychology can draw sustenance. In many cases the content of such study may itself prove invaluable. Such work is sufficiently well documented that elaboration is unnecessary at this juncture. However, special attention may be given to two more specialized forms of historiographic work. In the first instance, although most historians have avoided the use of general theoretical models, there are notable exceptions (including Spengler, Marx, & Toynbee). Such general theories of historical change have also been subject to wide-ranging criticism (cf. Popper, 1957). Given the social psychologist's frequent predilection for theoretical generalization, attention to such accounts and their shortcomings may be unusually edifying. A second specialized form of historical analysis is also of particular relevance for the social psychologist. As indicated, the vast share of historical work has focused on the actions of powerful or influential individuals or groups within various periods, while often treating ordinary social life as secondary (if not banal). However, there has been a steadily increasing interest, particularly among those identified with the New History in America, and those French historians comprising the *les Annales tradition* (see especially the works of Bloch, Braudel, Febvre, Goubert, and Le Roy Ladurie). Work within this latter tradition typically attempts to reconstruct the character of common life in earlier periods of French history. In this vein, social psychologists may also take special interest in Badinter's (1980) study of the historical relativity of mothers' love for their children, along with other treatments (Ariès, 1962; Peeters, 1974; van den Berg, 1961) of the changing conception of childhood over the centuries.

Is this to say that historical social psychology is in danger of becoming but a minor tributary of historical study more generally? It would not appear so. First one might argue with equal force that because historical work generally involves understanding human intention it is quintessentially a social psychological enterprise. History could thus be considered the more derivative discipline. In addition, both social psychology and history constitute separate guilds; each is a scholarly collectivity with shared values and conceptions. These shared perspectives differ considerably, and suggest that mutual interchange may be sought without special fear of incorporation. Most important, the two disciplines tend to differ significantly in (1) the focus of study and (2) the place of theory within the research process. In the case of research focus, traditional historians have often centered their concerns on incidents within the governmental, economic and military spheres; in contrast, the historical psychologist is typically more concerned with commonly shared psychological processes (perception, cognition, values, etc.) and their manifestations in social pattern. With the exceptions noted above, historians have tended to take a more aristrocratic view toward social life while psychologists have been more democratic. With respect to theory, historians have tended to leave theoretical predilections unarticulated, while attempting to vindicate a particular descriptive narrative. This goal of full and accurate description has foreshadowed concern with theoretical generalization. In contrast, for the historical psychologist theoretical concerns are generally paramount and often dictate the historical eras to be studied and the particulars under study within these eras.

Thus far we have only touched on several currents in historiography relevant to the development of historical social psychology. A second domain of special interest is that of historical sociology. The classic work in this case is that of Norbert Elias (1939), who masterfully explored the history of common customs and their social functions. However, in modern times historical sociology has forged a common bond with analytic or New History (cf. Lipset & Hofstadter, 1968). Historical sociology is now characterized by its strong emphasis on clearly defined variables, the numerical realization of these variables, and formalization with respect to the stated relationship among variables. Mention was earlier made to the pioneering work of Davies on revolution; such work may be usefully compared with Tilly's more recent *From Mobilization to Revolution,* a genre piece at its best. The combined efforts of sociologists, historians, and historically minded political scientists and anthropologists are currently represented within the Social Science History Association. Social psychology could add an important new voice to this colloquy.

Finally, the future development of historical social psychology stands to gain much by initiating dialogue with various philosophers, literary analysts, anthropologists and others centrally concerned with the problem of human understanding. The problem of how the contemporary scholar can comprehend the meaning or intention behind actions of the past has a long and distinguished history (cf. Mandelbaum, 1977). Similarly, debate continues over the problem of objectivity in interpreting human action (Gadamer, 1960/1975; Hirsch, 1976; Ricoeur, 1976), along with the extent to which concepts of human action are general or culturally specific (cf. Heelas & Locke, 1981; Shweder & Bourne, 1982). All are debates of critical relevance for the future direction of historical social psychology.

SUMMARY

The present chapter outlines the rationale, the origins, and the intellectual context for the development of a historical social psychology. As initially ventured, social psychology's traditional emphasis on synchronic forms of explanation, temporally delimited ranges of events and immutable patterns has each proved deeply problematic. Historical social psychology opens inquiry into diachronic theory, temporally extended patterns, and those aspects of human interchange which are in transformation. The roots of this enterprise were traced to the writings of Vico, Lotze and Wundt. As demonstrated, however, with the hegemony of the logical empiricist orientation in psychology, historical sensitivity was numbed. The more recent decay in confidence in this orientation has been accompanied by a renewed interest in cross-time processes. Three general lines of research in historical social psychology were then delineated: the stability, the ordered change, and the aleatory. As was shown, each approach harbors a particular view of human functioning and an associated concept of science. Finally, with respect to intellectual companionship, it was argued that for historical social psychology the reductionist preference of traditional psychology might usefully be replaced by an enhanced sensitivity to those disciplines concerned with understanding human action through time. Historical, sociological and philosophic studies were found to be particularly germane.

REFERENCES

Abelson, R. P. Psychological status of the script concept. *American Psychologist,* 1981, *36,* 715-729.

Adams, G. R. Physical attractiveness research: Toward a developmental social psychology of beauty. *Human Development,* 1977, *20,* 217-239.

Altman, I., & Gauvain, M. A cross-cultural and dialectic analysis of homes. In L. Liben, N. Newcombe, & A. Patterson (Eds.), *Spatial representation and behavior across the lifespan: Theory & application.* New York: Academic Press, 1981.

Altman, I., & Taylor, D. A. *Social penetration: The development of interpersonal relationships.* New York: Holt, Rinehart & Winston, 1973.

Anderson, J. W. Psychobiographical methodology: The case of William James. In L. Wheeler (Ed.), *Review of personality and social psychology* (Vol. 2). Beverly Hills, CA: Sage, 1981.

Apfelbaum, E., & Lubek, I. Resolution vs. revolution? The theory of conflicts in question. In L. Strickland, F. Aboud, & K. J. Gergen (Eds.), *Social psychology in transition.* New York: Plenum, 1976.

Argyle, M. Sequences in social behavior as a function of the situation. In G. P. Ginsburg (Ed.), *Emerging strategies in social psychological research.* London: Wiley, 1981.

Argyle, M., Clarke, D., & Collett, P. The social psychology of long term relations. Progress report to SSRC, August, 1982. Oxford University.

Ariès, P. *Centuries of childhood: A social history of family life.* New York: Vintage, 1962 (Originally published in 1960).

Bachman, J. G. & O'Mally, P. M. Self-esteem in young men: A longitudinal analysis of the impact of educational and occupational attainment. *Journal of Personality and Social Psychology,* 1977, *35,* 365-380.

Badinter, E. *Mother love, myth and reality.* New York: MacMillan, 1980.

Bakeman, R., & Ginsburg, G. P. The use of video in the study of human action. In M. Brenner & K. Knorr (Eds.), *Methods of social research.* London: Academic Press, in press.

Baltes, P. B., & Labouvie, G. Adult development of intellectual performance: Description, explanation and modification. In C. Eisdorfer & M. P. Lawton (Eds.), *The psychology of adult development and aging.* Washington, D.C.: American Psychological Association, 1973.

Baltes, P. B., & Schaie, K. W. On life-span developmental research paradigms, retrospects and prospects. In P. B. Baltes & K. W. Schaie (Eds.), *Life-span developmental psychology: Personality and socialization.* New York: Academic Press, 1973.

Bartholomew, D. J. *Stochastic models for social processes.* New York: Wiley, 1973.

Barzun, J. *Clio and the doctors' psycho-history, quanto-history and history.* Chicago: University of Chicago Press, 1974.

Basseches, M. Dialectical schemata: A framework for the empirical study of the development of dialectical thinking. *Human Development,* 1980, *23,* 400-421.

Berelson, B., Lazarsfeld, P. F., & McPhee, W. N. *Voting.* Chicago: University of Chicago Press, 1954.

Berlin, I. *Vico and Herder.* London: The Hogarth Press, 1976.

Birren, J. E., & Woodruff, D. S. Human development over the life span through education. In P. Baltes & K. Schaie (Eds.), *Life-span developmental psychology: Personality and socialization.* New York: Academic Press, 1973.

Blalock, H. M., Jr. Four-variable causal models and partial correlations. In H. M. Blalock, Jr. (Ed.), *Causal models in the social sciences.* Chicago: Aldine, 1971.

Blank, T. O. *A social psychology of developing adults.* New York: Wiley, 1982.

Brehm, J. W. *A theory of psychological reactance.* New York: Academic Press, 1966.

Brehm, S., Kassin, S. M., & Gibbons, F. X. *Developmental social psychology.* New York: Oxford University Press, 1981.

Brenner, M. (Ed.) *Structured actions.* Oxford: Blackwell, 1980.

Buss, A. R. *A dialectic psychology.* New York: Halstead, 1979.

Campbell, D. T. On the genetics of altruism and the counterhedonic components in human culture. In L. Wispé (Ed.), *Altruism, sympathy and helping.* New York: Academic Press, 1978.

Chandler, M. J. Relativism and the problem of epistemological loneliness. *Human Development,* 1975, *18,* 171-180.

Chapin, F. S. A theory of synchronous culture cycles. *Journal of Social Forces,* 1925, *3,* 596-604.

Clarke, D. D. The sequential analysis of action structure. In M. von Cranach & R. Harré (Eds.), *The organization of human action.* Cambridge: Cambridge University Press, 1982.

Collett, P., & Lamb, R. Describing sequences of social interaction. In M. von Cranach & R. Harré (Eds.), *The organization of human action.* Cambridge: Cambridge Press, 1982.

Collingwood, R. *The idea of history.* Oxford: Clarenden Press, 1946.

Comte, A. *The positive philosophy* V. 1 (Original French edition, 1830) Transl. London: Trubner, 1853.

Coulter, J. *The social construction of the mind.* London: Macmillan, 1979.

Cox, D. R., & Miller, H. D. *The theory of stochastic processes.* New York: Wiley, 1968.

Crosby, F. A model of egotistical relative deprivation. *Psychological Review,* 1976, *83,* 85-113.

Cunningham, M. R. Sociobiology as a supplementary paradigm for social psychological research. In L. Wheeler (Ed.), *Review of personality and social psychology* (Vol. 2). Beverly Hills, Calif.: Sage, 1981.

1. INTRODUCTION TO HISTORICAL SOCIAL PSYCHOLOGY 31

Danto, A. L. *Analytical philosophy of history.* Cambridge: Cambridge University Press, 1965.

Davies, J. C. Toward a theory of revolution. *American Sociological Review,* 1962, *27,* 5-19.

Dilthey, W. *Descriptive psychology and historical understanding.* The Hague: Martinus Nijhoff, 1977 (Originally published in 1894 and 1927).

Dray, W. Explaining "what" in history. In P. Gardiner (Ed.), *Theories of history.* Glencoe, Ill.: Free Press, 1959.

Eagly, A. H. Sex differences in influenceability. *Psychological Bulletin,* 1978, *85,* 86-116.

Elder, G. H. *Children of the great depression.* Chicago, Ill.: University of Chicago Press, 1974.

Elder, G. H. Social structure and personality: A life course perspective. In P. Baltes & O. Brim (Eds.), *Life-span development and behavior* (Vol. 2). New York: Academic Press, 1979.

Elias, N. *The civilizing process.* New York: Urizen Books. (Trans. Edmund Jephcott), 1978. (Originally published in 1939).

Farr, R. M. Sunk with hardly a trace: On reading Darwin & discovering social psychology. In R. Gilmour & S. Duck (Eds.), *The development of social psychology.* London: Academic Press, 1980(a).

Farr, R. M. Homo socio-psychologicus. In A. Chapman & D. Jones (Eds.), *Models of man.* Leicester: British Psychological Association, 1980(b).

Feldman, S., & Bush, D. (Eds.) *Cognitive development and social development.* Hillsdale, NJ: Lawrence Erlbaum Associates, 1976.

Festinger, L. A theory of social comparison processes. *Human Relations,* 1954, *7,* 117-140.

Festinger, L. *The human legacy.* New York: Columbia University Press, 1983.

Fierabend, I. K., & Fierabend, R. L. Aggressive behavior within politics, 1948-1962: A cross-national study. *Journal of Conflict Resolution,* 1966, *10,* 249-271.

Finison, L. J. Unemployment politics and the history of organized psychology. *American Psychologist,* 1976, *31,* 747-755.

Flavell, J. H., & Ross, L. (Eds.) *Social cognitive development: Frontiers and possible futures.* New York: Cambridge University Press, 1981.

Flavell, J. H., & Ross, L. (Eds.) *New directions in the study of social-cognitive development.* Cambridge: Cambridge University Press, in press.

Fox, R. The cultured animal. In J. F. Eisenberg & W. S. Dillon (Eds.), *Man and beast: Comparative social behavior.* Washington, D.C.: Smithsonian Institute Press, 1971.

Fromm, E. *Escape from freedom.* New York: Rinehart, 1941.

Gadamer, H. G. *Truth and method.* In G. Barden & J. Cumming (Eds.). New York: Seabury, 1975. (Originally published as *Wahrheit und methode.* Tubingen: J. C. B. Mohr, 1960).

Gadlin, H. Child discipline and the pursuit of the self: An historical interpretation. *Advances in child development and behavior* (Vol. 12). New York: Academic Press, 1978.

Gadlin, H., & Ingle, G. Through the one-way mirror: The limits of experimental self-reflection. *American Psychologist,* 1975, *30,* 1003-1009.

Gadlin, H., & Rubin, S. H. Interactionism. In A. R. Buss (Ed.), *Psychology in social context,* New York: Irvington, 1979.

Gallie, W. B. *Philosophy and the historical understanding.* London: Chatte and Windus, 1964.

Garfinkel, H. *Studies in ethnomethodology.* Englewood Cliffs, N.J.: Prentice-Hall, 1967.

Gauld, A., & Shotter, J. *Human action and its psychological investigation.* London: Routledge & Kegan Paul, 1977.

Gergen, K. J. Social psychology as history. *Journal of Personality and Social Psychology,* 1973, *26,* 309-320.

Gergen, K. J. Social psychology, science and history. *Personality and Social Psychology Bulletin,* 1976, *2,* 373-383.

Gergen, K. J. Stability, change and chance in understanding human development. In

N. Datan & H. Reese (Eds.), *Life-span developmental psychology: Dialectical perspectives on experimental research*. New York: Academic Press, 1977.

Gergen, K. J. Toward generative theory. *Journal of Personality and Social Psychology,* 1978, *36,* 1344-1360.

Gergen, K. J. *Toward transformation in social knowledge.* New York: Springer-Verlag, 1982.

Gergen, K. J., & Morawski, J. An alternative metatheory for social psychology. In L. Wheeler (Ed.), *Review of personality and social psychology* (Vol. 1). Beverly Hills, Calif.: 1980.

Gilligan, C. *In a different voice.* Cambridge, Mass.: Harvard University Press, 1982.

Ginsburg, G. P. (Ed.) *Emerging strategies in social psychological research.* Chichester, England: Wiley, 1979.

Gottman, J. M. *Time-series analysis: A comprehensive introduction for social scientists.* Cambridge, England: Cambridge University Press, 1981.

Graumann, C. F. Die Scheu des Psychologen vor den Interaktion. Ein Schisma und seine Geshichte. *Zeitschrift für Socialpsychologie,* 1979, *10,* 284-304.

Graumann, C. F. *Theorie und Geschichte.* Reihe Nr. 1, Archiv fur Geschichte der Psychologie, Psychologisches Institut, Universität Heidelberg, 1982.

Habermas, J. *Knowledge and human interest.* Boston: Beacon Press, 1971.

Hampden-Turner, C. *Radical man: The process of psycho-social development.* Cambridge, Mass.: Schenkman, 1970.

Harré, R. *Social being.* Oxford: Basil Blackwell, 1979.

Harré, R. Making social psychology scientific. In R. Gilmour & S. Duck (Eds.), *The development of social psychology.* New York: Academic Press, 1980.

Harré, R., & Secord, P. *Explanation of social behavior.* Oxford: Basil Blackwell, 1972.

Harris, A. E. Social dialectics and language: Mother and child construct the discourse. *Human Development,* 1975, *18,* 80-96.

Heelas, P., & Locke, A. *Indigenous psychologies: The anthropology of the self.* New York: Academic Press, 1981.

Helmreich, R. L., Spence, J. T., Beane, W. E., Lucker, G. W., & Matthews, K. A. Making it in academic psychology: Demographic and personality correlates of attainment. *Journal of Personality and Social Psychology,* 1980, *39,* 896-908.

Hempel, C. G. The function of general laws in history. In P. Gardiner (Ed.), *Theories of history.* Glencoe, Ill.: Free Press, 1959.

Higgins, E. T., Ruble, D. N., & Hartup, W. W. (Eds.) *Social cognition and social behavior: Developmental issues.* New York: Cambridge University Press, in press.

Himmelweit, H., Humphreys, P., Jaeger, M., & Katz, M. *How voters decide.* London: Academic Press, 1981.

Hirsch, E. D., Jr. *The aims of interpretation.* Chicago, Ill.: University of Chicago Press, 1976.

Hogan, R. T. Dialectic aspects of moral development. *Human Development,* 1974, *17,* 107-117.

Holzkamp, K. *Kritische Psychologie.* Hamburg: Fischer Taschenbuch Verlag, 1976.

Horkheimer, M. *Critical theory.* New York: Seabury Press, 1972.

Hovland, C. I., & Weiss, W. The influence of source credibility on communication effectiveness. *Public Opinion Quarterly,* 1951, *15,* 635-650.

Iggers, G. G. *The German conception of history.* Middletown, Conn.: Wesleyan University Press, 1968.

Israel, J. From level of aspiration to dissonance. In A. Buss (Ed.), *Psychology in social context.* New York: Irvington Publishers, 1979. (a)

Israel, J. *The language of dialectics and the dialectics of language.* New York: Humanities Press, 1979. (b)

James, W. *The principles of psychology.* New York: Henry Holt, 1890.

1. INTRODUCTION TO HISTORICAL SOCIAL PSYCHOLOGY 33

Janousek, J. On the Marxian concept of praxis. In J. Israel & H. Tajfel (Eds.), *The context of social psychology: A critical assessment.* London: Academic Press, 1972.

Jay, M. *The dialectical imagination.* London: Heinemann, 1973.

Jaynes, J. *The origin of consciousness in the breakdown of the bicameral mind.* New York: Houghton Mifflin, 1976.

Kendon, A., Harris, R. M., & Key, M. R. *Organization of behavior in face-to-face interaction.* The Hague: Mouton, 1975.

Kessler, S. J., & McKenna, W. *Gender: An ethnomethodological approach.* New York: Wiley, 1978.

Koch, S. Epilogue. In S. Koch (Ed.), *Psychology: A study of a science* (Vol. III). New York: McGraw-Hill, 1959.

Kreckel, M. A framework for the analysis of natural discourse. In M. Brenner (Ed.), *The structure of action.* Oxford, Blackwell, 1980.

Kroger, R. O. Explorations in ethogeny: With special reference to rules of address. *American Psychologist,* 1982, *37,* 810-820.

Kvale, S. Dialectics and research on remembering. In N. Datan & H. Reese (Eds.), *Life-span developmental psychology: Dialectical perspectives on experimental research.* New York: Academic Press, 1977.

Lana, R. E. Giambattista Vico and the history of social psychology. *Journal for the Theory of Social Behaviour,* 1980, *9,* 251-263.

Latané, B. Studies in social comparison: Introduction and overview. *Journal of Experimental Social Psychology,* 1966, *11,* 165-169.

Levinger, G. Toward the analysis of close relationships. *Journal of Experimental Social Psychology,* 1980, *16,* 510-544.

Levinger, G., & Huesmann, L. R. An "incremental exchange" perspective on the pair relationship. In K. J. Gergen, M. Greenberg, & R. H. Willis (Eds.), *Social exchange: Advances in theory and research.* New York: Plenum, 1980.

Levinger, G., & Snoek, J. D. *Attraction in relationships: A new look at interpersonal attraction.* Morristown, N.J.: Silver Burdett/General Learning Press, 1972.

Lipset, S. M., & Hofstadter, R. *Sociology and history: Methods.* New York: Basic Books, 1968.

Lonner, W. J. The search for psychological universals. In H. C. Triandis & W. W. Lambert (Eds.), *Handbook of cross-cultural psychology* (Vol. I). Boston: Allyn & Bacon, 1980.

Lotze, H. *Mikrokosmus Idean zur Naturgeschichte und Geschichte der Menscheit* (3 vols.). Leipzig: S. Hirzel, (1856-1864). English edition, New York: Scribner, 1897.

Lubek, I. A brief social psychological analysis of research on aggression in social psychology. In A. R. Buss (Ed.), *Psychology in social context.* New York: Irvington, 1979.

Mandelbaum, M. *The anatomy of historical knowledge.* Baltimore, Md: Johns Hopkins University Press, 1977.

Marsh, P. *Aggro, the illusion of violence.* London: J. M. Dent, 1978.

Marsh, P., Rosser, E., & Harré, R. *The rules of disorder.* London: Routledge & Kegan Paul, 1977.

Marx, K. *Capital: A critique of political economy* (Vol. I). New York: International Publishers, 1967.

McCleary, R., & Hay, R. A., Jr. *Applied time series analysis for the social sciences.* Beverly Hills, Calif.: Sage, 1980.

McClelland, D. C. *The achieving society.* Princeton, N.J.: Van Nostrand, 1961.

McGuire, W. J. The yin and yang of progress in social psychology: Seven koans. *Journal of Personality and Social Psychology,* 1973, *26,* 446-456.

McGuire, W. J. Historical comparisons: Testing psychological hypotheses with cross-era data. *International Journal of Psychology,* 1976, *11,* 161-183.

Meacham, J. A. A transactional model of remembering. In N. Datan & H. Reese (Eds.), *Life-span developmental psychology: Dialectical perspectives on experimental research.* New York: Academic Press, 1977.

Mink, L. O. Philosophical analysis and historical understanding. *Review of Metaphysics,* 1968, *21,* 667-698.

Morawski, J. G. On thinking about history as social psychology. *Personality and Social Psychology Bulletin,* 1982, *8,* 389-392. (a)

Morawski, J. G. Assessing psychology's moral heritage through our neglected Utopias. *American Psychologist,* 1982, *37,* 1082-1095. (b)

Moscovici, S. *Essai sur l'histoire humaine de la nature.* Paris: Flammarion, 1968.

Moscovici, S. Society and theory in social psychology. In J. Israel & H. Tajfel (Eds.), *The context of social psychology: A critical assessment.* New York: Academic Press, 1972.

Moscovici, S. *L'âge des foules.* Paris: Fayard, 1981.

Murchison, C. (Ed.) *A handbook of social psychology.* Worcester, Mass.: Clark University Press, 1935.

Nagel, E. Some issues in the logic of historical analysis. In P. Gardiner (Ed.), *Theories of history.* Glencoe, Ill.: Free Press, 1959.

Nesselroade, J. R., & Baltes, P. B. Adolescent personality development and historical change: 1970-1972. *Monographs for the Society for Research in Child Development,* 1974, *39,* (Ser. No. 154).

Ossorio, P. G. *What actually happens.* Columbia: University of South Carolina Press, 1978.

Overton, W. R., & Reese, H. W. Models of development: Methodological implications. In J. R. Nesselroade & H. W. Reese (Eds.), *Life-span developmental psychology: Methodological issues.* New York: Academic Press, 1973.

Pavlov, J. P. *Conditioned reflexes* (G. V. Anrep, trans.) London: Oxford University Press, 1927.

Pearce, W. B., & Cronen, V. E. *Communication, action and meaning.* New York: Praeger, 1980.

Peeters, H. F. M. *Kind en jeogdige in net begin van de moderne tijd.* Hilversum: Paul Brand, 1974.

Peeters, H. F. M. *Historische gedragswetenschap.* Meppel: Boom, 1978.

Pieterson, M., & van Hoorn, W. *Het technisch labyrint,* Amsterdam: Boom, 1981.

Porschnev, B. *Social psychology and history* (Trans. I. Savin). Moscow: Progress Publishers, 1970.

Psathas, G. (Ed.) *Everyday language, studies in ethnomethodology.* New York: Irvington, 1979.

Rappaport, L. On praxis and quasirationality. *Human Development,* 1975, *18,* 194-204.

Reese, H. W., & Overton, W. F. Models of development and theories of development. In L. R. Goulet & P. B. Baltes (Eds.), *Life-span developmental psychology: Research and theory.* New York: Academic Press, 1970.

Reis, H. T. An introduction to the use of structural equations: Prospects and problems. In L. Wheeler (Ed.), *Review of personality and social psychology* V. 3. Beverly Hills, CA: Sage, 1982.

Richardson, J., & Kroeber, A. L. *Three centuries of women's dress fashions, a quantitative analysis.* Berkeley, Calif: University of California Press, 1940.

Ricoeur, P. *Interpretation theory: Discourse and the surplus of meaning.* Fort Worth: The Texas Christian University Press, 1976.

Riegel, K. F. *Foundations of dialectical psychology.* New York: Academic Press, 1979.

Riley, M. W., & Nelson, E. E. Research on stability and change in social systems. In B. Barber & A. Inkeles (Eds.), *Stability and social change.* Boston: Little, Brown, 1971.

Rommetveit, R. *On message structure.* London: Wiley, 1974.

Rosnow, R. L. The prophetic vision of Giambattista Vico: Implications for the state of social psychological theory. *Journal of Personality and Social Psychology*, 1978, *36*, 1322-1331.

Rosnow, R. L. *Paradigms in transition.* New York: Oxford University Press, 1981.

Rowney, D. K., & Graham, J. Q. (Eds.) *Quantitative history.* Homewood, Ill.: Dorsey Press, 1969.

Ruble, D. N., & Rholes, W. S. The development of children's perceptions and attributions about their social world. In J. Harvey, W. Ickes, & R. Kidd (Eds.), *New directions in attribution research* (Vol. 3). Hillsdale, N.J.: Lawrence Erlbaum Associates, 1981.

Runyan, W. M. *Life histories and psychobiography: Explorations in theory and method.* New York: Oxford University Press, 1982.

Rychlak, J. F. (Ed.) *Dialectic: Humanistic rationale for behavior and development.* Basel: Karger, 1976.

Ryff, C. D. The phenomenological approach to personality development in adulthood and aging. In P. B. Baltes & O. G. Brim (Eds.), *Life-span development and behavior* (Vol. 6). New York: Academic Press, 1983.

Sabini, J., & Silver, M. *The moralities of everyday life.* New York: Oxford University Press, 1982.

Samelson, F. History, origin, myth and ideology: Comte's 'discovery' of social psychology. *Journal of the Theory of Social Behavior*, 1974, *4*, 217-231.

Samelson, F. Putting psychology on the map: Ideology and intelligence testing. In A. Buss (Ed.), *Psychology in social context.* New York: Irvington, 1979.

Sampson, E. E. Cognitive psychology as ideology. *American Psychologist*, 1981, *36*, 730-743.

Schlenker, B. R. On the ethogenic approach: Etiquette and revolution. In L. Berkowitz, (Ed.), *Advances in experimental social psychology* (Vol. 10). New York: Academic Press, 1977.

Serafica, F. C. (Ed.) *Social-cognitive development in context.* New York: Guilford, 1982.

Shaver, P., & Klinnert, M. Schacter's theories of affiliation and emotion: Implications of developmental research. In L. Wheeler (Ed.), *Review of personality and social psychology* (Vol. 3). Beverly Hills, Calif.: Sage, 1982.

Shotter, J. Vico, moral worlds, accountability and personhood. In P. Heelas & A. Lock (Eds.), *Indigenous psychologies.* New York: Academic Press, 1981.

Shweder, R. A., & Bourne, E. Does the concept of the person vary cross-culturally? In A. J. Marsella & G. White (Eds.), *Cultural conceptions of mental health and therapy.* Boston: Reidel, 1982.

Simonton, D. K. Socio-cultural context of individual creativity: A trans-historical time-series analysis. *Journal of Personality & Social Psychology*, 1975, *32*, 1119-1133.

Smith, M. B. Is experimental social psychology advancing? *Journal of Experimental Social Psychology*, 1972, *8*, 86-96.

Smith, M. B. A dialectical social psychology? Comments on a symposium. *Personality and Social Psychology Bulletin*, 1977, *3*, 719-724.

Smith, M. B. Attitudes, values and selfhood. In H. E. Howe & M. M. Page (Eds.), *Nebraska Symposium on Motivation.* Lincoln: University of Nebraska Press, 1980.

Spencer, H. *The principles of sociology* (Vol. 1). New York: Appleton, 1876-97, 3 vols.

Spengler, O. *The decline of the West.* New York: Knopf, 1926.

Stone, L. *The past and the present.* Boston: Routledge & Kegan Paul, 1982.

Sullivan, H. S. *The interpersonal theory of psychiatry.* New York: Norton, 1953.

Suls, J. M., & Miller, R. C. (Eds.) *Social comparison processes: Theoretical and empirical perspectives.* Washington, D.C.: Hemisphere, 1977.

Suls, J., & Mullen, B. From the cradle to the grave: Comparison and self-evaluation across the life-span. In J. Suls (Ed.), *Psychological perspectives on the self.* Hillsdale, N.J.: Lawrence Erlbaum Associates, 1982.

Sumner, W. G. *What social classes are to each other.* New York: Harper, 1883.
Swierenga, R. P. (Ed.) *Quantification in American history.* New York: Atheneum, 1970.
Taylor, C. *The explanation of behavior.* London: Routledge & Kegan Paul, 1964.
Taylor, C. Interpretation and the sciences of man. *The Review of Metaphysics,* 1971, *25,* No. 1.
Tesser, A. Self-generated attitude change. In L. Berkowitz (Ed.), *Advances in experimental social psychology* (Vol. 11). New York: Academic Press, 1978.
Thernstrom, S. Quantitative methods in history: Some notes. In S. M. Lipset & R. Hofstadter (Eds.), *Sociology and history methods.* New York: Basic Books, 1968.
Tilly, C. *From mobilization to revolution.* Reading, Mass.: Addison-Wesley, 1978.
van den Berg, J. H. *The changing nature of man.* New York: Norton, 1961.
van Hoorn, W. *As images unwind.* Amsterdam: Wutt Adams, 1972.
Veroff, J., Douvan, E., & Kulka, R. *The inner American: A self-portrait from 1957 to 1976.* New York: Basic Books, 1981.
Veroff, J., Kulka, R., & Douvan, E. Comparison of American motives: 1957 vs. 1976. *Journal of Personality and Social Psychology,* 1980, *39,* 1249-1262.
Vico, G. *Principles of the new science of Giambattista Vico* (1st edn. 1744). Ithaca, N.Y.: Cornell University Press, 1975.
Vygotsky, L. S. *Thought and language.* Cambridge, Mass.: MIT Press, 1961. (Originally published in 1934).
Wexler, P. *Critical social psychology.* Boston: Routledge & Kegan Paul, 1983.
White, M. *Foundations of historical knowledge.* New York: Harper, 1965.
Wicklund, R. A. *Freedom and reactance.* Potomac, Md.: Lawrence Erlbaum Associates, 1974.
Wilson, E. O. *On human nature.* Cambridge, Mass.: Harvard University Press, 1978.
Winch, P. *The idea of a social science.* London: Routledge & Kegan Paul, 1958. (Originally published in 1946).
Woodward, W. R. From the science of language to *Volkerpsychologie:* Lotze, Steinthal, Lazarus and Wundt. Archiv fur Geschichte der Psychologie, Reihe Nr. 2, 1982. Psychologisches Institut, Universitat Heidelberg.
Wundt, W. *Volkerpsychologie. Eine Untersuchung der Entwicklungsgesetze von Sprache, Mythus und Sitte* (10 vols.). Leipzig: Englemann, 1900-1920.
Wundt, W. *Elements of folk psychology* (trans. E. L. Schaub). New York: Macmillan, 1916. (Originally published as *Elemente der Völkerpsychologie,* 1912).

2 Historiography as a Metatheoretical Text for Social Psychology

J. G. Morawski
Wesleyan University

The linkages formed between history and psychology have consisted primarily of applying psychological theory and methods to historical inquiry. These have ranged from using traditional psychoanalytic models in historical interpretation to performing quantitative analyses on archival materials. Whatever the specific linkages, the general assumption has been that it is history that would benefit from any liaison with psychology. But this one-sided view of the relationship obscures both historical fact and future possiblities. The history of psychology, especially social psychology, reveals a number of significant attempts to bring historical theory and methods to research practices. Of particular note are Wilhelm Wundt's proposals for a social psychology (folk psychology) based on historical understanding (Blumenthal, 1975; Bringmann & Tweney, 1980), an entire section of the first *Handbook of Social Psychology* devoted to social histories (Murchison, 1935), and repeated efforts to establish historical social science (Barnes, 1925, 1948; Goldenweiser, 1933). The list of examples could be expanded considerably if one includes evolutionary models of social behavior, biographical or life-span studies, and the assorted archival methods for studying social phenomena.

Many of these projects to establish what may be called "historical thinking" in social psychology were short-lived, and their abandonment is closely tied to disciplinary politics. The attempted integrations of historical thinking have come precariously close to the practices of social historians, and the professional attitudes of disciplinary propriety and self-identity prevalent through much of the century discouraged such convergence

(Barnes, 1948). Perhaps even more important to ensuring disciplinary demarcations was the emerging isomorphism between a discipline and its methodological commitments. Once allied with psychology proper, social psychology adopted the rigorous methods associated with positivism while historians remained skeptical of that doctrine. Instead, historians permitted a certain methodological and epistemological pluralism, an attitude that has prompted continued reflection and that consequently has fostered something of a disciplinary autonomy and, more recently, what might even be called a "liberation" discourse on theory and practice.

As social psychologists have come to re-evaluate their experimental, specifically positivist heritage, the developments in historiography can no longer be considered patently irrelevant. Among the quandaries that have beset social psychology are several problems regarding the conventional presuppositions about human nature—the nature of both the investigator who is seeking knowledge and of the object of that knowledge search (Armistead, 1974; Gergen, 1973; Harré & Secord, 1972; Israel, 1972; Rosnow, 1981; Sarason, 1981). A number of these presuppositions have come under scrutiny, but the present discussion concerns three particularly germane ones. First, interests that inform the researcher's selection and conceptualization of subject matter have been held to be of minor, if any, importance to constructing and evaluating theory. Second, the transhistorical stability of social phenomena generally has been assumed without either empirical testing or critical assessment. Third, researchers have tried to locate explanations for social phenomena almost solely within a mechanistic model of sufficient or necessary causes and have disregarded other possible modes of explanation. Within social psychology there is now substantial research that recognizes the limitations of these presuppositions and that offers some metatheoretical alternatives. These developments clearly indicate a refusal to "lock up history in a museum" (Habermas, 1971, p. 316) or to disavow critical reflection whenever the phenomenon under study is psychological. Once social psychologists deliberate on such conventional assumptions, the commonalities between their pursuits and those of historians become even more striking.

The appearance of commonalities, however, can only be substantiated through better acquaintance with historical scholarship, and suggests the worth of assaying how historians have confronted the aforementioned problems. To do so, it is important to begin with a general account of the limitations of social psychology. Although many illustrative cases could be inspected, the recent research on sex roles is an exceptionally clear example for the perplexities in sex-role research provide multiple yet concrete grounds for earnest consideration of historiographic alternatives.

QUANDARIES IN THE STUDY OF MASCULINE AND FEMININE

Psychologists of varied theoretical orientations have sought to understand the dimensions that distinguish the personality and social psychology of males and females. These distinctions have been identified in the psychological concepts of masculinity and femininity and their concomitant social roles. Since the pioneering work of Terman and Miles in the thirties, numerous inventories assessing masculinity and femininity, or an individual's sex-role orientation, have been developed and utilized in psychological experiments and personality assessments. In the last ten years, critical studies of sex-role research have posed an increasingly serious challenge to the validity of this research program. The conventional models of sex roles have been found laden with normative values about the oppositional nature of these roles (Bem, 1972; Bernard, 1976; Carlson, 1972); differential evaluation of male and female attributes with preferred attributes generally associated with males (Favreau, 1977; Helson, 1972; Rosenberg, 1973); and with normative prescriptions for the desired consequences of sex-role acquisition (Bem, 1972; Block, 1973). Traditional theories were also found to assume stability of sex roles throughout adulthood and across historical periods despite substantial evidence of role flexibility, change, and context-dependence (Angrist, 1972; Emmerich, 1973; Hoffman, 1977; Maracek, 1979).

The major criticisms of sex-role research directly approached the problems of value stipulations, the temporality of social action, and the limits of acontextual causal explanations. A major attempt to rectify these problems occurred with formulation of the gender-fluid concept of androgyny. The new theorists postulated a mode of behavior where desirable masculine and feminine characteristics are adopted with reference to the situational demands, not in accordance with ascribed gender roles. In recognizing the normality of masculine and feminine traits within the same individual, the concept encompasses a broader range of "ideals" about appropriate behavior (Bem, 1974, 1977; Spence, Helmreich, & Stapp, 1975), and the concept has been anticipated as being sensitive to life-span and cultural transformations as well as specific contexts (Bernard, 1976; Maracek, 1979; M. White, 1979).

If judged by the volume of empirical research the concept of androgyny has satisfied many who found the conventional sex-role models inadequate. However, upon closer examination, its correctives prove to be somewhat illusory and, in fact, may not represent any exemplary improvements over previous models. In presenting androgyny as a superior or psychologically healthier mode of functioning, the problem of value assumptions is not alleviated. For instance, the "self-contained individualism" of the androgynous person also is a debatable yet essentially unquestioned attribute of mental health. Values associated with masculine and feminine are similarly retained, thus contributing to their ossification as universal characteristics (Lott, 1981; Rebecca & Hefner, 1979). The concept introduces problematic if not unrealizable prescriptions for psychological well-being (Kenworthy, 1979; Sampson, 1977), not to mention its neglect to attend to negative attributes and gender similarities (Rosen & Rekers, 1980; White, 1979). Although sensitive to change in gender-related actions within the individual, the model does not account for broader social transformations that affect these actions (Kaplan, 1979; Kenworthy, 1979; Worell, 1979). Thus, androgyny theory attempts to replace models that were circumscribed by history and culture but fails to confront its own historically constituted limitations by assuming transhistorical stability. The newer sex-role model renovates rather than replaces these two presuppositions about human nature and social inquiry that were criticized initially. It also suggests an absence of critical examination of the simple causal model which underlies the entire enterprise of explaining gender-related actions. Such renovations show the limitations of merely modifying the superficial manifestations of the constrictive presuppositions.

Some social psychologists have confronted these problems by positing a substantially different metatheory and consequently, different methods of inquiry (Brenner, Marsh, & Brenner, 1978; Gergen & Morawski, 1980; Gergen, 1978; Harre & Secord, 1972; Rosnow, 1981; Sampson, 1978; Sarason, 1981; Shotter, 1975). These alternatives demand a critical explication of the value bases of theory and the suspension of causal and mechanistic explanations of human action in order to consider the dialectical processes, intentional actions, and the social construction of rules and roles that may guide behavior. The alternatives often involve an interpretation of human action that would seek meaningfulness through understanding of the particular social and historical context.

Both the agenda for new metatheory and the failure of corrective revisions such as those attempted in sex-role research lend reasonableness to the ways that historians have confronted similiar problems. As it will become apparent, these historiographical issues do not address methodological concerns in the classical sense of engineering the experiment or maximizing dimensions of control and objectivity. Social psychologists have demonstrated sophistication at this level of methodological thinking. Where developments are now needed is in the decisions about the presuppositions or underlying assumptions which direct our theorizing and empirical inquiries. For instance, in deliberating plausible explanations for a given social phenomenon, concerted attention should be given to the basic premises about *what constitutes a good explanation or argument,* an essential question given the frequent inadequacy of engaging mechanistic or positivistic criteria for adequate explanation.

PLURALISM IN HISTORY

For present purposes, historiography can be defined initially by distinguishing it, on the one hand, from historical methods which involve locating, collecting, and editing evidence, and on the other hand, from the philosophy of history which typically entertains more speculative questions about the meaning of history and the development of human culture as a whole. Although in practice these distinctions are blurred, historiographical concern centers on the intervening processes between data collection and any final or synthesis of findings. Historiography, then, concerns how "historians put into written words what they already know experientially and diffusely about the past, to organize it into coherent and sequential statements in order to make it fully accessible first to themselves and then to others" (Hexter, 1968, p. 372). It explores the modes of explaining, narrating, interpreting, and generalizing from the collected records of events.

Through these functions, historiography has served as a central arena for ascertaining the nature of history, including its status as an art, science, and independent mode of inquiry (see Hughes, 1964), along with the decision rules for what makes a sound explanation of human events. A focal debate has continued around the claim that, like scientific statements, historical explanations must refer to a general law or law like regularity and employ deductive methods of inquiry. Historians' continual reluctance to endorse this claim indicates reservations toward positivist philosophy and has been instrumental in a developing sense of autonomy of history. The debate has prompted clarification of a number of approaches to historical explanations and, in turn, has engendered a certain pluralism in the practice of history.

HISTORICAL EXPLANATIONS

Despite historians' growing acquaintance with analytic and quantitative methods (Kammen, 1980), their discipline has maintained a comprehensive perspective on "explanation." Whereas social psychology has tended to follow the dictates of the conventional philosophy of science and to identify adequate "explanation" with a scientific, usually deductive strategy of locating causal relations, history has certified no singular model of explanations. Woven throughout discussions on historical explanation is a thread of tolerance that first, allows for the realization that models of explanation can not simply be imported from philosophy or any other discipline but should be compatible with indigenous practices in history, and second, entertains more than one form of what constitutes an adequate explanation. This does not mean, of course, that historians invoke anarchist principles in the selection and judgment of explanatory modes. On the contrary, discrepant positions have led to an extensive and animated literature on the virtues of various approaches to explanation. These very conditions have cultivated rich discourse on the possibilities for explaining the occurrence of human events.

Without delving into the intricacies of the ongoing debates or placing bets on the success of any model over the others, it is possible to delineate the variety of explanatory models. Three of these are of particular interest for psychology; positivist or law like, rational, and narrative. While the narrative type may be seen as a special case of rational explanations, the recent and innovative work on that type warrants special scrutiny.

Positive or Law Like Explanations

The most precisely defined yet probably most contested view holds that all real historical explanations are logically equivalent to explanations in natural science. The claim that historical explanations should be subsumed under the general rubric of scientific explanation represents an "assimilationist" position, which implies subsumption of historical explanations under those of the sciences. It can be contrasted with an "autonomous" position, which asserts the autonomy of historical explanations. Articulated in the most direct form by Hempel (1942, 1962), the covering-law model holds that a genuine explantion is deductive in form such that the event being explained (the explanandum) is deducible from a set of premises (explanans) or law like statements that describe the occurrence of certain events under certain circumstances. Hempel gave the following example: "Dust bowl farmers migrate to California 'because' continual drought and sandstorms render their existence increasingly precarious, and because California seems to them to offer so much better living conditions." A generalization supporting the explanation is that "populations will tend to migrate to regions which offer better living conditions" (1942, pp. 349–350).

The positivist, or "covering-law" model as it has been termed, is strongly criticized as being both limited and inappropriate for history (see Donogan, 1964; Dray, 1957; Mandelbaum, 1961; Scriven, 1966). The model poses several serious problems: that historical explanations rarely if ever can offer complete knowledge of the explanandum or explanans as is demanded, that no set of available deductive operations exists (or can exist), and simply that few historians' real explanations are in accord with the model. These criticisms have illuminated the difficulty and, frequently, the impossibility of exercising the model. These arguments subsequently influenced more concentrated study of other explanatory models and of the benefits of acknowledging the "autonomy" of historical understanding (Mink, 1965).

Rational Explanations

The "rational" form refers to those explanatory modes where the connections between events (or between dispositions, intentions, and events) require inferences other than those adduced empirically, but nonetheless form genuine explanations. It is important to note that arguments for rational explanations do not necessarily assume that empirical laws are not possible, but that they are not appropriate for all inquiries at hand or are not sufficient for the problem being investigated (see Atkinson, 1978; Mink, 1965). One such rational explanatory mode rests on an idealist base that asserts that historical explanation requires knowledge not merely of observable actions but also of the intentions and thoughts of the agents under study. R. G. Collingwood (1946) is representative of this stance in claiming that "for history, the object to be discovered is not the mere event, but the thought expressed in it. To discover that thought is already to understand it" (p. 214). Less extreme than Collingwood's idealism is the thesis that explanations should encompass the *reasons* behind the occurrence of a particular event: "Understanding is achieved when the historian can see the reasonableness of a man's doing what this agent did, given the beliefs and purposes referred to; his action can then be explained as having been an 'appropriate' one. . . ." Here "what is brought out by such considerations is a conceptual connection between understanding a man's action and discerning its rationale" (Dray, 1963, p. 108). Similar to this thesis of reasons is the position that historical explanations consist of identifying not simply observable relations, but also intrinsic relations between events. That is, the only way to account for the relations between events is by giving the fullest possible account of these events such that "The relation *between* events is always other events, and it is established in history by a full relation *of* the events. The conception of cause is thus replaced by the exhibition of a world of events intrinsically related to one another in which no *lacuna* is tolerated" (Oakeshott, 1966, p. 209).

This view, that genuine historical explanations depend on the various forms of relations perceived between events, or even between events and dispositions or intentions, resembles another view of rational explanation in which what counts as an explanation can only be made clear by reference to the broader context of the event to be explained. Explanation that depends on an exposition of the conditions particular to that event are the type that Pepper (1942) associated with the world view of "contextualism." It emphasizes the change and novelty in all events, and understanding is sought by re-presenting these *events* through examination of their texture, and the details and relations comprising their unique qualities.

Explanation of this form may be concerned with context in two ways: the context of the event to be explained and the context of the expositors of the account (historians, and their audience). In the former case it is contended that a coherent account of an event necessitates reference to the particular conditions—intentions, dispositions, perceived consequences surrounding its occurrence, as well as the immediate actions. Yet the task of contextual explanation is more complex than the weaving of coherent relations from the threads of the various conditions. It requires an unpacking of typical accounts by showing that "the distinction between cause and effect is itself a limited one, in the sense of being highly context-dependent. What is a cause in one context can be seen as itself a combination of cause and effect in another context" (Scriven, 1966, p. 241).

The second focus of a contextualist model is on the perspective or position of the expositor. As Pepper noted, contextualism embodies the rather blunt proviso that "we have to deal with the world as we meet it, and we meet it only in the events of the epoch in which we are living" (1942, p. 236). The concept of cause itself thus can be seen as dependent on the context of the researcher: "When we are looking for causes we are looking for explanations in terms of a few factors or a single factor; and what counts as an explanation is whatever fills the gap in the inquirer's or reader's understanding" (Scriven, 1966, p. 256). An explanation, then, depends on what is known and what one wants to know. The connections made in explaining must meet the attendant context-dependent criteria of intelligibility, adequacy, and correctness. These criteria command inspection of the conditions in which the expositor conceptualizes a question or puzzle and attains what is taken as a meaningful, adequate or correct solution (Passmore, 1962; Scriven, 1966; Wise, 1980). An explanation consequently must be understood in terms of the personal interests of the expositor, the perspective and contrasts signified by setting some event up as a "puzzle," and even the expositor's acceptance of the norms or rules of rationality held by the professional community.

Narrative Explanations

The idea of narrative as explanation is an extension of rational explanations. Here it is accepted that historical explanation is judged in terms of the development of a coherent story or narrative of past events. That is, the narrative constructed by the historian "is explanatory in itself, regardless of whether the events, actions, situations purportedly explained are connectable with antecedent events, etc., by laws or generalizations, or of whether they were the objects of anybody's rational endeavor" (Atkinson, 1978, p. 128). More than any of the other types, the narrative explanation acknowledges autonomous historical understanding, and although it is not generally presented as such, it does not necessarily obviate the possibility that history may entail multiple types of explanation (Atkinson, 1978; Dray, 1971).

The validity of narrative explanations obviously cannot rest on the simple assertion that the telling of a story, the development of some narrative account, in itself constitutes an adequate explanation. Investigations of the underlying structure of narrative explanations have located other requirements. Narrativists agree on the necessity for offering potentially "truthful" or verifiable evidence, and for reporting events in some chronological fashion. But they occasionally differ on the precise manifestation of these qualities in narratives. At least two positions have evolved from this questioning. The first, or what could be called a pluralist stance, claims that narrative explanations rely on the making of causal linkages, rational or lawlike, but still insist that narratives have properties which are unique to real historical understanding (Danto, 1965). These properties typically give coherence and intelligibility to the narrative as evidenced, for instance, in the manner that a "continuing central subject" structures the selection of salient facts and ordering of events (see Dray, 1971).

The stronger version of the narrativist claim is that the narrative *itself* is explanatory and thus has its own form of coherence and intelligibility (Gallie, 1964; Louch, 1969). This position has prompted considerable efforts to elucidate the characteristics that distinguish narrative explanation and the criteria by which it is judged as true or not true, coherent or incoherent. Mink (1978) has given a promising focus to these efforts by suggesting that the narrative be viewed as a cognitive facility: "a primary and irreducible form of comprehension that is used to give form to experience" (p. 132). In this case, narrative must be seen as a "cognitive instrument" deserving analysis on its own terms. Such recognition requires the development of approaches to issues of narrative objectivity, the truth value of complex wholes, and the relation of events or processes. Others have identified intelligibility in narrative with its "synthetic unity" or "delineation of a whole of nonsimultaneous parts" (Dray, 1971, p. 169). "Synthetic unity" may refer to the logical texture of contingencies in narrative (Gallie, 1964), the process of making continuity visible (Louch, 1969), the deployment of "process categories" (Mink, 1968), or to a type of synthetic understanding that may "presuppose" other models of understanding such as causal or rational ones (Dray, 1971). Attention also is being directed toward understanding in what ways the explanatory capability of narratives is dependent on the context of the historical question is asked. From this perspective, adequate accounts depend at least in part on the expectations in scholarship at that time and "can only be historically explanatory if they, and the questions which prompt them, can be felt to be in some way continuous with existing history" (Atkinson, 1978, p. 135).

Narrative explanations, then, while they have been long in use by historians and others (Butterfield, 1968; Scholes & Kellogg, 1966), are now receiving due hearing as a distinct explanatory form. And as the unique cognitive qualities of narratives are mined (Hull, 1975; Mink, 1978), their relevance to what have been seen as psychological questions emerges. Stipulating narrative structures requires consideration of experiences of time (Ricoeur, 1980), and of the objectives of the expositors whether they be historians (H. White, 1973, 1980), writers (Gossman, 1978), or psychologists (Schafer, 1980). Perhaps the most provocative stipulation is that a narrative, in accounting for real events, actually demonstrates that "the reality of these events does not consist in the fact that they occurred but that, first of all, they were remembered, and second, that they are capable of finding a place in a chronologically ordered sequence" (H. White, 1980, p. 23).

In summary, studies of explanatory models, while not conclusive, do, however, elucidate the possible forms that the explanation of human events can take and the assumptions about veridical testimony that underlie these forms. With these studies mechanistic concepts of causality and explanation can be situated within a variegated and complex mosaic of explanatory modes. Social psychologists, especially when attending to the temporality of social life, can find in the discourse on historical explanation a number of alternatives to a stark causal model of analysis. In offering other ways of accounting for social events, these models of explanation also show how any plausible account demands understanding of the multiple factors that render a given explanation adequate, coherent, and intelligible—they illustrate the possibilities for constructing new rules to guide social inquiry. However, such opportunities to expand our explanatory bases are but part of the characteristics of historical thinking, for the study of history also reveals varied approaches toward its subject matter. A compendium of such approaches might focus on the central subjects of historical inquiry and then would include such categories as biography, prosopography, political history and the history of ideas. These categories may inform the social psychologist of other possibilities for studying social life besides the cynosure of the individual. Beyond the question of central subject is another level of historical thinking about subject matter that is rarely developed in social psychological studies: the process of charting events across time and of making these temporally related events intelligible. At

MODELS OF CHANGE

> What was our fathers' chart of history? As they saw it, it was a tale told by God, unfolding itself from the creation through the Fall and the Redemption to the Last Judgment. As Professor Geyl says he sees it, it seems like a tale told by an idiot, signifying nothing. You may not agree with our father's view that history is a revelation of God's providence, but it is a poor exchange, isn't it, to swap their faith for the view that history makes no sense. (Gardiner, 1959, p. 313)

These words formed part of Arnold Toynbee's rejoinder to a critic, a defense of his seemingly pessimistic theory of the inevitable decline of civilizations. Although this particular debate is rather insignificant in the history of history, it illustrates the problems associated with identifying definitive patterns of change—from the simple question of whether or not such patterns exist (or persist) to the implications of viewing history as "determined," as adhering to regular tempos.

Despite an apparent disinterest in temporal regularities among contemporary historians, discernable patterns do appear, usually in less conspicuous forms, but remain, nevertheless, integral to the particular historical account. For instance, in a study of narrative forms of nineteenth-century histories, H. White (1973) noted various "prefigurations" regarding the direction of historical change, and in a study of psychohistorians, Pomper (1982) located "architechtonic principles" with which they structured continuity and change. Even purportedly atheoretical accounts, such as E. G. Boring's chronology of experimental psychology, wields a template for structuring change. His well-known text, *A History of Experimental Psychology* (1950), harbors a progressive model of change in which psychological science is depicted as advancing through cumulative contributions of knowledge towards some improved (alas, present) state (see O'Donnell, 1979).

The variety of such models, and the possibilities of others yet unrecognized, necessitates that their treatment here be limited to only the most prominent of them: uniformity and homeostasis, evolution and progress, crisis and revolution, cyclicity or recurrence, and decline or degeneration. These represent minimalist models in the sense that they indicate only directionality of change and will be described primarily as such. However, they could be evaluated in terms of other qualities such as *rate of change, spatial or subject characteristics* (reference to individual, nation-state or universal phenomena), *affective components,* or some combination of these. Thus the following taxonomy does not include the possible combinations and juxtapositions of models of time. For instance, as proposed by the *Annales* historian, Braudel (1956), there may be distinct structures or "conceptions" of time which can be associated with different events or entities in material culture. Also omitted is discussion of the recent objections to any manifestations of order in history. Foucault (1970) is perhaps the best exemplar of those who reject both notions of continuity of any unitary patterns in history; instead Foucault opts for a structural archaeology and the analysis of historical events on what may be conceived of as a vertical axis rather than a horizontal one. In describing the root modes for conceptualizing time, the following taxonomy opens way for further consideration of the permutations of as well as the contentions to those basic modes.

Uniformity and homeostasis. The view that humans or institutions remain uniform is complicated by the inevitable awareness of the passing of time. For this reason the idea of uniformity and continuity frequently has been associated with geological notions of time where change is admitted while constancy or stability also is recognized (Bochner, 1968). A stark model of homeostasis is apparent in Schopenhauer's assertion that "History shows on every side only the same thing under different forms.... The chapters of the history of nations are at bottom different only through the names and dates; the really essential content is everywhere the same" (quoted in Nisbet, 1980, pp. 319-320). The homeostatic model parallels a geological principle of uniformism where the causes of past geological change are identical to those of current change. The principle has been extended in the thesis that human knowledge or interests remains constant over generations, or alternatively, that change consists of minor fluctuations or perturbations within a particular system that remain constant over the longer course of time. The latter thesis is implied in contemporary cybernetic or systems models which describe homeostasis within an organism or system. The obvious difficulties inherent in any conjectures of stability explain why, besides a few religious or quasi-religious doctrines, uniformity models now are rarely found in historical accounts.

Evolution and progress. Modern accounts most commonly posit continuous change which ultimately demonstrates progress, or advancement over previous conditions. The model has been infused with biological images of growth and evolution as well as philosophical tenets of human perfectibility (Bury, 1920; Manuel, 1965; Nisbet, 1980; Passmore, 1970). Evolutionary models of human progress were shared among earlier social theorists and historians, even those as diverse as Auguste Comte, Herbert Spencer, Frederich Nietzsche, William James, and Henri Bergson. Such models have guided the work of many American historians, as evidenced in James Harvey Robinson's claim that "Society today is engaged in a tremendous and unprecedented effort to better itself in manifold ways. Never has our knowledge of the world and of man been so great as it now is...." For many historians this perspective mandated special responsibilities to promote a "historical-mindedness," which would contribute to intellectual life and "promote rational progress as nothing else can do" (quoted in Stern, 1956, p. 265).

The idea of continued advance dominated much of early twentieth century history of science such that science was dictated as progressing toward some true or final knowledge. Scholars have since challenged the presumption that progress inevitably proceeds from the use of scientific methods and the cumulation of experimental findings (Agassi, 1963; Teich & Young, 1973). However, some researchers continue to posit progressive models of the history of science by applying contemporary evolution theory to changes in scientific practices (see Richards, 1981).

Revolution and crisis. Both revolution and crisis refer to discontinuity or interruptions in ongoing patterns, but whereas the former model implies either transition to another state or a return to the starting point, the model of crisis does not convey any specific resolution of the discontinuity. These models consquently bear a complex relation to one another despite the fact that in historical usage they are sometimes juxtaposed, alternated, or conjoined. Whether used solely in reference to political programs or applied more generally to cultural, intellectual, or artistic conditions, models of revolutionary change encompass disruptions or irresolvable controversies between parts of a larger system; these disruptions typically result in decisive actions. Revolutionary models also can incorporate the idea of crisis, as in Marx's theory, by defining crises as periodic disturbances in equilibrium that eventually escalate to a critical condition for revolutionary change (Starn, 1971). Framed in this manner the enactment of crisis and/or revolution may be subsumed under a more integrative dialectic model where the discontinuity created by antithetical events, actions, or ideas precede sudden or dramatic turning points (Manuel, 1965). Thomas Kuhn (1962) described a somewhat different relation, proposing that in science, periods of intellectual stasis are interruped by anomalous findings and eventually brought to a "crisis" state. If the anomaly cannot be integrated harmoniously into the dominant paradigm, the disequilibrium engenders revolution.

Models of crisis without revolutionary consequences assume no simple or immediate resolution to tensions and disruptions, yet they allow for the possibility of other pronounced effects. For instance, Burton Bledstein (1976) has suggested that a cultural crisis was central to the development of professionalism in America. He argued that the abundance of reading materials and a growing literate population in mid-nineteenth-century America tended to "fragment the attention of the people, to encourage confusion and frustration that gave way to self-doubt and mistrust" (p. 78). This "crisis in confidence" strongly influenced the rise of the professions, as experts came to be seen as saviors, and "the citizen became a client whose obligation was to trust the professional. Legitimate authority now resided in special places, like the courtroom, the classroom, and the hospital; and it resided in special words shared only by experts" (Bledstein, 1976, pp. 78-79). Overall, the possible variations in the origins and eventual resolution or denouement of a crisis condition suggest the need for constructing a richer vocabulary for dealing with crisis models (see Ladurie, 1978, pp. 270-89; Mauser, 1968; Starn, 1971).

Cyclicity or recurrence. Any cyclical model of history holds that events undergo recurrent cycles of change, usually through repeated phases of growth and decay. While admitting reversal and recurrence in the process of human affairs, cyclical models do not necessarily include the prospect of eternal repetition. These models often assume that each cycle represents an improvement over the preceding ones. Such a variation endows recurrences with an ascending or spiral quality as seen in Giambattisto Vico's model of history (Capognigri, 1953; Rosnow, 1978). Some of the more recent historians who have employed cyclical models, such as Oswald Spengler and Arnold Toynbee, express less certainty about progressive elements in historical repetition. Even more recent and less optimistic is the cyclical model employed by the neurobiologist Gunther Stent (1978) to explain the ultimate limits of scientific advance. Cyclical models have also been utilized on scales considerably more modest than world history; for instance, one approach to the social history of the family develops a construct of a "family cycle" to assess changes in the collective family unit across time (Hareven, 1978).

Decline or degeneration. The idea of human history as a graph of continual decline is applied more often to particular periods than to entire civilizations. Further, since decline presumes some prior state, say that of a Golden Age or the Noble Savage, the model often is combined with progressive ones to portray cyclical or undulating patterns of change (Starn, 1975). Owing to the pessimism typically associated with models of decadence and decline, these models often receive adamant criticism (Winthrop, 1971) and are even labeled as cases of "moral terrorism" (Manuel, 1965). In addition to implications of deterioration found in the cyclical models of Spengler, Toynbee, and Stent, decline is prominent in the works of such twentieth-century figures as Jose Ortega y Gassett and Herbert Marcuse, as well as those historians who recognize progressive ideals as illusions (Nisbet, 1980; Winthrop, 1971).

The fact that few contemporary historians work to establish or articulate global models of change does not negate their importance for even historians dealing with restricted periods and subjects embrace models to comprehend change and, hence, rely on these often tacit guides for identifying, bracketing, and structuring materials into meaningful patterns. A singular benefit of delineating models of change is what these examinations give to an understanding of historical discourse. That is, identification of such basic models or structures opens the way for examining the rule systems by which historians make judgments about what constitutes a "decline" (Starn, 1975), or an adequate narrative account (Kellner, 1975). Although few historians work with an explicit and fully-developed model of change, it still remains that they nevertheless rely on informal models to structure or order events, and within this structure it may be possible to locate criteria with which to evaluate the coherence of that history (Humphreys, 1980; White, 1973).

SKEPTICAL OBJECTIVITY

The assumed dichotomy between facts and values that has purportedly excused many psychologists from arduously examining the limits of "objectivity" has not so misled historians. Historians' emancipation from simply endorsing positivism has prompted rigorous and continual reflection on the values, human interests, and subjectivity of their practices. However, intimating any degree of consensus among historians on these issues would be audacious as well as erroneous, for few historians even pretend any final closure on them. And as the discussions of explanation and models of change illustrate, the claim of objectivity can be queried at practically every stage of historical inquiry.

The virtue of the inquiries on objectivity resides not in any conclusiveness in the arguments but in certain general provisions that circumscribe these discussions. These provisions, sometimes appearing as caveats, distinguish historiographical discourse on objectivity from its counterpart in psychology in several important ways. First, because historians typically are separated from their subject by time, and from any "primary sense data" by two or more levels of evidence, they have developed fairly perspicacious positions regarding subject-object relations. Not the least of the resultant practices is an apparently successful avoidance of what William James called the "psychologist's fallacy": the confusion of the observer's standpoint with that of his or her subject (James, 1890, p. 196). To draw further analogies from psychological terminology, it can be said that historians have cultivated a form of "reflexive" and "reconstructive" theorizing through the realization that "The facts of history never come to us 'pure,' since they do not and cannot exist in a pure form: they are always refracted through the mind of the recorder. It follows that when we make up a work of history, our first concern should be not with the facts which it contains but with the historian who wrote it" (Carr, 1961, p. 22).

The second provision regarding objectivity is that selectivity is inherent in all inquiry and, therefore, its rationale and consquences require scrutiny. The implications of selectivity become an issue in choosing questions as well as answers. Except for rigidly theory bound studies such as those of orthodox psychohistory, selectivity in historical research is unlikely to be sanctioned by the official "blinders" of a research program in which the theoretical postulates justify or conceal innumerable forms of selectivity. For these reasons critical evaluation attends to those processes influencing the historians' determination of evidence; such evaluation ranges from examining the decisions about what constitutes adequate "facts" to the particular interests and context of historians themselves. These analyses enable conversations on the process of interpreting data as well as negotiations about their validity vis à vis the empirical findings (Atkinson, 1978; Hexter, 1971; Humphreys, 1980). Both of these provisions suggest a third: that the incalculable number of perspectives from which a past event can be observed and the hypothetically inexhaustible sources of evidence suggest that objectivity may involve pluralities, something not unlike James' postulate (1909). The possibility that there may be a number of incompatible yet objective accounts of an event is seriously contemplated, a possibility that can hold even for those who reject a staunch relativist stance (Atkinson, 1978; Hexter, 1971; Humphreys, 1980). This provision warrants some qualification for there have been notable attempts to avoid pluralism and its essential incompleteness. The *Annales* school represents one attempt to incorporate multiple perspectives and yet refrain from pluralist conclusions through a model of "total History"; however, the attempts are often cited as the source of diffuse and abstruse studies (Henretta, 1979, pp. 1297-1298).

Given the precepts outlined above, historians generally acknowledge that questions of objectivity are adjudicated through intellectually and professionally structured rules of discourse and argument. Whether philosophical pragmatists (Mandelbaum, 1977) or interpretivists (Humphreys, 1980) whether aligned with realist or idealist positions (Gilliam, 1976), they locate reasonable expectations for objective practices in the working rules of evidence, argument, and discourse. If the possible definitions of objectivity can be reduced equitably to two—objectivity as a correspondence with fact or reality and objectivity as a capability in principle of being accepted by any rational person (Atkinson, 1978, p. 70)—then in adopting the latter definition, historians depart furthest from conventional psychologists.

More closely resembling contextual or interpretive social science (see Kuklick, 1983; Rabinow & Sullivan, 1979), the latter position is clearly distinguishable from the conventional scientific one: "If the test of objectivity is that there are regular ways of settling issues, by the use of which men of whatever party can be brought to see what actually happened, then I do not see how one can doubt the objectivity of history. But if we are satisfied with nothing less than the productions of histories which all men the least rational will accept as final, then that would be a greater victory for the scientific spirit than we have any reason to expect" (Passmore, 1966, p. 91).

These four provisions have directed historians' commitments to objectivity in directions practically unexplored by psychologists, despite the latter's enduring investment in the issue. The possible consequences of psychologists doing so are tremendous, not only because such an exploration would probably open the way to methods that would be hastily discarded according to previous standards of objectivity but also because it might engender novel thinking about subject-object relations, something that would inevitably strengthen psychological theory (see Flanagan, 1981). Yet, in concluding, consideration should be given to the occasional claim that historians engage in analyses of "objectivity" more as a convention for criticism than as a constructive assessment of scholarship. If this is so, then perhaps it represents a case where virtue has transpired to vice. However, there remains the reasonable conjecture that social psychologists can find the historical perspective on objectivity valuable to their study of historical phenomena, gaining from the purported vice as from the virtues.

GENDER AND HISTORY REVISITED

The chapter has proceeded from a description of systemic problems in social psychology, illustrated with the case of sex-role research, to a review of similiar problems addressed in historiography, but it has offered no concrete demonstrations of the products of what might be called a historiographical consciousness. Some degree of parity on this matter can be attained by concluding with a note on recent historical studies of gender. Although it certainly cannot be claimed that gender issues have consistently received the most just or enlightened of historiographical treatment (see Carroll, 1976; Kelly-Gadol, 1975), the development of women's history has promoted substantial advances in this area of research.

A cursory screening of recent histories of gender-related phenomena in the nineteenth and twentieth centuries demonstrates the advantages of historical perspectives, particularly as they have incorporated advances in the historiography of the subject women. The resultant researches have challenged conventional perspectives, not only on gender but also on what counts as historical epochs, as notable events, and as subject matter generally. Thus, historians have begun to study what Smith-Rosenberg (1975) called "private places," that is, the world of intimate relations, kinship, household, and bedroom. But a more significant outcome of a broadened historical perspective are the substantive discoveries about the mutability, evolving functions, and the context meanings of gender, findings which are central to a social psychological understanding of gender relations.

These findings have proceeded, first, with recognition that gender-related actions and ideals are not necessarily stable, or even unidirectional in their modifications. Even prior to the rise of what can be called the new social history (see Kammen, 1980), notions like androgyny were traced through their recurrent appearances such as that of the late-nineteenth-century decadent movement (Praz, 1951), a period when transcendence of one's gender, or recognition of the opposite gender in oneself was attempted in art, philosophy, and everyday life of an elite minority. More recent studies have attended to both life cycle and generational transitions and are untangling the multiple relations between changing gender ideals and education (Lagemann, 1979; R. L. Rosenberg, 1982), feminism (Showalter, 1978), the state of medicine and birth control (Cott, 1978; Gordon, 1976) and labor conditions (Kennedy, 1979; Kessler-Harris, 1975). This wider basis for recognizing fluid and symbolically laden gender concepts has further indicated the reflexivity between cultural mores and the scientific "discoveries" about gender. Past scientific theories of sex and gender have been found to reflect cultural stereotypes as well as the researchers' ideals (Ehrenreich & English, 1978; Fee, 1974; Lewin, 1983; Shields, 1975). The other side of this reflexivity, that scientific ideas have influenced cultural thought and actions, has also been examined (R. L. Rosenberg, 1982; Smith-Rosenberg, 1974). Both the foci and findings of these projects reactivate questions of objectivity. Often guided by feminist theory and a broader conception of the "political" than is generally posited in history, the overall perspective, among other effects, "weakens any presumption that women were acted upon, rather than actors, and goes beyond objective appraisal to analysis from women's subjective point of view" (Cott & Pleck, 1979, p. 20).

Finally, perhaps the most valuable outcome of these histories is their interpretations of gender within particular and evolving contexts; these explanations move far beyond simple descriptions of gender manifestations. For instance, traditional feminine characteristics, a perennial subject of psychological research, have been analyzed within the social and political context that gave them meaning. Characteristics of nineteenth-century women such as passionlessness (Cott, 1978), idleness (Branca, 1974), emotionality (Smith-Rosenberg, 1974), distance in heterosexual relations

(Smith-Rosenberg, 1975), and the moral and psychological enactment of the "women's sphere" (Cott, 1977) have been made intelligible by examining them within the world of men's and women's experiences and expectations. Thus, the "passionless" women can be better understood in terms of their attempts to maintain familial and social power as well as to control the obvious consequences of sexuality (Cott, 1978). The stereotypically portrayed relationships between the sexes becomes intelligible with detailed knowledge of females' extended and intimate relations with one another and their limited relations with males (Smith-Rosenberg, 1975).

Understanding of gender states and transistions has been greatly expanded through a historiographical consciousness and even by a more critical self-reflection on historiography. The work cannot follow any hard and fast rules of methodology or pretend any final account of human actions. Yet judging from the results, these are, if anything, minor sacrifices. The results of using empirical procedures—the observation of real actions related to gender and sex—coupled with a grounded epistemology or philosophy of history, suggests that there is no reason why the questions of gender posed by psychologists cannot be given similar treatment.

Concluding this examination of historiography with substantive examples from the practice of history may produce a curious twist, for just as it has been argued that social psychologists freed from the conventional model of research share numerous metatheoretical interests with historians, so we have converging interests in understanding certain human events. And over the last several decades as many historians have moved away from constricted accounts of the "political" and "intellectual" past and toward more comprehensive "social" histories, the interests shared with social psychologists have become even more obvious (see Henretta, 1979; Vann, 1976). Historians have long studied psychologists' procedures for making human actions intelligible but the converse has rarely been done. In gaining acquaintance with those aspects of historiography that address issues of serious concern in social psychology, perhaps—as Wundt once proposed—social psychologists will make unique contributions to these issues. Perhaps historians and social psychologists will recognize their joint projects, a partnership with untelling possibilities.

REFERENCES

Agassi, J. Towards an historiography of science. *History and Theory,* 1963, Beiheft 2.
Angrist, S. The study of sex roles. In J. M. Bardwick (Ed.), *Readings on the psychology of women.* New York: Harper & Row, 1972.
Armistead, N. (Ed.) *Reconstructing social psychology.* Harmondsworth, England: Penguin, 1974.

Atkinson, R. F. *Knowledge and explanation in history: An introduction to philosophy of history.* Ithaca: Cornell University Press, 1978.

Barnes, H. E. *Psychology and history.* New York: Century, 1925.

Barnes, H. E. *Historical sociology: Its origins and development.* New York: Philosophical Library, 1948.

Bem, S. L. Psychology looks at sex roles: Where have all the androgynous people gone? Paper presented at the UCLA Symposium on Women, May, 1972.

Bem, S. L. The measurement of psychological androgyny. *Journal of Consulting and Clinical Psychology,* 1974, *42,* 155-62.

Bem, S. L. On the utility of alternative procedures for assessing psychological androgyny. *Journal of Consulting and Clinical Psychology,* 1977, *45,* 196-205.

Bernard, J. Change and stability in sex-role norms and behavior. *Journal of Social Issues,* 1976, *32,* 207-224.

Bledstein, B. J. *The culture of professionalism.* New York: W. W. Norton, 1976.

Block, J. H. Conceptions of sex role: Some cross-cultural and longitudinal perspectives. *American Psychologist,* 1973, *28,* 512-526.

Blumenthal, A. A reappraisal of Wilhelm Wundt. *American Psychologist,* 1975, *30,* 1081-1088.

Bochner, S. Continuity and discontinuity in nature and knowledge. *Dictionary of the History of Ideas* (vol. 1). New York: Charles Scribner's Sons, 1968.

Boring, E. G. *A history of experimental psychology* (2nd ed.). New York: Appleton-Century-Crofts, 1950.

Branca, P. Image and reality: The myth of the idle Victorian woman. In M. S. Hartman, & L. Banner (Eds.), *Clio's consciousness raised: New perspectives on the history of women.* New York: Harper & Row, 1974.

Braudel, F. Time, history, and the social sciences. In F. Stern (Ed.) *The varieties of history.* New York: Random House, 1956.

Brenner, M., Marsh, P., & Brenner, M. (Eds.) *The social contexts of method.* New York: St. Martin's Press, 1978.

Bringmann, W. G., & Tweney, R. D. *Wundt studies.* Toronto: Hogrefe, 1980.

Bury, J. B. *The idea of progress.* London: Macmillan, 1920.

Butterfield, H. Narrative history and the spadework behind it. *History,* 1968, *52,* 165-180.

Caponigri, A. R. *Time and idea: The theory of history in Giambattista Vico.* London: Routledge & Kegan Paul, 1953.

Carlson, R. Understanding women: Implications for personality theory and research. *Journal of Social Issues,* 1972, *28,* 17-32.

Carr, E. H. *What is history?* New York: Macmillan, 1961.

Carroll, B. A. (Ed.) *Liberating women's history: Theoretical and critical essays.* Urbana: University of Chicago Press, 1976.

Collingwood, R. G. *The idea of history.* Oxford: Claredon, 1946.

Cott, N. F. *The bonds of womanhood: "Woman's sphere" in New England, 1780-1835.* New Haven: Yale University Press, 1977.

Cott, N. F. Passionlessness: An interpretation of Victorian sexual ideology, 1790-1850. *Signs,* 1978, *4,* 219-236.

Cott, N. F., & Pleck, E. H. (Eds.) *A heritage of her own: Toward a new social history of American women.* New York: Simon & Schuster, 1979.

Danto, A. C. *Analytical philosophy of history.* Cambridge: Cambridge University Press, 1965.

Donogan, A. The Popper-Hempel theory reconsidered. *History and Theory,* 1964, *4,* 3-26.

Dray, W. *Laws and explanation in history.* New York: Oxford University Press, 1957.

Dray, W. The historical explanation of actions reconsidered. In S. Hook (Ed.), *Philosophy and history: A symposium.* New York: New York University Press, 1963.

Dray, W. H. On the nature and role of narrative in historiography. *History and Theory,* 1971, *10,* 153-171.
Ehrenreich, B., & English, D. *For her own good, 150 years of the expert's advice to women.* Garden City, N.Y.: Anchor, 1978.
Emmerich, W. Socialization and sex-role development. In P. B. Baltes and K. W. Schaie (Eds.), *Life-span developmental psychology: Personality and socialization.* New York: Academic Press, 1973.
Favreau, O. E. Sex bias in psychological research. *Canadian Psychological Review,* 1977, *18,* 56-65.
Fee, E. The sexual politics of Victorian social anthropology. In M. Hartman & L. W. Banner (Eds.), *Clio's consciousness raised: New perspectives on the history of women.* New York: Harper & Row, 1974.
Flanagan, O. J., Jr. Psychology, progress, and the problem of reflexivity: A study in the epistemological foundations of psychology. *Journal of the History of the Behavioral Sciences,* 1981, *17,* 375-386.
Foucault, M. *The order of things: An archaeology of the human sciences.* New York: Random House, 1970.
Gallie, W. B. *Philosophy and the historical understanding.* New York: Schocken, 1964.
Gardiner, P. (Ed.) *Theories of history.* Glencoe, Ill: The Free Press, 1959.
Gergen, K. J. Social psychology as history. *Journal of Personality and Social Psychology,* 1973, *26,* 309-320.
Gergen, K. J. Toward generative theory. *Journal of Personality and Social Psychology,* 1978, *36,* 1344-1360.
Gergen, K. J., & Morawski, J. G. An alternative metatheory for social psychology. *Review of Personality and Social Psychology,* 1980, *1,* 326-352.
Gilliam, H. The dialectics of realism and idealism in modern historiographic theory. *History and Theory,* 1976, *15,* 231-256.
Goldenweiser, A. *History, psychology, and culture.* London: Kegan Paul, Trench, Trubner, 1933.
Gordon, L. *Women's body, women's right: A social history of birth control in America.* New York: Viking/Grossman, 1976.
Gossman, L. History and literature. In R. H. Canary & H. Kozicki (Eds.), *The writing of history: Literary form and historical understanding.* Madison: University of Wisconsin Press, 1978.
Habermas, J. *Knowledge and human interests* (Trans. J. J. Shapiro). Boston: Beacon Press, 1971.
Hareven, T. K. (Ed.) *Transition: The family and the life course in historical perspective.* New York: Academic Press, 1978.
Harré, R., & Secord, P. F. *The explanation of social behavior.* Oxford: Basil Blackwell, 1972.
Helson, R. The changing image of the career woman. *Journal of Social Issues,* 1972, *28,* 33-46.
Hempel, C. G. The function of general laws in history. *Journal of Philosophy,* 1942, *39,* 35-48.
Hempel, C. G. Explanation in science and history. In R. G. Colodny (Ed.), *Frontiers of science and philosophy.* Pittsburgh: University of Pittsburgh Press, 1962.
Henretta, J. A. Social history as lived and written. *American Historical Review,* 1979, *84,* 1293-1333.
Hexter, J. H. Historiography. *International Encyclopedia of the Social Sciences,* 1968, *6,* 368-394.
Hexter, J. *The history primer.* New York: Basic Books, 1971.
Hoffman, L. W. Changes in family roles, socialization, and sex differences. *American Psychologist,* 1977, *32,* 644-657.

Hughes, H. S. *History as art and as science.* New York: Harper & Row, 1964.

Hull, D. C. Central subjects and historical narratives. *History and Theory,* 1975, *14,* 253-274.

Humphreys, R. S. The historian, his documents, and the elementary modes of historical thought. *History and Theory,* 1980, *19,* 1-20.

Israel, J. Stipulations and construction in the social sciences. In J. Israel & H. Tajfel (Eds.), *The context of social psychology: A critical assessment.* New York: Academic Press, 1972.

James, W. *The principles of psychology.* Boston: Henry Holt, 1980.

James, W. *A pluralistic universe.* New York: Longmons, Green, 1909.

Kammen, M. (Ed.) *The past before us: Contemporary historical writing in the United States.* Ithaca: Cornell University Press, 1980.

Kaplan, A. G. Clarifying the concept of androgyny: Implications for therapy. *Psychology of Women Quarterly,* 1979, *3,* 223-230.

Kelly-Gadol, J. The social relation of the sexes: Methodological implications of women's history. *Signs,* 1975, *1,* 809-824.

Kellner, H. D. Time out: The discontinuity of historical consciousness. *History and Theory,* 1975, *14,* 275-296.

Kennedy, S. E. *If all we did was to weep at home: A history of white working-class women in America.* Bloomington: Indiana University Press, 1979.

Kenworthy, J. A. Androgyny in psychotherapy: But will it sell in Peoria? *Psychology of Women Quarterly,* 1979, *3,* 231-240.

Kessler-Harris, A. Where are the organized women workers? *Feminist Studies,* 1975, *3,* 92-110.

Kuhn, T. *The structure of scientific revolutions.* Chicago: University of Chicago Press, 1962.

Kuklick, H. The sociology of knowledge: Retrospect and prospect. *Annual Review of Sociology,* 1983, *9,* 287-310.

Lagemann, E. C. *A generation of women: Education in the lives of progressive reformers.* Cambridge: Harvard University Press, 1979.

Ladurie, E. Le Roy, *The mind and method of the historian.* Trans. S. Reynolds and B. Reynolds. Chicago: University of Chicago Press, 1978.

Lewin, M. (Ed.) *In the shadow of the past: Psychology portrays the sexes.* New York: Columbia University Press, 1983.

Lott, B. A feminist critique of androgyny: Toward the elimination of gender attributions for learned behavior. In C. Mayo & N. M. Henley (Eds.), *Gender and nonverbal behavior.* New York: Springer-Verlag, 1981.

Louch, A. R. History as narrative. *History and Theory,* 1969, *8,* 54-70.

Mandelbaum, M. Historical explanation: The problem of "covering laws." *History and Theory,* 1961, *1,* 229-242.

Mandelbaum, M. *The anatomy of historical knowledge.* Baltimore: Johns Hopkins Press, 1977.

Manuel, F. E. *Shapes of philosophical history.* Stanford: Stanford University Press, 1965.

Maracek, J. Social change, positive mental health, and psychological androgyny. *Psychology of Women Quarterly,* 1979, *3,* 241-247.

Mauser, G. Crisis in history. *Dictionary of the History of Ideas* (Vol. 1). New York: Charles Scribner's Sons, 1968.

Mink, L. O. The autonomy of historical understanding. *History and Theory,* 1965, *5,* 24-47.

Mink, L. O. Philosophical analysis and historical understanding. *Review of Metaphysics,* 1968, *21,* 667-698.

Mink, L. O. Narrative form as cognitive instrument. In R. H. Canary & H. Kozicki (Eds.), *The writing of history: Literary form and historical understanding.* Madison: University of Wisconsin Press, 1978.

Murchison, C. (Ed.) *A handbook of social psychology* (2 vols.). Worcester: Clark University Press, 1935.

Nisbet, R. *History of the idea of progress.* New York: Basic Books, 1980.

Oakeshott, M. Historical continuity and causal analysis. In W. H. Dray (Ed.), *Philosophical analysis and history.* New York: Harper & Row, 1966.

O'Donnell, J. M. The 'Crisis of Experimentalism' in the twenties: E. G. Boring and his uses of historiography. *American Psychologist,* 1979, *34,* 289-295.

Passmore, J. Explanation in everyday life, in science, and in history. *History and Theory,* 1962, *2,* 105-123.

Passmore, J. The objectivity of history. In W. H. Dray (Ed.), *Philsophical analysis of history.* New York: Harper & Row, 1966.

Passmore, J. *The perfectibility of man.* London: Duckworth, 1970.

Pepper, S. *World hypotheses.* Berkeley: University of California Press, 1942.

Pomper, P. *The architectonic principles of psychohistory.* Unpublished manuscript, Wesleyan University, 1982.

Praz, M. *The romantic agony.* New York: Oxford University Press, 1951.

Rabinow, P., & Sullivan, W. M. (Eds.) *Interpretive social science: A reader.* Berkeley: University of California Press, 1979.

Rebecca, M., & Hefner, R. The future of sex roles. In M. Richmond-Abbott (Ed.), *The American woman: Her past, her present, her future.* New York: Holt, Rinehart & Winston, 1979.

Richards, R. J. Natural selection and other models in the historiography of science. In M. Brewer & B. Collins (Eds.), *Scientific inquiry and the social sciences: A volume in honor of Donald T. Campbell.* San Francisco: Jossey-Bass, 1981.

Ricoeur, P. Narrative time. *Critical Inquiry,* 1980, *7,* 169-190.

Rosen, A. C., & Rekers, G. A. Toward a taxonomic framework for variables of sex and gender. *Genetic Psychology Monograph,* 1980, *102,* 191-218.

Rosenberg, M. The biologic basis for sex role stereotypes. *Contemporary Psychoanalysis,* 1973, *29,* 374-391.

Rosenberg, R. L. *Beyond separate spheres: Intellectual origins of modern feminism.* New Haven: Yale University Press, 1982.

Rosnow, R. L. The prophetic vision of Giambattista Vico: Implications for the state of social psychological theory. *Journal of Personality and Social Psychology,* 1978, *36,* 1322-1331.

Rosnow, R. L. *Paradigms in transition: The methodology of social inquiry.* New York: Oxford University Press, 1981.

Sampson, E. E. Psychology and the American ideal. *Journal of Personality and Social Psychology,* 1977, *35,* 767-782.

Sampson, E. E. Scientific paradigms and social values: Wanted—a scientific revolution. *Journal of Personality and Social Psychology,* 1978, *36,* 1332-1343.

Sarason, S. B. *Psychology misdirected.* New York: The Free Press, 1981.

Schafer, R. Narration in the psychoanalytic dialogue. *Critical Inquiry,* 1980, *7,* 29-54.

Scholes, R., & Kellogg, R. *The nature of narrative.* New York: Oxford University Press, 1966.

Scriven, M. Causes, connections and conditions in history. In W. H. Dray (Ed.), *Philosophical analysis of history.* New York: Harper & Row, 1966.

Shields, S. A. Functionalism, Darwinism, and the psychology of women. *American Psychologist,* 1975, *30,* 739-754.

Shotter, J. *Images of man in psychological research.* London: Methuen, 1975.

Showalter, E. (Ed.) *These modern women: Autobiographical essays from the twenties.* Old Westbury, New York: The Feminist Press, 1978.

Smith-Rosenberg, C. Puberty to menopause: The cycle of femininity in nineteenth-century America. In M. Hartman & L. W. Banner (Eds.), *Clio's consciousness raised: New Perspectives on the history of women.* New York: Harper & Row, 1974.

Smith-Rosenberg, C. The female world of love and ritual: Relations between women in nineteenth-century America. *Signs,* 1975, *1,* 1-30.

Spence, J. T., Helmreich, R., & Stapp, J. Ratings of self and peers on sex role attributes and their relation to self-esteem and conceptions of masculinity and femininity. *Journal of Personality and Social Psychology,* 1975, *32,* 29-39.

Starn, R. Historians and 'crisis.' *Past and Present,* 1971, *52,* 1-23.

Starn, R. Meaning-levels in the theme of historical decline. *History and Theory,* 1975, *14,* 1-31.

Stent, G. S. *Paradoxes of progress.* San Francisco: W. H. Freeman, 1978.

Stern, F. (Ed.) *The varieties of history: From Voltaire to the present.* New York: World Publishing, 1956.

Teich, M., & Young, R. M. (Eds.) *Changing perspectives in the history of science.* London: Heinemann, 1973.

Vann, R. The rhetoric of social history. *Journal of Social History,* 1976, *10,* 221-236.

White, H. *The historical imagination in nineteenth-century Europe.* Baltimore: The Johns Hopkins University Press, 1973.

White, H. The value of narrativity in the representation of reality. *Critical Inquiry,* 1980, *7,* 5-27.

White, M. S. Measuring androgyny in adulthood. *Psychology of Women Quarterly,* 1979, *3,* 293-307.

Winthrop, H. Variety of meaning in the concept of decadence. *Philosophy and Phenomenological Research,* 1971, *31,* 510-526.

Wise, G. *American historical explanations: A strategy for grounded inquiry* (2nd ed.). Minneapolis: University of Minnesota, 1980.

Worell, J. Sex roles and psychological well-being: Perspectives on methodology. *Journal of Consulting and Clinical Psychology,* 1979, *46,* 777-791.

3 Theoretical Orientations in a Historical Psychology

Harry F. M. Peeters
University of Tilburg

Modern behavioral science is generally restricted to the study of the present. Shortly after its beginning, psychology defined its task in such a way as to make it impossible to discern to what extent human behavior is historically situated. Modeling itself after the natural sciences and a positivistic methodology, psychology came to view human behavior as independent of or detached from its historical surroundings. Over time the complexity of the present gradually proved too much of a challenge to trouble about the past. Thus, human behavior anchored in the past, and changes in behavior over time, were, and still are, generally disregarded. Naturally, this limited perspective has consequences for the terms, theory, and method used to describe and investigate behavior. Attention is distracted from the historicity of patterned action, the persistence of old behavior patterns, the historical contingency of behavioral determinants, and the processes and factors associated with these changes or constants. Further, this one-sided accentuation removes the possibility of discerning the interrelationship between the flexible and the more permanant aspects of human existence.

People also tend to perceive themselves as possessing a permanent identity, one that remains constant across circumstances. They believe that in spite of superficial changes in appearance they are fundamentally the same. This petrification of the internal leads to an acceptance of the "I" that—as an index word, registers all possible experience and bonds these experiences together like some sort of paper clip (Ryle, 1949). This "I" is perceived as something "inside," closed off from all other people and things (Elias, 1969). People do have a certain sense of change, but this sense is typically partial in character. The body grows and perishes to dust, is mortal, is changeable; the basic self, reasoning, or the soul, on the other hand, remains fixed. It is this fixed core of reason that, as it was ventured, elevated the human being over the animals and above time itself (Nauta, 1973, pp. 13–17). Such assumptions are virtually as old as philosophy itself. Reasonableness was always defined as an unchanging system of axioms. The only question was how to explain the origin of these universal principles; through eternal and unchangeable ideas beyond the human mind (Plato), through immanent but, at the same time, permanent form (Aristotle), through divine mind (Thomas), through innate ideas (Descartes), through a preordained harmony (Leibnitz), or through a priori categories inside the organization of our thinking (Kant).

To an important extent this cultural belief in the unchanging character of the internal has been incorporated by the field of psychology. One finds this position most fully articulated in the experimental domain, where psychological processes such as memory, perception, motivation, and the like are viewed as universal and transhistorical. A further manifestation may be discerned in personality concepts which belong to the so-called trait theories. In these theories, personality is seen as a structured cluster of traits, or inner behavioral positions, which determine certain forms of behavior in divergent situations, independent of external conditions. The situation and its historically specific distinguishing marks are left out of consideration, due to the belief that many situations are functionally equivalent against the background of a certain trait-structure. By these theories, the individual is truly lifted above his or her situation (Hettema, 1967). Finally, an ahistorical attitude in the behavioral sciences is facilitated by the position of static entities, the reification of concepts, the reducing of complex phenomena to simple metaphors, and by generalizing specific regularities to general laws.

Science and the Historicity of Human Behavior

Throughout the years, psychology has increasingly become an empirical-analytic science. The emergence of this orientation has been facilitated by: (1) the manageability of isolated behavioral elements in an experimental setting, and (2) the capacity of the orientation to yield products. Some behavioral variations are so obviously permanent (especially those biologically based processes) that they seem to justify the search for regularity. This search for regularity has yielded a number of general propositions from which, by manipulation of given conditions, a wide variety of concrete predictions can be derived (Homans, 1967; Schlenker, 1974). However, the problem with human beings is that they are not only regular and explainable creatures, but also social- and cultural-historical beings, characterized by continuous new adaptions to new information, products (Popper, 1973), social surroundings, and ecological settings.

Realization of the historicity of human behavior led Gergen (1973) to propose that social psychology is "primarily a historical inquiry," and that it, therefore, should not be devoted primarily to testing general principles of human interaction. Social psychology is limited to facts that are largely nonrepeatable; to surmount its own historical limits is largely futile. According to Gergen, most regularities of human behavior (and, therefore, the most important principles) are firmly bonded to historical circumstances. To support this opinion, Gergen, among others, refers to the different variables which predict various actions (e.g., political activism) over time, the historically based assumptions that underlie seemingly general theories (e.g., social comparison theory assumes that people want to evaluate themselves in comparison to others, and dissonance assumes that people cannot stand contradiction), and to the fact that reinforcers of human behavior do not remain stable (i.e., social approval and applause are not of equal value in all historical periods). In addition to these historical factors, social theories reaching common consciousness can neutralize each other, and prophecies fulfill or destroy themselves due to the fact that knowledge of the law leads to actions stated in the preconditions or to actions known to be countersuggestive (de Boer, 1975; Gergen, 1973). Gergen thus concludes that social psychology cannot be a nomothetical science in the traditional sense, but is primarily a historical endeavor.

Empirical relations change in every field. In psychology, J. W. Atkinson suggested that when a substantial relation is found between personality variables, it describes only "the modal personality of a particular society at a particular time in history" (1974, p. 408). Class differences observed in the 1950s were sometimes just the reverse of what had been observed in the 1930s (Bronfenbrenner, 1958). The empirical validity of any construct is temporary. With new times, the items carry new implications. Lee J. Cronbach once said;

> Generalizations decay. At one time a conclusion describes the existing variance, and ultimately it is valid only as history ... The half-life of an empirical proposition may be great or small. The more open a system, the shorter the half-life of relations within it are likely to be. We cannot store up generalizations and constructs for ultimate assembly into a network. It is as if we needed a gross of dry cells to power an engine and could only make one a month. The energy would leak out of the first cells before we had half the battery completed. So it is with the potency of our generalization. (1975, p. 123)

By reflection on their own results, psychologists are forced, at present, to reformulate the institutional rules of the science, to redivide the "reality domain," and to develop new forms of investigation.

Time Levels in the Analysis of Behavior

It is possible to distinguish among variations in the durability or longevity of various behavior patterns. For analytic purposes we may speak of these variations as time levels. Perhaps the most well-known set of time level distinctions is that of the French historian, Fernand Braudel. This classification distinguishes among events of brief duration, the conjuncture of medium duration, and the long duration of structure (Braudel, 1958).

Although imprecise, this distinction does illustrate the heuristic importance of time levels. For Braudel, the time span of short duration is comprised of multivarious and ever-changing events of daily life. Most research in modern behavioral science focuses on just such events. Conjuncture is a time span of medium duration, of decades, a quarter of a century, or, maximally, a half a century. Patterns of this variety are characterized by rhythm, repetition, and regularity. It is this time level that sciences such as economics and sociology are concerned with when they explore price curves, demographic progressions, developments in wage scales, and the like. Longitudinal studies in psychology are focused at this level as well.

Above these levels stands the time level of long duration, the time of structures, of organizations, or steady elements of society. Some structures are stable elements for countless generations; others pass more rapidly. According to Braudel, mental frameworks last for long durations. Patterns of long duration essentially enter into or structure the patterns of more circumscribed duration and are important for all behavioral sciences. They supply the structural framework for human behavior manifesting itself in the time tempi of shorter duration (molecular time units, events, conjunctures). These time tempi must be fitted on to more comprehensive and stable frameworks, in the interdependence of structures. Those structures precede, carry, and surround the elements and conjunctures, and often continue to exist when those elements and conjunctures have passed.

The classification of behavioral aspects by time levels has emerged several times in the history of psychology. For Freud, the most hidden element was also the most permanent one. The "id" retained its strength despite manipulations by the "ego." For Jung, the durability was identical to that of the archetypes; they were prototypes of the residues of all earlier generations' experiences. Others (Hermans, 1973; Popper, 1972; Rokeach, 1960; and Williams, 1971) have associated longer durability with values, institutions, and organizations rather than with attitudes and cognitions. In these cases, individual motives are the impulses for action. However, these motives are soon formalized and stabilized in institutions. Actions, first fed by the motives, derive increasingly more strength from the dictates of institutions and from what is perceived within that institution as valuable. The need for security and orientation ensures that these institutions, typically born out of an economic advantage, remain and become directives for human action.

Psychology in Three Dimensions

A consideration of both the historicity of human behavior patterns and variations in time levels invites the formulation of new rules for considering research domains, methods, and research outcomes in psychology. Recognizing that people are changeable does not mean that all searching for regularity is pointless. Surely the existence of various biologically based patterns indicates the value of continued concern with transhistorical principles. A structural psychology should be built upon these permanent behavioral conditions and forms of behavior. Methodologically, this could happen via natural scientific (biological, biochemical, or physiological) methods, via ethological observation and formal mathematical analyses, and/or via structuralistic (linguistic) research. One's search for laws, however, can only be conditionally formulated even in structural research. Only if certain earlier conditions are realized can certain consequences follow: should these conditions not exist, the results fail to appear (Popper, 1972). This means that it is not laws which are relative or temporary, but rather the conditions under which they are valid. The law is valid indeed, but only the applicability is relative. The historicity is, therefore, not in the law, but in the circumstances under which it is valid (de Boer, 1975).

A conjunctural psychology should study human behavior occurring in a medium term of duration. Its principal concern might be with patterns of social activity. Here, too, there are methodologically different possibilities: time series analysis, longitudinal research, cohort analysis, "figurative" research (Elias), and "orthodox" historical description. Such a science would be situated between other historical social sciences and so-called "mental history." Conjunctural psychology should not avoid the search for laws and regularities. A continuous radical change of action patterns is logically possible, but empirically, rather an exception. More than a structural psychology, conjunctural psychology would be a discipline of "shrinking application" (de Boer, 1980).

Contemporaneous and event-directed psychology would look at behavior as it manifests itself here and now. Methodologically, this psychology should be mainly guided by what Cronbach (1975) has called "the aspiration to assess local events accurately and develop explanatory concepts." Such ends might be achieved by the use of experimental research, field research, treatment, action research, and description. It is mainly the task of contemporaneous psychology to pin down the contemporary facts (Cronbach, 1975). The greatest theoretical challenge, however, would be to generate an understanding of the way in which patterns at each time level are related to one another. It is this form of integrated understanding that would inform one most fully of the roots and the destiny of contemporary existence.

Theoretical Frames for the Study of Long-term Behavior Change

Given the paramount need for a historically oriented psychology, the question rapidly emerges as to forms of understanding. How are changes in human activity over extended periods of time to be comprehended? Of course, the variety of such forms of understanding is basically limited only by the human imagination; many possibilities can be envisioned. At the same time there are several orientations to human change that have come to play an immensely important role in twentieth-century intellectual life. Any attempt to develop a sophisticated form of historical psychology would have to be developed against the backdrop of such analyses. It is to three of these orientations, the dialectic, the structural, and the evolutionary, that the remainder of this chapter is devoted. In each case major propositions will be sketched, and an attempt made to pinpoint existing shortcomings.

THE DIALECTIC FRAME

Dialectics is a method of seeing things as moments within their own development in, with, and through other things. The "dialectic vocabulary" itself shows this clearly: Terms such as moment, movement, contrast, mediation, determination, and proportion are critical to the perspective. In addition, dialectics is an approach to problems where one looks not only at the relation among different units (work, capital, exchange, competition, appearance, nature), but also at such relations as they change across time. Finally, dialectics is also a form of explanation (especially according to Marx) that allows one to discover hidden structures. This means that each focus of concern is subjected to differing viewpoints and the emergence of newly developing structures is accepted as the rule rather than the exception.

The dialectic perspective is often framed in terms of various laws or principles. Although there is frequent disagreement among dialecticians in the number and content of these laws, one of the most systematic and influential statements was published by Engels. According to Engles (MEW, band 20) the most important laws are:

Unit transformation. An increase or decrease in the number of units at a certain point transforms existing units into qualitatively different units.

Mutual penetration of contraries. Phenomena in nature possess internal contradictions; all have their negative and positive side, their past and their future, something that dies and something that develops. These contradictions essentially furnish the grounds for change,

Development by contradiction or negation of the negation. Existing phenomena are transformed and replaced with new ones, which in turn give way to new ideas and phenomena; development proceeds toward an increasingly higher level of integration.

Particularly important in the later development of dialectic psychology was Stalin's *About Dialectical and Historical Materialism*. (1947) In addition to the above principles, Stalin adds:

The Law of Coherence. All things and appearances are connected with each other; the world must be seen as a coherent unit where all phenomena are connected in an organic way, depending on each other and determining each other.

The Law of Necessity. All that is and becomes, is and becomes out of necessity; nature is seen as perpetual movement and change, renewal and development, wherein something always comes into existence, develops, and perishes in its transformations.

The Law of Leaps. Development is not gradual, but is brought about by sudden leaps through which new qualities emerge.

These various principles are usefully demonstrated in several treatments of psychological and social development. In the 1930s, the work of Vygotsky, the founder of the so-called "cultural-historical school," began to demonstrate how psychological processes were related in a dialectic way with sociohistorical conditions. His pupils, Luria, Galperin, and Leontiev, continued this work in Russia. However, with more recent experimental studies of Klaus Holzkamp (1975) in Germany, and the Marxist oriented personality theory of Lucien Sève (1969) in France, we find a significant broadening of interest in a dialectic psychology. In the United States such concerns are perhaps best represented by the developmental psychology of the late Klaus Riegel (1975, 1976) and his colleagues, and the social psychological inquiries of Alan Buss (1979).

Within the dialectic framework, the development of psychological phenomena is considered to be a historical process. Through an interaction of the environment with the activity of the organism, a natural historical process is set into motion, leading from a general responsivity of the organism to specific sensibilities, from active self-orienting activities to a growing differentation of receptor systems. Particularly within Marxist theory, societal labor becomes the chief bearer of social historical developments of psychological process. Human labor creates objects that change the environment. This altered environment, including the newly created environment, is then introjected and appropriated by the culture. People also interact within the structural systems necessary for production, and, therefore, again act upon themselves.

A special case of the dialectic connection between social and psychological phenomena is evident in bourgeois society. The structural characteristics of the labor system are manifest already in the child's experience of reality. For a child, objects such as a doll or a ball are not only playthings, but also come to reflect aspects of the economic system. That is, they are not only functionally useful items, but also come to possess an exchange value (in a derived form, a price). The latter is an expression of the structure of human labor required for their manufacture. They are introjected or appropriated, then, as subjects having a cost and a value within the system of exchange. Over time, it is argued, the attributes of price and/or exchange value come to be seen not as reflections of society, but as attributes that belong to things by nature. This discrepancy or contradiction will not itself be evident to the child. Through parents and other societal representations, money slowly gains its own place among things in a child's world. The child learns that money is a general medium of exchange, an abstract embodiment of an indefinite number of incompatible possibilities to use in exchange for desired objects. Finally, this view of objects as possessing value in a market of exchange comes to characterize the individual's view of other people. Performance, value, exchange, and consumption are seen as intrinsic to human relations when in fact they are historically situated economic configurations psychologically embodied.

This is only one illustration, a strongly Marxist one, of the more general dialectic view that psychological characteristics are interrelated with social context. Psychological processes and functions, such as needs, motivation, social perception, self-conception, observation, and thinking, change as human activity changes the environment and this altered environment acts upon people. Luria (1976) attempted to demonstrate that cognitive functions such as observation, generalization, abstraction, deductive inference, problem solving, self-analysis, and self-confidence are all altered as people find themselves in new socioeconomic surroundings. As Luria argued, such psychological aspects change (sometimes very quickly) not only in content, but in structure as well.

The Adequacy of Dialectic Theory

The present chapter is not the proper context for a full analysis of the dialectic orientation to social and personal change. However, it should prove useful to indicate certain problems inherent in the formulation in general and the Marxist perspective in particular. At the more general level we find at the outset the problem of the moving force in history from the dialectic perspective, namely, contradiction. Dialecticians seem correct in saying that contradictions can bring about changes or developments in the individual and/or society. Such change would seem essential only insofar as people are unwilling to tolerate inconsistency. When people decide to live with contradictions, the contradictions lose much of their capacity for change. Each contradiction or inconsistency can be answered with a "Why not?" and "So what?" (Popper, 1972). People of certain cultures can cope for centuries with what appear to be unimaginable social differences. They can lock themselves into a caste system (such as in India) without any anticipation of social or political action. The power that drives the dialectical movement forward, therefore, lies in the decision of people not to accept a contradiction. There is no mysterious strength within contradictory aspects of society or the individual that would seem to foster development.

Also at the general level, there is good reason for questioning the dialectic view of the necessity of development. In part, such questioning is grounded in the fact that the law of necessity can only be formulated post hoc. In other words, the law is based on a retrospective judgment about the result of events. The law thus seems no more than a post hoc means of putting the multifariousness of events into order. "Necessity" does not seem to be a distinguishing mark essential to the occurrence of events, or always intrinsically linked with events. Similar arguments can be raised regarding certain other dialectic essentials. For example, it has been asserted in the developmental sphere that contradictions fulfill a necessary function in inducing childlike and creative thinking (Riegel, 1975, 1976). However, the same assertion does not treat the fact that in creative thinking the child often "plays" with contradictions and thereby dissolves them.

We may now move from the more general dialectic perspective to Marxist assumptions in particular. As we have seen, structures, processes, and categories employed by Marxist theorists furnish the key to understanding all social forms across history. The category of "labor" especially seems always and everywhere to be the fundamental form of relation between the human being and nature and between humans themselves. Set above time, it becomes the "idea of ideas." As Marx himself said, "the labor process, as outlined in its simple and abstract phases, is an efficient activity for the manufacture of commodities and for making nature suitable for human needs; it is a general condition for the metabolism between people and nature, an eternal natural condition of human life, and is therefore independent from each specific form of this life. On the contrary, it is generally valid for all social forms of it" (MEW, band 23: 198).

Yet, to view labor as the critical fulcrum seems in itself peculiarly nondialectic. Labor itself would appear to be a historical category; its function and meaning change with the social and ecological situation in such a manner that it cannot be said in advance to represent "the fundamental form of relation" between human beings and nature or between human beings themselves. The idea of labor itself must be thought of differently within the different historical periods. To illustrate, according to Vernant (1971), for early Greeks a consciousness of labor in its general and abstract form did not exist. Societal labor did not yet have the universal character that it came to acquire in capitalist society. Labor was not an abstract category that included all professions; rather, each profession individually was considered a different form of activity. Social ties were formed in the nonprofessional and nonspecialized fields that constituted the political and religious life of the city. As a result, labor did not itself play an overarching role in fashioning psychological function.

Criticism of the prematurely arrested historicity of the term "labor" brings other Marxist terms, such as class and class struggle, into discussion. Disconnected from the term "work," these categories take on a different meaning. Within the Marxist system, knowledge and information become, for example, economical values. As a result, a class struggle takes place between laymen and experts, the trained and untrained, between experts with political power and economic power, and experts without, or, as in ancient Greece, between rich citizens with political power and rich "meteken" without political power. Yet, if we take a broader view of history, we find that class ties are not necessarily the only ties between people. Ties can also be based on individual self-interests that join members of different classes; further, effective ties can be based on nationalism, regionalism, or religion.

These various criticisms are hardly intended to portray dialectical theory (Marxist or otherwise) as irrelevant for a historical psychology. Through the years, many of Marx's concepts have "entered into the bloodstream of scientific life and, thus, ceased to distinguish Marx from others" as Kolakowski (1978) put it. Thus, it might be ventured, no behavioral science can permit itself to overlook either force of conflict or natural context in human history. Neither can a behavioral science permit itself to miss the heuristic implications of existing dialectical principles. These principles render processes and situations intelligible in a way unparalleled by competing theories. They call particular attention to the historicity of phenomena, the inherent contradictions within and mutual interdependence of social entities, and to the possibility of sudden transformation through conflict. A fuller appreciation may be obtained by a consideration of a second major perspective, the structural.

THE STRUCTURAL FRAMEWORK

A second major perspective from which to understand social life across time is furnished by the structural movement. It is chiefly within the present century that the world has come to be regarded as a well-regulated organization

3. THEORETICAL ORIENTATIONS 71

with an obvious hierarchy and internal self-regulating dynamics. Von Bertalanffy, one of the first to introduce the term "system" in biology, and who can be considered the pioneer of general system-theories, predicted the development of "an organismic revolution." Illustrating his thesis, this new paradigm appeared nearly simultaneously in such diverse domains as physics, biology, psychology, sociology, and cultural anthropology. The paradigm drew special attention not to the activity of specific entities, but to the functioning of systems as a whole. As it was optimistically ventured, it might be possible to develop principles governing the function of living systems in general. Such possibilities might be applicable at all levels of functioning, from the cell to society.

In Europe similar concerns were emerging in the form of structuralism. In the 1960s structuralism began to supersede existentialism in intellectual interest. The turning point came, according to Foucault (1966), when Lévi-Strauss (in the case of society), and Lacan (in the case of the unconscious) pointed out that sense and signification in human interaction, central concepts within existentialism, were only superficial epiphenomena. As it was argued, particular meanings in relationships were reflections of fundamental systems or clusters of elements within relations, the configuration of which is continually maintained and transformed. Further contributing to the rise of structuralism was undoubtedly the advent of the computer and the associated interest in data processing and cybernetics. Further, the feeling of helplessness to bring about reforms in social structure and political relations perhaps played a role in the shift to structuralism.

As it is usually maintained, structuralism is not a theory in itself, but an analytic instrument or method of research. As the ethnologist and cultural anthropologist Lévi-Strauss emphasized: structuralism, when practiced in a sensible way ("le structuralisme sainement pratiqúe") does not give a message, does not provide a key for every door. It does not pretend to formulate a new view of the world, or of the human being. It does not offer a philosophy or a therapy. It is chiefly concerned with locating the structures underlying the givens of daily life. For example, in the Greek, Scandinavian, and Celtic myths, different gods and heroes appear, but the social organization of the divine community possesses the same systemic features (e.g., hierarchy, rivalry).

Forms of structuralism have emerged in a variety of scientific sectors: in cultural anthropology (Lévi-Strauss), in literary criticism (Roland Barthes), in linguistics (George Dumézil), and in psychoanalysis (Lacan). However, most forms of structuralism demonstrate the same distinguishing characteristics:

> There is a search for stable and constant factors underlying human experience over time, and it is these factors that furnish the starting point for scientific investigation.

The number of these factors is limited due to the organization of the nervous system.

These factors form a structure that, as an autonomous entity, exists in reality.

This structure is not immediately visible but is hidden beneath the varieties and vagaries of human expression.

The structure can be demonstrated and made visible by revealing the processes of decoding (i.e., the relation between the visible actions and the underlying structure).

Elements or factors are not considered as independent entities, but as elements of a total system.

The system comes first and determines localized events.

Persons are generally unaware of the structured foundations of their actions; governing forces in social life are therefore unconscious.

Linear causal relations are considered one-sided and insufficient explanatory principles.

Lévi-Strauss frequently supports his structuralist theory with the results of linguistic study. According to him, the structures that shape a society are of the same kind that produce linguistic phenomena. The understanding of interpersonal relationships, economic systems, artistic expression, or myths, for example, must be done in the same way one uncovers grammatical rules. Social structures—as well as linguistic structures—are hidden, and they must be decoded by an objective "text" analysis. "If, as we believe, the unconscious activity of the mind exists because it imposes form on a meaning, and if the forms are basically the same for all minds (antique or modern, primitive or civilized), as the study of the symbolical function expressed in the language brilliantly demonstrates, then it is necessary and sufficient to come to an unconscious structure on which every attitude and every habit is thus based. Ultimately, therefore, an explanatory principle is reached that is also valid for other attitudes and other habits if the analysis is profound enough" (Lévi-Strauss, 1958 p. 28). With such an "in-depth" analysis, one reaches the core of certain social structures within a culture, and thereby, as well, similar structures in other parts of the world.

According to Lévi-Strauss, the structural analysis of the so-called primitive societies shows that the root of culture lies in the effort of humans to master the primary order of their existence and to free themselves from the inherent contradictions, such as life-death, male-female, and earth-heaven. The ancient order can be revealed by a structural analysis of language and the expression of art, religion, and myths. The incomprehensible and the contradictory data of human existence can, to a certain extent, be subdued or removed by such analysis. Relations between persons and between groups are also deviations from this sort of structure. The logic of social relations is essentially a realization of underlying structural logic. According to Lévi-Strauss, Rousseau and his contemporaries proved that they had a good structural understanding in their realization that cultural attitudes and elements such as "contract" and "consent" are not secondary formations, but, rather, are the foundation of social life. Cultural rules with respect to family and marriage govern the communication between different groups with regard to women, cultural and economic rules with respect to goods and services, and cultural and linguistical rules with respect to information. "Cultural structuralism," then, is directed toward discovering the elements and the relations between the elements of a basic system. It attempts to produce a syntax of transformation between the first elements or atoms and contemporary social patterns.

The Structural Archeology of Foucault

Although a critical intellectual movement in Europe, the structuralism of Lévi-Strauss and others of similar bent did little to explain cultural change, and it also, in effect, failed to recognize the historicity of social pattern. This outcome can be traced in large part to the structuralists' concern with human physiology as the generic source for fundamental structure. In the work of Foucault, the concern with basic physiology is eschewed and the historical transformation in pattern fully recognized.

Foucault traces the character of various social patterns to what he terms the "episteme." In his earlier work, especially in *Les Mots et les Choses,* Foucault defines episteme as the entirety of the fundamental codes of a culture, dominating the language, observation schemes, technology, and the hierarchy of the controlling power of that culture. This entirety constitutes the conditions making the evident manifestations of thinking and knowlege possible. For example, the search for likeness or similitude was a dominating and pervasive episteme during the sixteenth century. In the different forms of similitude—*convenienta* or neighborhood, *aemulatio* or competition, analogy, and sympathy—people, words, and things were connected with each other. The use of analogy in particular enabled people to create an unlimited number of reversible and polyvalent relations. People, animals, plants, planets, diseases, and natural phenomena were compared with each other in detail. Once a likeness was found, it determined practical actions. For example, due to the visual similarity between a walnut and a human head, the outermost thick green bark was considered suitable as a remedy for cranial membrane wounds; pain inside the head was prevented and cured by the nut itself, for it looked exactly like the brains.

Although the concept of the episteme seems to suggest that history be viewed as a series of static states, such a conclusion would disregard a central aspect of Foucault's work. Foucault described episteme as an "espace de dispersion," an open field, in which multiple relations can be generated. There is not a single code preferred by the biological system as such. As Foucalt says, "nothing is more strange to me than the search for a compelling sovereign and unique system" (1969, p. 850). In effect, for Foucault history is an open system in which the underlying codes rendering actions sensible are multiple and ever-changing. Instead of just one system, there are different systems present for each period. The same is true with the discontinuances in history: there is not one discontinuance (i.e., a break in all fronts at the same time), but rather many different discontinuances.

Foucault did not want to refer to the consciousness, the will, or the thoughts of the individuals in his work. He also did not want to write a history evaluating the mind according to its content or character. As he says, his attempt is to practice archeology; he wants to try to recover the cluster of rules that for a given period or a given society determined the boundaries and character of what could be said, what could be maintained (e.g., through a ritual or through education), of what was remembered and reactivated (e.g., by comment and exegesis), and of what became appropriated and how it happened (1968). This conception is also present in his studies of insanity (*Histoire de la Folie à L'âge Classique,* 1972), prison systems *(Surveiller et Punir. Naissance de la Prison,* 1975), and sexuality (*La Volonté de Savoir,* part I, 1976). People within a particular era are all subjected to the anonymous power of the unconscious structuration. This power determines what is insanity and what is sense, what is good and what is bad, what separates the insane from the sane, and what separates the criminal from the law-abiding citizen. It does not, according to Foucault, fall within the hands of the political and economic ruling class, the bureaucracy, or any other ruling institution. This power does not come from "above," but comes out of the miniscule and convergent actions which, together with one another, form the structural physiognomy of the era.

The Structural Orientation Scrutinized

With respect to the development of a historical psychology, what may be said of the structural orientation? At the outset it is clear that most system theories remain characterized by an ahistorical attitude and are primarily directed towards understanding the survival of a society rather than towards the changes of the society; they are directed more towards comprehending what blocks or hinders change than to what makes change possible. Analyses of structure and function do expand appreciation of social organization and the necessity of such divisions in society. However, at the same time such analyses often lose touch with the historicity of their subject. In many cases the systems in question (social and cultural, personality, etc.) consist of elements that remain constant and vary only in their differing combinations. Each type of society consists of the same elements or pattern of variables, and the selection of the elements seems to be both fixed and arbitrary.

In the case of Lévi-Strauss's structuralism, we further find an unwarranted and problematic bias that Moscovici (1972) has called the "hypothesis of the dominant reality": all that is universal with people or with societies is originally of a biological nature and, therefore, has to be understood or interpreted in biological terms. Whenever universals or generalities are demonstrated by structural analyses (i.e., in language, thinking, or relationships), biologists and geneticists take over. They provide explanations for the formation and working of genetical stuctures which are responsible for these generalities. At the moment that cultural and social generalities are detected, the research transfers from the social to the non-social sphere (Moscovici, 1972). This bias also means that a part of reality becomes placed outside of history; after that biological dynamic is exhausted, producing a creature equipped with a complex nervous system, language, and social relations, the genetic biological equipment becomes a static object that only serves to articulate the dynamic of social and cultural behavior. This view, however, ignores the influence of social behavior upon evolution. Social organizations vary with regard to their impact on various biological systems (e.g., the liver, the heart, etc.) and thus their effects on the survival value of various physical structures.

Although in later years Lévi-Strauss did reduce the stringent separation between nature and culture, he concluded that history cannot be an opponent of the strongly rooted structures of biology. Within linguistics, the preeminently structuralist domain, dynamic terms such as "structuring acting" (Guillaume) and "generative grammar" (Chomsky) also pointed to the possibility of new, derivative relations between the individual and the biological system, between what happens and the underlying structure. By noting a difference between competence and performance, between depth structure and surface formation, Chomsky suggested the possibility for sociocultural inputs to language. However, in spite of these possibilities, Chomsky's (1968) analysis remains finally inside the "hypothesis of the dominant reality:" transformations take place only within the framework of the depth structure. It is not surprising, therefore, that on the basis of Chomsky's theory, Lennenberg (1967) and McNeil (1970) again identified the universal forms of the depth structure with innate schemes of the organism. Thus biological structures were found capable of the only "performance" they are entitled to, that of a deus ex machina.

Foucault's form of structuralism does avoid major pitfalls of the kind here discussed. Unlike many systems theorists Foucault is concerned with historical change, and unlike Lévi-Strauss, Foucault does not treat biology as the "first reality." Yet, there remains a haunting problem with Foucault's work that remains to be resolved. If underlying codes universally fashion the process of making sense within a culture, then it is difficult to comprehend how one could discover this situational code outside the confines of these codes determining the art of comprehension itself. In other words, in the process of making sense of past historical periods, one could in principle only reveal the stuctures of the current episteme. The means by which one would transcend the present confines to comprehend previous epistemes remains unclear.

THE EVOLUTIONARY FRAME

The theory of evolution and psychology have met several times throughout their mutual histories. For Francis Galton and the early American functionalists, the idea of evolution served as an important theoretical justification of their pragmatic and instrumentalist attitude (Sanders, 1976). Evolutionary mechanisms of variation, selection, and retention can also be recognized in behaviorist theory, especially in operant conditioning. Lamarckian views may also be recognized in theories about the dangers of "social mixing" (van Hoorn & Verhave, 1977). After a temporary decline, the epistemological climate changed again in the 1950s and 1960s in favor of evolutionary thinking. Parallels have now been drawn between biological and cultural evolution (Campbell, 1975; Kluckhorn, Gerard, & Rapoport, 1956) and differences between the two examined in a variety of settings (Medawar, 1975; Tinbergen, 1976).

One of the most comprehensive and compelling views of evolution as applied to behavioral investigation over long duration has been proposed by Karl Popper. "When I was younger," he wrote in *Of Clouds and Clocks,* "I used to say very contemptuous things about evolutionary philosophies. When twenty-two years ago, Canon Charles E. Raven, in his *Science, Religion and the Future,* described the Darwinian controversy as 'a storm in a teacup,' I agreed, but criticized him for paying too much attention 'to the vapors still emerging from the cup,' by which I meant the hot air of the evolutionary philosophies (especially those which told us that there were inexorable laws of human evolution). But now I have to confess that this cup of tea has become, after all, my cup of tea; and with it I have to eat humble pie" (Popper, 1973 p. 241). More than any other scientific theoretician, Popper has not only applied evolutionary thinking to the sciences, but to virtually all other forms of cultural activity. Such activity constitutes what

3. THEORETICAL ORIENTATIONS

Popper calls the "third world." This world may be contrasted with the (first) physical world and the (second) world of subjective consciousness. The third world is one created by human interactions. In its own domain it generates new facts and problems; at the same time it creates new refutations. This third world is thus variable and changeable.

According to Popper, people's struggle for existence takes place mainly in the third world: Constantly emerging problems are approached and attempts are made to solve them by trial and error. New reactions, models, behavioral attitudes, and hypotheses are eliminated by refutation. Good solutions or those most suitable for the handling of a given problem, remain. At the same time, however, the initial problem becomes modified by this procedure, resulting in a new problem and a new hypothesis which needs to be tested anew. This all proceeds directly according to the formula:

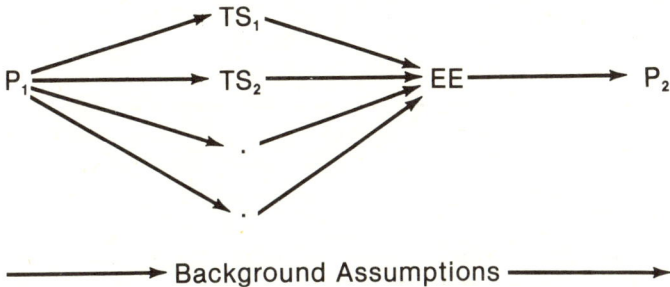

whereby P = problem, TS = tentative solution, EE = error elimination. P_1 is the first problem to which some solutions (TS_1, TS_1 . . .) are applied; as their application begins to offer a solution (EE), a new problem is created (P_2). All of this occurs against a background of general assumptions about the world.

Although some would disagree (De Mey, 1973), Popper argues that certain forms of stabilization are built into the evolutionary process. The third world does possess guiding mechanisms such as traditions and institutions which provide necessary stabilization of pattern. According to Popper, the evolutionary process does not at all lead to a chaos. His interpretation of the Darwinian theory of evolution suggests that the mechanisms of natural selection give a simulation of what could be in effect "the Creator's plan" or the essential goal of mankind. The continuous series of trials and error, and the confrontation with ever-emerging problems, make it possible, for example, for a complicated organ such as the eye to emerge in the human species as though created according to a well-considered plan. Analogous processes appear throughout the history of societies and human behavior.

Popper, along with Alister Hardy, Schrödinger, and Waddington, believes that evolution shows "orthogenetic trends," meaning that it shows successions of changes which go in the same direction. Popper explains this orthogenesis through the operation of internal as well as external selection mechanisms. These are based on an array of different sorts of genes including:

a-genes which mainly control anatomy,
b-genes which mainly control behavior, and which are divided into:
p-genes which control preferences or purposes, and
s-genes which control skills,

With these distinctions, Popper furnishes a conceptual ediface allowing interactions between the environment, genetic structure, and behavioral forms to be described. Changes in the environment can cause new problems and lead to the adoption of new preferences. These preferences manifest themselves first in the form of tentative behavior patterns. If these patterns are successful, changes are brought about in the s-structure, which in turn change the a-structure. Change thus follows the formula:

$$P \longrightarrow S \longrightarrow A.$$

Critique and Synthesis: Systems in Evolution

Whether in the hands of Darwin, Popper, or others, the theory of evolution is not essentially a scientific theory in the sense that it is subject to empirical refutation. Even if we found three species of bacteria on Mars tomorrow with a genetic make-up similar to that of three terrestrial species, Darwinism would not be refuted (Popper, 1973, 1972). A simple example would probably be given that these three species were the only forms among the many mutants which were sufficiently well adjusted to survive. The theory of evolution (in whatever form) is of a tautological kind. To say that species which adapt will be selected over others which do not is not a prediction but true by definition. The terms "adaptation" and "selection" presume one another. Adaptation or fitness is essentially a condition for survival and can be measured only by the success of survival.

Yet, although evolutionary theory should preferably be viewed as a metatheoretical orientation, it is nonetheless of great value for the behavioral sciences. It furnishes hope to the sciences that as its theories are developed, certain views shall be selected, chosen, and retained because, proportionally, they offer better solutions for existing problems. The evolutionary approach also offers a framework for research in human behavior. In terms of scientific activity, it suggests that the behavioral sciences can only unfold in a progressive way if they remain continuously sensitive to historically contingent forms of behavior. They must be continuously alert to the evolutionary changes in patterns of human interaction.

It is the opinion here that the theory of evolution also offers the best opportunity for connecting the historical long term to the biological phylogeny, and for researching the interaction between species-type and individual aspects of human behavior (Vossen, 1976) as well as culturally specific situations (Duijker, 1976). It also provides an opportunity to replace the traditional dichotomies between nature and culture or between human and animal behavior with new postulates such as "complementarity" and "transformation of totalities" (Moscovici, 1972).

At the same time, the evolutionary perspective would seem much enriched if it were to be combined with certain insights in the realm of systems theory. Such a possibility is already in evidence in the work of Parsons (1966) and Luhmann (1972) and this work has begun to open new theoretical perspectives. Systems theory furnishes a vocabulary for articulating the characteristics of the structures in evolution. It invites the investigator to differentiate among aspects of the systems under study and to evaluate the interdependency among the features.

Evolution is based on differentations within the mechanism of variation, selection, and stabilization. These functions must be divided among different vectors, and their coordination must be regulated. A good understanding of the nature of systems and the terms and methods of the systems theory seems essential if one wishes to penetrate the working of these processes (Luhmann, 1975, pp. 154–168). Further, by coupling the theory of evolution with systems theory, it becomes easier to understand why, at times, the genetic equipment is not sufficient for adaptation to the sociocultural or constructed world and vice versa.

More generally, then, if one accepts a world of a limited constancy, a world with specific conditions and creatures of limited variability living in it, then a situation is given in which the idea of trial and error elimination must be viewed as logically necessary. To be able to reduce the complex reality with manageable and representative models, by explaining continuities or hierarchic connections with other (sub) systems, and by developing and evaluating predictive formulations, a historical psychology may prove of considerable consequence to society.

REFERENCES

Atkinson, S. W. Motivational determinants of intellective performance and cumulative achievement. In S. W. Atkinson & S. O. Raynor (Eds.), *Motivation and Achievement.* Washington: Halsted, 1978.

Braudel, F. Histoire et sciences sociales. La longue durée. *Annales E.S.C.* 1958.
Bronfenbrenner, U. Socialization and social class through time and space. In E. E. Maccoby, T. M. Newcomb, & E. L. Hartley (Eds.), *Readings in social psychology* (3rd. ed.) New York: Holt, Rinehart & Winston, 1958.
Buss, A. R. *A dialectical psychology.* New York: Halsted Press, 1979.
Campbell, D. T. On the conflicts between biological and social evolution and between psychology and moral tradition. *American Psychologist,* 1975. *30,* 1103-1126.
Chomsky, N. *Language and Mind,* New York: Harcourt, Brace & World, 1968.
Cronbach, L. J. Beyond the two disciplines of scientific psychology. *American Psychologist,* 1975, *30,* 116-127.
de Boer, Th. Vooronderstellingen van een kritische psychologie. *Nederlands Tijdschrift voor de Psychologie,* 1975, *30,* 9.
de Boer, Th. Grondslagen van een kritische psychologie, Baarn; AMBO 1980.
de Mey, M. Paradigma's en Invisible Colleges. *Tijdschr. v. Geschiedenis;* 1973, 167-190.
Duijker, H. C. J. De psychologie en de psychologieen. *Nederlands Tijdschrift voor de psychologie,* 1976, *31,* 8.
Elias, N. *The civilizing process.* New York: Urizen Books, 1978. (trans. E. Jephcott).
Engels, F. *Marx-Engels Werke.* (MEW, band 20).
Foucault, M. *Les Mots et les Choses,* Paris: Gallimard, 1966.
Foucault, M. Réponse à une question, *Esprit,* 1969, *36,* 850-874.
Foucault, M. *Histoire de la folie à l'âge classique,* Paris: Plon, 1961.
Foucault, M. *Surveiller et punir. Naissance de la prison,* Paris, Gallimard, 1975.
Foucault, M. *La volonté de savoir,* Paris, Gallimard, 1976.
Gergen, K. J. Social psychology as history. *Journal of Personality and Social Psychology,* 1973, *28,* 309-320.
Hermans, H. J. M. *Op de valreep tussen rol en waarde.* Amsterdam: Swets § Zeitlinger, 1973.
Hettema, P. J. Trekken, processen en persoonlijkheidstests. *Nederlands Tijdschrift voor de Psychologie,* 1967, *22,* 618-641.
Holzkamp, K. *Sinnliche Erkenntnis. Historischer Ursprung und Gesellschaftliche Funktion der Wahrnehmung,* Frankfurt/Main: Atheneum Fischer Taschenbuch Verlag, 1975.
Homans, G. C. *The nature of social science.* New York: Harbrace J., 1967.
Kluckhorn, F., Gerard, R. N., Rapoport, A. Biological and cultural evolution, some analogies and exploration. *Behavioral Science,* 1956, 6-34.
Kolakowski, L. *Main Currents of Marxism,* (3 vols), Oxford: Clarendon Press, 1978.
Lennenberg, E. *Biological foundations of language,* New York: Wiley, 1967.
Lévi-Strauss *Anthropologie Structurale,* Paris: Plon, 1958.
Luhmann, N. Weltzeit and Systemgeschichte. Ueber Beziehungen zwischen Zeithorizonten und socialen Strukturen gesellschaftlicher Systeme. *Kölner Zeitschr. f. Soziologie u. Sozialpsychologie.* 1972, *16,* 81-115.
Luhmann, N. Systemtheorie, Evolutionstheorie under Kommunikationstheorie. *Sociologische Gids,* 1975, *22,* 154-168.
Luria, A. R. *Cognitive development. Its cultural and social foundations.* Cambridge, Mass.: Harvard Univ. Press, 1976.
Marx-Engels Werke, (MEW, band 23)
McNeil, D. *The acquisition of language,* New York: Harper Row, 1972
Medawar, P. W. *The frontiers of knowledge,* Allen & Urwin: 1975.
Moscovici, S. *Hommes domestiques et hommes sauvages.* Paris U.G.E., 1972.
Nauta, L. W. *De veranderbaarheid van de mens.* Kampen: 1973.
Parsons, T. *Societies; Evolutionary and Comparative Perspectives.* Englewood Cliffs, NJ: Prentice Hall, 1966.
Peeters, H. F. M. *Historische Gedragswetenschap,* Meppel: Boom, 1978.

Peeters, H. F. M. *Kind en Jeugdige in het Begin van de Moderne Tÿd* (1500—1650), Meppel: Boom, 1975
Popper, K. *Conjectures and refutations. The growth of scientific knowledge.* London: Routledge & Kegan Paul, 1972.
Popper, K. *Objective knowledge. An evolutionary approach.* Oxford: Oxford Univ. Press, 1973.
Riegel, K. Toward a dialectical theory of development. *Human Development,* 1975, 50-64.
Riegel, K. *Psychology of development and history.* New York-London, 1976. Plenum.
Rokeach, M. *The open and closed mind.* New York: Basic Books, 1960.
Ryle, G. *The concept of mind.* London: Harper Row, Hutchinson, 1949.
Sanders, C. Eisenga, L. K. A., & Rappard, J. F. H. van *Inleiding in de grondslagen van de psychologie.* Deventer: Van Loghum Slaterus, 1976.
Schlenker, B. R. Social psychology and science. *Journal of Personality and Social Psychology,* 1974, *29,* 1-15.
Sève, L. *Marxisme et théorie de la personalité,* Paris: Editions Sociales, 1969.
Stalin, Über dialektischen und historischen Materialismus Moskau, 1947 cit. in G. A. Wetter, *Philosophie and Natur, Wissenschaft in der Sowjetunion,* Hamburg.
Tinbergen, N. *Het dier in zijn wereld,* Utrecht: Spectrum, 1976.
van Hoorn, W., & Verhave, Th., Socio-economic factors and the roots of American psychology. In R. W. Rieber, & K. Salzinger, (Eds.), *The roots of American psychology.* New York: 1977.
Vernant, J. P. *Mythe et pensée chez les Grecs, II,* Paris: Maspéro, 1971.
Vossen, J. M. H. Verkenningen in de vergelijkende en fysiologische psychologie. *Nederlands Tijdschrift voor de Psychologie,* 1976, *31,* 69-86.
Williams, R. M. Change and stability in value and value systems. In B. Barber, & A. Inkeles, (Eds.), *Stability and change.* Boston: Little Brown, & Co., 1971.

4 Modern Dialectics in Social Psychology

Marianthi Georgoudi
Temple University

Over the past decade social psychologists have turned increasing attention to the concept of dialectics and to its potential utility in the construction of social theory. This concept has been employed to generate understanding of person-environment relationships (Altman, 1977; Altman & Gauvain, 1981), cognitive development (Basseches, 1980; Riegel, 1973), interaction (Ziller, 1977), ego development (Hogan, 1974; Meacham, 1975), interpersonal attraction (Adams, 1977), decision making (Mitroff & Betz, 1972), changes of family structure over time (Gadlin, 1978), and mother-child interactions (Harris, 1975; Riegel, 1973, 1976). A number of investigators have also contrasted the dialectic perspective with that of traditional positivism, and have seen within dialectics the possibility for a transformed social psychology (cf. Buss, 1979; Israel, 1979; Smith, 1977). Finally, a number of theorists have explored the methodological implications of dialectics (Cvetkovich, 1977; Hook, 1953; Kvale, 1976; Rychlak, 1976) and how it can be used in experimentation and research (Basseches, 1980; Kvale, 1976; Lourenço, 1976; Mancuso, 1976; Ziller, 1977). In effect, the concept of dialectics has played a catalytic role at the theoretical, metatheoretical, and methodological levels.

Yet, as one reviews these and other contributions to this emerging venture, it is apparent that the concept of dialectic remains ambiguous and unarticulated. The term is employed in a variety of ways for different purposes and with different degrees of sophistication. The present chapter is first an attempt to unpack the array of interdependent assumptions that appear to form the "deep structure" of the dialectic orientation. In doing so, theorists may grasp more clearly the broad implications of the perspective and discriminate among theories that are truly dialectic, as opposed to dialectic in name alone. Second, the attempt is made to show how the concept of dialectics resolves one of the most critical dualisms in social psychology, namely that of the individual versus the social. Finally, in light of these discussions a response can be formed to criticisms addressed to the current status of social psychology.

ASSUMPTIONS IN DIALECTIC THEORY

That the concept of dialectics has been differentially employed in social psychology has not only led to widespread confusion within the field, but has invited others to use the term in casual and trend-catching ways, while still others have come increasingly to view the term as little short of mystical incantation. To be sure, much would be lost in denying the concept variations in nuance or evolution in usage. At the same time, a careful tracing of the term as it has been developed by a number of more committed scholars (Adorno, et al., 1976; Cornforth, 1980; Engels, 1939; Howard, 1977; Israel, 1979; Jay, 1973; Kvale, 1976; cf. Marx, 1977 a, b, c) reveals a set of common assumptions. A coherent dialectic perspective emerges when these assumptions and their interrelationship are closely examined. Many social psychologists have found one or more of these assumptions useful thus far; in some cases one or another assumption has been misleadingly recontextualized within a positivist-empiricist framework. However, if a fully dialectic social psychology is to flourish, close attention must be paid to each and all of the following assumptions:

1. Dialectics Does Not Claim Ontological First Principles

The dialectic orientation in itself is opposed to all metaphysical conceptions that claim psychological processes, social structures, or material conditions as the primary cause of human activity. Thus, the concept of dialectics cannot be subsumed under any abstract metaphysical theory, claiming either a material or nonmaterial substance as the ultimate cause of existence. In this sense, dialectics does not lend itself uniquely to the interests of either behaviorist or cognitivist psychology; nor does it replace psychological reductionism with social structure or vice versa. Dialectics in its most general sense is the process of relating entailed in human activity.

2. Dialectics is a Form of Mediation

Dialectics is usually viewed as a process of relating or mediating between elements, such as subject and object or consciousness and being. Dialectics pertains neither to a theory of objects nor to a theory of subjects and does not postulate the ontological precedence of either subject or object; rather, it is the process of mediating the two and is, thus, entailed in their interrelatedness. Thus, dialectics cannot be treated as a category to be imposed on the world, that is, as a reified conceptual principle.

To illustrate, a common distinction is often made between the external or objective world and the psychological or subjective world. Each is treated as an independent, ontological domain possessing its own fundamental principles of operation. Yet, from a dialectic perspective neither of these so-called "ontological domains" possesses an independent status. Rather, they are mediated categories in the sense that neither can be defined apart from the other (Israel, 1979). Required for the definition of an objective world are observers who are apprehending from a subjective stance; required in the specification of a subjective world is a conception of an objective proposition. It is this form of mediation that is of central concern to the dialectician.

3. Dialectical Relations Are Founded on Negation

Negation or contradiction, as it is often called, is not viewed as a theoretical statement to be verified or falsified by empirical reality. Rather, it represents those antagonisms of life that cannot be removed by clear knowledge or formulation. At the most fundamental level, to recognize any existing entity is simultaneously to recognize its negation, that is, its state of nonbeing. The act of recognition itself demands negation. Thus, any stipulated entity exists in a condition that forms its negation. For example, to specify a world of actors is simultaneously to recognize their nonexistence, or a class of entities that stands in fundamental opposition to them. The dialectician would not, thus, view the world of subject and of object as two independent ontological categories, but as interlocking or related by mutual contradiction.

Two forms of contradiction may be distinguished. First, there is what Israel (1979) calls contradictions which are "mutually exclusive and exhaustive." For example, negating life implies (in a negative form) the affirmation of death, and vice versa. In this case, in denouncing the one we can only affirm the other and nothing else. If, in contrast, we denounce military dictatorship, we could be negatively affirming socialism, parliamentary democracy, or constitutional monarchy. That is, there is no necessary alternative entailed in the negation. This constitutes the second form of contradiction discussed by Israel, namely the "mutually exclusive but not exhaustive."

4. Negation Furnishes the Major Grounds for Transformation

Negation is essentially dynamic. Contradiction furnishes a primary impetus for the transformation of stipulated entities standing in such a relationship. The transformation is mutual: both entities are mutually altered so as to create a newly stipulated entity. However, in the recognition of the newly stipulated entity, the grounds are established for its own contradiction. Thus, contradiction does not entail negation in the sense of denunciation, but rather in terms of a negative affirmation. And the results of this affirmation are a synthesis that itself stands ready to undergo transformation. As Engels (1939) stated, " . . . I must not only negate, but also in turn sublate the negation. I must, therefore, so construct the first negation that the second remains or becomes possible" (p. 155).

To illustrate, the dialectician would not be content with the attempt of attribution theorists to explore the mechanistic principles governing the way people assign causes to others' behavior (cf. Jones & Nisbett, 1971; Kelley, 1971). Rather, the dichotomy between subject and object would first be collapsed; mediation would become focal (Lana & Georgoudi, 1982). Further, attributions would be viewed as in process, changing over time. And, critical to the present point, any given attribution would form the grounds for its own subsequent negation and transformation.

5. Transformations are Processual

Dialectics is concerned with activities of relating rather than frozen moments in time or static events; it is concerned not with states of being but the process of becoming. This follows readily from the above emphasis on contradictions and transformations, that is, on activities of relating (as a verb form) rather than on relationships (as a noun form) (Cornforth, 1980). If the central focus of dialectics is on contradictory relations, and such relations furnish the grounds for transformations, then from the dialectical perspective, the world of experience is in continuous motion. It is a world of relations in transformation, rather than static mechanisms or structures. The implications of this statement are accentuated when one takes account of the fact that most social psychological theories today are synchronic than diachronic in character. They isolate mechanisms such as dissonance, balance, reactance, equity, seeking, and self-awareness, which mechanisms are viewed as irrevocable and unchanging in their fundamental aspects across time.

6. Processes are Characterized by a Teleological Orientation

From the dialectic perspective, teleology is to be understood not as a property or a tangible aspect of the relations to be analyzed, but rather denoting a dynamic movement of created and recreated relations (Howard, 1977). As such, then, teleology exemplifies the processes' transformative potential. This teleology does not, for most dialecticians possess a fixed endpoint; its course is not predetermined. This follows from the earlier concern with avoiding metaphysical first principles (e.g., nature created by God, human action governed by biological process). For example, when examining interpersonal relations (e.g., attraction), the teleological orientation can be traced to the developmental process of forming a particular relationship (be it a friendship, an intimate relationship, or a mere acquaintance), which is never static, but is constantly *open* to new developments and transformations (e.g., a friendship might turn into an intimate relationship or vice versa). Teleology, in this sense, points at the open horizon of different forms of relating and underlines the dynamic character of the activities of relating.

7. Dialectical Relationships are to be Construed as Concrete Lived Experiences and Not as Reified Abstractions

The notion of "concreteness" denotes the existence of relations within the context of a totality, and emphasizes their motions and transformations in their concrete and multifaceted ways (Israel, 1979). As such, it is contrasted with abstraction and reification. It is also in this sense that dialectics can be viewed as a form of materialism (Cornforth, 1980). However, this does not imply that, in examining social relations, exclusive emphasis is to be laid on the material conditions of existence as often advocated by Marxist economists. Rather, materialism emphasizes the *concrete* reality of lived relationships. For example, in examining groups or group behavior, the dialectician would not treat the group as a static, reified entity, defining it either as a summation of its individual members or as having an identity of its own. Moving from the abstract to the concrete, the social psychologist would view the group in terms of dynamic developments and transformations of concrete social relations over time. Contrary to the dialectical position, traditional analysis might examine the group as an independent structure, subject to pressures both from *within* (individual members) and from *without* (societal conditions). In this sense, not only the group is treated as an abstract category, but its characteristics are the products of interactions between internal and external factors.

8. The Scientific Task of Generating Understanding is Historically Situated and Relational

For psychology in the positivist-empiricist mold, the scientist has been cast as an independent observer capable of extricating himself or herself from society, and assessing its characteristics from this independent and objective position. From the dialectic perspective this concept of separation is ill founded, an extension of the misleading subject-object dualism so central to traditional scientific beliefs. From the dialectic standpoint, scientist and society are bound together in an ongoing relationship, a relationship that is fundamentally contradictory, and which thrusts society and scientist toward mutual transformation. The implications of this view are far-reaching. Theory, from the dialectic perspective, is not to be viewed principally as a reflective device, mirroring aspects of a static reality. In opposition to this traditional view, there is no essential distinction to be made between theory and praxis, or active engagement in concrete relationships. Theoretical work enters into the sphere of social relationship and becomes an instrument of transformation (see also Gergen, 1982). Further, it is clear from the dialectic perspective that the traditional distinction between value-free and value-impregnated science is also misleading. The scientist is an active participant in the culture, and for this reason cannot escape the valuational grounds of his or her cultural activity. There is no warrant for the belief that through particular methods the scientist can transcend the subjectivity of the culture. As Adorno (1976) put it, " . . . Anyone who wishes to follow the structure of his object and conceptualizes it as possessing motion in itself, does not have at his disposal a method independent of the object" (p. 48). Methods are not independent of what are taken to be "the facts" and the facts are essentially a product of communal relations in which the scientist is fully engaged.

Having surveyed a number of core assumptions within the dialectic frame, we may better appreciate the strengths and failings of recent attempts to employ the concepts of dialectics in social psychology and related areas.

Perhaps one of the major confusions to have emerged is that of treating dialectics either as a metaphysical principle (ontological and/or epistemological) or a methodological tool. For example, Rychlak (1976) analyzes dialectics as a metaphysical construct emphasizing both its ontological (Many in One, World Principle) and epistemological (Valid Organon, Invalid Organon, Transcendence) aspects. Dialectics is claimed to be both a principle that accounts for the genesis and development of the world and a means for arriving at truth that transcends experience. Along similar lines, Hook (1953) distinguishes between two generic conceptions of the dialectic, namely, as a pattern of existential change or as a special method for analyzing such change. In the first case, the pattern can take the form of a pendular rhythm, a struggle, or a historical interaction; as a method it encompasses the characteristics of holism, interrelatedness among all things, and teleology. The argument is that using dialectics as a method does not necessitate the acceptance of existence as dialectic in nature.

Implicit in the above is the treatment of dialectics as a conceptual category or a special kind of logic separate from experience. Dialectics is,

4. MODERN DIALECTICS IN SOCIAL PSYCHOLOGY

thus, imposed upon reality either as a rational principle or simply as a methodological tool that best depicts it. In doing this, a fundamental dualism emerges between theory and method that places dialectics in the realm either of the former or of the latter. One is not denying that methods vary in the degree to which they incorporate the dialectic orientation and that some forms of analysis are more congenial with dialectics than others. However, to view dialectics *itself* as a method (e.g., to be contrasted with experimentation) or as an analytic tool (e.g., to be compared with structural analysis) would be to disregard a number of the basic assumptions outlined above. Methods of research or analysis presuppose particular kinds of worlds made up of particular kinds of entities. Experimentation as a method generally assumes a world of entities in causal relations; structural analysis presumes a fundamental structure beneath the transient givens. However, from the dialectic perspective one avoids metaphysical first principles; as scientist one engages in a mediated process. The scientist cannot abstract himself or herself from the process through analytic or methodologic means; he or she is fully absorbed in the process.

A second major confusion is derived from theorists' attempts (Basseches, 1980; Riegel, 1973) to view dialectics as a form of cognitive process, to argue that dialectics is simply a thought-form to be contrasted with formal operational thinking, logical inference, and the like. For example, Riegel (1973) has argued that dialectical thinking constitutes a cognitive developmental stage following Piaget's formal operational stage. Basseches (1980) has developed an array of 24 cognitive dialectical schemata said to represent various facets of dialectic thought, and attempted to show empirically that dialectical thinking is a more advanced form of cognitive processing. Although such arguments are both challenging and stimulating, it must be realized that the orientation which they represent is not itself fully dialectic. To hold that dialectics is a cognitive state or schema is to deny its existence in concrete social processes. That is, one should be careful not to confuse the mental representation of process with process itself. As we have seen, dialectics is to be found in concrete social relations and activities of relating and cannot be perceived apart from human praxis. Dialectics can be placed neither exclusively in the realm of ideas, as a preexisting thought schema, nor exclusively in the realm of the material, as an empirical description, but only with human action. It is neither a mental nor a situational phenomenon. To argue the existence of a schema does not demonstrate the existence of dialectics. Further, to argue for cognitive processes independent of the environment is itself to eschew critical features of the dialectic orientation. It is to adopt a traditional form of dualism which the dialectic orientation calls into question.

A third major confusion to have emerged is between interactionism and dialectics. The concept of interactionism has become particularly focal for investigators attempting to form a synthesis between situation-oriented, experimental social psychology and trait-oriented, personality psychology (cf. Bowers, 1973; Magnusson & Endler, 1977). Although the term interactionism has itself been employed in a variety of ways (Buss, 1980; Mischel, 1973), the most conceptually sophisticated view is one holding that the individual is both influenced by and acts upon the social situation. It is this form of two-way influence that Bandura (1982) has also incorporated in his concept of reciprocal interactionism. This view does furnish a welcome advance over the more traditional unidirectional S-O-R theories, and shares with the dialectic orientation a strong concern with process and cross-time transformation. It is perhaps for this latter reason that theorists such as Smith (1977) and Bowers (1973) have come to see the interactionist and dialectic orientation as virtually identical. As Smith argues, for example, "dialectics . . . is simply a thoroughgoing radical interactionism, an interactionism of developmental process" (p. 721).

Yet, as we have seen from the above analysis, to equate interactionism with dialectics is essentially to incorporate the latter into an extension of the traditional empiricist epistemology and thus to render it redundant. The interactionist orientation assumes the existence of independent, abstracted conceptual elements (viz. person, situation), each of which can be examined on its own. Further, it assumes a fundamental dichotomy between the observed entities and the observing scientist. As previously argued, a full dialectic orientation militates against separations; person and situation, scientist and society are all united in one ongoing process. Furthermore, the interactionist is principally concerned with frozen moments or static events, temporarily recovered from the sociohistorical context of which they are a part. One views the unidirectional impact of A on B at t_1, and then considers the unidirectional impact of B on A at t_2. There is essentially no concern with cross-time process itself. In contrast, the dialectician is principally concerned with the ongoing process of social relations as a whole and its continuous transformations. Lost, then, is the dynamic movement of created and recreated relations (teleology) which forms the basic orientation of the dialectical process.

Finally, other difficulties emerge when investigators take oppositions of any variety to be exemplars of dialectics. Thus, for example, Mancuso (1976) has argued that much of the empirical psychology has provided a sound basis for treating humans as if they were dialecticians. He gives as an example the use of bipolar semantic features as a recognition of dialectics in experimental social psychology. Yet, although contradictions are central to the dialectic orientation, they can hardly be equated with bipolar semantic features. Contradiction without the associated aspects of transformation and change is but a fractional accommodation. Further, contradictions in dialectics are exemplified in the process of concrete social relations; they do not represent abstract formulations subject to verification or falsification through empirical testing. As Adorno (1976) has stated, "... the dialectical contradictions express the real antagonisms which do not become visible within the logico-scientific system of thought" (p. 26). Contradictions, then, should not be loosely defined as a synonym for "difference" or "diametric opposite," as Rychlak (1976) points out. Such definitions would deprive dialectics of its essential emphasis on relatedness, transformation, and concrete process, and would reduce it to a principle in which dualisms are harbored.

THE PROBLEM OF THE INDIVIDUAL AND SOCIETY

Having laid out several grounding assumptions within the dialectic perspective, and discussed their partial realization in several aspects of current social psychology, we may usefully examine the application of dialectics to a major conceptual problem. In particular, one of the most basic and longstanding controversies in the field of social psychology has been that of the relation between individual (psychological) and social phenomena. Early social theorists such as Tarde, LeBon, and McDougall stressed the need for studying group phenomena. The crowd, mass phenomena, and the group mind were essential foci of concern, and individual psychological processes were interesting or important primarily as they related to or were derivative from group phenomena. Yet with the rise of behaviorism and the more recent hegemony of cognitivism, interest in group phenomena has largely been replaced by the investigation of psychological mechanism and process. It is in this context that many recent authors have despaired over the emphasis on the individual and the neglect of inter-individual processes; as it is argued, the wider social context within which psychological processes occur has been discarded (Argyris, 1975; Moscovici, 1972; Steiner, 1974; Israel & Tajfel, 1972). Many theorists now suggest that neither the individual nor the social should be given primary emphasis, but rather the major focus should be directed toward the interplay or interaction of the two (Deutsch, 1974, 1976; Stroebe, 1980).

How is this perennial antagonism to be regarded from the dialectic perspective? How promising are the present proposals for studying the interaction of the individual and the group? What solutions are offered to the traditional problems from a dialectic perspective? Answers to these questions begin to emerge when we first consider the initial dichotomy, that between individuals and groups. First, as argued above, the dialectical formulation views society as intrinsically related to the individual. Neither society nor psychological process is treated as a "static" entity, as abstract or pure concepts. Rather, the individual and the social are viewed as *intrin-*

sically related categories. Neither can be conceived as functioning or existing independently of each other nor can be defined without referring to the other. No form of interactionism could resolve the traditional controversy then, because interactionism maintains a fundamental dualism between the psychological and the social. By defining the individual and the social world independent of each other, and attributing to each an internal structure and lawfulness, interactionism establishes an *extrinsic* relationship between the two.

If individual and society are intrinsically related, what form is social psychology to take? From the dialectic perspective the study of independent entities and their interaction is replaced by a concern with concrete *relations* in a continuous process of creation, change, and transformation. Both the individual and society or the social world are, thus, fused in an ongoing dialectical process of created and recreated relations.

This line of argument may be demonstrated by reconsidering the psychological experiment. Traditionally the experiment has cast the subject in the role of independent entity, confronted by systematically controlled events and responding in psychologically determined ways. Similarly, the experimenter has been cast in the role of an independent observer, controlling, manipulating and measuring the subject's behavior. Implicit in this traditional view is the treatment of experimenter and subject as separate but interacting entities. In contrast, the dialectician would define both experimenter and subject in terms of their relations to each other. That is, the notion of an experimenter would necessarily demand the notion of an experimental subject and vice versa. The experimental situation then, would not be viewed as an independent structure with its own inner lawfulness or as comprised of the interactions between independent entities but rather as "relatedness" in Israel's (1979) terms. To clarify further, one might consider the movements of dancers in a pas de deux. A complete description of the actions of each dancer independently would fail to make the unity comprehensible. Nor could a description which concentrated on dancer A's actions and B's reactions. Rather, the dance itself is a coherent unity only as an ongoing set of coordinated movements. A vocabulary of "meeting hands," "lifting," "holding," and the like is required, a vocabulary that views the dancers as part of a singular, unified process.

No opposition exists, then, between the social world and the individual since, by definition, the two are interlocked in the process of concrete social relations. Marx, for example, has stated that, " . . . it is above all necessary to avoid restoring society as a fixed abstraction opposed to the individual" (1977a, p. 91), and also that, " . . . objectivism and subjectivism, spiritualism and materialism, activity and passivity lose their opposition and thus their existence as opposites only in a social situation" (1977a, p. 93). It is at this point that Marxist theory of society, as a historical anti-reductionist science (Fromm, 1961, 1966; Howard, 1977; McQuarie, 1978) becomes congenial for social psychology. Specifically, Marxist dialectics is principally concerned with the human beings as they relate to their concrete environment. In this sense, the theory is neither an empirical description of the social world, nor a Hegelian "Ideal"; rather, it is rooted in human praxis (Korać, 1965). The latter, as conceived by Marx, pertains specifically to the human mode of production which is not merely a response to physical needs, but a definite mode of activity characterizing people's life and their existence as social beings. Praxis, then, can be conceived as " . . . the concrete totality of interconnected activities in which socially productive activity or productive work are the point of departure" (Janoušek, 1972, p. 281). According to Marx, social production (referred to as "intercourse" or Verkehr) refers to a process of concrete *social relations* and activities in which the unity of individual and society is accomplished. The social process of production, thus, entails the creation and transformation of these relations as they unfold historically. These relations are not static events in time, but open, developmental, and transformative. This openness and transformative potential determine the directionality of the process, that is, its teleology. The teleology of historical materialism, then, is not to be understood as a tangible characteristic of the relations to be analyzed, but rather as emergent within the process (Howard, 1977).

Implicit in the Marxist notion of human praxis as social production is an emphasis on social relations as the human mode of being in the world. It should be emphasized, however, that in perceiving the individual and society as ongoing relations, one does not discard the person's "individuality." Rather, individuality gains its meaning from a consideration of the entire context. "Individuality" is not a characteristic of an individual standing separate from the social relations of which he or she is a part. It is a way of speaking about particular aspects of a larger configuration. As Marx said, "Man is in the most literal sense of the word a "zoon politikon," not only a social animal but an animal which can develop into an individual only in society" (1977c, p. 346). It is in this sense that Marx saw in the unity of man and society the "humanization of man" (Fromm, 1966). Since, then, individuality can only develop with the context of social relations, a person's activities are always "social" in nature even when they are not of a communal nature, that is, occuring within the presence of other human beings.

To recapitulate, social relations have been treated as an ongoing dialectical process that fuses the individual and the social. It is in this unity of individual and social and their concrete relatedness that a connecting line with Marxist social theory can be drawn. Furthermore, this approach has a series of fundamental implications for the social psychological domain, namely, (1) a basic reorientation toward an examination of concrete social relations as *processes* rather than as static moments. Implicit in this reorientation is the treatment of the vocabularies of individual psychology and of social groups as different forms of talk for an intrinsically coherent process, and the grounds for developing a vocabulary of the process itself. (2) A necessity for a *contextual developmental* perspective, that is, one that places these processes within a sociohistorical context (Gergen, 1973). Thus, social psychology would reject the restrictive use of the concept of law as applied to historically "neutral" quantities (e.g., law of gravity) (Adorno et al, 1976); rather it should employ "law" only in the sense of general principles, intelligible within particular sociohistorical periods (Lobkowicz, 1978); and (3) a reformulation of both the "individual" and "social world" as concrete activities of relating or *social relations*. Implicit in this conceptualization is the fundamental interconnectedness of individual and society as exemplified in human action.

THE DIALECTIC POSITION IN CURRENT CONTROVERSY

Within recent years a steadily increasing number of scholars have come to raise critical questions regarding traditional psychological investigation, its forms and its potential. Many have also begun to search for new forms of theory and metatheory to replace the old. Within this latter search, dialectics has been frequently cited as a viable alternative to the traditional orientation to social phenomena (cf. Buss, 1979; Israel, 1979; Gergen & Morawski, 1980). We have just seen how the dialectician might attempt to solve long-prevailing conceptual problems in social psychology. It remains in this final section to consider the adequacy of dialectics as a potential alternative to the hypothetico-deductive orientation of long standing. This evaluation may best proceed by evaluating the dialectic stance in light of major criticisms launched against the positivist-empiricist form of science. Four major criticisms are of particular concern:

1. Traditional science views the individual as a pawn to inexorable influences — both environmental (e.g., situational) and internal (e.g., personality, attitudes, cognitive patterns); it is important both intellectually and ethically to reintroduce the concept of the person as an active, intentional, and creative agent (Antaki, 1981; Brenner, 1980; Gergen, 1982; Harré, 1981; Israel, 1979; Pettit, 1981; Shotter, 1974, 1980, 1981).

2. Traditional science has placed almost exclusive reliance on the experiment. Not only does the experiment have little validity for understanding common patterns of action, but it has diminished the range of theoretical possibilities. Required is a psychology in which method, experimental or otherwise, is not the critical arbiter of value (Adorno, et al., 1976; Buck-Morss, 1977; Cvetkovich, 1977; Gergen, 1978; Lourenço, 1976; Moscovici, 1972; Rychlak, 1968).

3. Traditional science is ahistorical; it views various mechanisms and processes as trans-historically valid. Required is a science that recognizes the historical embeddedness of social phenomena (Gergen, 1973, 1982; Harre, 1980; Rosnow, 1978; Sampson, 1978).

4. Traditional science treats the scientist as an objective, nonpartisan bystander merely reporting the facts. Required is a conception of science recognizing the cultural embeddedness of the scientific process and the active role of the scientist within his or her cultural setting (Adorno, et al., 1976; Argyris, 1975; Asplund, 1972; Baumgardner, 1977; Cohen, 1973; Gergen, 1982; Samelson, 1974).

In light of these critical discussions what may be said about the position of dialectics? As will be ventured here, the principles of a dialectical social psychology do not only incorporate the above demands, but also point at new perspectives and directions that could enhance the field in a number of ways. A full elaboration on the above issues from a dialectical perspective goes beyond the scope of the present paper. The discussion that follows highlights the dialectic orientation toward these issues.

A. Human Agency and Action

A dialectical social psychology rejects the notion that the individual is a passive, receptive being, molded by the social world. However, it does not simultaneously enhance the notion that agency, intention, and creativity are a priori givens of human nature. That is, dialectic theory would not ascribe these characteristics to persons as traits, nor see them as the origins of behavior as many critics have wished to do. Rather, agency, intention, and creativity are removed from the realm of the individual and replaced as conceptual givens in the study of relationship. By fusing the individual and social in an ongoing dialectical process of created and recreated *relations,* a dialectical social psychology goes beyond the issue of an active versus passive human nature vis à vis the social world. Instead, it emphasizes activities of relating as entailing — by definition — agency, intentionality, and creativity. The latter, then, do not exist as characteristics of a person but rather characterize the *process* of relating. Thus, an individual is an origin of his or her activities in a relationship only when others in the relationship relinquish their agency over the individual. In this sense, agency is a derivative of a social arrangement and not, as traditionally believed, the source of these arrangements. In the same way, for an act to be "creative" it must be viewed against the backdrop of actions deemed noncreative. There is no creativity outside the juxtaposition or relationship of human activities one to another. Thus, the task of a dialectical social psychologist becomes not the examination of whether these features exist in persons as traits, how they function, and so on, but the examination of the development of the social relationships from which these features are derived.

B. From Facts to Processes

Since a dialectical social psychology defines as its subject matter processes of relating, "experimentation" in the strict use of the term is problematic. The experimental method is designed to capture cause-effect relations at a given moment, to furnish virtual snapshots of momentary mechanisms. It is almost unusable for purposes of elucidating the unfolding or alternation of pattern over extended periods of time. However, this does not imply that dialectics is nonempirical or that dialecticians are unable to construct theories of broad generality. On the contrary, it suggests that the interests of social psychologists are not to be defined so as to fit particular empirical methods, but rather such methods are to be redefined and expanded in order to incorporate the dialectic's mode of understanding. Thus, dialectics does not refute empirical exploration; it is the restrictive use of the latter that obscures the dialectic vision.

The task of the dialectician then, does not entail a continuous polemic against empirical work, but rather a constructive effort to expand the latter in ways that do not restrict his or her subject matter. In particular, efforts should be made towards the development of methodologies that tap social relations in their diachronic development. To this end, an examination of the *phases* that various relations go through in their genesis, development, and transformation acquires primary significance. Path-analysis, time-series, and cross-lagged correlations are all useful devices for a preliminary consideration of temporal phenomena. However, in their general concern with the relationship among particulate, abstracted variables, they are ultimately insufficient for demonstrating dialectic processes. Furthermore, the regularities that characterize these phases or the development of relations would be treated not as ahistorical laws, but rather as general principles of relating which become intelligible only within particular sociohistorical periods. Required in the future are methods that facilitate *understanding, describing,* and *synthesizing* social relations in their full unfolding within the culture.

C. Social Change and the Scientist's Role

As to the criticisms that traditional social psychology fails to take account of the historical change and the engagement of the scientist in that change, dialectics also furnishes useful insights. First, it is clear from the dialectical perspective that social psychology must be preeminently a historical undertaking. Social relations are inherently transformative, it is maintained, and to treat them as static entities is thus to obscure their most significant feature. However, dialectics also furnishes a means for understanding such transformations. The theorist is sensitized in particular to inherent negations or contradictions within relationships and to their potential in generating change.

Regarding the scientist's position within such change, dialectics is in full agreement with those who criticize traditional science for neglecting such considerations. However, an attempt is made to go beyond the common formulation that science and society are interdependent entities. The argument that sociohistorical conditions affect the subject matter and practice of social psychology or conversely, that the latter reflects dominant social issues, entails a dichotomy between social psychology as a scientific institutional structure and the social world. Within this formulation, sociohistorical conditions are, then, conceptualized as independent, reified entities, *external* to the scientific community, and exerting influence on it from the "outside." Social psychology is then perceived as exerting an influence on social conditions in the sense that its findings are potentially capable of changing social policy.

This orientation can be contrasted with a dialectical perspective in which societal structure or entities are understood as social relations and the particular mode that these relations take. Sociohistorical *conditions,* then, become sociohistorical and political *relations* and do no exist independently of or outside the practice of social psychology. Social psychology's practices are, thus, to be treated as modes of relationship. Society, the marketplace, industry, economic and political institutions once viewed as external influences upon the field are not thus, independent entities, but are comprised of ongoing social relations of which we, as social psychologists are a part. In other words, there is no overriding structure within which social psychology as a scientific institution is embedded. There are only ongoing social relations, and social psychology constitutes a particular *mode* that these relations take (other modes being religious, political, etc.).

From the dialectic standpoint, there are no external conditions, structures, or "interests" (often referred to as "status quo") that a social psychologist has to confront or overcome in order to implement change within the world. Instead, the possibility for social change is intimately connected with the conceptualization of professional practice as a *mode of relating* within the broader network of sociopolitical relations. Thus, in carrying out an experiment, conducting a survey, or even writing a theoretical paper, the scientist inserts himself or herself into the full schema of social relationships, and thereby transforms this schema.

This also means that self-critical assessment within social psychology cannot be separated from social critique more generally. As the profession continues to reevaluate its premises, goals, and accomplishments, it is also raising pertinent questions regarding the patterns of what it is a part. To voice concern over experimental manipulation, the lack of informed consent, or the use of scientific information as a source of social control is simultaneously to criticize manipulative, deceptive, and aggressive aspects of the society more generally. To alter such patterns of relating in the profession is simultaneously to engage in social transformation more generally.

REFERENCES

Adams, G. R. Physical attractiveness research: Toward a developmental social psychology of beauty. *Human Development,* 1977, *20,* 217-239.
Adorno, T. W. et al. *The positivist dispute in German sociology,* (G. Adey, & D. Frisby (trans.), London: Heinemann, 1976.
Altman, I. Privacy regulation: Culturally universal or culturally specific. *Journal of Social Issues,* 1977, *33,* 66-84.
Altman, I., & Gauvain, M. A cross-cultural and dialectic analysis of homes. In Liben, L., et. al. (Eds.), *Spatial representation and behavior across the life span: Theory and application,* New York: Academic Press, 1981.
Antaki, C. (Ed.) *The psychology of ordinary explanations of social behaviour,* New York: Academic Press, 1981.
Argyris, C. The incompleteness of social psychological theory. *American Psychologist,* 1969, *24,* 893-908.
Argyris, C. Dangers in applying results from experimental social psychology. *American Psychologist,* 1975, *30,* 469-487.
Asplund, J. On the concept of value relevance. In J. Israel & H. Tajfel, (Eds.), *The context of social psychology: A critical assessment,* London: Academic Press, 1972.
Avineri, S. *The social and political thought of Karl Marx,* Cambridge: The University Press, 1971.
Bandura, A. Self-efficacy: Toward a unifying theory of behavior change. *Psychological Review,* 1977, *84,* 191-215.
Bandura, A. The self and mechanism of agency. In J. Suls (Ed.), *Psychological perspectives on the self,* Hillsdale, N.J.: Lawrence Erlbaum Associates, 1982.
Basseches, M. Dialectical schemata: A framework for the empirical study of the development of dialectical thinking. *Human Development,* 1980, *23,* 400-421.
Baumgardner, R. S. Critical studies in the history of social psychology. *Personality and Social Psychology Bulletin,* 1977, *3,* 681-687.
Bowers, K. Situationism in psychology: An analysis and critique. *Psychological Review,* 1973, *80,* 307-336.
Brenner, M. (Ed.) *The structure of action,* Oxford: Blackwell, 1980.
Buck-Morss, S. The Adorno legacy. *Personality and Social Psychology Bulletin,* 1977, *3,* 707-713.
Buss, A. R. The emerging field of the sociology of psychological knowledge. *American Psychologist,* 1975, *30,* 988-1002.
Buss, A. R. Karl Manheim's legacy to humanistic psychology. *Journal of Humanistic Psychology,* 1976, *16,* 79-81.
Buss, A. R. In defense of a critical-presentist historiography: The fact-theory relationship and Marx's epistemology. *Journal of the History of the Behavioral Sciences,* 1977, *13,* 252-260.
Buss, A. R. Piaget, Marx and Buck-Morss on cognitive development. *Human Development,* 1977, *20,* 118-128.
Buss, A. R. *A dialectical psychology,* New York: Halsted, 1979.
Buss, A. H. *Self-consciousness and social anxiety,* San Francisco: Freeman, 1980.
Cohen, H. R. Dialectics and scientific revolutions. *Science and Society,* 1973, *37,* 326-336.

Cornforth, M. *Communism and philosophy.* N.J.: Humanities Press, 1980.
Cvetkovich, G. Dialectical perspectives on empirical research. *Personality and Social Psychology Bulletin,* 1977, *3,* 688-696.
Deutsch, M. The social psychological study of conflict: Rejoinder to a critique. *European Journal of Social Psychology,* 1974, *4,* 441-456.
Deutsch, M. Theorizing in social psychology. *Personality and Social Psychology Bulletin,* 1976, *2,* 134-141.
Dupré, L. *The philosophical foundations of Marxism.* New York: Harcourt Brace, 1966.
Engels, F. *Anti-Duhring: Herr Eugen Duhring's revolution in science.* New York: International Publishers, 1939.
Fromm, E. (Ed.) *Socialist humanism.* New York: Doubleday, 1961.
Fromm, E. *Marx's concept of man.* New York: Frederick Ungar, 1966.
Gadlin, H. Child discipline and the pursuit of self: An historical interpretation. *Advances in child development and behavior.* (Vol. 12). New York: Academic Press, 1978.
Garner, W. R. The acquisition and application of knowledge: A symbiotic relation. *American Psychologist,* 1972, *27,* 941-946.
Gergen, K. J. Social psychology as history. *Journal of Personality and Social Psychology,* 1973, *26,* 309-320.
Gergen, K. J. On taking dialectics seriously. *Personality and Social Psychology Bulletin,* 1977, *3,* 714-718.
Gergen, K. J. Experimentation in social psychology: A reappraisal. *European Journal of Social Psychology,* 1978, *8,* 507-527.
Gergen, K. J. Toward intellectual audacity in social psychology. In R. Gilmore, & S. Duck (Eds.), *The development of social psychology,* London: Academic Press, 1980.
Gergen, K. J. *Toward transformation in social knowledge,* New York: Springer-Verlag, 1982.
Gergen, K. J. & Morawski, J. An alternative metatheory for social psychology. In L. Wheeler (Ed.), *Review of Personality and Social Psychology.* Beverly Hills: Sage, 1980.
Glass, J. F. The humanistic challenge to sociology. *Journal of Humanistic Psychology,* 1971, *11,* 170-183.
Greenberg, D. S. *The politics of pure science.* New York: New American Library, 1967.
Harré, R. Making social psychology scientific. In R. Gilmour & S. Duck (Eds.), *The development of social psychology,* New York: Academic Press, 1980.
Harré, R. Expressive aspects of descriptions of others. In C. Antaki (Ed.), *The psychology of ordinary explanations of social behaviour,* New York: Academic Press, 1981.
Harris, A. E. Social dialectics and language: Mother and child construct the discourse. *Human Development,* 1975, *18,* 80-96.
Hogan, R. Dialectic aspects of moral development. *Human Development,* 1974, *17,* 107-117.
Hook, S. Dialectics in society and history. In H. Feigl, & M. Brodbeck (Eds.), *Readings in the philosophy of science,* New York: Appleton-Century-Crofts, 1953.
Howard, D. *The Marxian legacy.* New York: Urizen Books, 1977.
Israel, J. *The language of dialectics and the dialectics of language.* New York: Humanities Press, 1979.
Israel, J., & Tajfel, H. (Eds.) *The context of social psychology: A critical assessment,* London: Academic Press, 1972.
Janoušek, J. On the Marxian concept of praxis. In J. Israel, & H. Tajfel (Eds.), *The context of social psychology: A critical assessment.* London: Academic Press, 1972.
Jay, M. *The dialectical imagination.* Boston: Little, Brown & Company, 1973.
Jones, E. E., & Nisbett, E. R. The actor and the observer: Divergent perceptions of the causes of behavior. In E. E. Jones et al. (Eds.), *Attribution: Perceiving the causes of behavior.* Morristown: General Learning Press, 1971.
Jordan, Z. A. *The evolution of dialectical materialism,* New York: Macmillan, 1967.

Kelley, H. H. *Attribution in social interaction,* Morristown: General Learning Press, 1971.
Kolakowski, L. Responsibility and history. In G. Novack (Ed.), *Existentialism versus Marxism,* New York: Delta Books, 1966.
Korać, V. In search of human society. In E. Fromm (Ed.), *Socialist humanism.* New York: Doubleday, 1965.
Korsch, K. *Marxism and Philosophy,* London: NLB, 1970.
Kvale, S. Facts and dialectics. In J. F. Rychlak (Ed.), *Dialectic: Humanistic rationale for behavior and development.* Basel: Karger, 1976.
Lana, R. E., & Georgoudi, M. Causal attributions: Phenomenological and dialectical aspects. (unpublished manuscript).
Lobkowicz, N. *Theory and practice: History of a concept from Aristotle to Marx.* Notre Dame, Ind.: University of Notre Dame Press, 1967.
Lobkowicz, N. Historical laws. In D. McQuarie (Ed.), *Karl Marx: Sociology, social change and capitalism.* London: Quartet Books, 1978.
Lourenço, S. V. The dialectic and qualitative methodology. In J.F. Rychlak (Ed.), *Dialectic: Humanistic rationale for behavior and development.* Basel: Karger, 1976.
Magnusson, D., & Endler, N. S. (Eds.) *Personality at the crossroads: Current issues in interactional psychology.* Hillsdale, N.J.: Lawrence Erlbaum Associates, 1977.
Mancuso, J. C. Dialectic man as a subject in psychological research. In Rychlak, J.F. (Ed.), *Dialectic: Humanistic rationale for behavior and development,* Basel: Karger, 1976.
Manis, M. Is social psychology really different? *Personality and Social Psychology Bulletin,* 1976, *2,* 428-437.
Marx, K. Economic and philosophical manuscripts. In D. McLellan (Ed.), *Karl Marx: Selected writings,* Oxford: Oxford University Press, 1977a.
Marx, K. German ideology. In D. McLellan (Ed.), *Karl Marx: Selected writings,* Oxford: Oxford University Press, 1977b.
Marx, K. Grundrisse. In McLellan, D. (Ed.), *Karl Marx: Selected writings,* Oxford: Oxford University Press, 1977c.
McQuarie, D. (Ed.) *Karl Marx: Sociology, social change and capitalism,* London: Quartet Books, 1978.
Meacham, J. A. A dialectic approach to moral development and self-esteem. *Human Development,* 1975, *18,* 159-170.
Merleau-Ponty, M. *Adventures of the dialectic,* Evanston: Northwestern University Press, 1973.
Mischel, W. Toward a cognitive social learning reconceptualization of personality. *Psychological Review,* 1973, *80,* 252-283.
Mitroff, J. J., & Betz, F. Dialectic decision theory: A metatheory of decision making. *Management Science,* 1972, *19,* 11-24.
Moscovici, S. Society and theory in social psychology. In J. Israel & H. Tajfel (Eds.), *The context of social psychology: A critical assessment.* London: Academic Press, 1972.
Novack, G. Basic differences between existentialism and Marxism. In G. Novack, (Ed.), *Existentialism versus Marxism.* New York: Delta Books, 1966.
Pettit, P. On actions and explanations. In C. Antaki (Ed.), *The psychology of ordinary explanations of social behaviour.* New York: Academic Press, 1981.
Plon, M. On a question of orthodoxy. *European Journal of Social Psychology,* 1974, *4,* 457-467.
Rappoport, L., & Kren, G. What is a social issue? *American Psychologist,* 1975, *30,* 838-841.
Riegel, K. Dialectic operations: The final period of cognitive development. *Human Development,* 1973, *16,* 346-370.
Riegel, K. The dialectics of human development. *American Psychologist,* 1976, *31,* 689-700.
Rosnow, R. L. The prophetic vision of Giambattista Vico: Implications for the state of social psychological theory. *Journal of Personality and Social Psychology,* 1978, *36,* 1322-1331.

Rychlak, J. F. *A philosophy of science for personality theory.* Boston: Houghton Mifflin, 1968.

Rychlak, J. F. The multiple meanings of dialectic. In J. F. Rychlak (Ed.), *Dialectic: Humanistic rationale for behavior and development.* Basel: Karger, 1976.

Samelson, F. History, origin myth, and Ideology: Discovery of social psychology. *Journal for the Theory of Social Behavior,* 1974, *4,* 217-231.

Sampson, E. E. Scientific paradigms and social values: Wanted-A scientific revolution. *Journal of Personality and Social Psychology,* 1978, *36,* 1332-1343.

Schlenker, B. R. Social psychology and science. *Journal of Personality and Social Psychology,* 1974, *29,* 1-15.

Shotter, J. What is it to be human? In N. Armistead (Ed.), *Reconstructing social psychology.* Baltimore, Md.: Penguin, 1974.

Shotter, J. Acton, joint action and intentionality. In M. Brenner, (Ed.), *The structure of action.* Oxford: Blackwell, 1980.

Shotter, J. Telling and reporting: Prospective and retrospective uses of self-ascriptions. In C. Antaki (Ed.), *The psychology of ordinary explanations.* London: Academic Press, 1981.

Smelser, N. J. (Ed.) *Karl Marx: On society and social change.* Chicago: University of Chicago Press, 1973.

Smith, B. M. Social psychology, science, and history: So what? *Personality and Social Psychology Bulletin,* 1976, *2,* 438-444.

Smith, B. M. A dialectical social psychology? Comments on a Symposium. *Personality and Social Psychology Bulletin,* 1977, *3,* 719-724.

Steiner, I. D. Whatever happened to the group in social psychology?. *Journal of Experimental Social Psychology,* 1974, *10,* 94-108.

Stroebe, W. The critical school in German social psychology. *Personality and Social Psychology Bulletin,* 1980, *6,* 105-112.

Vigier, J. P. Dialectics and natural science. In G. Novack (Ed.), *Existentialism versus Marxism,* New York: Delta Books, 1966.

Ziller, R. C. Group dialectics: The dynamics of groups over time. *Human Development,* 1977, *20,* 293-308.

5 Dialectical Analysis and Psychosocial Epistemology

Leon Rappoport
Kansas State University

The Trouble with Dialectics is That it is too Dialectical

As a general mode of thought dialectical analysis is ubiquitous, since any comparison between opposed objects or concepts may be labeled "dialectical." In order to rescue the term from this anarchic condition and preserve its instrumental meaning in philosophy and social science, scholars have tried to either pin it down as a semantic *object* via formal definition: " . . . exposition based on juxtaposition of opposed or contradictory ideas"; or fence it in as a historical *subject* via chronology " . . . Socrates to Hegel to Marx to Critical Theory." Within the Wittgensteinian labyrinth so constituted, partisan scholars of the object (who recognize even language itself as problematic, a form of ideology) and of the subject (who recognize history as problematic, a form of ideology), frequently stalk each other in a ritual warfare of critique and counter-critique.

An exemplary demonstration of this linguistic tangle appears in Ollman's (1971) definitive study of Marx's theory of alienation. Before addressing the substantive topic, Ollman devotes over 70 pages to a clarification of the way Marx used language. That is, the semantic structure of his formulations, and the historical grounds upon which his ideas were developed. Consequently, readers must first negotiate a dialectical analysis of Marx's forms of expression, which is provided not in order to justify Marx, but simply to make his writing intelligible despite the linguistic and historical barriers surrounding it.

"Marx's relational conception of reality and corresponding use of language to convey relations make it necessary for any large scale examination of his work to proceed by piecing together what he is saying while simultaneously reconstructing the concepts with which he is saying it (Ollman, 1971, p. 71)." These difficulties, of course, are not limited to projects on Marx; any issue of *Telos* or *Theory and Society,* two of the major journal outlets for dialectical social analyses, will contain many other relevant examples. Such epistemological difficulties plaguing scholars committed to the development of dialectical perspectives have been exacerbated by their relative isolation from the ruling majority of mainstream scholars who see neither language nor history as intrinsically problematic, let alone ideological, and question the loyalty of those who do.

Furthermore, apart from the fact that dialectical thought does not express itself in uniform categories or speak with one voice, the established disciplines generally reject dialectical analysis because it is by its very nature invariably critical, revealing, and threatening: critical of established ideas and orthodoxies; revealing of implicit values within supposedly value-free forms of inquiry, and, therefore, threatening to the professional-academic hierarchies involved.

Within the specific context of contemporary psychology and sociology, moreover, dialectical thought generally violates the accepted premise that ideas are only as good as the empirical evidence supporting them. Like Socrates, Critical Theorists such as Adorno and Marcuse seemingly were delighted to curse the darkness while obstinately refusing to light any empiricist candles. This is clearly anathema to disciplines that have justified themselves to society by suggesting that in return for support, they can provide tangible means to solve or at least "manage" difficult social problems. The famous remark attributed to Kurt Lewin, "there is nothing so practical as a good theory," has served as a central element in the catechism of liberal-empiricist social science. Contrast this with the conclusion of Robert Heilbroner in a recent review of dialectics (1980):

> To use the language of discursive thought (that is, the language built on empirical generalizations and logic) is to use a language that rules out the very ambiguities, Janus-like meanings, and metaphorical referents that are the raisons d'etre for a dialectical view. Dialectics seeks to tap levels of awareness that defy the syntaxes of common sense and logic. To present dialectics as a set of generalizations derived from empirical observations, or as an exercise in logic, is to betray the very purpose for which dialectics exists. (p. 58)

Given all these considerations why "dialectics is too dialectical" for most scholars today, and accepting that still other, more concrete reasons might be added to the foregoing summary, why should the matter be pursued any further? Several thematic responses to this question will be developed in the following pages, but the overriding general answer I wish to propose is that there is really no other choice. The conventional objections to dialectical analysis noted above are valid enough as a description of the past and of many elements in the present not yet recognized as obsolete. It is quite evident, however (as will be argued), that in view of emerging trends of social philosophy, not to mention biology and physics, these objections are becoming, not invalid, but *irrelevant*. If it is accepted that social science cannot long stand still and will not move backwards, then the only metatheoretical orientation available for the future is in one form or another, "dialectics." The issue, in other words, is not whether social psychology, or psychology in general, will accept the dialectical orientation, but how this movement away from positivism will come about. As Royce has argued in his call for integrative and interpretative dialectics in psychology, time is running out on us.

"Psychology's past has caught up with its future. The focus on data gathering, research design, and statistical analysis, although necessary in the early phases of psychology's history, will not be sufficient to deal with psychology's future (Royce, 1982, p. 260)."

The conditions of obsolescence noted by Royce seem particularly relevant to the current status of social psychology, where most of the work is still carried on in accord with metatheoretical canons of the fifties, computer-based methods of the sixties, and explanatory, justificatory rhetoric of the seventies. Meanwhile, as we move further into the eighties, enrollments decline, research support dwindles, and the very subject matter of social psychology begins to migrate via secession aimed at forming new fields (e.g., environmental psychology; organizational psychology) or expanding older fields (social philosophy; psychosocial history).

Royce's arguments, however, like those of Alan Buss (1979) and others who have argued less explicitly for dialectical metatheory, are primarily based on conditions within psychology. The arguments to be developed in the present chapter will appeal to converging bodies of material both internal and external to psychology. To this end, the chapter is organized in three sections presenting (a) a discussion of some formal properties of dialectical thought with particular attention toward formulating the problem of psychosocial epistemology, (b) a descriptive summary suggesting how important but unresolved sociocultural and historical problems associated with the Holocaust may be opened up via dialectical analysis, and (c) some prospective discussion of the role of dialectics in the forseeable future of social psychology.

STRUCTURE AND DYNAMICS OF DIALECTICAL ANALYSIS

Over the past dozen or more years, the truism that has increasingly become characteristic of contemporary scientific and social thought is that "everything is related to everything else"; or, as Rifkin (1980) frequently observed in his review of energy systems, "there is no free lunch." Reflecting widening awareness of the ecological principles governing all human activities as well as nature-in-general, and serving as an important basis for what is often called the "holistic" world view, these slogans would have delighted Marx and Engels, whose formulation of the "dialectic of nature" was based precisely upon the assumption of a universe of relationships and interactions in constant flux.

As described by Engels, and later freeze-dried in philosophy textbooks, the modern dialectic consists of four central principles: (1) the transformation of quantity to quality, (2) the mutual penetration of polar opposites (i.e., things that appear separate and opposed are dependent upon each other for their meaning), (3) change and development via contradiction or negation, and (4) the spiral form of development (i.e., growth or progress via negation must be nonlinear).

Concrete examples of these principles (though of course usually not acknowledged as such) are plentiful throughout the life sciences. In psychology, one need look no further than to the familiar literature of human development, where Freud's psychosexual theory of personality development and Piaget's analysis of cognitive development both offer many cogent illustrations of all four principles. Parenthetically, it is noteworthy that the various branches of developmental psychology — life-span, childhood and adolescence, aging/gerontology — have been particularly receptive to explicit dialectical perspectives. This is partly owing to the intensive efforts of Klaus Riegel (1976) to promulgate "the dialectics of development," and partly to the inherent good fit between the dialectic and the manifestly spiraling, contradictory bio-social contours of life-span experience. It is significant, in this connection, that Hegel had already articulated a surprisingly modern sounding (Eriksonian) age-stage theory of personality development in 1830!

In addition to the four highly abstract principles of the dialectic, however, contemporary expressions of dialectical analysis frequently employ such psychosocial concepts as: (1) *alienation* (the tendency for people to become estranged from the products they create, the community they inhabit, and even their own conception of themselves); (2) *reification* (the tendency to treat abstractions as natural phenomena); (3) *inversion* (the tendency of ideas and social objects to turn into their opposite), and (4) *ideology* (ideas arrayed in explanatory frameworks wherein all elements appear self-evident and the whole tends to provide imperative justifications for action).[1]

---

[1] Most readers will know that each of these concepts has been the subject of extensive scholarly discourse as to their multiple historical and sociopolitical meanings. Ollman, for example, indicates that thirteen different meanings of "ideology" may be found in Marx. The parenthetical descriptions offered above are merely rough common sense abbreviations.

The primary function of these concepts in dialectical analyses of nature and history is to describe the mechanisms governing the social construction of reality that occurs when the underlying dynamics of flux, growth, and decay in the world system, as it were, are not recognized. A summary appreciation of this point may be attained via an oversimplified reconstruction of the Marxian analysis strategy. It begins with a fundamental question: If the dialectic is a valid description of the principles governing nature, including human nature, how is it that human social life appears to operate in such a contrary fashion? Aside from oppression of the weak by the strong, the Marxian answer to this question was to trace the impacts of prevailing modes of production upon the whole spectrum of social life, ranging from the level of the individual to that of international trade. In this context, ideologies geared to the interests of the ruling elements in society are seen to arise in order to conceal the actual conditions of life from the rest of society. Then an artificial or false structure of reality is built up via the mechanisms of alienation, reification, and inversion. Alienation saps creative energy and impedes cooperative action; reification supports perception of the status quo as unproblematic and prevents critical self-awareness; and inversion permits the assimilation of critique, and critics, into the established order.

Of course, the foregoing scan of dialectical analysis ignores vast areas for the sake of immediate didactic convenience, but it is by no means entirely arbitrary (cf. Heilbroner, 1980, Ollman, 1971, and Seigel, 1978). More to the point of the present volume, however, dialectical analyses conducted within the field of psychology have begun to approximate the foregoing Marxian model of ideology-critique. Sampson's (1981) analysis of cognitive psychology, for example, follows the pattern of ideology-critique insofar as it suggests how ostensibly objective, value-neutral theories of cognition can mask and divert attention from important social problems, thus serving to support the sociocultural status quo. Cognitive psychology, therefore, is perceived by Sampson as an ideology in service of "the given," which he labels "cognitivism." In a similar vein, critiques of social issues research (Rappoport, 1980; Rappoport & Kren, 1975) have suggested that applied studies purportedly aimed at resolving or correcting social problems may be no more than limited exercises of social science expertise carried out according to an implicit "ideology of understanding." That is, they may constitute routinized forms of research planning and analysis in which the existing social structure and dominant cultural values are taken for granted, and problems tend to be "understood" in terms of inadequate knowledge and/or failures of communication.

Briefly then, the argument up to this point is that despite many apparent difficulties and disagreements concerning dialectics, the basic principles involved are eminently well suited to the bio-social subject matter of psychology. Indeed, as the holistic, ecological orientation of research and theory in the natural as well as the social sciences continues to grow, the formerly dominant principles of reductionistic positivism appear increasingly naive and inadequate, whereas the principles of the dialectic become more and more compelling. The various types of dialectically informed critique already becoming available within psychology indicate the necessity for a deeper exploration of thought and behavior than has previously been the case. This will entail development of a larger and more complex framework of theoretical discourse in which the origins and modes of production of knowledge may be engaged as part of the subject matter of social science. It is this relatively unknown, intimidating domain, where philosophy, psychology, and the other social sciences converge upon one another to form the ground of contemporary social knowledge, that is considered next under the heading of psychosocial epistemology. It is noteworthy, furthermore, that working from a very different perspective, Royce (1982) has reached similar conclusions about the necessity to utilize dialectical thought in order to clarify both the epistemology of psychology and the sociology and psychology of epistemology.

PSYCHOSOCIAL EPISTEMOLOGY

The problem of psychosocial epistemology stands at the center of what is often referred to as "post-Marxist dialectics," that is, the extension of dialectical analysis beyond the now-questionable material-economic and positivist science assumptions of Marxian thought. Psychosocial epistemology is, in its more familiar form, concerned with the historically and culturally rooted psychological and sociological forces influencing the "discovery" or production of knowledge. It is in many ways similar to Weber's "sociology of knowledge," but differs by embracing linguistic and psycho-historical factors that were at best peripheral to Weber's socio-economic analysis. Still more important: The conceptual tools accepted as unproblematic by Weber and his followers (rationality, efficiency, economic interest, etc.) become matters of inquiry in the larger context of psychosocial epistemology.

The so-called critical historians and philosophers of science tend to work on the problem of knowledge employing Freudian, Marxist, Weberian, Kuhnian, or other theories as tools for revealing the previously unknown or unexamined role of psychosocial and economic factors in scientific work. A good example of such efforts is Mitroff's aptly named study of moon research investigations, *The Subjective Side of Science* (1974). However, some noteworthy studies of this type specific to psychology have also appeared. Salient among these — to name a few — are Apfelbaum and Lubek's (1976) critical review of conflict research; Baumgardner's (1977) revisionist discussion of themes in the history of social psychology; and Samelson's (1977) archivally based reinterpretation of World War I intelligence testing. All too often, such critical works are of necessity published in the guise of routine historical and/or philosophical inquiries, although from the standpoint of the present discussion, since they tend to reveal the play of ideology and related mechanisms in the development of knowledge, they may be characterized as dialectical analyses of psychosocial epistemology. An outstanding case in point is Samelson's paper, noted above, which ends with the comment (p. 280), "What, then, is this piece of history about: an episode in the success story of empirical science, or a horror story of scientific ideology?"

But aside from the critical history meaning associated with psychosocial epistemology, there is another, more immediate and as yet much more obscure way to understand it, as indicated by the following question. How can we gain knowledge about the psychosocial factors that influence the production of knowledge when these psychosocial factors are themselves problematic? Thus, although the theories of Freud, Marx, Weber, and even Jung (as employed by Mitroff), clearly serve as excellent instruments for the critical historical studies constituting a form of psychosocial epistemology, these theories are no more absolute, no more above critical epistemological suspicion than the reified, positivistic fields and structures of knowledge they are used against. In sum, lest we deceive ourselves, it is ultimately necessary to recognize that critically useful psychosocial, economic and historical theories can become, and inevitably must become, *objects* of psychosocial epistemological analysis as well as *instruments* for its accomplishment.

One historically imperative basis for the formulation of this issue will be taken up below in connection with long-standing problems of Holocaust interpretation. Abstractly, however, and considered in connection with contemporary philosophy of science, the questions of how to deal with the apparent infinite regress of dialectical critique, of how to avoid becoming the victim of implicit, not-yet-realized ideology while attempting to reveal ideology elsewhere, force recognition of the fact that psychosocial epistemology cannot be indifferent to issues of ontology. That is, once the knowledge processes of psychology are recognized as problematic and open to critique, then the ontological basis, or "ground of being" for the critique itself becomes questionable. Ultimately (as the saying goes), what we have here is a problem concerning the *existential status* of social science! It seems very important to emphasize, furthermore, that in many ways it was exactly this problem that logical positivism attempted to deal with, or to be more precise, eliminate, via development of empirical rules-of-the-game for science. In other words, an oppressively rule-bound empiricism, grounded on operationism and given direction by reductionism, came to be thought of as offering the best way out of the existential dilemma. (See Gergen, 1982, for a thorough discussion of why this rules-of-the-game approach is ineffectual except in very limited circumstances.)

Some alternative approaches to this problem based on dialectical assumptions have already been put forward within philosophy and psychology. The philosophers of science Mitroff and Feyerabend, for instance, have called for the institution of radical pluralism in science. Mitroff argues that dialectical inquiry systems are required in order to prevent the hegemony of ruling ideas or ideologies. Such systems would demand that every important formulation be challenged by its opposite; put to test against its dialectical contradiction. Feyerabend (1975) suggests a more sweeping "epistemological anarchy," meaning formal recognition and encouragement of the idea that in science, "anything goes." Moreover, since science is a reflection of society, society itself must be freed from the domination of rationalized, positivist science, and all alternative views—witchcraft, astrology, various religions—should be given free reign in the marketplace of ideas. Under some such conditions as these, ideology-based orthodoxies would be more difficult to establish and maintain because, as a matter of principle, all relevant formulations would either be required from the outset to acknowledge their conditionality, their contextual limitations, or else have to face constant, diverse critique aimed at revealing this conditionality, forcing it to the surface, as it were.

Within psychology, one counterpart to the Mitroff and Feyerabend positions is the argument by Loftus-Senders (1978) for a radical change of epistemological consciousness emphasizing a holistic, dynamic, dialectical view of nature and human behavior. Her suggestion is accompanied by very clear demands for ontological changes on the part of social scientists themselves, that is, in the way they think of and relate to their subject matter, including their "subjects," clients, and students. These ideas are similar to those independently proposed by Sampson (1978), as part of his suggested new paradigm, "paradigm 11," for psychology. And Gergen (1982), after pointing out the necessity for "generative" theories aimed at breaking through rather than maintaining prevalent sociocultural viewpoints, has suggested a "sociorationalist" metatheoretical orientation which has many of the same characteristics indicated by Sampson, Loftus-Senders, and the position of Royce noted earlier.

In general, therefore, it seems roughly correct to say that the multifaceted problem of psychosocial epistemology and related matters of ontology, whether labeled as such or not, are now taking on recognizable form among philosophers and social scientists. This condition has already stimulated proposals for a much broader and critically self-aware view of knowledge processes than has previously existed in psychology. Of course, such proposals are at present only outlines on our theoretical-philosophical horizon, and there is no guarantee that if they were actually put into general practice, all the difficulties discussed above would disappear. There are, however, good reasons to believe that at least some of these difficulties could be resolved. The present tendency of established social science to sink into ideology by supporting or even joining with the ideology structures that demand critical investigation (health, welfare, and education bureaucracies, (cf. Illich, 1976, Lasch, 1978), might be corrected "from above" when the positivist rules-of-the-game are transcended.

In this connection, it should be apparent that the case for dialectically oriented metatheory has an important basis outside of social science as well as inside. The arguments thus far have mainly been from the inside, appealing to certain philosophical principals and some of the ways they have been employed for purposes of internal critique. But social science exists in order to study and interpret social phenomena; insofar as it cannot do this effectively, its failure provides the basis for analysis and critique from the outside, as will be shown below in the context of Holocaust studies.

THE EPISTEMOLOGICAL INSTRUCTION OF HOLOCAUST INTERPRETATION

The "instruction" gained from intensive analysis of the Holocaust (Kren & Rappoport, 1980) concerned the necessity of finding not merely new forms of psychosocial, historical knowledge, but new *ways* of finding such knowledge, because we discovered that the old ways were blatantly inadequate. We began our project believing that contemporary social and psychohistorical theories could be used to penetrate and assimilate major aspects of the Holocaust; we ended by realizing that the Holocaust had penetrated and assimilated major aspects of contemporary social and psychohistorical theories. The Holocaust phenomena, in other words, turn out to be an immanent, powerful critique of social science because they defy interpretation according to established principles. This point has been elaborated elsewhere (Kren & Rappoport, 1982), emphasizing its historiographic and social-philosophical implications.

The problem here is not that all social science theories are useless for Holocaust interpretation, but rather that when they are confronted, "tested," against the mass murder that occurred at the center of European civilization, some very strange, unexpected conclusions begin to emerge. These involve clear and unavoidable indications that the very same logic structures and instrumental rationalities (or *èpistemes*, à la Foucault) by which one attempts the diagnostic/interpretative *unveiling* of the Holocaust, *are themselves implicated* in its constructions and its subsequent obscurity. To be more concrete: As this obscurity is to some extent penetrated by breaking conventional unities and cutting across the familiar categories of both theory and subject matter, what eventually is glimpsed underneath the masks of conventional analyses are some of the very same thought structures — turned a little askew, to be sure — that one has been using to try to get through them.

The odd progression or "movement of thought" underlying this realization involves a sequence whereby the subject matter of the analysis initially only seems resistant to the instruments employed. Yet, as these instruments are increasingly deformed by the unyielding material they were supposed to penetrate, the unexpected results are first, dawning awareness that the instruments are inadequate; second, deeper awareness that the instruments have been transformed to the point of becoming, in themselves, subject matter for analysis; and finally, a still-deeper, hardly nameable awareness that the original subject matter and the instruments it has transformed are not separate at all, but really constitute one more general problem.

Merely to formulate such statements as the foregoing is to risk serious confusion; to try to briefly convey the deep structure basis for them is almost impossible since we do not yet have appropriate language terms for such things, except perhaps in poetry. This is a situation in which epistemology meets ontology, for one is speaking here of something like a conversion experience: the realization in historical-psychosocial terms, of something like a gestalt reversible figure. However, a few thematic examples may indicate how certain prior, inadequate social science interpretations of the Holocaust can be traced back to the more abstract issues of dialectical analysis and psychosocial epistemology.

The criminal psychopathology of the SS. The two major sources for the idea that the SS was made up of men who were psychopaths, had "criminal superegos," nurtured pathological hatred of the Jews, were sadists, or psychosexual deviants, and so forth, were first of all the Nazi propaganda itself, which aimed to portray the SS as an instrument of implacable terror in order to better intimidate all opposition (hence the black uniforms and death head insignia), and second, concentration camp and death camp survivors who described incidents of extraordinary torture and brutality. To focus on this sort of material is to leave aside the fact that by 1941–42, and afterwards, the SS had become a huge multifaceted organization with far more personnel in military combat units and administrative bureaucracies than could ever be employed to operate the camps. However, even when analysis is limited to the guards and officers manning the camps, the notion that they had volunteered for, or welcomed, such service as a means of gratifying abnormal psychogenic needs turns out to be false.

Many of the camp personnel were, in fact, like Franz Stangl, who commanded Treblinka, or the notorious Henrich "Gestapo" Mueller, originally members of civilian police forces that had been administratively absorbed into the SS. Because of the chronic shortage of manpower in wartime Germany, and an arrangement whereby Himmler was not allowed to siphon off recruits from the military age pools jealously claimed by the Wehrmacht, men like Stangl were assigned to special service under real or implied threats of severe punishment if they refused.

Detailed case studies now available (e.g., Boehnert, 1977; Sereney, 1974; Segev, 1977; Sydnor, 1977; Dicks, 1972; Weingartner, 1968) show that SS men who participated directly in mass killings or served in major death camps tended, if anything, to be conformists with weak ego strength before authority rather than pathological killers. Many found their duties to be appalling and were just barely able to carry them out. Among the killing units (Einsatzgruppen) sent into Poland and the Soviet Union in 1940-41, drunkenness, narcotics use, and suicides became significant problems. It was after Himmler toured some of his units "at the front" and realized their condition that efforts were made to set up the more systematic death camps, beginning with the primitive diesel-exhaust gas chambers at Sobibor and Treblinka. After the war, moreover, virtually all of the men who had been closely involved in the mass murders, including many who were wanted for trial as war criminals, lived unexceptional, "normal" lives. The decisive fact, usually ignored in the early Holocaust literature circa 1945-65, is that the death camp and concentration camp personnel were not primarily psychopaths, neurotics, nor even passionate haters of Jews, Gypsies, or Slavs, but were specific, *contextual* killers: Their killing was restricted to categories of victims selected for death at a place and in a manner chosen by superiors who had the legal and customary authority to issue such orders.

As for the horrors and atrocities reported by survivors, they were real enough, although it is noteworthy that in this memoir literature one also finds a great many accounts of SS men who helped Jews. Himmler specifically complained during the war that too many of his men were trying to keep their "good" or pet Jews alive, and after the war, during war crimes trials, it became a cliché that every former SS man could produce at least one former Jewish prisoner who would testify in his favor. Finally, to the question "how could normal people do such things?" all that one can say, based on the evidence of the Holocaust, and subsequent relevant events in Algeria, Vietnam, Nigeria, Uganda, Iran, Cambodia, Chile, and lately El Salvador, is that normal people can do such things. Even Jewish and Polish prisoners in the camps participated in killing their own people — under threat of death, of course, but nevertheless, they could do it, and as Tadeusz Borowski (1967) showed in *This Way for the Gas, Ladies and Gentlemen,* these people were not abnormal; instead, the real horror was that brutality, torture, and murder had become normal.

It is just at this point that we begin to meet the problem, or actually glimpse the abyss, usually concealed by rationalizations based on the prevailing, designed-for-comfort positivist epistemology; namely, that people who commit horrible actions must be certifiably abnormal. Instead, the radical truth of the social construction of reality revealed in the Holocaust is that when powerful local norms define murder and torture as normal, then only those who are eccentrically abnormal will not follow them. The real problem of interpretation here — the reversible figure — is not "how could normal people do such things?" but "how could normal people defy the horrors of the situation and *not* do such things?" (See our chapter "Resistance," Kren & Rappoport, 1981).

A direct illustration of the epistemological problem at stake here was given by Jean Amery when discussing the SS men who tortured him (1980):

> Were they sadists, then? According to my well-founded conviction, they were not sadists in the narrow sexual-pathological sense. In general, I don't believe that I encountered a single genuine sadist of this sort during my two years of imprisonment by the Gestapo and in the concentration camps. But probably they *were* sadists if we leave sexual pathology aside and attempt to judge the tortures according to the categories of, well, the philosophy of the Marquis de Sade. Sadism as the dis-ordered view of the world is something other than the sadism of the usual psychology handbooks, also other than the sadism interpretation of Freudian analysis. (p. 34).

But what is it, this non-sexual, dis-ordered view of the world? Amery has no answer other than to appeal to existentialist notions concerning negation of "the other." He, like all the rest of us, simple runs into the epistemological entropy prevailing at those frontiers of modern social experience where the normatively defined "normal" meets the non-clinically definable "abnormal." What ends up being problematic, therefore, is not the horrible behavior of the Nazis in the camps, but the epistemological status of currently accepted, empirically based (cf. the MMPI), concepts of psychopathology.

Contemporary public manifestations of this situation can be seen in court cases such as the trial of Patty Hearst for crimes committed after being kidnapped, and the trial of John Hinckley for his attempt to kill President Reagan. In both, contradictory testimony by well-credentialled psychiatric experts reveal the severe limits of psychopathology as an explanation for violent criminal behavior. A similar conclusion may be drawn from social psychology, where the Milgram experiments on obedience to authority, and the Zimbardo study of behavior in simulated prison conditions, provide comparatively mild but convincing demonstrations that depending upon contextual circumstances, normalcy is irrelevant to inhumane conduct. The point to be emphasized, however, is that although the evidence from the Holocaust is affirmed by many sorts of contemporary material calling into question the epistemological basis for psychiatric categorizations of behavior, this evidence is either ignored or narrowly construed to minimize its contradiction of prevailing social theory. (If widely accepted constructs of psychopathology and behavior are seriously brought in question, is it not possible that the whole psychiatric-social science category superstructure might begin to fall?)

Victimization and resistance. Another aspect of the immanent epistemology critique emerging from the study of the Holocaust may be seen when we turn from the perpetrators to consider the situation of their victims. The prevalent metaphor-myth about the Jews and the other millions of Nazi victims is that they all, especially the Jews, went "like sheep to the slaughter." On this subject, even after almost 40 years of archival research and theoretical analysis, the dominant theme eloquently described by Dawidowicz (1981) is still paradox, confusion, and angry arguments among various scholarly and sociopolitical factions. The reasons for this, aside from the diverse vested interests of the parties involved, are not hard to find. At the very outset, there is the problem of how to define victimization as a mass social process in a modern nation. Certainly the Jews were victims of anti-Semitism throughout European history, but until the advent of Hitler, they were less so in Germany than in many other countries. Moreover, even in Germany up through 1940-41, anti-Semitism was not mass murder; was not a rationalized social policy of genocide conducted with the resources of a mobilized modern state. Hence one striking paradox is that anti-Semitism, as such, loses much of its psychosocial and historical meaning once the Holocaust, as such, begins.

Questions about the causal status of anti-Semitism are not merely a matter of academic hairsplitting, for until the period 1940-41, the German and other European Jews defined their situation, quite correctly, to be one of coping with a harsh, politically inspired form of anti-Semitic scapegoating, and they followed the traditionally effective Jewish strategy of compromise, passive resistance, and emigration, which in fact worked. (All through the late thirties Hitler complained that the Jews seemed to persist in Germany despite all the Nazi threats, repressions, and pressures to force emigration.) It was only after anti-Semitism was secretly changed to genocide that the Jewish response became a disastrous failure, which in some respects facilitated the mass destruction. In a number of cases Jewish community leaders who initially believed the SS cover stories encouraged their people to go quietly to trains leaving crowded ghettos for "new settlements in the East."

The victimization of the Jews also remains debatable at a more abstract level of analysis, where the epistemological question centers on whether the Holocaust was unique, or a genocide in which European Jews were historical victims "like all the others": Albigensians, Armenians, American Indians, and the like. The analytical advantage of the latter view is that it opens the way for comparative, normal science studies which may then provide a general model of genocide. One such study (Dadrian, 1976) provides a descriptive, ahistorical theory of genocide based on the case of the Armenian destruction at the hands of the Turks, and another, more philosophical discourse (Horowitz, 1976) links the potentialities for mass murder to the power of the modern state.

The disadvantage of assimilating the Holocaust to other historical genocides is that this obscures its genuine particularity. As Bauer (1978) and others (including Kren and Rappoport) have argued, the policies leading to the destruction of the European Jews and the historical circumstances under which it was carried out are profoundly different from all other cases of genocide. The question of uniqueness, then, is very significant for scholars: Since it cannot be resolved by appeal to conventional historiographic research or psychosocial analyses, it forces recognition of epistemological limitations that might otherwise be ignored. The conditionality of positive social science is forced to the surface.

Problems arising from unrecognized or deliberately avoided epistemological issues are if anything more pronounced in the area of resistance than victimization, although the two are in many respects coterminous. Prior to the Second World War, when the allied governments sanctified the term resistance in order to encourage irregular civilian groups to gather intelligence, harass, and sometimes attack German occupying forces, such forms of partisan or guerilla warfare were considered to be essentially criminal and punishable as such. (e.g., Quantrell's guerillas in the American Civil War; the Boer commandos; the Philippine "insurrectionists" circa 1900; the Irish Republican Army; and many others.)

There is, in general, no clear line or formula by which outlawry may be separated from resistance, or banditry from revolution. Historically, these distinctions are made after the fact, depending on who wins. The Mexican leader Pancho Villa is exemplary: In official histories he is described as having been first a bandit, then a genuine revolutionary, and then a bandit again. He may yet be transformed into a hero of reflexive anarcho-communalism. (cf. the Womack biography of Emiliano Zapata 1969.) The point is that "resistance" has no independent meaning. During World War II irregular warfare was legitimized under this heading via improvised legalisms centering upon the existence of governments in exile, although these were often fragile affairs. Poland had two such governments, one in

England and one in the Soviet Union; Jugoslavia had one in England and two more contesting the ground in Jugoslavia; for a time the French had one in England and another in North Africa.

Tenuous as they were, however, these political formations were able to authorize and organize acts of resistance. The European Jews had no such alternative authority structures available. In fact, the Jewish communities were fragmented along religious and political lines. The religious spectrum included atheists, converts, the reformed, conservative, and the orthodox; politically, there were communists, socialists, social democrats, liberals, and conservatives, and all of these categories were divided into factions over questions concerning Zionist emigration or assimilation. Jews as such, moreover, were never recruited or encouraged towards resistance by the Allied powers. Many Jews joined national resistance groups, mainly in Western Europe, but these groups all had strategic and tactical aims which did not usually include protecting Jews as a salient objective.

Given these conditions, and adding in native European anti-Semitism ranging from moderate in the West to extreme in the East, as well as the traditional Jewish cultural bias against outlawry and personal violence, the fact that so many Jews could be killed without offering significant resistance has appeared quite understandable to many scholars. Yet this is only one side of the issue. Once the mass killings became known during 1942–43, fighting Jewish resistance groups were formed in almost all of the remaining ghettos of Eastern Europe and violent rebellions occurred even in the major death camps (see Kren & Rappoport, 1981, for a general review of these matters).

Aside from the Warsaw ghetto uprising, however, knowledge of widespread Jewish resistance during the latter part of the war has only begun to accumulate since the late 1960s when survivors who were unwilling or unable to speak earlier began to do so, and when a new generation of Holocaust scholars began to discover relevant evidence in recently opened archives or previously neglected Polish, Russian, and Yiddish language sources. The chief result of this new information has been to undermine the prior historical consensus that resistance was virtually impossible, thus leaving the whole question even more problematic than it was before. Lest there be any doubt, it bears emphasis that the epistemological dilemma here follows from the fact that we now have bodies of theory and empirical evidence providing a good basis of support for either side of the resistance question. In the face of this contradiction, one may finally encounter the extraordinary irony of coming full circle back to the themes of racist social Darwinism, with the thesis that Jewish resistance increased as more and more of those incapable of resisting were killed, and that the Nazis had unwittingly created a "survival of the fittest" environment for the European

Jews. (It is not unusual, I am told, to hear variations of this notion repeated in contemporary Germany whenever the Israelis score a military success against one of their enemies.)

Holocaust analyses as detoxification. The problematic issues described above constitute only a few of the many uncertainties emerging from Holocaust study and leading to epistemology critique. As Friedlander (1979) has suggested, serious scrutiny of the Holocaust forces reexamination of the whole Enlightenment ideal of progress, but social scientists have preferred to "make adjustments" while maintaining the ideal. Thus, instead of searching for underlying flaws in the Enlightenment ideal, and tracing their manifestations in modern European culture, the general trend of scholarship has been to make excuses for it. The present argument is similar but more specific: If the Holocaust horrors have not provoked much reexamination of the civilization that "could do such things," nor of the epistemological framework supporting the social and physical technologies which made such things possible, it is because elements of this framework and of these technologies have been employed to ward off the horrors they helped to create. Working in a different but relevant context, Maslow (1966) accurately described one of the root psychosocial sources for this epistemology critique of social science:

> What looks . . . like an interest in the nature of the object being studied . . . may be primarily an effort by the organism to calm itself down and to lower the level of tension, vigilance, and apprehension. The unknown object is now primarily an anxiety producer, and the behavior of examination and probing is first and foremost a detoxification of the object, making it into something that need not be feared. (p. 20)

By labeling the SS as psychopaths, therefore, reified notions of psychiatric nosology and clinical symptomology can be kept safe from the radical epistemological critiques developed by Zsasz, Laing, Fanon, Foucault, and others who have discussed the pathological nature of the normatively "normal" conditions and institutions (not excluding psychiatry) of modern societies. More personally, the attribution of pathology allows us to maintain our illusions about our own culturally defined values and self-concepts. From the SS to the Jim Jones Guyana "cult," individuals and groups remain open to condemnation, courtesy of modern social science, while the culture fostering their creation goes free and social science looks the other way.

Similarly, when the Holocaust victims are hypostasized as martyrs or heroes, this diverts attention from the social power factors underlying their destruction at the hands of a modern state bureaucracy: Realities of sociopolitical power allowing a state to decimate populations under its control are not brought into question, and the concurrent impotence or indifference of other nations is hardly noticed except as a regrettable "reality principle" of the international system. (Cf. Jimmy Carter's failed effort to make concern with human rights a significant dimension of U.S. foreign policy.) For most social scientists, moreover, it is apparently easier to go on seeking funds from the state than to examine its internal contradictions and risk association with those, like Kafka and Nietzsche, whose visions of the state were confirmed by the Holocaust.

In sum, however, what Maslow could see, and what our studies of Holocaust problems seem to further affirm is that when faced with the threatening pressure of events, such as Auschwitz, which it cannot assimilate, the structure of contemporary social psychological knowledge processes begins to fail, and its limitations begin to reveal themselves. The presently established psychosocial rationality then, instead of serving to expose the anxieties hidden behind projections, denials, rationalizations, and other defense mechanisms, becomes itself a defense mechanism blocking out those anxieties which threaten to overwhelm it. This is a fundamental source of what the philosopher of epistemology Garelick (1971) has called "the irrationality of reason," which " . . . consists of its final dependence upon directions imposed by the temperament, by the body (p. 94)." It also helps to explain why so many otherwise sophisticated, articulate Holocaust survivors could not speak of it except to warn that the camps were "another universe," and no one who did not experience it could know what it was like. Even when some few, such as Elie Wiesel, persisted in attempts to describe that universe, they usually failed because their messages fell on the ears of listeners who were epistemologically unprepared to hear them.

When Bruno Bettelheim (1960), for example, spoke in depth about prisoner and SS behavior based on his experiences in the Buchenwald camp, he became the center of a storm of criticism. And E. A. Rappaport, who was also a psychoanalyst and former prisoner, has discussed in detail his gradual realization that the assumptions of psychoanalytic theory virtually guarantee false interpretation of the so-called "traumatic neurosis" underlying the emotional problems of survivors. In the following passage he refers to life in the world after the camps as the "trauma after the trauma," and notes that for many years he was unable to speak openly of his experiences for fear of seeming abnormal (1968):

> Actually, it was the trauma after the trauma which weakened my determination to write and to publish. My expectation . . . was thoroughly frustrated from the beginning. Instead, there was the fear of appearing perhaps "abnormal" and of having not worked through my own inner conflicts. Even Sperling (an analyst colleague, L. R.) who opened his discussion with declaring how

necessary it was that I wrote this paper, referred to my "conflict" about faith in humanity and accusations about humanity's lack of interest as a reflection of a conflict with a parent figure in my childhood. (p.730)

Aside from the cruel ontological irony conveyed by this statement, in which the psychoanalyst Holocaust victim finds that he must defend himself against psychoanalytic reductionism, the issue manifestly dramatized here concerns the epistemological limits of psychoanalytic theory in relation to the Holocaust.

In this connection one thinks of the famous epigram by Karl Krauss: "Psychoanalysis is that spiritual disease of which it considers itself to be the cure (Janik & Toulmin, 1973, p. 20)." It may be premature to claim that much of mainstream social science is today symptomatic of those diseases of modern societies for which it purports to offer diagnoses and cures, but an increasing number of social thinkers have argued precisely in this direction. Relevant examples include MacIntyre's (1981) critique of moral philosophy; Lasch's (1978) critique of social service systems; Illich's (1971, 1976) critiques of education and medical practice; Feyerabend's (1975) critique of scientific methodology; Gouldner's (1970) critique of sociology; Sampson's (1981) critique of psychological reification; Rappoport and Kren's (1975) critique of social issues research. The forthcoming Kren and Rappoport (1983) review of Holocaust research, elements of which have been briefly noted above, stands in line with the other critiques just noted insofar as it too discovers in the prevailing modes of explanation and interpretation, reflections of the same thought processes that helped to create the problems they now presume to clarify.

It is, however, one thing to maintain that pre-Holocaust epistemology is inadequate for interpretation, and another to argue that it is implicated in that catastrophe. Concerning the latter point, it has only been possible here to describe how critical scrutiny of certain key issues such as the presumed pathology of the SS and the apparent passivity of their victims indicates problems of epistemology that are hidden underneath the horrors of the events. Hence the conventional but failed social rationality:

Human beings should not be able to do such things unless they were lunatics; lunatics should not be able to do such things with sustained efficiency; consequently, not to worry.

Larger scale inquiry along these lines is needed but remains beyond the scope of the present paper. Among other things, such an inquiry would require further development of the dynamics of psychosocial epistemology in relation to ontology, something akin to Foucault's "knowledge/power" project. The foregoing discussion merely offers a preliminary move in that direction. The Holocaust was not only a catastrophe for its victims, but also for the thought and knowledge processes which made it seem impossible before it happened, unbelievable while it happened, and incomprehensible after it happened. Those processes still constitute the bulk of our established epistemology even though they are no longer trustworthy. In the end, it is just because the conceptual tools needed to clarify this argument are not readily available that the argument must be made. This may sound like an epistemological *Catch 22,* but the Holocaust material does not lend itself to formulation of more comfortable intellectual positions.[2]

SUMMARY AND FUTURE PROSPECTS

If, as noted as the outset of this paper, dialectics is too dialectical for many scholars today, it is largely because they have quite properly come to embody the culture processes their disciplines represent. That is, they have based their work upon the empiricist logic systems and quantitative epistemologies that have been the main force behind the rise of Western civilization in this century. As we approach the end of this century, however, and can begin to look upon it in a more historical perspective, its accomplishments seem increasingly dubious; the advances of twentieth-century industrial civilization are the main sources of threat to its continued existence. The accelerating internal and external difficulties facing the modern societies today further emphasize the challenge to reexamine their underlying epistemologies.

The present argument has been that in one form or another, dialectical analyses provide us with a formal, knowable means of attempting critical scrutiny of our culturally established knowledge processes while remaining — as necessarily we must — a part of them. Those of us primarily concerned with social and psychological domains are thus faced with the problem named here as psychosocial epistemology.

This problem has emerged within psychology in forms such as critical history research and ideology critique of prominent theoretical positions. But dialectically oriented concern with psychosocial epistemology also grows out of critical scrutiny of the failures of social science to develop meaningful interpretations of important social phenomena, such as the Holocaust. In sum, it appears that independent lines of argument based on

---

[2]This general perspective on the significance of the Holocaust for social science epistemology is better seen and appreciated by scholars of philosophy than most others. I am indebted to the following for encouraging correspondence and/or conversations: Antonio de Nicolas (SUNY Stony Brook), Paul Feyerabend (U.C. Berkley), J. Glenn Gray (Colorado Coll., deceased), Richard Rubenstein (Florida State), and Albert Franklin (Kansas State, emeritus).

conditions both inside and outside of psychology can be cited as converging to support the importance of psychosocial epistemology. On the basis of this analysis, future prospects for social psychology would appear to depend upon the following considerations.

First, there is no doubt that the study of epistemology has (to coin a phrase) become too important to be left to the philosophers. Pushed by a growing awareness of how their disciplines have been formed by unexamined epistemological assumptions, social psychologists and other social scientists are reentering the domains of philosophy, and as Royce (1982) suggests, are in some instances beginning to dominate them. Viewed in this perspective, it seems likely that if the theoretical work of social psychology becomes more historical and philosophical, it may blend with elements of these disciplines to form a new, pluralistic field of psychosocial and historical studies.

Second, whether or not dialectical thought and consequent concerns with psychosocial epistemology become explicit conceptual features of future social science, they are already being accepted, de facto, as part of the movement toward "holistic," "contextual," and/or "ecological" models of behavior. This movement is well advanced in areas such as environmental psychology, stress and health management, life-span development, and the study of consciousness. As these areas continue to expand, the dialectical orientations imposed by the demands of their subject matter can be expected to expand with them.

Third, the necessity for generative theory work along the lines stipulated by Gergen receives important support from the epistemology critique constituted by Holocaust studies. The terrible events of the Holocaust have for many years been either unspeakable or expressed inadequately because pre-Holocaust language and epistemology could not grasp them. Generative theory efforts grounded on dialectical schemes of inquiry seem to offer the only plausible means of forging the tools required to engage the deep structure crises of our times.

Finally, it should be apparent that many of the perspectives articulated in this paper connect very closely with the metatheoretical paradigm Gergen has introduced under the title of *socio-rationalism*. If our Holocaust analyses have anything to add to this paradigm, it is a value orientation emphasizing that future social science cannot place any considerations of objectivity, logic, reason, or method, no matter how these may be defined, above the guiding ideal of a unitary, indivisible humanity. A social science ungrounded in these terms is simply too dangerous according to Kren and Rappoport (1980):

> . . . the history of European racism shows that with the rise of science during the Enlightenment, preexisting mythic racist traditions were not truly repudiated but simply assimilated into the new context of "reason."

It should be clear that the mental splitting which separates emotionality from rationality is deliberately inculcated by science oriented Western culture in order that people may repress or suspend reflexive emotions that might block achievement of abstract, distant goals. The ability to categorize objects, to then perform mental (imaginary) operations upon these objects, and thus transform the meaning of the objects into something other than what one started with is fundamental to all science . . . Yet this capacity for scientific-intellectual functioning in Western culture is what can make extraordinary horrors possible (pp. 134-135).

What seems to be required, then, is nothing less than the avowal of a frankly untestable metaphysical proposition, something akin to the "golden rule." One way to promulgate such a rule is by *expanding* the scope of freedom of science, not, as many might fear, by curtailing it. If social science expands to include dialectical analyses of psychosocial epistemology as a fully acceptable activity, this could provide the means of ensuring awareness of the wider human implications of all science and technology.

REFERENCES

Amery, J. *At the mind's limits: Contemplations by a survivor of Auschwitz and its realities.* Bloomington, Ind.: Indiana Univ. Press, 1980.

Apfelbaum, E., & Lubek, I. Resolution vs. revolution: The theory of conflicts in question. In L. Strickland, F. E. Abaud, & K. J. Gergen (Eds.), *Social psychology in transition.* New York: Plenum, 1976.

Bauer, J. *The holocaust in historical perspective.* Seattle: University of Washington Press, 1978.

Baumgardner, S. E. Critical studies in the history of social psychology. *Personality and Social Psychology Bulletin,* 1977, *3,* 681-687.

Bettleheim, B. *The informed heart.* Glencoe: The Free Press, 1960.

Boehnert, G. C. *A sociography of the SS Officer Corps, 1925-1939,* Unpublished Ph.D. Thesis, University of London, 1977.

Borowski, T. *This way for the gas, ladies and gentlemen.* London: Jonathan Cape, 1967.

Buss, A. R. *A dialectical psychology.* New York: Halsted Press, 1979.

Dadrian, V. N. A theoretical model of genocide. *Sociologica Internationalis,* 1976, *14,* 99-126.

Dawidowicz, L. S. *The holocaust and the historians.* Cambridge: Harvard University Press, 1981.

Dicks, H. *Licensed mass murder: A socio-psychological study of some SS killers.* New York: Basic Books, 1972.

Feyerabend, P. *Against method.* London: Humanities Press, 1975.

Friedlander, H. Toward a methodology of teaching about the Holocaust. *Teachers College Record,* 1979, *80, 3,* 519-542.

Garelick, H. M. *Modes of irrationality: Preface to a theory of knowledge.* The Hague: Martinus Nijhoff, 1971.

Gergen, K. J. *Toward transformation in social psychology.* New York: Springer Verlag, 1982.

Gouldner, A. W. *The coming crisis in western sociology.* New York: Basic Books, 1970.

Heilbroner, R. L. *Marxism: For and against,* New York: W. W. Norton, 1980.

Horowitz, I. L. *Genocide: State power and mass murder.* New Brunswick: Transaction Inc., 1976.
Illich, I. *Deschooling society.* New York: Harper & Row, 1971.
Illich, I. *Medical nemesis,* New York: Pantheon, 1976.
Janik, A., & Toulmin, S. *Wittgenstein's Vienna,* New York: Simon & Schuster, 1973.
Kren, G. M., & Rappoport, L. *The Holocaust and the crisis of human behavior.* New York: Holmes & Meier, 1980.
Kren, G. M., & Rappoport, L. Resistance to the Holocaust: Reflections on the idea and the act. In Y. Bauer & N. Rotenstreich (Eds.), *The Holocaust as historical experience.* New York: Holmes & Meier, 1981, 193-222.
Kren, G. M., & Rappoport, L. Failures of thought in Holocaust interpretation. In W. Dobkowski & I. Walliman (Eds.), *Towards the Holocaust.* New York: Greenwood Press, 1983.
Lasch, C. *The culture of narcissism: American life in an age of diminishing expectations.* New York: W. W. Norton, 1978.
Loftus-Senders, V. Psychology and the future. *American Psychologist,* 1978, *33,* 7, 643-644.
MacIntyre, A. *After virtue.* Notre Dame, Ind.: University of Notre Dame Press, 1981.
Maslow, A. *The psychology of science: A reconnaissance.* New York: Harper & Row, 1966.
Mitroff, I. *The subjective side of science.* New York: American Elsevier, 1974.
Ollman, B. *Alienation: Marx's conception of man in capitalist society.* Cambridge: Cambridge University Press, 1971.
Rappaport, E. A. Beyond traumatic neurosis. *The International Journal of Psychoanalysis,* 1968, *49,* 719-730.
Rappoport, L. *Three theses on the ideology of understanding.* Paper given at the American Psychological Association Convention, Montreal, September, 1980.
Rappoport, L., & Kren, G. M. What is a social issue? *American Psychologist,* 1975, *30,* 838-841.
Riegel, K. F. The dialectics of human development. *American Psychologist,* 1976, *31,* 689-700.
Rifkin, J. *Entropy: A New World view.* New York: Viking Press, 1980.
Royce, J. R. Philosophic issues, division 24, and the future. *American Psychologist,* 1982, *37,* 258-266.
Samelson, F. World War I intelligence testing and the development of psychology. *Journal of the History of the Behavioral Sciences,* 1977, *13,* 274-282.
Sampson, E. E. Scientific paradigms and social values: Wanted—A scientific revolution. *Journal of Personality and Social Psychology,* 1978, *36,* 1332-1343.
Sampson, E. E. Cognitive psychology as ideology. *American Psychologist,* 1981, *36,* 730-743.
Segev, T. *The commanders of the Nazi concentration camps.* Unpublished Ph.D. dissertation, Boston University, 1977.
Seigel, J. *Marx's Fate: The shape of a life,* Princeton, N.J.: Princeton University Press, 1978.
Sereny, G. *Into that darkness: From mercy killing to mass murder.* New York: McGraw-Hill, 1974.
Sydnor, C. W. *Soldiers of destruction: The SS Death's Head Division 1933-1945,* Princeton, N.J.: Princeton University Press, 1977.
Weingartner, J. *Hitler's guard: The story of the LeiBstandarte SS Adolf Hitler 1933-1945.* Carbondale and Edwardsville, Ill.: Southern Illinois University Press, 1968.
Womack, J. *Zapata and the Mexican Revolution.* New York: Knopf, 1969.

6 Methodological Considerations in the Analysis of Temporal Data

David A. Kenny
University of Connecticut

Donald T. Campbell
Lehigh University

The analysis of temporal data whether it be many persons measured a few times (longitudinal data) or a few persons measured many times (time-series data) has over the past few years received careful attention. Numerous books and articles have described many available alternative analysis strategies that are available (e.g., Kessler & Greenberg, 1981; Nesselroade & Baltes, 1980). However, it is our belief that many of the procedures that have been proposed for the analysis of temporal data are procedures that were developed for the analysis of cross-sectional data and then were applied to temporal data. For instance, a common analysis strategy for over-time data is to use multiple regression by regressing the time-two variables on the time-one variables. Multiple regression and analysis of variance are analytic tools developed for cross-sectional data. Moreover, most of the problems discussed in the analysis of temporal data (e.g., multicollinearity, measurement error) are general problems of data analysis and not problems unique to temporal data. In sum we see little in the analysis of temporal data that capitalizes on the over-time nature of the data. Just as substantive work in social science has an implicit static orientation, methodology also seems to have a static orientation.

The one very important exception to this rule is time-series analysis. The problem of serial dependency is almost uniquely a problem of temporally structured data. (Serial dependency is the fact that observations closer in time tend to be more related than observations further apart in time.) This serial dependency invalidates the use of standard techniques such as analysis of variance for time-series data. One can view the time-series literature as basically an attempt to understand and correct for serial dependency.

This chapter outlines the rationale for four methodological orientations particularly relevant to the analysis of longitudinal data. We do not present a set of statistical methods as most review papers on longitudinal analysis do, but rather a set of methodological approaches unique to the analysis of temporal data. These four approaches are time-reserved analysis, temporal invariance, stability, and cross-lagged correlation. As will be seen, these notions are only relevant to temporal data and not cross-sectional data.

TIME-REVERSED ANALYSIS

One useful but rarely utilized approach to temporal data is a time-reversed analysis. The purpose of time-reversed analysis is to reanalyze temporal data to check for artifactual effects. The idea of a time-reversed analysis is a reanalysis of the data in which the temporal ordering of the data is reversed. So, for instance, if in the original analysis all time-two measures are treated as dependent variables and all time-one measures as independent variables, the time-reversed analysis would repeat the same analysis but make the time-one variables the dependent variables and the time-two measures the independent variables. A time-reversed analysis obeys the biblical declaration that, "the first shall be last and the last shall be first."

Imagine the following temporally ordered readings of some physiological variable:

53, 56, 59, 52, 55, 57, 75, 76, 73, 71, 78.

Note that there is a sharp jump from 57 to 75 in the data. This jump from 57 to 75 is readily apparent when the numbers are reversed:

78, 71, 73, 76, 75, 57, 55, 52, 59, 56, 53.

However, instead of the jump in the first series, we now have a drop. In this simple analysis, reversing the flow of time reverses the direction of the effect. This is the motivating idea behind a time-reversed analysis. Reversing the temporal ordering of the data and reanalyzing the data should reverse the direction of the effect.

Thus, a time-reversed analysis involves reversing the flow of time. Such a reanalysis may not yield the opposite result but rather can yield the same result. When both the original and the time-reversed analysis yield the same result, we should lose confidence in the original analysis. Thus, if self-esteem "causes" academic achievement with a causal lag of one year but a time-reversed analysis, in which prior achievement is "caused" by later self-esteem, yields the same conclusion, we would view the former result with suspicion. Logically a time-reversed analysis is a nonsensical analysis. By itself it does not deserve serious study or attention. But its very "nonsensicalness" provides a rationale for the analysis. If the original analysis yields essentially the same results as the nonsensical time-reversed analysis, then perhaps the original analysis is as nonsensical as the time-reversed analysis.

There are two ideal results of a time-reversed analysis. We have already discussed the first ideal result: essential agreement. In this case the time-reversed analysis calls into question the validity of the conclusions of the original. (There is one exception. If there is "nothing going on in the data," then both the original and time-reversed analysis should give the same result. When nothing is happening over time, the same result should emerge whether we look forward as the original analysis does or if we look backward as the time-reversed analysis does.) The second ideal result is one in which the time-reversed analysis yields results of roughly equal but of opposite sign. In this case the time-reversed analysis supports the conclusions of the original analysis since looking backward in time produces a "backward" result.

Time-reversed analysis was perhaps first used by Campbell and Clayton (1961). They examined among other things the effect of seeing the movie *Gentleman's Agreement* on anti-Semitic attitudes. Glock (1951) examined differences between groups (those who viewed the movie and those who did not) at various levels of initial attitude. Attitude was measured before and after viewing the movie. Campbell and Clayton (1961) suspected that the "effect" of the motion picture on attitudes was, in part, an artifact of regression toward the mean. To demonstrate their point, they argued that, "if the apparent effect were only this simple regression [toward the mean], then one should get a similar picture by reversing the temporal arrangement of the table." They thus performed what we would call a time-reversed analysis and found essentially the same result when they reversed the flow of time.

Campbell and Clayton (1961) were not only the first to perform a time-reversed analysis, but they also provided a rationale. They noted that regression toward the mean works both forward and backward in time. Tall fathers have shorter sons (forward regression) and tall sons have shorter fathers (backward regression). Thus, if a statistical procedure is biased due to regression toward the mean (that is, the effect "estimate" is nothing more than regression toward the mean), then a time-reversed analysis should produce an effect estimate with the same sign. If the effect estimate in the original analysis is not due to regression toward the mean, then the effect estimate in the time-reversed analysis should reverse the sign. Thus, a time-reversed analysis can be viewed as a procedure for rendering regression toward the mean implausible.

A second use of time-reversed analysis was by Simonton (1974). In an analysis of archival data, Simonton investigated among other things the effects of political instability on creativity through a series of multiple regression analyses. He used the political instability of the prior generation to predict the number of eminent creators in the current generation. Then the regression analysis was repeated, but instead of using the political instability of the *previous* generation he used the political stability of the *next* generation. He thus predicted backward in time. He found that the "effect" of political instability was much greater when the previous generations were used to predict subsequent events than the reverse.

Certain data analytic procedures have built into them the principles of time-reversed analysis. That is, these procedures guarantee that the time-reversed analysis will have exactly the opposite results of the original analysis. Moreover, these procedures will, when the original analysis shows no effect, also show no effect with a time-reversed analysis.

The simplest of methods that satisfy the time-reversal criteria is McNemar's test of change (Hays, 1963) for a dichotomy. Given a dichotomy measured at two points of time, the test examines only the "changers." For instance, Chevrolet claims that a greater percentage of persons stick with their product than any other product. Such a claim is common for a brand that has the largest share of the market. In Table 6.1 we present artificial data that support Chevrolet's claim. At time two, of the 146 respondents who purchased a new car, Chevrolet held 78% of its owners while Ford retained only 69% of its previous owners. However, a time-reversed analysis yields similar results. Chevrolet "retained" 82% and Ford 63%. The time-reversed analysis calls into question Chevrolet's claim since the time-reversed analysis also illustrates Chevrolet's "success." If we look more closely at the data we see that the percentage of Chevrolet owners actually declined: from 64% at time one to 61% at time two. Although more people stay with Chevrolet, this is practically a statistical necessity since Chevrolet has a larger share. To test whether the percentage share is constant we employ McNemar's test. We compare only the changers: the 16

TABLE 6.1
Illustration for McNemar's Test

TIME ONE	TIME TWO		
	Chevrolet	Ford	
Chevrolet	73	21	94
Ford	16	36	52
	89	57	146

persons who switched to Chevrolet versus the 21 who switched away, the difference is -5. The appropriate test is $\chi^2(1) = (16 - 21)^2/(21 + 16 = .68$ which is not significant. The results of McNemar's test satisfy the time-reversal criteria. In particular, the results of a time-reversed analysis by designating time one as time two and vice versa will always be the opposite of the original analysis; that is, those who "switched" to Chevrolet is 21 and 16 "switched" away, a difference of 5. Also when the original analysis indicates no change, so will the time-reversed analysis.

A number of other statistical procedures can be shown to satisfy the time-reversal criteria. That is, when the flow of time is reversed, effect estimates reverse in sign and zero effect estimates remain as zero. They are raw change score analysis, standardized change score analysis, and cross-lagged panel correlation.

We wish to emphasize that we do not feel that a time-reversed analysis is a cure-all for the analysis of longitudinal data. It represents an intriguing idea that we feel deserves further attention. We should add one word of caution. In certain cases a time-reversed analysis will yield inappropriate conclusions. If the regression-discontinuity design is employed and one uses the techniques discussed by Reichardt (1979) or Judd and Kenny (1981), a time-reversed analysis will yield the inappropriate conclusion. Needed is careful study about when a time-reversed analysis is valid and when it is not.

Time-reversed analysis provides the researcher with a simple way of ruling out regression artifacts as a plausible alternative explanation of the results. To some it may seem to be an unjustifiable strategy since it supports what they see as questionable analysis strategies such as change score analysis and cross-lagged panel correlation analysis. Rather, we believe that the notion of time reversal provides these procedures with a rationale for their usefulness. We believe that employing a time-reversed analysis can provide an intuitive rationale for complex statistical analyses of over-time data especially when regression toward the mean is a likely problem.

TEMPORAL INVARIANCE

It is a seeming paradox that the only way to identify change is within a background of stability. The motion of the planets in the heavens is only recognizable given the background of the stability of the stars. We cannot learn about changes unless we first understand the things that do not change. It may even be that a feature that does not change is the most interesting aspect of the data.

When we look at data over time there is almost always change. The scores of a person do not remain constant over time. Although the numbers may change, the relationship between the numbers may be invariant. A simple example will illustrate the point. When a square that is anchored in the center is rotated, the corners have all moved. However, their positions in relation to each other have not changed. The same often holds with longitudinal data. The numbers change but their relation to each other remain invariant.

Virtually every analysis strategy for temporal data makes stationarity or equilibrium assumptions about processes over time. These assumptions essentially are assumptions of temporal invariance. But the spirit of these assumptions does not seem to us to be in the same spirit as those by astronomers who used the stars as a baseline for the movement of the planets. That is, assumptions of stationarity are made, but one cannot actually observe the invariance in the data. They are assumed only to justify the data analysis.

We have in our work on longitudinal data analysis suggested three possible types of invariance and urged others to look for them. First, Campbell and Fiske (1959) as well as Campbell and O'Connell (1967, 1982) in their discussion of the multitrait-multimethod matrix considered time as a method. They proposed that one criterion of test validity be that the pattern of correlation between traits be invariant across time. That is, the correlation between a pair of traits should not change dramatically over time. An invariant correlational structure over time is taken as evidence that the same constructs are being measured at both points in time.

Although working in a very different context of cross-lagged panel correlation, Kenny (1975, 1979; Kenny & Harackiewicz, 1979) has also discussed this notion of the stability of correlational structure over time. Kenny refers to such stability of structure as *stationarity*. Kenny extended the notion to allow for stationarity to exist after adjustments have been made for changes in communality. Correlations may change over time because some variables may have more or less variance over time that is potentially "correlatable" with other variables. Once corrections for changes over time in communality are made, an invariant correlational structure may more clearly emerge; that is, the correlations between pairs of variables do not change.

Kenny and Cohen (1980) have proposed a related invariance. They argued that the pattern of relationships between an outcome measure and background variables may be invariant over time. Given the proposed invariance if the effect of age doubles from time one to time two, the effects of the other variables should also double. Thus, what is assumed to be invariant is the *relative* effect of the background variables over time. Kenny and Cohen proposed this invariance can be used as a background to detect the effects of planned social interventions.

It strikes us that researchers are so eager to measure what it is that has changed that they have failed to step back and try to see what has not changed. We can only see change in the figure by noticing the stability in the background.

STABILITY

One purpose of a longitudinal study is to measure the stability of scores on a variable. Stability refers to lack of change in the scores whereas temporal invariance refers to a lack of change in association over time. Social scientists are keenly interested in the stability of variables over time. In particular, the classical trait conception of personality presumes that the traits that make up a person's personality are relatively stable over time. To measure the stability of a variable, the standard practice is to compute the autocorrelation or test-retest correlation. However, the autocorrelation measures more than just the stability of a variable. It also measures reliability. Mathematically we can express this relationship as

$$\text{Autocorrelation} = \text{Stability} \times \text{Reliability}$$

These two factors multiply. For example, if reliability is perfect then the autocorrelation exactly estimates stability. If the reliability is zero, then the autocorrelation is also zero. Thus, two factors contribute to a low autocorrelation: low stability and low reliability. Since these two factors combine multiplicatively, low reliability is sufficient to explain a low test-retest correlation. It may be that the often reported disappointingly low autocorrelations reflect low reliability and not stability.

As pointed out in Kenny (1979) there is another explanation of low autocorrelations: changes in factorial composition. Consider a variable X that is determined by two uncorrelated factors A and B. In equation form, at time one

$$X_1 = .98A_1 + .20B_1$$

and at time two

$$X_2 = .20A_2 + .98B_2$$

where all variables are standardized. As can be seen from the equations, at time one X is primarily determined by A and at time two by B. Even if A and B have autocorrelations of one, the correlation of X_1 with X_2 is only .39. Even though none of the determinants of X change, the variable X appears to change because its factorial composition changes.

Even if we ignore changes in factorial composition, to measure stability, we need to correct autocorrelations for unreliability. Below we will discuss three different correction strategies: disattenuation, autoregressive models, and multiple indicator models.

Disattenuation

Given a variable X measured at times 1 and 2 with reliabilities of r_{11} and r_{22}, respectively, the disattenuated stability of X is defined as

$$\frac{r_{x_1 x_2}}{\sqrt{r_{11} r_{22}}}.$$

To disattenuate an autocorrelation, reliabilities need to be derived. They can be obtained by various methods. In the absence of any data, they can be derived by theoretical speculation. Better would be to use reliability estimates of previous researchers. However, it is more likely that the standard error of measurement is invariant across populations rather than the reliability. Consider the reliabilities in Table 6.2 taken from Adorno, Frenkel-Brunswik, Levinson, & Sanford, (1950). For four samples the reliability, the standard deviation, and the standard error of measurement, $s\sqrt{1-r}$, where s is the standard deviation and r the reliability, are featured. Note that the standard error of measurement is relatively more stable than the reliability. If r_A (reliability) and s_A^2 are from the original study and if s_B^2 is the standard deviation of the sample for which reliability is to be estimated, the inferred reliability, r_B, assuming constant standard errors of measurement across the samples is

$$r_B = \frac{s_B^2 - s_A^2 (1 - r_A)}{s_B^2}.$$

Again referring to Table 6.2, if we use the first sample to establish the standard error of measurement and forecast reliability, we see that we are better able to estimate reliability of the other three samples than we would if we simply assumed equality.

TABLE 6.2
Reliability of Ethnocentrism Measure for Four Samples:
Predicted Reliability Using the Public Speaking Class Women

	Reliability	Standard Deviation	Standard Error of Measurement	Predicted Reliability
Public Speaking Class Women	.80	1.07	.48	—
Public Speaking Class Men	.74	1.04	.53	.79
Extension Psychology Class	.80	1.13	.51	.82
Professional Women	.88	1.21	.42	.84

Data taken from Adorno et al. (1950) p. 119.

If possible, the researcher should estimate reliability directly from the data. Generally preferable is to estimate some form of internal consistency reliability, normally coefficient alpha or as it is sometimes called Cronbach's alpha.

Autoregressive Model

Internal consistency estimates of reliability are not possible if there is only a single measure of if the measures need not theoretically be internally consistent to be reliable. In such cases reliability estimation is still possible. We assume that the reliable part of X, X', is determined only by prior values of X'. Thus, X_3' is caused by X_2' and not X_1'. A model with these assumptions is called an autoregressive model. If X is measured at three time points, X_1, X_2, and X_3 and given this autoregressive model, the reliability at time two, r_{22}, is estimated by

$$\frac{r_{x_1 x_2} r_{x_2 x_3}}{r_{x_1 x_3}}.$$

If we assume that the reliability at the three time points does not change over time, the stability between times one and two is estimated by

$$\frac{r_{x_1 x_3}}{r_{x_2 x_3}}$$

and between times two and three, the stability is estimated by

$$\frac{r_{x_1 x_3}}{r_{x_1 x_2}}.$$

More details are given in Kenny (1979) as well as a procedure for assuming a constant standard error of measurement instead of reliability. The autoregressive model requires a minimum of three waves of measurement and even with three waves the researcher must make assumptions about the process of change.

Multiple Indicator Model

The multiple indicator approach is similar to the disattenuation method but it makes a more realistic assumption concerning measurement error over time. The items, raters, or subtests that provide a measure of internal consistency are called indicators. They indicate the true variance of the construct that they purport to measure. We can view the data from the same set of indicators at two or more time points, as a multitrait-multimethod matrix (Campbell & Fiske, 1959). The time points are the "traits" and the measures of indicators are different methods. Viewing the data in this way would lead us to interpret large same-indicator, different-time correlations as pointing to method variance. These correlations reflect not only the stability of the trait over time but correlated measurement error over time.

We should expect then that if the same indicators are used at both time points, the stability will be artificially inflated because of autocorrelated measurement error. This problem is akin to bias in correlations computed from rating data because of halo effects. We can use in this case a solution for the biasing effect of halo presented in Kenny and Berman (1980). Let us denote X_{1i} as the time one measure for indicator i and X_{2i} as the time two measure. The estimate of the stability for k indicators, controlling for measurement error is

$$\frac{\sum_{i=1}^{k-1} \sum_{j=i+1}^{k} |r_{X_{1i}X_{2j}} r_{X_{1j}X_{2i}}|}{\sum_{i=1}^{k-1} \sum_{j=i+1}^{k} |r_{X_{1i}X_{1j}} r_{X_{2i}X_{2j}}|}$$

where the vertical lines mean absolute value. Ordinarily this measure of stability will be somewhat lower than the simple disattenuated estimate which ignores correlated measurement error.

Not one of these three methods provides us with an estimate of stability that can be tested for significance. However, latent-variable causal modeling methods can be used to estimate stability correlations as well as test their significance (Kenny, 1979). Latent variable causal model is a version of factor analysis applied to hypothesis testing.

CROSS-LAGGED CORRELATIONS

We can not only compute correlations of the same variable over time, but we can correlate two different variables. Such correlations have been called cross-lagged correlations. Both of us have suggested that a comparison of cross-lagged correlations can be useful, and we have called this technique cross-lagged panel correlation analysis.

Recently cross-lagged panel correlation analysis has been criticized by Rogosa (1980). His major criticism is not a new one but one articulated at least a decade earlier (e.g., Bohrnstedt, 1969; Duncan, 1969; Goldberger, 1971; Heise, 1970). These authors and Rogosa have shown that a comparison of cross-lagged correlations may not be indicative of relative causal effects. Let us state their arguments.

Let us assume that there are two constructs, X and Y, measured at two points in time, 1 and 2. We assume that both X_2 and Y_2 are caused by X_1 and Y_1. In equation form

$$X_2 = aY_1 + bX_1 + U$$
$$Y_2 = cY_1 + dX_1 + V$$

where X_1 and Y_1 are uncorrelated with U and V and X_1, X_2, Y_1, and Y_2 are all standardized. The cross-lagged correlations can be shown to equal

$$\rho_{X_1Y_2} = d + c\rho_{X_1Y_1}$$
$$\rho_{X_2Y_1} = a + b\rho_{X_1Y_1}.$$

The difference between cross-lags equals

$$\rho_{X_1Y_2} - \rho_{X_2Y_1} = d - a + (c - b)\rho_{X_1Y_1}.$$

The cross-lag difference measures not only the relative causal impact, $d - a$ but also the relative stability of the variables $c - b$. Thus, the cross-lagged difference is a misleading measure of relative causal impact. Does this mean that cross-lagged panel correlation analysis is useless? Not at all!

As early as 1963, Campbell pointed out that third variables must be ruled out of a plausible rival explanation of causal effects. By causal effects we mean that either X causes Y or Y causes X or both. Rozelle and Campbell (1969) see ruling out third variable effects a purpose of cross-lagged analysis: "'Third-variable' and 'co-symptom' effects over and beyond any mutual causal relation are assumed. Thus, in the present case it had been expected that all cross-correlation, both synchronous and lagged, would be substantially positive." Kenny (1973, 1975) in his work has developed a model of no causal effects or as he has called it a model of spuriousness. His work has shown that a necessary assumption to test a model of spuriousness is that the spurioius factor equally affects X at times 1 and 2 and similarly equally affects Y. Given the model of no causation developed by Campbell and Kenny, unequal cross-lags under certain conditions indicate that spuriousness is not plausible. Although originally developed to pinpoint causal direction, cross-lagged panel correlation is currently used for ruling out spuriousness.

This aim of providing evidence that is inconsistent with spuriousness is rather unique. Most contemporary work in causal analysis involves the estimation of the causal paths of a stated causal model. Thus, in causal analysis we directly measure the causal impact of X on Y. In cross-lagged analysis, we assume that X and Y are not causally related and no causal paths are estimated. It would seem that the utility of cross-lagged analysis is for exploratory analyses in which the variables are likely not to causally affect one another. Given a large number of variables for which there is no postulated causal network, cross-lagged analysis may pinpoint key relationships. If the interest is explicitly testing causal relationships, then cross-lagged analysis is clearly inappropriate.

However, the cross-lagged difference can be informative in some very special circumstances even if X and Y are known to cause each other. When the variables X and Y are measured with error and it is not possible to control for measurement error through the use of multiple indicators or instrumental variables, a cross-lagged comparison may be informative if the variables are equally stable. For instance, consider the following hypothetical example.

There are large amounts of measurement error in Y (reliability equal to .25 at both times 1 and 2) and not X and the stabilities of true X and Y are equal (.8). Variables X_1 and Y_1 are correlated .30 and true Y_1 causes X_2 with a value of .1. (All variables are standardized.) The cross-lagged comparisons correctly indicate Y as having more causal impact ($\rho_{X_1Y_2} = .24$, $\rho_{X_2Y_1} = .29$) while the beta weights, distorted by measurement error in Y call X the winner ($\beta_{Y_2X_1 \cdot Y_1} = .198$, $\beta_{X_2Y_1 \cdot X_1} = .035$). As Rogosa (1980) correctly points out, one can control for the biasing effects of measurement error through the use of multiple indicators. Such procedures are preferable to a cross-lagged panel analysis; however, if multiple indicators are not available, cross-lagged correlations *may* be more valid than cross-lagged regression coefficients.

There are probably other cases in which the standard model of X_1 and Y_1 causing X_2 and Y_2 is incorrectly specified but the stabilities are equal. In these cases a cross-lagged comparison may be more valid than a comparison of regression coefficients. It would be beneficial if these conditions could be determined.

Our point is not that cross-lagged correlations are infallible. In determining causal predominance, they make a dubious assumption of equal stabilities. However, if such an assumption is nearly true, then conclusions drawn from cross-lagged panel correlation analysis can be closer to the truth than the cross-lagged regression coefficients when the standard multiple regression model contains certain specification errors.

Rogosa (1980) has helped us to understand the major difference between the approach of cross-lagged correlations and cross-lagged regression coefficients. To determine the causal predominance, cross-lagged panel correlation presumes equal stabilities of the variables. It makes this questionable assumption because it does not "trust" the autocorrelations to estimate the stabilities. They can be distorted by measurement error, autocorrelated measurement error, and "stable implicit variables" (Heise, 1970). The multiple regression approach takes the autocorrelations as reliable indicators of stability and adjusts for the differential stability of the variables.

The two methods then approach the stability issue very differently. One method makes a strong assumption of equality and the other makes strong assumptions that permit estimation of causal effects.

In sum, cross-lagged panel correlation analysis is a viable analytic procedure. Its major utility is not to diagnose causal relations but rather to rule out spuriousness. It can be used to measure causal predominance when multiple regression cannot be used and the variables are equally stable. Rogosa's (1980) conclusion that "cross-lagged correlation is best forgotten" is best forgotten.

SUMMARY

We have four possibilities that over-time data afford. The first is a time-reversed analysis. The analysis is reoriented by a temporal reordering. This approach can be used to rule out the plausible rival hypothesis of regression toward the mean. The second is an examination of temporal invariance. The researcher examines whether the structure of relationships remains stable over time. Third, longitudinal data allows us to measure the stability of variables over time. Such measurements need to be adjusted for the attenuating effects of measurement error. Fourth, cross-lagged comparisons can be made. Although such cross-lagged correlations can be misleading concerning causal predominance, they are useful in ruling out spuriousness.

We feel that the analysis of temporal data has been guided by ideas oriented to the analysis of cross-sectional data. The analysis of temporal data has been fitted into the mold of cross-sectional data. We have tried to present some ideas and techniques uniquely tied to the analysis of temporal data. We hope that these ideas may prove fruitful to the development of future methods for the analysis of temporal data.

REFERENCES

Adorno, T. W., Frenkel-Brunswik, E., Levinson, D. J., & Sanford, R. N. *The authoritarian personality*. New York: John Wiley & Sons, 1964.

Bohrnstedt, G. W. Observations on the measurement of change. In E. F. Borgatta (Ed.), *Sociological methodology 1969*. San Francisco: Jossey-Bass, 1969.

Campbell, D. T. Form description to experimentation: Interpreting trends as quasi-experiments. In C. W. Harris (Ed.), *Problems in measuring change*. Madison: University of Wisconsin Press, 1963.

Campbell, D. T., & Clayton, K. N. Avoiding regression effects in panel studies of communication impact. In *Studies in public communication*. Chicago: University of Chicago Press, 1961.

Campbell, D. T., & Fiske, D. W. Convergent and discriminant validation by the multitrait-multimethod matrix. *Psychological Bulletin*, 1959, *56*, 81-105.

Campbell, D. T., & O'Connell, E. J. Methods factors in multitrait-multimethod matrix: Multiplicative rather than additive? *Multivariate Behavioral Research,* 1967, *2,* 409-426.

Campbell, D. T., & O'Connell, E. J. Methods as diluting trait relationships rather than adding irrelevant systematic variance. In D. Brinberg & L. Kidder (Eds.), *Forms of validity in research.* San Francisco, Jossey-Bass, 1982.

Duncan, O. D. Some linear models for two-wave, two-variable panel analysis. *Psychological Bulletin,* 1969, *72,* 177-182.

Glock, C. Y. Some applications of the panel method to the study of change. American Society for Testing Materials, Symposium on Measurement of Consumer Wants. *Special Technical Publ. No. 117,* 1951, 46-54. Reprinted in P. F. Lazarsfeld & M. Rosenberg (Eds.), *The language of social research.* Glencoe, Illinois: Free Press, 1955.

Goldberger, A. S. Econometrics and psychometrics. A survey of communalities. *Psychometrika,* 1971, *36,* 83-107.

Hays, W. L. *Statistics.* New York: Holt, Rinehart, & Winston, 1963.

Heise, D. R. Causal inference from panel data. In E. F. Borgatta & G. W. Bohrnstedt (Eds.), *Sociological methodology 1970.* San Francisco: Jossey-Bass, 1970.

Judd, C. M., & Kenny, D. A. *Estimating the effects of social interventions.* Cambridge, England: Cambridge University Press, 1981.

Kenny, D. A. Cross-lagged and synchronous common factors in panel data. In A. S. Goldberger & O. D. Duncan (Eds.), *Structural equation models in the social sciences.* New York: Seminar, 1973.

Kenny, D. A. Cross-lagged panel correlation: A test for spuriousness. *Psychological Bulletin,* 1975, *82,* 887-903.

Kenny, D. A. *Correlation and causality.* New York: John Wiley & Sons-Interscience, 1979.

Kenny, D. A., & Berman, J. S. Statistical approaches to the correction of correlational bias. *Psychological Bulletin,* 1980, *88,* 288-295.

Kenny, D. A., & Cohen, S. H. A reexamination of selection and growth processes in the nonequivalent control group design. In K. F. Scheussler (Ed.), *Sociological methodology 1980.* San Francisco: Jossey-Bass, 1980.

Kenny, D. A., & Harackiewicz, J. M. Cross-lagged panel correlation: Practice and promise. *Journal of Applied Psychology,* 1979, *64,* 372-379.

Kessler, R., & Greenberg, D. Linear PANEL analysis: *Quantitative models of change.* (*Studies in social relations.*) New York: Academic Press, 1981.

Nesselroade, J. R., & Baltes, P. B. (Eds.). *Longitudinal research in the study of behavior and development.* New York: Academic Press, 1979.

Reichardt, C. S. *The design and analysis of the nonequivalent group quasi-experiment.* Unpublished doctoral dissertation, Northwestern University, 1979.

Rogosa, D. A critique of cross-lagged correlation. *Psychological Bulletin,* 1980, *88,* 245-258.

Rozelle, R. M., & Campbell, D. T. More plausible rival hypotheses in the cross-lagged panel correlation technique. *Psychological Bulletin,* 1969, *71,* 74-80.

Simonton, D. K. *The social psychology of creativity: An archival data analysis.* Unpublished doctoral dissertation, Harvard University, 1974.

7
Generational Time-Series Analysis: A Paradigm for Studying Sociocultural Influences

Dean Keith Simonton
University of California, Davis

The concept of "generation" frequently emerges in discussions of historical change. Such entities as "generations of peace and prosperity," "generations of creative giants," "generations of civil chaos," and the like are frequent constituents of talk about the past. Historical generalizations, in particular, are often expressed in generational terms. Thus one may hear statements such as "generations plagued by political oppression or religious intolerance tend to produce fewer cultural innovators than generations which enjoy ideological freedom." Yet despite the ease with which one can lapse into such phrases, a systematic generational methodology has yet to be developed in the social sciences (Mannheim, 1952). This lack is unfortunate insofar as the generation may provide a natural analytical unit for discovering the many "lessons of history" that supposedly lie buried beneath the morass of dates and proper names. To be sure, social scientists have evolved a number of perspectives that have some claim to being called generational analyses (Marias, 1968; McClelland, 1961; Ortega y Gasset, 1958; Sorokin, 1937–1941). Of these approaches, cohort analysis is probably the best known and most adequately developed (Ryder, 1965). Yet the analysis of cohorts is not designed to answer the kind of questions for which a true generational procedure appears appropriate. Therefore, in this chapter I develop a research paradigm that may be termed a "generational time-series analysis." In the first section I discuss the theoretical and methodological assumptions of the paradigm. In the second section I delineate the methodological problems and kinds of statistical inferences that characterize generational time-series designs.

THE RESEARCH PARADIGM

The Longitudinal Model

The most fundamental assumption of generational analysis is that an individual's life can be subdivided into three major phases (cf. Beard, 1874; Ortega y Gasset, 1958). The first phase of life may be called the *developmental period*. During this time span the individual is exposed to all sorts of environmental influences that may have a lasting impact on personal growth and maturity (Simonton, 1978a). Some of the developmental period influences can be more individual in character, such as educational experiences and socialization practices (e.g., McClelland, 1961; Simonton, 1976a). Still other influences, no less vital, may concern larger sociocultural events, such as political disturbances or ideological conflicts (e.g., Simonton, 1976g). In either case, one may presume that some environmental influences may have a permanent impact on the development of basic needs, abilities, motives—in a word, of personality. To illustrate, exposure to need for achievement themes may have a lasting effect on adulthood success in business (McClelland, 1961), formal education may have a debilitating effect on leadership ability (Simonton, 1976a, 1981b), or cultural diversity may nurture the development of creative potential (Simonton, 1976d).

After the development of more or less stable personality traits has taken place, the individual may proceed to the *productive period*. Here the person realizes the possibilities established in the developmental period. If an entrepreneur, the basic need for achievement will manifest itself in appropriate risk-taking investments and decisions; if a leader, the earlier developed need for power will become more fully activated; or if a creative individual, productivity will begin in the chosen field. Needless to say, from a substantive standpoint any division between the productive and the developmental periods is likely to be somewhat arbitrary. Mozart began composing at the age of 6 years, for example, and thus to dichotomize his efforts into developmental and productive phases may at first appear to be a mere methodological exercise. Despite such problematic special cases, however, there can be no doubt that, on the whole, the division between the two longitudinal periods is justified. For instance, empirical research has shown that some factors may operate only on one or another of the two life phases (e.g., McClelland, 1961; Simonton, 1975d, 1978a). So when does development end and productivity begin? Some researchers have taken the division point to be around the 25th year (e.g., Cox, 1926), and some empirical research seems to suggest that such a cut-off point may not be far off the mark (e.g., Albert, 1975). On the other hand, productivity may not get fully started until around age 30 for the vast majority of persons (Dennis,

1954, 1966; Lehman, 1953; Simonton, 1977c). In any case, somewhere in the late twenties or early thirties we may assume that productivity becomes much more prominent than development in a person's life.

The third and final longitudinal period is more conceptually and empirically arbitrary than the previous two; for the lack of any better term it has been styled the *consolidative period.* At this phase of life, productivity either slows down or becomes more or less routinized. If the individual remains still rich, powerful, or famous, it may be because past productivity has built a huge nest of laurels on which to rest. Or it may be the case that the person is actively engaged in consolidating past achievements to put them on a firmer footing—a commendable and probably essential enterprise for enduring eminence. Although this division between productive and consolidative periods is partly dictated by methodological considerations to be discussed later, there is ample empirical evidence to prop up the assumption. Thus, there appears to be an almost universal convention that the peak productive age—sometimes referred to as the "acme" or "floruit"—lies around the 40th year of a person's life (e.g., Gray, 1966; Kroeber, 1944). Moreover, research conducted by Lehman (1953) supports this convention in almost every field of human activity. A number of psychologists, especially Dennis (1956, 1958), have challenged the methodological soundness of Lehman's results (cf. Lehman, 1956, 1960). Nevertheless, more recent investigations that exploit the full panoply of multivariate methods have adequately demonstrated that the 40th year still provides the optimum all-weather estimate of the "center of mass" for an individual's career (Simonton, 1975a, 1977a, 1977c, 1980b, 1980c). Since the peak productive period seems to extend from around the 30th to the 50th year of life, the half-century point seems to mark a reasonable, even if approximate, dividing point between productive and consolidative phases of a career.

Despite the schematic approximations of the longitudinal model, there can be no question that it contains enough truth to provide the basis for defining a generational unit—an endeavor to which we now turn.

The Generational Unit

In the broadest possible terms, a "generation" can be considered to be a cluster of near contemporaries. In other words, individuals may be said to constitute a generation if they live about the same time and place. To pin this down a bit more precisely, we need to examine both the cross-sectional and the temporal boundaries of the generational unit.

Cross-sectional definition. What do we mean when we assert that a group of historical persons live in "about the same place"? Some researchers have found it necessary to use a whole civilization area as the spatial delimiter (e.g., Gray, 1958; Kroeber, 1944; Naroll, Benjamin, Fohl, Fried, Hildreth, & Schaefer, 1971; Simonton, 1975d, 1976f), while still others find the national unit more appropriate (e.g., McClelland, 1961; Simonton, 1976b). Or the sphere of interest can be subdivided yet further by restricting the unit to subcultures or traditions within a nation or civilization. For example, one may limit one's study to successive generations of scientists within a civilization (e.g., Simonton, 1976e) or within individual nations (e.g., Simonton, 1976b). In effect there is no absolute criterion for selecting one spatial definition over another: The decision may rest principally on the particular substantive issue at hand. Some variables, such as the achievement motive or economic prosperity, may be best defined according to national units, whereas other variables, such as philosophical activity or political fragmentation, may be best defined in the context of an entire civilization. To be brief, the cross-sectional definition of the generational unit is more effectively made after the formal statement of the hypothesis to be tested.

Temporal definition. Past generational investigations have used or recommended temporal units ranging in length from 15 to 30 years (e.g., Mannheim, 1952; Ortega y Gasset, 1958). Let me defend the choice of 20 years (or a fifth century) as the methodologically and conceptually most useful. Unlike 15 or 30 years, a fifth century obviously goes into 100 years an even amount of times. And unlike 25 years, a fifth century is itself divisible by 2, 4, and 10 (as well as the 5 years which is the common denominator of both). This demonstration is not a numerological exercise, for the foregoing facts mean that a researcher who employs fifth centuries can easily collapse his or her own units or those of others in order to make comparisons, especially reliability checks, between different data sets (e.g., Simonton, 1975b, 1975d). But the most persuasive reason for choosing a fifth century is that generations having this length are highly compatible with the longitudinal scheme discussed earlier. The logic behind this application proceeds as follows. Assign each individual, whether leader or creator, to each 20-year period according to when his or her 40th birthday was attained. Call the interval to which the individuals are assigned "generation g." Then any events occurring within generation g can be said to be possible *productive period influences*. That is, since the persons placed in generation g will average about 40 years, they will be at their respective peak productive age, and hence subject to whatever happens to characterize their environment in that particular time interval. Now what about events occurring in generation $g - 1$? Individuals who, on the average, were 40 years old in generation g will be, also on the average, 20 years old at generation $g - 1$. Since this latter age falls within the developmental period of a person's life, we may infer that events occurring during generation $g - 1$

are potential *developmental period influences*. Hence the distinct advantage of a 20-year definition of the generation is that a direct equivalence can be established between a longitudinal model on the individual level and a generational aggregate of near contemporaries suitable for transhistorical studies.

This equivalence between individual and aggregate levels is particularly desirable under the two following conditions. First, it is useful when the researcher is interested in developmental period influences. For example, the commitment in much of my previous work was to discover how certain critical sociocultural events affect the early development of potential leaders or creators. If the hypotheses to be tested involved only productive period effects, then it would often be better to employ yearly intervals and tabulate actual products or events rather than individual historical figures (e.g., Simonton, 1980a). The second condition favoring generational analysis is that one has a large number of sampled individuals to spread over a relatively small number of consecutive 20-year time units. As a rough rule of thumb, there should be an average of at least five persons assigned to each generational unit. The rationale for this requirement is simple: Not all historical figures will have their 40th birthdays fall right in the middle of the appropriate 20-year interval. But if there are enough persons to allot to the various units, for every person whose 40th year comes early in the generation there will be another whose 40th year comes late in the same generation, so that the average age of the individuals in that generation will remain around the presumed peak productive age. The more individuals who are so aggregated, the better is the approximation to the developmental model. Having reviewed the logic of generational classification, we are now in a position to examine methodological aspects of its application.

METHODOLOGY

In this section I explore three major issues: the collection and quantification of data for generational analyses; the reliability and validity of the resulting measures; and, the appropriate statistical analysis for testing various types of research hypotheses.

Data Collection and Quantification

Once the relevant hypotheses are formed, generational analysis should begin with two preliminary steps: (a) the location or formation of a chronological arrangement of the raw transhistorical data and (b) the operational definition and quantification of the variables of interest.

Chronology construction. Any transhistorical study must be based on some underlying chronological listing of events or persons. Such a chronology greatly facilitates the eventual tabulation of the separate historical items into generational time series. Thus the first question concerns how to go about obtaining an appropriate chronology. The initial step is to locate the secondary sources. Any good university or college library is replete with a large number of histories, biographical dictionaries, and similar materials, and so it would seem on first blush that the construction of a useful chronology would not be that difficult—but such is not the case. The chief difficulty is that there are frequently *too many* sources to choose from, and consequently one must establish a set of criteria which establishes beforehand what should be considered as adequate secondary sources of information. For most purposes the "standard reference works" in a given historical domain, such as encyclopedias and biographical dictionaries, serve as optimal sources of data. Particularly valuable are sources that contain comprehensive chronological tables of political events, life histories, or major cultural contributions. Such tables have the special asset of lending themselves to the construction of an extensive index-card file containing all the relevant historical data for the study (Gray, 1958, 1966; McGuire, 1976; Simonton, 1974). By judicious use of a photocopy machine, scissors, and glue, the researcher can compile a flexible chronology that holds more information than can be found in any single source, that permits cross-checks of data from different sources, and that allows the insertion of new chronological facts as they are found. But most importantly, the resulting chronological arrangement of data immensely simplifies quantification of the key variables. Variable quantification is reduced to a mere process of counting index cards that have already been clustered into generational sections.

Variable operationalization. After an extensive chronology has been constructed containing all the persons and events under study, the next step is to define the variables so that the information can be quantified in a form appropriate for hypothesis testing. Generally speaking, the kinds of enumerations available for transhistorical data are very similar to those deployed in content analytical and cross-cultural research (Holsti, 1969; Naroll, 1968). But the most broadly applicable type of quantification is the "frequency" measure. A good example is the tabulation of a sample of eminent persons into "generations" according to the 40th-year floruit rule (Simonton, 1975d). In other words, one merely counts the number of creators or leaders who celebrated their 40th birthday (or would have done so) in each 20-year period. But many events besides creators can be tallied into the temporal units: One can tabulate wars or civil disturbances or natural disasters—virtually anything that can be reduced to a mark on a tally sheet (e.g., Naroll et al., 1971; Simonton, 1975d; Sorokin, 1937–1941).

Of course, the researcher must seriously consider whether the tabulations should consist of unweighted raw tallies or more elaborately weighted quantifications (see, e.g., Gray, 1958; 1966; Sorokin, 1937–1941). To give the most frequent instance of the problem, how should one go about tallying creative individuals into generation-sized intervals? Should all creators be counted equally no matter what the difference in fame or should such differences be taken into account? For instance, should a philosopher as eminent as Aristotle be counted with no greater weight than, say, his comparatively unknown contemporary thinker Xenocrates? To be sure, research has indicated that weighted and unweighted measures tend to be very similar (e.g., Sorokin & Merton, 1935). And both measures have their justification: Unweighted measures of creativity put greater stress on quantity of representatives per generation whereas weighted measures stress quality. Nevertheless, the choice of weighted versus unweighted measures makes a difference on the results (Simonton, 1975b). Political instability, for example, displays a negative lagged relationship with a weighted creativity count but not with an unweighted one, signifying that only the creative development of the most renowned geniuses is adversely affected by political anarchy and chaos. So unless one has some a priori rationale for selecting one or the other, analyses probably should be run for both to see if the outcome differs (e.g., Simonton, 1975d). Other measures besides those of creative activity can be weighted as well. For instance, wars may be weighted according to the number of battles, the number of casualties, and so forth.

Once we have operationalized the generational variables, we should ask about their adequacy before we subject them to statistical analysis, which brings us to the next methodological issue.

Measure Quality

It is common practice to distinguish between two questions concerning the adequacy of any set of measures. The first question concerns "reliability," that is, the extent to which the empirical concepts are measured consistently and without error. The second issue involves "validity," or the degree to which the indicators are actually measuring the constructs they purport to measure. Since reliability is a necessary but not sufficient requisite for validity these two problems are frequently intertwined. Still, for the sake of convenience we will discuss each separately.

How reliable? Measurement error is clearly an extremely critical consideration when evaluating the quality of any given investigation. This question becomes especially crucial for historical information which, on the face of it, appears a relatively error-ridden data source. Some of these errors can be remedied somewhat by only using the "hardest" forms of this otherwise "soft" data. For example, by restricting attention to "names, dates, and places" and avoiding speculations regarding vague social "trends" or personal "motives," one can make the most out of a less than optimal situation. Additionally, dating ambiguities can be alleviated by judicious comparisons of several sources. It should also be pointed out, finally, that dating difficulties are frequently curtailed when the tabulations pertain to 20-year units of analysis. For example, a person indefinitely dated "in the early fifth century A.D." would confound a yearly analysis, but using fifth centuries, such an individual can be confidently placed in the generation 400-419. In fact, it is a general rule that the reliability of event tabulations always increases as the length of the temporal unit is enlarged (Allison, 1977).

Whatever efforts are made at mitigating error, they do not obviate the need for quantitative reliability checks whenever feasible. The usual procedure is to estimate the rank-order or product-moment correlation between two independent measures of the same construct. If several measures are available, a factor analysis can be used to establish a composite indicator for which coefficient alpha may be calculated (Simonton, 1980a). Whatever the details, the reliability of generational measures cannot be fairly criticized (Simonton, 1981a, 1981c, 1984). Despite the common opinion regarding the accuracy of archival materials, objective evaluations have almost always found extremely respectable reliabilities (e.g., Naroll et al., 1971; Simonton, 1975d, 1976f, 1977c, 1979, 1981d). For example, the product-moment correlations between independent transhistorical measures of scientific productivity tend to range from the .80s to the .90s (Simonton, 1975c, 1976b, 1976e, 1980a). Such a degree of agreement compares quite favorably with other measures in the social and behavioral sciences.

How valid? The question of validity plagues all research in the behavioral sciences. Seldom do we have access to "reality" or "things-in-themselves" and thus we must begrudgingly accept mere "indicators." Within the context of generational time-series analysis, however, one issue deserves special attention, namely, the question of transhistorical validity (cf. Naroll, 1968). That is, in defining a transhistorical measure one must arrive at a variable operationalization which is valid across vastly different time periods. Is a battle a battle whether it takes place at Marathon or at Waterloo? Is a scientist a scientist whether the name be Ptolemy or Einstein? Clearly in some respects "history never repeats itself," and accordingly every transhistorical variable must be an abstraction that but crudely fits the particular names, dates, and places (McClelland, 1961). At the same time, even historians use certain general labels—such as "battle" or "scientist"—over and over in their historical narratives and chronologies. So at least in principle, transhistorical measures can be reasonably justified.

However, this justification requires a thorough familiarity with the historical period under investigation. This familiarity can be acquired both by compiling one's own raw data and by running several pilot inquiries to see if a given operationalization is feasible. In addition, the researcher can frequently exploit various data transformations in order to improve the transhistorical validity of the measures. To offer an illustration, any measure of the number of creators over historical time is very likely to exhibit a salient exponential trend over the last few centuries. Even though an upward trend probably cannot be denied (see Price, 1963, chap. 1), there is sufficient cause for believing that its explosive facet is exaggerated (e.g., Simonton, 1976a). In other words, more recent creators probably do not have to be as "great" as those living a long time ago in order to get into the sample (Gray, 1966; Taagepera & Colby, 1979). It is standard practice to combine a logarithmic transformation with a time-control variable to temper this temporal bias down to more realistic proportions (see Simonton, 1975b, 1975c, 1975d, 1976g, cf. 1976c).

Statistical Analysis and Causal Inference

After the researcher has gathered and quantified data, the final step is to test one or more hypotheses. An impressive array of statistical techniques is available for this purpose, the precise one chosen depending, naturally enough, on the propositions to be tested. Here we can do little more than briefly survey the principal possibilities (Simonton, 1978c).

Correlational analyses. Although many exploratory investigations simply examine correlation matrices, the following three types of correlational techniques can be more fully exploited within a hypotheses-testing framework.

1. The simplest correlational technique is probably *autocorrelation analysis.* An "autocorrelation" is a correlation of a variable with itself across time, for which purpose the usual product-moment coefficient is most often used. For example, Kroeber (1944) hypothesized that geniuses are not randomly distributed over time but rather they tend to cluster into what he called "configurations." Kroeber's hypothesis could be tested as follows. Tally a sample of highly eminent persons into 20-year periods according to the 40-year floruit rule and then calculate the product-moment correlation between the number of geniuses at generation g and the number at generation $g + 1$ (where $g = 1, 2, 3,...N$). If the resulting autocorrelation is statistically significant and positive, then Kroeber's hypothesis is substantiated (see Simonton, 1974, 1976b, 1976e). Moreover, since a genius who is productive in generation $g + 1$ is in his or her developmental period at generation g, such an autocorrelation can be interpreted in terms of per-

sonal creative, leadership, or entrepreneurial growth. For example, a significant positive autocorrelation might be interpreted to indicate that the availability of role models during the developmental period can have a beneficial effect on subsequent adulthood achievement. If, in contrast, the autocorrelation is *negative,* then one might infer a "pendulum swing" or oscillation due to, perhaps, the detrimental effect of one generation aping the achievments of the previous generation (Kroeber, 1944; cf. Simonton, 1976f, 1981d).

2. An explicitly multivariate approach is *P-technique factor analysis* (Cattell, 1953; Cattell & Adelson, 1951; Simonton, 1975b, 1975c, 1980a). In this case, if one has measurements on several variables across a generational time series, one can execute a factor analysis in much the same fashion as in the standard R-type technique. The extracted factors can then be interpreted as indicating which events or people tend to cluster together over time. For example, if the variables concern the fluctuations of creators in different scientific disciplines, then a single "science" factor will emerge if creative scientists in all disciplines tend to be contemporaries. On the other hand, if the scientific enterprise actually consists of two independent components, such as "basic" and "applied" research, then two orthogonal factors may be extracted. It is even possible to extract bipolar factors if, say, "basic" researchers are very *unlikely* to be contemporaries of "applied" researchers (Simonton, 1975c).

3. The final correlational technique is *trend analysis.* Essentially, this technique entails the estimation of the major movements across time of one or more generational variables. For instance, if one wishes to show that the number of eminent persons has been increasing as a linear function of time, one can simply calculate the product-moment correlation between the number of persons per generation and the *time* (or date) at which each generation begins (e.g., Simonton, 1976b). The latter variable can also be squared and even cubed to test for higher order time functions, such as the third-order polynomial time trends mentioned earlier (e.g., Simonton, 1975d; cf. Simonton, 1980b). However, to fully evaluate nonlinear time trends, it is best to use a multiple regression procedure, regressing the generational variables on linear, quadratic, and cubic functions of time.

Quasi-experimental designs. If the researcher wants to test some causal hypotheses relating to two or more substantive variables, the above three correlational techniques offer little help. However, causal inferences in generational analyses may exploit one of the so-called "quasi-experimental" designs (Campbell, 1969; Campbell & Stanley, 1966). The following two methods are especially valuable.

First, the researcher may use some kind of *interrupted time-series* design (Campbell & Stanley, 1966, pp. 34-64.) This design aims at discovering whether some event or "intervention" interrupts or changes the direction of a time series in some conspicuous way. Campbell (1969) has discussed how such designs can be applied to transhistorical data, and Buss (1974, pp. 65-66) has suggested that they might be usefully applied in generational analyses. Although such applications are as yet rare, the following example illustrates how interrupted time-series designs may lead to causal inferences in generational data. To offer a hypothetical example, say one wished to test whether the Black Plague had a catastrophic effect on European creativity in the generation 1340-1359. One could tally the number of eminent persons in each 20-year period for a few hundred years before and after that dramatic event. Using the appropriate procedures one could then test if this natural "intervention" had a negative impact on the number of creators for the period in question. In order to help rule out rival explanations, other cultures not exposed to the Black Plague (e.g., China) could be used as controls (see Campbell, 1969). Alternately, one may employ a cross-sectional time-series design: By splitting Europe into separate nations (France, Italy, England, Germany, Spain, etc.), the general effect of the Black Plague can be assessed across diverse national conditions (Simonton, 1977b).

A second quasi-experimental design possibility is the *cross-lagged correlation technique* (Campbell & Stanley, 1966). Although some of the prototypes of this technique involved transhistorical data (e.g., McClelland, 1961; Schmookler, 1966), the methodology has been most extensively developed for use in panel data (Kenny, 1975). Nonetheless, cross-lagged correlations are particularly useful in generational analysis since the longitudinal model described earlier can then be fully exploited, especially for verifying hypothesized developmental period influences. For instance, cross-lagged correlation analysis could have been used to test the hypothesis that the achievement motive is causally antecedent to economic growth and prosperity (cf. McClelland, 1961). Such a test would have argued that the number of famous entrepreneurs at generation g is a positive function of the amount of achievement themes in literature or children's readers at generation $g - 1$ (i.e., when the adult entrepreneurs were youths). Therefore, the cross-lagged correlation from the number of entrepreneurs at generation g to the amount of achievement imagery at generation $g - 1$ should be significantly more positive than the reverse cross-lagged correlation from the amount of achievement imagery at generation g to the number of entrepreneurs at generation $g - 1$ (cf. DeCharms & Moeller, 1962). To extend this argument, if 20-year intervals are used to define the generational unit, and if 20 years closely approximates the true causal lag, then the cross-lagged correlation from the number of entrepreneurs at generation g to the amount of achievement imagery at generation $g - 1$ should be more positive than either of the synchronous correlations (see Simonton, 1976g,

1978b). Such a pattern might lead to the inference that the amount of achievement imagery during the developmental period of an individual's life may affect the probability of entreprenuerial behavior during the individual's productive period.

Even though cross-lagged correlation analysis has not been used for studying the relation between the achievement motive and economic prosperity, the technique has been employed in the investigation of other potential intergenerational influences such as those among political events (Simonton, 1976g), among various kinds of creativity (Simonton, 1975b, 1976d), among diverse ideologies (Simonton, 1978b), between political events and creativity (Simonton, 1976b, 1976e), between political events and philosophical beliefs (Simonton, 1976g), and between creativity and ideological diversity (Simonton, 1976d). The application of cross-lagged correlation analysis to generational time series appears to have considerable research potential. Yet, one must be cautioned that the technique is relatively insensitive to causal relationships within a multivariate framework. Because cross-lagged correlation analysis is essentially a bivariate method, it may be most valuable when supplemented by the next set of statistical tools.

Multiple regression time-series designs. One has only to peruse the econometrics literature to become convinced that multiple regression models have the greatest potential utility for generational analysis. Four assets of this technique are particularly noteworthy. First of all, multiple regression permits the simultaneous estimation and test of several influences while controlling for possible spurious relationships, whether substantive or methodological. One often hears the historical generalization hedged with the phrase "all other factors remaining constant": Multiple regression can convert this indefinite qualification into an empirically testable proposition. For instance, one study of creativity used multiple regression to evaluate the effects of role-model availability, cultural diversity, political instability, and war while controlling for a linear time trend and potential dating biases (Simonton, 1975d; cf. Naroll et al., 1971). In this way it could be shown that certain predictor variables, such as role-model availability exerted a positive effect on creativity even after holding many other variables constant. A second asset of multiple regression is that by incorporating product terms, multiple regression equations can estimate complex interactions and curvilinear relationships (e.g., Simonton, 1975a, 1976a). For example, the historian Arnold Toynee (1946) held that a "moderate challenge" is needed for the emergence of a generation of creative individuals; such a hypothesis can be subjected to an empirical test through the use of what is called a quadratic term (Simonton, 1975d; cf. McClelland, 1961; Naroll et al., 1971). Third, multiple regression is advantageous because temporal information contained in any generational time series can be utilized for the estimation of dynamic or distributed lag regression models in which variables are introduced that are measured at different generational points in time. For example, one generational analysis used a dynamic model to show how the number of creators in generation g is a positive function of the number of creators in generations $g - 1$ and $g - 2$ (Simonton, 1975d, 1981a). Finally, multiple regression is useful because regression equations can be embedded in a whole system of equations, which permits the estimation of more sophisticated causal models using such techniques as path analysis and structural equation modeling (Heise, 1975; Kenny, 1979). To my knowledge there has been no attempt so far to apply these much more elaborate techniques to generational data, but the potential value of such an application would be immense.

CONCLUSION

Given that generational time series invariably utilize historical data, why not let the historian inform us what truths lie hidden in the experiences of past generations? There can be no doubt that the historian's inductive generalizations frequently provide provocative insights of great potential value. Still, historical generalizations are so much more easily ventured than demonstrated that there seems to be little consensus about what constitutes the true "lessons of history" (e.g., Durant & Durant, 1968). In this sense it should not be surprising that many historians despair of ever finding universal laws (Norling, 1970). Yet the difficulty of locating nomothetic principles may result not from the historical data but rather from the historian's method of drawing general conclusions. Human affairs are far too intricate to permit viable qualitative insights. Hence it is at this juncture that generational time-series analysis comes into the fore. Because the present paradigm can test hypotheses in a multivariate framework, the complexity of the real world can be retained while concomitantly sorting out the various influences in a quantitative and objective manner. Additionally, because statistical analyses invariably incorporate a stochastic or "error" term, hypotheses can be confirmed even in the face of occasional "exceptions to the rule" (cf. McClelland, 1961). Historical laws, if they exist at all, must admit some amount of "chance," whether it be attributed to the indeterminacy of human activities or to the ignorance of the social scientist (see Simonton, 1979). Hence, in comparison to the historian's intuitive impressions, generational time-series analysis offers what in many respects is a superior approach to the scientific study of sociocultural influences operating on the individual members of successive generations.

Norling (1970) concluded his exhaustive summary of historical generalizations with the remark: "If laws governing the appearance of geniuses in history do exist, they remain undiscovered" (p. 279). The generational analyses that have been done in the past decade already render this conclusion obsolete. Inquiries using autocorrelations have shown that creators in any discipline are prone to cluster into flourishing "Golden Ages" separated by "Dark Ages" (Simonton, 1974, 1975d). Creativity is thus nonrandomly distributed over time. Moreover, P-technique factor analysis has indicated that creators in certain disciplines are also likely to appear together: Distinguished "discursive" creators—scientists, philosophers, writers, and composers—have a high probability of being contemporaries, and so do "presentational" creators—painters, sculptors, and architects—though discursive and presentational disciplines form two orthogonal dimensions (Simonton, 1975b). Focusing on just philosophy, cross-lagged correlation technique has revealed how the emergence of key philosophical beliefs in one generation results from both philosophical movements (Simonton, 1978b) and political events (Simonton, 1976g) in the preceding generation. To illustrate, 20 years after empiricism reigns supreme in intellectual debate, we see the growth of materialism, individualism, skepticism, and fideism, while a score years after civil disturbances, such as rebellion and revolution, we witness an extremist polarization of the stands taken by thinkers on the major philosophical questions of ethics, epistemology, ontology, and the like (the "law of polarization"). Finally, multiple-regression time-series analysis of generational data has isolated several variables pertinent to the emergence of historical genius (Simonton, 1975d). Famous creators have a greater likelihood of developing when many role-models are available in the previous two generations. In addition, certain key historical events, such as political anarchy, tend to discourage creative development, whereas other events, such as nationalistic revolts, tend to encourage such development. Many other generational analyses have demonstrated how the individual personality is embedded in the ideological, cultural, and political zeitgeist in which it developed, but it is impossible in this short space to inventory all the chief research findings—and even less to provide extensive substantive interpretations. All that has been done elsewhere anyway, both in the original publications and in more general reviews (Simonton, 1978a, 1981c, 1984). Still, the small list of relationships that I have just provided should suffice to contradict Norling's negativistic remark. Laws determining the emergence of historical genius do indeed exist, and many of these laws have already been discovered using generational time-series analysis.

REFERENCES

Albert, R. S. Toward a behavioral definition of genius. *American Psychologist,* 1975, *30,* 140-151.

Allsion, P. D. The reliability of variables measured as the number of events in an interval of time. In K. F. Schuessler (Ed.), *Sociological Methodology 1978.* San Francisco, Calif.: Jossey-Bass, 1977.

Beard, G. M. *Legal responsibility in old age.* New York: Russell, 1874.
Buss, A. R. Generational analysis: Description, explanation, and theory. *Journal of Social Issues,* 1974, *30,* 55-71.
Campbell, D. T. Reforms as experiments. *American Psychologist,* 1969, *24,* 409-442.
Campbell, D. T., & Stanley, J. C. *Experimental and quasi-experimental designs for research.* Chicago: Rand McNally, 1966.
Cattell, R. B. A quantitative analysis of the changes in culture patterns of Great Britain, 1837-1937, by P-technique. *Acta Psychologica,* 1953, *9,* 99-121.
Cattell, R. B., & Adelson, M. The dimensions of social change in the U.S.A. as determined by P-technique. *Social Forces,* 1951, *30,* 190-201.
Cox, C. *The early mental traits of three hundred geniuses.* Stanford, Calif.: Stanford University Press, 1926.
DeCharms, R., & Moeller, G. H. Values expressed in American children's readers: 1800-1950. *Journal of Abnormal and Social Psychology,* 1962, *64,* 132-142.
Dennis, W. Bibliographies of eminent scientists. *Scientific Monthly,* 1954, *79,* 180-183.
Dennis, W. Age and achievement: A critique. *Journal of Gerontology,* 1956, *11,* 331-333.
Dennis, W. The age decrement in outstanding scientific contributions: Fact or artifact? *American Psychologist,* 1958, *13,* 457-460.
Dennis, W. Creative productivity between the ages of 20 and 80 years. *Journal of Gerontology,* 1966, *21,* 1-8.
Durant, W., & Durant, A. *The lessons of history.* New York: Simon & Schuster, 1968.
Gray, C. E. An analysis of Graeco-Roman development: The epicyclical evolution of Graeco-Roman civilization. *American Anthropologist,* 1958, *60,* 13-31.
Gray, C. E. A measurement of creativity in Western civilization. *American Anthropologist,* 1966, *68,* 1384-1417.
Heise, D. R. *Causal analysis.* New York: Wiley, 1975.
Holsti, O. R. *Content analysis for the social sciences and humanities.* Reading, Mass.: Addison Wesley, 1969.
Kenny, D. A. Cross-lagged panel correlation: A test for spuriousness. *Psychological Bulletin,* 1975, *82,* 887-903.
Kenny, D. A. *Correlation and causality.* New York: Wiley, 1979.
Kroeber, A. L. *Configurations of culture growth.* Berkeley, Calif.: University of California Press, 1944.
Lehman, H. C. *Age and achievement.* Princeton, N.J.: Princeton University Press, 1953.
Lehman, H. C. Reply to Dennis' critique of age and achievement. *Journal of Gerontology,* 1956, *11,* 333-337.
Lehman, H. C. The age decrement in outstanding scientific creativity. *American Psychologist,* 1960, *5,* 128-134.
Mannheim, K. The problem of generations. In P. Kecskemeti (Ed.), *Essays on the sociology of knowledge.* London: Routledge & Kegan Paul, 1952.
Marias, J. Generations. I. The concept. In D. L. Sills (Ed.), *International encyclopedia of the social sciences (Vol. 6).* New York: Free Press, 1968.
McClelland, D. C. *The achieving society.* New York: Van Nostrand, 1961.
McGuire, W. J. Historical comparisons: Testing psychological hypotheses with cross-era data. *International Journal of Psychology,* 1976, *11,* 161-183.
Naroll, R. Some thoughts on comparative method in cultural anthropology. In H. M. Blalock & A. B. Blalock (Eds.), *Methodology in social research.* New York: McGraw-Hill, 1968.
Naroll, R., Benjamin, E. C., Fohl, F. K., Fried, M. J., Hildreth, R. E., & Schaefer, J. M. Creativity: A cross-historical pilot survey. *Journal of Cross-Cultural Psychology,* 1971, *2,* 181-188.
Norling, B. *Timeless problems in history.* Notre Dame, Ind.: University of Notre Dame Press, 1970.
Ortega y Gasset, J. *Man and crisis* (M. Adams trans.). New York: Norton, 1958.

Price, D. *Little science, big science.* New York: Columbia University Press, 1963.
Ryder, N. B. The cohort as a concept in the study of social change. *American Sociological Review,* 1965, *30,* 843-861.
Schmookler, J. *Invention and economic growth.* Cambridge, Mass.: Harvard University Press, 1966.
Simonton, D. K. *The social psychology of creativity: An archival data analysis.* Unpublished doctoral dissertation, Harvard University, 1974.
Simonton, D. K. Age and literary creativity: A cross-cultural and transhistorical survey. *Journal of Cross-Cultural Psychology,* 1975, *6,* 259-277. (a)
Simonton, D. K. Interdisciplinary creativity over historical time: A correlational analysis of generational fluctuations. *Social Behavior and Personality,* 1975, *3,* 181-188. (b)
Simonton, D. K. Invention and discovery among the sciences: A p-technique factor analysis. *Journal of Vocational Behavior,* 1975, *7,* 275-281. (c)
Simonton, D. K. Sociocultural context of individual creativity: A transhistorical time-series analysis. *Journal of Personality and Social Psychology,* 1975, *32,* 1119-1133. (d)
Simonton, D. K. Biographical determinants of achieved eminence: A multivariate approach to the Cox data. *Journal of Personality and Social Psychology,* 1976, *33,* 218-226. (a)
Simonton, D. K. The causal relation between war and scientific discovery: An exploratory cross-national analysis. *Journal of Cross-Cultural Psychology,* 1976, *7,* 133-144. (b)
Simonton, D. K. Does Sorokin's data support his theory?: A study of generational fluctuations in philosophical beliefs. *Journal for the Scientific Study of Religion,* 1976, *15,* 187-198. (c)
Simonton, D. K. Ideological diversity and creativity: A re-evaluation of a hypothesis. *Social Behavior and Personality,* 1976, *4,* 203-207. (d)
Simonton, D. K. Interdisciplinary and military determinants of scientific productivity: A cross-lagged correlation analysis. *Journal of Vocational Behavior,* 1976, *9,* 53-62. (e)
Simonton, D. K. Philosophical eminence, beliefs, and zeitgeist: An individual-generational analysis. *Journal of Personality and Social Psychology,* 1976, *34,* 630-640. (f)
Simonton, D. K. The sociopolitical context of philosophical beliefs: A transhistorical causal analysis. *Social Forces,* 1976, *54,* 513-523. (g)
Simonton, D. K. Creative productivity, age, and stress: A biographical time-series analysis of 10 classical composers. *Journal of Personality and Social Psychology,* 1977, *35,* 791-804. (a)
Simonton, D. K. Cross-sectional time-series experiments: Some suggested statistical analyses. *Psychological Bulletin,* 1977, *84,* 489-502. (b)
Simonton, D. K. Eminence, creativity, and geographic marginality: A structural equation model. *Journal of Personality and Social Psychology,* 1977, *35,* 805-816. (c)
Simonton, D. K. The eminent genius in history: The critical role of creative development. *Gifted Child Quarterly,* 1978, *22,* 187-195. (a)
Simonton, D. K. Intergenerational stimulation, reaction, and polarization: A causal analysis of intellectual history. *Social Behavior and Personality,* 1978, *6,* 247-251. (b)
Simonton, D. K. Time-series analysis of literary creativity: A potential paradigm. *Poetics,* 1978, *7,* 247-259. (c)
Simonton, D. K. Multiple discovery and invention: Zeitgeist, genius, or chance? *Journal of Personality and Social Psychology,* 1979, *37,* 1603-1616.
Simonton, D. K. Techno-scientific activity and war: A yearly time-series analysis, 1500-1903 A.D. *Scientometrics,* 1980, *2,* 251-255. (a)
Simonton, D. K. Thematic fame and melodic originality: A multivariate computer-content analysis. *Journal of Personality,* 1980, *48,* 206-219. (b)
Simonton, D. K. Thematic fame, melodic originality, and musical zeitgeist: A biographical and transhistorical content analysis, *Journal of Personality and Social Psychology,* 1980, *39,* 972-983. (c)

Simonton, D. K. Creativity in Western civilization: Intrinsic and extrinsic causes. *American Anthropologist,* 1981, *83,* 628-630. (a)

Simonton, D. K. *Formal education, eminence, and dogmatism: The curvilinear relationship.* University of California, Davis, 1981. (ERIC Document Reproduction Service No. ED 201-276.) (b)

Simonton, D. K. The library laboratory: Archival data in personality and social psychology. In L. Wheeler (Ed.), *Review of Personality and Social Psychology* (Vol. 2). Beverly Hills, Calif.: Sage Publictions, 1981. (c)

Simonton, D. K. Presidential greatness and performance: Can we predict leadership in the White House? *Journal of Personality,* 1981, *49,* 306-323. (d)

Simonton, D. K. *Genius, creativity, and leadership.* Cambridge, Mass.: Harvard University Press, 1984.

Sorokin, P. A. *Social and cultural dynamics* (4 vols.). New York: American Book, 1937-1941.

Sorokin, P. A., & Merton, R. K. The course of Arabian intellectual development, 700-1300 A.D. *Isis,* 1935, *22,* 516-524.

Taagepera, R., & Colby, B. N. Growth of western civilization: Epicyclical or exponential? *American Anthropologist,* 1979, *81,* 907-912.

Toynbee, A. J. *A study of history* (abridged by D. C. Somervell). New York: Oxford University Press, 1946.

II DIACHRONIC INQUIRY: FROM THE MICRO-SEQUENCE TO THE LIFE-SPAN

8 The Sense of Closure

Stuart Albert
University of Minnesota

Consideration of the temporal dimension of human experience directs our attention to certain categories of events: beginnings and endings, entrances and exits, pauses, gaps, interruptions, and temporally ordered sequences of all kinds. A subset of these phenomena might be considered issues of temporal punctuation which address the question of how events in time are segmented or partitioned so that one event is perceived as over (the issue of closure), and another event is perceived to begin.

The concept of closure is essential to the concept of change, for given the finite capacity of human beings, some sense of closure seems to be necessary to make possible new activities. But a sense of psychological closure to temporal events implies more than that they have ended; it implies a sense of harmonious completion. It is this sense of harmonious completion, of balance and equilibrium restored, of tension reduced that allows the pursuit of new challenges and activities.

A thought or action, encounter or relationship, task or objective, may end or terminate without a sense of closure, or may even continue after one has been reached. In some cases closure may not occur for a long time after the event or relationship has been terminated. Moreover, in some cases it is not expected to. Mourning the death of another is an example. On the other hand, if an encounter or relationship continues past the point where closure has been achieved, the result is usually unpleasant. The person feels bound to an encounter that is over and wishes to escape.

Thus, although the fact of termination is by itself insufficient to create a sense of closure, which may be achieved, if at all, long before or after the point of termination has been reached, the fact of termination and the sense of psychological closure are closely linked: the occurrence of one creates the need, although not the requirement, for the occurrence of the other.

This chapter is concerned with four approaches to the question of how closure to temporal events is achieved. Each approach is presented in the form of a model, but a model that is less a predictive theory than a point of view by which we might make sense of the concept of closure. For the most part, the four models take their illustrations from the domain of social interaction, but the intent is to present each in the most general form so that the range of potential applications is as large as possible.

In considering the issue of closure, nothing is more common than to think in terms of the ultimate categories of death and dying, and to imagine that we can understand other instances of closure as pale copies of these. The four models presented in this chapter make the reverse assumption. Each model addresses common and frequent instances of closure, and we propose that it is the nature of these frequent events that condition our view and understanding of death and dying rather than the reverse.

The four models to be presented do not exhaust the ways in which a sense of closure may be achieved. They do, however, bring together a collection of ideas and approaches by which the subject might be approached.

MODEL I. SEQUENCE COMPOSITE ANALYSIS: SYNCHRONOUS TERMINATION AS A DETERMINANT OF CLOSURE

The world of human action as it is phenomenally presented to us is rarely simple. Even the simplest action, plot, occasion, are intuitively perceived to be a bundle of dimensions, aspects, properties, events, episodes, and so forth. Model I (Albert & Jones, 1977) invites us to view each distinguishable aspect of an ongoing scene or universe of observation as a set of directed sequences each of which has a beginning and ending. The model utilizes the assumption (stated in the introduction) that there is a tendency to derive the experience of closure from the fact of termination, for in the absence of exceptional circumstance, such as when an event is interrupted, the termination of an event typically confers at least some minimal degree of closure. The basic idea of the model is that a sense of closure is achieved for a given universe of observation when all the sequences that compose it terminate simultaneously. Consider the following example. I open and close my briefcase; I open and close a conversation; a car enters, traverses, and exits a bridge across the Mississippi; a sentence begins and ends. Were those the only events in our universe of observation, the sequence composite analysis model proposes that their synchronous *termination* would create in the viewer a sense of closure even, and perhaps, in spite of the fact that the events have little or no organic connectiveness. The sequence composite analysis model was originally developed by Albert and Jones (1977) as a way to understand the endings of children's bedtime stories. The basic four properties of the model can be developed using that context. In a child's bedtime story entitled *Ten Bears In My Bed* (Mack, 1974), a small boy comes into his bedroom and finds that there are ten bears in his bed. There is a look of displeasure on his face as he begins to order the bears out of his bed one by one. After all of the bears have left through a window, the little boy takes a teddy bear that was in the corner of the room and falls asleep on the bed. On the final page of the book the little boy is seen dreaming of all the bears happily playing with his toys. This story can be anlayzed as a set of sequences as shown in Fig. 8.1.

The first sequence is a descending counting structure starting with ten and proceeding to zero. The second sequence is defined by the properties, rested and tired. The boy is rested at the beginning of the story, but becomes tired as he attempts to get the bears to leave. The third sequence of this story is defined by the terms awake and asleep. The boy is awake in the beginning of the story and asleep at its conclusion. The fourth sequence is defined by the terms light and dark. The story begins with the light on. At the conclusion of the story the boy's mother enters and turns the light off. The fourth sequence is defined by the terms unhappy and happy. The boy is unhappy at finding the bears in his bed, but happy once they have left. For each of the

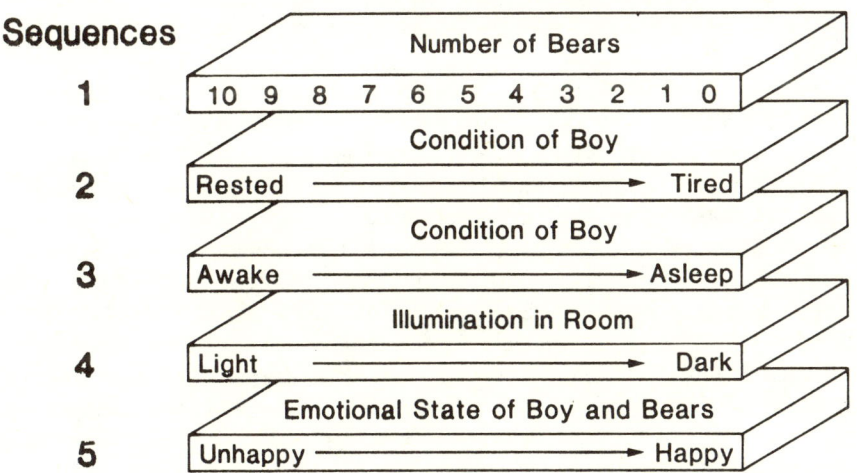

FIG. 8.1

above sequences, the first term of the sequence is typically associated with a beginning state, and the second term, with a state of termination (a state of balance, equilibrium, tension reduction, etc.). The structure of the first sequence assures a sense of closure by virtue of the properties of the number system. The central proposition of the model is that the greatest sense of closure is achieved when all of the constituent sequences of the narrative terminate at the same time.

As Albert and Jones (1977) noted, there is no mechanical discovery procedure for analyzing narrative action into a set of sequences, but for a given set of sequences, it is possible to determine both whether they are synchronized or not, and whether they are independent of each other.

The first proposition of the model is that the greater the proportion of sequences describing the structure of a given encounter that are synchronously terminated, the greater the sense of closure. We define the property of *thickness* as the number of independent directed sequences that comprise the structure of action. Since each independent sequence has a beginning and an ending state, each is assumed to contribute to a sense of closure. The greater the number of such sequences (provided that they are synchronized) the greater the feeling of closure.

In this model it is important to determine not only the number of sequences and the degree to which they are synchronized but also the order of each sequence. *Normal order* is defined as a sequence that progresses from a state associated with a beginning to a state associated with an ending. *Inverted order* is the reverse. An example of inverted order within the child's bedtime story would be a version in which the story took place in darkness and ended with the boy's mother turning on the light just as he fell asleep. Furthermore, there may be some sequences whose beginning and ending points have little to do with what is commonly thought to be a beginning or ending. For example, if instead of turning the light on and off in the child's bedroom, the light were to switch from red to blue, there would be no implications for closure. We therefore say that sequence is either *strongly or weakly ordered,* or in the example of a red-blue shift, not ordered at all, relative to conventions of what is associated with a beginning or an ending state. Such conventions, of course, are context specific and may well be expected to vary in different cultures and at different periods of history.

Once narrative action is decomposed for purposes of analysis into a set of directed sequences, it is possible to create alternative plots or narrative forms by putting these sequences in and out of synchrony with one another, by adding or deleting sequences, and by inverting them. And for each of the resulting stories or narratives it is possible to empirically access the extent of closure that seems to be achieved.

Albert and Krakow (1983) provide preliminary evidence that asynchronized stories are rated as less satisfying by adults than a synchronized

8. THE SENSE OF CLOSURE   163

version of the same story. Two examples of synchronization are given in Fig. 8.2 for the *Ten Bears* story. In one the child falls asleep before all the bears have left the child's bed, and in the second, all the bears have left for some time before the child enters his bed and falls asleep; and in neither case is the ending of the story rated as satisfactory on a set of dimensions as the original version.

A final conjecture of the model, which remains to be tested, is that even if the degree of closure that is evoked or conferred by the termination of a given event within the universe of observation is minimal, the synchronous termination of all events within the universe of observation will lead to a sense of closure that is more substantial than a purely additive model would predict.

In summary, the sequence composite model proposes that a sense of closure for ongoing events is created to the extent that the terminal points of the sequence that constitute its structures are all totally synchronized, provided that each sequence is strongly directed in the normal order (beginning to ending state). Although illustrated by a child's bedtime story, the model should be applicable to a wide variety of phenomena.

In a sense, Model I is the most general of the models to be presented in that it is a way of aggregating whatever sense of closure is obtained when multiple events within the same universe of observation are terminated, but it does not indicate how a sense of closure might be constructed over time within each event. This is the subject of the following model.

MODEL II. THE JANUS SEQUENCE

The elements of the sequence that define Model II were first developed in the context of analyzing the endings of social encounters, but the principles discovered in that context appear to be readily generalizable to many other

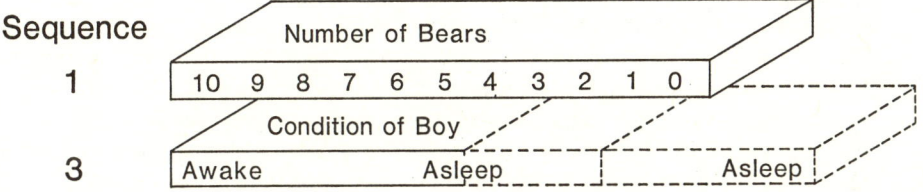

FIG. 8.2 An example of sequence asynchronization.

domains. We develop the model in its originating context, and then briefly illustrate its principles in a very different context.

Model II defines five processes and their sequential ordering that characterize the terminal phase of many social encounters and that, when present, tend to confer a sense of psychological closure. The sequence is named the Janus Sequence after the Roman god Janus, the god of gates and transitions, who was said to look with one face into the past and with the other into the future. The sequence begins with an examination of the past, the summary process, justifies the termination of the past as it extends into the present, and concludes with a set of processes that look to the future (processes of continuity and well wishing).

We consider each of the five elements of the sequence separately.

The process of summarization (S). A summary is a symbolic and selective statement of all or part of the cognitive or affective history of an encounter, an event, a task, and so forth.

There are a number of possible reasons why the presence and construction of a summary may create a sense of closure. First, a summary is by definition a form of redundancy; it replaces new information with information that is old and familiar, thereby challenging at least one justification for continuing any past activity, namely, that its continuation will reveal something new and potentially valuable.

Second, a summary is a historicizing act; that is, it refers to the encounter, activity, and so forth, as something that happened, and in doing so creates a sense of closure by making the event part of past history.

Third, and perhaps most important, a summary is a form of historical concept formation that makes the past better able to be stored and retrieved. As a result, a summary makes it possible for the past event to be symbolically retained, a point that is more fully developed in the fourth term of the model which deals with the process of creating continuities between past and future.

The question of how extensive or detailed or complete a summary must be to create a given degree of closure is unknown. However, we propose that the more complete, detailed, extensive, complex, a summary, the greater the resulting sense of closure that is created. One possible reason is that a longer, more complex summary may be taken as evidence that what is being summarized has gone on for a long time (in order to make such detail possible) and therefore might be nearing its natural termination.

The process of justifying termination (J). Most encounters, tasks, and so forth, require a justification for their interruption or termination. Closure typically requires a reason for discontinuing the past activity. The reason may be internal, for example, the claim that the encounter's task is over, or external, for example, that other more pressing matters are at hand.

The expression of positive sentiments (P). The analysis of positive statements is considered in section III as part of a general model that deals with the expression of attraction, liking, and cohesiveness.

Continuity (C). Within the domain of social interaction, a statement of continuity creates a sense of closure by relating the social encounter to overarching social relationship that survives physical separation. In fact, the affirmation of continuity denies that the essential meeting of the encounter is one which requires physical presence. An example of a continuity statement is "See you tomorrow," which affirms that the relationship endures while the encounter does not. Thus, a successful statement of continuity creates a sense of present closure by denying its finality even as it creates and expresses its present necessity.

The process of well wishing (W). The expression of well-wishing statements such as "take care," or "have a safe trip," represents the projection of positive feelings into the departing person's future.

Albert and Kessler (1978) demonstrated not only that all of the elements in this sequence are more frequent during the terminal phase of a social encounter, but that these elements tend to occur in the order presented. To give an illustration of the sequential ordering of the SJPCW sequence, consider the following series of statements that might characterize the end of conversation between two individuals. "Well, we talked about X, Y and Z (S), but listen, I have to go. I have an appointment at 3: P.M. with the Vice-President" (J). "I really enjoyed talking this over with you" (P), and "I do hope that we'll have a chance to talk about this in the future" (C). "Take care" (W).

In general, the order in which these processes occur is probably a weaker determinant of a sense of closure than the fact that the individual elements of the sequence occur. However, some orders are more likely to create a sense of closure than others. For example, if we simply reverse the SJPCW order and end a conversation as follows: "Well, take care (W). We'll have to talk again (C). It was nice talking to you (P). By the way, the reason we have to end our conversation now is that I have an appointment with the Vice-President (J), and listen, we talked about X, Y and Z (S). Bye," closure is less likely than were the sequence in its normal order.

The SJPCW model proposes that the processes of summarization, justification, the expression of positive affect, and the expression of continuity can generally be applied to the endings of tasks, encounters, games, policies, and the like, and that their construction and presence create a sense of closure. Well-wishing statements seem more restricted to interpersonal separation.

The presence of all five elements of the model creates the feeling that what has preceded them has been an upper temporal bound. They create a sense of the temporal embeddedness of an event, and therefore can be regarded as part of the process by which the temporal context of an event is defined and constructed.

MODEL III. THE EMBRACE, A MODEL OF INTENSIFIED POSITIVE AFFECT (IPA) FOR THE OBJECT, PERSON, OR EVENT THAT IS BEING TERMINATED

Model III presents one possible elaboration of the expression of positive sentiments indicated by the (P) term of the SJPCW sequence. The IPA model may operate within that sequence, but it may also stand independently of it and create a sense of closure in the absence of processes of summarization, justification, continuity and future well wishing.

The model can be developed in an interpersonal context by means of a particular theoretical curve that we label a temporal cohesiveness function. A temporal cohesiveness function is either a theoretical or an empirical curve, that plots the level of expressed mutual cohesiveness between two individuals as a function of the history of their encounter from beginning to end. A hypothetical curve is given in Fig. 8.3. This curve illustrates a hypothetical conversation between a man and a woman. The begining portion of the curve (t_1) illustrates the increased display of cohesiveness associated with the ritual of greeting. The conversation or encounter then proceeds as the individuals discuss matters of substance. At the conclusion of the encounter and depending on the circumstances, the two individuals might hug and kiss each other goodbye as might be appropriate if one of the individuals were leaving for a long trip. This increase in the display of mutual cohesiveness during the terminal phase of the social encounter is defined as ΔC. The magnitude of ΔC is determined by the following three functional equations:

1. $\Delta C = f(W, N, O)$.
2. $W = f(R, e)$
3. $N = f(D, T)$

Equation 1 proposes that the magnitude of cohesiveness displayed between two individuals is a function of whether it is warranted (W), whether it is necessary (N), and whether there is opportunity (O) for it to occur. As

TEMPORAL COHESIVENESS FUNCTIONS

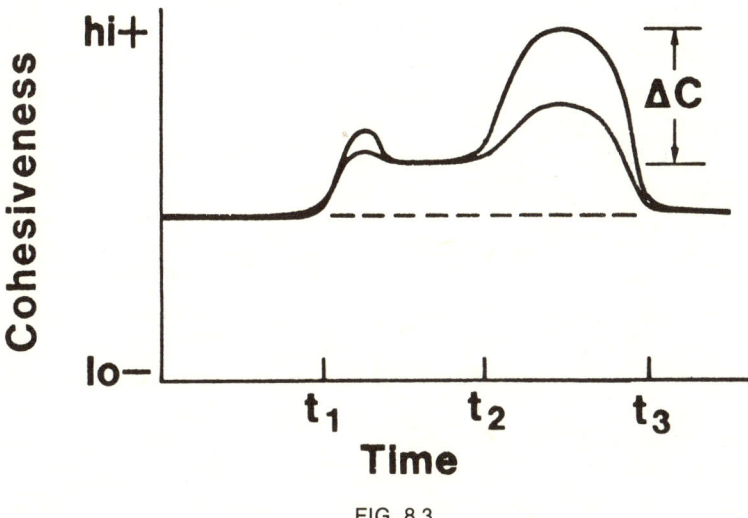

FIG. 8.3

stated in Equation 2, whether a display of cohesiveness is warranted or not depends on at least two factors. The first is the relationship between the two individuals, and the second is the nature of their encounter. In general, friends have a basis for expressing cohesiveness, whereas strangers do not. We add the term e to Equation 2 to indicate that there are situations in which the intimacy or setting of the encounter (e) may cause strangers to act as friends. Equation 3 proposes that cohesiveness will be displayed when it is perceived as necessary, which in turn depends upon the expected duration of the separation (D), and the potential threat (T) the separation holds for both individuals once separated.

We can illustrate these equations by examining the magnitude of ΔC that is appropriate for pairs of friends and pairs of strangers who are separating for a long or a short period of time. ΔC is both warranted and necessary for friends separating for a long time. If they are separating for a short time, ΔC will be absent, since although warranted, it is unnecessary. ΔC will rarely be displayed beyond some minimal level during the separation of strangers.

A final comment is needed with respect to the term O in Equation 1. The display or expression of mutual cohesiveness will occur provided that time and circumstances permit it. The model suggests that part of the agony of unexpected separation, as in the case of an unexpected death, is that the individuals have not had an opportunity to display the level of cohesiveness that was warranted on the basis of their past relationship and made necessary by the permanence of the separation.

The simplicity of functional Equations 1–3 disguises a rather difficult and perplexing problem, which, because it is so well solved in the normal course of events, is rarely seen as a problem. The problem is how attraction can be expressed in such a way that it frees the interacting participants rather than binds them more tightly together. One might have expected that separation would proceed by a ritual in which the bonds of relationship were momentarily weakened so as to permit separation. Why doesn't the expression of cohesiveness present separation from occurring? One can best appreciate the seriousness of this problem by considering some of its solutions.

The first is to utilize a vehicle for expressing attraction that is self-terminating. Consider a hug. A hug is physically intense, but time limited. If a person hugged another with less intensity, he might be able to sustain the hug for a long time, but rather than engaging in a hug he would be accused of holding. Thus, a tight hug facilitates interpersonal separation because it is an expression of attraction that is self-terminating if it is to retain its identity as a hug rather than as something else. Thus, it is clear that there are certain modes of expressing attraction that are time limited both because of the energy involved in producing them, and because they would be redefined as another class of behaviors if their temporal properties were altered.

A second way to solve the problem of how to express attraction that facilitates separation rather than hinders it is to choose an appropriate level of attraction. If an expression of attraction is both warranted and necessary and does not occur, the probability of successful separation will be quite low, as when friends leave for a long trip without saying good-bye. On the other hand, if the magnitude of ΔC is excessive, that is, if it exceeds what is warranted and necessary, if the individuals tell each other how wonderful it has been, how much they value their relationship, how pleasant the conversation has been, they might conclude that there is no reason for ending the encounter. Thus, if the magnitude of ΔC is inappropriately large or small, successful separation will not occur, and the appropriate sense of psychological closure will not be achieved, for our thesis is that the expression of ΔC at the appropriate level as defined by Equations 1–3 is a necessary condition for a sense of closure to be realized.

Thus far, cohesiveness has been illustrated by means of the expression of positive emotions such as a hug. Cohesiveness, however, can also be expressed by statements of the loss that will result when separation has taken place, an example of which is the statement, "I will miss you." Statements of anticipatory loss follow the same rules as statements of positive attraction. Thus, when an expression of anticipatory loss is warranted and necessary, but does not occur, the offended party may complain, "You mean you won't even miss me," a complaint which delays at least for the moment the possibility of a smooth and successful separation.

The problem we have posed, namely, how attraction can be expressed in such a way that it does not force, even by implication, the continuation of the encounter, is solved in part when attraction is expressed in a ritual mode. Despite the fact that there is no generally agreed upon definition of ritual, one commonly accepted component is the ability of ritual behavior to be divorced from its original function. Probably the best example is ritual fighting in animals in which no lasting physical harm results. In effect, the teeth have been removed from an otherwise aggressive act by expressing it in a ritual mode. The proposition we advance is that when attraction is expressed in a ritual mode the usual consequence of attraction, namely continued physical proximity, is eliminated. Thus, ritual attraction facilitates separation by expressing the desirability of continued physical contact in such a way as to permit its opposite. Just as ritual aggression does not harm, ritual attraction does not detain. The possibility that attraction may be expressed divorced from its original function is not without cost however. It means that attraction expressed in a ritual mode may be suspect. A ritual kiss between two individuals, for example, may imply less about their mutual affection than about their joint obedience to the customs of society. Thus, to be successful and facilitate separation, attraction expressed in a ritual mode must also include evidence of its genuineness.

To illustrate the model in a completely different context, consider an organization that must decide whether to terminate a particular product. Model III suggests a procedure for creating a sense of closure that will both reflect the decision to do so and/or make such a decision easier. If the product were to be permanently eliminated, and if it had been central to the identity of the organization, then an expression of the importance of the product to the organization, the way the hopes and dreams of its membership were involved in its success, would be both warranted and necessary. The organization would, however, have to prevent the celebration of the historical significance of the product from creating false reasons for its continuation. In short, the organization would have to solve the problem of how to celebrate the importance of the product in the lives of its members without having that celebration prevent separation.

In all three models that we have presented, our thesis is that the conditions that typically result in successful separation are the same conditions that create a sense of closure, that the principles of those occasions can be employed quite generally, and that they help create a sense of closure even when the satisfactory termination of an event, relationship, and so forth, is impossible. Thus, an analysis of the conditions of frequent successful separation (a separation that occurs on time, with mutual intent and with little or no emotional stress) provides an analysis of the conditions for creating a sense of psychological closure.

MODEL IV. A MODEL OF RETROSPECTIVE CLOSURE

An ending in which there is no summary, no adequate justification, no source of continuity; an ending in which there is a clear interruption of action rather than its completion, an ending in which the sequences that define the action are out of synchronization; an ending in which there is no expression of attachment or cohesiveness despite the necessity for providing such a statement; in short, an ending that has violated many of the prescriptive features that we have enumerated, can nonetheless, with the passage of time, achieve a certain sense of closure. How this is possible is the study of finished unfinished business, and is the topic of Model IV (Albert, 1978). The basic premise of the model is that the occurrence of almost any event has future as well as present implications. We call the perceived future implication of a stimulus of an event its forecast. The interval in which a forecast may be realized we label its opportunity interval, and any prior interval in which such a forecast is not expected to occur its incubation period. The duration of both intervals may vary independently. The model proposes that the more historically remote an event, the more likely the opportunity interval for its future consequences has been exceeded. The more intense an event, particularly if it is negative, the more the individual will monitor its future to determine whether a forecast was implied, and what its nature might be. Thus, the complete evaluation of an intense negative event will always be partially postponed pending an examination of its future.

The model we are proposing is of interest in part because it challenges the dominant psychoanalytical position. According to the psychoanalytical view, past events grow more positive with the passage of time because negative aspects are repressed, denied, or selectively forgotten. Model IV takes an alternative position, that the reevaluation of a negative event over time represents a rational process rather than an irrational or defensive one. When an event ends in an unsatisfactory way, a question arises. Is such an ending an anomaly or does it signal a more profound and disquieting alteration in the normative patterns that govern social action? No answer is possible until the unfolding future provides a context against which any possible forecasts implied by the discomforting event can be judged.

The model we have presented is one of a number of models that deal with the retrospective construction of meaning, in this case the evaluation and acceptance of an unsatisfactory ending. The model suggests that although the ending will not achieve a sense of closure for the reasons specified in

Models I, II, III, it may, with the passage of time, come to be accepted as finished in the sense that no future forecasts of any danger seem to be implied. The absence of such forecasts confers upon the ending a sense of closure. Despite the fact that the ending may never have been satisfactorily resolved, it becomes in such cases finished unfinished business.

For convenience, and because it is required by our theory of closure, we summarize the concepts that we hypothesize are involved in the construction of a psychological sense of closure to ongoing temporal events:

Model I: Sequence Composite Analysis

The properties of sequence synchronization, thickness, strong versus weak versus no order, normal versus inverted order.

Model II: The Janus Sequence

The processes of summarization, justification, the expression of positive affect, the discovery and statement of dimensions of continuity.

Model III: The Embrace

The concept of ΔC, and the three functional equations that describe its magnitude.

Model IV: A Model of Retrospective Closure

The concepts of stimulus forecast, incubation period, and opportunity interval.

As a set, the four models present complementary rather than competing viewpoints. The elements of each can be varied to create different degrees of closure in different contexts and in different circumstances. The relative contribution, and indeed, the applicability of each model to a given situation, have yet to be investigated beyond a few illustrative cases.

The possibility of varying all elements of all four models simultaneously to achieve different degrees of closure in a given context affords us at least a beginning technique of investigation. Some modifications may make sense in a given context, and others may not. Indeed, whether certain combinations of modifications are logically compatible has yet to be determined.

Closure is so general a psychological state that no set of models is likely to exhaust the domain of theoretically relevant approaches. The limited scope of this essay, however, derives not merely from limitations of time and space, but from the difficulty of bounding the field in any sensible way, of arguing on principled grounds, for example, that certain approaches are relevant and others are not, or that certain are more important than others. The aim of this essay has therefore, of necessity, been more limited. What we have done is to present four models that are not generally available, that capture some aspects of common experiencce, that at least in one case (Model IV) provide an alternative to dominant patterns of thinking, and that suggest ways to imaginatively modify the taken-for-granted temporal landscape so that things not only end, but come to be felt as over.

REFERENCES

Albert S. Time, memory, and affect: Experimental studies of the subjective past. In J. T. Fraser & N. Lawrence (Eds.), *The study of time,* (Vol. 3). New York: Springer-Verlag, 1978.

Albert, S., & Jones, W. The temporal transition from being together to being alone: The significance and structure of children's bedtime stories. In B. Norman & A. Wessman (Eds.), *The personal experience of time.* New York: Plenum Press, 1977.

Albert, S., & Kessler, S. Six processes for ending social encounters: The conceptual archeology of a temporary place. *Journal of the Theory of Social Behavior,* 1976, *6,* 147–170.

Albert, S., & Kessler, S. Ending social encounters. *Journal of Experimental Social Psychology,* 1978, *14,* 541–553.

Albert, S., & Krakow, M. Preferences for synchronized vs. asynchronized endings. (manuscript in preparation, 1983).

Mack, S. *Ten bears in my bed: A goodnight countdown.* New York: Pantheon Books, 1974.

9 The Social Construction of Narrative Accounts

Mary M. Gergen
Kenneth J. Gergen
Swarthmore College

Writers of fiction, philosophy, and psychology have frequently portrayed human consciousness as a continuous flow. One does not confront a series of segmented snapshots, as it is said, but an ongoing process. Similarly, in our experience of self and others we seem to encounter not a series of discrete movements, endlessly juxtaposed, but coherent sequences, cross-time patterns, and overall directionality. This characteristic of flow, of cross-time process, poses particular difficulties at both the level of daily life and science alike. To describe or give an account of continuously emerging motion is no simple matter (cf. Kress, 1970). Segmented and static words do not easily map continuous change. How is understanding of this temporal character of human activity achieved? What particular forms of human accounting are required in order to establish comprehension of persons in process? It is to just such forms of accounting, their characteristics and their genesis, that the present chapter is directed.

Initial insight into the manner of understanding unfolding action may be gained by consulting people's daily accounts of themselves. It may be argued that one's view of self in a given moment is fundamentally nonsensical unless it can be linked in some fashion with his or her past. Suddenly and momentarily to see oneself as "aggressive," "poetic," or "male," for example, might seem mere whimsy unless such concepts could be secured to a series of earlier events. Some account must be available as to why these concepts are relevant and not others. Elsewhere we have spoken of these accounts of self-relevant events across time as *self-narratives* (Gergen & Gergen, 1983); however, narrative accounts are no less essential in comprehending the actions of others. In developing narratives one attempts to establish coherent connections among life events (Cohler, 1979; Kohli, 1981). Rather than seeing one's life as simply "one damned thing after another," the individual attempts to understand life-events as systematically related. They are rendered intelligible by locating them in a sequence or "unfolding process" (DeWaele & Harré, 1976). Most events are thus not sudden and mysterious revelations, but the sensible sequence of ongoing stories. As Bettelheim (1976) has argued, such creations of narrative order may be essential in giving life a sense of meaning and direction. As evidenced in the chapters of the present volume, they are also essential to the scholar attempting to render broad patterns of human activity sensible.

In the present chapter we open consideration on the problem of narrative forms. First we consider the basic components of the narrative account, that is, the specific characteristics that an account must possess in order to qualify as a narrative. Then we ask whether there are certain inherent restraints placed over this form of accounting. That is, are there commonly shared rules that limit how it is we can communicate about life across time? What are the boundaries within which one can make sense to one's fellow creatures? This analysis will set the stage for considering the relationship between narrative and drama, along with the connection between narrative accounts and objective events. With these considerations in mind we can finally turn to the process of narrative construction. As will be contended, narratives are preeminently communal products. They are not the possession of single individuals, but are the byproducts of social interchange. One's "life story" is thus not truly one's own, but a social property. Throughout these analyses, however, we sustain a dual concern, on the one hand with understanding an important aspect of daily life and on the other with the process of explanation within the behavioral sciences.

THE VARIETIES OF NARRATIVE FORM

An understanding of narrative explanation in social life requires at the outset a differentiated vocabulary of narrative form. Without distinctions among narrative forms, detailed inquiry into the functions, generation, and erosion of narrative is constrained. Although a full elaboration of narrative form is beyond the scope of this chapter, it is particularly useful to distinguish among a variety of prototypes and their variants. We may then consider the dramatic aspects of such forms along with the problem of truth through narrative.

Perhaps the most essential aspect of narrative is the capability to generate directionality among a series of otherwise isolated events. The narrative essentially structures events in such a way that they demonstrate first, a connectedness or coherence, and second, a sense of movement or direction through time. What are the critical ingredients of the narrative that enable it to succeed in achieving these ends? Or to put it another way, what is it about a "story" that makes it identifiable as such? An earlier discussion of literary narratives (Gergen & Gergen, 1983) suggests two related ingredients which together foster such ends. To succeed as a narrative, the account must first *establish a goal state* or valued endpoint. For example, it must succeed in establishing the value of a protagonist's well-being, the destruction of an evil condition, the victory of a favored group, the discovery of something precious, or the like. With the creation of a goal condition, the successful narrative must *select and arrange preceding events in such a way that the goal state is rendered more or less probable*. A description of events unrelated to the goal state detracts or dissolves the sense of narrative. In effect, all events in a successful narrative are related by virtue of their containment within a given evaluative space. Therein lies the coherence of the narrative. As one moves from one event to another, one also approaches or moves away from the desired goal state. Through this latter means, one achieves a sense of directionality.

Given that it is primarily the narrative account that is employed in rendering the comprehension of life across time, how are we to understand its various forms? What are the constraints on our means of explaining life through narrative explanation? An answer to this question is furnished by elaborating the logic of our preceding account. That is, if the successful narrative is one that arranges a sequence of events as they pertain to the achievement of a particular goal state, there are only three prototypical or primitive narrative forms: those in which progress toward the goal is enhanced, those in which it is impeded, and those in which no change occurs. The last of these prototypical forms may be termed the *stability narrative*, that is, a narrative that links incidents, images or concepts in such a way that the protagonist remains essentially unchanged with respect to evaluative position. As depicted in Fig. 9.1, we also see that the stability narrative could be struck at any level along the evaluative continuum. At the upper end of the continuum the individual might conclude for example, "I am still as attractive as I used to be," or at the lower end, "John continues to be haunted by feelings of failure." As can also be seen, each of these narrative summaries possesses inherent implications for the future. That is, they furnish an indication or anticipation of the coming events. In the former case the individual might conclude that he or she will continue to be attractive for the foreseeable future, and in the latter, that John's feelings of failure will persist regardless of circumstance.

This rudimentary narrative may be contrasted with two other prototypical forms based on linking events in such a way that either increments

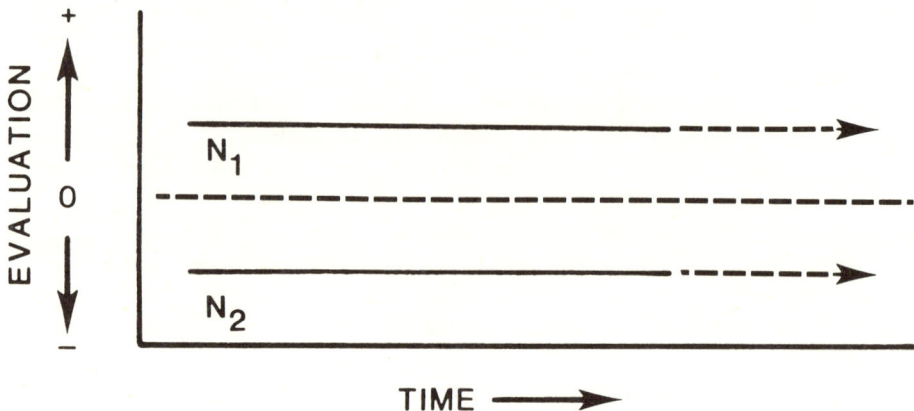

FIG. 9.1 Positive (N_1) and negative (N_2) stability narratives.

or decrements characterize movement along the evaluative dimension over time. In the former case we may speak of *progressive,* and in the latter *regressive,* narratives (see Fig. 9.2). For example, the individual might be engaged in a progressive narrative with the surmise, "She is really learning to overcome her shyness and be more open and friendly with people," or a regressive narrative with the thought, "He can't seem to control the events of his life anymore." Directionality is also implied in each of these narratives with the former anticipating further increments and the latter further decrements.

As indicated, these three narrative forms, stability, progressive and regressive, exhaust the fundamental options for the direction of movement in evaluative space. As such as they may be considered rudimentary bases for other more complex variants. Theoretically one may envision a potential infinity of variations on these rudimentary forms. However, for reasons of social utility, aesthetic desirability, and cognitive capability, the culture may limit itself to a truncated repertoire of possibilities. For example, of prime interest within this limited set is the *tragic narrative.* In the present framework such a narrative would possess the structure depicted in Fig. 9.3. The tragedy, in this sense, would tell the story of the rapid downfall of one who had achieved high position. A progressive narrative is thus followed by a rapid regressive narrative. This common narrative form may be contrasted with that of the *happy ending* or *"comedy,"* as it was termed by Aristotle. The comedy is the reverse of the tragedy: A regressive narrative is followed by a progressive narrative. Life events become increasingly problematic until the denouement, whereupon happiness is rapidly restored to the major protagonists. (See Fig. 9.3.) Further, if a progressive narrative is

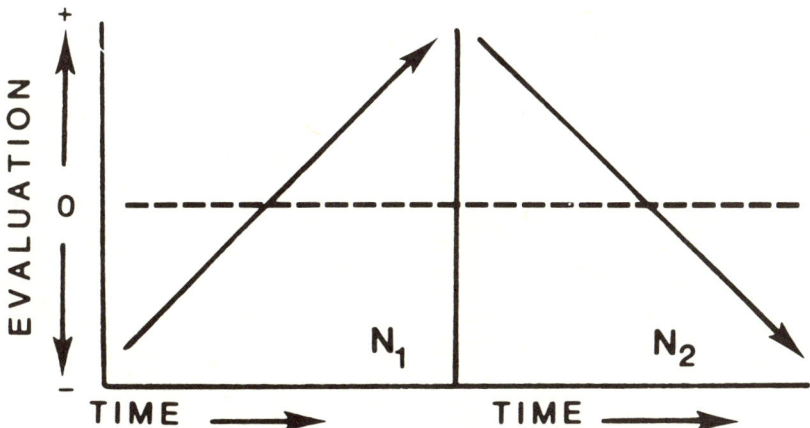

FIG. 9.2 Progressive (N_1) and regressive (N_2) narratives.

followed by a stability narrative (see Fig. 9.4), we have what is commonly known as the *"happily-ever-after"* myth widely adopted in traditional courtship. And we also recognize the *romantic saga* as a series of progressive-regressive phases. In this case, for example, the individual may see life as a continuous array of battles against the powers of darkness.

These narrative forms not only serve to structure one's personal accounts. They also enter into, and are informed by, the process of scholarly accounting. Consider Morawski's (Chapter 3) analysis of the models of change most frequently employed by historians. For the most part such models may be viewed as a rendering of a prototypical narrative form. For example, the *uniformity* model of historical explanation holds that institutions remain fundamentally unchanged regardless of alterations in localized visage. As can be seen, this model essentially adopts a stability narrative. Within historical analysis, *evolutionary* theories are those in which society is viewed as evolving continuously toward a more enhanced state of adaptation. Such an explanation is clearly a form of progressive narrative. In contrast, *revolution* and *crisis* models of history frequently employ the regressive prototype (unless the crisis is viewed as a critical integer in a progressive narrative). Somewhat more sophisticated in form is the *homeostatic* model of historical accounting. In this case, a positive steady state is punctuated by negative deviations and adjustments. This account seems more akin to the romantic saga narrative in which the protagonist (in this case the valued society) undergoes various calamities, only to emerge victorious.

As is also apparent, scholarly accounts can furnish alternative forms of accounting to the culture more generally. One of the most pertinent of these

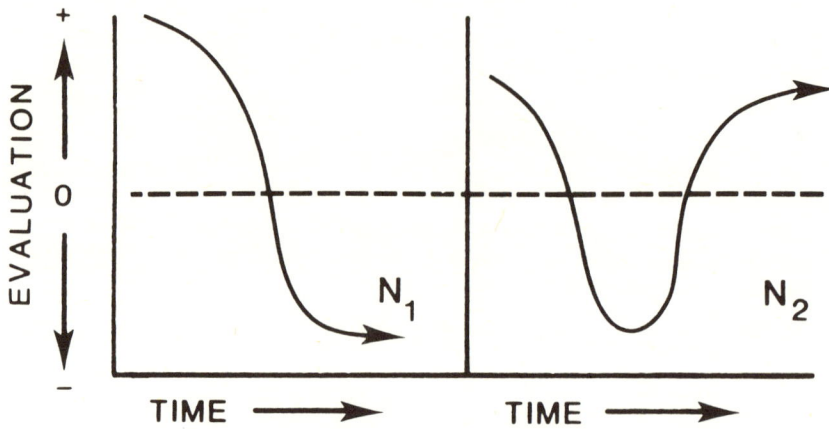

FIG. 9.3 Tragic (N_1) and comic (N_2) narrative.

cases is the dialectic form of narrative (see Chapters 3, 4, and 5), a form employed with increasing frequency in the social sciences but not yet absorbed by the culture more generally. The dialectic narrative may be viewed as the most complex variant of the basic prototypes thus far discussed, for it requires not one but two simultaneous narrative lines. As depicted in Fig. 9.5, these two lines progressively arrive at a point of conflict or mutual exclusivity. (The choice of progressive narratives in the present figure is incidental. In fact many other narrative forms could act in an antagonistic fashion to any other.) At the point of conflict transformation occurs, typically treated by dialecticians as embodying certain elements of the antagonistic tendencies but in a way that represents an advance over either alone. In this sense the prototypical form of dialectic theory is progressive. However, unlike preceding accounts, conflict is held essential to increments in evaluative space. As dialectic theory becomes increasingly elaborated in the scholarly realm, the assumption of progress through conflict may gain momentum in the culture more generally.

Dramatic Engagement in Narrative Form

We now see how coherence among events may be produced through evaluative contrasts. However, we have said little about one of the most phenomenologically salient aspects of narrative form: the capacity to create feelings of drama or emotion. We may refer to this aspect of narrative form in terms of *dramatic engagement*. In the same way that theatrical productions vary in their capacity to arouse and compel an audience, so may the

9. SOCIAL CONSTRUCTION OF NARRATIVE ACCOUNTS

narrative forms of daily life and of science vary in their dramatic impact. How are we to understand the elements giving rise to these variations? Of course, dramatic engagement cannot be separated entirely from the content of a given narrative. Yet, segmented events in themselves appear limited in their capacity to sustain engagement. For example, a film depicting the continuous, random juxtaposition of startling events (an auto crash, circus acrobats, a passionate embrace, a dog fight) would soon produce tedium. It is the *relationship* among events, not the events themselves, that seems chiefly responsible for sustaining dramatic engagement, and a theory of narrative form is essentially concerned with such relationships. What characteristics of narrative form are necessary then to generate dramatic engagement?

At this preliminary juncture, one must consider the dramatic arts as a source of insight. In this case, it is of initial interest that one can scarcely locate a theatrical exemplar of the three rudimentary narratives proposed above. A drama in which all events were evaluatively equivalent (stability narrative) would scarcely be considered drama. Further, a steady but moderate enhancement (progressive) or decrement (regressive narrative) in a protagonist's life conditions would also seem to produce ennui. At the same time, it is also interesting to observe that the tragic narrative depicted in Fig. 9.3 bears a strong resemblance to the simpler, but unarousing regressive narrative (Fig. 9.2). How does the tragic narrative, with its consistently powerful dramatic impact, differ from the more rudimentary regressive narrative? Two characteristics seem particularly significant.

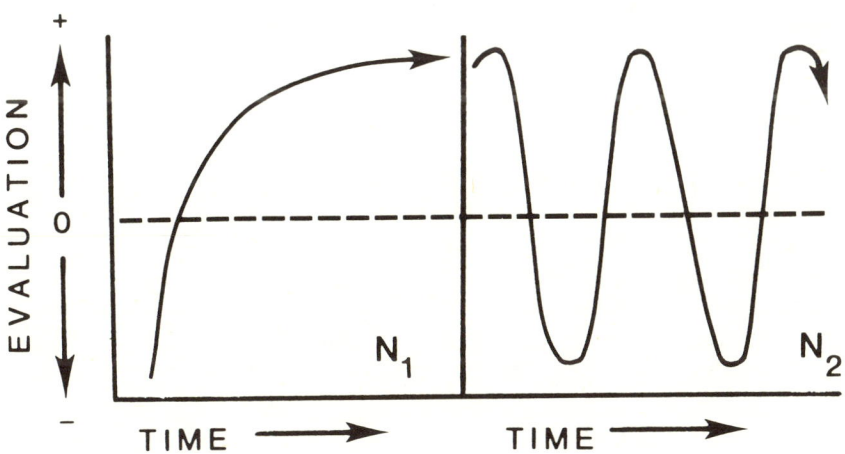

FIG. 9.4 "Happily-ever-after" (N_1) and romantic saga (N_2) narratives.

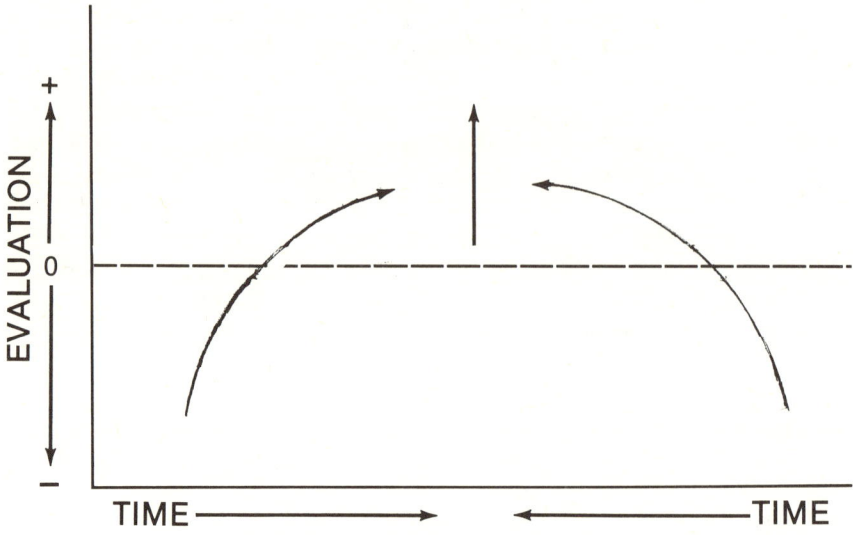

FIG. 9.5 The dialectic narrative.

First, we note that the relative decline in events is far less rapid in the prototypical regressive narrative than it is in the case of the tragic narrative. Whereas the former is characterized by moderate decline over time, the latter organizes events in such a way that decline is precipitous. In this light one may conjecture that the rapidity with which events deteriorate in such classic tragedies as *Antigone, Oedipus Rex* and *Romeo and Juliet* may be essential to their dramatic impact. More generally, it may be suggested that the rate of change, or more formally *the acceleration of the narrative slope,* constitutes one of the chief components of what is here termed dramatic engagement.

A second major component is also suggested by the contrast between the regressive and the tragic narratives. In the former case (see Fig. 9.2) there is unidirectionality in the slope line, whereas in the tragic narrative (Fig. 9.3) we find a progressive narrative (sometimes implied) followed by a regressive narrative. It would appear to be this "turn of events," or more precisely, the change in the evaluative relationship among events, that contributes to a high degree of dramatic engagement. It is when the individual who has attained high goals, has reached the apex of ecstasy, or has at last discovered life's guiding principle, is brought low that drama is created. In more formal terms, the *alteration in the direction of narrative slope* may be considered a second major component of dramatic engagement.

In this light it is interesting to consider a case in which individuals have been confronted with the task of accounting for their personal histories.

9. SOCIAL CONSTRUCTION OF NARRATIVE ACCOUNTS 181

Twenty-seven undergraduate students were asked to draw a continuous line depicting their feelings of generalized well-being from their childhood to the present. Although there were marked variations in the resulting trajectories, it was possible by converting graphic points to numerical values (at each 5-year interval) to compute an average account for the group. This composite is featured in Fig. 9.6. As is clear, the average college student in this sample accounts for his or her general life pattern (within this research setting) as a dramatic affair. Essentially the composite approximates the "comedy" form of narrative. The individual says, in effect, "life was good in the early days, then it collapsed several years ago, but now I have regained (or surpassed) the early years." Of course, each student employs a different array of events to construct the comedy narrative. When asked to describe high points, mention was made, for example, of visiting another country, the recovery of a sister from a serious illness, falling in love, and

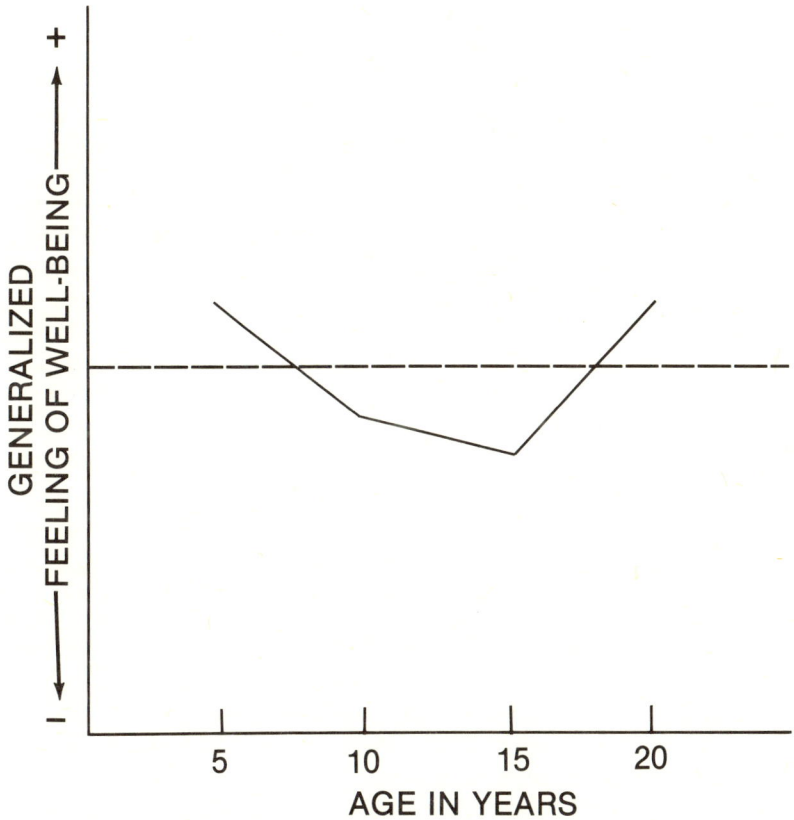

FIG. 9.6 Self-narrative trajectories of college students.

walking in the woods. When asked about the lowest points in the narrative line, students described their parents' divorce, moving residences, fights with parents, jealousies, and being excluded from peer groups. In effect, by focusing on certain events and not others, the students injected drama into their life accounts.

TRUTH AND MULTIPLICITY IN NARRATIVE

When Joyce Carol Oates was challenged to describe her development as an author, she despaired. No single, coherent account seemed to furnish "the truth." Rather, as she lamented, she found herself developing countless miniature stories. "Each angle of vision, each voice, yields . . . a separate writer-self, an alternative Joyce Carol Oates," each of these "contains so small a fraction of the truth, it is untrue." (*New York Times,* July 11, 1982). This account raises a question of critical importance in understanding narrative constructions. Narratives may be used by novelists to frame compelling stories, but in both science and everyday life they are treated as windows on the truth. When one recounts the party of the previous evening, tells a life story, or furnishes a scholarly account of the rise of slavery, for example, each is typically treated as a candidate for veracity—subject to challenge by others who might have "seen more accurately or objectively." Yet such claims would appear to be unwarranted, and their problematic aspects lay the grounds for understanding a final aspect of narrative formulation.

The assumption of truth through narrative rests on two subpropositions: first, that one can be accurate or inaccurate with regard to reporting facts, and second, that one can be correct or incorrect with respect to the relationship among facts. Space limitations prevent a full discussion of the complexities of objectivity in reports of human action. However, the strongest argument made by a historian against this initial proposition is that of Collingwood (1946). As he demonstrates, historians concerned with human activity are not concerned with people's bodily movements. Rather, historians furnish accounts of what people are attempting, trying, intending, or thinking they are doing. The history of bodily movements would be an absurdity; history is written in terms of *meanings* assigned to movement. This argument has more recently been extended (Gergen, 1982) to show how such meanings are themselves unverifiable outside the framework of another meaning system. To say that in 1215 King John sealed the Magna Carta at Runnymede makes reference to intentions, and not to the actual movements of pressing wax to parchment. If John's hands had been pressed to paper by his companions, or he had accidentally sealed the document while believing it was some other, one would be disinclined to say that he had sealed the

9. SOCIAL CONSTRUCTION OF NARRATIVE ACCOUNTS

Magna Carta. In effect the description refers not to the spatio-temporal event, but to the intentions underlying the movement. For further discussion of the interpretive basis of social knowledge the reader should consult Gadamer (1975), Gauld & Shotter (1977), Rabinow & Sullivan (1979) and Giddens (1976).

The second relevant proposition, that there is an objective relationship among events, proves equally, if not more, problematic. As we saw, narratives gain their coherence through the establishment of a goal state. Whether event A (falling from a horse) is better or worse than event B (mounting and galloping into the distance) depends on the endpoint served. Thus if the protagonist were a heroic marshal in a Western novel, the narrative relationship would be considered progressive; if the protagonist is a heinous villain, the narrative reverts to a regression. Yet the establishment of the goal state in itself is a matter of value. One is ill put to establish value stipulations objectively. In effect, narrative relationships are perspectival, and there would appear to be no limit, in principle, over perspective.

This latter emphasis on multiplicity in perspectives furnishes an additional insight of significance. As we saw, Joyce Carol Oates found herself confronting a multiplicity of life accounts. Even though it is common practice to speak as if each individual possesses *a* "life story," in fact there would appear to be no *one* story to tell. People appear capable of adopting multiple perspectives and selecting events so as to justify the selected narrative. Common experience in the culture will typically offer the individual exposure to a wide variety of narrative forms, from the rudimentary to the complex. Thus, the individual typically enters relationships with a potential for using any of a wide number of forms. In the same way an experienced skier approaches a steep incline with a variety of techniques for effective descent or a teacher confronts a class with a variety of means for effective communication, so the individual can usually construct the relationship among life experiences in a variety of ways. At a minimum, effective socialization should equip the person to interpret life events as consistencies, as improvements, or as decrements. And, with little additional training, the individual should develop the capacity to envision life as tragedy, comedy, or romantic saga.

To illustrate, in our research we have asked participants to draw graphs indicating their feelings of satisfaction over the years in their relationship with their mother, their father, and their academic work. These graph lines pose a striking contrast to the "generalized well-being" account depicted in Fig. 9.6 above. In that case the students portrayed their general life course as a "comedy"—a positive childhood, followed by an adolescent fall from grace, and capped by a postive retrenchment. However, in the case of both father and mother, participants tended most frequently to select progressive narratives, slow and continuous for the father, but more sharply accelerated in the most recent time period for the mother. Thus, they portrayed their relationships with each parent as showing increasing improvement. Yet, although attending one of the most competitive colleges in the country, the students tended to depict their feelings of satisfaction with their academic work as one of steady decline—a regressive narrative that left them in the present on the brink of dissatisfaction.

THE SOCIAL NEGOTIATION OF NARRATIVE

Narrative construction can never be entirely a private matter. In the reliance on a symbol system for relating or connecting events one is engaging in an implicitly social act. A concept acquires status as a symbol by virtue of its communicative capacity; that is, its position within a meaning system must be shared by at least one other person. A movement of the hand is not in itself a symbol, for example, unless it has the capacity to be understood by at least one other person. Thus, in understanding the relationship among events in one's life, one relies on symbols that inherently imply an audience. In the same sense, not all symbols imply an identical audience; narratives possessing communicative value for certain audiences will be opaque to others. In effect, narratives as linguistic devices are inherently a product not of individuals but of interacting persons.

The clearest cases of social interdependency are perhaps born of people's attempts to construct accounts of their experiences together—the events of their vacation, the evening before, or even the few preceding moments. For example, one member of the relationship might venture that the evening's party became increasingly enjoyable, and in doing so establishes the valuational endpoint (the goal against which things are to be evaluated as good or bad) along with a preliminary sketch of the narrative. However, this preliminary statement is but a proposal and is not typically treated as an "objective reality" until a good deal of interpersonal work has transpired. The other member of the relationship is free to propose both an alternative valuational yardstick (e.g., "it may have been fun for you, but we hardly saw each other the whole night"), or to disagree with regard to the narrative form (e.g., "I think it was good fun, but don't you really think it dragged a bit toward the end?"). At this point the chief issues become pragmatic in nature. Who gains superiority, in what manner, and for what purpose become paramount to the resolution of conflicting narratives. In any case, the emerging reality is a joint or communal product.

More ambiguous as communal products are self-narratives, or autobiographical accounts. In this case it appears at the outset that the individual's "life story" is his or her own independent construction. Yet, such a conclusion is altogether unwarranted. The individual is limited at the outset to a vocabulary of action that possesses currency within the culture. One cannot compose an autobiography of cultural nonsense. One is also constrained by the demands for narrative coherence. An autobiography typically tells a story of a particular form. Beyond these social constraints, however, the dependency of the narrative on social interchange is demanded by the public realization of the narrative.

As indicated earlier, narrative constructions frequently possess behavioral implications. To maintain that one has always been an honest person (stability narrative) suggests that one will avoid temptation when it is subsequently encountered. To construct one's past in such a way that one has overcome increasingly greater obstacles to achievement (progressive narrative) suggests that one should treat oneself with a certain degree of respect. Or, to see oneself as losing one's abilities because of increasing age (regressive narrative) is to suggest that one should attempt to accomplish less. Most important for present purposes, as these behavioral implications are realized in action they become subject to social evaluation. Others can accept or reject such actions; they will find them credible or misleading. And, to the extent that such actions are rejected or found improper, doubt is cast upon the relevant narrative construction. If others express doubt about one's honesty, suggest that one's pride is unmerited, or find one's reduction in activity unwarranted, revisions may be necessitated in the narrative construction. Thus, as narratives are realized in the public arena, they become subject to social sanctioning.

Active negotiation over narrative form is especially invited when the individual is asked to justify his or her behavior, that is, when he or she has abrogated common frames of understanding. However, the process of social negotiation need not be solely a public one. People appear generally to avoid the threat of direct negotiation by taking prior account of the public intelligibility of their actions. They may select in advance actions that can be justified on the basis of an intelligible or publicly acceptable narrative or may privately justify questionable acts when they suspect that they will have to account for behavior. In this sense the bulk of the negotiation process is anticipatory or implicit; it takes place with an imaginary audience prior to actual confrontations. In this way most human interaction proceeds unproblematically.

Reciprocity and the Interknitting of Narrative Construction

The social generation of narrative construction hardly terminates with the negotiation process in its implicit and explicit forms. An additional facet of narrative construction throws its communal basis into vivid relief. Thus far we have spoken of narratives as if solely concerned with the temporal trajectory of individual protagonists. This conception must now be expanded. Frequently, the narrator stands as the chief protagonist in the narrative construction. However, such constructions typically make reference as well to relations with others. Others' actions contribute vitally to the events to be linked in narrative sequence. For example, in justifying his continuing honesty, an individual may point to an instance in which another person has tempted him; to illustrate, an achievement may depend on showing how another person was vanquished in a particular competition; in arguing that one's skills are on the wane it may be necessary to point to the alacrity with which a younger person performed a particular task. In all cases, the action of the other enters as an integral part of the narrative construction. In this sense, such constructions typically require a *supporting cast*. The implications of this fact are broad indeed.

First, in the same manner that the individual feels that he or she has priority in self-definition, others also feel themselves to have primary jurisdiction over the definition of their own actions. Thus, one's understanding of the supporting role played by another cannot easily proceed without the acquiescence of the other. If others are not willing to accede to their assigned parts, then one can ill afford to rely on their actions within a narrative. If another fails to see his or her actions as "offering temptation," the actor may be unable to conclude that he or she has displayed honesty; if the other can show how he or she was not really vanquished in a given competition, one can scarcely use the episode as a stepping-stone in a progressive narrative; if the younger person can demonstrate that his or her alacrity was only an apparent one, far overestimating true qualities, then one can ill afford to weave the incident into a regressive narrative.

This reliance on others' definitions of their actions places the narrator in a precarious position. As we have seen, people possess a variety of narrative forms, any one of which may be used in a particular circumstance. At the same time, members of a supporting cast may choose at any point to reconstruct their actions in opposing ways. Thus, an actor's success in sustaining any given narrative is fundamentally dependent on others' willingness to play out certain parts in relationship to the actor. In Wilhelm Schapp's (1976) terms, each of us is "knitted" into others' historical constructions, as they into ours.

This delicate interdependence of constructed narratives suggests that a fundamental aspect of social life is a reciprocity in the negotiation of meaning. Because one's narrative constructions can be maintained only so long as others play their proper supporting roles, and in turn because one is required by others to play supporting roles in their constructions, the moment any participant chooses to renege, he or she threatens the array of interdependent constructions. For example, an adolescent may reveal to his mother that he believes she has been a very bad mother, thus potentially destroying her continuing self-narrative as a "good mother." Yet, at the same time, the son risks his mother's reply that she always felt his character was so inferior that he never merited her love. His continuing narrative of self as valued person is thus thrown into jeopardy. A lover may announce that she has begun to feel her male partner no longer interests her as he once did, thus potentially crushing his stability narrative; however, she does so at the peril of his replying that he has long been bored with her, and happy to be relieved of his lover's role. In such instances the parties in the relationship each pull out their supporting roles, and the result is a full degeneration of the narratives to which they contribute.

Mechanisms for Narrative Sustenance

It would appear that most relationships are not under the immediate threat of mutual withdrawal. In part this is because many people are content with existing reciprocity. There is little to gain in abandoning the support roles that in turn also serve one's own constructions. However, there are three particular mechanisms that can insulate members of a relationship from quixotic resignations, and the resulting "collapse of reality." Reciprocity is protected first by the *incorporation of others' narrative into one's own.* That is, the other's self-construction and one's place in the supporting cast can be integrated into one's own self-narrative. Thus, people do not merely rely on the supporting roles that others play, but come to believe in others' beliefs in these roles. One may not only see his or her mate playing a supporting role as "loving helper" in one's upward route to success, but also comes to believe that the other possesses a private narrative in which this role has a major place. The attempt is thus not only to weave into one's own narrative others' actions, but their underlying narrative constructions as well. The individual thus shelters his or her own constructions by including within them the constructions of others.

A second means of protecting oneself from ontological abandonment is to engage in an *objectification of the "relationship,"* thus shifting concern to the history of this emergent entity. Rather than each individual seeing himself or herself as an independent entity requiring support, individuals may decide that together they create a new entity—that of the relationship itself. Once objectified ("we have a relationship") the participants can shift to the simpler task of negotiating one narrative rather than two. Rather than concerning themselves with such issues as whether each individually is "growing as a person," for example, they can negotiate about the trajectory of the mutually created relationship. "Is our marriage failing?" "Is the team's desire to win growing stronger?" or "What is happening to the morale of this organization?" are all relevant questions to ask once the relationship has become objectified and the relevant narrative created (see also Shuster, 1982).

Finally, one cannot underestimate the *power of affective control* in maintaining reciprocity in narrative construction. Guilt, for example, may be invoked when one party of an interdependent unit accuses another of falling short of his or her history, of failing to live up to the narrative that has been agreed upon as objective. A comment such as "you said you were my close friend, but no friend could ever . . ." implies that the accused has failed in playing out a part that was implied by a previous narrative construction. A common reaction to such accusations may be a restorative negotiation in which the accused person attempts to demonstrate the falsity of the accusations, or to counter with accusations of one's own. In a more positive vein, participants may mutually sustain various narratives by calling attention to the various positive emotional states with which they have been associated. People often speak, for example, of the "happiness," "fulfillment," and "joy" derived from a given relationship, or the "security," "relief from anxiety," and "optimism" drawn from a given history. When narratives are abandoned, so are the linguistic buttresses to their credibility. Thus, by employing various rhetorical devices members of a relationship can ensure that collective or reciprocal agreements are maintained over extended periods of time.

SUMMARY

The argument was initially advanced that the description of social conduct across time generally takes the form of narrative. Narrative constructions possess certain necessary properties and their basic forms are limited in number. These basic forms are pervasive within daily life as well as the social sciences, and differ systematically in their capacity to generate a sense of drama. Narrative constructions must be considered products of social interchange and not essentially subject to correction through observation. Such interchange may be viewed as a negotiation process in which participants propose, adjust, and interweave narratives. Any existing narrative thus stands in a reciprocal relationship with other narratives, and a variety of social mechanisms may be used to sustain the balanced array.

REFERENCES

Bettelheim, B. *The use of enchantment.* New York: Knopf, 1976.
Cohler, B. J. *Personal narrative and life-course.* Unpublished manuscript. University of Chicago, 1979.

Collingwood, R. G. *The idea of history.* Oxford: Clarendon Press, 1946.
DeWaele, J. P., & Harré, R. The personality of individuals. In R. Harré (Ed.) *Personality.* Oxford: Blackwell, 1976.
Gadamer, H. G. *Truth and method.* G. Bardun & J. Cumming (Eds.), New York: Seaburg, 1975.
Gauld, A., & Shotter, J. *Human action and its psychological investigation.* London: Routledge & Kegan Paul, 1977.
Gergen, K. J. *Toward transformation in social knowledge.* New York: Springer-Verlag, 1982.
Gergen, K. J., & Gergen, M. M. Narratives of the self. In K. Scheibe & T. Sarbin (Eds.), *Studies in social identity.* New York: Praeger, 1983.
Giddens, A. *New rules of sociological method.* New York: Basic Books, 1976.
Kohli, M. Biography: account, text, method. In D. Bertaux (Ed.), *Biography and society.* Beverly Hills, Calif.: Sage, 1981.
Kress, P. F. *Social science and the idea of process. The ambiguous legacy of Arthur F. Bentley.* Urbana: University of Illinois Press, 1970.
Rabinow, P., & Sullivan, W. (Eds.) *Interpretive social science: A reader.* Berkeley: University of California Press, 1979.
Schapp, W. *In Geschichten Verstrickt zum Sein von Mensch und Ding.* Wiesbaden: B. Heymann, 1976.
Shuster, R. G. *Applying an alternative social psychology metatheory: Discovering and sharing stories of friendship.* Unpublished manuscript. Wesleyan University, 1982.

10 Diverging Life Paths: Their Probabilistic and Causal Structure[1]

William McKinley Runyan
University of California, Berkeley

> Two roads diverged in a yellow wood,
> And sorry I could not travel both
> And be one traveler, long I stood
> And looked down one as far as I could
> To where it bent in the undergrowth;
> . . .
> Two roads diverged in a wood, and I—
> I took the one less traveled by,
> And that has made all the difference.
>
>   Robert Frost

The life course can be defined, most simply, as the sequence of events and experiences in a life from birth until death, a sequence which is generated through a continuing interaction of persons with their social and historical worlds. The life course has been conceptualized in a great variety of ways, each revealing and obscuring parts of the process. For example, the life course has been conceptualized as a sequence of episodes and proceedings (Murray, 1938, 1959); a sequence of tasks or issues (Erikson, 1963); a sequence of stages (Levinson, Darrow, Klein, Levinson, & McKee, 1978; Loevinger, 1976); a sequence of transitions (Lowenthal, Thurnher, & Chiriboga, 1975); a sequence of personality organizations (Block, 1971); a sequence of changing environments and organismic responses (Skinner, 1953); a sequence of dialectical operations (Riegel, 1975); a sequence of

---
[1]Portions of this material appeared previously in Runyan (1980, 1982b).

person-situation interactions (Baltes & Schaie, 1973); and a sequence of behavior-determining, person-determining, and situation-determining processes (Runyan, 1978). The life course has also been conceptualized from sociological and social structural perspectives that focus more on roles, lifelong socialization, age norms, and the flow of populations through socially and historically structured pathways (e.g., Clausen, 1972; Elder, 1975, 1981; Neugarten & Datan, 1973; Riley, Johnson, & Foner, 1972).

In spite of these extensive conceptual developments, there is still a need for conceptualizations which reveal the immense variety of life paths followed by individuals, and which indicate the substantial possibilities of experience open to individuals. This chapter argues that a conceptualization of the probabilistic and causal structure of the life course, and more particularly, a stage-state analysis of this structure, can be a useful approach to these issues. The intent is to develop a conceptualization of diachronic or cross-time processes which can be used for analyzing the divergent life paths followed by groups of individuals and for analyzing the array of life paths open to single individuals.

In recent years, the concept of "development," particularly when applied to adult and life-span development, has come to be defined very broadly (Baltes, Reese, & Nesselroade, 1977; Neugarten, 1982) to include not only sequential, undirectional, and universal patterns of change in behavior but also "any age-related change that is not random, short-term, or momentary" (Baltes, Reese, & Nesselroade, 1977, p. 82). This broadened conception of development recognizes both inter-individual differences in the course of development and the contingency of developmental trajectories upon social and historical conditions. A conception of the probabilistic and causal structure of the life course pursued here directs attention to questions such as: What are the consequences of a current action or event for the probabilities of occurrence of an array of possible future events? What are the effects of a given decision, action, or set of experiences upon the future life course?

This conception of the causal and probabilistic structure of the course of experience has particular relevance from the perspective of persons considered as conscious self-directing agents (Gergen, 1982; Tyler, 1978), whose decisions and actions are inevitably dependent upon assumptions about the causal structure of the course of experience and about the likely effects of different courses of action upon this experience.

There are, of course, limits in the extent to which the life course has a tightly knit causal and probabilistic structure. Meehl (1978), for example, has suggested that "a human being's life history involves . . . something akin to the stochastic process known as a 'random walk' . . . Luck is one of the most important contributors to individual differences in human suffering, satisfaction, illness, achievement, and so on" (p. 811). Gergen (1977,

1982) has also argued for an aleatory model of development, in which the course of experience is open-ended and largely chance-dependent. The virtue of this perspective in my view is that it stresses the flexibility, open-endedness, and context-dependence of the life course. But if the course of life was totally determined by chance and luck, this would vitiate the possibilities for any rational decision making or goal-directed action in relation to major life outcomes. Chance factors unquestionably do impinge upon the life course, but they don't wash out all regularities and structured relationships.

At the other extreme, it is difficult to defend the position that the life course has a fully determinant causal and probabilistic structure, in which the consequences of particular events or actions can be traced through a life-long sequence of contingent events and processes. The chain of consequences from particular life events often quickly disappears into mists of obscurity.

The precise extent to which the causal and probabilistic structure of the course of lives is determinate and knowable cannot and need not be resolved here. Discussion can proceed with the assumption that at least some aspects of the course of experience are ordered in a probabilistic and causal structure that can be revealed through empirical research.

This chapter presents stage-state analysis as a method for studying the probabilistic and causal structure of the course of lives and for examining individual differences in the course of experience. This framework can be used for identifying types of life courses and their relative frequency, analyzing the routes or processes connecting initial states with a variety of potential outcomes, and visualizing an array of possible life paths for individuals at different points in the life course.

This conceptual framework, like each of the others mentioned earlier, has a particular "range of convenience" and is useful for only a particular range of theoretical and practical purposes. It does not allow us to analyze the process of living in all its complexity, but it does provide a method for studying the sequential structure of person-situation interactions. In particular, it provides a way for investigating the alternative routes, or sequences of processes, through which initial person-situation configurations may be linked with an array of potential outcomes, and for analyzing aspects of the probabilistic and causal structure of the course of lives.

Stage-state analysis makes the simplifying assumptions that the life course can be divided into a sequence of stages, and that a person can exist in one of a limited number of states within each stage. For example, if the course of early experience is divided into Freud's psychosexual stages, then individuals can be characterized according to whether they have been excessively frustrated, excessively gratified, or normally satisfied at the oral or anal stage. Conditions of inadequate or excessive gratification may be conceptualized as possible states (or outcomes) within each psychosexual stage. If the life course is divided according to Erikson's eight psychosocial stages, then persons can presumably be characterized by their ratios of basic trust versus mistrust experienced or acquired at the oral-sensory stage, of identity versus role confusion in adolescence, intimacy versus isolation in young adulthood, and so on. In both examples, potential differences in experience can be conceptualized as possible states within relatively common stages.

The stage-state approach combines aspects of the search for common sequential order pursued in stage theories, along with a concern for individual differences in the way that stages are negotiated and experienced. As expressed by Levinson et al. (1978, p. 41), "Everyone lives through the same developmental periods in adulthood, just as in childhood, though people go through them in radically different ways."

Both stages and states can be defined by personal, situational, or behavioral-experiential variables, or by combinations of the three. The concept of "stage" is being defined here in a broad way to indicate periods in a process, and not necessarily in the more technical sense used in developmental psychology of a hierarchy of qualitatively different structures (Kitchener, 1978; Kohlberg, 1969). The most sophisticated conceptualizations of states within a stage will identify specific kinds of persons behaving in particular ways in particular social and historical circumstances. Although this chapter focuses on a stage-state analysis of the life course, stage-state analyses may also be made of the course of experience within more specific domains, such as within educational careers, occupational careers, or interpersonal relationships.

A particular set of stage and state definitions permits an exhaustive classification of possible life courses, with a life course defined by a person's movement through a particular sequence of states. The empirical distribution of people among alternative life courses can be computed. This provides a way of thinking about types of life courses, and about their relative frequency within a population. In some cases, it would be possible to compare the frequency of different types of life courses across age cohorts, or across cultures and ethnic groups.

By studying the movement of numbers of people through a sequence of stages, multi-stage flow tables or transition matrices can be constructed which indicate the probabilities of a person moving from any given state through an array of possible future states. These multi-stage flow tables can also be used to identify the variety and likelihood of routes between a given early state, or origin, and a specific later state, or destination. This specification of routes provides a way of analyzing one class of life history processes.

This chapter presents a quantitative illustration of a stage-state analysis of the life course and suggests that empirical data from a stage-state model can be examined in relationship to the three reference points of statistical independence, complete predictability, and implicit theories about the course of lives. Finally, there is a brief discussion of the ways in which data from stage-state analyses can and cannot be used by conscious agents in thinking prospectively about the course of life experience.

TYPES OF LIFE COURSES AND THEIR DISTRIBUTION

For this initial exposition of the stage-state approach, I use a relatively simple set of four stages, with four possible states within each stage. The analysis focuses on transitions between type of family background, level of educational attainment, type of first job, and type of last job. It cannot be emphasized too strongly that the stages and states proposed here are illustrative, and in no sense final. They are used to give a quantitative illustration of a form of analysis which can be applied to a range of substantive phenomena, and which may employ a variety of alternative conceptualizations of stages and states.

The data come from the Occupational Changes in a Generation data file (Blau & Duncan, 1967), which is a representative national sample of more than 20,000 American men between the ages of 20 and 69, taken in 1962. The present analysis uses a random subsample of 614 men between the ages of 35 and 45.

The four stages are family background (indicated by father's occupation), level of educational attainment, type of first job, and type of last job (most recent job as of 1962). Occupations are divided into four levels or states: Professional and executive, skilled, semi-skilled, and unskilled and farm (hereafter abbreviated as unskilled). Educational attainment is also divided into four states: Elementary school, some high school, high school graduation, and college or higher.

What are the possible courses among these stages? The number of possible courses can be calculated by multiplying the number of states within each stage; so, in this case, there are $4 \times 4 \times 4 \times 4 = 256$ possible life courses. Life courses are defined by a pattern of movement through a sequence of states, rather than by characteristics at any single stage, and a life course can be identified or classified according to any one of these 256 possible state sequences.

This set of stages and states, and the variety of courses through them, are illustrated in Fig. 10.1. Out of the 256 possible paths, Person A followed the particular course of movement from unskilled family background, to some high school, to an unskilled first job, to a semi-skilled last job; and Person B the path from skilled family background, to a college or higher education, to a professional or executive first and last job. (The model could be made

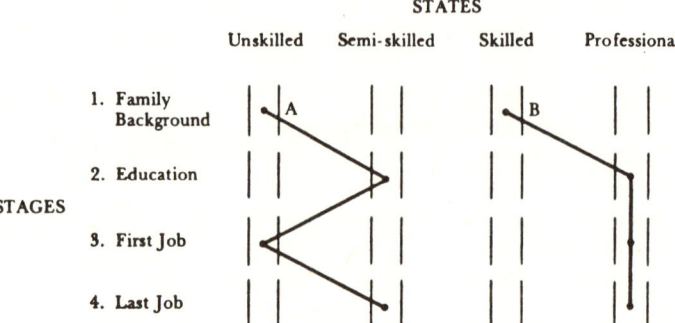

FIG. 10.1 Alternative paths through a sequence of stages and states. (Note: The four states for stage 2-education, are, respectively, elementary school education, some high school, high school graduation, and college or higher.)

more complex by considering changes in personal characteristics and behaviors as different kinds of people moved along the various paths.)

What is the empirical distribution of people in this sample among each of the possible life courses? If people were distributed randomly among each of the 256 possible courses, there would be 1/256, or approximately 0.4% of the population within each life course. The single most frequent course, containing 5.8% of the population, is defined by movement from family background with an unskilled father to elementary education, to unskilled first job, to unskilled last job. The second most frequent course, containing 5.1% of the sample, consists of movement from a family with an unskilled father, to elementary education, to unskilled first job, to semi-skilled last job; while the third most frequent course, followed by 3.0% of the sample, is defined by movement from a family with a professional or executive father, to college education, to professional first job, to professional last job.

To account for the majority of men, it is necessary to consider only a small portion of the theoretically possible life courses. Out of 256 possible courses, 27 courses, or 11% of the total, have been pursued by 1% or more of the population. These 27 courses account for 54% of the population. The other 46% of the men are distributed among the remaining 229 possible courses.

Not all of the theoretically possible courses have actually occurred. Of the 256 possible courses, 99 have not been followed by any member of the sample. For example, there is no one who had a professional father, got a college education, a professional first job, and an unskilled last job. Neither is there anyone in the sample who had an unskilled father, received an elementary education, and ended up in a professional or executive last job. There are 62 other possible courses which have been followed by only one person, or by 0.2% of the sample.

10. DIVERGING LIFE PATHS

Why are some life courses so much more common than others? Why, for example, were there so many sons of unskilled workers who received an elementary education, and got unskilled first and last jobs? Was upward mobility prevented by deficits in skills or intelligence, by low levels of aspiration and expectation, by class biases of schools or employers, by an interaction of social structural constraints with deficits in personal and economic resources, or by other factors and processes? A detailed answer will probably require different explanations for different individuals and groups and will need to consider the sequential interaction of persons with their social environments (Runyan, 1982b). In any case, the discovery of nonrandom transition probabilities suggests questions about the causal structure of the course of lives which can then be investigated through experimental, quasi-experimental, and naturalistic research methods (Blalock, 1964; Campbell & Stanley, 1963; Cook & Campbell, 1979).

MULTISTAGE FLOW TABLES

Using a stage-state analysis of the life course, a set of multistage flow tables or transition matrices can be constructed which allow us to estimate the probabilities of a person moving from any given state through an array of future states, to see how these transition probabilities are affected by prior background, and to estimate the probabilities of taking different routes from a given origin to a particular destination. Thus, multistage flow tables allow us to address a set of questions which cannot be handled through the use of base rates or standard two-stage flow tables.

The base rates or population percentages for each state within each stage are contained in Table 10.1. Out of the entire sample, 15% of the men had fathers with professional jobs, and 26% had fathers with skilled jobs. As for education, 27% of the sample received a college education, and 25% obtained an elementary school education.

In the absence of any other information, these base rates can be used for making predictions. With base rates alone, it would be estimated that a per-

TABLE 10.1
Population Percentages for Each State

	Education[a]		Father's Job	First Job	Last Job
College	27	Professional	15	10	30
High School	29	Skilled	26	28	30
Some H.S.	19	Semi-skilled	17	28	23
Elementary	25	Unskilled	42	34	17

[a]Each cell contains a percentage of the column total.

son would be most likely to receive a high school education, to get an unskilled first job, and to get a professional or skilled last job. Base rates have the limitation of not indicating the differential probabilities of outcome dependent upon the values of earlier states. For example, men from professional versus unskilled families could be expected to have significantly different educational and occupational careers. To examine differential probabilities, a set of flow tables is needed. For a model with four stages, there are six possible two-stage flow tables (e.g. stage 1 to 2, 2 to 3, or 1 to 4), one of which is produced in Table 10.2.

These percentages are significantly different than those that would be expected on the grounds of base rates alone. Knowing father's occupation is of substantial help in predicting a man's likely level of education. For example, men with professional fathers had a 63% chance of attending college, while men with unskilled fathers had only a 10% chance. Similarly, knowing a person's level of education helps in predicting his type of first job and type of last job.

Two-stage flow tables are common analytic tools in the social sciences, yet there are several important kinds of questions that they cannot answer, and for which the multistage tables in a stage-state analysis are required. First, can life courses be regarded as Markov processes, in which transition probabilities are contingent only upon current states (Tibbitt, 1973), or does knowledge of previous states aid in predicting? For example, of all those holding a skilled first job, do men with different family backgrounds have equal chances of attaining a professional last job? Second, by what processes or routes have people moved from their initial family background to their last job? For example, what variety of routes or state sequences were followed by men moving from families with unskilled fathers to professional last jobs?

Questions about differential transitions from one stage-state to later ones depending upon previous background, and questions about intervening

TABLE 10.2
Father's Job to Education:
Outflow Percentages

Father's Job	Level of Education			
	Elementary	Some High School	High School	College
Professional	3	11	23	63
Skilled	8	16	34	42
Semi-skilled	21	24	34	20
Unskilled	43	21	26	10

10. DIVERGING LIFE PATHS

processes can be answered by flow tables containing three or more stages. In this case, we can construct a multistage flow table which indicates movement through a sequence of four stages, and which represents all of the 256 possible sequences of state transitions. This complete table can be broken down into sixteen 4 × 4 subtables, each of which has a fixed level of family background and of educational attainment. One of these subtables, describing the experience of men from unskilled family backgrounds with elementary educations, is presented in Table 10.3.

The meaning of these figures can be illustrated by consideration of the lower right-hand cell. The top figure is the percentage of the column total, and indicates that 80.2% of men with unskilled last jobs came from unskilled first jobs. The second figure is the percentage of the row total and indicates that 46.0% of men with unskilled first jobs ended up in unskilled last jobs. The third figure is the number of men in the cell over the subtable total, and tells us that 33.1% of men from unskilled family backgrounds ended up in unskilled first and last jobs. The fourth figure is the number of men in this cell over the total for the inclusive table, and indicates that 5.8% of the sample followed the particular life course from unskilled family background, to elementary education, to unskilled first job, to unskilled last job. The bottom figure is the cell total and indicates the number of men in the sample following this particular life course.

What are the effects of background states upon transition probabilities? As indicated by data from the comprehensive multistage flow table which Table 10.3 was drawn from, men with skilled first jobs have widely different chances of attaining professional last jobs depending upon their preceding history. For men having skilled first jobs, even with family background held constant at the level of unskilled fathers, those with elementary educations have little or no chance of getting a professional last job, those with some high school have a 16% chance, those graduating from high school have a 30% chance, and those with at least some college have a 43% chance of attaining a professional last job. In short, previous background has a substantial effect upon later state transitions, and these data cannot be accurately fitted by a Markov model.

Second, what variety of routes were used by people moving from a given family background to a particular type of last job? With this particular model, there are 16 different ways such transitions may be made. Let us consider, for example, the 41 men in the sample who moved from an unskilled family background to a professional last job. Altogether, 14/41, or 34% of these men got college educations, and 13/41, or 32%, got a professional first job. The chances are 9/41, or 22%, that a man making this transition followed the specific route of going to college *and* getting a professional first job. The chances are 0/41 that he followed the specific route of getting an elementary education and a professional first job. The probabili-

TABLE 10.3
Example of a Multistage Flow Table (Subtable for Men with
Unskilled Fathers and Elementary School Educations)

Type of first job	Type of last job				
	Professional	Skilled	Semi-skilled	Unskilled	Total
Professional					
N	—	—	—	—	0
% column total	—	—	—	—	
% row total	—	—	—	—	
% subtable total	—	—	—	—	0
% grand total	—	—	—	—	
Skilled					
N	—	3	2	1	6
% column total	—	24.7	3.8	2.3	
% row total	—	56.6	27.3	16.1	
% subtable total	—	3.3	1.6	.9	5.8
% grand total	—	.6	.3	.2	
Semiskilled					
N	—	4	10	7	21
% column total	—	33.7	25.6	17.6	
% row total	—	20.1	47.3	32.5	
% subtable total	—	4.5	10.5	7.2	22.3
% grand total	—	.8	1.8	1.3	
Unskilled					
N	4	5	28	31	68
% column total	100.0	41.7	70.6	80.2	
% row total	5.8	7.7	40.5	46.0	
% subtable total	4.2	5.6	29.1	33.1	71.9
% grand total	.7	1.0	5.1	5.8	
Total N	4	12	40	39	95
%	4.2	13.3	41.2	41.3	100.0

Note. This is a weighted sample, so there is sometimes a discrepancy between the number of persons in a cell and their percentage of the sample total.

ty of following any of the 14 other routes between an unskilled family background and a professional last job can also be calculated.

In general, given a transition between any two nonadjacent states, a stage-state model can indicate the number of possible transition routes, and the probability that each of these routes was followed.

So far, the discussion has considered probabilistic transitions between a sequence of states, but a stage-state model can also be used to study causal chains. Working with this same set of stages and states, causal inferences could be made about chains of effects by introducing treatments such as special educational programs or family financial assistance to a sample of children, and then examining the sequence of effects upon educational attainment, first job, and last job. A quasi-experimental study tracing the effects of an early life experience, in this case economic deprivation, upon a sequence of later life stages is reported by Elder (1974).

COMPARISON WITH A PATH ANALYTIC APPROACH

Multiple regression and path analytic techniques are frequently used in the analysis of quantitative life course data, so it may be useful to briefly compare the issues addressed by these techniques with those addressed by the multistage transition matrices presented here.

A path analysis of the relationships between family background, level of education, first job, and last job in this sample is presented in Fig. 10.2. The straight lines connecting one variable with another show the magnitude of the direct relationship between the two variables. For example, the magnitude of the direct influence of education upon last job is .36. These path coefficients are partial regression coefficients, with the other variables in the system controlled for. The lines with no sources indicate the residual paths, standing for all other influences on the variables, such as unmeasured causal variables, errors of measurement, and departures of the relationships from additivity and linearity.

What kinds of questions can be addressed with a path analytic model versus a multistage conditional probability model? Path analysis allows us to give quantitative interpretations to the causal relationships among variables in a system. "The technique of path analysis is not a method of discovering causal laws but a procedure for giving a quantitative interpretation to the manifestations of a known or assumed causal system as it operates in a par-

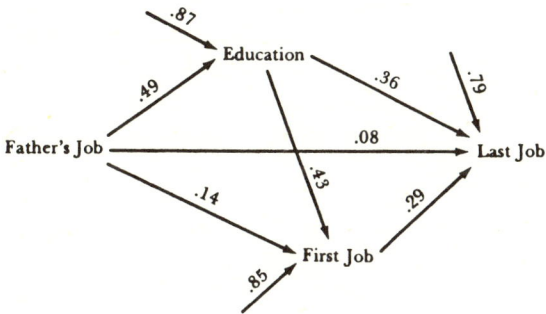

FIG. 10.2 A path analysis of occupational attainment.

ticular population" (Blau & Duncan, 1967, p. 177). Path analysis permits the calculation of the magnitude of direct and indirect effects of earlier variables upon later ones, such as the influence of educational attainment upon level of last job. The data in Fig. 10.2 indicate that an increase of one standard deviation in education should lead to an increase of .36 (direct effects) plus .43 × .29 (indirect effects) = .48 standard deviations in level of last job.

The advantages and uses of path analysis are considerable, yet it seems that a stage-state analysis provides access to a somewhat different set of questions. In general, a path analytic model elucidates the quantitative relationships among variables and reveals variable-to-variable relationships that can be abstracted across contexts, or across person-situation configurations. On the other hand, a stage-state model allows us to think more easily about persons in situations, and about different processes or different sequences of conditions which may emerge from these person-situation configurations.

In particular, a stage-state model allows us (1) to calculate the probabilities for an array of qualitatively different outcomes, (2) to estimate the probabilities of particular sequences of states, or sequences of person-situation configurations, and (3) to analyze the variety of routes or processes connecting initial states with later outcomes. These are three kinds of questions that seem to be handled more effectively by a stage-state approach than by a path analytic approach.

On the other hand, one of the limitations of a stage-state analysis is the large number of cases required to fill in the cells for complex sets of stages and states. When a large number of personal and situational variables are considered in the definition of stages and states, it may be necessary to find ways, perhaps through factor analysis or cluster analysis, of reducing the number of discrete stages and states.

A second limitation of the stage-state approach, which is shared by path analysis, is that it can be applied only under conditions where the course of experience can be divided into a relatively common sequence of stages. The stage-state model is only one approach to finding order in the probabilistic and causal structure of the course of experience, and for studying less structured sequences, other models, such as stage-state-sequential approach mentioned further on, will need to be developed.

COMPARISON WITH STATISTICAL NORMS AND IMPLICIT THEORIES

In this stage-state model, statistical significance of the results can be assessed by comparing expected with observed transition frequencies from one stage-state to later stage-states. Expected transition probabilities are calculated on the assumption of random movement between stage S and stage S + 1, or in other words, on the assumption that all of the states in stage S have equal access to the array of states at stage S + 1. The χ^2-test provides a simple method for comparing the information in flow tables to the null hypothesis of statistical independence between stages.

A second reference point to use in assessing the information in these conditional probability tables is that of total predictability or total regularity. Complete regularity is approached as each of the transition probabilities approaches .00 or 1.00. An index, or "hit rate," varying from zero to 100% can be used to assess the degree of predictability permitted by the data. Prediction is used here in the sense of estimation from known to unknown variables within a population. Due to the pace of social and historical change (e.g. Cronbach, 1975; Gergen, 1973), generalization to other cohorts and predictions to future time periods can be made only with considerable caution.

To illustrate the index of predictive efficiency, consider the problem of predicting an individual's last job. On the basis of population percentages alone, the best strategy for each individual is to predict a professional last job, which will be accurate 30% of the time, and inaccurate 70% of the time.

What happens to predictive accuracy if information about an earlier stage, such as father's occupation, is made available? This can be calculated according to the following formula, where A_i represents each category of father's occupation:

Prob. of Hit = ΣP (hit/A_i) • $P(A_i)$.

Drawing upon the two-stage table relating father's occupation to last job, and from Table 10.1, which gives the likelihood of each category of father's occupation, we get:

Prob. of Hit = (.57) (.15) + (.46) (.26) + (.36) (.17)
             + (.30) (.42)
           = .40   .

Knowing father's occupation has raised accuracy in predicting last job from 30% to 40%.

If information about several previous stages, such as father's occupation and level of education, is made available, then predictive accuracy can be computed according to a similar formula, where A_i represents each level of father's occupation, and B_j represents each level of education:

Prob. of Hit = ΣP (hit/$A_i B_j$) • $P(A_i B_j)$
             = .503   .

Given knowledge of father's occupation and of level of educational attainment, type of last job can be accurately predicted 50% of the time, rather than the 30% accuracy obtainable through base rates alone. By defining more stages, and differentiating more states within each stage, predictive accuracy can often be increased so that it rises progressively farther above base rates. This same index of predictive accuracy can also be used to assess predictions about *sequences* of future states.

As a third reference point, observed probabilities can be compared to "common knowledge," or to individuals' implicit theories about the course of lives. For example, people could be asked to estimate the proportion of men with college educations who ended up in each job level, or about the frequency with which given routes connected a particular origin, such as unskilled family background, with a particular outcome, such as professional last job. Using alternative conceptions of stages and states, respondents could be asked to estimate the likelihood of orally deprived children ending up with different types of adult character, or to estimate the likelihood of generative older adults having successfully mastered identity and intimacy at earlier life stages, and so on.

As well as having implicit theories of personality (Schneider, 1973), of personality development (Ryff, 1982), and of events (Ajzen, 1977), people also have implicit theories of the life course, or implicit theories about the structure of the course of experience, and about the probabilities and processes of moving from one state to a set of later ones. Implicit theories about the life course undoubtedly influence the ways in which individuals plan, make decisions within, and conduct their lives. It would be valuable to investigate the implicit theories of life courses that people hold, and the processes through which these theories are constructed and revised in changing social and historical circumstances.

GENERALIZATION AND APPLICATIONS

Stage-state analyses are not restricted to any particular substantive domain but may be applied to the analysis of sequences of state transitions within parent-child relationships, educational careers, occupational histories, interpersonal relationships, and the "natural histories" of psychological disorders, criminal behavior, or drug abuse. Most generally, stage-state analyses can be used for examining the temporal course of classes of behavior, personality characteristics, encountered situations, or sequences of person-situation interaction. The minimal requirements are that there be individual differences in the course of the phenomena under investigation, and that there be enough comparability across cases to permit quantitative analysis.

If, for example, one were interested in the temporal course of aggressive behavior, a stage-state framework could be used to divide the relevant time period into a number of stages (such as childhood, adolescence, early adulthood, and middle adulthood), to identify three or four levels or states within each stage, and to trace the relative frequency of different diachronic patterns (such as continual antisocial aggression, high-level aggression only in adolescence, or high-level aggression in childhood gradually tapering off). Kagan and Moss (1962) have data on variables such as compulsivity, social spontaneity, passivity, and aggression, assessed over four time periods, which could be analyzed in this fashion.

A related analysis, focusing on sequences of person-situation interaction in careers of heroin use, examined probabilities of changes in personal characteristics, behaviors, and encountered situations through the four stages of initial use, occasional use, addictive use, and termination of heroin use (Runyan, 1978).

For some analytic purposes, it may be advantageous to relax the assumption of a set of common stages, and to examine instead sequences of selected states and events, and the relative likelihood of alternative sequences, which could be termed "state-sequential" analysis. For example, one might want to examine the probability of alternative sequences of events such as finishing formal education, starting a full-time occupation, getting married, and having a first child. In studying the sequential arrangement of the first three of these events, Hogan (1978) found that 45.7% of his sample of men followed the particular sequence of completing formal education, starting first full-time job, and then getting married; 4.6% followed the sequence of completing education, marriage, and first full-time job; 6.0% the sequence of full-time job, completing education, and marriage; and so on. The probability of different event sequences varied depending upon conditions such as birth cohort and ethnic background.

Evaluation Research

A stage-state framework may also be employed in evaluation research for assessing the sequential effects of intervention programs. The net value of an intervention is determined not by its effects at a single point in time, but by its effects on a sequence of future experiences. Insofar as possible, this sequence of effects needs to be considered in assessing the desirability of alternative forms of treatment (Runyan, 1977). In the short term, thalidomide may have been quite effective as a sleeping aid, but in the long term, if taken in the first trimester of pregnancy, it could also lead to deformed babies. In the realm of psychosocial intervention, the Cambridge-Somerville delinquency prevention program appeared to have few short-term effects, but a 30-year follow-up (McCord, 1978) indicated that men who had been in the treatment group were more likely than controls to commit a second crime, show signs of alcoholism and serious mental illness, have occupations with lower prestige, and to report high blood pressure or heart trouble, without any compensating advantages.

In these two examples, negative long-term effects clearly outweigh short-term benefits, but in other cases, such as the use of psychotropic drugs with potentially damaging side effects (Klein & Davis, 1969), more differentiated knowledge about short- and long-term risks and benefits for different kinds of patients is needed for making informed treatment decisions.

THE RELATIONSHIP OF CONSCIOUS AGENTS TO STUDIES OF STATE SEQUENCES

Stage-state and state-sequential analyses provide a framework for analyzing sequences of states and events through the life course. The study of extended sequences of states and events raises questions about the relationships between empirical inquiry and our status as conscious agents with particular force; in a way that is not as immediately apparent in correlational, experimental, or case study research.

Can the study of state sequences lead to knowledge about sequences of events and processes that will inevitably unfold in the course of lives? Are we helplessly embedded in an unfolding sequence of events that is beyond our conscious control? To some extent, we undoubtedly are. The course of biological aging, the process of balding, the course of untreatable diseases, and age-related changes in social constraints and expectations are all pretty much beyond individual control.

In many other ways, however, the course of life experience is at least partially under conscious control. As conscious agents, we have at least some control over choice of an occupation, what we will do with our vacations, or whom we decide to marry. To the extent that people function as rational agents (as at least some of us do some of the time), the analysis of state sequences can be used not only for providing a glimpse of what is to come but also for visualizing an array of possible paths and outcomes, designing plans and strategies for the pursuit of desired goals, and for making decisions in light of the expected short- and long-term consequences of alternative courses of action.

Consider, for example, a college student worrying about getting into medical school, a graduate student thinking about the prospects of getting an academic job, or a cancer patient faced with choosing among alternative forms of treatment. In each case, a rational actor needs to estimate the likelihood of alternative outcomes, to identify or generate methods believed to increase the probabilities of desired outcomes, and to make decisions and pursue courses of action in light of these considerations. Stage-state or state-sequential analyses of the experiences of other applicants to medical school, other aspiring professors, or other cancer patients can provide information about what those in similar situations, who may have been more or less knowledgeable about the structure of their worlds, attempted to do, and were or were not able to do. Such information can, at least in principle, be of use to those engaged in planning and decision making in similar circumstances.

There are two related questions which need to be distinguished. Descriptively, how *do* conscious agents make use of the experience of others in thinking prospectively about the course of their own lives? (Studies of social cognition suggest that there may be substantial errors and biases in such processes, e.g., Nisbett & Borgida [1975], Ross [1977], Tversky & Kahneman [1974].) Second, normatively or rationally, what inferences *should* be made from the experience of others in thinking prospectively about the course of one's own life? Both of these questions deserve investigation in their own right, but the more specific point being made here is that stage-state analyses of the life course are at least potentially useful to conscious agents in thinking prospectively about the course of life experience.

CONCLUSION

In summary, stage-state analysis provides a method for analyzing aspects of the probabilistic and causal structure of diverging life paths. Stage-state analysis makes the simplifying assumptions that the course of experience can be divided into a sequence of common stages, with a limited number of possible states within each stage. This approach provides a method for examining the relative frequencies of different courses of experience, estimating the probability of movement from given states through a sequence of future states, and analyzing the routes or processes connecting initial states with a variety of potential outcomes.

There are opportunities for applying such an analytic framework to research on the temporal course of behaviors, personal attributes, encountered situations, and interaction processes within a wide range of substantive areas, such as parent-child relationships, stability and change in personality characteristics, histories of deviant behavior, or assessment of the sequential effects of intervention efforts.

Studies of the structure of the course of life experience may be used by individuals in looking prospectively at the future course of their own lives, visualizing an array of possible futures—with regard to educational career, occupational career, relationships, or parenting—and attempting to anticipate the sequential effects of different decisions or courses of action. This may be done either intuitively, trying to imagine the likely outcomes of different decisions or actions, or also more systematically and empirically, by attempting to draw inferences from the life experiences of those in similar circumstances. The group studies discussed here will need to be supplemented by intensive studies of the structure of single lives (Runyan, 1982a, 1982b).

Due to factors such as the pace of historical change, the operation of random processes, and even the transforming effects of inquiry itself, there are real limitations in the extent to which the sequential structure of the course of lives can be known. Within these limits, however, stage-state and state-sequential analyses can be of use to conscious agents attempting to foresee, make decisions within, and intentionally direct the course of life experience. The choice among diverging life paths will remain a gamble in many respects, but studies of the probabilistic and causal structure of the life course can sometimes extend the horizon of knowability, or throw a light that penetrates a few feet further into the fog.

REFERENCES

Ajzen, I. Intuitive theories of events and the effects of base-rate information on prediction. *Journal of Personality and Social Psychology,* 1977, *35,* 303–314.

Baltes, P. B., Reese, H. W., & Nesselroade, J. R. *Life-span developmental psychology: Introduction to research methods.* Monterey, Calif.: Brooks/Cole, 1977.

Baltes, P. B., & Schaie, K. W. *Life-span developmental psychology: Personality and socialization.* New York: Academic Press, 1973.

Blalock, H. *Causal inferences in nonexperimental research.* New York: Norton, 1964.

Blau, P. M., & Duncan, O. D. *The American occupational structure.* New York: Wiley, 1967.

Block, J., in collaboration with N. Haan. *Lives through time.* Berkeley, Calif.: Bancroft, 1971.

Campbell, D. T., & Stanley, J. C. *Experimental and quasi-experimental designs for research.* Chicago: Rand McNally, 1963.

Clausen, J. The life course of individuals. In M. Riley, M. Johnson, & A. Foner (Eds.), *Aging and society* (Vol. 3). New York: Russell Sage, 1972.

Cook, T. D., & Campbell, D. T. *Quasi-experimentation.* Chicago: Rand McNally, 1979.

Cronbach, L. J. Beyond the two disciplines of scientific psychology. *American Psychologist,* 1975, *30,* 116–127.

Elder, G. H., Jr. *Children of the Great Depression.* Chicago: University of Chicago Press, 1974.

Elder, G. H., Jr. Age differentiation and the life course. *Annual Review of Sociology,* 1975, *1, 165*–190.

Elder, G. H., Jr. Social history and life experience. In D. Eichorn, J. Clausen, N. Haan, M. Honzik, & P. Mussen (Eds.), *Present and past in middle life.* New York: Academic, 1981.

Erikson, E. H. *Childhood and society* (2nd ed). New York: Norton, 1963.

Gergen, K. J. Social psychology as history. *Journal of Personality and Social Psychology,* 1973, *26,* 309–320.

Gergen, K. J. Stability, change, and chance in understanding human development. In N. Datan & H. Reese (Eds.), *Life-span developmental psychology: Dialectical perspectives on experimental research.* New York: Academic Press, 1977.

Gergen, K. J. *Toward transformation in social knowledge.* New York: Springer-Verlag, 1982.

Hogan, D. P. The variable order of events in the life course. *American Sociological Review,* 1978, *43,* 573–586.

Kagan, J., & Moss, H. A. *Birth to maturity.* New York: Wiley, 1962.

Kitchener, R. F. Epigenesis: The role of biological models in developmental psychology. *Human Development,* 1978, *21,* 141–160.

Klein, D. F., & Davis, J. M. *Diagnosis and drug treatment of psychiatric disorders.* Baltimore: Williams & Wilkins, 1969.

Kohlberg, L. Stage and sequence: The cognitive-developmental approach to socialization. In D. Goslin (Ed.), *Handbook of socialization theory and research.* Chicago: Rand McNally, 1969.

Levinson, D. J., Darrow, C., Klein, E., Levinson, M., & McKee, B. *The seasons of a man's life.* New York: Knopf, 1978.

Loevinger, J. *Ego development.* San Francisco: Jossey-Bass, 1976.

Lowenthal, M., Thurnher, M., & Chiriboga, D. *Four stages of life.* San Francisco: Jossey-Bass, 1975.

McCord, J. A thirty-year follow-up of treatment effects. *American Psychologist,* 1978, *33,* 284–289.

Meehl, P. E. Theoretical risks and tabular asterisks: Sir Karl, Sir Ronald, and the slow progress of soft psychology. *Journal of Consulting and Clinical Psychology,* 1978, *42,* 806–834.

Murray, H. A. *Explorations in personality.* New York: Oxford, 1938.

Murray, H. A. Preparations for the scaffold of a comprehensive system. In S. Koch (Ed.), *Psychology: A study of a science* (Vol. 3). New York: McGraw-Hill, 1959.

Neugarten, B. L. *Dilemma in developmental psychology.* Invited Address, American Psychological Association, Washington, D.C., August 23, 1982.

Neugarten, B. L., & Datan, N. Sociological perspectives on the life cycle. In P. Baltes & K. Schaie (Eds.), *Life-span developmental psychology: Personality and socialization.* New York: Academic, 1973.

Nisbett, R. E., & Borgida, E. Attribution and the psychology of prediction. *Journal of Personality and Social Psychology,* 1975, *32,* 932–943.

Riegel, K. F. Adult life crises: A dialectic interpretation of development. In N. Datan & L. Ginsberg (Eds.), *Life-span developmental psychology: Normative life crises.* New York: Academic Press, 1975.

Riley, M. W., Johnson, M. E., & Foner, A. (Eds), *Aging and society: A sociology of age stratification* (Vol. 3). New York: Russell Sage, 1972.

Ross. L. The intuitive psychologist and his shortcomings: Distortions in the attribution process. In L. Berkowitz (Ed.), *Advances in experimental social psychology* (Vol. 10). New York: Academic, 1977.

Runyan, W. M. How should treatment recommendations be made? Three studies in the logical and empirical bases of clinical decision making. *Journal of Consulting and Clinical Psychology,* 1977, *45,* 552–558.

Runyan, W. M. The life course as a theoretical orientation: Sequences of person-situation interaction. *Journal of Personality,* 1978, *46,* 569–593.

Runyan, W. M. A stage-state analysis of the life course. *Journal of Personality and Social Psychology,* 1980, *38,* 951–962.

Runyan, W. M. In defense of the case study method. *American Journal of Orthopsychiatry,* 1982, *52,* 440–446. (a)

Runyan, W. M. *Life histories and psychobiography: Explorations in theory and method.* New York: Oxford University Press, 1982. (b)

Ryff, C. D. Self-perceived personality change in adulthood and aging. *Journal of Personality and Social Psychology,* 1982, *42,* 108–115.

Schneider, D. J. Implicit personality theory: A review. *Psychological Bulletin,* 1973, *79,* 294-309.

Skinner, B. F. *Science and human behavior.* New York: Macmillan, 1953.

Tibbitt, J. E. A sociological comparison of stochastic models of social mobility. *Sociological Review Monographs,* 1973, *19,* 29-44.

Tversky, A., & Kahneman, D. Judgment under uncertainty: Heuristics and biases. *Science,* 1974, *184,* 1124-1131.

Tyler, L. E. *Individuality: Human possibilities and personal choice in the psychological development of men and women.* San Francisco: Jossey-Bass, 1978.

11 Homes and Social Change: A Case Study of the Impact of Resettlement

Mary Gauvain
Irwin Altman
Hussein Fahim
University of Utah

INTRODUCTION

The present chapter examines how people respond to and cope with dramatic changes in their home environments. A central theme of our analysis is that the design and use of a home is closely linked with cultural values and practices, as well as with politics, economics, technology, and a variety of pragmatic issues (Altman & Chemers, 1980; Rapoport, 1969). The home is a "window" to a culture in that it displays religion and cosmology, sex roles, family organization, and a variety of aspects of a culture. Homes also often serve as vehicles of cultural change, as people incorporate new technologies in their dwellings. And, sometimes new home designs are forced upon people, as in cases of resettlement and relocation.

This chapter focuses on the way in which homes are used to manage social relationships among dwelling occupants and between occupants and others in the community, especially under conditions of imposed changes in home design. We will adopt the framework of Altman and Gauvain (1981), who proposed that homes can be described in terms of two dialectic dimensions: *openness/closedness* and *identity/communality*. These social psychological dimensions will be used to examine the effects of social change on the home-culture linkage. To ground this analysis we shall focus on the Nubian people of Egypt and Sudan. The case is particularly noteworthy inasmuch as this culture was forced to relocate from their centuries-old dwellings as a result of the construction of the Aswan High Dam.

A PLACE-PROCESS APPROACH TO HOMES

A Transactional Perspective

One reason for the emergence of the field of environmental psychology in the 1970s was an increasing awareness that traditional research, especially in social psychology, had neglected the relationship between the physical environment and social behavior. Aside from the work of Barker (1968) and a handful of others, the physical contexts of behavior were neglected, were treated as variables to be controlled, or were relegated to error terms of statistical analyses. If the physical environment entered at all into theory and research, it was frequently based on Lewin's (1964) approach, namely to deal primarily with features of the environment that affect subjective psychological processes.

During the past decade psychologists have adopted a variety of perspectives about the physical environment in relationship to behavior. (See Stokols, 1980, and Stokols & Shumaker, 1981, for a description of some of these different approaches.) Some researchers treat environmental factors as totally separate and independent entities from psychological processes. Thus, one can describe a home or other setting in terms of the physical density of its occupants, the configuration of rooms, and the like. In this approach, properties of settings are specified in physical terms, although the expectation is that they may influence psychological processes. This approach is *objectivist,* in that attention is given to the unique and independent characteristics of physical environments (Stokols, 1980; Stokols & Shumaker, 1981).

A second approach may be termed *subjectivist.* Here the environment is defined strictly in terms of the perceptions, feelings, and subjective processes of those in the setting. Lewin's (1964) concept of psychological environment typifies this orientation, as does certain research on cognitive maps, perceptions of crowding, and so forth. Although a given piece of research may relate objective characteristics of the environment to subjective processes, the person and environment are considered to be separate, with each defined in its own terms.

In the present analysis we adopt a different perspective on place-process relationships. Our view, perhaps best termed a *transactional* perspective, proposes that physical environments and psychological processes need not be separated; rather they can be treated as an integral unit. In other words, this orientation assumes that physical settings and psychological events can be viewed as inseparable, as mutually defining and as intrinsic aspects of person-environment units. This approach is an alternative way to study environment and behavior relationships and synthesizes the objectivist and the subjectivist orientations by calling for the study of a different unit of analysis—a place/process unit. Instead of dimensionalizing physical environments and psychological processes separately and then studying their *inter*-action, as if they were different entities, a *trans*-actional approach suggests that a useful strategy may be to treat environments and psychological processes as a single unit of analysis. (See Dewey & Bentley, 1949, for a philosophical analysis of transactional and other perspectives.)

To achieve a transactional perspective, we believe that it is first necessary to develop conceptual dimensions that apply simultaneously to both psychological processes and physical settings. If physical places, such as homes, can be described in terms that also apply to psychological processes and, conversely, if psychological processes can be described in terms of the contexts in which they occur, then a first step toward a transactional perspective will be achieved. That is, if one identifies a single conceptual framework for describing *both* places and processes, then one can in effect, treat them as an integral unit. The idea of studying characteristics of the physical environment and psychological processes within the same conceptual framework is not new. (See Ekehammar, 1974, for a review of literature in this area, particularly in reference to personality theory.) However, our approach applies a transactional perspective to the cross-cultural analysis of homes.

Place/Process Dimensions of Homes

In a prior analysis Altman & Gauvain (1981) used a dialectic framework to compare homes in different cultures. There have been many approaches to dialectics throughout history (for a discussion of these, see Altman, Vinsel & Brown, 1981), and our version centers around three themes: (1) Social and psychological processes are characterized by polarities and oppositions, (2) oppositions form a unified system, and (3) oppositional processes are dynamic and change over time and in relation to one another. We do not assume that these oppositional processes are directed toward stability, balance, or consistency. Instead, we assume that people exhibit *both* stability and change in their relationships and that oppositions display differential strength vis a vis one another at different times and in different circumstances.

In applying a dialectic approach, Altman & Gauvain (1981) theorized that homes involve the interplay of the individual and society. They suggested that dwellings mirror the degree to which cultures and their members must cope with the dialectic oppositions of individual desires and motives versus the demands and requirements of society at large. Several aspects of the individual/society opposition fit with the general features of dialectics described above. While cultures probably vary in the extent to which individual versus societal factors predominate, it is expected that both exist to some extent in all cultures. In addition, we do not assume that social systems strive toward perfectly balanced relationships between individuals and society. A great range of possible relationships exist, any of which may be viable, as long as some amount of both oppositional processes exist in the system. Also in accord with general dialectical reasoning, we assume that there are dynamic and changing relationships between individual and societal factors. Thus, there are likely to be shifts in the strength of individual and societal processes on both a long- and a short-term basis.

The individual/society dialectic has many specific forms, for example, independence/conformity, competition/cooperation, self-gain/altruism, many of which have been discussed by philosophers and social scientists over the centuries. Altman & Gauvain (1981) proposed that homes reflect at least two particular aspects of the individual/society dialectic: (1) openness/closedness, and (2) identity/communality.

Openness/closedness. One facet of the individual/society dialectic involves the ways in which homes reflect the openness and closedness of occupants to social interaction with one another and with outsiders. This dialectic draws upon recent theorizing about privacy as a boundary regulation process (Altman, 1975, 1977; Altman & Chemers, 1980; Altman, Vinsel, & Brown, 1981). On some occasions people or groups are open to others and on other occasions they are closed or inaccessible. We propose that the home serves as one of several behavioral mechanisms used by people to regulate openness/closedness. This is accomplished by means of the location and siting of homes, exteriors, thresholds and entranceways, and interior design and use. We also hypothesize that the home serves both poles of the openness/closedness dialectic, although perhaps to different degrees in different cultures. For example, in Tarong (Nydegger & Nydegger, 1966), a kin-based hamlet in Northern Luzon, Philippines, neighborhood living groups are connected by footpaths. These paths make all the homes in the village readily accessible to almost anyone in the community. However, the paths near houses are controlled by the household residents, and passersby are obliged to greet the houseowner and request the right to pass. These procedures allow for simultaneous public access to homes along with individual control over accessibility.

Houses in Tarong have a front porch which serves as a focus of daily activity and is in constant use by family, neighbors, and visitors. The porch is raised approximately 5 to 6 feet off the ground and is reached by a bamboo ladder. In the evening or when no one is home, the ladder is pushed away from the porch, thereby discouraging visitors. The ladder serves, therefore, as a formal entranceway and provides cues regarding the accessibility of a family to outsiders.

The interior of the home is also used to regulate social contact with outsiders. For example, Errington (1978) described how the Buginese house is divided into a front and a rear area. The front area of the house is a public place where guests are entertained. On the other hand, the rear door and rear area are used by family members and are inaccessible to visitors. The front and rear areas are also separated by a partition of woven cane or rattan, and sometimes a sign is placed above the doorway that declares the rear area to be "off limits" to guests. Thus the Buginese home is clearly marked in terms of its openness and closedness.

In summary, these few examples illustrate that homes in a variety of cultures reflect the accessibility, as well as inaccessibility, of occupants to social interactions with one another and with outsiders.

Identity/communality. It is hypothesized that homes simultaneously depict the uniqueness of their residents, as well as the bonds that residents have with their larger community and culture. Throughout the world people often use their dwellings to display their identity and to make themselves distinct from others. Yet at the same time people often design, decorate, and use their homes in ways that portray their communality and ties to their neighbors and culture. Altman & Gauvain (1981) used ethnographic evidence to demonstrate how cultures vary in the ways that identity and communality are simultaneously reflected in different areas of the home—the exterior, the entranceway, the threshold, and the interior. For example, nomadic North African Berbers pitch their tents in a sacred order—the *douar,* or circle—around which related families gather, suggesting communality in the siting of homes (Faegre, 1979). Wealthier and more important families have larger and more elaborate tents, thereby reflecting their status and identity. Regardless of its size, however, each tent faces the center of the *douar,* where the mosque tent is located. Thus, the siting, size, and elaborateness of the tent simultaneously represent the traditions of the large community, and the uniqueness and individuality of the family.

Thresholds and entranceways also often display the identity/communality dialectic. For example, the Tlingit Indians of Northwestern North America place totem poles that are carved with figures of animals, humans, and mythological creatures near the entrances to their dwellings. The carvings on totems may contain symbolic and historical events unique to the life of the dwellers, indicating personal identity. They also often have figures that apply to the clan or to the larger culture, thereby signifying communality. In this way, the totem poles and entranceways simultaneously depict both aspects of the dialectic.

The interior arrangements and decorations of homes also reflect the desire of occupants to appear different from others, but still express their affiliation with the customs and values of the community. For example, the skin tents of the Tuareg people, who live in the Southern Sahara Desert, are similar in color and shape, with low flat roofs to withstand sand storms

(Faegre, 1979). Despite the lack of individual expression on the exteriors of the tents, the interiors are quite decorative. Tuareg women are skilled artisans and the entire interior of the tent exhibits their work. The fact that all of the women decorate their tents suggests community acknowledgement of the importance of the inside of the tent. Yet, within such displays of communality, one sees the unique skills of individuals exhibited.

These and other examples provided by Altman & Gauvain (1981) illustrate that openness/closedness and identity/communality can be used to study social behavior and home use and design in a variety of cultures. The home is not only a repository of general cultural and environmental influences; it is also a setting within which people can display openness/closedness and identity/communality. In other words, the home can be viewed as a direct manifestation of social psychological processes, and as inseparable from such processes. In a transactional perspective, therefore, places such as homes and social psychological processes such as openness/closedness and identity/communality can be defined and studied within a common conceptual framework.

Homes and Social Change

Of central interest to this chapter is how place/process units operate in relation to social change. The patterns of openness/closedness and identity/communality displayed in homes represent a form of adaptation or coping by a family, community, or culture to its situation. In other words, the home reflects a complex behavioral pattern designed to facilitate a family's or culture's social organization and social stability. However, cultures are not static; they evolve and change continuously. Social changes occur for a variety of reasons, such as contact with other cultures, exposure to new technology, changes in climate, depletion of natural resources, disease, and population changes. And, social change can affect many aspects of a culture—values, attitudes and beliefs, customs, practices, norms and rituals, and places, such as religious, educational and work settings. Of particular interest to us are the ways in which an externally imposed, sudden, and extensive social change impinges upon the openness/closedness and identity/communality characteristics of homes.

The research literature indicates several major types of imposed, sudden, and pervasive social changes: (1) relocation or resettlement of people because of urban and rural housing programs; (2) resettlement of rural/agricultural people as a result of large-scale public works projects, such as dam construction and water control programs; (3) settlement of nomadic people on reservations or in established communities; and (4) resettlement of people as a result of natural disasters or political upheavals.

Particularly vivid examples of externally imposed, sudden and extensive changes occur in some urban renewal projects. Oftentimes, United States government-sponsored housing for the poor involves high-density, high-rise buildings. For people accustomed to using streets and areas outside the home for socializing, childrearing, and community activities, high-rise housing designs can create many problems. The classic case of the Pruitt-Igoe housing development in St. Louis indicates how sudden and dysfunctional changes in housing design can create severe social disruption. Residents were unable to control semipublic space, it was difficult to supervise children, access to public toilets was restricted, and limited contact with neighbors created a climate of suspicion that led to increase dependence on legal authorities to resolve community disputes (Rainwater, 1970; Yancey, 1971).

When people are resettled because of large-scale public works projects, the social impact is usually enormous due to the large number of people who are relocated and the accompanying scope of the change. There is considerable literature on resettlement, particularly in relation to large-scale water development projects in Africa, the Middle East, and Asia (Scudder, 1973, 1975, 1976; Stanley & Alpers, 1975. For example, in Africa alone, 56,000 people were resettled during the 1950s in connection with the Kariba Dam project in Zambia and Rhodesia; in the 1960s, 70,000 people were resettled as a result of Nigeria's Kainji Dam. In the 1970s approximately 80,000 people were moved from their homes because of the Kossou Dam program in the Ivory Coast, and, as discussed later, 100,000 Nubians in Egypt and the Sudan were relocated in 1963–64 in connection with the development of the Aswan High Dam on the Nile River. These represent but a few of the resettlement and relocation projects that have occurred or are in various stages of planning in different parts of the world.

In a theoretical analysis Scudder (1973) hypothesized the occurrence of physiological, psychological, and sociocultural stresses during the initial stages of relocation (up to 2 years). Physiological stresses and disease result from poor, insufficient or strange foods, inadequate water supplies, population density, and climatic and ecological changes. Psychological stresses involve individual effects of relocation such as grieving for the lost home, feelings of loss of kin and community, a sense of displacement, confusion regarding new sex role responsibilities and freedoms, fear of strange and harmful "spirits" and other forces, and general anxiety and malaise. At a more macro level, Scudder described numerous sociocultural stresses associated with relocation. These include the undermining of local leadership as group composition shifts, the breakup of extended kin and neighboring patterns, the alteration of sex role and parent-child relationships, changes in religious rituals as sacred shrines and sites are lost, and disruptions of the economic structure of the culture.

Several analyses of resettlement programs have found that new homes are often incompatible with those in the original communities, thereby interfering with the adjustment process. For example, Algerian people who were resettled in 1954-1961 were given homes built of corrugated iron and cement (Sutton, 1977). Such materials, in contrast with mud that had been traditionally used, were unsuited for temperature control. In addition, cement floors were not appropriate for people who were accustomed to being barefoot and who slept on the floor. European style homes that were close to one another and that had small rooms were provided to relocatees who were accustomed to homes that were more dispersed and that had larger interior spaces to accommodate extended kin. This caused disruptions in customary practices inside and outside the home. Furthermore, unlike the traditional communities where women were free to move about and to visit in public, the higher density and close proximity of homes resulted in women being confined indoors in order to protect their privacy.

Because the relocation of the Egyptian Nubian people has been thoroughly studied, and because of our access to information about homes before and after their resettlement, we will examine in detail this exemplar of externally imposed, sudden and pervasive change.

Aspects of the Nubian Culture in Egypt

In 1963-64, in preparation for the construction of the Aswan Dam, the Egyptian government resettled 5,000 Egyptian Nubians into new communities in Kom Ombo, north of the city of Aswan and about 800 kilometers south of Cairo. The government of Sudan also resettled 50,000 Sudanese Nubians during this same period. The original Nubian communities in Egypt had extended along the Nile River shoreline for approximately 350 kilometers (2 km. wide), starting at Aswan and extending south. The new settlements occupied a much smaller area, 60 kilometers long x 3 kilometers wide. The relocation also involved the consolidation of some 600 hamlets, each housing approximately 100 people, into 43 villages of about 2,000 people each, resulting in a considerable increase in population density (Fernea, 1973).

Throughout the centuries Nubia was rarely in contract with other cultures. According to Fernea (1973), Nubia was composed of a number of small hamlets located along both banks of the Nile. Because this section of the Nile offered an inhospitable desert environment, limited natural resources and impassable stretches of the river, Nubia never became a main thoroughfare between Egypt and Africa nor was it ever subjected to extensive colonization. Consequently, the traditional Nubian culture changed very little over the centuries.

With resettlement, the centuries-long lifestyle of the Nubians changed drastically. The shift from isolated and dispersed communities threatened numerous traditions, especially those related to village and family life. There were significant changes in land use and farming practices, problems of food supply and distribution, consolidation of people into larger and more dense villages, and greater accessibility of social services and education, all of which paved the way for cultural upheaval. The following analysis of the dimensions of openness/closedness and identity/communality in relation to traditional and new Nubian homes illustrates how the sudden and pervasive changes imposed on the Nubian people affected their culture. The analysis is based on the writings of Fahim (1979, 1981), Fernea (1973), and Fernea and Kennedy (1966), and on field observations by Fahim.

The Home in Old and New Nubia

The traditional Nubian home was located within a small hamlet having a population of about 100 people, many of whom were relatives, and many of whom had lived in the community for generations. Individual homes were actually compounds that sheltered an extended family (see Fig. 11.1). The compounds were built about a quarter of a kilometer apart, and as a family grew, the compound was enlarged. For example, when a son married, he and his new wife often lived in a bridal area that was added to his parents' compound (Fernea, 1973). In spite of the continued growth of a compound, some degree of separation and distance was always maintained between adjacent dwelling units. A family compound contained a guest area, courtyard, bridal hall, cooking, storage, sleeping and living areas, an open covered *loggia* or outside work area, and a stable for animals.

Openness/closedness. The traditional Nubian home can be analyzed in relation to the dimension of openness/closedness. For example, the separation of compounds ensured that occupants could avoid interactions with others if they so desired. This was further aided by high (approximately 4–5 meters) and thick (approximately 1/3–2/3 meters) exterior walls. These walls were also important for temperature control, since they enclosed high-vaulted rooms that were ventilated by numerous openings along the upper part of the walls (Fernea, 1973). In addition, thick interior walls helped protect the privacy of household members from one another.

Other effective privacy regulation mechanisms included the use of a single main entranceway to the compound (a second entrance was sometimes added, permitting separate entry into the bridal hall area) and the custom of not entering a compound without permission. In addition, a guest room for overnight visitors was always located to the immediate left of the entranceway, away from the activities of the compound, thereby providing mutual privacy.

The traditional Nubian residence also had a number of design features that facilitated openness and social interaction. For example, the interior of

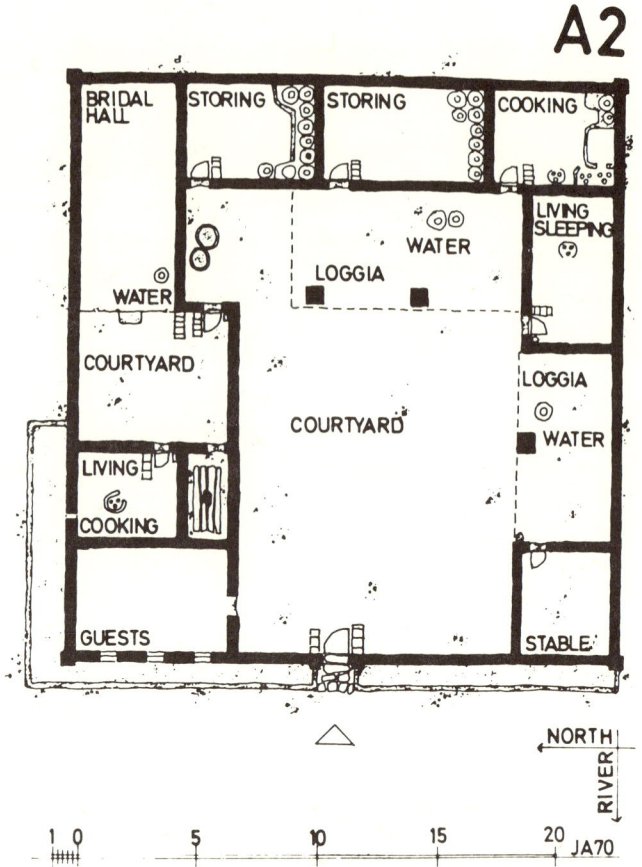

FIG. 11.1 Floorplan of traditional Nubian compound. From Fernea, R. A. *Nubians in Egypt: Peaceful People.* Austin, Texas: University of Texas Press, 1973.

the compound contained open shaded areas where family members could work or interact, and the guest room was often used as a family gathering place when there were no visitors. Also, directly outside the compound, attached to the front wall, was a benchlike sitting area, called a *mastaba*. Children often played on the wide *mastaba* and adults would frequently sit on it and converse with neighbors and passersby. As such, the *mastaba* was a design feature of homes that enabled contact and openness among residents of the community.

Another way that people made themselves accessible to others was through decorating and painting the walls on the outside and inside of compounds (see Fig. 11.2). Individualized decorations, some of which depicted previous experiences, for example, visits to Mecca, work in cities or on

FIG. 11.2 Front facade and entranceway of traditional Nubian compound with individualized decorations and Mastaba. From Fernea, R. A. *Nubians in Egypt: Peaceful people.* Austin, Texas: University of Texas Press, 1973. Photograph by Georg Gerster.

ships, hunting skills of the occupants, provided residents with a socially acceptable mechanism for revealing their accomplishments, skills, and interests to others. These examples illustrate how the traditional Nubian compound had a variety of means by which people could make themselves differentially accessible to one another.

The initial phases of relocation created a number of problems—settlement into densely populated villages, difficulties with food and water supplies, shifts in land distribution practices, inaccessibility to the Nile River, close contact between different ethnic groups, and so on. Of particular interest to this chapter are the ways in which the new homes and communities violated traditional Nubian expressions of openness/closedness and identity/communality and thereby may have interfered with adjustment to the new setting.

In order to accommodate large numbers of people and reduce building costs, the new Nubian villages were arranged around straight, Western style streets, with houses sharing adjoining walls. The shift from small dispersed hamlets to large, almost contiguous villages resulted in far more contact among strangers, and more noise, activity, and congestion than the Nubians were accustomed to. Homes in the new settlements varied in size and had anywhere from one to four rooms in addition to a small courtyard and a bathroom. People were assigned to homes according to the size of their nuclear families, which resulted in the fragmentation of traditional extended kin units. Along with the increased population density in the new villages, the small number and size of rooms in dwellings resulted in an increase in household density. In fact, household density doubled following the relocation and was associated with an increase in communicable diseases such as dysentery, measles, and encephalitis. As a consequence, mortality rates rose for children and for the elderly (Fahim, 1979).

Traditional patterns of home design and use which previously helped regulate the openness/closedness of household members, families, and neighbors to one another were not available in the new communities. Fewer rooms meant that family members were forced into more interaction with one another. The absence of a guest room often resulted in mutual intrusions by guests and the host family. During his field observations in New Nubia, Fahim observed that in some instances, in order to provide a guest with privacy, a family would move in with a neighbor or kin. This arrangement was not wholly satisfactory, since it resulted in greater contact between neighbors and kin than had been the case in traditional Nubia.

Other features of the new home design interfered with traditional practices of privacy regulation. For example, neighbors shared a common wall between dwellings, thereby eliminating a traditional barrier. Furthermore, walls around homes and the openings used for ventilation were much lower than had been customary in Old Nubia, which according to Fahim's observations, made it difficult to maintain privacy from neighbors and passersby. And, many new homes had windows in the fronts of dwellings, whereas in Old Nubia windows faced onto the courtyard and the outer walls had no windows or openings other than for ventilation. As a result of these new design features, passersby could easily hear household conversations and arguments. This, says Fahim, led to strains in community relations, as gossip heightened, and as people had more than normal access to activities within a household.

The new dwellings also made it difficult to achieve desired contact with others. Extended kin and friends did not always live near one another, making it difficult for them to interact on a daily basis. This was particularly troublesome for women. Because of congestion, crime, and a general loss of feelings of security, women were no longer free to move about the community and exchange information with friends and relatives. Fahim observed that women became restricted to their homes and were increasingly isolated from others and from activities in the community. In addition, the absence of a guest room led to less interaction with visitors, resulting in further isolation and loss of contact among people.

Another factor that affected social interaction in the new communities was the absence of a *mastaba,* the low benchlike structure in front of dwellings. Without a *mastaba,* it was difficult for people to interact with neighbors in a socially acceptable and informal way. If a person wished to sit in front of a dwelling, he or she would have to sit on the ground. According to Fahim, this behavior was frowned upon, because it was considered unclean, and because it was a practice of Egyptians peasants with whom the Nubians did not wish to be identified.

Identity/communality. The homes of New Nubia also affected many of the traditional channels used to express identity/communality. In Old Nubia, the ties of residents to their community and culture were evident in the widespread practice of decorating the outside and interior walls of compounds and rooms. By means of paintings, carved reliefs, or decorative additions, residents displayed their bonds with the local community and with the larger cultures of Egypt and Islam. For example, elaborate and colorful paintings of the national flag sumbolized bonds with Egypt. Paintings of stars and crescents reflected adherence to Islamic principles, as did the special door decorations that symbolized that the occupant had made a pilgrimage to the holy city of Mecca. Common values and beliefs were reflected in paintings of hands, eyes and other symbols, which were designed to protect occupants from the "evil eye" and other forms of harm. Such paintings appeared in different parts of the home, for example, evil eye and protective symbols were drawn around entranceways and living areas; scorpions were drawn near storage and water containers in order to protect the contents from contamination. Another common practice was to display china plates on the front facade of compounds, as a symbol of the hospitality of the master of the household to the community.

In addition to community bonds, traditional Nubian homes depicted the individuality and uniqueness of the occupants. The paintings and decorations on the outside and inside walls of the compound displayed the distinctive artistic talents of their creators, usually women. Furthermore, unique spects of the lives of the residents were often displayed. A steamship painted on a wall symbolized the fact that the owner had worked on ships; a decorated door indicated that the male of the house had made a pilgrimage to Mecca; a carved relief of a man shooting an alligator identified the occupant as a noted hunter. Such displays not only reflected the unique qualities of the occupants but, as noted earlier, they also served as a vehicle for self-disclosure.

Decorative practices in the interior of the compound also depicted the unique identity of the occupants. For example, the guest room was kept very clean and was decorated with wall hangings, handmade baskets, china plates suspended from the ceiling (these were also used for food storage) and elaborate articles of furniture (see Fig. 11.3). Much like the formal living rooms of the American suburban culture, the Nubian guest room displayed the unique talents, hospitality, and tastes of the hosts, especially the women. Other rooms in the courtyard were also decorated with handicrafts, souvenirs, personal mementos, photographs, and cherished family heirlooms that were unique to the occupants.

The new homes and villages violated many aspects of community bonds and inhibited expression of individual uniqueness. Because the new homes were small, it was difficult to adhere to the Nubian values of cleanliness and tidiness, especially in relation to storage and the maintenance of livestock. Consider the early months of adjustment to the typical new village. The Nubian people had moved from clean, well-decorated, spacious communities into high-density homes, communities with littered streets, housing with cramped interiors that had little room to store food and supplies, no place to keep animals that traditionally had separate areas in the compound, no guest space, and no room to expand (see Fig. 11.4). To solve some of these problems, dried food, fuel and other materials were stored on the roofs of dwellings or were placed in the middle of the streets. These practices proved to be frustrating and humiliating to the Nubian sense of group identity, however. Nubians traditionally distinguished themselves from the average Egyptian peasant, who stored belongings on the roof and kept animals in the home. To be forced to live as if they were poor peasants was an insult and an embarrassment to the Nubian cultural identity and esteem.

The sense of community fostered by the small hamlets of Old Nubia was seriously disrupted in the large villages where there were many strangers and

FIG. 11.3 Elaborately decorated guestroom in traditional Nubian home. From Fernea, R. A. *Nubians in Egypt: Peaceful people*. Austin, Texas: University of Texas Press, 1973. Photograph by Georg Gerster.

where people were separated from their extended kin and close friends. The fact that homes were built side by side and had common walls prevented the organic growth of the traditional compound, did not permit the housing of newly married children in the compound, and made it difficult to have a guest room. As mentioned above, when guests did visit they were housed in the family living area, which meant that family members had to stay with friends or relatives so that guests would have privacy and comfort. Thus the extended family configuration and strong norms about hospitality to visitors, central features of the Nubian sense of community, were severely affected by the design of the new dwellings.

The design of the new communities and homes also interfered with traditional expressions of individuality and uniqueness. Row after row of similar homes, the plain cinderblock construction, the disruption of status relationships regarding homes (e.g., landlords and well-to-do families lived side by side and in the same quality of housing as their former tenants and employees), all contributed to a loss of individual identity and esteem. The new homes had no decorations, were poorly constructed, and had no distinguishing qualities. Even the traditional guest room, a vehicle by which a family displayed its unique artistic and decorative talents, was missing. To make the situation worse, the authorities prohibited major modifications of homes, since many communities were considered temporary settlements.

Reactions to the resettlement. Although the disruptions and stresses of the relocation were severe, the Nubians responded in ways that demonstrated their sensitivity to the importance of openness/closedness and identity/communality. Shortly after the relocation, the Nubians began to modify the government houses in accordance with their traditional practices and in spite of government prohibitions (see Fig. 11.5). Although this may have been partly an intuitive and unconscious process, it was also often done deliberately. For example, one Nubian said, "If we want to maintain our old customs, we must maintain our Nubian architecture." (Fernea & Kennedy, 1966).

In some cases the traditional sense of community was reflected in cooperative projects. Streets were cleaned and annexes were built to house animals. Groups of neighbors sometimes plastered the front facades of their homes, and in some instances neighboring families undertook cooperative decorating efforts in an attempt to make a row of homes appear unique and attractive. Many families began to paint the exteriors of their homes soon after relocation, using traditional techniques and symbols. Paintings of Egyptian flags, the symbolic crescent of Islam, and decorations of honor were added to the fronts of homes. Residents also decorated (see Fig. 11.6.)

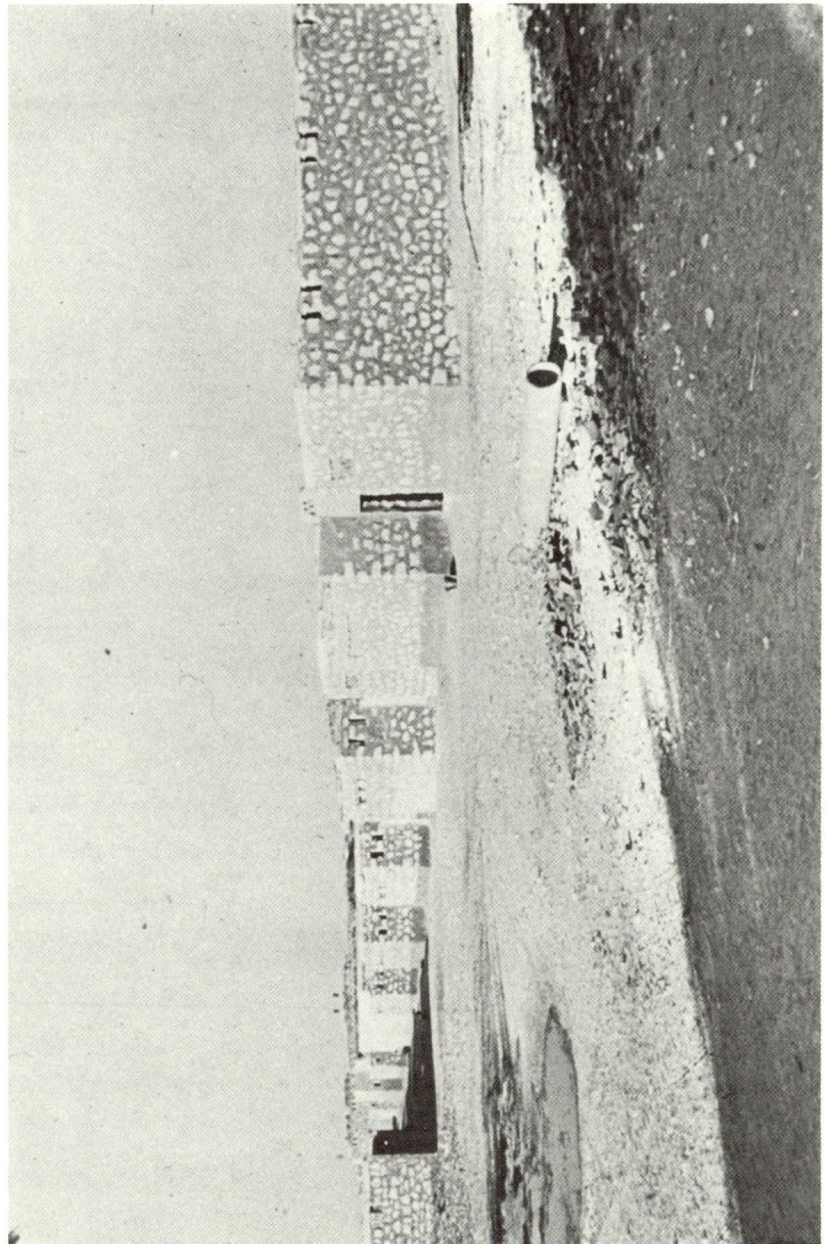

FIG. 11.4 New Nubia at time of relocation. Photograph by Hussein Fahim.

FIG. 11.5 Beginning stages of alteration of the government houses. Photography by Hussein Fahim.

FIG. 11.6 Interior decorations in a home in New Nubia. Photograph by Hussein Fahim.

the interiors of their homes. Floors were tiled, small rooms were added where possible to create spaciousness, walls were painted with traditional symbols such as scorpions, hands, eyes, and flowers. The color, design, and location of decorations varied by household, reflecting individuality, but traditional community symbols were present in many homes.

The Nubians attempted to overcome features of the new homes that interfered with the regulation of openness and closedness. Some families raised the height of the front walls of dwellings, not only to restore the traditional form but to permit greater privacy. In addition, low ventilation outlets were blocked and front windows were boarded up in order to restore privacy. Some families built a traditional *mastaba*, so that children could play outside and adults could sit in front of their homes and interact with others in the community. Many families also hung china plates over their front entranceways as a traditional symbol of their hospitality and accessibility.

These renovations, although not done by everyone, illustrate how the Nubians attempted to incorporate traditional values with respect to openness/closedness and identity/communality in their new homes. To some extent they were successful in reproducing important facets of traditional practices in the new communities. But it was also the case that the expression of many traditional values was not possible, thereby setting the stage for permanent changes in the culture. For example, although the front walls of homes could be raised higher to reestablish privacy, side walls were shared with neighbors, and there was not always mutual agreement or resources available to make alterations. In addition, the cramped quarters and arrangement of homes in the resettlement villages did not allow for expansion. As a result, one community built a communal guest house to accommodate visitors. Although this solved the physical problem of housing visitors, it was not wholly satisfactory because of the impersonal nature of the arrangement. In another case, a family solved the problem of limited space by adding a second story onto their home. However, they were criticized by others because the side windows of the second story overlooked the courtyards of adjoining homes, thereby violating others' privacy. The problem was resolved by closing and permanently locking the shutters of the windows that overlooked neighboring homes. In another instance a family moved out of the village and built a larger home. Although this arrangement provided more space and expressed individuality and status, the family was also isolated from the community to a greater extent than had been customary in traditional Nubian hamlets. In summary, although the Nubians were able to deal with certain problems associated with their new homes and communities, not all problems could be resolved.

IMPLICATIONS AND CONCLUSIONS

We have attempted to demonstrate that social upheaval often involves changes in homes, and that the dimensions of openness/closedness and identity/communality can be used to describe some of these changes. The design, use, and modification of dwellings serve as a vehicle for establishing and maintaining cultural values, not only in times of stability, but also during periods of social change. A comparison of the Nubian home before and after relocation illustrated this theme. The resettlement of the Nubians created a number of stresses associated with the move itself—shifts in agricultural styles, food and water problems, and the general upheaval of the social structure. It also seriously interfered with the ability of people to regulate openness/closedness and identity/communality in the ways that had been customary in their traditional hamlets and homes. One can only speculate as to whether the stresses of relocation would have been reduced if the new homes permitted appropriate expressions of cultural values associated with openness/closedness and identity/communality. In the case of the Nubians, and in several other instances noted in the chapter, the new homes of relocatees impaired the ability of people to express themselves with respect to these dimensions, and therefore may have interfered with their adjustment to the new environment. We do not mean to suggest that the best solution to the Nubian case, or to other instances of radical social change, is to simply reproduce the traditional home in the new environment. Instead, our analysis suggests that environmental designers and planners should attend to the underlying social psychological dimensions of openness/closedness and identity/communality when designing new homes and communities, especially in cases of sudden and pervasive social changes. The planner or designer, ideally in collaboration with residents, should address a number of questions in relation to the new homes and communities: How are values associated with openness/closedness and identity/communality expressed in the traditional homes of a culture? What is the relative importance of expressing openness versus closedness, or of communality versus identity in the homes of a specific culture? What are the likely consequences if people are unable to express these values in the new setting? What compensatory ways does a culture have for exhibiting a particular value?

Answers to diagnostic questions of this type can serve as the basis for development of alternative designs for homes and communities. According to the logic of this chapter, it would be crucial to assess the degree to which alternative designs are compatible with cultural values embodied in traditional home designs. This does not mean that the new and old designs should be identical. It is usually impossible to recreate traditional designs in an exact fashion in a new setting, due to space restrictions, population density, limitations of technology, and a host of other factors. The thrust of our analysis is not to require the physical duplication of traditional home designs. Instead, we call for *functional equivalency* between old and new homes. Thus efforts should be made to incorporate in new homes the functional capability for people to express cultural values associated with openness/closedness and identity/communality. For example, in the Nubian case it may not have been physically possible to create large separate compounds in order to insure privacy. However, there may have been compensatory design features that would have permitted an equivalent level of privacy even though the physical setting was different. Similarly, in urban renewal programs, it may be necessary to radically alter the living arrangements of people, for example, from low- to high-rise buildings. Nevertheless, the incorporation of relevant social psychological dimensions into the design process in a functionally equivalent way may assist in the adjustment of people to new settings. Based on the present and earlier analyses (Altman & Gauvain, 1981), we believe that openness/closedness and identity/communality are useful dimensions for describing and designing homes in a variety of cultures. We do not suggest, however, that they are the only relevant dimensions, social psychological or otherwise. In fact, it may be useful to extend this approach to include other dimensions of homes, such as sex-role differentiation, efforts to master or be subjugated to natural forces (Triandis, 1981), or the home as a place of security or insecurity (Dovey, 1978).

An important aspect of our analyis is that social change is an intrinsic aspect of culture. Change is neither necessarily good nor bad, and planners and environmental designers should not have as a goal the prevention of social change. Instead, it is important to recognize the occurrence and the potential effects of social change. The outcomes of social change can vary considerably, depending upon the nature of the change in relation to the culture. The thrust of our approach is to provide a conceptual framework for tracking the consequences of social change, so that policy makers, environmental designers, and community members can anticipate likely consequences and develop constructive means for dealing with change.

There are three capstone themes to this chapter—one is pragmatic, one is theoretical, and one is both pragmatic and theoretical.

An important pragmatic conclusion is that environmental designers, planners, and policy makers should assess the implications of social change in relationship to homes. Because the home is a crucial site of cultural activity and cultural expression, its compatibility with cultural and individual factors must be considered when new social policies are formulated and implemented. Although this theme has been stated many times by various environmental researchers, designers, and policy makers, the present approach is different in that we propose specific concepts to use in the design process: the social psychological dimensions of openness/closedness and identity/communality. Although these dimensions may not be easy to quantify, and although they may not be the only relevant dimensions, we believe that they reflect important social psychological processes that apply to homes in a variety of cultures and in different circumstances.

At a theoretical level, the present chapter examined the transactional unit of psychological processes and places. On the one hand, our analysis suggests that the physical setting of the home can be defined, in part, by using the social-psychological processes of openness/closedness and identity/communality. Similarly, explicit in the theme of transactional unity is the idea that these (and other) social psychological processes occur in physical settings, and that it is useful to examine these processes in the context of places and settings. In so doing we have linked places and processes in terms of a common set of descriptive dimensions, and applied this place analysis to describe some of the environmental and psychological dynamics of adjustment and reaction to resettlement.

The final theme of this chapter is both pragmatic and theoretical. We believe that perhaps one way of bridging the traditional schism in orientations and goals of social science researchers and environmental designers is by means of a transactional perspective. A transactional approach may be useful in avoiding many of the central differences between these disciplines, that is, that environmental designers focus on places and social science researchers focus on processes, and that designers are interested in applied research and social scientists are interested in basic research (Altman, 1973). Instead, we have proposed that one try to understand places in terms of psychological processes, and psychological processes in relationship to the characteristics of places. Thus, the differences between theoretical and problem-solving perspectives may be reduced by an approach that incorporates places and processes within a common conceptual framework. It is the unification of the pragmatic and the theoretical that we see as one potential of our cross-cultural and dialetic analysis of homes in relationship to social change.

ACKNOWLEDGMENTS

An extended version of this chapter appears in N. R. Feimer and S. Geller (Eds.), *Environmental psychology: Directions and perspectives.* New York: Praeger, 1983. Permission for this adaptation has been granted by Praeger Publishers. We are indebted to several colleagues who commented on earlier versions of the manuscript: Robert Bliss, Richard Brislin, Gerald Davis, Kim Dovey, Nickolaus Feimer, Sandra Howell, Joseph E. McGrath, Barbara Rogoff, Harry Triandis.

REFERENCES

Altman, I. Some perspectives in the study of man-environment phenomenon. *Representative Research in Social Psychology,* 1973, 4(1), 109-126.
Altman, I. *The environment and social behavior.* Monterey, Calif.: Brooks/Cole, 1975.
Altman, I. Privacy: Culturally universal or culturally specific? *Journal of Social Issues,* 1977, 33, 66-84.
Altman, I., & Chemers, M. M. *Culture and environment.* Monterey, Calif.: Brooks/Cole, 1980.
Altman, I., & Gauvain, M. A cross-cultural and dialectic analysis of homes. In L. Liben, A. Patterson, & N. Newcombe (Eds.), *Spatial representation & behavior across the life span: Theory and application.* New York: Academic Press, 1981.
Altman, I., Vinsel, A., & Brown, B. B. Dialectic conceptions in social psychology: An application to social penetration and privacy regulation. In L. Berkowitz (Ed.) *Advances in experimental social psychology* (Vol. 14). New York: Academic Press, 1981.
Barker, R. G. *Ecological psychology.* Stanford: Stanford University Press, 1968.
Dewey, J., & Bentley, A. F. *Knowing and the known.* Boston, Mass.: Beacon, 1949.
Dovey, K. *The dwelling experience: Toward a phenomenology of architecture.* Unpublished Master of Architecture thesis. University of Melbourne, Australia, 1978.
Ekehammar, B. Interactionism in personality from historical perspective. *Psychological Bulletin,* 1974, 81, 12, 1026-1048.
Errington, S. *The Buginese house.* Unpublished manuscript. University of California, Santa Cruz, 1978.
Faegre, T. *Tents: Architecture of the nomads.* New York: Anchor Books, 1979.
Fahim, H. Field research in a Nubian village: The experience of an Egyptian anthropologist. In G. M. Foster, T. Scudder, E. Colson, & R. V. Kemper (Eds.), *Long-term field research in social anthropology.* New York: Academic Press, 1979.
Fahim, H. *Dams, people and development: The Aswan High Dam Case.* New York: Pergamon Press, 1981.
Fernea, R. A. *Nubians in Egypt: Peaceful people.* Texas: University of Texas Press, 1973.
Fernea, R. A., & Kennedy, J. G. Initial adaptations to resettlement: A new life for Egyptian Nubians. *Current Anthropology,* 1966, 7, 349-354.
Lewin, K. *Field theory and social science.* New York: Harper & Row, 1964.
Nydegger, W. F., & Nydegger, C. *Tarong: An Ilocos barrio in the Philippines.* New York: Wiley, 1966.
Rainwater, L. *Behind ghetto walls.* Chicago: Aldine Publishing Co., 1970.
Rapoport, A. *House form and culture.* Englewood Cliffs, N.J.: Prentice Hall, 1969.
Scudder, T. The human ecology of big projects: River basin development and resettlement. In B. J. Siegel, A. R. Beals, & S. A. Tyler (Eds.), *Annual Review of Anthropology* (Vol. 2). Palo Alto, Calif.: Annual Reviews, Inc. 1973.
Scudder, T. Resettlement. In N. F. Stanley & M. P. Alpers (Eds.), *Man-made lakes and human health.* London: Academic Press, 1975.
Scudder, T. Social impacts of river basin development on local populations. In *River Basin Development: Policies and Planning.* Proceedings of the United Nations Interregional Seminar on River Basin and Interbasin Development (Vol. 1). Budapest: Institute for Hydraulic Documentation and Education, 1976.
Stanley, N. F., & Alpers, M. P. *Man-made lakes and human health.* London: Academic Press, 1975.
Stokols, D. *The relationship between environmental psychology and applied social psychology.* Paper presented at Conference on Applied Social Psychology, Center Interdisciplinary Research, University of Bielefeld, Bielefeld, West Germany. 1980.

Stokols, D., & Shumaker, S. A. People in places: A transactional view of settings. In. J. Harvey (Ed.), *Cognition, social behavior, and environment.* Hillsdale, N.J.: Lawrence Erlbaum Associates, 1981.

Sutton, K. Population resettlement: Traumatic upheavals and the Algerian experience. *The Journal of Modern African Studies,* 1977, *15,* 279-300.

Triandis, H. C. *Some dimensions of intercultural variation and their implications for interpersonal behavior.* Technical Report No. 2, Contract N 0014-80-C-0407; NR 170-906. Urbana-Champaign, Illinois, May 1981.

Yancey, W. L. Architecture, interaction and social control. *Environment and Behavior,* 1971, *3,* 3-21.

12 The Changing Character of Cultural Dispositions: A Social Indicators Approach

Joseph Veroff
University of Michigan

Survey research has often been accused of being more journalism than science. To know about consumer attitudes, political orientations and voting propensities, job satisfaction, or the general quality of one's life makes for good feature stories, and radio or T.V. highlights. But where is the science? The recent introduction of fancy multivariate analyses (curve fitting and causal modeling) into survey research deflects the accusation to some extent, but the fact remains that results from survey research are usually basically descriptive and become interesting largely because of their potential implications for public policy. Will consumers spend more in a given year becomes a critical question to answer if the federal government tries to regulate interest rates. Are people voting with commitment to their party identification is an important issue for political parties to consider. To know whether men and women are satisfied with their work or happy about the general quality of their lives tells us about how restless the natives are. We are gradually becoming as involved in these indicators as we are in economic indicators of productivity and the consumer price index. But again, where is the science?

I do not wish to trivialize the journalistic value or interest in survey research. Enlivened by a social issue much as a journalist would be, many a survey researcher is driven to gather data about a topic for which there is no good information. And unlike most journalism, such data gathering would be systematic and open to public scrutiny. Furthermore, the results of such data gathering will not necessarily correspond exactly to the observations of a popular journalist. Well-done representative surveys fulfill systematic observational needs of science that even the best of journalists cannot meet.

Studs Terkel had much leeway in describing working people's feelings about their work (Terkel, 1974) and their dreams for the good life (Terkel, 1980); he selected, juxtaposed, and edited what people said with considerable liberty. In this journalistic freedom Terkel profoundly affected a reader of *Working* and *American Dreams*. One comes away from these books convinced that Americans of the 1970s may be gutsy, but certainly a fairly frustrated people. His journalism thus became a call to change our work lives and to balance our burdensome goals for achievement with more humane ideals for our lives. By contrast, survey researchers who have looked at problems similar to the ones Terkel addressed but who have studied them by asking representative samples about the quality of their lives have come up with a much more positive portrayal of our satisfactions (see Campbell, 1980). As an admirer of Terkel's journalism, I have learned much about unfulfilled Americans from his work, but as a scientist, I have to accept the survey researchers' conclusions as being closer to the general reality of the American experience. Thus, survey research is a very special brand of journalism. It gives a democratic accounting of people's behavior and feelings. As such, it begins to be science. Its observations permit us to deal systematically and fairly with social issues that could otherwise be distorted by people with zealous social or political goals.

And yet, as science, such accounting is just a beginning. We need something more than just record keeping if we are going to contribute to the understanding of social phenomena. It is the contention of this paper that the introduction of repeated representative surveys over time gives the survey researcher a unique opportunity to expand scientific ventures. When the social indicators movement was first launched with vigor (see Bauer, 1966; Campbell & Converse, 1972; Duncan, 1974), our first thoughts were not with respect to social science but with respect to social policy. Now that this movement has been thriving for a while, it has become increasingly apparent that what's good for social policy might also be extremely good for social science. As social history becomes deeply embedded in our systematic data gathering through surveys, we have begun to think differently about the critical social psychological variables that affect people and how these variables might be best conceived. As we have begun to see how people change or don't change over a given historical time period, we have begun to consider such topics as a person's birth cohort, processes of life cycle adaptation, adult socialization, group diffusion, and social comparison processes in ways we had not considered before. Forced into the role of social historian, survey researchers have had to become more articulate social scientists and not merely systematic journalists. After all, social historians and social scientists both deal with factors that affect what happens next in the flow of human behavior.

There are many examples of the use of over-time replications of surveys that have begun to make such theoretical contributions. Let us look at some of them.

With regard to economic behaviors, George Katona has helped fashion a long-term series of studies on consumer attitudes and how they affect the economic behaviors of the American people (see Katona, 1960). Basically the ideas that Katona tested were founded on a simple social psychological idea that expectations for purchase can distinctly affect actual purchasing behavior. Katona was linking attitudes to behavior. While this may seem to be a straightforward proposition, social psychologists have commonly discovered considerable lack of correspondence between attitudes and behavior in empirical studies. Katona's work in consumer studies provided no exception. There is no one-to-one correspondence between an individual's expectation to purchase and his or her actual purchasing behavior. So what do we find special in Katona's analysis? An exciting theoretical contribution came from his discussion of macropsychology (Katona, 1979), which suggested that although the connections between consumer attitudes and behaviors for a given individual are not powerful, the *aggregate* connections between attitudes and behavior are. This phenomenon has interesting social psychological theoretical value, for it suggests that perhaps one can talk about the contagion or diffusion of attitudes in a group, which have more stability at that aggregate level than any given enactment of an attitude in the behavior of an individual. While individuals may change their mind about purchasing, in the process they may have discussed the matter with many others who, in turn, may decide to make the purchase rather spontaneously. This diffusion takes time to develop. Only cross-time surveys could illustrate the phenomenon.

Similarly, by examining attitudes towards various objects of a political nature in replicated surveys of voter behavior, Converse has developed an important conceptual basis for thinking about the meaning of "centrality of attitudes" and what such centrality implies for attitude structure (see Converse, 1964, 1970). From an original study comparing an elite group of candidates for the United States Congress in 1958 with a national sample of adults, Converse concludes that among people for whom political issues were central (such as the candidates) there were higher inter-attitude correlations and greater stability, especially for abstract ideological issues. These results also implied that only for very concrete political issues would people with less central concerns about politics show any stability in their attitudinal structures over time. Converse confirmed this hypothesis in a panel survey study of American population for 1958 to 1960. These over-time surveys thus were used to test our general theoretical idea about the structure of attitudes.

Surveys on the quality of employment have been conducted at various points of time during the 1970s (Quinn & Staines, 1979). Most of the results are merely descriptive of the changes in the qualities of satisfactions and dissatisfactions expressed by American workers in three different surveys in 1969, 1973, and 1977. Towards the end of this important monograph, *The 1977 Quality of Employment,* however, there exists a test of a clear theoretical hypothesis that job satisfaction is contingent upon expectations for work. This hypothesis assumes that during the 1970s people began to develop higher expectations for what their jobs would be like, and because these higher expectations were largely unmet, dissatisfactions mushroomed. This hypothesis can be used to explain the disgruntlements that occurred from the early 1970s to the late 1970s with regard to people's quality of employment. The hypothesis was not confirmed using measures of underutilization of educational attainment or skills as measures of dashed expectations. In this particular case a favorite hypothesis of casual journalists and even a Presidential Commission (*Work in America,* 1973) was not substantiated. Perhaps the hypothesis should not be totally discarded, but remain open for further testing as more subtle measures of dashed expectations are devised. Nevertheless, this research is greatly enhanced by considering the theoretical issues of how expectations lead to satisfactions or dissatisfactions.

How people use their time has also been explored in two national surveys, one in 1965 and the other in 1975 (Robinson, 1977). Using a systematic diary technique, people described events during a day in their lives. This survey technique allows a comparison of how people allot their time: in work, family care, free time, and so forth. Previous studies (Robinson & Converse, 1972) have suggested that in industrialized countries, people, given labor-saving devices, begin to fill up their free time with work-related activities. Thus a very important theoretical hypothesis about Western industrial peoples is that they are motivated to maintain a constant balance of work and leisure, and that they are highly regulated by norms to work. This hypothesis, however, was not borne out in the 1965-1975 comparisons (Robinson, 1977) where we find there is a considerable shift away from time spent at work to time spent in so-called free time. Thus, these data from replicated surveys allow us to test the relationship between work and leisure in modern industrial society.

Duncan, Schuman, and Duncan (1973) documented the changes in attitudes expressed in a variety of topics from a set of social studies done in the Detroit area series dating from 1953 through 1959, and replicated in a 1971 omnibus survey. Most of this work is frankly journalistic, albeit very scholarly and systematic. Some of the analyses, however, indirectly pose theoretical questions. For example, Duncan, Schuman, and Duncan note that communalism in religious groups (that is, the tendency to maintain contact primarily with people of the same religious faith) was considerably reduced between 1958 and 1971. They find that this reduction was not due to a presumed reduction in children attending parochial schools. They note that there was no clear change in parochial school attendance. It would thus be hard to argue that religious communalism in adults is highly dependent on earlier socialization to the church. Duncan (1975) has also used some of these data from the comparison of the 1950s and the 1970s in the Detroit area to show that people's satisfaction with income is dependent not on an absolute amount of buying power they have but on the social comparisons they make with other incomes at that time. His results confirm ideas raised by Easterlin's (1974) analysis of happiness in 19 countries, which showed that reported happiness has more to do with respondents' relative income in their own country than to their absolute income.

In this very brief excursion through some notable social indicator studies that employed over-time assessment, I have tried to pull out instances where data were used to test out a theoretical idea. Social history is thus used to theoretical advantage. Again, I do not wish to undermine the use of these surveys in their obvious descriptive utility. Both functions are important.

To amplify the value of over-time surveys for these two functions, the rest of this paper is devoted to my own contact with two surveys separated by 19 years, one done in 1957 (Gurin, Veroff, & Feld, 1960) and the other done in 1976 (Veroff, Douvan, & Kulka, 1981; Veroff, Kulka, & Douvan, 1981). For most of the material, identical procedures and questions were used. These surveys dealt with how people describe their own subjective mental health, how they react to various life roles, and how they cope with life problems. In addition, these surveys assessed motives through content analysis of imaginative stories told in response to pictures—standard assessments of needs for achievement, affiliation, and power developed by McClelland and his colleagues (see Atkinson, 1958; Veroff, Depner, Kulka, & Douvan, 1980). Although each of these surveys was journalistically and theoretically interesting about each of the time periods, the most exciting aspects of these surveys arise from their comparison over time.

SOCIAL HISTORY AND SOCIAL PSYCHOLOGY: A TALE OF TWO SURVEYS

We have recognized that in survey research there can be two very different important scientific objectives, sometimes blended and sometimes not: (1) systematically describing individuals within given social historical contexts; (2) using data to test social psychological propositions that focus on processes occurring during that particular historical context. These two functions are sometimes difficult to separate but I will attempt to do so in our analysis of the 1976 replication of the 1957 survey of subjective mental health.

Descriptive Utility of Replicated Surveys

Having the subjective reactions of two national representative samples of adults separated by 19 years, we are obviously in a very good position to talk about the country as a whole during each of those 2 years and especially about changes that have occurred over the time period. As such, we have the potential to plot "social indicators" that are highly useful in outlining systematic social history. Because these are national studies, results are important with regard to federal policy matters aimed at coping with changes detected in the country across the time span in the country at large, or in any large subgroup.

Social indicators of change and stability. The volume, *The Inner American* (Veroff, Douvan, & Kulka, 1981), pulls together results from the two surveys that describe what factors in social experience remained constant and what factors changed from 1957 to 1976. The volume, *Mental Health in America* (Veroff, Kulka, & Douvan, 1981), does the same for help-seeking patterns assessed in the two surveys. Some of the results represent important social indicators of the quality of social life. We found, for example, that people's answers to questions about the nature of their experience in work shifted substantially over the generation. As a specific instance of this, we found that men and women in their work lives were more likely in 1976 to report achievement satisfaction (e.g., a sense of accomplishment, having a chance to express one's skills and talents) than they were in 1957, while they were much *less* likely to speak of their work as interesting. This led us to talk of an important shift in the quality of work—from a more task-centered outside-self focus to a more individual, self-actualizing focus. Another example. Men and women in the 1970s were more likely to speak of their own independence as a source of happiness. These and other results suggested that the qualitative bases of experiences shifted considerably over the generation. In *The Inner American,* we conclude that people in 1976 were more reliant on their own personal reactions to experience and less reliant on the social world's expectations of what they are supposed to be. This shift from a role-based to a self-based anchor of experiences is a critical change in psychological structuring of experience. We found such restructuring in many subtle social indicators. Knowing that this change came about can be useful in social forecasting for the future, as well as understanding the past.

Not all important social indicators showed change. Particularly critical was the fact that summary evaluations of well-being—such as evaluation of happiness/unhappiness—showed little change. The latter might argue that overall evaluations of well-being remain relatively constant. Perhaps people's feelings of happiness/unhappiness depend so much on social comparison with others at a particular moment in history that they are little guided by the intrinsic characteristics of their experience. Similarly we find that there are really no dramatic shifts in overall experiences of job satisfaction, although sources of satisfaction have shifted. Again one could argue that job satisfaction remains relatively stable as a social indicator because people adapt to whatever currently realistic expectations for work are like. One should not second-guess too quickly what indicators are inevitably going to be stable. When we first designed the questionnaire for the 1957 study, we ruled out certain questions because we assumed that they would produce a skewed distribution. For example, we had asked people in a pretest to the 1957 survey what were the things that were not so nice about raising children. Very few people in the pretest were able to give us any response to that question whatsoever. The norm for childrearing was so strongly positive that people were loath to admit to *any* negative experiences with the regard to raising kids. We thus did not include that question in the 1957 survey. Had we known that in the future there would be another survey and that the social changes after the 1950s would make a deep impression on the experience of parenting, we might have wanted to include such a question. In other words, social changes can sometimes produce remarkable shifts in social indicators, even when the scientist does not expect them. To cite another example, one of the most provocative results in the replicated political surveys has been the sharp rise in alienation people feel from their political leadership. Back in the early 1950s there was a very skewed distribution of responses to questions of political orientation. Everyone avowed trust in government. Political scientists were beginning to think that they should omit such questions in further studies because they were not giving any information. During the 1960s there was a sharp increase in the experience of alienation of government which was accounted for by the particular social conditions occurring during the 1960s. The political scientists were very pleased to have included the measures over time because they then could study factors contributing to rising political alienation.

At a more abstract level, Bryant and Veroff (1982) have discussed ways in which the factor structure of different measures of well-being changed or remained stable from 1957 to 1976. The paper documents ways in which year differences can be seen in the *structure*. The research also controlled for sex differences in structure within and between years. In these analyses, the data clearly show that the year differences are more striking than the sex differences and that sex differences are more apparent in 1957 than they were in 1976. An example of a year difference in structure concerns the importance of marital unhappiness to an overall factor of general happiness. Bryant and Veroff find that one's marital happiness or unhappiness was less related to a factor of overall feelings of happiness in 1976 than it was in

1957. These results suggest that the marital role has become a little less critical to feelings of general well-being than it once was.

What of the changes in sex differences in the structure of well-being? Bryant and Veroff find that compared to 1957, in 1976 there was a muting of differences between men and women in how they structure their well-being. These results are important documentation for social indicator purposes; they show that men and women are becoming more alike in the way they think about themselves and their well-being than they once were. Furthermore, this change seems to be primarily due to shifts in the structures of men from 1957 to 1976 in the direction of the structure of women. For example, more men in 1976 than men in 1957 are like women in both 1957 and 1976 in the following way: their concerns about parental adequacy are part of a more general dimension of self-adequacy. In 1957 feeling inadequate about being a parent was evidently much more compartmentalized from a man's general self-evaluation. By 1976, it was more tied to his general self-concept, as always had been the case for a woman. When Veroff, Douvan, and Kulka (1981) looked at the absolute differences between men's and women's responses on the various indices of well-being from 1957 to 1976, they failed to see many results that suggested this growing similarity between men and women. In other words, Bryant and Veroff's more abstract analysis of the *structure* of well-being gave us information about social indicators different from the frequency distributions themselves. The historical shifts noted in the Bryant and Veroff study speak to a deeper level of change or stability than ones documented in *The Inner American*.

Thus, whether one looks at direct assessments of responses of people to a question in one time period as opposed to another or at the more subtle interrelationships of the responses, as in the factor analytic study, one gets at very important aspects of changes in the social responses of people over time. Such studies help document the nature of social change with systematic social psychological assessments.

Cohort analysis. In the process of working out social indicators from replicated surveys, we soon discovered an additional methodological possibility that having only one cross-sectional sample lacks. An important rationale for following national samples over time is to be able to plot *cohort effects* that may not be as easily obtained from a more limited cross-sectional sample. People born at the same time, identified as a *birth cohort,* often migrate to other geographic locations and to other organizational settings. Following up a cohort in a longitudinal study sometimes presents some extraordinary problems. To have replicated *national* samples, however, more easily permits one to follow a birth cohort over time with respect to a certain attitude or with respect to a particular behavioral disposition. If we can assume that in- and out-migrations from the country, and also that movements out of households to living arrangements not sampled in our household interview (e.g., hospital, prison, barracks) and vice versa apply equally to all cohorts, we can feel confident that a national cross-sectional sample of a given birth cohort in one year safely reflects that cohort in another year. In our two national studies, people who were young, 21-29 in the 1957 study, were people who were approximately 40-49 in the 1976 survey. One can compare those groups to see whether they showed any similarity in their responses, especially in comparison to other cohorts. If we found people of a given cohort were more like each other over time then they were to other cohorts, we could begin to identify a *cohort effect*. For example, are people socialized at some early point in their lives to view marriage in a certain way? Are the attitudes of middle-aged people in 1976 about their marriages more like the attitudes they held when they were younger or more like middle-aged people in 1957? Those are the kinds of questions one can discover in a cohort effect.

Our two national surveys permitted us to look at cohort phenomena. At the start of our investigation we anticipated finding many cohort phenomena. Other researchers led us to believe we would. Baltes, Cornelius and Nesselroade's (1976) discussion of cohorts suggested that we would obtain clear-cut cohort phenomena on personality-related factors such as the motives (see especially, Nesselroade & Baltes, 1974). Elder's work (1974) impressed us with the fact that children born in the depression would demonstrate particular coping styles—such as, those reflecting realistic planning for the future. We were thus surprised by finding little evidence for stable cohort effects in most of the results. There is much more evidence either for historical effects (e.g., 1957 vs. 1976 differences in *all* people) or for age effects (i.e., differences attributed to being of a certain age regardless of year). A few pieces of evidence seemed interpretable as cohort effects. We discuss these below. Nevertheless, to discover the absence of any cohort effects with respect to certain dispositions was also exciting. We also discuss these below.

What were some of the cohort phenomena that did exist? Being of a certain birth cohort tells us to some extent about the styles of coping that people use to handle periods of worry, or periods of unhappiness. Respondents were asked:

> If something is on your mind that's bothering you or worries you, and you don't know what to do about it, what do you usually do?

> And one of the things we'd like to know is how people face the unhappy periods in their lives. Thinking of unhappiness you've had to face, what are some of the things that have helped you in those times?

We find that people of a given birth cohort seem to be alike both in 1957 and in 1976 in how often they mention either praying or turning to loved ones, friends, and family for support during such times of distress. Those born during a particular decade speak of using such support at the same rate in both 1957 and 1976. These rates differ in different cohorts, but remain relatively stable over the generation for any given cohort. Thus, a person's help-seeking style may be guided by some early socialization, perhaps during adolescence or even earlier, that remains with that person as he or she moves through the life cycle.

Another birth cohort phenomenon was detected in people's commitment to parenthood. In particular we found that the young parents in the fifties, who were progenitors of the baby boom, were highly committed to that parenting role, not only in the 1950s when they were young, but also in the 1970s when they were middle-aged. One theoretical explanation for this is that as that cohort's contribution to overpopulation became frowned on by other members of society then the cohort became defensive and hence ever more committed to the products of their fertility. Other explanations are possible. With whatever explanation, it seems to be a clear cohort phenomenon.

We also have evidence that the very young people in the 1970s seem to be quite different in many attitudes from young people either in the 1950s or any other group at either time period. This may be a long-lasting phenomenon for the cohort born in the 1950s and 1960s. I refer particularly to three striking orientations found in this cohort: an extremely tolerant attitude toward not marrying; a negative attitude toward the effects of becoming a parent; and, among women, a strong commitment to work. While each generation may have comparatively greater openness during early adulthood, many observers of the new generation's views on family roles and work for women suggest that these may be very persistent dispositions (see Hacker, 1982). Only future replicated surveys will tell.

It is important to note with respect to each of these cohort findings that had we had only one cross-sectional survey, we could not have easily attributed the result to a possible cohort effect but would have been strongly tempted to attribute each phenomenon to a person's age. Even with two replicated surveys what we interpret as a cohort effect can be reinterpreted as an age x year interaction. Nevertheless, we can begin to interpret data about a potential cohort effect with two sample points. With any additional sample points our confidence would of course be further raised.

The absence of strong cohort effects in our projective assessment of motives is very illuminating. From numerous theories of personality based on neo-Freudian principles, one would assume that men and women, having developed strong or weak achievement affiliative or power motives either in early childhood or, at the latest, adolescence, would show some constancy about such motives for the rest of their lives. If that were the case, one would have expected that different socialization practices pertinent to the various birth cohorts during their childhood or adolescence would have produced significant and stable differences in motives among varying cohorts. As we looked at the motive scores of people in 1957 and 1976, we expected much of the variance to be due to cohort differences. Such was not the case. Except for a few instances, a birth cohort that was particularly high in 1957 in a given motive was not any more or less likely to be high in that motive in 1976. These results suggest that the social motives we have assessed—needs for achievement, affiliation, and power—are largely conditioned by adult experience. The socialization encountered as people move through the life cycle effects changes in motives. In addition, particular historical phenomena that occur to all or only certain age groups at a given time can effect motive changes. I discuss some of these phenomena in a later section. For now it is important only to realize that cohort socialization does not seem to be a strong basis for individual differences in the motives for social interaction that were measured in our surveys. Since we had a sample of very important motives, one might be tempted to generalize and say that strength of important social motives may not be forged as enduring characteristics in early development and remain at that level over the life cycle. Rather, adult socialization of motive can occur at *any* point over the life cycle.

National character analysis. Our capacity to compare the motive scores between 1957 and 1976 illustrates the potential in having two surveys that was not available in having only one. In being able to explore stability or change in these motives over time surveys, we can better speak of a national modal character analysis than we could with results from only one slice of time. That is, in the assessment of achievement, affiliation, or power motives in 1957 we had no idea how high a particular motive was for American society, compared to other societies past or present. For example, it could very well have been that the achievement motive scores that we had for the 1957 American sample came from a very limited range of potential scores for all people everywhere. The whole culture might be modally high or low. We only had Americans and no other comparison groups to serve as a baseline for thinking about the strength of Americans' achievement motives. With the introduction of the second survey, we still had no way of knowing the absolute strength of the mean American achievement motive score, but we could feel more confident about talking about increases, decreases, or stability in the achievement motive among Americans over time. For example, we find that there is a considerable increase in fear of weakness (one assessment of the power motive) in both men and women from 1957 to 1976.[1] Regardless of what the absolute value of the power motive was in either year for either sex, this pattern of change that exists from 1957 to 1976 is striking and has important implications. If Americans are becoming more power motivated, it suggests a very new structure to social life. Indeed, power motivational issues may become more and more to define the way we evaluate our marriages, the way we consider our work. Veroff, Douvan, and Kulka (1981, p. 166) speak of the relationship model of marriage as being new in 1976 compared to 1957. The power motivational rise may have spearheaded this change.

This type of national character analysis led us to see some other important shifts in disposition in American society. There are striking increases in women's achievement motive and men's hope of power motive, a second assessment of the power motive.[2] Furthermore, there is a decrease in men's affiliation motive. The increase in hope of power accompanied by a decrease in the affiliation motive in men is disturbing in light of McClelland's (1961) research which suggests that the pattern of low affiliation, high power exists in countries prior to the rise of totalitarianism. McClelland had previously analyzed cultural documentations to assess national levels of motives. In this instance, we have direct assessment of a national change in motives.

It would be erroneous to cite only the 1957-1976 comparison of motive scores as data from the surveys that could be used to assess national character. After all, various facets of human dispositions go into making "character." Other information from the two surveys could be used in this way: modal responses to ways of defining happiness, job and marital satisfaction, general styles of perceiving one's self or one's future, styles of coping with problems, and many other characteristics. As noted above with regard to the motives, there was no way we could have used the 1957 survey alone to get a confident assessment of national character. We had used the 1957 survey alone to make national character statements about these matters in previous reports but it was a risk. For example, we found that when people were asked the following question, most people gave us an optimistic response:

---

[1] One should note that in examining modal changes in motive scores from 1957 to 1976 we took account of large scale demographic shifts that have occurred in the country in that time period. That is, the country as a whole has become more educated and has become more bimodal in the age distribution (i.e., there were relatively more very young and very old people in the 1976 sample than there were in the 1957 sample). The year differences in fear of weakness are *net* of changes that occur in both education and age distributions.

[2] Two types of power motives were assessed; one based on Veroff and Veroff's (1972) work describing a projective instrument that assesses a person's concern with not losing power (fear of weakness) and the other based on Winter's (1973) work describing an instrument that reflects a person's positive interest in having impact (hope of power).

Compared to your life today, how do you think things will be 5 or 10 years from now? Do you think things will be happier for you than they are now, not quite as happy, or what?

It was very tempting to conclude, and we did, that dispositionally we are an optimistic people. But suppose we had worded the 1957 question not in comparison to life today but in regard to getting all that people had hoped for. A different type of distribution of responses might have occurred, and perhaps we would have been led to a different conclusion about American optimism. However, having a 1976 replication of the question about the future, we can in the 1957-1976 comparison feel very confident about any stability or change in the modal responses to this question. We thus can draw more substantial conclusions about national character. As it turns out, as a nation in 1976, we remained about as optimistic on this question as we were in 1957, but when we instituted age and education controls, we discovered that there was a net shift toward greater pessimism in 1976. With respect to optimism or pessimism what then can we say about our national character? As a nation we are just as optimistic in 1976 as we were in 1957, but, *considering the demographic shifts in the country,* we are getting more pessimistic. Both pieces of data seem to be important for a complete assessment of our character for social historical analyses. In any case, such 1957-1976 comparisons can be used with greater justification than single surveys to assess national character.

Replicated Surveys for Theoretical Analysis

Beyond the descriptive virtues of replicated surveys lies their potential for generating tests of social scientific explanations for social behavior. There are clear-cut theoretical contributions to be made to social psychology by the investigations possible in anlayzing responses of survey samples over time. The most exciting contributions come from panel or longitudinal survey samples. Social scientists most easily confront issues about social causation if they can talk about changes that occur *within* the individual from one time period to another. For example, a recent longitudinal survey study of well-being in a Chicago representative sample (Pearlin, Lieberman, Menaghan, & Mullar, 1981) is able to map and test causal links between disruptive life events (job loss) and depression. It examined intervening processes that focused on how people cope (e.g., whether they use social support to reduce strain; whether they distort the events they experience to minimize their impact). The study found, among other things, social supports cushion a person's loss of self-esteem after a disruptive life event, and it is this loss in esteem that seems to induce depression. Thus, social support seems to buffer a person's interpretation of himself or herself after a negative event, rather than mitigating one's depression directly. These results could be clearly analyzed given replicated individual data from surveys. But because longitudinal surveys are extraordinarily difficult and expensive, we usually content ourselves with only replicated cross-sectional surveys to approximate issues of social causation when doing large-scale studies of representative samples over time.[3]

The search for conceptual bases for group difference. One approximation to the analysis of social causation in replicated cross-sectional surveys comes in the form of theoretical explorations of subgroup differences. Whenever groups differed significantly from one another in an important social psychological dimensions, in either or both of our surveys, we had the opportunity to consider theoretical explanations for the result. To do so, we might offer a theoretical speculation and then either go back to the data to test out deductions drawn from our explanations or look for parallel evidence in other results from the survey. Obviously, we had to make sure that critical controls were also imposed before we attributed the results to the group difference in consideration. In this process there were distinct advantages to having replicated surveys. If any group difference was stronger in one year or the other, social history would become part of the theoretical understanding of the group difference. Or, if the group difference transcended social historical considerations, then certain other deductions were possible. Furthermore, some of the differences may be very small even if significant in one year but become much more impressive when repeated again in the second survey. Let me illustrate such attempts at theory construction and testing when replicated survey data point to subgroup differences in one or both of the surveys.

1. Sex differences in symptomology. Men and women differed in both 1957 and in 1976 in the ways they responded to questions about symptoms of distress including both physical (e.g., headaches and stomach-aches) and psychological (e.g., feeling nervous) complaints. Women reported more symptoms than men. The favored theoretical argument for the 1957 data had been that women are more prone to admit to weaknesses than men, because there is an important sex role expectation about such matters. While men are supposed to appear invulnerable in responding to questions of weakness, women are not only permitted to report that they feel vulnerable, they may be encouraged to do so. There is, of course, another conceptual analysis of these results. Some theorists (see Gove & Tudor,

---

[3]Kulka (1978) cogently argues for instances where replicated cross-sectional surveys might be preferable to panel data. These occur when repeating the measure might challenge its validity. For example, repeating the projective assessment of motive may be invalid because once having responded with given thematic contents to a picture, respondents may purposely think up new materials in order to avoid the stigma of seeming uncreative.

1973) have suggested that women in fact lead more stressful lives that make them actually feel more vulnerable. Women may experience more actual role overload. Thus we have two competing explanations: one depending on a sex role response bias; another depending on role overload differences. The fact that in 1976 we replicated these sex differences *with no interaction by year* makes us favor the role overload hypothesis more than the response bias hypothesis. There were lots of reasons to think that in the interim between 1957 and 1976 men and women were moving closer together with respect to their self-presentation styles. Women should have begun to feel more comfortable about appearing invulnerable, and men more comfortable about appearing vulnerable. The fact that the sex difference in symptom reporting remained fairly stable suggests the response bias interpretation is perhaps less critical than the role overload hypothesis. Indeed we draw on that hypothesis in some detail in *The Inner American.* We suggest that because women more often than men assume the responsibility for other people's lives in their interpersonal relationships, they are more prone to experience many more stresses than men would. We argue that women accrue empathic strain resulting from other people's crises, more so than men.

2. *Age differences in motives.* The 1957 survey produced many differences in mean motive scores among various age groups. For example, middle-aged men were particularly high in the achievement motive. At that time we had life cycle developmental interpretations of these data. In most instances we were in considerable error, for we found that for the most part the age trends were not replicated in 1976. Only two age results were strikingly consistent in both years. Both pertain to women and not men. First, the affiliation motive is highest in young women, moderately high in middle-age women, and lowest in old women. Second, the achievement motive of elderly women was decidedly lower than the achievement motive in younger or middle-aged women. Because we had little evidence for stability in motive scores for cohorts, as already mentioned, and because we had no consistency in age trends between the 2 years, aside from the two mentioned, we have begun to theorize that at each point in social history, there are role expectations for people of different age groups which act as strong conditioners for the development of strong motives. Each historical era may have its particular expectations for particular age groups. For example, higher achievement motives in middle-aged men in 1957 contrasted to 1976 suggest that career building was a more gradual expectation for men in the 1950s than in the 1970s. Men in 1957 were probably expected to work themselves slowly into more achieving and responsible positions. The pinnacle of expectation for them was at mid-life. By contrast, in the 1970s expectation for orbiting into such positions existed at a much younger age.

Given these ideas about social historical conditioning factors that directly or indirectly affect people's strength of motives at different ages, what would we say about the two aforementioned cases of *consistent* age trends in motives in both 1957 and 1976? We would suggest that age-related expectations were similar for these motives in 1957 and 1976. For example, the fact that achievement motive scores are consistently high in younger women of both social eras and more consistently low in elderly women suggests that career investments were consistently more tied to being young in both 1957 and 1976. We could imagine a social era when older women were expected to enter the labor force with extraordinary high work commitment. Indeed we may be moving in that direction during the 1980s. In that case, these age trends would shift.

These are important theoretical conclusions. They suggest that life-span developmental changes in motives are not forged by different cohort experiences, nor by universal ontological consequences of adult development, but are by and large conditioned by historical cultural contexts. The fact that middle-age men in 1957 were particularly high in achievement motive rests not on something special about middle-age demands on men in all historical eras, nor by the peculiar socialization of these men in their childhood or adolescence, but by the social factors operating about age norms for men in 1957. While any consistent age results discovered may reflect some generalized ontological phenomena, we should also consider alternative social historical explanations for these results. For example, the decline over age found in women's need for affiliation in both 1957 and 1976 does not exist for women highly committed to prestigeful work, although this group is not particularly high or low in this motive. We would thus argue that as women become more engaged by meaningful work, their affiliation motive will not decline over the life cycle as it has for most women in both years. And, as a result, we can read the general decline in affiliation motive as a reflection of the more general sex-role expectations about family centered life for women, which become less and less focused on affiliative concerns as women mature.

In summary, we have used our analysis of cohorts, age, and year differences in motives to help us fashion a new framework about motive change over the life cycle. While we cannot entirely rule out early socialization factors, we have moved toward a theoretical scheme that puts major emphasis on social historical interpretations of age norms for men and women as the critical, causal determinants of motive development and change in adulthood.

Avenues for direct hypothesis-testing. Exciting survey research often reflects a researcher's attempt to test implicitly or explicitly a specific conceptual scheme. Most typically it involves comparing critical demographic groups, as we indicated in the prior sections. Frequently it involves using a theory to explore the correlations between responses. With the introduction of historical change into the determination of such correlation, theory testing becomes even more exciting, because *change in correlations* can sometimes be predicted or accounted for by a theoretical conception.

An example from *The Inner American* is warranted. Lasch (1979) has proposed that Americans have over time become more "narcissistic" implying that they are more dependent on their own self-fulfillment and personal characteristics as a source of their overall well-being than they once were. As a result, he would argue, they are less committed to others, less socially integrated. For each year, we examined the correlations between the evaluation of happiness and each of the major sources of reporting happiness or unhappiness. The years were then compared, and we looked carefully for any shifts showing higher correlations in 1957 between happiness and *socially* centered sources of happiness or unhappiness (e.g., community or family satisfactions or difficulties) and higher correlations in 1976 between happiness and very *personally* relevant characterizations of happiness and unhappiness (e.g., a person's own virtues or faults). No such shifts could be detected. We thus argued that some conceptual scheme other than the one that involves a process of increased narcissism as a focus for well-being ought to be used in exploring some of the clear breakdown in social integration occurring in American society.

Another example of hypothesis testing in replicated surveys was our implicit use of role theories to help account for some of the changes in social indicators of reactions to marriage, parenthood, and work. With regard to marriage, for example, we discovered a general loosening of the imperatives of marriage for everyone and a more diffuse set of expectations about the consequences of marriage for both men and women. This lack of clarity about the role and diminution of explicit expectation should have very interesting consequences on peoples' feelings about marriage, according to many role theories. We looked for such consequences in changes from 1957 to 1976 in how people reacted to their own marriages. The most interesting was a greater focus on relationships in 1976 and less blaming of one's self or one's spouse for problems in a marriage. Diffuse roles, we would reason from role theory, produce less direct personal blame for difficulties encountered in the role.

With the regard to the work role, we found a very interesting set of results that confirm conceptual ideas about a reciprocal relationship between obligations to self and obligations to the group. I mentioned earlier the qualitative shift in work satisfaction that has occurred between 1957 and 1976: from a more task-centered, outside self-focus to a more self-actualizing focus. In specific terms this means people were thinking of their work as being more achievement gratifying but less "interesting." One view of this result is that people have become more absorbed in personal competition and fulfillment and in the process have come to ignore the effects of such personal orientations on others. They become less group minded. This conceptual opposition of the individual and the group is a common theoretical scheme for thinking of social interaction. A support for such a view came in the findings that compared to 1957 workers, the 1976 population, while finding their work more self-actualizing, was finding their social community at work more dissatisfying. Many more people in 1976 talk of affiliative difficulties at work. Thus, posing individual achievement versus group gratification goals as an inevitable conflict in social life gets some corroboration in these historical changes in people's orientation to work. Once again, we find the analysis of replicated surveys helpful in delineating and testing a theory.

SUMMARY

This discussion has focused on ways in which replicated surveys can be helpful for both descriptive and theoretical social research. We have highlighted a set of data having to do with subjective mental health and human motives that were obtained in both 1957 and 1976. Social history had to be considered. This social historical analysis has value at a merely descriptive level. Clearly, systematic assessment of the changes or lack of changes in American life is informative in and of itself. Furthermore, as we saw, the responses to questions shift or remain stable over the past generation; we have become more fully cognizant of how the year of measurement provides a context for understanding the meaning of the measure. A social historical approach to surveys has also helped us understand some of the potential dynamics of change in certain groups and not others. At a more theoretical level, looking for subgroup differences over time allows us to test out potential causal explanations for why certain social psychological phenomena change and why others do not. Furthermore, explicit theory testing occurred in these replicated surveys that could not have come about in a single-time study. Our investigations of role theory in the social historical perspective of the two surveys allowed us to see the effects of weakened roles on people over time.

In all of these analyses, however, we should realize that these replicated surveys are rich material for investigations of social policy to be used for both social diagnostics and social forecasting. And they will be used that way. To the extent that social scientists commit themselves to investigating the general conceptual problems of social psychology and formulate proper conceptual schemes to explain the social history being documented, the social policy issues ought to be better understood. Needless to say, social psychology is also enriched. Certain hypotheses about the effects of social history on psychological processes can be tested in no other way.

REFERENCES

Atkinson, J. W. *Motives in fantasy, action and society.* Princeton, N.J.: D. Van Nostrand, 1958.

Baltes, P. B., Cornelius, S. W., & Nesselroade, J. R. Cohort effects in developmental psychology: Theoretical and methodological perspectives. In W. A. Collins (Ed.), *Minnesota Symposium on Child Psychology* (Vol. 11). Minneapolis Institute of Child Development, University of Minnesota, 1976.

Bauer, R. A. (Ed.) *Social Indicators.* Cambridge, Mass.: MIT Press, 1966.

Bryant, F. B., & Veroff, J. The structure of psychological well-being: A socio-historical analysis. *Journal of Personality and Social Psychology,* 1982, *43,* 653–673.

Campbell, A. *Sense of well-being in America: Recent patterns and trends.* New York: McGraw-Hill, 1980.

Campbell, A., & Converse, P. E. *The human meaning of social change.* New York: Russell Sage, 1972.

Converse, P. The nature of belief systems in mass publics. In D. Apter (Ed.), *Ideology and discontent.* Glencoe, Ill.: The Free Press, 1964.

Converse, P. Attitudes and non-attitudes: Continuation of a dialogue. In E. Tufte (Ed.), *The quantitative analysis of social problems.* Reading, Mass.: Addison-Wesley, 1970.

Duncan, O. D. Developing social indicators. *Proceedings of the National Academy of Sciences* (Vol. 71) 1974, *12,* 5096–5102.

Duncan, O. D. Does money buy satisfaction? *Social Indicators Research,* 1975, *2,* 267–274.

Duncan, O. D., Schuman, H., & Duncan, B. *Social change in a metropolitan community.* New York: Russell Sage, 1973.

Easterlin, R. A. Does economic growth improve the human lot? Some empirical evidence. In P. A. David & M. W. Reder (Eds.), *Nations and households in economic growth.* New York: Academic Press, 1974.

Elder, G. *Children of the Great Depression.* Chicago: University of Chicago Press, 1974.

Gove, W. R., & Tudor, J. Adult sex roles and mental illness. *American Journal of Sociology,* 1973, *78,* 50–73.

Gurin, G., Veroff, J., & Feld, S. C. *Americans view their mental health.* New York: Basic Books, 1960.

Hacker, A. Farewell to the family? *The New York Review of Books,* 1982, *19,* 37–44.

Katona, G. *The powerful consumer.* New York: McGraw-Hill, 1960.

Katona, G. Toward a macro psychology. *American Psychologist,* 1979, *34,* 118–126.

Kulka, R. *Monitoring social change via survey replication.* Paper presented at Radcliffe Conference on Methods for Studying Women and Social Change, 1978.

Lasch, C. *The culture of narcissism.* New York: Norton, 1979.

McClelland, D. *The achieving society.* Princeton, N.J.: D. Van Nostrand, 1961.

Nesselroade, J. R., & Baltes, P. B. Adolescent personality development and historical change: 1970–1976. *Monograph of the Society for Research in Child Development,* 1974, *39.*

Pearlin, L. J., Lieberman, M. A., Menaghan, E. G., & Mullar, J. T. The stress process. *Journal of Health and Social Behavior,* 1981, *22,* 337–356.

Quinn, R. P., & Staines, G. L. *The 1977 Quality of Employment Survey: Descriptive statistics with comparison data from the 1969-1970 and 1972-1973 surveys.* Ann Arbor, Mich.: Survey Research Center, Institute for Social Research, 1979.

Robinson, J. Changes in Americans' use of time: 1965-1975: A progress report. Cleveland: John Robinson, 1977.

Robinson, J., & Converse, P. Social change as reflected in the use of time. In A. Campbell & P. Converse (Eds.), *The human meaning of social change.* New York: Russell Sage Foundation, 1972.

Terkel, S. *Working.* New York: Pantheon, 1974.

Terkel, S. *American Dreams.* New York: Pantheon, 1980.

Veroff, J., Depner, C., Kulka, R., & Douvan, E. A comparison of American motives: 1957-1976. *Journal of Personality and Social Psychology,* 1980, *39,* 1249-1262.

Veroff, J., Douvan, E., & Kulka, R. *The Inner American: A Self-Portrait from 1957 to 1976.* New York: Basic Books, 1981.

Veroff, J., Kulka, R., & Douvan E. *Mental health in America: Patterns of help-seeking from 1957-1976.* New York: Basic Books, 1981.

Winter, D. B. *The power motive.* New York: Free Press, 1973.

Work in America: Report of a special task force to the Secretary of Health, Education and Welfare. Cambridge, Mass.: MIT Press, 1973.

III HISTORICAL INQUIRY

13 Love, Misogyny, and Feminism in Selected Historical Periods:* A Social-Psychological Explanation

Paul F. Secord
University of Houston

Since historical method is as controversial as psychological method, there are no clear guidelines for doing historical social psychology. Because of this, it is important for investigators who follow this new path to identify their assumptions and to spell out their procedures. First, let me emphasize that I am not writing history. The history of the times and places examined here has already been written, by others infinitely more competent than I. My reason for examining selected historical periods was to ascertain whether demographic and associated social conditions found in a contemporary setting were also present in the past. The periods examined were not selected randomly, but were deliberately chosen because they were times when members of one gender group were greatly in abundance over the other. The social effects that this imbalance in sex ratios produced is the focus of this chapter.

Certain background assumptions underlie my thinking here. I share with Hexter (1971) the belief that natural science is not the correct model for doing history. In social science, we only have full explanations of social behavior when we are able to articulate the relationships between individual behavior, interactions among individuals, and the relationship of these to

---

*The sex ratio thesis which is the central topic of this investigation was initially conceived by the late Marcia Guttentag. At the time of her death, she had completed, in rough unpublished form, an examination of the thesis among shtetl Jews in eastern Europe and in two medieval populations and had done some work on the classical Greeks and the contemporary United States black population. I have finished the work on these populations and carried out my own investigations of early and contemporary white populations in the U.S.A., and have produced the theoretical work pertaining to the research. The completed project is reported in a book-length monograph (Guttentag & Secord, 1983).

various social structural features of society. The problems in constructing such explanations have been spelled out elsewhere (Manicas & Secord, 1983; Secord, 1982), and here I will only pause to point out that such explanations go well beyond experimentation and beyond the methods used in the natural sciences. They require an attention to the actions of human agents described in a manner that takes seriously their own accounts of what they were doing, to historical description (even if only of events that took place yesterday, last week, last month, or decades ago), to underlying social structures that may have been created by human agency, albeit unintentionally, as well as to the social context or circumstances within which the social phenomena to be explained were exhibited. It is within this framework that the present study is undertaken.

The aim of the present discussion is to describe the profound effects that follow from imbalanced sex ratios in a population in various historical periods. The larger project (Guttentag & Secord, 1983) on which the present discussion is based, used both contemporary and historical materials to develop extensive accounts of these social effects and ultimately to fashion relevant social psychological explanations. Our understanding of these social effects was enormously enhanced and enriched by the use of historical documents along with contemporary data.

STAGES OF THE SEX RATIO PROJECT

Because use of historical data is rare for social psychologists, it may be helpful to indicate the several stages of the sex ratio project. In its earliest phases, a rudimentary sex ratio thesis was the guiding idea which led to examination of both contemporary and historical phenomena. The kernel of this thesis was that a shortage of young unmarried men (or women) in a population would have a strong impact on relationships between men and women and on the institutions (e.g., family) associated with these relationships. The sex ratio is a standard demographic index, defined as the number of males per 100 females in a population or in some specified cohort of a population. Thus a ratio of 110 would mean that there are 110 males for every 100 females in the population: high ratios represent an excess of males, and low ratios, a female surplus. The sex ratio question asks what happens to relations between men and women at ages when they most commonly form enduring relationships, under conditions where there is a shortage of either male or female partners suitable for marriage. Our thesis was that certain common processes would be set in motion by each form of sex ratio imbalance, but that their effects on relationships between men and women would depend upon the varying customs and practices prevailing in different societies.

Marcia Guttentag and I were living on the Harvard campus at the inception of this project; we thus had an opportunity to discuss this thesis extensively with faculty members and other interested friends and colleagues, most of whom were from disciplines other than psychology. These discussions were invaluable and led us to data sources ordinarily undreamed of by social psychologists. What became apparent almost immediately was that several populations from past times provided almost ideal circumstances for examining the implications of the thesis and especially for detailing the kinds of social effects that might be anticipated. This first stage of the overall project, which extended over several years, and to which Marcia Guttentag was the principal contributor, was one of gathering a good deal of *descriptive* material concerning several societies from the past, as well as some data from the contemporary United States.

Our search was much encouraged by the early discovery of the work of two historians, each of whom had anticipated a part of the sex ratio thesis. Herbert Moller (1958–59) attributed the "courtly love complex" to a shortage of upper-class women in Moorish Spain in the ninth, tenth, and eleventh centuries, in southwestern France in the twelfth century and southern Germany in the twelfth and thirteenth centuries. In another publication, he called attention to the great value placed on women in frontier America, where they were very scarce (Moller, 1945). This is only a part of our sex ratio thesis; the other side concerns what happens when there is an abundance of women. Here, a German scholar (Bucher, 1882) linked the great surplus of women in the later medieval period to loose sexual morals, to the disparagment of women and the family, to misogyny, and to *Die Frauenbewegnung* (women's movements). The discovery of the work of these historians provided tremendous impetus to further examination of the sex ratio thesis in historical periods.

One other early finding is worth noting, because it underscored the relevance to the thesis of contemporary conditions in the United States. This was the phenomenon of the *marriage squeeze,* first reported in those terms by Glick, Heer, and Beresford (1963). This condition is brought about by a steadily rising birth rate combined with the practice of women marrying men 2 or 3 years older than themselves. The birth rate in the United States rose steadily for 12 years from 1945 to 1957. So when women born between 1947 and 1957 reached a marriageable age, they had to find a male partner from a birth cohort appreciably smaller than their own, so long as they continued to look for a man older than themselves.

The first stage of the project, then, was a descriptive one guided by a rudimentary sex ratio thesis which held that a persistent shortage of unmarried men (or women) would have a dramatic impact on the way that men and women related to each other, and that it would in time bring about changes in related social institutions. As more data accumulated, the nature of these anticipated changes became clearer. Ultimately it became possible to describe a kind of *ideal type* or *model* for each of the two sex ratio conditions, high or low. The forms they take in particular societies always differ somewhat from the ideal and depend upon other features of those societies.

The descriptive work of the first stage imperceptibly led into an intermediate stage where it became necessary to formulate more clearly the nature of the demographic indices that produced the social effects; the concept of *marital opportunities* based upon sex ratios for certain selected age cohorts emerged. Along with this, an effort was made to specify the conditions in the societies examined that caused the social effects to occur or that modified or even prevented them from occurring, even though sex ratios were considerably out of balance.

The final stage of the project required developing an explanation for the relationship between the demographic conditions and the social effects. Social exchange theory proved to be extremely helpful in achieving this goal, and with the completion of the project a somewhat different kind of investigation becomes possible. An investigator can now start with a developed theory and apply it either to contemporary society or to earlier historical periods to ascertain its applicability and generate new insights into relationships between men and women characterizing that society or period.

The following sections briefly illustrate these various stages of investigation and conclude with a highly plausible social psychological explanation of the forms that relationships between men and women take.

SEX RATIO EFFECTS IN SELECTED TIMES AND PLACES

As every demographer knows, only three general sources can upset the balance of males and females in a population: differential birth rates, differential mortality, and differential migration. As we will see, the sources creating imbalances in the societies discussed varied from one to another society. Moreover, examining the effects of sex ratios for any point in time requires careful consideration of all those social conditions and practices that might combine with gender imbalances to affect relationships between men and women. Space limitations here do not permit extensive discussion of each society; instead, brief sketches of the salient features are included (see Guttentag & Secord, 1983, for more complete presentations). Sketches to be presented are of classical Athens and Sparta, and the early and late medieval period in selected areas of Europe. A caveat is stressed here: as is well known to historians, the kind of social history dealt with here can only be known to apply to the upper classes, since "ordinary" people, and especially women, are almost invisible in traditional historical accounts.

Classical Athens and Sparta

What is not well known is that Athens and Sparta differed markedly in their population sex ratios. The Spartans were much concerned with rearing sturdy citizen-soldiers, and so male infants were often killed or neglected if they did not show such promise. The frequent absence of men on military service also created a de facto low sex ratio. Spartan couples did not live together for the first 12 years of their marriage; although Spartan boys married at the age of 18 years, they went on living with their sex-segrated army group until the age of 30 (Weldon, 1907).

In contrast, sex ratios in Athens were very high. A unique demographic study of sex ratios among Athenians in the fourth century B.C. was stimulated by our sex ratio thesis (Harward, 1976). A random sample of 1,500 funerary inscriptions was used to determine male-female ratios, and this was compared with the ratio of male to female names cited in court orations made on inheritance, abuse of guardianship, or attempts to recover dowries. An explicit set of rules was used to infer sex ratios from the inscriptions or orations, in order to avoid bias of any kind. These two independent analyses yielded only a 2 to 3% discrepancy in sex ratios, which were estimated to range from 143 to 174 for the Attic population during the fourth century. Clearly, then, in these two city-states we have the contrasting high and low population sex ratios required for examining our thesis.

The *social* status of women in classical Greece, especially Athens, has been the subject of a lively controversy among scholars, but they agree reasonably well on their political and legal status. The status of Athenian women varied drastically depending upon whether they were citizens, courtesans, noncitizens, concubines, servants, or slaves (Pomeroy, 1975). But in any case, women were much lower in status than men. Athens was a very traditional high sex ratio society. Athenian women had domestic roles as wives and mothers, and were subservient to their husbands. They were tied to the household and did not participate in business, professional, political, or legal activities. A citizen-wife could bear a citizen child who would hopefully perpetuate the family line, and this form of motherhood was the highest honor for an Athenian woman.

Citizen girls of Athens received little education and were wholly outside of the active intellectual and cultural life of Athens. They were socialized in traditional feminine values. Strong protective controls were exercised over Athenian women. Both fathers and husbands were masters of their households and were highly paternal toward their wives. Girls were married at puberty to a man who was considerably older and who had more education and more worldly knowledge. Legally, wives were "minors" in the care of their husbands; children were the legal property of their father, but not their mother. Marriages of daughters were arranged by the father, and if a husband died, the widow's son would often arrange a marriage for his mother. Divorce was an easy male prerogative; the husband need only expel his wife from the household. The extremely rare instances of divorce initiated by a wife were negotiated exclusively by her male relatives.

In spite of its low sex ratios, Sparta was like Athens in one respect. Spartans placed great emphasis on women as bearers of children who would become warrior-citizens. This emphasis on motherhood is uncharacteristic of low sex ratio societies but is understandable in view of Sparta's military requirements. As in other low sex ratio societies, the family as a unit was not especially valued, with the male segregated in military service for a period of 12 years.

Except for childbearing, Spartan women contrasted strongly with Athenian women, in a manner consistent with a low sex ratio society. They had greater economic, educational, and sexual opportunities than Athenian women. Their education was equal to that of Spartan boys; traditional female domestic training was minimized, and they had the same physical training as Spartan boys. With their greater education and some economic power, Spartan women were noted for being outspoken and witty. Their witticisms and their poetry have been praised and quoted, but no comparable female poet has been found among Athenian women (Pomeroy, 1975).

The Spartan legal code was far more favorable toward women than the Athenian code. When divorced, a woman took her own property and half of the produce of the household. Moreover, if a father, husband, or son violated the regulations concerning the property of children, control passed to the mother or wife. A woman's work was even recognized as producing wealth to which she was entitled in the event of divorce. Spartan women could possess and inherit property and could even dispose of it in their husband's absence. In the fourth century B.C., Spartan women actually controlled two-fifths of the land and property in Sparta (Pomeroy, 1975).

The protective sexual morality for Athenian women was essentially absent in Sparta, a feature we have come to contrast in high and low sex ratio societies. In Athens, the husband of a wife who was seduced or raped was compelled to divorce her; in Sparta, adultery and rape carried only monetary fines. Lesbianism apparently also flourished in Sparta, as might be expected in a sex-segregated society, but there is no mention of homosexuality among Athenian women. The widely reputed prevalence of male homosexuality in classical Greece might be thought to be inconsistent with the purported characteristics of a high sex ratio society. One such characteristic is a protective morality for women, particularly to preserve privileged sexual access to them. If the dominant sexual outlet of males were homosexual, such protection would be unneeded. Historical accounts indicate that Greek men were bisexual; moreover, the importance of having *legitimate* heirs required appropriate sexual constraints on women. The widespread belief that the Greeks of classical times were rampantly homosexual may in large part have been created by the contrast between the ascetic attitudes of the Christian civilization that followed in later centuries and the casual acceptance of bisexuality among the classical Greeks.

Courtly Love in the Medieval Period

In the United States and in some other Western countries, relationships between young men and women have often been associated with love and romance. During the first half of the twentieth century this was vividly reflected in popular songs, in fiction, and in film romances created in Hollywood. This set of beliefs and practices emphasizes the unique desirability of the woman loved, as well as her goodness and purity. Often the male has experiences of self-deprivation and sacrifice for his loved one, in exchange for a fantasied final state of unending bliss in marriage to her. Since the romantic complex appears only in some societies, it has been something of a mystery to scholars, who have speculated endlessly about its origins. But only one scholar, Herbert Moller (1958–59), has made an extensive effort to link this complex to a shortage of women, and his work was an important impetus to our sex ratio project.

Our view is that this romantic complex is especially impelled by high sex ratios created by a scarcity of women. Its appearance in certain places and times in the medieval period, as well as in colonial and early America, supports this idea. In Moorish Spain in the ninth, tenth, and eleventh centuries sex ratios were high, and upper-class women were especially scarce. This condition was brought about by population shifts resulting from wars and the migration of males. During these centuries, Hispanic-Arabic love poems similar to later troubadour lyrics appeared and became prominent among the upper classes. The poetry of Muslim Spain expressed themes of the spiritualized love of women by men, emphasizing restraint, tenderness, the avoidance of gross satisfactions, and devotion to their beloved. In some parts of southwestern France and southern Germany, upper-class women were also scarce, and it was then that the courtly love tradition became an important cultural theme within the upper classes.

The great value of these women was also illustrated by the custom in some places of *bride-price,* where either the bride or her family had to be paid handsomely for the privilege of marrying her. During this later period, much of Europe shifted toward low sex ratios, with men in short supply, and women in excess. According to our argument, when sex ratios are low, women are not supposed to be valued, so how is this intensely romantic culture to be explained? In this historical instance it turns out that high sex ratios prevailed for limited subgroups of the population. The kinds of social constraints that prevail over the pairing of men and women can determine whether a de facto undersupply or oversupply exists. In southwestern France in the 12th century, and in Southern Germany in the later 12th and 13th centuries, the emergence of a courtly love tradition coincided with social conditions that created intense competition among men for a small group of noble women. Political and economic changes in both locales created a need for a larger secular class of heavily armed knights and lay administrative personnel. Many of these men were needed because of the building boom in castles occurring from the eleventh to the thirteenth century. Thus, the nobility became an open class. A class of men known as ministeriales emerged, men of uncertain origin, who were needed by and acceptable to the nobility. Many achieved wealth and power. By marrying noble women, they could climb still higher, consolidating and confirming their new upper-class status. Below the ministeriales were other aspiring, ambitious men, many of whom moved upward through being knighted.

This influx of men into upper-class status created an extraordinarily high sex ratio in that status. But this made it difficult to find a woman of noble status, even for a man with genuine noble origins, and marriage downward could result in a serious loss of status. A good marriage meant superior social status, more property, and secure status for one's children. The inevitable intense competition for a suitable bride created the exaggerated wooing that characterizes the courtly love tradition. Moller describes the essence of this theme:

> In the classic version of courtly love, . . . the male lover presents himself as engrossed in a yearning desire for the love of an exceedingly beautiful and perfect woman whose strange emotional aloofness and high social status make her appear hopelessly distant. But the frustrated and sorrowful lover cannot overcome his fascination and renders faithful "love service" to this "high-minded" and exacting lady who reciprocates in a surprising manner: she does not grant him the amorous "reward" which he craves, but she gives him what immeasurably increases his "worth": she rewards him with approval and reassurance. The great lady accepts him as being worthy of her attention, but only at the price of behavioral restraint and refinement of manners, that is, at the price of courtois (courteous) behavior. . . . The fantasy content of the courtly love complex was not altogether pleasurable: to crave against hope the possession of an inaccessible woman, who usually was understood to be already married, to suffer agonizing fears of rejection, and to gain the coveted approval of a protecting figure only at the cost of self-denial and frustration. (1958–59, p. 137)

Misogyny in the Late Medieval Period

Herbert Moller (1958-59) wrote only of the social effects of a scarcity of women but apparently did not consider the reverse phenomenon. However, a nineteenth-century German scholar took note of the overabundance of women in the late medieval period, and described many social effects emanating from this demographic condition (Bucher, 1882). The year A.D. 1000 was a pivotal point for changes in medieval society. During the next two centuries, the European population began to grow rapidly, and spread out across distant frontiers. Towns and cities emerged. Two factors contributed to lower sex ratios, representing a surplus of women. The increasing urbanization favored the longevity of women by reducing the hard physical labor of farm work; and, with more adequate food supplies, the middle and higher classes expanded, with more women members. Also single women and widows migrated to the town or city.

Consistent with the sex ratio thesis, the reduced value of women when they are abundant drove down the exorbitant bride-price characteristic of the earlier medieval period to a point where the bride and the groom were expected to make equal contributions to a marriage. But, starting in the twelfth century, the increasing surplus of women steadily eroded the marriage rights of women. Limits were imposed on the groom's contribution, and the wife's right to a portion of the household property on the death of her husband was reduced. Analyzing thousands of marriage agreements, Herlihy (1974) traced the decline of the bride-price or reverse dowry from earlier centuries until it virtually disappeared and noted that it was followed by a rise in the dowry to be paid by the bride's family. The dowry increased during the 13th and 14th century and eventually became so large as to document Dante's remark in his *Divine Comedy* that the birth of daughters struck terror into their fathers' hearts.

Rulers and legislators attempted to control the sizes of dowries, without much success. The age at first marriage was driven ever downward, a result of the anxiety of parents to get their daughter properly betrothed: this simply increased the pressures further, by reducing the supply of eligible men. That men had to be paid to marry young women was not the only measure of the low value of women in this low sex ratio society. In such societies, we expect males to be reluctant to make a marital commitment and some public disparagement of marriage itself to occur. The easy availability of women increases brief sexual encounters and licentiousness. The literature of the late medieval period illustrates these themes. The earlier sympathetic views toward women held by the Church shifted to a negative stance. Women themselves often questioned the value of marriage.

Since in low sex ratio societies many women cannot acquire status through making a good marriage, they attempt to gain an economic, cultural, and sexual existence for themselves outside of marriage; to some extent this puts them in competition with men for scarce resources. One such result in the medieval period was the emergence of the *Frauenbewegung,* or women's movements, noted by Bucher (1882). No longer was there sufficient accommodation for women in religious orders and convents. Some helped to form and became a part of heretical groups. Many women emerged as spokeswomen for their cause and sharply questioned traditional female roles. A common theme was the disparagement and hatred of the family.

Especially notable were the communal settlements of women, usually in towns. The numerous settlements in northern Europe, especially in Flanders, called *Beguines,* were lay organizations rather than religious ones. The antagonism toward them is partly shown by the fact that, in the early fourteenth century, the canon law of the Clementine decrees defined the Beguines as an "abominable sect of women." Despite such official opposition, these communal settlements continued to grow. Especially notable is that these Beguines produced a radical feminist literature suited to the conditions of the times: they argued that women could commune *directly* with God, without going through a *male* priest! (Manz, 1975; McConnell, 1969; Tarrant, 1974).

The numbers of "independent" women were so great that many, often surreptitiously, entered the trades through their families or other benefactors. Widows, wives, and daughters participated in work with husbands or fathers. Increasingly, they were hired outside of their own families. Trade unions that were exclusively female, in occupations such as weaving, sewing, and working with textiles, were formed. Even prostitutes formed a powerful guild, complete with their own pension plans. Thus, the low sex ratio condition drove women to seek economic parity with men, in a fashion similar to contemporary times.

Now that we have sketched sex ratio effects in several historical periods, it seems desirable to present brief descriptions of our "ideal types" or "models" of high and low sex ratio societies.

High Sex Ratios: An Undersupply of Women

Where young adult women are in undersupply, they would be more highly valued. What they would be valued for would depend upon the society. Most often, single women would be valued for their beauty and glamour and their company would be coveted. Married women would be valued as wives and mothers. Men would extend themselves in the competition for wives and would be willing to make and keep a commitment to remain with them. In such societies, women would largely achieve their satisfactions through assuming traditional domestic roles and would be less interested in achieving economic or sexual independence. They would experience a subjective sense of power deriving from their scarcity, power that would be expressed largely through traditional female roles rather than in political or economic realms.

Both men and women would stress sexual morality involving monogamous relationships, especially for women. This arises from the male desire to possess his own partner and to protect himself from competition with other men. Thus, virginity in potential wives is apt to be prized. But this morality does not prevent a double standard; males might be promiscuous while females would be expected to be chaste. Especially where women had some freedom in choosing a mate, the competition among men for a female partner would often produce a romantic tradition. Being deprived of female company would stimulate male longings and fantasies and would encourage the elaboration of a romantic love tradition with its songs, poetry, and other customs.

Low Sex Ratios: An Oversupply of Women

When young women are in relative oversupply, the social, cultural, and economic trends would, in some respects, be opposite to those of an undersupply. Women would have a subjective sense of powerlessness and would be devalued by the society. They would be apt to be treated as mere sex objects. Marriage would be less valued by men; it would not have to be offered in exchange for acquiring a sex partner.

Sexual libertarianism would be the prevailing ethos, shared by men and women alike, although the options would be much greater for men. Liaisons would be briefer than in high sex ratio societies, and adultery would be commonplace. Love and romance itself would be devalued. Women would react to these circumstances in various ways. Some might redouble their efforts to attract or keep a man, making sacrifices and going out of their way to please him. Other women would rebel, feel resentful, rejected, and angry. They would reject the traditional feminine role and would be impelled to strive for various forms of feminine independence, particularly of an economic and sexual nature. Feminist movements appropriate to the society in question would be likely to be launched.

EXPLAINING SEX RATIO EFFECTS

The final task is to explain why these differences exist, how these social changes come about, and to identify the conditions that are responsible.

Marital Opportunity Ratios

In dealing with contemporary populations, ordinary sex ratios proved to be too gross for specifying the conditions under which social effects would occur, especially where imbalances were not very great. Consider a sex ratio for a total population. It includes children and the elderly, and married as well as unmarried individuals. Thus the overall ratio might be biased by a vast difference in the numbers of elderly men and women, while younger single men and women might be present in equal numbers. Further, the inclusion of married couples greatly attenuates sex ratios. They must be excluded in order to obtain the correct perspective on the proportion and number of unattached persons lacking a potential partner in the population.

Our interest was particularly in relationships between young men and women during the time that they were still single, in the kinds of relationships that are formed in marriage during the childrearing years, and in the duration and stability of marriages. So it was important to develop an index that would bear more directly on those selected cohorts of the population. This led to the concept of *marital opportunity*. This condition affects not only opportunities for marriage but also for casual contacts and nonmarital living arrangements. Moreover, it may well have an impact on family stability because it provides a provocative opportunity for extramarital affairs.

Earlier I called attention to the common practice of men marrying women who are 2 or 3 years younger than themselves, and the "marriage squeeze" on women that is produced if these male and female cohorts were born at a time of steadily rising birth rates. This suggested that marital opportunities could be measured more precisely by looking at ratios for male and female cohorts that were suitable for each other with respect to age. In the United States, the average difference in age at first marriage has been about 2.5 years. So a crude index of marital opportunities for particular cohorts could be formed by comparing numbers of women with numbers of men 2 years older.

These opportunity indices for White Americans are shown for a range of ages in Fig. 13.1, for 1960 and 1970. The marriage squeeze is dramatically illustrated. Women who were eventually to be caught in the marriage squeeze were in 1960 still too young to be affected, and so nearly all age categories of women have more than enough potential partners in the marriage pool. But by the 1970 census, those born during the rising birth rate (ages 23 to 35 years) were eligible for marriage. As shown in Fig. 13.1, their marital prospects were precipitously lower than those of women in the same age category in 1960. Marital opportunity indices can only be calculated where modern census data are available. They require marital status information by single-year ages rather than the more commonly reported age intervals, and so we have used them primarily for our analysis of white and black populations in the contemporary United States.

These indices proved essential to constructing and testing a theoretical explanation of the links between sex ratio imbalances and relationships be-

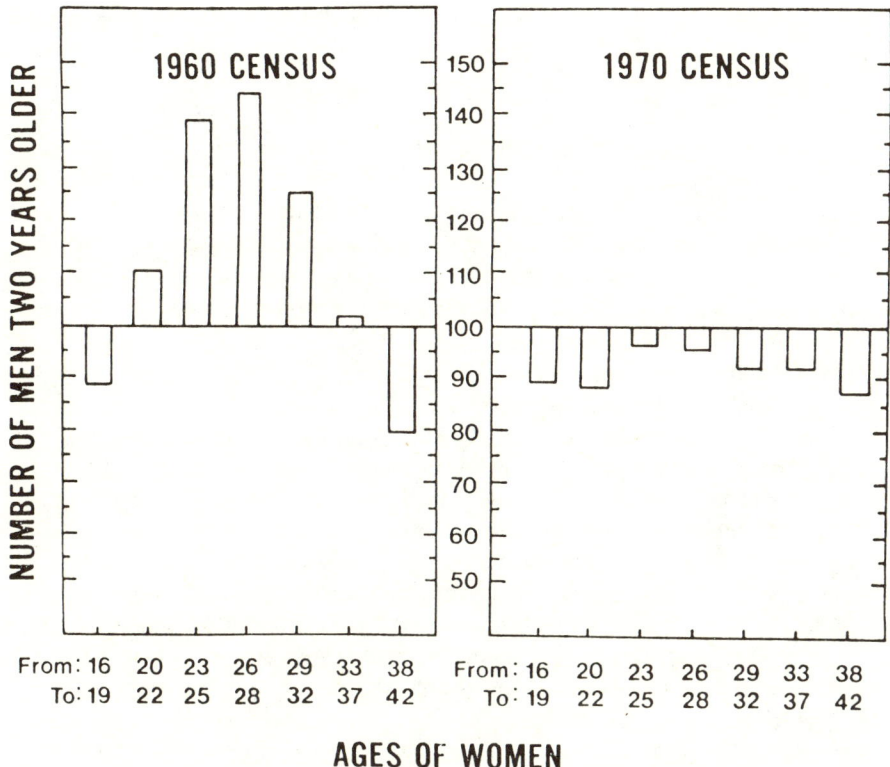

FIG. 13.1 Marital opportunity indices for white women in 1960 and 1970, by age.

tween men and women. The use of the gross sex ratio in historical periods, however, can be defended. To solve the problem of dealing with population sex ratios rather than marital opportunity indices, we limited ourselves to historical periods where the imbalance was so apparent and so gross that it had to include men and women in the age cohorts of interest, and where the imbalance persisted for many years. A fortuitous condition actually reduces the risk appreciably: the life span in the earlier historical periods examined was far shorter than it is today, and so a much greater proportion of the population automatically would be in the appropriate age cohorts.

Asymmetry in the Sex Ratio Models

Looking at the gender roles and associated attitudes and behaviors that characterize our sex ratio models, a curious asymmetry becomes immediately apparent. When men are in short supply and women are in abundance, men take advantage of the situation by "playing the field." They are apt to have simultaneous and successive relationships with more than one woman, and they are wary about committing themselves to a monogamous relationship. Further, women are more independent and more sexually permissive.

But now consider the reverse situation where women are scarce and men are abundant. Symmetry would prevail if women had simultaneous and successive relationships with more than one man, and if women were cautious about commitment to a man. But just the opposite happens! In societies where women are scarce, women form monogamous relationships, brides are expected to be virgins, and sexual constraints on women are often written into a moral code. So, clearly, imbalanced sex ratios have asymmetrical effects which depend upon which gender is scarce. One or more powerful conditions *other than the sex ratio imbalance* must therefore be operating to bring about this ubiquitous asymmetry.

The asymmetry may be further demonstrated by attempting explanations of sex ratio effects in terms of certain principles. A simple *supply principle* might be tested: a scarce supply of the opposite sex makes it more difficult to find a suitable partner. So in low sex ratio societies, where women are in excess and suitable men are hard to find, we would expect women to marry at a later age, to obtain more divorces, to constitute a larger pool who are single or divorced at any one time, to delay longer before remarrying, and so on. Census statistics for the 1970s, when men were scarce, compared with 1960, when they were not, strikingly confirm all of these statistics (Guttentag & Secord, 1983, Chap. 7).

What about high sex ratio societies, where men are in excess, and women are scarce? If the sex ratio had symmetric effects, and the supply principle held, we would expect men to marry at a later age, to have more divorces, to have a larger proportion who are single or divorced at any one time, and so on. But just the opposite is true, according to census statistics (Guttentag & Secord, 1983, Chap. 7)! Compared with 1970, in 1960 when women were harder to find, men married at an *earlier* age, obtained *fewer* divorces, and a *smaller* proportion remained single. So, plainly, an explanation in terms of supply works for women, but not at all for men, and so must be rejected.

Inconsistent results are also obtained if, following economics, we look at a more sophisticated *supply and demand* principle. When a commodity is in abundant supply, its price falls and it is less desired. This principle fits the value placed upon women in high and low sex ratio societies, where the value of women is high and low, respectively, and corresponds directly with their scarcity. But the value of men does not seem to shift in a comparable manner. In low sex ratio societies, where men are scarce, women are apt to have more cynical attitudes toward them and, in high sex ratio societies, where men are in excess, to have more favorable attitudes toward them.

These simple principles will not suffice. An adequate explanation must not only account for the two kinds of models, but must also explain the asymmetry of these models. I have suggested that a powerful condition is interacting with sex ratio imbalances to produce the observed effects. A careful study of the two kinds of societies points to this condition and explains the asymmetry at the same time. It suggests that two kinds of power are operating here, and that the distribution of these powers between the two genders account for all of the findings. One form of power is *dyadic power,* which derives from sex ratio imbalances via processes of social exchange. The other is *structural power,* which is a relatively invariant condition that has prevailed throughout recorded history. The latter form of power especially accounts for the asymmetry of the two sex ratio models through its impact on the exercise of dyadic power.

Before moving on to discuss the explanation of asymmetry in terms of social powers, some alternative explanations should be mentioned. Some might argue that the asymmetry between the two sex ratio models is quite simply explained by assuming that men have a much stronger sex drive than women. Women are passive and leave sexual initiatives to men. Hence, when men are in surplus supply, women, unlike men, do not go out and find more than one partner. But this assumption is contrary to the evidence. While women in many societies may behave in accordance with it, this is more apt to be culturally conditioned than to be a result of female biology. For example, an intensive review of sexuality among female primates, emphasizing the more careful, less biased observations of the last decade or so, makes clear that female primates of many species are sexually aggressive and seek multiple matings (Hrdy, 1981). Although the inference to human females constitutes a giant leap, the primate evidence puts the burden of proof on anyone who wants to assert that sexuality among human females is the opposite to that of several of the primate species closest to humans.

But there are some obvious and undisputed differences between men and women: Men have greater muscular strength and women bear and suckle children. In the past, given the primitive nature of warfare, hunting, agricultural production, and other important pursuits of society, these biological differences meant that men and not women gained political and economic control. These observations are consistent with and lead into our explanation of asymmetry between the two sex ratio models in terms of the two forms of social power.

Dyadic Power

I assume that readers are relatively familiar with social exchange theory (Becker, 1975; Blau, 1964; Thibaut & Kelley, 1959; Kelley & Thibaut, 1978) and so only briefly show how the dyadic power of men and women in relation to each other derives from it.

Dyadic power is derived from sex ratio imbalances as a result of applying the following propositions from social exchange theory:

1. Two persons in a dyad strive to maximize their *outcomes,* which are the net effect of the psychological *benefits* and *costs* associated with social exchanges or interactions.
2. Their *satisfaction* with or *attraction* to the relationship depends upon the degree to which their outcomes are above what they expect to experience—their *comparison level.*
3. Their *dependency* on the relationship and their willingness to remain in it is a function of the extent to which their outcomes remain above what they expect they would experience in alternative relationships—their *comparison level for alternatives.*

The comparison levels are based upon previous experience in similar relationships, and even on imagined relationships. The term *dyadic power* is apt because it pertains to power over one's partner and holds only so long as both partners stay in the two-person relationship.

To apply these propositions to imbalanced sex ratio conditions, consider circumstances where there are appreciably more single women than men. Individuals do *not* need to be aware of this; their attitudes and actions are shaped by their previous experiences in successive dyads. Because, compared with their female partners, men have had more choice in the dyads they have formed, their comparison level within an existing dyad is higher—they expect higher outcomes than their partner does. Second, they have more social power in the dyad. Dyadic power in essence stems from an individual's resources for satisfying a partner and the dependency of that partner on those resources. Of course, the relative powers and dependencies of individuals in dyads depends partly on the manner in which their personal characteristics create resources or dependencies. A handsome or wealthy man has more resources for satisfying a woman—if she values (is dependent on) those characteristics—while a beautiful or vivacious woman has more resources than a plain or dull woman.

But what is important to note is that when women are more abundant than men, men will be better able to form more satisfying dyads than women will. They can choose among women, selecting those who provide the highest outcomes in a dyadic relationship. Since women's choices are limited, their comparison levels decline; they expect less from a relationship with a man. He expects more from the same relationship, since his options—his comparison level for alternatives—are much greater. By the same token, women are more dependent than their male partner on an existing relationship, for their alternative options are fewer. Thus to maintain the relationship, they must provide outcomes for their partner that are at least equal to the best alternative relationship available to him. While this principle also applies equally to the male partner, the outcomes that need to be provided for her by her male partner to keep her in the relationship are lower because her comparison level for alternatives is lower.

Very important is an underlying assumption here: For these inferences to be valid, individuals must be able to make their own decisions about staying in a dyad, leaving it, or entering a new one. So sex ratio imbalances would function very differently in societies where matches are arranged by one's family. And even in a relatively free society like ours, some constraints on movement do emerge. A strong commitment, perhaps best illustrated by marriage, greatly increases the costs of leaving the dyad, as experienced in guilt feelings, leaving the children, giving up one's property in a divorce settlement, financial costs, and so forth. So alternative options would have their strongest impact on individuals who are not deeply committed to a particular monogamous relationship.

In sum, dyadic power enables its possessor to negotiate more satisfying outcomes in a relationship, to choose partners who can provide more satisfaction, and to be less dependent on the relationship. It encourages movement from an existing relationship to one with higher outcomes, and it weakens commitment to any particular partner. As we have seen, when men are in short supply, they exercise their dyadic power to fit these principles, but women do not.

Structural Power

Nothing I have said so far explains the asymmetry between high and low sex ratio situations. If dyadic power alone were the determining factor, men and women could use it in exactly the same way as men do. But in fact they cannot, because of the structural power that men hold. Men use this structural power to shape male-female relationships to their relative advantage in *both* high and low sex ratio societies. But they apply their structural power very differently, depending upon whether their dyadic power is low or high.

Structural power is a reflection of the many social structures that enable a category of individuals to have a part in shaping the behavior of other individuals. Thus its sources are economic, political, and legal. Economic resources can be used to exact compliance, political ones to establish social policy, and legal ones to pass laws controlling certain actions. But structural power is more than any of these because its consistent use leads to established social practices and to the acceptance of selected social values congruent with the exercise of such power. These are reflected in the kinds of age-sex roles that are maintained for males and females (Secord, 1982). Ultimately, some of the pressures are further enhanced because they become associated with moral values. It is this entire complex that I call structural power.

No one can doubt that men have held an overwhelming advantage in structural power. Societies throughout history have been male dominated. In this light we may look again at high and low sex ratio societies to see how they differ, and how male structural power has shaped male-female relationships in these two kinds of societies. When women are scarce, their increased dyadic power should enable them to pick and choose so as to achieve the best alternative relationships. And that potentially could include more than one relationship, in or out of marriage. In high sex ratio societies where single women are free to choose a mate, they are able to exercise their dyadic power. Its exercise may often lead men to woo a woman, showering her with gifts, and professions of undying love. And even in marriage, if women are free to divorce their husband, their dyadic power may exact favorable exchanges from their spouse.

But *exactly the opposite* often happens. Women are often *not* free to exercise their dyadic power. Men use their structural power to place economic, legal, or moral constraints on women's use of dyadic power. What happens is that, in high sex ratio societies, women are more sheltered—protected from contact with men. Virginity becomes a moral value for single women, and adultery an immoral act or even a crime for married women. Other constraints may arise through divorce laws that favor husbands rather than wives, as we found in Athens but not Sparta. These constraints are created by men to protect the relationships they have formed with women and to exclude from competition men who are outside of the relationship. With sustained social practice, the constraints acquire the force of morality and are often accepted by women themselves.

Such constraints on women, particularly on their sexual behavior, have been exercised in a multitude of ways. Although we do not have sex ratio data on the particular tribes that practice it, clitoridectomy, infibulation, and other related practices to destroy a woman's sexual pleasure represent extreme examples of control. But constraints extend well beyond direct sexual behavior and generally involve sheltering or cloistering. The relative strength of the structural power of men can often intensify the extent to which women are controlled. A case in point is the Chinese-Americans in the nineteenth century.

One of the highest sex ratios in all history was that of Chinese-American laborers brought to the United States in the nineteenth century to build the railroads. At one point the ratio was 2,000 men per 100 women. Unlike many frontier immigrants, Chinese-Americans brought with them their traditional social structures, which consisted of clans, tongs, and communal associations. Since these were exclusively male, Chinese-American men had enormous structural power, while women had virtually none. Consequently, a vast proportion of the women were locked into brothels controlled by the powerful tongs. Those few women who were not forced into prostitution were often married to wealthy Chinese-Americans, but even they were sheltered and protected almost to the point of being kept prisoners (Lyman, 1970, 1974). This is a striking example of how the potential dyadic power of women can be crushed by the overwhelming structural power held by men.

This argument for the role of structural power in creating asymmetry between high and low sex ratio societies would be greatly reinforced if a society could be found where women had the power. In that instance, women should behave as men do in a low sex ratio society where women are abundant. Women should take advantage of the abundance of men and have multiple relationships with men, either simultaneously or successively. So far as I know, no full-fledged society of that sort exists. But I did discover a report on the Bakweri, who in 1950 lived in a cluster of villages in Cameroon, West Africa, in a plantation economy. The native social order had been shattered by the imposition of a British protectorate, which established a judicial system to maintain order among natives according to British norms. The Bakweri had a sex ratio of 236, with an extremely high divorce rate and great instability in relationships between men and women (Ardener, Ardener, & Warmington, 1954).

Bakweri women were highly valued, both as wives and for casual sex, and the family of the bride had to be paid substantial sums for their daughter in marriage. But most notable was that Bakweri women had considerable structural power—mostly economic. Both single and married women gained this power through engaging in casual sex with the large number of single men who migrated to the area. Many Bakweri women earned enough through casual sex to have an independent income, and some paid off their own bridewealth in order to be free of their husband. Husbands were deeply unhappy about this, but were powerless to act, given their meagre income. Wives often changed husbands if they found a man who could pay a larger bridewealth and repay the earlier bridewealth. So here is a society where the superior economic power of women gained through casual sex enables them to exercise their dyadic power to their own considerable advantage. They use their economic power in much the same way that men do in low sex ratio societies.

I have been discussing how structural power is used by men to constrain dyadic power in high sex ratio societies. Now let's turn to low sex ratio conditions. Here, men instead of women are scarce, and men combine their dyadic power with their structural power to gain even more advantage, just as the Bakweri women did when they held both sources of power. Unlike men when women are scarce, women in a low sex ratio society where men are scarce ordinarily have very few means of countering the dyadic power of men. Since women are plentiful, men no longer need to compete with each other for possession of them, and constraints on the sexual behavior of women weakens, and permissiveness is the rule. Men become more reluctant to commit themselves to one woman in a monogamous relationship, and they are more apt to leave such a relationship for a more attractive alternative.

The behavior of women under these disadvantageous conditions is striking. Some women choose to better their status through a relationship with a man, and so are apt to cater to him, to maximize his outcomes to the extent of their capabilities. But others, many of whom may have bitter experiences in relating to men, do strive to constrain the dyadic power of males. First they stress female independence. This includes striving particularly for economic independence—an attempt to alter the balance of structural power. This is illustrated in our own society. Women at the highest occupational level or the highest income bracket are much more likely than other women to be single or divorced, presumably because this is an option they can afford (Carter & Glick, 1976). Feminist movements are apt to arise, which through organizational means increase the structural power of women and help to develop an ideology which counters male-oriented ideologies and which stresses independence and equality for women in all realms of life. The consciousness raising that accompanies this kind of movement is apt to draw in many women who had previously defined their relationship with a man as satisfactory, but who became willing to work for the cause of other women, and who may even eventually redefine their present relationship as unsatisfactory. Still another solution is to adopt Lesbianism as a life style: this totally eliminates a woman's dependence on a man for sexual satisfaction and compansionship.

CONCLUSIONS

Social psychologists whose training has been almost exclusively in psychology are all too often oblivious to the impact of social structure on human behavior and to the part that social structure must play in providing adequate explanations of social behavior. Treatments by psychologists of social exchange theory, for example, view parties to an exchange as free agents who can negotiate for themselves the best possible outcomes. But this conception is badly mistaken in the case of many kinds of social exchanges that take place in life settings, and it is especially misleading when the exchange process takes place between men and women.

Social structure may have an impact on social exchanges in many different ways. In the present study, a demographic condition, the imbalanced sex ratio, has been shown to affect exchanges in a rather direct fashion, by modifying alternative comparison levels. But social structures also impact in various other ways. They can readily produce differences in the relative power of the parties and thereby upset the balance of their negotiating power within the dyad. Various kinds of enduring social structures, such as gender roles and moral values impact in somewhat more complex ways on exchange processes. The more structured the gender roles, the less free the role actors are to engage in negotiations.

Knowledge of the manner in which social structural processes interact with psychological processes can only be gained through the study of human behavior in its natural context. The investigation reported here demonstrates that this need not be limited to one's own contemporary society, but that the examination of appropriate historical periods and settings may greatly enrich our understanding of social psychological phenomena and may even provide substantive evidence in support of a theory.

REFERENCES

Ardener, E., Ardener, S., & Warmington, W. A. *Plantation and village in the Cameroons: Some economic and social studies.* London: Oxford University Press, 1960.

Becker, G. S. *The economic approach to human behavior.* Chicago: University of Chicago Press, 1975.

Blau, P. M. *Exchange and power in social life.* New York: Wiley & Sons, 1964.

Bucher, C. *Die Frauenfrage im Mittelalter.* Tubingen: Verlag Der H. Laupp'schen Buchhandlung, 1882.

Carter, H., & Glick, P. C. *Marriage and divorce: A social and economic study.* Revised edition. Cambridge, MA: Harvard University Press, 1976.

Glick, P. C., Heer, D. M., & Beresford, J. C. Family formation and family composition: Trends and prospects. In M. B. Sussman (Ed.), *Sourcebook in marriage and the family* (2nd ed.). Boston: Houghton Mifflin, 1963.

Guttentag, M., & Secord, P. F. *Too many women? The sex ratio question.* Beverly Hills, Calif.: Sage Publications, 1983.

Harward, J. *Report on an investigation of the ratio between men to women in the Athenian population of the fourth century.* Draft 2. Cambridge, Mass.: Unpublished manuscript, October, 1976.

Herlihy, D. The medieval marriage market. In D. B. J. Randall (Ed.), Medieval and renaissance studies, *Procedings of the Southeastern Institute of Medieval and Renaissance Studies, Medieval and Renaissance Series No. 6,* Summer, 1974.

Hexter, J. H. *The history primer.* New York: Basic Books, Inc., 1971.

Hrdy, S. B. *The woman that never evolved.* Cambridge, Mass.: Harvard University Press, 1981.

Kelley, H. H., & Thibaut, J. W. *Interpersonal relations: A theory of interdependence.* New York: John Wiley & Sons, 1978.

Lyman, S. *The Asian in the west.* Reno, Nev.: Social Science and Humanities Publication No. 4, Western Studies Center, Desert Research Institute, University of Nevada System, 1970.

Lyman, S. *Chinese Americans.* New York: Random House, 1974.

Manicas, P. T., & Secord, P. F. Implications for psychology of the new philosophy of science. *American Psychologist,* 1983, *38,* 399-413.

Manz, R. *Historiography of the Beguine movement.* Unpublished paper, July, 1975.

McConnell, E. W. *The Beguines and Beghards in medieval culture.* New York: Octagon Books, 1969.

Moller, H. Sex ratios and correlated culture patterns of Colonial America *The William and Mary Quarterly,* 1945, *2,* 113-153.

Moller, H. The social causation of the courtly love complex. *Comparative Studies in Society and History,* 1958-59, *1,* 137-163.

Pomeroy, S. B. *Goddesses, whores, wives, and slaves: Women in classical antiquity.* New York: Schocken Books, 1975.

Secord, P. F. (Ed.). *Explaining human behavior: Consciousness, human action and social structure.* Beverly Hills, Calif.: Sage Publications, 1982.

Tarrant, J. The Clementine decrees on the Beguines: Conciliar and Papal versions. *Archivum Historiae Pontificiae,* 1974, Vol. 12.

Thibaut, J. W., & Kelley, H. H. *The social psychology of groups.* New York: John Wiley & Sons, 1959.

Weldon, J. E. C. (transl.) *Aristotle's politics.* London: Macmillan, 1907.

14 Family Life and the Marketplace: Diversity and Change in the American Family[1]

Jan E. Dizard
Amherst College

Howard Gadlin
University of Massachusetts/Amherst

The family is a universal institution—present in all societies. It is in the family that certain transhistorical features of human life are most clearly and unambiguously illustrated. At the same time, when we examine the family historically we are struck by how familial activities and relations are intertwined with many other kinds of activities and relations. Family life must be understood as part of the cultural life as a whole. Among the most important features of society which interact with family is the organization of work and production and consumption. We shall call this constellation of forces the marketplace. Indeed, while sociologists have for many decades been studying the relationship between the economy and the family, psychological research, with a few exceptions (e.g., Piotrkowski, 1978) is noteworthy for the absence of a serious consideration of the world of work as it affects people's lives, directly or indirectly.

In the present chapter we propose to outline a scheme within which we can understand the changing forms of family structure as attempted adaptations to changes in the marketplace over the past three centuries. For the most part we will limit ourselves to a discussion of the American family. Discussions of the American family almost always have an evaluative tone. For much of the past century, observers of the American social scene have been debating putative changes in the nation's families. Popular commen-

---

[1]This essay is the first of several projected essays by the authors on the American family. Our work has been collaborative in every sense and the order in which authorship is listed is simply alphabetical.

tators, religious leaders, social scientists and social critics, each for different reasons, have bemoaned or decried the passing of the stable family; the family that included a rather extensive array of kin and was oriented to the succor of its members. Repeatedly, from the 1880s on, a moral crisis has been announced and its locus has been the family. The current generation, it has been argued regularly, no longer follows their parents' advice or example, but, instead, impetuously follows their own path. Absorbed in strivings and pleasures of the moment, the young have been portrayed as ignoring the responsibilities of marriage and parenthood and turning a deaf ear to the needs of the elderly and children.

Though negative analyses have struck a resonant chord, suggesting some truth to such portraits of family life, others have been quick to rise to the defense of the family. Although changing, these analysts claimed, the family was not facing extinction but, rather, was adapting to changing circumstances. This debate continues today, in terms scarcely changed from those of the late nineteenth and early twentieth centuries. Responding to the mounting voices of alarm in the sixties and early seventies, Mary Jo Bane, in a book entitled *Here to Stay* (1976), reviewed the critics' case and proceeded to argue that both census reports and surveys show Americans have an undiminished propensity to marry and bear children. While the divorce rate is high and rising, Bane points out that nearly 4/5 of all divorced persons in fact remarry. Indeed, Bane sees divorce as a kind of emotional safety valve, allowing people to terminate unhappy marriages, freeing them to be able to begin again, hopefully on a happier, more fulfilling course with a new spouse. Though divorce is no doubt difficult—or worse—for children, in the past, children were much more often faced with the death of a parent, arguably an even more traumatic disruption of family life. She concludes that, overall, Americans are more satisfied with the institution of marriage than ever before.

After careful review of the evidence, noted economist Sar Levitan, in a volume written with fellow economist Richard Belous, *What's Happening to the American Family?* (1981), reaches similar conclusions. Though the bonds between husband and wife are clearly more fragile, marriage is the overwhelming choice of living arrangement. Caplow, Bahr, Chadwick, Hill, and Williamson (1982) reach the same conclusion after their updating of the Lynds' classic study of Middletown (Muncie, Indiana). Rather than decay and fragility, they were surprised to discover a high degree of marital satisfaction and an equally high commitment to the norms of a stable family.

In spite of these closely reasoned and carefully researched reassurances about the basic integrity of the family, doubts persist. Certainly, marriage is still popular: most couples still look forward to bearing children, and nuclear families are not totally atomized. People still rely on kinfolk for emotional support, financial assistance, and for a diffuse sense of "connectedness." But equally clearly, marriage does not mean the same thing to contemporary couples as it did to couples even two generations ago. Divorce is more likely, by a considerable factor (Cherlin, 1981); with a divorce rate above 40%, one has to believe that the meaning of the marriage vow is changed, however much the wording may have stayed the same. In these circumstances it is the very commitment of each of the marriage partners that must be suspect. Indeed, recent survey studies show substantial consequences of the instability of marriages for attitudes toward marriage.

Veroff, Douvan, and Kulka (1981) note that for all the professions of contentment in marriage that appear in surveys, there is still the nagging problem of divorce and a "greater tolerance of people who reject marriage as a way of life." They continue:

> This loosening of the normative necessity of being someone's wife or husband in order to be a valid adult undoubtedly has had and will continue to have profound effects on other reactions to marriage . . . . Divorce has become more than a peripheral institution. It has come to be a much more viable alternative to marriages that are not successful. (p. 191-192)

But it is not just the availability and viability of divorce that indicates a change in the meaning of marriage and family. Conceptions of both parent and partner roles have been transformed and other areas of identification have emerged that make the family less and less the exclusive source of emotional gratification that it once purported to be, especially for women. Though children are still desired by most couples, the interactions between parents and children are increasingly informed by new values and structured by new modes of childrearing. Parents who are more protective of their own autonomy and less inclined to bend every personal resource to their children's needs turn to day care and other hired help for assistance with the care and rearing of infants and preschool children. And interaction with kin beyond the immediate nuclear family has also undergone change—a weakened, much more circumscribed interaction.

At least some of the confusion and divergence of views may be derived from a simple misunderstanding borne of casual use of terms, "The Family" as an institutionalized expression of attachment between two adults is, in all likelihood, in Bane's words "here to stay." Institutionally, although there are alternatives in the abstract (casual liaisons, nursery-reared children, communal arrangements, etc.), our society gives no evidence of sustaining a massive defection from committed coupling with the blessings of state and/or church. But taken individually, families, as opposed to THE FAMILY, can be seen to be in considerable disarray. In the absence of widely acceptable alternatives, divorce does not threaten to undermine our commitment to familial life, but it surely creates havoc with the lives of individual family members. And it breeds cynicism in the young. Veroff et al. (1981) remark:

> Indeed, in questions dealing with norms, and general attitudes toward marriage, we find that the young are distinguished by their skepticism toward marriage and their neutrality and tolerance toward alternative life paths. (p. 182)

Clearly, families can be in considerable trouble without jeopardizing the stability of the family as an institution. If the two levels of analysis are conflated, confusion will result.

The situation is made more confusing because most discussions of the family overlook the obvious fact that there are many kinds of families. Some are large; others small. Some consist of a highly autonomous husband-wife pair, with or without a child, quite remote from relatives; others consist of a thick network of kin, linking individual nuclear families tightly together into a sprawling ensemble. In some families, husband and wife adhere to traditional roles of breadwinner and homemaker; in increasing numbers, others are moving toward more egalitarian divisions of roles. All are families, but their differences may overwhelm their similarities. Before we can even begin to reach a clear determination of the condition of the family in modern America, we have to attempt to discern the varieties of family styles extant and attempt to assess the particular dynamics of each of them. To discuss the variety of family styles, we must understand family life in terms of attempted adaptation to changing social and economic circumstances. These adaptations are best illustrated through a comparison of modern and preindustrial families.

It has long been commonplace for commentators on the family to note the differences between the typical family of preindustrial societies and that of modern, industrial societies. The preindustrial—or traditional—family is large and complex. Individual households generally contained one or more persons in addition to the nuclear family comprised of husband, wife, and their children. Even when nuclear units lived in separate households, individual households were enmeshed in an elaborate and dense network of kin relations. Often, the relations between kin were paramount, eclipsing the bonds that held husband and wife together. The requirements of subsistence discouraged, if they did not preclude altogether, impulses that husband and wife might have had to withdraw from the inclusive network of kin. Life was simply too precarious to turn one's back on the support offered by the expanse of relatives, even when maintenance of kin relations required the dramatic subordination of personal wishes to the needs of the larger unit. Relatives looked out for one another in a context in which there were few other sources of solace. To be sure, along with support and comfort came considerable intrusions on personal autonomy: parents ruled on matters of mate selection, timing of marriage, land tenure, and a host of decisions affecting the life of the young couple. Individual needs were, except for the patriarch, routinely subordinated to the needs of the larger family unit. The sharing and cooperation, which in our own day looks so noble and attractive, was less freely given than it was constrained by economic necessity, superstition, and fear (Colson, 1974).

Although some aspects of the traditional arrangement persist, at least in some quarters, families today are generally organized quite differently. Normally, the nuclear unit is much more clearly demarcated and the couple is much more autonomous. Bonds between spouses are both more intense and more volatile, and bonds to relatives less intense and less pervasive. The couple is usually expected to be much more self-sufficient, emotionally and financially. Households are typically small and simple—that is, consist only of members of the nuclear family. The needs of individuals are by no means automatically subordinated to the needs of the larger family ensemble and the needs of the couple are routinely given precedence over the claims of relatives.

The demise of the traditional family has been gradual and even in the most highly developed of industrial societies is by no means complete. This unevenness, coupled with the complexity of the process of change itself, has shaped much of the disagreement that persists among analysts of the family. For some, the weakening of connections between kin signals the "end of the family." But the dilution of kin ties needs to be understood in terms of the process of industrial development. It is in the very nature of the transformation from a subsistence, preindustrial society to a consumer-oriented, industrial society, that increasing numbers come to rely not on kin but on the impersonal artifices of the marketplace and the bureaucracies that service this marketplace.

The growth of the marketplace—both for jobs and for goods and services—made it possible for large numbers of people to reduce their reliance on kin. Though the actual historical process was very halting, over time, as occupations grew more numerous and as products available for purchase grew in both volume and diversity, there were more possibilities for the bold and the disgruntled to leave the network of kin, the world of subsistence, and strike out on their own. Indeed, one of the striking features of the changes in family life in American history is the degree to which changes which seem required by altered economic circumstances, quickly appear among the aspirations of those affected by transformation in economic conditions. For example, at that period in the mid-nineteenth century when many people were forced economically to abandon rural for urban life, there surfaced in considerable numbers people who aspired to and advocated the very new modes of city life which necessity required of them. In agriculture, the shift came with the move toward producing crops for cash, which slowly but inexorably led to the decline of the family farm, classical locus of the traditional virtues of familism. In the cities, the shift came with the gradual rise of the middle class dependent upon occupational success, rather than on kinfolk, for their satisfactions in life.

In the early stages, when the needs of the economy were for capital goods, rather than consumer goods, the fact that most people remained thoroughly embedded in familial networks of exchange was highly significant. In that context, low wages and long hours would be tolerated. The expanse of kin provided a buffer for the ill and disabled and, until the 1930s, the family, again in its expanded form, could absorb the unemployed in hard times. They could be reassimilated into the land-based system of subsistence. This "reabsorption" was by no means easy, materially or psychologically. But in the absence of alternatives (unemployment compensation, etc., which came late to the United States, compared to Europe), families provided for the general welfare as best they could. In a sense, the traditional family form helped subsidize the development of industrial capitalism.

By the late 1800s and early 1900s, however, the economy underwent a decisive change. Heavy investment in capital goods—factories, railways, and so on—was diminishingly profitable in the absence of a lively and growing consumer market; without consumers willing and able to buy, there would be no point in producing and there would be no freight to carry. Again, haltingly, occasioned by tumultuous conflict between employer and employee, producer and consumer, the United States slowly shed the culture of frugality and thrift, the culture of homespun, and moved toward a culture of ever higher levels of consumption. Workers demanded higher wages and shorter hours. New, more romantic, images of marriages began to be promoted in order to add encouragement to accentuating the nuclear family, and to downplay the virtues of homemade, the wisdom of elders, and the authority of tradition. Store-bought was better: more modern, more efficient, more stylish, more nutritious, more rational. The advice of experts, whether in nutrition or child rearing or homemaking, was preferable to the advice of parents (Ewen, 1976).

Though there had been movement away from the traditional family and toward the modern, nuclear family for many years, even centuries, the changes described above did not become widely generalized until quite recently. The force of inertia is not to be underestimated and the attractions of the new way should not be overestimated, particularly since these attractions were mitigated by the instabilities of the market. In good times, the traditional family "exported" members to the modern arrangement; in bad times, the net flow was in the opposite direction. This unevenness meant that only those most insulated and protected from the fluctuations of the economy could sustain a fully modern family—a family comparatively remote from kin, focused in on itself, heavily dependent upon the marketplace for its material needs and for its emotional needs as well. For a considerable span of time, then, the modern family had a stable social composition only in the middle class. By the 1950s, however, the middle class itself began to undergo rapid change. Not only did it begin to expand at an unprecedented rate, but its composition changed as well. Technical, professional, and bureaucratic occupations came to predominate over entrepreneurial modes (C.W. Mills, *White Collar,* 1951).

To add to the confusion of family analysts, the postwar developments added a new consideration: the nature of the modern family itself began to be diversified. The ideals of the nuclear family, long nurtured in a small-town, entrepreneurial middle class, exploded into contradictions just at the moment when they seemed to be astonishingly successful. Those scholars who had deftly shown that earlier concerns for the family were misplaced, that families were adapting to new styles that promised greater personal satisfaction were suddenly confronted with soaring divorce rates, ideological challenges to prevailing sex roles, and increasingly bold assertions of individualism that separated sexuality from marriage and that even sought to put marriage on a par with any number of alternatives.

We have already enumerated some reasons for the persistence of disagreements on the health of the family. As is clear, there is little or no consensus among family experts on how to characterize the current status of the family. It is our belief that many of the current contradictions may be resolved by moving beyond the singular concept of "The Family" to a consideration of multiple family forms. Most treatments of the family, whether critical or not, do not even acknowledge the possibility that a range of family forms exist. Rather, there has been a steady effort to force families into the traditional/modern dichotomy. Young and Willmott (1973) are an important exception here. Much of the social science literature takes the nuclear family form which has been dominant mainly in the middle class as normative. What we propose below is a typology of family styles that will help make clear both the strengths and weaknesses of the contemporary family, while allowing us to see more clearly the ways that family life and the broader, more impersonal factors of economy and politics interact to produce the particular dynamic that is so much of concern today. Having done this, we will then examine several outcomes in contemporary society. Let us first examine the diversity of families that now constitute "The Family" in the United States.

I. VARIATIONS IN THE CONTEMPORARY FAMILY

As has been noted, virtually all commentators on the family agree that the traditional family has been superseded. Most argue that the processes of modernization, whether undertaken under private or public sector auspices, has led to an autonomous nuclear family unit at the expense of the tightly knit extended family. Agreement ends here. Yet, not only are there differing accounts of the process, there are also widely differing accounts of the outcomes. Part of this confusion seems to stem from a desire to see the process of change as both one way and largely complete, ending in as much normative uniformity as prevailed when the traditional family held sway. When Parsons (Parsons and Bales, 1955) asserted that the contemporary American family was a nuclear unit, isolated from relatives, that was predicated on emotional and material self-sufficiency, critics (cf. Litwak, 1960) were quick to point out that many nuclear families maintain close ties to relatives and depend on an intrafamilial flow of resources. Not all families, it seems, are "modern," in Parsons' terms at least. Parsons' "typical" family, it turns out, was typical of but a slice of Americans, predominantly an upper-middle-class slice. Moreover, as we shall endeavor to demonstrate, there are several forms that the modern, isolated nuclear family can take—there is no one, widely accepted family style, if there ever was one.

Though the determinants of change that have resulted in the present situation are indeed complex, one feature stands out as especially crucial for shaping family life. As we suggested above, modernization has meant that the face-to-face dependencies upon which traditional societies were based have been progressively replaced by increasingly impersonal, formal dependencies. Few members of contemporary society any longer directly produce their own means of subsistence. Instead, people enter the labor market, earn a wage, and exchange that wage for the goods and services they can afford. To the extent that this arrangement works smoothly, people will come to depend less on family ties and connections and more on market. But this "arrangement" seldom works smoothly—there are many rough spots: Depressions and recessions are the most obvious. Even in prosperous times, particular occupations or industries may be failing, whole regions may be declining. Until public programs (welfare, unemployment, etc.) were enacted, such misfortune almost invariably occasioned a flow of people back toward the venerable reliance on kin. Even today, in part because public policy is inadequate and welfare programs miserly, hard times cause many to drift back toward greater reliance on family-based support. These features of American modernity, when coupled with nostalgia for the traditional family, mean that there has remained a social base for reproducing a version of the traditional family.

The persistence of poverty produces a variant of the traditional family—what we call the Expanded Family. Like the traditional family, relations with kin are intense and extensive, often competing directly with ties between spouses (Stack, 1975, pp. 111–115). Unlike the traditional family, however, marriages tend to be quite unstable, largely because under modern, urban, industrial conditions the male head of household is a problematic figure. Stripped of the capacity to earn a living, males tend to become peripheral and females tend to dominate the family network. The instability of the husband-wife bond has often been interpreted as a signal of familial disintegration, but among the poor, it now seems clear that the expanded network of kin is more often than not quite stable. Although disagreement on this topic is widespread and heated, the volatility in relations between men and women is not to be ignored and, most probably, contributes to the array of miseries that afflict the poor. However, it is still the case that women, young children and at least some adult males find in their expanded families whatever comfort, joy, and strength there is to be found among the poor in our society.

The expanded family is, in effect, an adaptation to a market-oriented society by those who are disadvantaged, for whatever reasons, in the market—those who are regularly unemployed and/or poorly paid. What they cannot claim in the market must either be done without or, in some form, provided for outside the domain of the market. Exchange within networks of relatives is the time-tested alternative. Clothing, furnishings, food, money, and services are all exchanged in family networks. Households are permeable, able to absorb new additions or temporary residents in need of shelter. Though young people pair off, fully as affected by the romantic ideals of marriage as any others in our society, economic forces and public policy itself greatly limit the extent to which the poor can even hope to realize the ideal of nuclear family self-sufficiency. In such circumstances, the husband-wife bond is frail and expectations are frequently frustrated. The result is dependence upon kin and reduced emphasis on family and personal autonomy.

Some observers of the expanded family celebrate its capacity to persevere and buoy its members up under conditions of extreme deprivation and humiliation (Aschenbrenner, 1975). These strengths are not to be gainsaid. But it must be remembered that its virtues are largely born of cruel necessity. Given realistic choice in the matter, few would deliberately choose the expanded family over what is by now the conventional nuclear family. While the self-oriented upper middle class may find valued expressiveness in "creative divorce" and "open marriage," it is clear that among the poor and near poor, obliged by circumstance to endure high rates of divorce and infidelity, the prosaic attractions of a stable marriage in which spouses are trusted and where the nuclear couple can stand on its own is clearly preferred (Scanzoni, 1977).

In contrast to the expanded family is what may be called, after Burgess' (Burgess and Locke, 1950) pioneering work, the Companionate Family. The companionate family is distinguished from the expanded family (and from the traditional family) by its relative autonomy from kin and the correlative emphasis placed upon the relationship between husband and wife. Until very recently, the companionate family came as close as any to a society-wide normative ideal: husband and wife are more than simply partners, they are supposed to be "best friends," sharing activities, and intimate feelings as well as the more mundane joys and sorrows of life. Husbands are expected to be the main provider, though of late it has become widely acceptable for the wife to work as well. But, classically, neither spouse was to be preoccupied with his or her work. The companionate family is family centered. Fathers become dads who are pals to their sons and (more problematically) daughters; moms are at the center of family life, omnipresent and resourcefully sympathetic. Ties to relatives are present and strong, especially to immediate relatives, but unlike the traditional and the expanded families, households are decidedly not permeable: the home is for the nuclear family. Relatives can visit but are not expected to remain. Children are rarely moved from one household to another as personal circumstances and economic exigencies change.

The companionate family emerged historically as the first successor to the traditional family and was then, as we have already noted, largely a middle-class possibility. To even approximate the level of emotional and financial self-sufficiency offered by the companionate ideal requires a reasonably secure position in the economy. Today, the companionate family prevails among the stable working class and the lower middle class. In the nineteenth century, the companionate family was the epitome of integration into the market, buying more goods and services than it produced on its own or exchanged within the orbit of kin. This was also the family form that was hailed as a "haven in a heartless world" (Lasch, 1977). Today, its relationship to the market seems less thoroughgoing, largely because others have dramatically increased their dependency upon the impersonal apparatus of market exchange.

Long accustomed to working outside the home and to purchasing most goods and services, we tend now to see the familism of the companionate family as partaking of tradition. Indeed, the companionate family sits somewhere midway between a kin orientation and a market orientation. And therein lies its particular instability. The companionate family requires that partners provide for each other much of the mutuality and support which in the traditional was supplied by a diversity of kinfolk. In order for companionship to flourish, especially after the first romantic blushes have faded, at least two conditions must be met: the couple must be able to spend considerable time together and husband and wife must see one another as substantively equal. In mutuality, both conditions are difficult to sustain over time, making the companionate family less stable than it might otherwise be.

As the homespun philosopher of the market, Ben Franklin, knew, time is money. Leaving the traditional family greatly increases the couple's need for income. A home of one's own, by mid-twentieth century, required considerable income, amounts that were beyond the reach of the vast majority of Americans until the post-World War II boom. A home also meant a car, and often two cars, not to mention the refrigerator, washer-dryer, TV, and on and on. To keep up with this rising standard of living, many felt compelled to work overtime, get second jobs, or upgrade skills and commitments to work in order to increase earning power (Oppenheimer, 1982). Economic pressures, now focused predominantly on the couple, rather than the larger array of kin, consistently emerge as a source of tension and disruption in the accounts of contemporary studies of the family. These pressures on the breadwinner tend, over time, to produce the characteristic division of labor that yields separation between the "man's world" and the "woman's world" (Rubin, 1976). This separation into different spheres reduces the mutuality of interest and perspective necessary for companionship.

This tendency for husband and wife to grow apart, and thus to experience declining companionship, is exacerbated by the persistent legacy of patriarchal traditions. Typically, early marriage is a period in which husband and wife can achieve a modest utopia of equality. Even doing household chores together can be romantic and fun. But over time, especially after the birth of the first child, sex roles become more assertive and sharing and companionship begin to erode. Feelings are hurt or blunted; routine replaces adventure; commitment wavers and misunderstandings grow (Komarovsky, 1962; Rainwater, 1962; Rubin, 1976).

Under such circumstances, some families drift back toward an involvement with kin, back toward an assertion of traditional patterns. Others strive for even greater involvement in the marketplace, making a virtue of the separation of husband and wife roles. Others find themselves in tumultuous relationships. Still others hang on and make do, maintaining respectability and suffering stoically the absence of involvement and affection that follows the decline of companionship.

The companionate family, with its emphasis on the relationship between husband and wife, is in tension both with kin and the marketplace. One way of resolving this tension is to embrace even more fully the institutions and rhythms of the market. Families that do so might well be called Professionalized Families. The professionalized family looks like the companionate family with one crucial difference: It is largely organized around the principal task of maintaining the husband's high level of occupational commitment. The asymmetries in sex roles that the companionate family inherits become deliberate and explicit features of the professionalized family. The wife is expected to invest the same kind of talent and energy in her household tasks as her husband invests in his occupational endeavors. The result, supposedly, is a well-run, efficient family in which all prosper (Fowlkes, 1980).

Given the world of careers, the professionalized family is necessarily mobile. Its roots in a community are shallow, its ties to kin are subordinate to career contingencies. The husband is often a shadowy presence, at least insofar as young children are concerned, since major portions of the waking day find him occupied away from the home. Even at home, the husband often is preoccupied with work-related matters. The wife is expected to keep the children and home well ordered, posing as few distractions for her husband as possible. In exchange, the husband is expected to earn a handsome income, supporting the family at a high level of comfort, if not affluence.

Needless to say, such families are heavily dependent on the marketplace. Occupational success defines the family's success. Standing in the community is indicated by the quality of home, as well as the variety of accompaniments to upper-middle-class family living: elaborate electronic devices, home hobby supplies, expensive lessons for children, and so on. There may be some residual exchanges within narrow circles of relations—help with an initial down payment, a college fund for grandchildren—but the nuclear couple is essentially on their own, setting their own goals and plans largely in terms of their own immediate needs and aspirations.

The professionalized family comes as close as any to being the family that Parsons (Parsons and Bales, 1955) described as quintessentially modern. Though he acknowledged that it was subject to many strains and stresses, he believed it best adapted to the requirements of a modern industrial society. Insulated from the often harsh impersonality of the marketplace, children could flourish under the watchful and informed guidance of mothers, assisted at each turn by a host of professionals. Well educated and securely employed, with comfortable income and thus able to avail themselves of modern conveniences and the best advice of experts, this type of family seemed ideally suited to lay to rest fears that the companionate family was intrinsically fragile.

Parsons (Parsons and Bales, 1955) clearly saw a tension between the values of the marketplace (rationality, impersonality, self-interest) and traditional familial values (love, sharing, cooperation). So long as humans required the comfort and emotional security that seems still to be best provided in a nurturant—that is, family—setting, the values of the marketplace must somehow be kept at bay. The companionate family, to the extent that it could do so, achieved this distance by moderating its expectations, both for occupational advancement and for consumption, ideally balancing market forces with a commitment to family. But the most rapidly increasing occupations, the technical, managerial, and professional jobs of the postwar era, seemed to require levels of commitment not easily reconcilable with either companionate or traditional family life. The perfect solution seemed to merge the old with the new—the wife would sustain the old, presiding over the world of familism, albeit with modern technical and expert assistance; the husband would pursue the new. Together, the family would enjoy the best of both worlds.

In theory, the professionalized family appeared sound. Limited historical experience with high status families of this modern sort also suggested stability and well-being. However, it was not long after the professionalized family began to proliferate that problems emerged. After WWII, the ranks of the upper middle class began to swell—the demand for technical skills, for managerial talent and for professional services simply exploded. Suburbs grew and became the locus of the rapidly expanding ranks of the professionalized family.

It wasn't long before reality overtook theory. Intimations of difficulties appeared in a variety of critiques of the suburbs, where one found hesitant and muted concern for family life (cf. Seeley, Sim and Coopley, 1956). Many questions revolved around the absence of the husband. Beneath the civic activism and the hectic schedules of shopping, lessons for kids, and meetings, some detected malaise among the wives. The heralded stability of this family form was exploded with the publication of Betty Friedan's *The Feminine Mystique* (1963), the rightly famed critique of the place accorded the women in the society. While aspiring to a general critique of patriarchy, in fact Friedan was almost exclusively concerned with the problems of college-educated, upper-middle-class women: women whose husbands are absent for most of the day, working in the city, women whose education and talents are now to be totally devoted to keeping husband actively and enthusiastically career oriented and rearing children to assume their rightful places in this world. While many aspired to the affluence and comfort, once there, no small number of wives discovered emptiness and frustration. It was not long before sons and daughters of the upper middle class discovered alienation. Together, given the struggle against racism started in the south by blacks and, a bit later, the outrage of a criminal war, mothers, sons and daughters helped create the cultural and political upheavals of the sixties and early seventies (cf. Evans, 1979; Flacks, 1971).

By now, after nearly two decades of analysis and commentary, the weaknesses of the professionalized family have been well rehearsed. Wives were, simply put, in an untenable position. That many managed to maintain themselves and their marriages does not detract from the indictment, it only indicates that humans can adapt. Many refused, implicitly or explicitly, to adapt. In some instances, often associated with a husband's flagging occupational commitment, a couple would move back toward a more companionate form of marriage. The husband would disengage from intense job involvement and pursue more family-oriented undertakings. In some instances, the marriage collapsed.[2] In others, wives began to respond to the asymmetries between themselves and their husbands by deciding to enter the world of the market themselves.

Wives, beginning almost unnoticed in the 1950s, began to seek employment outside the home. Unlike early times, though, when poverty was the spur, this time middle- and upper-middle-class wives sought jobs. In part this reflected the enormous pressures on income that are posed by suburban living and the disengagement from kin. Even moderately successful breadwinners faced more expenses than income, as appetites simply expanded beyond anyone's imagination.[3] But equally important, the increased labor force participation of wives represented the growing realization among women, especially college-educated women, that their sense of self-worth, like their husband's, needed confirmation in the public arena, in the marketplace.

What mothers were doing hesitantly and often guiltily, daughters began to pursue explicitly and even insistently. If the idealized equality of the companionate ideal could not be realized, then a new understanding of equality was called for: Let husband and wife be equally engaged in occupational endeavor, sharing the breadwinning and, presumably, the household chores as well. A new family form emerged from the tensions and contradictions between family and marketplace: the Dual Career Family. The dual career family represents an even fuller realization of the tendency to rely less on kin and more on the market. It is, in this sense, the family form most explicitly organized around the central task of maximizing occupational involvement of both spouses. Highly mobile—indeed, it is no longer uncommon for spouses to maintain two residences in separate cities in order to accommodate career contingencies that take them in separate directions—and affluent, the dual career family has little room for family life that is distinct from the marketplace. If the dual career couple has a child (more than two

---

[2]Surprisingly, we can find no current census data with which to fully substantiate this assertion. While marital disruption still is inversely related to status, indications abound that divorce is rapidly becoming common to high-status groups. An inkling of this is provided in Glick and Carter (1976, pp. 402–406). The very rapid rise in divorce in the last two decades could only have occurred if strata heretofore relatively "immune" from divorce had contributed disproportionately to the swelling ranks of the divorced.

[3]One measure of the growth in appetite and the consequent stress on family income can be found by comparing the growth in disposable income to the expansion of home buying and the expansion of consumer credit. Sweezy and Magdoff (1970) report that between 1946 and 1969, disposable family income rose by a factor of 3.9. At the same time, outstanding home mortgage indebtedness expanded by a factor of 11.6. And, futher, short-term consumer credit (revolving charges, credit card balances, and the like, including automobile loans), expanded by a factor of 14.6. In other words, Americans were accumulating indebtedness far more rapidly than their incomes were increasing.

14. FAMILY LIFE AND THE MARKETPLACE 295

is highly uncommon), it is cared for outside the home; or by hired help; experts are heavily relied upon, for advice about childrearing, careers, and crises in personal relations (Rapoport & Rapoport, 1976).

Divorce, as near as we can tell, tends to be quite high among dual career couples, not simply because the wife's career allows her greater freedom and independence, though obviously it does, but also because both husand and wife have heightened senses of individuality and of their own personal needs. However flexible and adaptable they may be (or however hard they may try to master one or another of the several pop psych strategies for ensuring adaptability), this heightened sense of individuality makes it harder to mesh smoothly with each other's needs. Deferral of gratification is more difficult, taking cognizance of others' wishes more abrasive, autonomy more tempting. The satisfaction of needs within the constraints of a relationship with another autonomous person is not terribly efficient when calculated from the individual's point of view. The market is preferable: There you need not take others' needs into account, except indirectly and abstractly.

As long as one's job is engaging and satisfying, as long as it provides a large enough income, the market can be very satisfying. Indeed, so much is this the case that increasing numbers of young men and women are postponing marriage itself in order to better avail themselves of the pleasures our society offers, unencumbered by having to take a spouse or child's needs into account. Single-person households are now the third most frequent household and their numbers continue to soar. While technically not a family at all, the rapid growth of single men and women needs to be taken into account, if only because they point to the possibility that growing numbers may choose to do without family life altogether.

In a sense, young singles represent the culmination of the trends we've been describing—in the abstract, they suggest the realization of *homo economus* in the private as well as the public sphere. Single-person households (exclusive of the lonely aged, mostly widows, who now constitute on the order of 7 to 10% of all households) seem to represent a form of defamilization and integration into the marketplace. Emancipated from their parents, and not committed to a family of their own, singles must rely almost exclusively on their job and their ability to purchase commodities and services as sources of identity and satisfaction.

Before we turn our attention to several particular features of the upheaval in the family that this proliferation of family styles represents, let us draw out and make explicit the general features of the dynamic we have sketched. As we do so, it would perhaps be helpful if we graphically set out the range of family styles we see extant in America today (see Fig. 14.1).

In a very real sense, each of the successive types of family represents an attempt to balance family and market forces, private and public spheres.

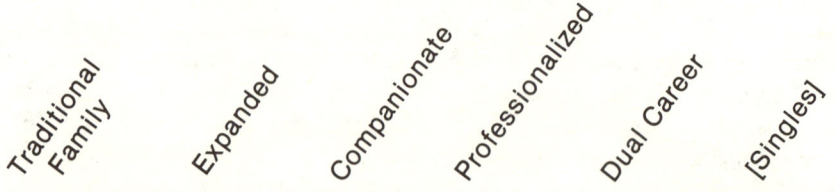

-low integration into marketplace   high integration into marketplace

FIG. 14.1

None is abstractly more suitable than another, none more adapted to modern society. Indeed, it is quite probable that in the course of a life cycle, two individuals could "experiment" with each of these styles, finding each in some sense a resolution of particular dilemmas. Each of these styles, then, represents individual action in the face of pressures on living standards and attempts to adjust traditional conceptions of family life with current realities. None is likely to become as widespread and consenually accepted as was the traditional family precisely because the family is no longer an imperative, and there are systemic forces producing incentives to retard if not altogether dissolve family ties.

II. AUTONOMY AND THE MARKET

The present analysis has emphasized a felt increase in autonomy and a proliferation of choice resulting from integration into an expanding market. To be sure, putting matters this way ignores other effects of the spreading market—alienating work; disruption of communities; increasing materialism and secularism, to name only a few of the more important effects. All bear on the family, but they do so insofar as these associated changes all lead to enlarged ranges of personal choice. Of course, the range of choice is not the same for everyone. Persons in the lower classes have greatly circumscribed choice, at least compared to their upper-middle-class counterparts. But compared to their ancestors, even the very poor have a range of choices—a range of personal identities, as it were, that would have been unthinkable not too many generations ago. In traditional societies, and for most people in our own society as recently as 80 years ago, people were woven together in a complex fabric of personal dependencies. It was virtually impossible to ignore or be oblivious to the immediate consequences of one's actions in the social surround. If your crop was a good one, and your cousin's was not, you would be expected to share your bounty. Over time, the market dissolves these kinds of bonds, and with this disappearence individuals are freed to pursue their own designs. The flow of goods and services, once largely directed by sprawling families, seems increasingly regulated by the impersonal marketplace and by equally impersonal bureaucracies. The range of people on whom one directly depends narrows, allowing individuals to focus more of their resources—material and emotional—on this shrinking circle of associates. The result is a sharply elevated feeling of independence and individuality.

To be sure, members of the society do remain fundamentally interdependent. However, these interdependencies are largely formal and fleeting: they are literally faceless multitudes who collect the tolls, make the clothing and food, repair the telephones, and so on. With others no longer directly implicated in one's lives, we become content to pursue our own narrow interests, trusting that everyone else is doing likewise. The larger outcomes—poverty for some, affluence for others, and so on—are not felt to be of one's making and, thus, one does not ordinarily feel responsible. Over time, accustomed to thinking of oneself and the narrow circle of family around one, dependencies become irritating, constricting, even threatening. There are enormous temptations to shed even more of them—narrowing still futher the circle of interdependencies. Families become smaller. More and more wives become restive in their dependent role and begin to seek ways of being more autonomous.

And what becomes of the children in this process? At the outset it is clear that there are simply fewer of them. The child poses a threat to the personal autonomy of both mother and father. Moreover, children face a very different emotional and developmental milieu than heretofore. First of all, parental authority is vastly altered. In traditional societies, children were largely obliged to follow in the footsteps of parents—there were simply few alternative paths to follow. As a consequence, parental authority was ineluctable: parents possessed the skills and aptitudes that children needed to acquire if they were to take their rightful place as adults in the society. Children no doubt resented this state of affairs and some inevitably rebelled against their parents. But for the most part, the combination of limited options and the parents' monopoly of skills weighed heavily in favor of parental dominance.

By contrast, with the onset of the industrial revolution, and with accelerating speed thereafter, parental monopoly was broken. New skills were demanded, skills that parents did not possess. For a time, parental control was maintained by parents actively choosing the person a child would be apprenticed to. But as the pace of industrialism quickened, even this was rendered impossible. As development proceeded, schools began to attract the young and soon became compulsory. Parents' views gradually ceased to be the last word—children came to have first-hand acquaintance with plural sources of authority.

To the extent that parents insist on obedience and insist that children follow their prescriptions and proscriptions, the parents are increasingly cast in the role of being authoritarian, rather than authoritative. If parents cling to their traditional forms of domination, they increasingly appear to their children as capricious and arbitrary. But if they yield to the authority of teachers and employers, they come to be seen as extensions of a larger public authority, rather than as buffers between the child and the larger world. Either way, relations between parents and children become strained and the child's dependency on parents increasingly likely to be experienced as vulnerability.

This sense of vulnerability has been heightened by a correlative development. One of the standard instruments that parents use to socialize children is the threat to withdraw love and approval, a deliberate play on the child's dependent status and emotional needs. In most societies, and in our own until the early 1900s, this dependence was mitigated by the many tasks, concrete and practical responsibilities, that children carried out for the well-being of the family. For example, being sent to bed without supper one night would be softened in the morning by the fact that parent and child resumed a round of tasks that placed them working side-by-side: after rejection came the reaffirmation of interdependence.

Modern conditions alter this exchange significantly by drastically reducing the practical, cooperative tasks that require a child's participation, that reassure the child of his or her value to the family. Increasingly, the threat to withdraw love ("go to your room," or "if you do not get good grades, Daddy will think less of you") is not as readily buffered by the continual affirmation of reciprocation. Children today do not experience themselves as useful members of a household; their dependence on parents is not mitigated by their ability to contribute materially to the welfare of the family. Sometimes explicitly, often implicitly, children are reminded how much their parents have done for them. This in turn ramifies to the experience of love and emotional dependency: to be emotionally dependent upon someone, to love or need someone, is to become vulnerable to manipulation by that "someone."

It is in this nexus of relations that we think the quest for autonomy lies. To be free of direct dependencies is to be freed of the vulnerability that opens one to being manipulated. As increasing numbers of families move along the continuum we have just described, more of them approximate the conditions in which the threat to withdraw love is the major instrument of socialization, unalloyed by reaffirmations of being needed. This in turn produces, in the extreme, a reluctance on the part of the child to become emotionally dependent. Later this same aversion may become manifested in an avoidance of intimate relations; one fears recapitulating as an adult the vulnerability one experienced as a child. Thus we find an increase in the numbers of young people who profess no desire to become married, who indicate in word and deed a resolve to remain autonomous from the emotional commitments that would, from their point of view, compromise and restrict their freedom of action.

This outcome, it should be quickly noted, is not simply a function of changes in childrearing occasioned by industrialism. The conditions of adult life amplify the importance of this dynamic which originates in childhood.

Paradoxically, this same dynamic may be the source for a directly opposite phenomenon as well: the desire among some, especially middle-and upper-middle-class youth, for complete absorption in communal experience. From the few published reflections of former cult members now available (cf. Richardson, 1978) one theme frequently is mentioned: the young person experienced parental love as conditional upon his or her performance. Feelings of inadequacy and anger surfaced, followed by a longing for acceptance without conditions. One or another cult seemed to offer just such an arrangement. Instead of becoming wary of love and dependency, some seek total submission, a startling complete rejection of autonomy.

Both of these responses to the altered interaction between parents and children are far from common. Most people grow up neither fearful of forging loving relationships nor interested in total submersion in one or another cult. But, the pressures that incline some to one or another extreme are no doubt widely felt, contributing to the paradoxical findings of social research on the family with which this essay began. Most desire loving intimacy (though increasing numbers evince reticence on this score) at the same time that it is clear that fewer are willing to make the sacrifices and compromises that are required to sustain such a relationship over a long time period.

Care needs to be taken here to avoid the conclusion that the desire to remain single, cult membership, and the rising divorce rate are all to be laid at the doorstep of parent-child interaction. What we are suggesting is that the broad structural trends, summarized under the rubric "industrialization," do two things more or less simultaneously and that, together, they come to produce the changes we have been describing. First, an array of unprecedented options emerge: new jobs, new commodities, new possibilities for fashioning a life for oneself and one's immediate family. Second, traditional patterns are slowly discredited or undermined: parental authority is undercut as the resources monopolized by parents are devalued, kin networks are supplanted by markets, thrift and frugality are replaced by increased appetite and officially sanctioned appeals to spend. As the internal dynamic of the family is changed, largely in the direction of making dependencies more abrasive, more capricious, the external world is changing in ways that offer the individual alternatives for autonomy.

III. FAMILY, AUTONOMY, AND THE PUBLIC ORDER

The process by which people have become progressively less dependent on family members has been complex, halting, and unsynchronized. The move away from a heavy reliance on family relationships exposes the individual to considerable risk—the risk of rebuff, the risk of failure, and the risk of loneliness. But when the prospects for the individual are bright, when choices proliferate, the risks of staying at home become palpable. In the extreme, parents' expectations become oppressive: some offspring directly rebel while others are propelled toward an avoidance of dependencies as adults. Apart from the extremes, contemporary families have gradually lost their resemblance to traditional families. They are smaller, more remote from kin, increasingly shaped by the demands of occupational life. Throughout, individual considerations become more salient, the family as an integral unit becomes less salient.

This process of modernization, like all social phenomena, varies in specifics from one culture to another. Even now, amongst those societies commonly regarded as fully modernized, there are significant differences in family life to be observed. In Japan, for example, the traditional authority of parents remains strong—the majority of marriages are still arranged by parents for their children, for example—and the closely knit kin network remains an important force in most people's lives. This may be one of the contributing reasons for the much higher rate of savings of the average family in Japan as compared to western Europe and, even more dramatically, to the United States. On the average, the Japanese family saves nearly three times more of every earned dollar than its American counterpart (Kuttner, 1981).

As we have argued above, an expansive and vigorous kin network is inversely related to reliance on the market. This reliance on the market has proceeded furthest in the United States, with the consequences of lower savings rates, higher levels of personal consumption, and greater isolation from kin. In virtually all western European societies, the state has long been an explicit force, not only in fostering economic growth but also in cushioning the harshest consequences of reduced levels of familism. The welfare state, so called, is not simply an anti-poverty instrument, as it tends to be characterized in the United States, but is, much more importantly, an agency that at once sustains the tendency toward autonomy while reducing the likelihood that an individual's drive for autonomy will leave aging parents, a no-longer-loved spouse, or single parent bereft of dignity and freedom of maneuver.

Just as the United States has the lowest rates of personal savings and the highest levels of personal consumption, so too do we have the lowest levels of state spending on welfare. We depend very heavily on markets, celebrating the emancipation of the individual that this form of dependency makes possible. Therein lies the particular recurrent urgency of the fears for the family: Americans have found no way, other than familial, to ensure that persons look out for one another. As the family withers in the face of the imperatives of a commanding market, we are left with a particularly bourgeois version of autonomy: an exaggerated, possessive self with a greatly reduced sense of responsibility for one's fellows. Yet if persons are to be free of the parochial constraints of family, it would seem imperative to find the means of ensuring that some institution other than the family be developed to protect the individual.

In a profound and increasingly troubled sense, the United States is in the worst of two worlds: The traditional familial networks of support have largely been decimated and the public sector is weak. The result bears in on everyone: women who wish to balance career and family life are left to their own devices, devices that even the affluent have difficulty discovering; fathers who wish to share more equally in the tasks of homemaking and childrearing risk being judged inadequately motivated in their jobs, or outdistanced in their careers; growing old threatens even the well-to-do with having to rely on children whose own lives may not be accommodating.

Ironically, it is the political right wing that has mobilized sentiment around the family issue, relying heavily on our lingering nostalgia for an earlier era of family solidarity. The irony lies, of course, in the fact that it has been the unfettered economy, not welfare programs or Equal Rights Amendments or federally supported birth control programs, that appears to have dissolved the family bonds that the right professes such attachment to. By reducing the already miserly supports, family crisis will be exacerbated, not ameliorated. It appears that our nation might be better served by pressing for a more responsive public order, for public policy that restrains the excesses of the market, that encourages autonomy while balancing it with a pervasive sense of social responsibility.

The family, in Bane's words, may be "here to stay," but its meaning for people's lives has not been and will not likely be constant. The tension between individual needs and family integrity will remain with us, making many marriages conflictual and impermanent. It will do little good to bemoan the decline of familism, especially as long as one is committed to high levels of personal consumption and the spread of commodification. Instead, we would be well advised to seek in enlightened and humane public policy those virtues that were once necessarily found only in family life.

REFERENCES

Aschenbrenner, J. *Lifelines: Black families in Chicago.* New York: Holt, Rinehart & Winston, 1975.

Bane, M. J. *Here to Stay: American Families in the Twentieth Century.* New York: Basic Books, 1976.

Burgess, E. W., & Locke, H. J. *The family: From institution to companionship.* New York: American Book Company, 1950.
Caplow, T., Bahr, H. M., Chadwick, B. A., Hill, R., & Williamson, M. H. *Middletown families: Fifty years of change and continuity.* Minneapolis: University of Minnesota Press, 1982.
Cherlin, A. *Marriage, divorce, remarriage.* Cambridge: Harvard University Press, 1981.
Colson, E. *Tradition and contract: The problem of order.* Chicago: Aldine, 1974.
Evans, S. *Personal politics: The roots of women's liberation in the Civil Rights Movement and the New Left.* New York: Knopf, 1979.
Ewen, S. *Captains of consciousness: Advertising and the social roots of the consumer culture.* New York: McGraw-Hill, 1976.
Flacks, R. *Youth and social change.* Chicago: Rand McNally, 1971.
Fowlkes, M. *Behind every successful man: Wives of medicine and academe.* New York: Columbia University Press, 1980.
Friedan, B. *The feminine mystique.* New York: Norton, 1963.
Glick, P., & Carter, H. *Marriage and divorce: A social and economic study.* Cambridge: Harvard University Press, 1976.
Haraven, T. K., & Langenbach, R. *Amoskeag: Life and work in an American factory-city.* New York: Pantheon Books, 1978.
Komarovsky, M. *Blue-collar marriage.* New York: Vintage Books, 1962.
Kuttner, B. Growth with Equity. *Working Papers.* September-October, 1981, pp. 32-43.
Lasch, C. *Haven in a heartless world: The family besieged.* New York: Basic Books, 1977.
Levitan, S., & Belous, R. *What's happening to the American family?* Baltimore: Johns Hopkins University Press, 1981.
Litwak, E. Occupational mobility and extended family cohesion. *American Sociological Review,* 1960, 25, 9-20.
Mills, C. W. *White collar.* New York: Oxford University Press, 1951.
Oppenheimer, V. K. *Work and the family: A study in social demography.* New York: Academic Press, 1982.
Parsons, T., & Bales, R. F. *Family, socialization, and interaction process.* New York: The Free Press, 1955.
Piotrowski, C. S. *Work and the family system: A naturalistic study of working-class and lower middle-class families.* New York: Free Press, 1978.
Rainwater, L., Coleman, R. P., & Handel, G. *Workingman's wife.* New York: MacFadden Books, 1962.
Rapoport, R., & Rapoport, R. *Dual-career families re-examined: New integrations of work and family.* New York: Harper & Row, 1976.
Richardson, J. T. (Ed.). *Conversion careers: In and out of the new religions.* Beverly Hills, Calif.: Sage Publications, 1978.
Rubin, L. *Worlds of Pain.* New York: Basic Books, 1976.
Scanzoni, J. H. *The black family in modern society: Patterns of stability and security.* Chicago: University of Chicago Press, 1977.
Seeley, J. R., Sim, R. A., & Loosley, E. W. *Crestwood Heights: A study of the culture of suburban life.* New York: John Wiley & Sons, 1956.
Stack, C. *All our kin: Strategies for survival in a black community.* New York: Harper & Row, 1975.
Sweezy, P., & Magdoff, H. The long run decline in liquidity. *Monthly Review,* 22 (September, 1970), 1-17.
Veroff, J., Douvan, E., & Kulka, R. A. *The inner American: A self portrait from 1957 to 1976.* New York: Basic Books, 1981.
Young, M., & Willmott, P. *The symmetrical family.* London: Routledge & Kegan Paul, 1973.

15 Traditional, Present Oriented, and Futuristic Modes of Group-Environment Relations

Daniel Stokols
Maryann Jacobi
University of California, Irvine

As abruptly as the "crisis in social psychology" subsided during the mid-1970s, the domain of applied social psychology emerged. The establishment of two annual monograph series (Bickman, 1980; Kidd & Saks, 1980), the development of a new journal, *Basic and Applied Social Psychology,* in addition to the more established *Journal of Applied Social Psychology,* and the publication of several related textbooks (e.g., Perlman & Cozby, 1983) all attest to the rapid growth of applied social psychology in recent years. The explicit emphasis on community problem solving and field research methods within this literature seemed to respond to many of the concerns raised during the 1960s and early seventies about the relevance of social psychology to contemporary societal issues (cf. Elms, 1975; Ring, 1967; Smith, 1973).

The systematic application of social psychological theory to the analysis of community problems such as energy conservation (Stern & Gardner, 1981), family planning (Oskamp, Mindick, Berger, & Motta, 1978), and urban stress (Cohen, Evans, Krantz, & Stokols, 1980) has led researchers from their laboratories into the field and has promoted a more eclectic approach to research methodology than was reflected in earlier, predominantly lab-oriented studies. Despite these developments, however, many observers contend that the "crisis" in social psychology has not subsided. Specifically, the shifts from basic to applied research, and from laboratory toward field studies, have failed to address certain fundamental, theoretical dilemmas (cf. Gergen, 1982; Pepitone, 1981). These dilemmas relate to the restricted temporal, spatial, and cultural scope of much social psychological theory. In an effort to develop parsimonious explanations of social behavior, social psychologists have emphasized narrowly reductionistic analyses while avoiding broader, contextual formulations of social phenomena.

In this discussion, the term "reductionism" refers not to an alleged hierarchical relationship among scientific disciplines (cf. Jessor, 1958, for a discussion and critique of this doctrine), but rather to the restricted contextual scope of many social psychological theories. Social psychological phenomena (e.g., attribution processes, helping behavior, attraction, aggression) are often examined in a de-contextualized manner, as if they can be understood apart from the historical, geographical, and cultural contexts in which they occur. The restricted temporal scope of such research is reflected in its emphasis on short-term situations and events and its neglect of the social psychological dimensions of time (cf. Gergen, 1976; Jacobi & Stokols, 1983). Similarly, much social psychological research is of limited spatial scope in the sense that physical objects and places are viewed as an inert or neutral backdrop for individual and collective behavior. Although the material features of environments have been examined in social psychological studies of noise, density, heat, and air pollution, little attention has been given to the symbolic significance of objects and places for individuals and groups (cf. Stokols & Shumaker, 1981). Finally, social psychological research has all too often treated interpersonal behavior as culturally universal, while neglecting the cultural bases of social behavior (cf. Pepitone, 1981; Triandis, 1978).

The reductionist bias of earlier social psychological theory poses an important challenge for future research: namely, the development of theories that are of broader contextual scope. By developing concepts that encompass the historical, spatial, and cultural underpinnings of social behavior, we can begin to address a diversity of questions that previously were ignored by social psychologists: for instance, (1) In what ways do the symbolic meanings associated with objects and places affect patterns of social behavior? Do groups with enduring traditions, for example, behave differently toward outsiders and toward their own physical surroundings than do those without such traditions? (2) Do symbolically meaningful objects and places serve as social surrogates (e.g., by promoting a sense of security or support) in lieu of more direct interpersonal encounters? (3) Do the physical arrangements of buildings and neighborhoods affect observers' attributions about the occupants of those places? (4) What geographic and cultural factors affect the strength of individual and group ties to specific places?

The present chapter offers a framework for analyzing the temporal dimensions of group-environment relations. The assumptions and emphases of our analysis are directly relevant to the theoretical issues mentioned above. First, we offer a set of terms for describing the ways in which group members construe their collective history as well as their aspirations for the future. Specifically, we distinguish among four different temporal orientations of groups: traditional, present-focused, futuristic, and coordinated (the latter involving a balance of traditional and futuristic orientations). These terms provide a basis for analyzing the historical dimensions of group experience and, at a practical level, are immediately relevant to several community problems including intergroup conflict, health consequences of residential mobility, conservation of environmental resources, and the psychosocial impacts of modern technology.

Second, our analysis emphasizes the symbolic aspects of physical objects and places and the role of environmental symbolism in facilitating group cohesion and continuity. By focusing on the "social imageability" of physical environments (i.e., their capacity to evoke vivid and widely held social meanings among group members; Stokols, 1981), our analysis gives explicit attention to important social psychological functions of objects and places that have been neglected in prior research.

Third, our analysis focuses on group members' collective representations of their shared history and future, rather than on individuals' perceptions of time in relation to strictly personal events (cf. Albert's 1977 discussion of personal time perspectives). Thus, we emphasize processes of social perception or the ways in which group members collectively perceive and ascribe meaning to their activities and material surroundings. Our concern with the social meanings that often become associated with and symbolized by physical environments reflects a group level of analysis—a perspective that for many years appeared to have been replaced by a predominantly "person-centered" approach to the study of social behavior (cf. Gergen, 1982; Steiner, 1974).

PSYCHOLOGICAL PERSPECTIVES ON TIME

Our analysis of the temporal orientations of groups offers an alternative conceptualization of time than is reflected in earlier psychological research. Generally, temporal concepts and measures have been used in psychological studies to describe dispositional attributes of persons or objective features of environments. Examples of the *trait* perspective on time include recent research on personal dispositions toward the past (Taylor & Konrad, 1980), future time perspective (e.g., Albert, 1977; Oskamp et al., 1978), and time urgency as a component of the coronary-prone behavior pattern (e.g., Glass, 1977). Examples of *environmentalist* conceptions of time include analyses of commuting distance and time as a source of personal stress (e.g., Cullen, 1978; Stokols, Novaco, Stokols, & Campbell, 1978); studies of the relationship between spatial and temporal constraints on daily activity patterns and family interaction (e.g., Michelson, 1982); and research in which the attractiveness or aversiveness of stimuli and events are examined in relation to the individual's length of exposure to those events (e.g., Cohen et al., 1980; Stokols, Shumaker, & Martinez, 1983; Zajonc, Crandall, Kail, & Swap, 1974).

The trait and environmentalist conceptions of time are often combined within analyses of the interactions between temporally related dispositions and objective measures of time. This *interactionist* perspective is illustrated by Krantz, Glass, & Snyder's (1974) study of stress reactions among Type-A (coronary prone) and Type-B (non-coronary prone) individuals in relation to the duration of their exposure to random bursts of noise. Similarly, Stokols et al. (1978) found that long distance automobile commuting and frequent exposure to commuting delays were associated with different levels of stress among Type-A and Type-B individuals.

In earlier psychological research, then, temporal variables usually refer to characteristic attributes of individuals or environments; and often, the interactive relationships among these personal and situational variables are assessed. In the present analysis, however, we introduce a set of temporal concepts that refer not to the independent attributes of persons and environments, but rather to various forms of interdependence that arise among people and their sociophysical milieu. For example, the concept of tradition as it is developed below does not refer to the characteristics of *either* persons *or* environments. Rather, it represents an important and enduring form of interdependence that can exist between particular groups and places. Thus, whereas trait or environmentalist perspectives construe time as an independent component of situations, our analysis relies heavily on "composite" terms (such as tradition) which emphasize the inherent interdependencies among multiple components of a particular situation (see Stokols [1982] for a further discussion of component and composite analyses of people-environment transactions).

Temporal Orientations of Groups

A distinguishing feature of organized groups, which is absent among noninteracting or co-acting aggregates, is the shared perception of interdependence among individual members (cf. Thibaut & Kelley, 1959). This perceived interdependence is reflected in group members' awareness of their common goals and activities. Generally, social psychological research on group dynamics has focused on short-term, experimental groups whose common goals and experiences are quite temporary (e.g., Berkowitz, 1978; Hare, Borgatta, & Bales, 1965; the longitudinal research of Sherif and Sherif [1953] on intergroup conflict is an exception to this trend). Yet, the perception of interdependence among members of naturally occurring groups often encompasses the cumulative experience of earlier and current generations of members, as well as their present plans and aspirations about future activities and outcomes.

We propose that groups can be usefully differentiated in terms of the *temporal depth* of their shared experience, that is, the extent to which group members perceive their current goals and activities to be linked to past and/or future shared events (cf. Stokols, 1982). Considering that group experiences can encompass both *past* and *future* events, and that the temporal extension of these events can be either *shallow* or *deep,* four distinct temporal orientations of groups are suggested: namely, *present-focused* (shallow past/shallow future), *traditional* (deep past/shallow future), *futuristic* (shallow past/deep future), and *coordinated* (deep past/deep future).

The four temporal orientations suggested above are hypothetical constructs intended to identify important patterns of interdependence among current, previous, and future generations of group members (social bonding), and between group members and their material surroundings (sociospatial bonding). To be useful, the proposed constructs must be clearly differentiated and the social psychological phenomena that they suggest should be amenable to precise measurement. In an effort to address these definitional and measurement concerns, we suggest five basic criteria for distinguishing among different temporal orientations of groups. Specifically, the proposed temporal orientations can be differentiated in terms of at least five major components, including: (1) a *group referent,* consisting of earlier and/or future generations of the group with whom current members perceive themselves to be linked (also, the current group sometimes serves as its own self-referent, as in the present-focused orientation); (2) *environmental referents,* consisting of objects and places that have functional and symbolic significance for the group, and with which group members perceive themselves to be linked; (3) *cognitive processes,* such as reminiscence about the past, short-term planning of current activities, and anticipation of the future, which reflect the temporal depth of group experience; and shared informational content consisting of the beliefs and values held by current and previous generations of the group; (4) *affective tone* reflecting the emotional valence and significance of attachments among group members and between group members and their material surroundings; and (5) *behavioral patterns,* such as the preservation of historically significant places, utilization of present resources, or investment in the development of future environments; these activity patterns reflect the predominant temporal orientation of group members toward their material surroundings.

The five components, or distinguishing features, of the temporal orientations of groups are summarized in Table 15.1. These features provide a

TABLE 15.1
The Temporal Depth of Environmental Experience: Distinguishing Features of Traditional, Present-Focused, Futuristic, and Coordinated Orientations of Groups

	FUTURE ORIENTATION	
	Shallow	Deep
	Present-Focused	*Futuristic*
Shallow	*group referent:* current group as self-referent	*group referent:* future generations
	environmental referent: objects, places that have current functional significance for the group; example: Las Vegas	*environmental referent:* objects, places that symbolize links between current and future generations; example: Three Mile Island
	cognitive processes: focus on current activities; short-term planning	*cognitive processes:* focus on the connections between current and future events; longrange planning, envisioning, anticipation
	affective tone: satisfaction/dissatisfaction with current situation	*affective tone:* hope/anxiety about the future
	behavioral patterns: consumption, utilization of environment	*behavioral patterns:* investment, development of environment

PAST ORIENTATION

	Traditional	*Coordinated*
Deep	*group referent*: past generations	*group referent*: past and future generations
	environmental referent: objects, places that symbolize links between current and past generations; example: Wailing Wall in Jerusalem	*environmental referent*: objects, places that symbolize links between past, present, and future generations; example: "People Tree" sculpture in Columbia, Maryland
	cognitive processes: focus on connections between current and historical events; reminiscence	*cognitive processes*: focus on the connections between past, current, and anticipated events; remembrance of the past, envisioning of the future
	affective tone: nostalgia/regret about the past	*affective tone*: nostalgia/regret about the past and hope/anxiety about the future
	behavioral patterns: ritual, preservation of environment	*behavioral patterns*: ritual, preservation of environment; investment in and development of the environment

basis for comparing and contrasting present-focused, traditional, futuristic, and coordinated orientations. A comparative analysis of these orientations is presented below. Before turning to that discussion, however, we note two general measurement issues raised by our proposed typology. The first issue is that of finding meaningful, valid measures for identifying the temporal orientation of a particular group. In other words, what methods can be used to assess the construct validity of our typology of temporal orientations (cf. Cook & Campbell, 1979)? Assuming that valid and reliable measures of the proposed constructs can be developed, a second issue arises concerning the strategic use of these measures to examine the antecedents and consequences of temporal orientations in groups.

The focus of this chapter is on theoretical rather than methodological concerns. Therefore, we will not address the above measurement issues in detail. We do, however, suggest a general methodological strategy for examining temporal orientations in groups: namely, *measuring the functional and symbolic meanings of objects and places that are closely associated with current, prior, and future phases of group existence*. By observing the material context of a group, and by probing the perceived significance of that context for collective identity and continuity, it should be possible to identify the predominant temporal orientation of the group. More specifically, a representative sample of group members can be presented with actual, simulated, or imagined environments, and with structured interview items designed to assess their cognitive, affective, and behavioral orientations toward the target environments. Strategies for measuring the symbolic meanings of objects and places are discussed in greater detail in Appleyard (1979), Broadbent, Bunt, and Llorens (1980), Jacobi & Stokols (1983), and Lym (1980).

Our emphasis on the environmental dimensions of temporal orientations derives from the assumption that the material surroundings of groups serve important symbolic functions, including the enhancement of collective identity and continuity. The temporal meanings associated with objects and places constitute a subset of the "perceived social field of the physical environment," or the totality of sociocultural meanings that have become associated with a particular place and are widely recognized by group members (cf. Stokols, 1981). The explicit measurement of the temporal meanings associated with objects and places, we believe, offers a rich but as yet untapped source of information about group formation, conflict, cohesion, and continuity. Our comparison of the different temporal orientations of groups, therefore, will give particular emphasis to the environmental referents and symbolism associated with each orientation.

Present-focused orientation of groups. The temporal orientations of groups reside not in the physical characteristics of the environment, alone, nor simply in the social organization of the occupants themselves—but rather in the *actual and perceived links between past, present, and future generations of group members; and between the group and particular environments.* According to our analysis, present-focused groups relate to their environment in terms of its functional significance for the accomplishment of immediate goals and plans. Connections between the current group and earlier or future generations are either absent or nonsalient. Thus, the material surroundings of present-focused groups have little (if any) historical significance and convey weak or negligible images of the group's future existence.

Lacking strong connections to either past or future generations, present-focused groups exhibit cognitive, affective, and behavioral patterns that reflect members' predominant concern with the "here-and-now" of their immediate goals and activities. Thus, the cognitive processes of group members reveal a preoccupation with short-term decision making and a lack of historical ideals or aspirations for the future. Similarly, affective reactions of group members focus on the favorable or unfavorable quality of immediate environmental conditions in relation to short-term needs and impulses and are not tempered by past experiences or the anticipation of future events. Also, the predominant behavioral orientation of present-focused groups is toward consumption and utilization of existing environmental resources, rather than toward historic preservation or future-oriented investment of those resources.

The Las Vegas "Strip" represents an environmental exemplar of the present-focused orientation (see Fig. 15.1). For many Americans and non-Americans, as well, Las Vegas has come to symbolize a preoccupation with immediate gratification, unencumbered by the Early American ideals of frugality, piety, and family cohesion; or by anticipated regrets about one's current impulsive behavior. The physical structure and symbolism of Las Vegas are a celebration of the here-and-now, with little reference to the past or future. Less dramatic representations of the present-focused orientation are revealed in other commercial areas, such as shopping malls, which are often designed to showcase current fashions and intensify consumer experience of immediate need.

A present-focused orientation is likely to be most apparent during the early stages of group formation, and particularly among the members of "defined-duration" behavior settings (i.e., those that have prescribed termination dates; Stokols & Shumaker, 1981). Yet, in those settings where group members continue to interact over extended periods, they may begin to acquire a sense of their own history, reflected in the accumulation of collectively held information about earlier shared events. Previous and present phases of group existence are compared in an effort to strengthen collective identity and to gauge progress toward the accomplishment of mutual goals.

FIG. 15.1 Las Vegas epitomizes a present-oriented setting. (From Las Vegas News Bureau; reproduced in Toll, D. *The complete Nevada Traveler: A guide to the state.* Gold Hill, Nevada: Gold Hill Publishing Company, 1981, p. 138.)

Furthermore, group members may commemorate portions of the physical environment associated with significant prior events to concretize and symbolically convey their shared identity. This phase in the group's existence, when members acquire images and information about their collective past, reflects the transition between a preoccupation with present activities toward the cultivation of group traditions.

Traditional orientation of groups. As in the case of present-focused groups, the physical environment of traditional groups is directly relevant to the accomplishment of everyday goals and activities. But besides having functional significance or behavioral "affordances" (Gibson, 1977), traditional objects and places have historical value as well. That is, they symbolize important aspects of a group's history to its members (and often to outsiders).

An essential function of tradition is to strengthen and preserve the ties between current and past generations of group members. The perceived connections between the current generation and the *historical referent group,* to which their activities and surroundings are symbolically linked, are based on a set of shared values and experiences (Jacobi & Stokols, 1983). The values and experiences symbolized by traditional behavior and places (e.g., commemorative environments such as the Lincoln Memorial in Washington, D.C.) may relate to religious beliefs, ethnic ties, national history, or any other widely held meanings that serve to bind group members with each other.

To the extent that the traditional significance of an activity or an environment endures, it can be inferred that some group is committed to the maintenance of that tradition. It is important to note, however, that traditions are not invariably associated with positive emotional reactions among group members. While one individual may identify positively with a particular tradition and experience a nostalgic appreciation of the past, another member may feel detached from the tradition and express bitterness about certain aspects of the group's history.

Affective response to traditional referents also may vary in relation to the level of external threat, increasing in intensity when the referents (such as symbolically meaningful places) are facing modification or destruction. In these instances, the salience of traditional meanings increases and group members become more aware of the importance of tradition as a basis for preserving their collective identity and survival. Within the group, variation in members' affective responses may be related to group role, such that those individuals who hold positions of responsibility and authority will be most committed to the preservation of traditional behavior and environments. The centrality of traditional meanings to an individual's or group's identity, then, is a major determinant of the affective and symbolic significance of those meanings.

The symbolic and affective dimensions of tradition are overtly manifested through social behavior and environmental design. Many religious settings, for example, are associated with traditional activities and architectural elements. The Wailing Wall in the Old City of Jerusalem is a preserved remnant of the Second Temple, most of which was destroyed in A.D. 70 (See Fig. 15.2). To this day, Jews from all over the world come to this place to reaffirm their collective identity and their ties to earlier generations of fellow Jews. Daily religious rituals that have survived the ages are enacted. Although the same rituals are carried out in numerous other locations within Israel and throughout the world, the Wailing Wall is an especially holy and significant place for it constitutes an objective manifestation of Jewish history and a symbolic link with ancient Jewry.

The Wailing Wall in Jerusalem and the behavioral patterns associated with it illustrate the five components of tradition outlined in Table 15.1. The affective significance of the Wall is evident in the emotional reactions

FIG. 15.2 The Western Wailing Wall exemplifies a traditional setting symbolizing the history and continuity of cherished religious values. (From Kollek, T. & Perlman, M. *Jerusalem sacred city of mankind: A history of forty centuries.* Jerusalem: Steimatzky's Agency, Ltd., 1968.)

of visitors who often kiss and caringly touch the ancient stones. A vivid demonstration of the importance of the Wall occurred immediately after the June 1967 Six Day War when thousands of Israelis visited the Old City to commemorate the return of the Wailing Wall to Israeli sovereignty.

For many Jews, the Wailing Wall symbolizes the perseverance of Judaism throughout the ages, despite recurring tragedies and adversity. Yet the particular values and symbolic meanings attached to the Wall may vary depending on the religious fervor of its visitors. For orthodox Jews, the preservation of the Wailing Wall signifies the continuity of religious ritual and values. For nonreligious Israelis, however, the Wall symbolizes the preservation of the Jewish nation and its ties to the land of Israel, rather than the continuation of religious rituals and values.

Finally, the physical qualities of the Wall (e.g., its geographical location, the texture of its stones) and the behavioral patterns associated with it (e.g., daily prayers, ceremonial events) exemplify the objective manifestations of Jewish history and tradition. These physical symbols of Judaism derive their significance and power from the collective experiences and perceptions that are associated with them.

The Wailing Wall exemplifies a traditional behavior setting in which recurring patterns of group activity perpetuate the ties between current members, a historical referent group, and a specific location (cf. Jacobi & Stokols, 1983). At a more micro level of group-environment interaction, individual artifacts and structures (even when placed within relatively nontraditional settings) can evoke a sense of history and symbolize the enduring values of a particular group. Family heirlooms exemplify traditional artifacts. These cherished objects link family members to their ancestors and reflect family values (cf. Csikszentmihalyi & Rochberg-Halton, 1981). Important chapters in the family's history are evoked by the heirlooms. The artifacts help the family retain a sense of connection to their past and an understanding of their current identity.

Family heirlooms may convey meanings and significance other than traditional ones. For instance, the heirlooms may be sold to outsiders who value them for their aesthetic qualities or monetary worth. In such a case, their traditional meaning will be modified or lost, since the new owners lack the insider's knowledge of the historical referent group.

Tradition is only one element of the multiple and complex meanings contained within the physical environment. The traditional referents in the physical environment, rather than promoting a constant awareness of historical links, carry important meanings that are accessed by group members as needed. The physical manifestations of tradition comprise a repository of latent meanings which group members draw on to reaffirm their links with the past. The salience of such meanings may be higher, for example, during holidays, commemorative anniversaries, or when the group is facing some threat to its existence. At other times, however, the aesthetic, functional, and nonhistorical features of the environment may be more salient to group members than traditional meanings.

To this point in the discussion, we have emphasized the role of traditions in linking previous and current members of the group. Although traditions sometimes reflect a rigid preoccupation with the past, they are often associated with group aspirations for the future and emphasize the enduring connections between past, present, and future generations. The confirmation ceremony in Catholicism or the Bar Mitzvah ceremony in Judaism, for example, not only mark personal developmental transitions, but also symbolize the perpetuation of a religious heritage from one generation to the next. In such instances, the temporal orientation of the group reflects a balanced blend of historical and futuristic perspectives, rather than an exclusive emphasis on past or future events. Before discussing this *coordinated* temporal perspective in further detail, we examine the predominant elements of a *futuristic* orientation.

Futuristic orientation of groups. Certain objects and places become strongly associated with group members' hopes and concerns about the future. Consider, for example, the nuclear reactor at Three Mile Island (TMI). As a result of the malfunction and near-catastrophe that occurred at TMI during 1979, the images of the TMI reactor towers have become indelibly ingrained in the minds of many residents and nonresidents as a symbol of future technological disasters (see Fig. 15.3). These visions of an uncontrollable future have been linked in recent research to anxiety and physiological stress among TMI residents (Baum, Grunberg, & Singer, 1982). Moreover, pictures of the TMI reactor and images of the near-disaster that occurred there have provided a concrete, symbolic focus to the anti-nuclear movement in the U.S.A., whose political objectives are to close existing reactors and to prevent the construction of new ones. For the members of these social movements, the vision of an alternative, non-nuclear future and concerns about the safety of current and future generations have prompted substantial investments of time, energy, and funding—all directed toward the protection of environmental quality and collective security.

A preoccupation with the future is often evident in geographical areas associated with rapid technological change. During the early 1960s, thousands of scientists and professionals migrated to Cape Canaveral, Florida, in response to the career opportunities afforded by the sudden expansion of the United States' space exploration program. The growth and prosperity of Cape Canaveral during the Sixties was viewed by many as the beneficial by-products of the nation's investment in space technology. Moreover, physical elements of the Cape Kennedy Space Center (e.g., ma-

FIG. 15.3 The nuclear power plant at Three Mile Island, Pennsylvania illustrates an environment with futuristic connotations. (By Margaret Smyser; reporduced in Corbett, M., *A better place to live: New designs for tomorrow's communities*. Emmaus, Penn.: Rodale Press, 1981.)

jestic missiles resting on elaborate launch pads) became symbols of a new era in human history—interplanetary exploration and colonization.

Mission-oriented groups, such as the scientific teams associated with the lunar landing of 1969, typically disband once the mission has been completed. Yet, even before their major goals are accomplished, groups may face coordination and resource constraints that threaten internal cohesion and task completion (Bales, 1965). During these crisis periods, the survival of the group may depend as much on the availability of enduring traditions and values as on the strength of collective goals for the future. A group that can view present problems from a broad, historical and futuristic perspective may be better equipped to cope with immediate constraints than those that remain exclusively oriented toward either the past or the future. This temporally coordinated orientation is described below.

Coordinated orientation of groups. The combination of traditional and futuristic perspectives within the same group can be distinguished from the three temporal orientations outlined earlier, in which group members are predominantly oriented toward present, past, *or* future events. In many (and perhaps most) groups, all three of these temporal perspectives (traditional, present-focused, futuristic) are jointly operative, with the relative salience of each depending on situational factors such as the nature of group goals and the duration of members' shared experience.

One example of a combined or "hybrid" orientation is the temporally coordinated perspective in which group members ascribe *equal* significance to past, present, and future events. The members of these groups perceive themselves as linked to both earlier and future generations, and they measure the quality of their current situation in relation to previous and anticipated experiences. The activities of temporally coordinated groups reflect a blend of traditional and innovative behavior. Furthermore, the use and investment of existing resources are balanced by a concern for the preservation of historically significant areas (cf. Firey, 1945).

The evolution of a coordinated temporal orientation occurs gradually as group members acquire a sense of collective history, as well as shared images and ideals about the future. During the early stages of group formation, when present and future concerns are more predominant among group members than images of their collective past, the yearning for a sense of tradition and shared identity among members may be especially acute. To hasten the development of traditional bonds between themselves and their surroundings, group members often decorate and embellish their environments with symbols of group identity. After moving into a new home, for example, family members are often eager to display cherished objects evocative of their shared past, thereby establishing a sense of continuity with past homes and experiences (Altman & Gauvain, 1981; Vinsel, Brown, Altman, & Foss, 1980).

In many of the planned communities, or "new towns," that have developed in the United States during the last 10 years, planners have incorporated environmental symbols to promote shared identity and cohesion among residents (cf. Burby & Weiss, 1976). An example of these symbols is the "People Tree" sculpture designed for the community of Columbia, Maryland (see Fig. 15.4). This sculpture, situated in the Village Center of Columbia, symbolically conveys the importance of family ties and friendship bonds among all members of the community. As symbolized by the *People Tree* (Fig. 15.4), Columbia was intended to be a melting pot of diverse individuals and groups, all of whom are linked by a common respect for the value of the individual and a reverence for the community as a whole. Although Columbia is a relatively new town, the "People Tree" provides a visible and succinct summary of the traditional American values shared by residents of the community. Thus, an attempt seems to have been made by the planners of Columbia to link the futuristic ideals of the new community with enduring cultural traditions.

IMPLICATIONS OF THE PROPOSED TYPOLOGY FOR SOCIAL PSYCHOLOGICAL RESEARCH

Kurt Lewin (1936) introduced the term "social power field" to describe the direct influence of group members on each other that occurs by virtue of their co-presence. The present analysis suggests that the physical environments of groups gradually acquire a *symbolic* power field of social meanings through their association, over time, with group activities and experiences. Once established, the symbolic meanings of places influence the thoughts and actions of their occupants even when other group members are not immediately present. The perceived social field of the physical environment becomes, in effect, a surrogate source of social influence—its impact on individuals occurs even in the absence of direct interpersonal contact.

Previous research on social influence has given little attention to the symbolic properties of physical environments. For instance, Latané (1981) defined "social impact" as the various changes that occur in an individual (e.g., physiological, emotional, behavioral) as a result of the "real, implied, or imagined presence" of other persons. Latané's integrative review of the literature reveals that empirical studies of social impact have focused almost exclusively on the influence of *co-present* individuals. *Little if any attention has been given to the social influence of persons who are physically and*

FIG. 15.4 The "People Tree" sculpture in Columbia, Maryland reflects a coordinated temporal orientation, representing community continuity and cohesion. (Photograph by Irwin Altman)

temporally distant from the target individual. Our analysis of temporal orientations in groups suggests that the symbolism of physical environments serves as a vehicle of social influence by making past and future generations of the group more salient to its current members.

Assuming that symbolic objects and places transmit the influence of spatially and temporally distant persons, and that these implicit processes of influence can be reliably measured, the present analysis suggests some new directions for social psychological research. Studies of conformity, altruism, and aggression, for the most part, have emphasized immediate situational variables such as the number and relative status of interacting persons. Yet the *environmental and symbolic context* of social interaction may also affect individuals' tendencies toward compliant, altruistic, or aggressive behavior. The environmental symbols of traditional groups, for instance, may encourage prosocial behavior by making shared values and ideals more salient to group members. The surroundings of present-focused groups, on the other hand, may be less promotive of prosocial behavior due to the relative lack of traditional environmental symbolism.

At the same time, symbolic environments may play a prominent role in promoting or sustaining intergroup conflict, particularly when opposing groups lay claim to the same historically significant areas. The Middle East conflict exemplifies an enduring struggle among diverse political and religious groups, all of whom view themselves as historically tied to the same geographical region. The old sector of Jerusalem, for example, contains several shrines and holy objects that are associated with strong, but often conflicting, symbolic meanings for Moslems, Christians, and Jews. Closer to home, the discovery of natural resources in locations considered sacred by some Native American groups has resulted in conflict between industry, with a predominantly futuristic orientation, and Native Americans, with a strong traditional orientation (U.S. Forest Service, 1981). The role of environmental symbolism in promoting or reducing intergroup conflict is an issue that warrants further attention in social psychological research.

The relationship between environmental symbolism, psychological stress, and health is another topic that has received little attention among social psychologists. Futuristic symbols, for example, may help to promote a sense of optimism among group members in the face of immediate environmental constraints and hardship. An optimistic perspective on the future has been linked in many studies to enhanced coping and the reduction of stress (Caplan, 1983; Kobasa, 1979; Stokols, 1982). Also, the presence of environmental symbols that signify individuals' connections to past and future generations has been found to be associated with enhanced emotional well-being among elderly persons (Csikszentmihalyi & Rochberg-Halton, 1981; Rowles, 1978). Future research on the functions of environmental symbols in providing surrogate (noninteractional) social support could have important practical implications for community planning and urban design.

Finally, an emerging area of psychological research concerns the social impacts of technological change (cf. Ittelson, 1980). Here again, environmental symbols of the future may play a crucial role in mobilizing social movements (as in the case of TMI nuclear reactor; see Fig. 15.3) and collective efforts to ensure group continuity and well-being. A short-sighted, temporal perspective (one that gives disproportionate emphasis to current environmental conditions) may inhibit group members' capacity for long-range planning and, ultimately, impair their collective survival (cf. Kaplan, 1972). The visual imagery conveyed by futuristic environmental symbols, thus, may serve the crucial function of reminding group members about future contingencies and constraints.

SUMMARY

Much social psychological research reflects a restricted temporal scope (emphasizing short-term situations and events) and neglects the symbolic significance of the physical environment for individuals and groups. In this chapter, we have presented a framework for analyzing the temporal orientation of a group and the role of the environment in conveying temporal and other symbolic meanings that are closely associated with group identity and continuity. A major purpose of the chapter is to offer a typology of different temporal perspectives in groups and to identify some of the distinguishing features of these perspectives. Accordingly, the various temporal orientations have been portrayed in the preceding discussion as static or "ideal" types. A more complete analysis would address the dynamic nature of temporal orientations in groups and give explicit attention to the evolution and change of these orientations as a result of factors internal and external to the group. Thus, an important research direction suggested by our typology is the analysis of circumstances associated with the development and social psychological consequences of temporal orientations in groups.

REFERENCES

Albert, S. Temporal comparison theory. *Psychological Review,* 1977, *84,* 485–503.

Altman, I., & Gauvain, M. A cross cultural and dialectic analysis of homes. In L. Liben, A. Patterson, & N. Newcombe (Eds.), *Spatial representation and behavior across the life span.* New York: Academic Press, 1981, 283–320.

Appleyard, D. The environment as a social symbol: Within a theory of environmental action and perception. *American Planning Association Journal,* 1979, April, 143–153.

Bales, R. F. Adaptive and integrative changes as sources of strain in social systems. In A. P.

Hare, E. F. Borgatta, & R. F. Bales (Eds.), *Small Groups: Studies in social interaction.* New York: Alfred A. Knopf, 1965.

Baum, A., Grunberg, N. E., & Singer, J. E. The use of psychological and neuroendocrinological measurements in the study of stress. *Health Psychology,* 1982, *1,* 217-236.

Berkowitz, L. (Ed.). *Group processes.* New York: Academic Press, 1978.

Bickman, L. (Ed.). *Applied Social Psychology Annual* (Vol. 1). Beverley Hills, Calif: Sage Publications, 1980.

Broadbent, G., Bunt, R., & Llorens, T. (Eds.). *Meaning and behavior in the built environment.* New York: John Wiley & Sons, 1980.

Burby, R., & Weiss, S. *New Communities U.S.A.* Boston: D.C. Heath, 1976.

Caplan, R. Person environment fit: Past, present and future. In C. Cooper (Ed.), *Stress research: Issues for the eighties.* London: Wiley, 1983, 35-78.

Cohen, S., Evans, G. W., Krants, D. S., & Stokols, D. Physiological, motivational and cognitive effects of aircraft noise on children. *American Psychologist,* 1980, *35,* 231-243.

Cook, T. D., & Campbell, D. T. *Quasi-experimentation: Design and analysis issues for field settings.* Chicago: Rand McNally, 1979.

Csikszentmihalyi, M., & Rochberg-Halton, E. *The meaning of things: A study of domestic symbols and the self.* Cambridge University Press, 1981.

Cullen, I. G. The treatment of time in the explanations of spatial behavior. In T. Carlstein, D. Parkes, & V. Thrift (Eds.), *Human activity and time geography.* New York: John Wiley & Sons, 1978, 27-38.

Elms, A. C. The crisis of confidence in social psychology. *American Psychologist,* 1975, *30,* 967-976.

Firey, W. Sentiment and symbolism as ecological variables. *American Sociological Review,* 1945, *10,* 410-418.

Gergen, K. J. Social psychology, science and history. *Personality and Social Psychology Bulletin,* 1976, *2,* 373-383.

Gergen, K. J. *Toward transformation in social knowledge.* New York: Springer-Verlag, 1982.

Gibson, J. J. The theory of affordances—Toward an ecological psychology. In R. Shaw & J. Bransford (Eds.), *Perceiving, acting and knowing.* Hillsdale, N.J.: Lawrence Erlbaum, 1977.

Glass, D. C. *Behavior patterns, stress and coronary diseases.* Hillsdale, N.J.: Lawrence Erlbaum Associates, 1977.

Hare, A. P., Borgatta, E. F., & Bales, R. F. *Small groups: Studies in social interaction.* New York: Alfred A. Knopf, 1965.

Ittelson, W. H. Environmental psychology: Past accomplishments and future prospects. In G. Hagino & W. H. Ittelson (Eds.), *Interaction processes between human and environment: Proceedings of the Japan-United States Seminar, Tokyo, September, 1980.* Tokyo, Japan: Bunsei Printing Co., 1980.

Jacobi, M., & Stokols, D. The role of tradition in person-environment transactions. In N. R. Feimer & E. S. Geller (Eds.), *Environmental psychology: Directions and perspectives.* New York: Praeger, 1983, 157-179.

Jessor, R. The problem of reductionism in psychology. *Psychological Review,* 1958, *65,* 170-178.

Kaplan, S. The challenge of environmental psychology: A proposal for a new functionalism. *American Psychologist,* 1972, *27,* 140-143.

Kidd, R. F., & Saks, M. J. What is applied social psychology? An introduction. In R. F. Kidd & M. J. Saks (Eds.), *Advances in applied social psychology:* (Vol. 1). Hillsdale, N.J.: Lawrence Erlbaum Associates, 1980.

Kobasa, S. Stressful life events, personality, and health. *Journal of Personality and Social Psychology,* 1979, *37,* 1-11.

Krantz, D. S., Glass, D. C., & Snyder, M. L. Helplessness, stress level and the coronary prone behavior pattern. *Journal of Experimental Social Psychology,* 1974, *10,* 284-300.

Latané, B. The psychology of social impact. *American Psychologist,* 1981, *36,* 343-356.

Lewin, K. *Principles of topological psychology.* New York: McGraw-Hill, 1936.

Lym, G. R. *A psychology of building: How we shape and experience our structural spaces.* Englewood Cliffs, N.J.: Prentice-Hall, 1980.

Michelson, W. *The impact of changing women's roles on transportation needs and usage.* Unpublished research report available from the Institute of Transportation Studies, University of California, Irvine, 1982.

Oskamp, S., Mindick, B., Berger, D., & Motta, E. A longitudinal study of success versus failure in contraceptive planning. *Journal of Population,* 1978, *1,* 69-83.

Pepitone, A. Lessons from the history of social psychology. *American Psychologist,* 1981, *36,* 972-985.

Perlman, D., & Cozby, P. (Eds.). *Social psychology: A social issues perspective.* New York: Holt, Rinehart, & Winston, 1983.

Ring, K. Experimental social psychology: Some sober questions about some frivolous values. *Journal of Experimental Social Psychology,* 1967, *3,* 113-123.

Rowles, G. D. *Prisoners of space? Exploring the geographic experience of older people.* Boulder, Colo.: Westview Press, 1978.

Sherif, M., & Sherif, C. *Groups in harmony and tension.* New York: Harper & Row, 1953.

Smith, M. B. Is experimental social psychology advancing? *Journal of Experimental Social Psychology,* 1973, *8,* 86-96.

Steiner, I. D. What ever happened to the group in social psychology? *Journal of Experimental Social Psychology,* 1974, *10,* 94-108.

Stern, P. C., & Gardner, G. T. Psychological research and energy policy. *American Psychologist,* 1981, *36,* 329-342.

Stokols, D. Group × place transactions: Some neglected issues in psychological research on settings. In D. Magnusson (Ed.), *Toward a psychology of situations: An interactional perspective.* Hillsdale, N.J.: Lawrence Erlbaum Associates, 1981, 393-415.

Stokols, D. Environmental psychology: A coming of age. In A. Kraut (Ed.), *The G. Stanley Hall Lecture Series* (Vol. 2). Washington, D.C.: American Psychological Association, 1982, 155-205.

Stokols, D., Novaco, R., Stokols, J., & Campbell, J. Traffic congestion, Type-A behavior and stress. *Journal of Applied Psychology,* 1978, *63,* 467-480.

Stokols, D., & Shumaker, S. A. People in places: A transactional view of settings. In J. Harvey (Ed.), *Cognition, social behavior, and the environment.* Hillsdale, N.J.: Lawrence Erlbaum Associates, 1981, 441-488.

Stokols, D., Shumaker, S. A., & Martinez, J. Residential mobility and personal well-being. *Journal of Environmental Psychology,* 1983, *3,* 5-19.

Taylor, S. M., & Konrad, V. Scaling dispositions toward the past. *Environment and Behavior,* 1980, *12,* 283-307.

Thibaut, J., & Kelley, H. *The social psychology of groups.* New York: John Wiley & Sons, 1959.

Triandis, H. C. Some universals of social behavior. *Personality and Social Psychology Bulletin,* 1978, *4,* 1-16.

U.S. Forest Service. *Inventory of Native American religious practices, localities, and resources: Study area on the Mount Baker-Snoqualmie National Forest.* Seattle, Wash.: Mount Baker-Snoqualmie National Forest, 1981.

Vinsel, A., Brown, B. B., Altman, I., & Foss, C. Privacy regulation, territorial displays, and effectiveness of individual functioning. *Journal of Personality and Social Psychology,* 1980, *39,* 1104-1115.

Zajonc, R. B., Crandall, R., Kail, R. V., & Swap, W. Effect of extreme exposure frequencies on different affective ratings of stimuli. *Perceptual and Motor Skills,* 1974, 38, 667-678.

16 The Temporalization of the Self

Thom Verhave
Queens College, City University of New York

Willem van Hoorn
University of Amsterdam, The Netherlands

The modern sciences of human affairs became professionalized investigations during the course of the nineteenth century. The American and French Revolutions had then already taken place and the industrial revolution was in full swing. Compared with the biological sciences, as these developed during the same century, one can point to two similarities. Both shared a preparatory eighteenth-century prehistory in which *temporalization* as an historical process has played a major role. By "temporalization" we refer to the subjection of things and processes including human thought and conduct to the uniform, linear, quantified time of the mechanical clock. Linear, Absolute Newtonian Time, had come to rule triumphant during the nineteenth century (Buckley, 1966). H. Meyerhoff points out that in the nineteenth century "all the sciences—biology, anthropology, psychology, even economics and politics—became 'historical' sciences in the sense that they recognized and employed a historical, genetic, or evolutionary method" (1955, p. 97). To the list of sciences he enumerated one can add linguistics and such natural sciences as geology and cosmology; they were busy formulating secular accounts of the development of languages, the earth and the universe as natural events and processes taking place in time (Lovejoy, 1936). The belles-lettres of the Victorian period reflect a similar concern with time. "The Victorians," writes J. H. Buckley in *The Triumph of Time,* "at least as far as their prose and verse reveal them, were preoccupied almost obsessively with time and all the devices that measure time's flight" (1966, pp. 1–3). "Time's flight," alludes to another aspect of the nineteenth-century concern with time: a preoccupation with death

(Morley, 1971). Personified, death even shows up in *Alice in Wonderland:* "If you knew Time as well as I do," the Mad Hatter tells Alice, "you wouldn't talk about wasting *it*. It's *him*" (Carroll, 1865).

The second way in which, towards the end of the nineteenth century, the human sciences were similar to geology and the biological sciences is that one could in the case of all of them distinguish between a historical and an ahistorical branch. Our use of the word "branch" should not be taken to imply, however, that the ahistorical and historical components were necessarily offshoots of the same tree. In biology, evolutionary theory was a development out of natural history, whereas physiology developed out of medicine and anatomy. Whatever their origins and differences in methodology, such as "genetic," "comparative," or "experimental," it is important to realize that both branches were considered legitimate and of more or less equal importance. It would seem that, from a theoretical point of view, the historical and the empirical or experimental branches are indeed complimentary rather than antithetical. Wundt certainly thought so (van Hoorn & Verhave, 1981). In practice, however, due to differences in methodology, vocabulary, and specialization, it has been different, both in biology and the social sciences. The paleontologist and the experimental physiologist seem to have as little in common in terms of how they think and what they do, as clinical psychologists and psychophysicists. Wundt's version of an historical psychology did not survive him. Psychophysics did. In 1940 Karl Mannheim could ask why it was that there was no historical psychology (Mannheim, 1940). Even today we still have a more or less flourishing historical economics but hardly a historical sociology, historical psychology, or historical social psychology (van den Berg, 1956).

It is not the purpose of this essay to describe how this odd state of affairs has come about (cf. Braudel, 1979; Harris, 1968; Nisbet, 1969; Peeters, 1978). We do wish to explore what it could mean to engage in a historical (social) psychological inquiry and to delineate what, if any, the special contribution of the historical psychologist to the *scientiae humanae* could be. To do so, we have focused on two basic psychological and social categories, the *Self* and *Time* (cf. Verhave & van Hoorn, 1977). In tracing the historical emergence of contemporary ideas of self in relation to changes in temporality as a societal and psychological dimension, we may illustrate how a historical approach may enrich our understanding of the social life and sciences of our own time.

To answer such historical questions one needs an explicit historiography to organize and guide one's thought. Elsewhere one of us has presented a summary statement describing the main features of our *Transformational Contextualism* as a general model for the development of psychology (van Hoorn, 1981). In this essay, we apply a similar historiographic approach to the transformations of the self during the modern transition period that

16. THE TEMPORALIZATION OF THE SELF 327

began with the breakdown of the feudal order and the concomitant revival of trade between 950 and A.D. 1350 (Braudel, 1979; Feddema & Tichelman, 1978; Ferguson, 1963; Hale, 1971; Huizinga, 1924; Lopez, 1971; Mumford, 1934; Polanyi, 1944). Transformational contextualism insists on placing individuals in the societal context of their own time. It looks for "the social aspect of every psychological phenomenon, and . . . interpret(s) it in terms of a continual interaction between individual and society" (Mannheim, 1940, p. 17). One implication of our historiographical approach is that the history of social psychology itself is to be analyzed within the context of other "larger" societal developments. The demise of Wundt's *Völkerpsychologie* is related to the transition from a linear to a multidimensional, relativist temporality. Linear models of "social evolution" and the "genetic method," came to be seen as irrelevant and discredited (Harris, 1968; Nisbet, 1969).

In its general form, transformational contextualism employs three planes, each of which itself can consist of as many dimensions as are needed or useful. As far as the three multidimensional planes are concerned, imagine a cube somewhat like Rubik's. Fortunately, we need only three sides each of which is divided into a number of rows only. Each of the rows of the *frontal* surface represents a distinct and specific *societal conflict*. As Heraclitus taught, "strife is the father of all things." The transformations in these societal conflicts are some of many which investigation has shown to be relevant and appropriate to a set of "target transformations" such as the transformations in the self concept. The *top* surface of the cube represents transformations in the domain of discourse as represented by scientific theories, philosophies, and literature. The *lateral* surface represents the outcome of the interacting transformations of the other two planes. In a Marxian sense, it represents the fields of praxis. However, the resultant behavior patterns can also, once established, modify the then existing "fields" of societal conflict and discourse. As generations of cohorts succeed each other within any culture, new institutions, behavioral patterns, or "selves" emerge at the *intersections* of transformations which take place in *each* of the three multidimensional fields of analysis. What could be termed an *historical social psychology* of the self, should be regarded as the attempt to unravel the interactions of each of these transformations taking place among all three levels of analysis. An historical sociology would work with a similar set of three dimensions but take the transformations of our frontal plane for its field of focus.

Within our contextualist framework, we use the term *transformation* in a special way to refer to a particular kind of historical change. In the case of a transformation, one does not deal with one-dimensional, qualitative or quantitative, changes only, but rather with a multidimensional number of either or both of these two kinds of change. In our analysis of the self we will discuss qualitative changes only. What then is a transformation? Any process or thing at a particular moment in time has a distinct number of specific properties or characteristics. When sampled for their presence or absence at various later moments in time, some of these properties may no longer be there. Other novel features, drawn from other historical sources, may have replaced them. The terms accretion and deletion, fusion and separation, or conflation and spinoff suggest some of the basic ways in which a transforming cultural matrix can change over time. There exists the possibility that at a later time, all properties or elements of a matrix that were present initially, have been completely replaced by others. In that case a total transformation has taken place. If one or more elements remain present throughout the entire process of transformation from the first to the last sample, however, one could speak of a metamorphosis or partial transformation.

That changes have taken place in the concept of the self we take for granted, in general agreement with Burckhardt (1860), Ortega y Gasset (1930), Gusdorf (1948) and a number of recent scholars (Benton, 1970; Goodheart, 1968; Lyons, 1978; Morris, 1972; Perkins, 1969; Sebba, 1972; Ullmann, 1966). "The breakdown of the medieval world view," writes G. Sebba, "initiated a radical change in the Western concept and experience of self. The question: 'What am I?' can no longer be answered by defining man's status and destiny within the 'primordial community of being', . . . Now a sovereign self stands in isolation over and against all that is outside it, and the question must read: 'But I, detached from all other human beings and from everything—what am I myself?' This is how Jean-Jaques Rousseau had formulated it when he was almost at his life's end. It is the question of the modern self" (Sebba, 1972, p. 452). The seventeenth century, according to Georges Poulet, "is the epoch in which the individual discovers his isolation. The medieval edifice of the world, in which all forms of created beings were ordered in a system of permanent relations, no longer exists" (1956 edition, page 13). The "Great Chain of Being" was no more.

There have been equally profound changes in the concept and personal experience of time (Hale, 1971; Le Goff, 1980; Poulet, 1950) as well as in temporality as a societal dimension. For an anthropolgoical analysis of the structures of a society and its reckoning of time, there is the work of Evans-Pritchard (1940). It and the suggestive sociological work by Halbwachs (1950) were recently reviewed by Douglas (1980a). Other literature can be found in the books on time, written and edited by J. T. Fraser (1981) under auspices of *The International Society for the Study of Time*. Time, writes R. J. Quinones (1975), "has been, and should be, treated as an *indicator-theme,* one that clearly points to and is even instrumental in the surges and sags of Western Society" (p. 122).

In the remaining pages of this chapter, we argue that with respect to the transformations of the self:

1. Different societal contexts (technological, economic, and the like) produce qualitatively different, and thus uniquely new kinds of selves. Changes in selves over time are discontinuous.

2. Attitudes towards time as lived, and opinions about time as conceived, make up a fundamental component of each self. It is for this reason that time is a basic societal category in terms of which to distinguish between qualitatively different kinds of selves as they appear in history.

3. Three different kinds of time may be distinguished, each characteristic of a given historical phase in human cultural development. These are (a) the cyclical time of the archaic phase, (b) the linear and one-dimensional time of the modern phase, and (c) the relative and multidimensional time of the contemporary phase. Each is connected with a new and uniquely different kind of self, not found during prior pretransitional stages. Each of these new selves has its own distinguishing attitude toward and conception of time and therefore also toward life and death.

4. This does not mean that the kinds of selves that flourished before a transformation occurred, can not be found after that transformation has taken place. Different selves belonging to different times can, and do, in our contemporary world live side by side. Our three phases represent "telescoping" temporal or cultural strata, which since the beginning of the "expansion of the West," have interacted and intermingled in complex ways. Novel kinds of selves should not, however, occur before the appropriate transformations have taken place. It is in this regard, that our theses can be disproven by historical evidence.

It is obvious that it is not possible in this chapter to present all the evidence for or against the above theses; that must await another occasion.

The familiar historiographic distinctions between Middle Ages, Renaissance, Reformation, Baroque, Enlightenment, Romanticism, and Victorianism all belong, as far as the transformation of the self is concerned, to the transitional "modern" stage. As is to be expected during the very phase when temporalization took hold, they suggest a simple linear one-dimensional succession of distinct periods. They need not and should not be so interpreted. Like the three macro-temporal phases outlined above, they should all be interpreted as "socioecological" or cultural niches. They provide useful historiographic labels for fragmentary time samples of the complex transformations of the self that took place after about A.D. 1450 in Western Europe. For these transformations must be mapped against the societal changes that took place as the isolated, ancient, sacred circular polis surrounded by an agricultural community with its cyclical time evolved into the contemporary world of interconnected urban, commercial, industrial, and technological centers within separate national states. It is a contemporary world in which there are, simultaneously, many times (Brumbaugh, 1978). Contemporary time is relativized "Einsteinian" time, it varies with location and perspective (Ortega y Gasset, 1930).

The contemporary man, who wrote *Borges and I,* ironically emphasizing the gap between his public and private selves, is historically a quite different man from the man who wrote "I think, therefore I am" (Borges, 1962; Descartes, 1637). Unlike Descartes, we and Borges live in contact with many different social selves representative of many different cultural histories. All these contemporary selves live, still uneasily, side by side, as so many types and layers of rocks in a societal Grand Canyon. The island of Manhattan is its concrete embodiment.

The historical changes in the nature and concept of the self are here related to *temporalization* as a historical and societal process. By this we do not mean modernization, secularization or historization, a metaphorical "falling into secular time" (Cioran, 1964). There is also a clearcut difference between Lovejoy's concept of the "temporalizing" of *The Great Chain of Being* and our definition of temporalization. Lovejoy's work was a cross-disciplinary study in the "history of ideas" (Lovejoy, 1936). Temporalization is a *societal* process. It is the subjection of things and processes, including the life of the mind, to uniform, linear, and irreversible time, the modern secular time introduced by the mechanical clocks of the first commercial centers of the North Italian Renaissance. Unlike the Cartesian version of a static unmoving substance, the world of the communities of the archaic agricultural societies was ever changing, like our own contemporary world. Yet, time was different then. Their view of time and change is still beautifully expressed by John Dryden (1631-1700) in his Preface to *Fables, Ancient and Modern,* "For Mankind is ever the same and nothing is lost out of Nature, though every thing is alter'd" (Dryden, 1700, 1978 edition, p. 531). That statement still reflects the cyclical cosmic visions of the ancient agricultural communities of the Old as well as the New Worlds (Brandon, 1965; Dumont, 1966, Eliade, 1958; Evans-Pritchard, 1940; Griaule, 1965; de Solla Price, 1975; Waters, 1963). It was a world in which the motions of the heavens were circular and thus, as for Aristotle, "divine," that is, eternal. Time's arrow, by contrast, is the apt metaphor of secular, linear, "scientific" time: its essential aspect is *irreversibility.* It is also the time of modern biology, once Darwin had sealed the fate of divine purpose or god's design (Haber, 1972). The immutable Cartesian soul is an anachronism, an illusion without a future. The crucial transition phase, as far as the temporalization of the self is concerned, runs from Petrarch's fourteenth century until well into the Victorian era. This is the "modern" transition phase during which the sacred cyclical time of the medieval agricultural communities was replaced by secular, mercantile, capitalist, and successional time (Le Goff, 1980). Social life fell under the yoke of the clock. The transition from a closed and finite planet to an infinite universe, was matched by the transformation of the timeless soul into a restless and mere finite self on a rather small planet (Poulet, 1950).

Unlike any human population before the Renaissance, contemporary selves in the large commercial urban centers of the world, live in an ever expanding, industrializing and technological world of relativized time. Since the collapse of the Western colonial empires after World War II, that world has been penetrating the still extant pre-modern as well as still modern societies. The Muslim world did not become aware that something momentous had happened among the infidels of Europe until long after Napoleon occupied Egypt in 1798. "The feeling of timelessness, that nothing really changes, is a characteristic feature of Muslim writing about Europe—as, indeed it is of their writings about other times and places." As in medieval Europe, "a physician . . . is content to translate a book on medicine . . . written 50 or 100 years earlier" (Lewis, 1982). Flying around the globe today, one does not just pass through different geographical time-zones; one traverses different societal and psychological time-warps.

The beginnings of the modern metamorphosis of the concept of the self can be traced to early treatments of the self's theological alterego, the soul. To ordinary Christians of the middle ages, the "soul" was whatever survived the body after death; "it" could go to either heaven, hell, or purgatory. What a person did or did not do during the brief sojourn on earth might seal the soul's eventual fate, but neither his mortal body nor his fleeting thoughts made up his eternal soul. Since time was not perceived to be continuous and irreversible, the continuity of soul or consciousness was not a problem. A serious concern with the immortality of the individual soul did not appear until the Renaissance through the efforts of Marsilio Ficino (1433-1499) and others (Kristeller, 1972). At an abstract level, Ficino's concerns are those of a Platonic Humanist, the societal context is the wealthy city of Florence where the Medici had come to power, the center of artistic individuals who signed their own creations. The concern with the survival after death of the individual soul and its continuity in successional time became a major concern among Protestants after the Reformation and thus, among Catholics too (Lovejoy, 1961; Poulet, 1950).

According to Descartes, in the *Discours de la Méthode* (1637), the soul (l'âme), by which I am what I am, "is entirely distinct from the body, and is even more easily known than is the body, and even if the body did not endure, the soul would remain what she is" (1953, p. 148). Descartes as well as Pascal were battling an already prevailing atheism, their own intellectual doubts and their fear of death. Their quest was for an Absolute Truth beyond all doubt which would resolve not only their own personal crisis but end the religious strife of the period as well. "We burn with desire to find solid ground, a steady base on which to build a tower that rises to Infinity," wrote Pascal (Kahler, 1957). For Descartes that "solid ground" was his immortal soul. Its essence was thought (penser).

The soul was not to be equated with mere fleeting thoughts, however. Wrote Bishop Berkeley in 1710:

> But, besides all that endless variety of ideas on objects of knowledge, there is likewise something which knows or perceives them and exercises diverse operations, as willing, imagining, remembering, about them. This perceiving, active being is what I call "mind," "spirit," "soul," or "myself." By which words I do not denote any one of my ideas, but a thing entirely distinct from them, wherein they exist or, which is the same thing, whereby they are perceived . . . We have shown that the soul is indivisible, incorporeal, unextended, and it is consequently incorruptible. Nothing can be plainer than that the motions, changes, decays, and dissolutions which we hourly [sic] see befall natural bodies . . . cannot possibly affect an active simple, uncompounded substance; such a being therefore is indissoluble by the force of nature; that is to say, the soul of man is naturally immortal (1734 edition, pp. 22-23 & 92-93).

To a twentieth-century social psychologist, the most striking thing about the Cartesian Cogito, when taken at face value as pure "meditation," is the total lack of concern with the social origin and context of thought and of the "I" in "I think, therefore I am." Thought, in the general sense of "anything private which may pass through one's head" could, after Descartes, be that much more readily equated with one's immortal soul. It was he who set the stage for the ready equation of "soul," "mind," "self," and, somewhat later, "consciousness" as practically synonymous terms. We just saw the first of these three words so used by Berkeley in 1710, even though the good Bishop still believed that he possessed an eternal soul, outside of time. Once those modern equivocations had become common usage, they became the vehicles which lead to further changes in the concept of the self. According to F. W. J. Schelling (1795), "Because the Ego is indivisible, it is likewise incapable of change. For it can not be changed by anything external." Elsewhere he asserts that "it is *through* self-consciousness that all limitation, and so all time, arises; that original activity, therefore, cannot fall within time; the Ego as Ego is absolutely eternal; i.e., outside of time altogether," (In Lovejoy, 1961, p. 77). The problem of one's personal death, the limitations of the finite self in a temporalizing society, is the hidden agenda of Schelling's "Transcendental Idealism." Since the self could "not be changed by anything external," it lacked a social dimension. That is a lingering legacy of Cartesian Dualism. It split the created world into two exclusive substances, a natural body and a soul outside time without a natural history. The absence of the historical dimension of human life in contemporary social psychology is an example of "learned categorical inattention," an inattention which hs been transmitted across successive generations of university graduates (cf. Proffitt & Halwes, 1982). Towards the end of the nineteenth century, as the inadequacy of Cartesian dualism became more and more glaring, a growing specialization and professionalization in the *scientiae humanae,* has made it possible for this general neglect of the historical dimension, to continue unabated among social psychologists until this very day.

During the eighteenth century, the increasingly more desperate "Cartesianism" of philosphers such as Schelling was one consequence of the relentless temporalization process. The "temporalizing" of the "great chain of being" was another. (Lovejoy, 1936). The related developments of Philosophical Associationism and the modern novel were still another consequence of the growing dominance of linear or successional time. "The primary temporal sequence of *Tristram Shandy,"* a novel by Laurence Sterne (1713–1768) written between 1759 and 1767, "is based . . . on the flow of association in the consciousness of the narrator" (Watt, 1957, p. 332). By the middle of the century, Sterne could poke fun at the English bourgeoisie who let their lives be run by the clock. "In counting house and shop, [they had] reduced life to a careful, uninterrupted routine: so long for dinner: so long for pleasure—all carefully measured out, as methodical as the sexual intercourse of Tristram Shandy's father, which coincided, symbolically, with the monthly winding of the clock. Timed payments, timed contracts . . . from this period on nothing was quite free from the stamp of the calendar or the clock" (Mumford, 1934, p. 42). Clocks now were everywhere and in a society where religious faith had become shaky, they had become, as elsewhere in Western Europe, the grim symbols of approaching death (Maurice & Mayr, 1980). The "ideal man of the new order," as Mumford (1934, p. 42) and Quinones (1972) point out, was Daniel Defoe's (1660–1731) *Robinson Crusoe* (1719). "It is the middle-class book *par exellence,* showing [its] dearest values . . . in the process of formation" (Quinones, 1972, p. 501). Time was scheduled carefully even on Robinson's island: ". . . I kept my calendar, or weekly, monthly, and yearly reckoning of time." Time was money; time wasted, diminished a finite life, as the Mad Hatter was to remind Alice.

The "whistling-in-the-dark" style of philosophizing of Schelling hid a "deep-structured" motive, to borrow a fashionable phrase, "behind" German Idealism. Claims about the uninterrupted nature of self-awareness or the temporal continuity of the soul, now equated with thought or consciousness, had been asserted long before Schelling. They led David Hume in 1739 to ask disturbing questions. "There are some philosophers," wrote Hume, "who imagine we are every moment intimately conscious of what we call our *self*; that we feel its existence and its continuance in existence; and are certain, beyond the evidence of a demonstration, both of its perfect identity and simplicity" (1961, p. 227). Hume, however, was not so certain and thus called the beliefs in the soul's immortality and its continuity in time into question. Where was Berkeley's immutable soul or the Cartesian "substantial" self to be found, a self the existence of which is "never interrupted"? Hume denied "the strict and proper identity and simplicity of a self or thinking being" and suggested that the mind "is a kind of theatre, where several perceptions successively make their appearance . . . ," a stage show without an audience and director (1961, pp. 553 and 229). Hume was devoid of Schelling's beleaguered Ego.

There were two different, although not necessarily incompatible, ways in which individuals reacted to the increasing subjection of the self to successional and irreversible time. On the one hand, finite selves turned inward and sought their bearing by means of reminiscence, the writing of personal diaries or memoirs, recollections. Schelling's "Idealismus" and a more sedate, petit bourgeois, sentimental subjectivism are all representative. An introspective psychology was beginning to replace piety as the favored "opium" to deal with religious distress (Sommer, 1892). Writes Poulet, "the great discovery of the eighteenth century is the phenomenon of memory" (Poulet, 1950, pp. 23-24). "Without memory," wrote François Quesnay, "the sentient human being would have only sensation, or the idea of the actual instant . . . All his ideas would be consumed by forgetfulness as fast as they were born; all the instants of his duration would be instants of birth and . . . death" (In Poulet, 1950, p. 24). To think, and towards the end of the eighteenth century, to *feel* incessantly and excessivley, to recollect past experiences was to reassure oneself of one's continued existence. It was one way of coping with the fear of death and the retreat of God from a heliocentric Newtonian clockwork universe (Lovejoy, 1961; Maurice & Mayr, 1980; Poulet, 1950). Other selves, such as David Hume, for similar reasons "went public" and immersed themselves in historical investigations and the daily affairs of life. The second "discovery" of the eighteenth century was the social origin of the finite self, and not just the self, but mind, consciousness, language, and all literature. The "Wild Boy of Aveyron" (1799) was no fortuitous discovery (Lane, 1976). The beginning of the now tiresome nature versus nurture debate was another legacy of that "social awakening." The beginnings of the "modern" study of history date back to this century also; represented by the work of Vico, Gibbon, Hume, and Herder, it would lead eventually to the "acceptance of history" (Bock, 1956).

The Cartesian soul was a private preserve, outside time and beyond the reach of authorities in an authoritarian age. The more worldly self, during the course of the eighteenth century, became increasingly defined in terms of public life. It remained, however, like the soul, a reified entity. For Descartes language was "the window of the soul." By the middle of the eighteenth century, the *origin* of language was hotly debated by such authors as Condillac, Diderot, Hartley, Maupertuis, La Mettrie, Rousseau, Turgot, and Adam Smith (Stam, 1976). J. D. Michaelis (1717-1791) published his *Dissertation on the Influence of Opinions on Language and of Language on Opinions* in 1760 in response to an essay contest sponsored by the Berlin Academy of Science. In 1800 Mme. de Staël (1766-1817) published her *De la littérature considérée dans ses rapports avec les institutions sociales,* "revolutionary for its view that all literature reflects the social background which produced it" (Thorlby, 1969, p. 738). Adam Smith published *The Theory of Moral Sentiments* in 1759, 40 years after *Robinson Crusoe* by Daniel Defoe. Wrote Smith:

> Was it possible that a human creature could grow up to manhood in some solitary place without any communication with his own species, he could no more think of his own character, of the propriety or demerit of his own sentiments and conduct, of the beauty or deformity of his own face. All these are objects which he cannot easily see, which naturally he does not look at; and with regard to which he is provided with no mirror which can present them to his view. Bring him into society, and he is immediately provided with the mirror which he wanted before. It is placed in the countenance and behavior of those he lives with, which always mark when they enter into, and when they disapprove of his sentiments (1777 edition, pp. 180-181).

The quoted passage suggests that although an isolated "human creature" might not be able to "think of his own character," such a creature might, even so, still be able to think about things other than himself. Could the passage also, one cannot help but ask, be the remote source of C. H. Cooley's "Looking-glass Self" (1902)? The word *social* is not used in the quotation. During the seventeenth century, according to Raymond Williams, that word "could mean either associated or sociable." By the last third of the eighteenth century, however, it had become "mainly general and abstract: 'man is a Social creature; that is, a single man, or family, cannot subsist, or not well, alone out of all Society'..." (Williams, 1976, p. 246). For many eighteenth-century authors, however, language as well as private thought, due to the historical identification with the soul, were not conceived to be socially derived at all. For some, language, like the soul, was a gift of God; for others, the individual act of a mysterious Ego behind phenomena and beyond time. The still prevalent lack of full insight into the social origin of "solitary thoughts" is strikingly demonstrated in Thomas Reid's work of 1785.

Thomas Reid's *Essays on the Intellectual Powers of Man* were published 4 years before the French Revolution; the last section of the *Preliminary*

Essay is entitled *Of the social operations of the mind.* That section is of interest for two reasons. There is a notable emphasis on the "social operations" of the mind as a new abstract category (cf. Williams, 1976, p. 246), but the discussion shows that Reid still thought it possible for a person "to understand, and will . . . ; to apprehend, . . . judge, and reason," even if he would somehow manage to survive just by himself since birth. Reid, like Rousseau, belongs to the complex transition phase from the supposedly solitary Cartesian ego that existed outside time in a social vacuum to a temporalized social self that develops and changes over time. According to Reid (1785):

> All languages are fitted to express the social as well as solitary operations of the mind . . . to express the former, is the prime and direct intention of language. A man who had no intercourse with any other intelligent being, would never think of language. He would be as mute as the beasts of field . . . When language is once learned, it may be used even in our solitary meditations; and by clothing our thoughts with words, we may have a firmer hold of them. But this was not its first intention; and the structure of every language shows that it was not intended for this purpose (p. 73).

Reid, it would appear, was aware of the importance of the immediate social setting of our "non-solitary mental operations." Unlike Mme. de Staël, however, he was not aware of their inescapable social or cultural origin.

According to Marx and Engels in an often quoted passage, "Life is not determined by consciousness, but consciousness by life" (In Feuer 1959, p. 247). For Marx and Engels, as for Mme. de Staël, there can be no "pure" or "solitary" consciousness without social life. For "from the outset 'spirit' is cursed with the 'burden' of matter, which appears . . . [as] . . . language. Language is as old as consciousness, language is practical consciousness, as it exists for other men, and thus as it really exists for myself as well. Language, like consciousness, only arises from the need, the necessity, of intercourse with other men . . . Consciousness is therefore from the very beginning a social product, and remains so as long as men exist at all" (Marx & Engels, 1845/1846, in Bottomore, 1956, pp. 70-71).

The self was now fully temporalized as well as secularized. It was recognized as an "ideological" product subject to historical change as new social developments emerged. The poor soul was ready for the scrapheap of intellectual history (cf. Brittan, 1977). Although God had not spoken directly to Descartes in his dreams of 1619, he had given them a religious interpretation (Poulet, 1950); not so Marx. "Society is thinking through me," wrote the young Karl Marx two centuries later (Braudel, 1982 p. 458). The transformation from an eternal soul into a finite, culturally sustained, self-referential verbal repertoire, to mix Marx and Skinner, was complete. The reflexive modern self of the phenomenologist is an eighteenth-century societal and cultural development. Its nineteenth-century mental agonies, the opposition between temporal existence and eternal truth, became a "sickness unto death" (Kierkegaard, 1846).

After Marx come seemingly endless rearguard battles against his basic truth about "Man's Place in Society." The idea, like its counterpart in biology, the theory of evolution, is still controversial in many religious, philosophical, and political circles and stirs excitement in others (Bain, 1983). The social origin and context of consciousness, the realization that "the self represents the interface between the individual and social reality," as a recent text puts it, can hardly remain a secret in a secularizing, industrializing and pluralizing society (Wegner & Vallacher, 1980, p. 28).

One way to demonstrate that secularization and temporalization are distinct though related historiographical categories is to point to secularizing thinkers who fought temporalization. Nietzsche, like Georg Hegel and Heinrich Heine before him, announced "the death of God," but was unable to resign himself to the implications of irreversible time. Nietzsche, as Kaufman points out, is "one of the first thinkers with a comprehensive philosophy to complete the break with religion" (Kaufman, 1954, p. 17), itself a major milestone in the secularization of the West. He is also the harbinger of what J. Ortega y Gasset in 1916 called *perspectivismo* (1961 edition, p. 90). Even so Nietzsche, like Marx and Freud, was unable to resign himself to the irreversibility of secular time. Freud placed the unconscious beyond time, a notion which "forms *the* core-concept of the entire edifice of theoretical psychoanalysis" (van Hoorn, 1982; cf. Feffer, 1982). Marx proclaimed the end of societal change after the successful dictatorship of the proletariat. In Nietzsche's case, it was the self-contradictory doctrine of "The Eternal Return," which was a desparate attempt to reassert the "reality of being," its victory over "process." "That everything recurs, is the maximum approximation of a world of becoming to a world of being! The height of contemplation, . . . To *stamp* becoming with the character of being—this is the *highest Will to Power*" (In Dauer, 1975, p. 94). It is also, to us, a transparent, all too transparent equivocation. Time will not have a stop. Nietzsche, often shrill and overwrought, remains a fascinating and important thinker partially because he belongs to the late nineteenth-century phase of the philosophical battle against temporalization. To find nonmorbid "perspectival selves" with the same intellectual vigor as Nietzsche, one must go to the twentieth century (Quinones, 1975; Zurcher, 1977).

The metamorphosis of the eternal soul into a temporalized social self had set the stage for the next development in the temporalization of the self. Although more secular, it still was conceived to be an unanalyzable whole or unity; in that way it was still similar to its predecessor, the soul. The more mundane self as a participant in social life, however, was vulnerable to the ever increasing segmentation and pluralization of society. In an increasingly industrializing and upwardly mobile society, the social self thus eventually came to be recognized as a set of multidimensional processes. The self consists, we might now say, of multiple and temporalized social roles enacted in many distinct social contexts. Braudel, searching for words to sum up his analysis of the development of commercial and capitalist activities in Western European societies from the fifteenth through the eighteenth centuries, described society as an "ensemble des ensembles," a "set of sets" (1982 edition, p. 459). According to William James, the individual not only possessed a "social self," but had "as many social selves as there are individuals who recognize him and carry an image of him in their mind" (James, 1890, p. 294). Social selves, according to current textbooks which take their cues from G. H. Mead, H. S. Sullivan, R. Linton, and M. Sherif, emerge through interaction with "significant others" as members of social "reference groups" (Gordon & Gergen, 1968; Sahakian, 1974). "The movement from unity into multiplicity, between 1200 and 1900, was unbroken in sequence, and rapid in acceleration. Prolonged one generation longer, it would require a new social mind," wrote Henry Adams in 1904 (In 1918, p. 498). Adams was correct.

Within the context of our contemporary "pluralistic" society, to steal a term from William James (1909), a qualitatively new kind of self has emerged in connection with the transition from linear to multidimensional, relative time. Following up on a suggestion by Ortega y Gasset, one may refer to it as the "perspectival self" (Quinones, 1975). Like any fledgling, it is still an endangered breed. It is a self that recognizes and has accepted the multiplicity of the individual's social roles as well as the irreversibility of time in a secular world. It is a "mutable self" (Zurcher, 1977). Wrote Ortega y Gasset in 1916, "since there can be no absolute beholder, there can be no absolute time; instead we have changing perspectives. Consequently, perspective itself must enter into the picture of reality" (In Quinones, 1975, p. 130). J. Duvignaud, in a preface to the first edition of *La Mémoire Collective* by M. Halbwachs (1950), wrote that "time recollected" was a specially important cultural theme of the first quarter of this century. He mentioned Henry James, Joyce, and Proust as novelists who experimented with new ways to use the resources of memory. That cultural theme developed in fact during the eighteenth century as documented by Poulet (1950) for France, Lovejoy (1961) for Germany, and Watt (1957) for England. The turn of this century, however, marks, as Duvignaud recognized, the transition from linear Newtonian to multidimensional relative time. It was Halbwachs, initially a student of H. Bergson and E. Durkheim, who "so well adapted sociological thinking . . . to an Einsteinian relativism that nothing can be said on the subject of memory now that does not owe him a debt" (Douglas, 1980b, p. 19). In the arts, one need only refer to the work of Picasso and Stravinski. Perspectival selves are as multiple as the availability of differential social and intellectual perspectives which they have incorporated and *integrated*.

Zurcher, who with the aid of the Twenty Statements Test, uncovered the "mutable self," suggested that "the acceleration of social change" has influenced its development (Zurcher, 1977). A more extended historical perspective reveals a more complex situation. The increasing potential for upward mobility for continuously increasing numbers of individuals since the rise of a mercantile society in the Italian city states, has been viewed correctly, as a breaking up of the ancient structure of society, the social and political equivalent of the great chain of being. Nobody "knew his rightful place" anymore. Hereditary claims to power, prestige, and respect were in decline.

Concurrent with the great societal transformation which, at a seemingly ever accelerating pace is now sweeping the globe, there have been recurrent complaints from individuals about "being unsettled," "set adrift," and the like. These are indeed reactions to social change and what Henry Adams called "The Acceleration of History" (1918). Wrote Adams "in the nineteenth century, society by common accord agreed in measuring its progress by the coal output . . . [It had] . . . doubled every ten years between 1840 and 1900" (p. 490). Such complaints of individuals can best be understood as a psychological contrast effect. Consider the plight of an aging historian like Henry Adams (1838–1918). He grew up in an agricultural and largely rural democracy without trains, telegraphs, and electricity. The first electric lights lit a few office buildings in Manhattan on September 4, 1882 while the world's coal output "was doubling every ten years." The frequency of such complaints over time can be expected, taking social phase lag into account, to be correlated with the spurts and sags of temporalization and its economic, political, industrial, and technological concomitants (cf. Ogburn, 1964). All spread like the shock waves of an earthquake out of the Italian Renaissance as its geographical and temporal epicenter. The mutable self is hardly as "recent" as Zurcher seems to believe. Nor is it "correlated" in any simple way with the "acceleration of social change" as a phenomenon of recent origin. Contemporary "mutable perspectival selves" are most directly a product of the diversification of contemporary society.

At a risk of stating the obvious we suggest that the emergence of perspectival selves has been enhanced, synergistically, by:

1. The increasing potential for upward mobility of larger numbers of people and the increasing pluralization of society, factors which together expose individuals to a greater range of different significant others and reference groups.

2. The increase in general literacy almost everywhere. This was initially

made possible by the invention of the printing press. It now enhances symbolic contact among individuals in widely disparate geographical and cultural contexts.

3. The "quantum jump" in increased interpersonal contacts, made possible by contemporary technology: means of travel, telegraph, telephone, radio, television, and now interactive computer based communications.

The notion of the soul was an archaic and culturally sustained fictitious self-image, that flourished during the still predominantly agricultural stage of Western societal development. During the extended transition phase between approximately A.D. 1450 and A.D. 1900, the simple supernatural soul, "beyond time," was transformed into a multifaceted, worldly, and temporalized social self. Death's sting thereafter, could no longer be deflected by means of traditional Christian religious pieties and waves of religious revivals. Many ways of coping with this loss of faith were invented and found wanting during this extraordinary transition phase which culminated in the *Spiritual Crisis of the Gilded Age* (Carter, 1971). The hunger for cosmic support (Otto, 1949, p. 127) and the yearning for permanence of selfhood seems "instinctive" and relentless. So is the denial of death (Becker, 1973). As uniquely human traits these are a consequence of the origin of language. Writes Lovejoy, "a great part of the history of Western, as of Eastern, philosophy . . . has been a persistent flight from the temporal to the eternal, the quest of an object on which the reason or the imagination might fix itself with the sense of having attained to something that is not merely perduring but immutable, because the very notions of 'before' and 'after' are inapplicable to it" (1961, pp. 75–76). The same is true for all religions (Brandon, 1965). In Moscow, where the political vested interests promote the state cult of a safely dead Lenin, the slogan holds that "Lenin is more alive than the living."

"One of the more persistent factors in the existence of humankind," writes Carl Eisdorfer, "has been thanatophobia, the fear of death." It is a fear which is currently influencing our attitudes towards and our care of an increasingly aging population, "the bittersweet legacy" of our recent medical and nutritional "miracles" (Eisdorfer, 1983). To what extent the new types of "perspectival selves" that have emerged here and there with the rather recent transition from the linear, one-dimensional time of a "simpler society," to the relativized time of our contemporary technological and pluralistic society, can cope in new and creative ways with such "ultimate" human problems, Time, the Daughter of Truth, will in due time reveal.

Summary

The self has undergone radical transformations since the Middle Ages. These have been related to changes in temporality as a societal and psychological category. Three different kinds of time were delineated, each characteristic of a phase in the transformations of self and society: the cyclical time of the still predominantly agricultural medieval period, the linear and one-dimensional "modern" time of the mechanical clock, and the relative and multidimensional time of contemporary, non-authoritarian, pluralistic societies. Each of these concepts of time has had profound implications for the self. During the medieval period, the soul was viewed as an indivisible eternal entity beyond the finite bounds of the material world and the circular time of the planets and seasons. The world was "timeless" for nothing really changed, social change was inconceivable. These interrelated conceptions of self, time, and society were gradually replaced by a concept of the self as a private, publicly inaccessible preserve yet subject to the secular, irreversible, quantified time of the marketplace and natural philosophy. The self came to be recognized as a social product, subject to social moulding processes. With increased industrialization, and the technological revolution of the past hundred years, the concepts of time and self were relativized. With this last shift, the self has come to to be seen as multidimensional, constrained by a multiplicity of distinct social contexts, a product of social interaction. Contemporary study in psychology as yet only partially and reluctantly reflects these social realities of the contemporary world. Contemporary cognitive psychology, for example, still treats intellectual processes as if they occur in a social, political, economic, cultural, and thus, historical vacuum.

Current psychological literature on the self, although it appears to confirm our analysis, generally ignores the historical dimension of the self we have sketched in outline (Babad, Birnbaum, Benne, 1983; Rosenberg, 1979; Wegner and Vallacher, 1980; Zurcher, 1977). As our discussion of the "acceleration of history" indicates, the "mutable self," which Zurcher (1977) identifies as a recent social phenomenon, has instead an extended prehistory. Personality theory as well as social psychology, as this dissenting volume attests, have stubbornly remained ahistorical.

The self is now conceived as "the interface between the individual and social reality." The concrete context and precise specification of the nature of the *interactive, cultural* and therefore historical processes that constitute that "social reality" remain ignored. It is the task of the historical social sciences to contribute to our understanding of social change and cultural transmission. These terms point to a central theoretical problem of the *scientiae humanae* which must still be solved in detail at both a qualitative and quantitative level. To that task, historically oriented social science investigations must make as essential a contribution as historical geology, paleontology, and natural history still make to the theory of evolution in biology.

REFERENCES

Adams, H. *The education of Henry Adams.* Boston: Houghton Mifflin, 1974 (first published in 1918).
Babad, E. Y., Birnbaum, M., & Benne, K. D. *The social self.* Beverly Hills, CA.: Sage Publications, 1983.
Bain, B. *The sociogenesis of language and human conduct.* New York: Plenum, 1983.
Becker, E. *The denial of death.* New York: Macmillan, 1973.
Benton, J. F. (Ed.). *Self and society in medieval France.* New York: Harper & Row, 1970.
Berkeley, G. *A treatise concerning the principles of human knowledge.* Indianapolis, IN.: Bobbs-Merrill, 1965 (first published in 1710).
Bock, K. E. *The acceptance of history: Toward a perspective for social science.* Berkeley, CA.: University of California Press, 1956.
Borges, J. L. Borges and I. In *Labyrinths: Selected stories and other writings.* New York: New Directions, 1962.
Bottomore, T. B. (Ed.). *Karl Marx: Selected writings in sociology and social philosophy.* New York: McGraw-Hill, 1964 (first published in 1956).
Brandon, S. G. F. *History, time and deity.* Manchester: Manchester University Press, 1965.
Braudel, F. *The wheels of commerce.* New York: Harper & Row, 1982 (first published in 1979).
Brittan, A. *The privatised world.* London: Routledge & Kegan Paul, 1977.
Brumbaugh, R. S. Metaphysical presuppositions and the study of time. In J. T. Fraser, N. Lawrence, D. Park (Eds.). *The study of time III.* New York: Springer-Verlag, 1978.
Buckley, J. H. *The triumph of time.* Cambridge, MA.: The Belknap Press, 1966.
Burchkhardt, J. *The civilization of the Renaissance in Italy.* New York: Harper & Row, 1929 (first published in 1860).
Carter, P. A. *The spiritual crisis of the Gilded Age.* Dekalb, IL.: Northern Illinois University Press, 1971.
Cioran, E. M. *La chute dans le temps.* Paris: Gallimard, 1964.
Cooley, C. H. *Human nature and the social order.* New York: Scribner's, 1922 (first published in 1902).
Dauer, D. W. Nietzsche and the concept of time. In J. T. Fraser & N. Lawrence (Eds.), *The study of time II.* New York: Springer-Verlag, 1975.
de Solla Price, D. Clockwork before the clock and timekeepers before timekeeping. In J. T. Fraser & N. Lawrence (Eds.), *The study of time II.* New York: Springer-Verlag, 1975.
Descartes, R. *Oeuvres et lettres.* Paris: Gallimard, 1953.
Dodgson, C. L. (Lewis Carroll) *Alice in wonderland and through the looking-glass.* London, Pan Books, 1947 (first published in 1865).
Douglas, M. *Evans-Pritchard.* London: Fontana, 1980a.
Douglas, M. Introduction. In M. Halbwachs, *The collective memory.* New York: Harper & Row, 1980b.

Dryden, J. *The poems and fables of John Dryden* (J. Kinsley, Ed.). Oxford: Oxford University Press, 1970 (first published in 1700).
Dumont, L. *Homo Hierarchicus*. Chicago: University of Chicago Press, 1970 (first published in 1966).
Eisdorfer, C. Conceptual models of aging. *American Psychologist,* 1983, *38,* 197-202.
Eliade, M. *Patterns in comparative religion*. Cleveland: World, 1963 (first published in 1958).
Evans-Pritchard, E. E. *Nuer*. London: Oxford University Press, 1940.
Feddema, R., & Tichelman, F. *De doorbraak van het kapitalisme*. Meppel: Boom, 1978.
Feffer, M. *The structure of Freudian thought: The problem of immutability and discontinuity in developmental theory*. New York: International Universities Press, 1982.
Ferguson, W. K. *Renaissance studies*. New York: Harper & Row, 1970 (first published in 1963).
Feuer, L. S. (Ed.) *Marx and Engels: Basic writings on politics and philosophy*. Garden City, N.Y.: Doubleday, 1959.
Fraser, J. T. (Ed.) *The voices of time* (2nd ed.). Amherst, MA: University of Massachusetts Press, 1981.
Goodheart, E. *The cult of the ego*. Chicago: University of Chicago Press, 1968.
Gordon, C., & Gergen, K. J. *The self in social interaction*. New York: Wiley, 1968.
Griaule, M. *Conversations with Ogotemmêlli*. New York: Oxford University Press, 1979 (first published in 1965).
Gusdorf, G. *La découverte de soi*. Paris: Gallimard, 1948.
Haber, F. C. The Darwinian revolution in the concept of time. In J. T. Fraser, F. C. Haber, & G. H. Müller (Eds.), *The study of time*. New York: Springer-Verlag, 1972.
Halbwachs, M. *The collective memory*. New York: Harper & Row, 1980 (first published in 1950).
Hale, J. R. *Renaissance Europe*. New York: Harper & Row, 1971.
Harris, M. *The rise of anthropological theory*. New York: Thomas Y. Crowell, 1968.
Huizinga, J. *The waning of the Middle Ages*. Garden City, N.Y.: Doubleday, n.d. (first published in 1924).
Hume, D. *A treatise of human nature*. Garden City, N.Y.: Doubleday, 1961 (first published in 1739).
James, W. *The principles of psychology*. New York: Henry Holt, 1890.
James, W. *A pluralistic universe*. London: Longmans, Green, 1909.
Kahler, E. *The tower and the abyss*. New York: Viking Press, 1967 (first published in 1957).
Kaufman, W. (Ed.). *The portable Nietzsche*. New York: The Viking Press, 1954.
Kierkegaard, S. *Samlede Vaerker*. Kopenhagen: Gyldendal, 1920-1936 (15 volumes).
Kristeller, P. O. *Renaissance concepts of man and other essays*. New York: Harper & Row, 1972.
Lane, H. *The wild boy of Aveyron*. Cambridge, MA: Harvard University Press, 1976.
Le Goff, J. *Time, work, & culture in the Middle Ages*. Chicago: University of Chicago Press, 1980.
Lewis, B. *The Muslim discovery of Europe*. New York: Norton, 1982.
Lopez, R. S. *The commercial revolution of the middle ages, 950-1350*. Englewood Cliffs, N.J.: Prentice-Hall, 1971.
Lovejoy, A. O. *The great chain of being*. New York: Harper & Row, 1960 (first published in 1936).
Lovejoy, A. O. *The reason, the understanding, and time*. Baltimore, MD: Johns Hopkins University Press, 1961.
Lyons, J. O. *The invention of the self*. Carbondale: Southern Illinois University Press, 1978.
Mannheim, K. *Man and society in an age of reconstruction*. New York: Harcourt, Brace & World, 1940.

Maurice, K., & Mayr, O. *The clockwork universe.* New York: Neale Watson, 1980.

Meyerhoff, H. *Time in literature.* Berkeley: University of California Press, 1955.

Michaelis, J. D. *A dissertation on the influence of opinions on language, and of language on opinions.* London: W. Owen, 1769 (first published in 1760).

Morley, J. *Death, heaven and the Victorians.* Pittsburgh: University of Pittsburgh Press, 1978 (first published in 1971).

Morris, C. *The discovery of the individual 1050-1200.* New York: Harper & Row, 1972.

Mumford, L. *Technics and civilization.* New York: Harcourt, Brace & World, 1963 (first published in 1934).

Nisbet, R. A. *Social change and history.* New York: Oxford University Press, 1969.

Ogburn, W. F. *Social change.* New York: B. W. Huebsch, 1922.

Ogburn, W. F. *On culture and social change.* Chicago: University of Chicago Press, 1964.

Ortega y Gasset, J. *The modern theme.* New York: Harper & Row, 1961 (first published in 1916).

Ortega y Gasset, J. *The revolt of the masses.* New York: W. W. Norton, 1932 (first published in 1930).

Otto, M. *Science and the moral life.* New York: New American Library of World Literature, 1949.

Peeters, H. F. M. *Historische gedragswetenschap.* Meppel: Boom, 1978.

Perkins, J. A. *The concept of the self in the French Enlightenment.* Genève: Librairie Droz, 1969.

Polanyi, K. *The great transformation.* Boston: Beacon Press, 1957 (first published in 1944).

Poulet, G. *Studies in human time.* Baltimore, MD: The Johns Hopkins University Press, 1956 (first published in 1950).

Proffitt, D. R., & Halwes, T. Categorical perception: a contractual approach. In Weimer, W. B. & Palermo, D. S. (Eds.), *Cognition and the symbolic processes* (Vol. 2). Hillsdale, N.J.: Lawrence Erlbaum Associates, 1982.

Quinones, R. J. *The Renaissance discovery of time.* Cambridge, MA: Harvard University Press, 1972.

Quinones, R. J. *Four phases of time and literary modernism.* In J. T. Fraser & N. Lawrence (Eds.), *The study of time II.* New York: Springer-Verlag, 1975.

Reid, T. *Essays on the intellectual powers of man.* Cambridge: The M.I.T. Press, 1969 (first published in 1785).

Rosenberg, M. *Conceiving the self.* New York: Basic Books, 1979.

Sahakian, W. S. *Systematic social psychology.* New York: Intext, 1974.

Sebba, G. Time and the modern self. In J. T. Fraser, F. C. Haber, & G. H. Müller (Eds.), *The study of time.* New York: Springer-Verlag, 1972.

Smith, A. *The theory of moral sentiments* (6th ed.). Dublin: J. Beatty & C. Jackson, 1777 (first published in 1759).

Sommer, R. *Geschichte der Deutschen Psychologie und Aesthetik.* Amsterdam: Bonset, 1966 (first published in 1892).

Stam, J. H. *Inquiries into the origin of language.* New York: Harper and Row, 1976.

Thorlby, A. (Ed.). *The Penguin companion to European literature.* New York: McGraw-Hill, 1969.

Ullmann, W. *The individual and society in the middle ages.* Baltimore: Johns Hopkins University Press, 1966.

van den Berg, J. H. *The changing nature of man.* New York: Dell, 1964 (first published in 1956).

van Hoorn, W. Transformational Contextualism as a general model for the development of psychology. Rome: CNR—Conference on the historiography of psychology, 1981.

van Hoorn, W., & Verhave, T. Wundt's changing conception of a general and theoretical psychology. In W. Bringmann & R. Tweney (Eds.), *Wundt Studies*. Toronto: C. J. Hogrefe, 1980.

van Hoorn, W. Psychoanalysis, romanticism and biology. *Storia e Critica della Psicologia*, 1982, *3*, 5-25.

Verhave, T., & van Hoorn, W. The temporalization of ego and society during the nineteenth century: a view from the top. *Annals of the New York Academy of Sciences*, 1977, *291*, 140-148.

Waters, F. *Book of the Hopi*. New York: Ballantine Books, 1963.

Watt, I. *The rise of the novel*. Harmondsworth: Penguin Books, 1972 (first published in 1957).

Wegner, D. M., & Vallacher, R. R. *The self in social psychology*. New York: Oxford University Press, 1980.

Williams, R. *Keywords*. New York: Oxford University Press, 1976.

Zurcher, L. A., Jr. *The mutable self*. Beverly Hills, CA: Sage Publications, 1977.

17 The Evolution of Aesthetic Taste

Colin Martindale
University of Maine

AESTHETIC EVOLUTION

Art and literature exhibit such profound historical changes that it is often difficult to find much in common between works in the same medium produced during different eras. Consider, for example, the following excerpts of French poetry:

> Beneath your fair head, a white delicate neck
> Inclines and would outshine the brightness of snow.
> *Chénier,* "Les Colombes"

> The violin quivers like an afflicted heart;
> Melancholy waltz and languid vertigo!
> *Baudelaire,* "Harmonie du soir"

> I love you opposite the seas
> Red like the egg when it is green
> *Breton,* "Tiki"

The lines by Chénier, written in the late eighteenth century, are perfectly consistent and understandable. The simile in the excerpt from Baudelaire, who wrote in the mid-nineteenth century, is remote, and the adjectives used to modify "waltz" and "vertigo" are incongruous. Breton's simile, written in the early twentieth century, is so incongruous that it violates conventional logic. In a variety of poetic traditions, there seems to be a historical movement of similes and metaphors away from consistency toward remoteness and incongruity. Similar historical trends can be found in other artistic media as well. For example, it is generally agreed that Western music has become more dissonant across the last several centuries.

What has caused such trends? If we believe that art reflects society, we would attribute the historical trends to social changes. However, there are a variety of reasons to question the belief that art does reflect society. Furthermore, it would, if possible, be more parsimonious to attribute artistic trends to evolutionary forces endogenous to the social systems that produce art. Evolutionary theories have recently been suggested with increasing frequency in the explanation of sociocultural change (e.g., Boulding, 1978; Cavalli-Sforza, & Feldman, 1981; Pulliam & Dunford, 1980). I have elsewhere proposed an evolutionary theory of change in the arts and presented quantitative evidence pertaining to the history of poetry that is supportive of the theory (Martindale, 1973a, 1975, 1978, 1981a, 1981b). In this chapter, I first describe the theory and then present quantitative evidence from studies of British poetry, music, and painting that is consistent with predictions derived from the theory.

In order for evolution of any sort to occur, three factors must be present over a period of time (Campbell, 1965): variation, selection criteria, and mechanisms for the retention of selected variations. In the case of art, variation is certainly present (i.e., different contemporary poets do not all write the same or even similar poems, different painters do not duplicate each other's work, etc.). This variation can be either inadvertent or due to conscious striving for novelty. Mechanisms for retention are also clearly present. Retention mechanisms can be indirect (e.g., printed books) or they can take the form of direct personal contact. These retention mechanisms allow the work of past artists to influence the work of future artists. They serve the same function as does sexual reproduction in biological evolution.

Selection criteria refer to the reasons why a work of art is selected for retention. The more consistent such criteria are over time, the more orderly and predictable we may expect an evolutionary process to be. By analogy with biological evolution, we may conceive of two general types of selection criteria. First, there is "fitness" for the environment in which a work of art is produced. Thus, for example, a licentious poem has low fitness in a puritanical society, while a moralistic poem has high fitness. The selection criterion of fitness gives us little hope for developing a general theory of aesthetic evolution, since fitness varies widely in different times and places, just as in the case of biological evolution. The second selection criterion has to do with preference or liking. In his theory of sexual selection, Darwin (1871) explicitly proposed such a purely aesthetic or hedonic selection mechanism. At first glance, it is not apparent that hedonic selection criteria are consistent for very long, in that taste seems to show marked historical fluctuations. However, an examination of the general bases for aesthetic preference reveals that, in fact, at least one basic law of hedonic selection appears to have been present ever since art has been produced. This raises the exciting possibility that we might find very orderly evolutionary trends in the history of art.

Determinants of Aesthetic Preference

According to Berlyne (1971), aesthetic preference is determined by the arousal potential of a work of art. Arousal potential refers to the amount of arousal or tension that the work induces. Preference or liking is a curvilinear function of arousal potential. Berlyne reviews extensive experimental research showing that people prefer aesthetic and other stimuli having medium arousal potential and find stimuli with either less or more arousal potential boring and/or unpleasant. Arousal potential is determined by three aspects of a work of art: psychophysical properties (e.g., intensity, color, pitch), ecological properties (e.g., signal value, meaningfulness), and collative properties (e.g., novelty, complexity, incongruity). The more of these properties that a work of art has, the more arousal potential it has.

Habituation

The subjective arousal potential of a work of art—or of any stimulus for that matter—is not constant so far as any given observer is concerned. Each exposure of the stimulus tends to elicit less arousal than previous exposures. This is the phenomenon of habituation (Thompson & Spencer, 1966). The subjective arousal potential of a work of art will gradually decline with repeated exposures. Because of stimulus generalization, this decline in arousal potential will spread to other similar works of art. Habituation, of course, has consequences for aesthetic preference, since arousal potential is the determinant of such preference. If a work of art is maximally liked on the first exposure, it will be liked less and less with each repetition, as its arousal potential declines (Berlyne, 1971). It should be noted that habituation seems to be a universal process of nervous tissue (Thompson, Berry, Rinaldi, & Berger, 1979). Although rate of habituation may vary with a number of factors (e.g., stimulus intensity, exposure frequency), habituation has certainly been present ever since people began perceiving art. It thus serves as the basis for a long-lasting and consistent selection criterion.

Habituation means that an audience confronted with a series of works of art will tend to shift preference toward those with more objective arousal potential[1] over time. In other words, there is a consistent selection pressure

---

[1] Operationally, objective arousal potential is defined as the arousal potential of an art work for a person who has not been exposed to prior "habituation trials." By subjective arousal potential is meant the arousal potential of the work for a person who has been exposed to habituation trials.

for increasing objective arousal potential. If a series of artists kept producing works with the same objective arousal potential, liking for these works would decline since the subjective arousal potential of each successive work would decline because of habituation. This process will operate on both the consuming audience and upon artists themselves, but the consequences are generally similar in either case. (Possible dissimilarities in speed of habituation are discussed in Martindale, 1975.) In order to compensate for habituation, successive artists must increase the objective arousal potential of their productions. This cannot very well be done by increasing intensity or other psychophysical variables. Successive painters could paint larger or brighter pictures, or successive composers could compose louder and louder compositions. However, there are rather severe limits as to how large and bright a painting can be, just as there are limits as to how loud a piece of music can be. Poets cannot vary the physical intensity of their poetry at all. Thus, increasing arousal potential by increasing intensity or related variables is, at best, a limited and short-term strategy. There are also limits on how meaningful something can be, and since what is meaningful for one person may not be meaningful for another, it would be difficult for successive artists to imbue their works with more and more meaning for very long. Thus, the pressure for increased objective arousal potential comes down to a pressure for increasing novelty, complexity, and other collative variables.

Consequences of Habituation

The theory thus leads to the prediction that, in any artistic tradition, successive productions should show increases in complexity, novelty, incongruity, variability, and similar variables. Rather similar predictions were made by the Russian and Czech formalist theorists (e.g., Mukařovský 1940; Shklovsky, 1919; Tynjanov, 1929) as well as by a number of other thinkers (e.g., Cohen, 1966; Göller, 1888; Kubler, 1962; Laver, 1950; Peckham, 1965). However, these theorists failed to realize that the predicted changes are "linked" with other less obvious but more interesting changes. If we stop to think how successive artists could manage to keep increasing the novelty and variety of their art, we discover that the selection pressure on the arousal-producing aspects of art indirectly but inexorably constitutes a selection pressure on apparently unrelated aspects of artistic style and content. That is, changes in collative variables are linked, as will be explained below, to changes in other aspects of art. The reason is that artists must systematically change their mode of production in order to keep increasing arousal potential. These changes leave their mark on artistic products. It is these changes that constitute the basis for the more interesting and nonintuitive predictions arising from this evolutionary theory of aesthetic preference.

Production of Novel Responses

According to Kris (1952), novel responses arise from a biphasic process of inspiration and elaboration. Inspiration hypothetically involves a movement from secondary process cognition (sane, logical, reality-oriented thought) toward primary process cognition (the free-associative, irrational, and primitive thought found in dreams, reveries, and drug-induced states). The secondary process-primary process continuum is the fundamental axis along which type of cognition or state of consciousness varies (Fromm, 1978). Inspiration produces the raw material of the work of art. The act of creative inspiration involves the combination of elements (ideas, words, images) in new ways. Primary process thought allows this, since it involves quasi-random combinations of mental elements as opposed to the learned and logical combination of mental elements in secondary process cognition. The more thought becomes primary process in nature, the more it approaches randomness and, thus—other things being equal—the more it facilitates the production of novel combinations of mental elements (Martindale, 1981a). Elaboration involves a movement back toward secondary process thought. In the stage of elaboration, the work of art is put into its final form. That is, it is put into communicable form, made to conform with current rules of style, and so on. Other currently accepted theories of creativity are essentially the same as Kris' but are phrased in quite different terminology (see Martindale, 1981a).

In order for successive artists to increase the novelty or variability of their works, they may engage in two strategies: (1) changes in inspiration or (2) changes in elaboration. Essentially, a change in elaboration means a change in artistic style. The first method seems empirically to be much more common. Thus, we shall first discuss how originality could be increased within the confines of a given style.

Trends in Primary Process Content

In order to produce increasingly novel or variable works of art, successive poets working within the same style should have to engage in increasingly deeper regression (movement toward primary process cognition) during inspiration. Depth of regression should be reflected in the content of the works of art produced. Thus, a historical series of poems produced in the same style should show content increasingly reflective of primary process cognition. An example of this sort of progression can be seen if we compare the content of early and late English metaphysical poetry. Consider the intellectual or secondary process emphasis in Donne's poetry—for example,

> If they [our souls] be two, they are two so
> As stiffe twin compasses are two,

> Thy soule the fixt foot, makes no show
> To move, but doth, if the 'other do.
> *Donne;* "A Valediction: Forbidding Mourning"

as compared with the unrealistic, oral, and sensuous quality of Crashaw's poetry—for example,

> Upwards thou dost weepe,
> Heav'ns bosome drinkes the gentle streame,
> Where the milky Rivers creepe
> Thine floates above and is the creame.
> *Crashaw,* "The Weeper"

It should be noted that the secondary process-primary process dimension is isomorphic with dimensions such as classic versus romantic, ethos versus pathos (Sachs, 1946), abstraction versus empathy (Worringer, 1957), or ideational versus sensate (Sorokin, 1937), that hypothetically describe the major dimension along which works of art vary. Thus, the evolutionary theory gives promise not only of explaining changes in artistic variability and novelty but also of explaining other basic changes in artistic content.

Trends in Elaboration: Stylistic Change

There is a second method besides increased regression by which successive artists can make their works more novel. This is by creating a new artistic style; that is, by changing what is done during the process of elaboration. Generally, a new style involves a loosening of the rules governing what is appropriate for a given art form. This allows more novelty to be gained with less regression than was previously required. The clearest example of this is the style change in French poetry at the turn of the present century. Until 1900, the elements joined in poetic similes had to be alike in at least some manner. By the late nineteenth century, this had become rather difficult, since the "obvious" similes had all been used. Thus, the similarity of elements joined in similes tended to be rather arcane; for example,

> This evening a done-for sun lies on the top of the hill,
> Lies on its side, in the straw, on its overcoat.
> A sun white as a gob of spit in a tavern
> On a litter of yellow straw,
> *Laforgue,* "L'Hiver qui vient"

Around 1900 this rule was explicitly abrogated: *Any* words could be joined by the word "like." The result was that the construction of similes became quite easy for a period of time. Poets could combine close word associates that the previous stylistic rules had disallowed (Martindale, 1975). For example, Eluard could write, "The earth is blue like an orange," and Soupault could observe that, "A church rose striking like a bell."

In terms of style and content, the present theory makes the prediction that the works of art produced in a given tradition (e.g., English poetry, Italian painting) will be grouped into a series of styles (i.e., sets of rules). While any given style is in effect, primary process content should increase over time. With the introduction of a new style, primary process content should decline. However, it should begin to increase once the new style has come into effect. While primary process content should thus show an oscillating or sinusoidal trend, indices of arousal potential should show a monotonic increase over time so long as the tradition remains unperturbed by extreme external influences. For example, in the case of Italian painting, we would expect that while the Renaissance style was in effect, primary process content of successive paintings should increase. With the introduction of the subsequent baroque style, we would expect a decline in primary process content. However, once the baroque style was firmly established, primary process content should begin to increase again. Across the entire time span, however, the objective arousal potential of successive paintings should show a monotonic increase.

Strong and Weak Versions of the Theory

The general theory outlined above can be construed in two ways. The weak version would hold that the sorts of changes postulated occur, along with many others, in the history of an art form. Thus, there might be unrelated trends in style or subject matter going on simultaneously with the trends predicted by the theory. Furthermore, these trends might be due to extra-artistic causes such as changes in cultural values, economic conditions, and so forth. The strong version would be that evolutionary theory accounts for all or most changes in style and content.[2] In this version, any major trends

---

[2] In discussing strong and weak versions of the theory, I am considering art produced in an "average, expected" social environment. An art-producing system can, of course, be destroyed by politicians. In this extreme case, the strong version of the theory would obviously not hold. However, short of this, the strong version can hold even in the presence of political or other controls, subsidies, and pressures. Even in the case of extreme pressures of this sort, it seems to be generally the case that the most the extra-artistic system can do is to favor one already existing style over another. Control of art by political or other extra-artistic institutions tends to focus on the meaning of art works, since it is often completely unclear how psychophysical or collative variables would be related to political or other ideologies. In order to evade such control, artists may stabilize meaning (e.g., everyone paints the crucifixion) or neutralize it (e.g., everyone paints still-lifes). Pursuit of increasing arousal potential may then proceed via uncontrolled (i.e., psychophysical or collative) means. Finally, as Sorokin (1937) remarked, if a patron or politician wants to exercise anything other than rather indirect control over art, he will end up having to produce the art himself.

in the content or style would be subsumed by the general trends in arousal potential and primary process content. Espousal of the strong version of the theory is not altogether unreasonable. The two basic axes along which works of art are held to vary by many theorists are the arousal potential dimension and the primary process-secondary process dimension.[3] According to the strong version of the theory, whatever changes are seen as constituting the history of an art form ultimately reduce to changes along the arousal potential and the secondary process-primary process continua. Thus, for example, styles such as mannerist, romantic, or expressionist are essentially mere "local realizations" of primary process style that differ only in their surface details but not in their deep content and structure. Although using other terms, a number of theorists (e.g., Ehrenzweig, 1953; Kahler, 1968; Maritain, 1953; Ortega y Gasset, 1948) have indeed argued that movement along the primary process dimension does constitute the major trend in the arts over at least the last several centuries.

In a study of English metaphysical poetry (Martindale, 1982a), the poetic texts were analyzed with the Harvard Third Psychosociological Dictionary (Stone, Dunphy, Smith, & Ogilvie, 1966). This is a very general content analysis dictionary designed to tap a wide variety of types of textual content. Thus, it might be expected to show up trends unrelated to the theoretically predicted ones. Only 8 of the 55 Harvard Third Dictionary categories exhibited significant linear trends over time. All 8 categories were highly intercorrelated with one another, and all were significantly correlated with the index of primary process content described below. Correlations ranged from .48, $p < .05$ to .67, $p < .01$. Thus, so far as can be determined from this analysis, there were no historical trends in poetic content that could not be explained by or reduced to the predicted trends in primary process content. Based upon scores on all 55 of the Harvard Third categories, a similarity matrix of the poets included in the study was created. That is, for each pair of poets, a score was computed indicating how similar the content of their poetry was. Statistical analyses of the similarity matrix indicated that 67% of the similarity among poets could be attributed to similarity in the indices of arousal potential and primary process content. Thus, about two-thirds of the general variation among the poets in the sample could be accounted for by the two theoretical variables.

The strong version of the theory has the corollary that the influence of extra-artistic forces (e.g., social or economic variables) on the arts is minimal, that art does not reflect society. A necessary further corollary is that reflectionist theories of artistic change—theories that ascribe artistic change to social, economic, or political changes—are incorrect. In an earlier work (Martindale, 1975) logical difficulties with reflectionist theories of ar-

---

[3]A variety of quite different labels have, of course, been used to describe these dimensions.

tistic change were discussed. It might be noted that even most Marxist theorists (e.g., Trotsky, 1924) concede such a high degree of autonomy to artistic systems that they see only a small portion of artistic change as mirroring or reflecting social or economic change. Empirical evidence against reflectionist theories of several sorts has been gathered. A number of social, economic, and other time-series have been gathered for the time span covered by the study of British poetry described below. Neither strong nor consistent correlations with the theoretical variables have emerged (Martindale, 1981b). Second, it is possible to produce, in a laboratory setting, patterns of the sort predicted by the theory (Martindale, 1973b). Given that it is possible experimentally to simulate artistic change with extra-artistic variables held constant, the principle of parsimony suggests that we disregard such variables in explaining artistic change.

Range of the Theory

The evolutionary theory described above applies only to a series of artists working within the same tradition. In the same way that biological evolution is species-specific, aesthetic evolution is tradition-specific. Thus, an evolutionary change in kangaroos has no direct implications for elephants. However, traditions are not as clearly defined as species. What, exactly, is evolving? It is an empirical question whether it is a specific tradition within a specific medium, the entire medium, or perhaps all artistic media. If the last possibility were correct, then we should expect that primary process cycles in all artistic products would be synchronized or otherwise systematically related. If the first or second possibility is correct, then we should expect the cycles to be randomly related. The question is of interest since historians of art and literature have been asking for at least two centuries whether the arts change in synchrony or not. Perhaps because of the lack of quantitative investigations, two centuries of humanistic inquiry have produced no generally agreed upon answer to the question.

Martindale and Hasenfus (1978) and Hasenfus, Martindale, and Birnbaum (1983) undertook a study of British period styles. The time span from 1600 to 1839 was divided into six 40-year periods. For each of four media (poetry, painting, architecture, and music) two artists born within each period were selected on the basis of eminence. For each artist, two works were selected on the basis of a predetermined order of search through a set of sources. In this way, 96 works by 48 artists were selected. Eight-line excerpts from poems were typed on index cards; color photographs of paintings were made; black and white photographs of architecture (a front facade and an interior view of the same building for each architect) were made; and 30-second excerpts of musical compositions were recorded on cassette tapes.

Subjects with minimal training in the arts were confronted with these stimuli. Their task was to sort the 96 stimuli into groups on the basis of style. On the basis of these sorts, a 96 × 96 similarity matrix was constructed. An odd-even reliability check revealed good intersubject agreement ($p < .001$) in sorting. The similarity matrix was analyzed with a multidimensional scaling program, MINISSA (Lingoes, 1967, 1973). In multidimensional scaling, similarities are represented by distances in space, with more similar stimuli being closer together and more dissimilar stimuli being further apart. The question of interest is how many spatial dimensions are necessary to accomplish this representation. For 96 stimuli, a maximum of 95 dimensions would be needed. The results suggested that the similarity matrix could best be represented by a five-dimensional space. That is, subjects were hypothetically arriving at their categorization decisions by discriminating the works of art along five orthogonal dimensions. The coordinates for each dimension were analyzed with Medium × Period × Artist within Medium × Period analyses of variance. One dimension exhibited a significant main effect for Period, $F(5,48) = 3.63$, $p < .05$, with no other significant effects. This represents a cross-media period-style dimension where artists are grouped on the basis of period rather than medium or the interaction of period and medium. Thus, the artistically untrained subjects did in fact tend to group together works of art produced during the same period. When average values on the cross-media dimension of the works of art for each period were graphed, they showed an irregular cyclical trend. This suggested that the dimension might have to do with the primary process-secondary process dimension.

In order to help in labeling the period-style dimension, other subjects were asked to rate each of the stimuli on a variety of 7-point rating scales. An art work's position on the period-style dimension correlated with several scales seemingly indicative of the primary process-secondary process dimension (see below): e.g., strange, unnatural, meaningless, imagination important, and otherworldly. These results thus suggest a cross-media synchronization of primary process cycles. A possible implication of this finding is that the evolutionary forces described above may operate not on medium-specific traditions but upon the entire art-producing system in a given society.

EVOLUTIONARY TRENDS IN BRITISH ART

Several quantitative studies have been conducted to test predictions derived from the evolutionary theory described above. These include studies of French poetry (Martindale, 1975), Italian painting (Martindale, 1982b), Japanese prints (Martindale, 1982c) and French, German, British, and

Italian music (Martindale & Uemura, 1983). These investigations have yielded results consistent with theoretical predictions. However, the most extensive work has been done with British poetry (Martindale, 1975, 1978, 1981b). In order to provide more details concerning empirical support for the theory, this work will be described and then related to work in progress on British painting and music.[4]

British Poetry

In order to have a systematic method of sampling British poets, the time span from 1490 to 1949 was divided into 23 periods of 20 years each. For each of these periods, the poets born during the period were ranked on the basis of number of pages devoted to them in the relevant Oxford anthology of English verse. For each period, the five most eminent poets were selected.[5] Once poets had been selected, the most complete and recent available edition of their poetic works was obtained. Fifty random samples were taken by drawing 50 page numbers from a table of random numbers. The first eight lines were counted off and the sample for each page was terminated at the first phrase delimiter at or after the end of the eighth line. The mean number of words per poet was 2980 (SD = 272). Before putting the samples into machine readable form, some editing was done in order to make the texts compatible with the programs used: Contractions and abbreviations were spelled out, and all hyphens and dashes were deleted. Old spellings were consistently modernized in order to facilitate dictionary lookups (see below). Modernization was confined to minor spelling changes. The texts were analyzed with several computer programs written by the author: COUNT (Martindale, 1973b), SEMIS (Martindale, 1975), and LEXSTAT (Martindale, 1974).

The Regressive Imagery Dictionary, used with COUNT, contains 2900 words assigned to 43 categories. Of these categories, 29 measure primary process content, 7 measure secondary process content, and 7 measure references to emotion. The 29 categories designed to measure primary process content are subsumed under 5 summary categories: Drives (references to oral, anal, and sexual content), Sensation (references to touch, taste, odor, etc.), Perceptual Disinhibition (references to uncontrolled motions and chaotic percepts), Regressive Cognition (direct references to alteration in consciousness or to attributes of primary process cognition—e.g., timelessness), and Icarian Imagery (references to fire, water, rising, and

---

[4]In order to save space, minor methodological details are omitted. The reader is referred to the references cited above for details.

[5]For the first two periods only two poets were available. Thus, the total sample consists of 109 poets.

falling; based on the contention of Murray, 1955, and Ogilvie, 1968, that such references relate to preverbal symbolization of drives and emotions). The Secondary Process summary category subsumes the categories Abstraction (e.g., "know," "thought"), Social Behavior (e.g., "tell," "call"), Instrumental Behavior (e.g., "make," "work"), Restraint (e.g., "stop," "bind"), Order (e.g., "simple," "measure"), Temporal References (e.g., "now," "then"), and Moral Imperatives (e.g., "should," "virtue"). For any document, COUNT produces a tally of the percentage of text words falling into each of the categories. The categories and more examples of the words in each are listed in Martindale (1975, 1976, 1978, 1981a). The dictionary was constructed by searching the theoretical literature for aspects of primary process and secondary process cognition that might be indicated by word usage (see Martindale, 1975).

Evidence for the construct validity of the dictionary has come from a number of studies where dictionary categories have yielded results consistent with theoretical expectations. For example, more primary process content has been found in the poetry of writers exhibiting signs of psychopathology than in the poetry of writers not exhibiting such signs (Martindale, 1975), in folktales of more primitive as opposed to more advanced preliterate societies (Martindale, 1976), in the fantasy stories of younger as opposed to older children (West, Martindale, & Sutton-Smith, 1980), in verbal productions of hypnotized as opposed to nonhypnotized subjects (Comeau & Farthing, 1982), and in verbalizations of people under the influence of psilocybin (Martindale & Fischer, 1977) and marijuana (West, Martindale, Hines, & Roth, in press).

Depth of regression should hypothetically be measured by amount of primary process content and (inversely) by amount of secondary process content. A summary measure, Primary Process,[6] was computed as follows: Standard scores (with a mean of 0 and standard deviation of 1) were obtained for the primary process summary categories Drive, Sensation, Perceptual Disinhibition, Regressive Cognition, and Icarian Imagery. These were added together and the sum restandardized. Then the standardized Secondary Process score was subtracted. The purpose of the standardizations was to allow equal weighting, first, of the primary process summary categories and, second, of the contribution of primary process and secondary process categories.

Martindale (1978) constructed a Composite Variability Index to measure the complexity, ambiguity, and variability of texts. Essentially, it is intended to be a measure of the arousal potential or impact value of a text. It

---

[6]In previous publications, this measure was labeled Net Regression. However, since a variety of statistical regression procedures are reported below, the two uses of the term "regression" would prove confusing.

is composed of several relatively nonredundant measures computed by SEMIS and LEXSTAT. The index is composed of the following scores:[7] Polarity (extremity of a word's rating in semantic differential space; hypothetically a measure of semantic intensity), Meaningfulness (number of word-associates given to a word in a one-minute period: hypothetically a measure of use of multiple-meaning or ambiguous words), Hapax Legomena Percentage (percentage of words occurring only once in a text; hypothetically a measure of difficulty or complexity), Mean Word Length (hypothetically a measure of difficulty), Coefficient of Variation of Word Frequency, Coefficient of Variation of Word Length, and Coefficient of Variation of Phrase Length (hypothetically measures of variability). For each of these measures, residual scores removing any effects of number of words and number of phrases in the document were computed. These were then standardized (to a mean of 0 and a standard deviation of 1) in order to give each equal weight. Finally, the standard scores were added together to yield a Composite Variability Index for each poet.

As predicted by the evolutionary theory, the Composite Variability Index varies across periods in a statistically significant way; $F(22,86) = 9.16$, $p<.0001$. These differences are due to the predicted monotonic uptrend over time, $F_{lin}(1,86) = 178.32$, $p<.0001$, while $F_{higher-order}(21,86) = 1.11$, ns. The theory merely predicts a monotonic uptrend rather than a specifically linear one. However, some nonlinear trends would be contrary to theoretical expectations. Thus, the absence of higher-order trends is gratifying.

Primary Process rises over time, but a cyclical trend is superimposed on the linear increase. It is the cyclical trend that is of most theoretical interest: The basic prediction is one of oscillation rather than one of a necessary long-term rise in primary process content. Results of the analysis of variance suggest that both trends are real ones. For the overall analysis of variance, $F(22,86) = 5.71$, $p<.0001$; $F_{lin}(1,86) = 88.58$, $p<.0001$; $F_{higher-order}(21,86) = 1.76$, $p<.05$. Figure 17.1 presents mean values of Primary Process for each period. (For purposes of comparability, the autocorrelation analyses reported below were done on detrended and standardized scores: Both linear and quadratic trends were removed from all of the series illustrated in Fig. 17.1, and each was restandardized to have a mean of 0 and a standard deviation of 1.) As may be seen, the Primary Process cycles are not all of equal duration. The time from one valley to the next (ignoring the slight decline in Period 11) is four periods (80 years) in four cases and five periods (100 years) in one case. Primary Process does decline during periods commonly seen as involving initiation of a new style

---

[7]The first two measures are based on text words found in a dictionary based on normative ratings. The remaining scores are computed on the basis of all of the words in a text.

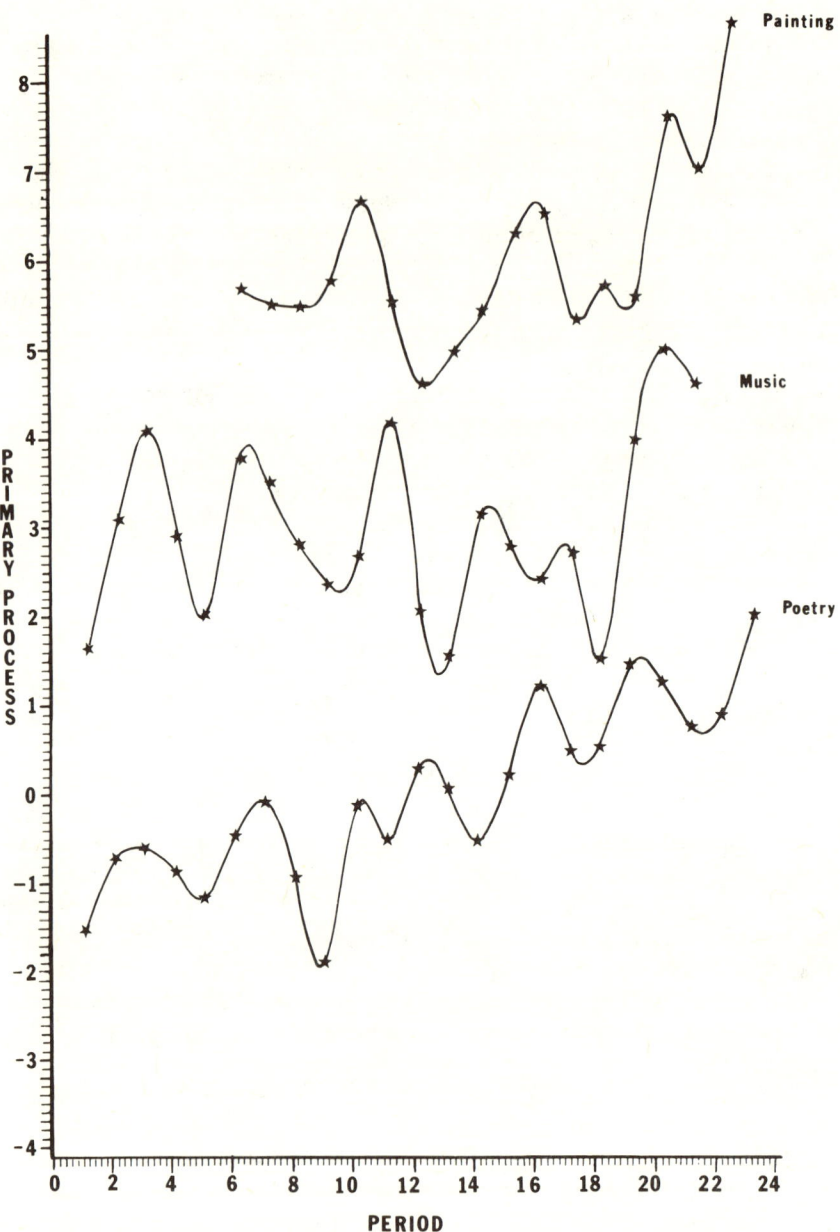

FIG. 17.1 Primary process content in poetry, music, and painting. Values for music are shifted upward three points and those for painting are shifted upward six points.

(see Martindale, 1978, 1981b) and begins to rise once the new style is established.

Spectral analysis of the means shown in Fig. 17.1 shows a clear peak indicating the existence of a four-period cycle. Both theoretical considerations and the fact that the cycles vary somewhat in their periods suggest that they arise from a stochastic rather than a deterministic cause. Cycles of this sort can arise from a second-order autoregressive process; that is, the mean value for a given period is determined by the value for the prior two periods plus random error (Gottman, 1981). Autocorrelation analysis of the detrended Primary Process mean scores supports this notion: Autocorrelations at lags from 1 to 10 exhibit a damped sinusoidal pattern. On the other hand, partial autocorrelations (the autocorrelation at a given lag partialling out the effect of autocorrelations due to earlier lags) fall to essentially zero after a lag of two. This is the pattern expected with a second-order autoregressive process (Gottman, 1981). It is of less than incidental interest that a quite different pattern should be found if the reflectionist theory (primary process content in a given period is due to extra-literary "shocks" in the current and/or prior periods) were true (Gottman, 1981). Since the first autoregressive parameter is insignificant, the best autoregressive model for Primary Process in a given period (PP_t) is

$$PP_t = -.48\, PP_{t-2}$$

That is, amount of primary process content in the poetry of a given period is a function primary process content two periods prior (PP_{t-2}) to the period. The autoregressive parameter is significant, $t(22) = 2.63$, $p < .05$. When Primary Process scores are regressed on predictions from this model, a significant fit is achieved, $F(1,19) = 6.89$, $p < .05$, $r^2 = .27$. The fact that the first autoregressive parameter is insignificant suggests that we are dealing with a "seasonal" rather than a second-order autoregressive process. Both processes can produce periodic trends.

In summary, theoretical predictions concerning both arousal potential and primary process content are supported by the statistical analyses. The index of arousal potential exhibited a monotonic increase with no evidence of cyclic oscillation across the entire time span. The index of primary process content showed the predicted cyclic trend. Autocorrelation analysis of the primary process scores indicated that—as expected from the evolutionary theory—amount of primary process content in a period could be predicted by amount of primary process content in a prior period. The autocorrelation analysis produced results contrary to those that would be predicted by reflectionist theory.

Specificity of the Linguistic Trends to Poetry

Although intuitively unlikely, it is possible that the trends reported above are characteristic of changes in the English language in general rather than being specific to poetry. To explore this possibility, an analysis of prose samples from the *Annual Register* was conducted (Martindale, 1978). The *Annual Register* has appeared yearly since the mid-eighteenth century. It includes a narrative description of world events for the year. For the period from 1770 to 1970, 10 samples from the *Annual Register* for every twentieth year (i.e., 1770, 1790, etc.) were drawn at random. The mean number of words per volume sampled was 2687 ($SD = 281$). The Composite Variability Index was computed for each sample. It showed no interperiod differences, $F(10,99) = .76$, *ns,* and no linear trend over time, $F_{lin}(1,99) = 1.61$, *ns.* Likewise, there were no interperiod differences for Primary Process, $F(10,99) = 1.10$, *ns,* nor any linear or higher-order trends. Thus, the trends found in poetry do not appear to be reflective of general trends in the English language.

Application of the Theory to Other Arts

In order to test the evolutionary theory on other art forms, such as painting or music, it is necessary to find nonlinguistic operationalizations of the key variables, arousal potential and primary process content. The approach taken in regard to studying painting and music has been to have subjects rate colored slides or musical excerpts on 7-point rating scales. Based on the work of Berlyne (1974), there is good reason to believe that arousal potential can be measured with scales such as simple-complex, relaxed-tense, and passive-active. Indeed, in studies of Italian painting (Martindale, 1982b), Japanese prints (Martindale, 1982c), and French, German, British, and Italian music (Martindale & Uemura, 1983) these scales have loaded highly on the same factor in factor analyses and have generally behaved as theoretically predicted.

In these studies, scales, such as photographic-nonphotographic, natural-unnatural, meaningful-meaningless, this world-other world, and representative-nonrepresentative have tended to load highly on another factor presumably indicative of primary process content. In one study (Martindale, Ross, & Miller, in preparation), subjects wrote TAT stories to a set of nine paintings in a variety of nineteenth- and twentieth-century styles, while other subjects rated the paintings on the natural-unnatural, representative-nonrepresentative, meaningful-meaningless, and photographic-nonphotographic scales. The TAT stories were analyzed with the Regressive Imagery Dictionary and an average primary process score for each painting was computed. Spearman correlations with above named scales were .62, .80, .70, and .65, all $p < .05$. These results support the contention that these scales are valid measures of primary process content.

British Music

In order to test predictions derived from the evolutionary study, Martindale and Uemura (1983) conducted a study of musical themes from the works of French, German, British, and Italian composers born between 1490 and 1909. This time span was divided into 21 periods of 20 years each. For each country, the three most eminent composers born during each period were selected by consulting a series of standard reference works in a specified order. One theme (usually three to six bars) was selected for each composer by a systematic search of a series of standard musical theme dictionaries and collections of compositions. Each theme was played by a violinist and tape-recorded. Because of the large number of themes, three sets of raters each rated one-third of the themes, which were presented to them in random order. The themes were rated on 13 seven-point bipolar scales designed to measure the two theoretical constructs.

After assessment of reliability, an average rating was obtained for each theme and a factor analysis was performed. Three factors with eigenvalues greater than 1.00 were obtained. The first showed high loadings on the scales Tense, Strong, Complex, and Active. The second showed high loadings on the scales Meaningless, Unnatural, Disorderly, and Dislike. The first factor seems to measure arousal potential, while the second seems to measure primary process. Factor scores on each factor were obtained for each theme. Arousal potential was also measured by the melodic originality procedure used in an earlier study (Simonton, 1980). The first 10 notes of each of the 292 themes were keypunched and note-to-note transitional probabilities were computed for each pair of notes. Then, for each composition, the sum of its two-note transitional probabilities was computed. This gives an (inverted) measure of the originality or improbability of the theme. This measure was reversed so that higher numbers indicated greater originality, standardized, and combined with first-factor scores to yield an index we shall call Arousal Potential.

In this section we consider only the results for the British series of composers. Arousal Potential exhibited a significant linear increase over time, $F_{lin}(1,42) = 13.63$, $p < .001$ but no nonlinear trends, $F_{higher-order}(19,42) = .85$, ns. Results for Primary Process in music are illustrated in Fig. 17.1 above. The overall analysis of variance was not significant; however, a glance at Fig. 17.1 shows that the predicted oscillatory pattern is clearly present, so the analysis was pursued further. Spectral analysis of the means indicated a periodicity at four periods per cycle. Autocorrelations exhibited a pattern similar to that found with poetry. The best model was

$$PP_t = -.40\, PP_{t-2}$$

with the autoregressive coefficient significant at $p<.06$, $t(20) = 1.98$. Regressing the original means on predicted scores yielded $r^2 = .20$, $F(1,17) = 4.34$, $p<.06$.

In summary, the results of the study of British music were in conformity with theoretical predictions. Arousal potential increased monotonically, while the index of primary process content exhibited an oscillatory pattern. Autocorrelation analysis yielded results contrary to those that would be expected by a reflectionist theory but consistent with the prediction of evolutionary theory. Primary process in a given period could be predicted from primary process in prior periods, as was the case with poetry.

British Painting

Additional research, as yet unpublished, focused on paintings by French and British painters born between 1590 and 1919. This time span was divided into 17 periods of 20 years each. For each country, the three most eminent painters born during each period were selected in a manner similar to that used for the selection of composers. Then, one color reproduction of a work containing human figures by each painter was systematically selected. Color slides of each painting were made and the slides were rated on 10 seven-point bipolar scales. After assessment of reliability, average ratings were obtained for each painting and a factor analysis was performed. Two factors with eigenvalues greater than 1.00 emerged. Unfortunately, the variables supposedly tapping both arousal potential and primary process all loaded highly on the first factor, while the second factor tapped hedonic tone. The cause of the problem would seem to be that the fairly nonrepresentative paintings from the last three periods showed extremely high scores on both of the theoretical variables. The first factor scores exhibit a positively accelerated uptrend, $F_{lin}(1,34) = 4.50$, $p<.05$, $F_{quad}(1,34) = 5.44$, $p<.05$, without higher-order trends, $F_{higher-order}(14,34) = .62$, ns. Thus, arousal potential as well as primary process does seem to increase. Of the individual rating scales, only the dimension Orderly-Disorderly yielded a significant overall analysis of variance, $F(16,34) = 2.35$, $p<.05$. Since this scale has loaded with primary process indices in other studies, there is some at least tentative support for taking it as an index of primary process content in painting. Means for each period are illustrated in Fig. 17.1 above. Spectral analyses of these means indicated a clear five-period cycle. Autocorrelation analysis yielded results similar to those found for both poetry and music. In this case, the best prediction equation was

$$PP_t = -.61\ PP_{t'3},$$

with the coefficient significant at $p<.01$, $t\,(16) = 3.21$. Regression of observed scores on predicted scores yielded $r^2 = .47$, $F\,(1,12) = 10.55$, $p<.01$.

In summary, the study of British painting yielded results in general conformity with theoretical predictions. Because of high intercorrelations among the scales, the index of arousal potential was contaminated by scales usually tapping primary process content. The index did, however, exhibit a monotonic increase across time. The index of primary process content showed the expected oscillations, and autocorrelation analysis yielded results consistent with evolutionary theory and inconsistent with reflectionist theory.

Synchronicity of Evolution

To what extent have British poetry, music, and painting evolved together? Has British art in general evolved or has each of the arts evolved in essential isolation from the others? Examination of Fig. 17.1 does not yield a clear answer to this question. The cycles are obviously not completely in phase. It is logically impossible for painting to be in phase with poetry and music because the latter exhibit four-period cycles, while painting has a five-period cycle. Poetry and music, however, do move together across at least parts of the time span studied. However, primary process in poetry and music are both autogregressive processes with similar parameters. If both started out by chance at the same point, they could appear to be cross-correlated even if they were not (Jenkins & Watts, 1968). In order to test for cross-media influences, we must first remove the autoregressive influences. For each series, residual scores (the difference between the observed score for the period and the score predicted by the autogressive equation) were obtained. Then, for each series, stepwise regression was used to relate the residual score for the series to the residual scores from the other two series for the current period and the prior four periods. If a real cross-correlation existed, this analysis should reveal it. The reasoning is the same as that behind partial correlation. If two series are in fact cross-correlated, this cross-correlation should remain once autoregressive factors capable of inducing a spurious correlation are removed (Haugh, 1976; Pierce, 1977).

The results for primary process in poetry and painting were clear. No variable or combination of variables yielded a significant ($p<.05$) correlation. On the other hand, the results for music were different. The best predictor is summarized in the following equation,

$$M_t = -.47 - 1.01 \, Pt_{t-2}$$

where M_t is the residual primary process score for music in period t, and Pt_{t-2} is the residual primary process score in painting in period t − 2. For this regression, $r^2 = .56$, $F(1,7) = 8.77$, $p < .05$. In order to work with a somewhat longer time series, primary process in music was regressed on only the poetry primary process scores. In this case the best set of predictors is summarized in the following equation,

$$M_t = -.09 - .39 \, P_t + .47 \, P_{t-4},$$

where P_i is the residual poetry primary process score for period i. For this regression, $r^2 = .44$, $F(2,12) = 4.73$, $p < .05$. (On the other hand, stepwise regression of poetry scores on music scores alone yields insignificant results.) Thus, music does seem to be influenced by prior developments in both poetry and painting. Not only is music influenced by these arts but, as has often been suggested, it tends to lag behind them. That is, earlier values of primary process in poetry and painting are most important in determining later values of primary process in music.

Why this pattern of results emerges is not completely clear. It is certainly reasonable to think, however, that it is easier to "translate" a theme or idea from poetry or painting to music than to perform the reverse "translation." The reason for this is that it is easier to understand what a poem or a painting is about than to understand what a piece of music is about. Given this, a poet or painter has a better chance of influencing a composer than vice versa.

A study in progress on the "sociometry" of the British poets reported on in this chapter shows that they form a remarkably interconnected series. That is, poets in the series tended to know personally at least some other contemporary poets in the series. This is so much the case that we might think of British poetry as having been passed on as an oral tradition. Though the study is not complete, it is already quite clear that poets and composers tended not to be personally acquainted. It is almost certainly the case that the composers were not in general personally acquainted with contemporary painters either. Given this, it would be more likely that a composer would be influenced by earlier poets or painters, who had already attained fame, than by contemporaries who would be more likely to be working in comparative obscurity. Though poets and painters did occasionally know one another, a similar line of reasoning could be evoked to explain the independent evolution of poetry and painting.

SUMMARY

The theory of aesthetic evolution presented in this chapter makes two basic predictions about the history of any artistic tradition. The objective arousal potential of the artifacts produced by the tradition should increase over time, and primary process content of the artifacts should exhibit a cyclical pattern over time. The cyclic pattern is caused by periodic stylistic changes. It is held that these trends are produced by an evolutionary process intrinsic to the artistic tradition. Of course, profound social, political, or economic changes could disrupt this evolutionary process or end it altogether by destroying the tradition. In regard to the two basic predictions, evidence supportive of both arose from studies of British poetry, painting, and music. The evolutionary theory essentially says that artistic content is due to autocorrelation within an artistic tradition (i.e., current content is determined by prior artistic content). Thus, it is encouraging that statistically significant autoregressive models could be fit to the indices of primary process content in all three media, and that the autocorrelation analyses produced patterns contrary to those that would be found if artistic content were caused by nonartistic social forces. The latter finding is consistent with the strong version of the evolutionary theory—that the theory accounts for all or most of the trends to be found in the history of an art form. Also consistent with the strong version are findings that at least two-thirds of the overall similarity among a group of poets is accounted for by similarity in the theoretical variables, that art history can be experimentally simulated in the laboratory, and that it has so far been impossible to find extra-artistic time series that correlate with artistic time series in a consistent manner.

Since it is important to know the level at which aesthetic evolution operates, we asked whether evolution in British poetry, painting, and music is coordinated or synchronized. The statistical analyses yielded clear results: poetry and painting seem to evolve independently, whereas change in music is somewhat dependent upon present and prior changes in both poetry and painting. A set of independent autoregressive series each having about the same periodicity would be expected to drift in and out of phase in a more or less random manner. Thus, if we asked whether period styles exist in the case of poetry and painting, we would get contradictory answers depending upon the epoch we considered. However, the general answer for British art is clear: Poetry and painting evolved independently, and any similarity during a given epoch probably arose purely by chance.

The specificity of aesthetic evolution is rather surprising. Consider the history of British poetry. We have seen that the content of British poetry cannot be predicted from the content of British painting or music. It cannot be predicted from the content of French poetry, either (Martindale, 1975). Nor can it be predicted from British social, economic, or political time series. Indeed, after 15 years of looking, I can find no consistent predictor other than the content of prior British poetry. For almost five centuries then, British poetry seems to have been driven by evolutionary forces the operation of which was impervious to factors we might have thought would be important—what was occurring in the other arts; whether poets were courtiers or paupers; whether they wrote during war, peace, revolution, plague, famine, inflation, or depression. Perhaps this is an anomalous case, but results to date with other artistic series suggest that it is not. Artistic traditions seem to be much less interconnected with other artistic traditions, let alone with the larger society, than is commonly thought. This leads one to wonder whether other social institutions are as interdependent as we think them to be. Social, political, judicial, and economic institutions may also be subject to powerful independent evolutionary processes the strength of which is currently underestimated.

REFERENCES

Berlyne, D. E. *Aesthetics and psychobiology.* New York: Appleton-Century-Crofts, 1971.
Berlyne, D. E. (Ed.). *Studies in the new experimental aesthetics: Steps toward an objective psychology of aesthetic appreciation.* Washington, D.C.: Hemisphere, 1974.
Boulding, K. E. *Ecodynamics: A new theory of societal evolution.* Beverly Hills: Sage, 1978.
Campbell, D. T. Variation and selective retention in sociocultural evolution. In H. R. Barringer, G. I. Blanksten, & R. W. Mack (Eds.), *Social change in developing areas.* Cambridge: Schenkman, 1965.
Cavalli-Sforza, L. L., & Feldman, M. W. *Cultural transmission and evolution: A quantitative approach.* Princeton, N.J.: Princeton University Press, 1981.
Cohen, J. *Structure du langage poétique.* Paris: Flammarion, 1966.
Comeau, H., & Farthing, G. W. *An examination of language content for manifestations of primary and secondary process during the hypnotic and awake states.* Unpublished paper, University of Maine, 1982.
Darwin, C. *The descent of man and selection in relation to sex.* New York: D. Appleton, 1896. (Originally published, 1871).
Ehrenzweig, A. *The psycho-analysis of artistic vision and hearing.* New York: Braziller, 1953.
Fromm, E. Primary and secondary process in waking and in altered states of consciousness. *Journal of Altered States of Consciousness,* 1978, *4,* 115-128.
Göller, A. *Entstehung der arkitektonischen Stilformen.* Stuttgart: K. Wittwer, 1888.
Gottman, J. M. *Time-series analysis: A comprehensive introduction for social scientists.* Cambridge: Cambridge University Press, 1981.
Hasenfus, N., Martindale, C., & Birnbaum, D. The psychological reality of cross-media artistic styles. *Journal of Experimental Psychology: Human Perception and Performances,* 1983, *9,* 841-863.
Haugh, L. D. Checking the independence of two covariance stationary time series: A univariate residual cross-correlation approach. *Journal of the American Statistical Association,* 1976, *71,* 378-385.
Jenkins, G. M., & Watts, D. G. *Spectral analysis and its applications.* San Francisco: Holden-Day, 1968.
Kahler, E. *The disintegration of form in the arts.* New York: Braziller, 1968.
Kris, E. *Psychoanalytic explorations in art.* New York: International Universities Press, 1952.
Kubler, G. *The shape of time: Remarks on the history of things.* New Haven: Yale University Press, 1962.
Laver, J. *Dress.* London: John Murray, 1950.
Lingoes, J. C. An IBM-7090 program for Guttman-Lingoes configurational simularity-I. *Behavioral Science,* 1967, *12,* 502-503.

Lingoes, J. C. *The Guttman-Lingoes nonmetric program series.* Ann Arbor: Mathesis Press, 1973.

Maritain, J. *Creative intuition in art and poetry.* Cleveland: Meridian, 1965. (Originally published, 1953).

Martindale, C. An experimental simulation of literary change. *Journal of Personality and Social Psychology,* 1973, *25,* 319-326. (a)

Martindale, C. COUNT: A PL/I program for content analysis of natural language (abstract). *Behavioral Science,* 1973, *18,* 148. (b)

Martindale, C. LEXSTAT: A PL/I program for computation of lexical statistics (abstract). *Behavioral Research Methods and Instrumentation,* 1974, *6,* 571.

Martindale, C. *Romantic progression: The psychology of literary history.* Washington, D.C.: Hemisphere, 1975.

Martindale, C. Primitive mentality and the relationship between art and society. *Scientific Aesthetics,* 1976, *1,* 5-18.

Martindale, C. The evolution of English poetry. *Poetics,* 1978, *7,* 231-248.

Martindale, C. *Cognition and consciousness.* Homewood, Ill.: Dorsey, 1981. (a)

Martindale, C., & Uemura, A. Stylistic evolution in European music. *Leonardo,* 1983, *15,* 225-228.

Martindale, C. Evolutionary trends in poetic style: The case of English metaphysical poetry. Paper in preparation, 1982. (a)

Martindale, C. *Stylistic evolution in Italian painting.* Paper presented at American Psychological Association convention, Washington, D.C., 1982. (b)

Martindale, C. Unpublished data. 1982. (c)

Martindale, C., & Fischer, R. The effects of psilocybin on primary process content in language. *Confinia Psychiatrica,* 1977, *20,* 195-202.

Martindale, C., & Hasenfus, N. *The psychological reality of cross-media period styles.* Paper presented at Semiotic Society of America meeting, Providence, October 6, 1978.

Martindale, C., Ross, M., & Miller, I. Stylistic evolution in modern painting: A preliminary study. Paper in preparation, 1982.

Martindale, C., & Uemura, A. Stylistic evolution in European music. *Leonardo,* 1983, *15,* 225-228, (in press).

Mukařovský, J. *On poetic language.* Lisse: Peter de Ridder, 1976. (Originally published, 1940).

Murray, H. American Icarus. In A. Burton & R. E. Harris (Eds.), *Clinical studies of personality* (Vol. 2). New York: Harper & Row, 1955.

Ogilvie, D. The Icarus complex. *Psychology Today,* 1968, *3*(7), 30-34.

Ortega y Gasset, J. *The dehumanization of art.* Garden City, N.Y.: Doubleday, 1956. (Originally published, 1948).

Peckham, M. *Man's rage for chaos.* Philadelphia: Chilton, 1965.

Pierce, D. A. Relationship—and the lack thereof—between economic time series, with special reference to money and interest rates. *Journal of the American Statistical Association,* 1977, *72,* 11-26.

Pulliam, H. R., & Dunford, C. *Programmed to learn: An essay on the evolution of culture.* New York: Columbia University Press, 1980.

Sachs, C. *The commonwealth of art: Style in the fine arts, music, and the dance.* New York: Norton, 1946.

Shklovsky, V. Der Zusammenhang zwischen den Verfahren der Subjetfügang und den allgemeinen Stilverfahren. In J. Štriedter (Ed.), *Texte der Russichen Formalisten.* Munich: Fink, 1969. (Originally published, 1919).

Simonton, D. K. Thematic fame, melodic originality, and musical Zeitgeist: A biographical and transhistorical content analysis. *Journal of Personality and Social Psychology,* 1980, *38,* 972-983.

Sorokin, P. A. *Social and cultural dynamics.* New York: American Book Company, 1937.

Stone, P., Dunphy, D., Smith, M., & Ogilvie, D. *The general inquirer: A computer approach to content analysis.* Cambridge: MIT Press, 1966.

Thompson, R. F., & Spencer, W. A. Habituation: A model for the study of neuronal substrates of behavior. *Psychological Review,* 1966, *173,* 16–43.

Thompson, R. F., Berry, S. D., Rinaldi, P. C., & Berger, T. W. Habituation and the orienting reflex: The dual process theory revisited. In H. D. Kimmel, E. H. van Olst, & J. F. Orlebeke (Eds.), *The orienting reflex in humans.* Hillsdale, N.J.: Lawrence Erlbaum Associates, 1979.

Trotsky, L. *Literature and revolution.* Ann Arbor: University of Michigan Press, 1968. (Originally published, 1924).

Tynjanov, J. *Archaisten und Neuerer.* Munich: Fink, 1967. (Originally published, 1929).

West, A., Martindale, C., Hines, D., & Roth, W. Marijuana-induced primary process content in the TAT. *Journal of Personality Assessment,* in press.

West, A., Martindale, C., & Sutton-Smith, B. *Age trends in content and lexical characteristics of children's fantasy narrative productions.* Paper presented at Eastern Psychological Association convention, Hartford, 1980.

Worringer, W. *Form in Gothic.* London: G. P. Putnam's Sons, 1957.

18 History and the Study of Expressive Action

Peter Collett
Oxford University

Of all the disciplines that are concerned with human affairs, social psychology is probably the most ahistorical. Other disciplines such as sociology, cultural anthropology and linguistics have enjoyed a long flirtation with history, as well as the occasional union. But social psychology has chosen to play the part of the wallflower. So far we have been largely unaware of the interdisciplinary dance going on around us, or if we have known about it we have decided not to join in. Sociology, on the other hand, has had a long and profitable association with history. Comte and Marx were equally at home in either discipline, and Durkheim and Weber had a profound impact on the course of historical studies—in particular on historians such as Febvre, Bloch and the *Annales* school in France. Durkheim was of course both a sociologist and an anthropologist, and in his latter capacity he was able from the beginning to claim a special place for history in the study of other societies. The role of history has since been reinforced by such diverse anthropologists as Evans-Pritchard (1961), Harris (1968), and Lewis (1968). Of the recent anthropologists, Evans-Pritchard has probably been the most adamant in insisting on the importance of history. He makes the point that just as culture offers a way of testing theories and models in different societies, so too history affords a laboratory for testing their validity in different ages. That is, it offers the kind of diversity that the anthropologist finds in different cultures.

Social psychologists have also been quick to appreciate the value of comparative studies, but they seldom put their theories to the test in time as well as culture. A brief examination of the history of social psychology reveals, however, that this was not always the case. For example, Wundt (1911) drew heavily on historical evidence in his discussion of language, custom and gesture, as did Le Bon (1895) in his seminal work on crowds. But today's social psychologists are quite unmoved by history, and so, it seems, are most linguists. At the turn of the century linguistics was devoted almost entirely to questions surrounding the evolution of language and the laws which govern its development over time. Today the historical linguist is in a minority, and history, which once enjoyed the limelight, has been relegated to a dim corner of the linguistics stage. When we examine the casting practices of the various disciplines we notice that while sociology and anthropology have happily offered history a leading role, and linguistics has grudgingly given it a minor supporting part, social psychology has not even allowed it the briefest audition. It sometimes seems that social psychologists are content to behave as though the world only came into existence a few decades ago.

In this chapter we shall explore some of the ways in which the social psychologist can draw on observations of the past in order to chart certain historical constancies and changes in behavior. In so doing we shall focus our attention on the expressive domain of action, particularly the gestures, signs, and symbols that people use to announce their relationships to each other. Broadly speaking, there are two reasons for drawing on historical material. In the one case the psychologist may have established that a particular practice is presently being employed by a group of people and he or she may now wish to know whether it was employed in the past. In the other case the psychologist may simply be concerned to discover whether a practice was employed in the past, irrespective of whether it is used today. Here the psychologist may also be involved in the exegetic task of trying to reconstruct a practice on the basis of some extant description or depiction.

TRACING THE ORIGINS OF SOCIAL PRACTICES

Some years ago we embarked on a study of European gestures which, among other things, looked at the ways in which people signal "yes" and "no" with their heads (Morris, Collett, Marsh & O'Shaughnessy, 1979). During the Italian phase of the project we found that while the headshake was used throughout the whole of Italy, southern Italians either shook their heads from side to side or tossed them back to signal negation. Traveling north, we found that people employed both the headshake and the headtoss as far up as Naples, but that by the time we had arrived in Rome (which is about 200 kilometres further north) only the headshake remained. In other words, the headtoss had disappeared somewhere between Naples and Rome. To determine the exact location of the boundary which separated people who use the headtoss from those who do not, we returned to the area between Rome and Naples and travelled from village to village until we had mapped the headtoss in that region. When we came to examine the areas in which the headtoss was used most frequently we discovered that it began at a small range of hills just north of Naples and extended south, hugging the coastline. It also appeared on the eastern coast near the Gargano peninsula and extended south past Bari. The question before us was, why should the headtoss be found in just these areas?

The clue to this question was found in the fact that the headtoss is also the gesture for negation in Greece. Southern Italy was known to the ancient Greeks during the time of the Odyssey. We are told, for example, that Odysseus braved the dangerous channel between the mainland and Sicily, and that the siren Parthenope, who lived on the site of present-day Naples, flung herself into the sea for his love. In the first millenium B.C. the Greeks established trading posts at Ischia and Cumae. Very soon afterwards, *Magna Graecia* expanded to include Neopolis, Metapontum and Tarentum on the mainland, and Catane and Syracuse in Sicily (Boardman, 1964). All the Greek trading posts, and the cities into which they subsequently grew, were located along the coast, and their situation on the mainland corresponds very closely to the present-day location of the headtoss along the coast of southern Italy. On the west coast the Greeks settled at places like Cumae, Neopolis, Paestum and Agropoli, and it just so happens that it is precisely here that the highest concentrations of the headtoss are to be found today. Even though the early Greeks did not establish permanent trading posts on the east coast, their contact with this area was considerable. During the expansion of *Magna Graecia* the east coast was invaded by the Iapygi. The Iapygi came from what is now Albania and South Dalmatia, and as the present inhabitants of this region also employ the headtoss there is a strong possibility that the Iapygi were importing the gesture into the east coast while the Greeks were introducing it to the west and the south. Alternatively the headtoss could have been brought to the east coast when the Greeks hellenised that area a few centuries later.

We know that modern Greeks use the headtoss, and there is ample proof that their ancestors colonized southern Italy, but how can we be sure that the ancient Greeks employed the same gesture for negation as their descendants? The information that is required to complete this story comes from an examination of the verb *ananeuo,* which is the common classical Greek expression for negation and refusal. There are two sources of evidence which show that ananeuo refers to the act of tossing rather than shaking the head. First, its etymology reveals that while the stem *neuo,* refers to "nodding movement", the prefix, *ana,* means "up". Second, there are documents which report that the Greeks "aneneuo'd" during the first millenium B.C., as well as several metaphorical uses of the term which indicate that the gesture involved an upward movement of the head. The earliest documentary evidence that the Greeks ananeuo'd for negation comes from Homer. In book six of the *Iliad,* Hecuba and a group of Trojan women enter the temple, place gifts on the knees of the statue of the goddess Athene, and pray for a Trojan victory. The Goddess is reported to have refused their prayer by ananeuo'ing. There is always the possibility that this reference to ananeuo was intended figuratively rather than literally, in other words that it was used to refer to negation rather than to the gesture of tossing back the head. This suggestion, which is voiced by people like Sittl (1890), can in fact be discounted by looking at the ways in which the term has been applied metaphorically. For example, Galen (6:83) refers to the eyes ananeuo'ing and kataneuo'ing like a shaduf, which is a device that is

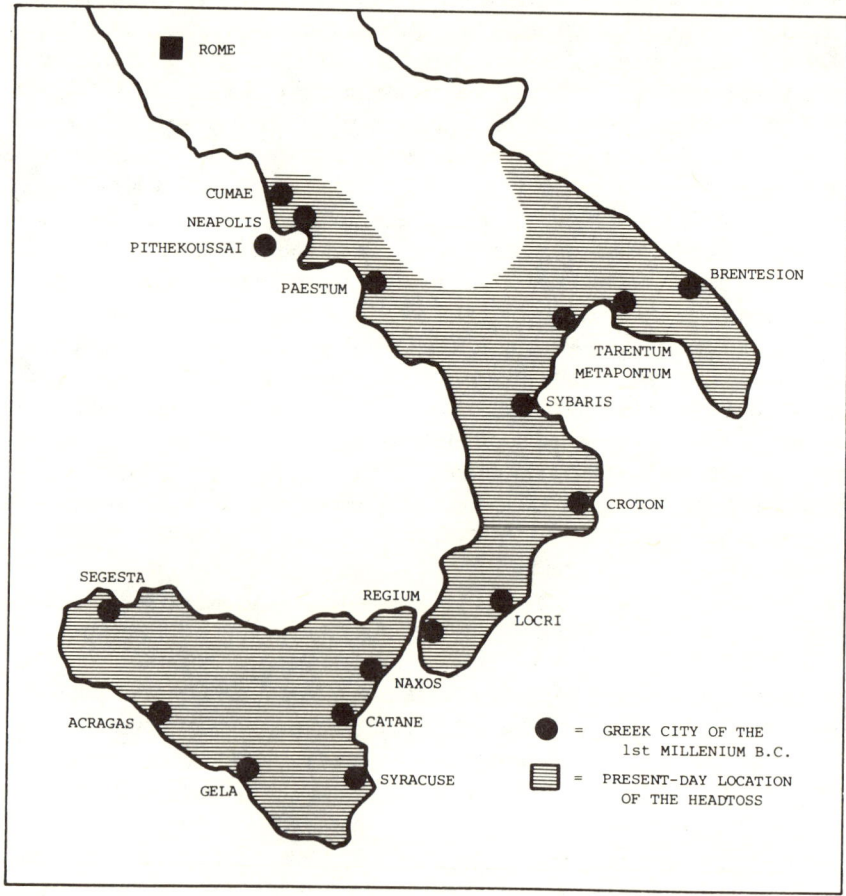

FIG. 18.1 The Headtoss in southern Italy.

moved up and down to draw water from a well. Pollux (1:219) describes horses as ananeuo'ing as they rear up, and Dionysius the Areopagite (15,3:166) talks of people ananeuo'ing toward the heavenly bodies.[1] The etymology of ananeuo, and its denotative and metaphorical uses, all point to the fact that the ancient Greeks tossed their heads back to signal negation. Their descedants also employ the gesture for the same purpose, as do the inhabitants of southern Italy where the ancient Greeks settled during the first millenium B.C.

This shows that the headtoss is extremely conservative. Despite the disappearance of the Greek language from Italy, the unification of the country, the advent of mass communications and a thousand other ravages of time, the headtoss is still to be found in the same region where it was first introduced more than two thousand years ago. But apart from revealing the remarkable tenacity of the headtoss, this illustration also serves to show how it is necessary to consult historical materials in order to explain contemporary practices. Originally we discovered that the headtoss is used in southern Italy, and later on that it is employed most frequently along the coast. This raised the possibility that the headtoss was a vestige of some earlier age. In order to explore this we were forced to consider the history of the region. This led us to the ancient Greeks and the documentary evidence relating to their gesture for "no". Only by examining the history of the region and the documents left by the Greeks was it possible to explain why southern Italians use the headtoss today.

There are two main sources of evidence that the social psychologist can consult when he or she wishes to know how people behaved in the past. The first is the written word, which includes documents in all their various forms, and the second is the visual image, which comprises painting, drawing, sculpture, photography and film.[2]

---

[1] See Stephanus (1831) for references to Galen, Pollux and Dionysius the Areopagite.

[2] There are of course other sources of historical material such as artefacts and oral records, but these have little bearing on the issue of expressive behavior. For example, flints, pots, and domestic utensils are useful indicators of technology, mode of subsistence and even the social organization of prehistoric peoples, but they seldom offer a basis for reconstructing their expressive behavior. Oral records are also disqualified from serving a useful purpose. Oral records can provide information on things like King-lists, genealogies and population movements, but even here they are subject to various types of chronological distortions such as telescoping, lengthening and outright fabrication (see Henige, 1974; Vansina, 1965). But for our purposes the important feature which distinguishes the oral tradition from writing and the visual media is the fact that while the latter speak to us directly across the chasm of time, oral accounts are always decoded and encoded at each link in the chain of transmission. As a result they are liable to the distortions and refinements associated with each new hearing and each new telling. This is not the case with written documents, except where they have passed through translation or been copied. Nor is it the case with painting, drawing, photography or film.

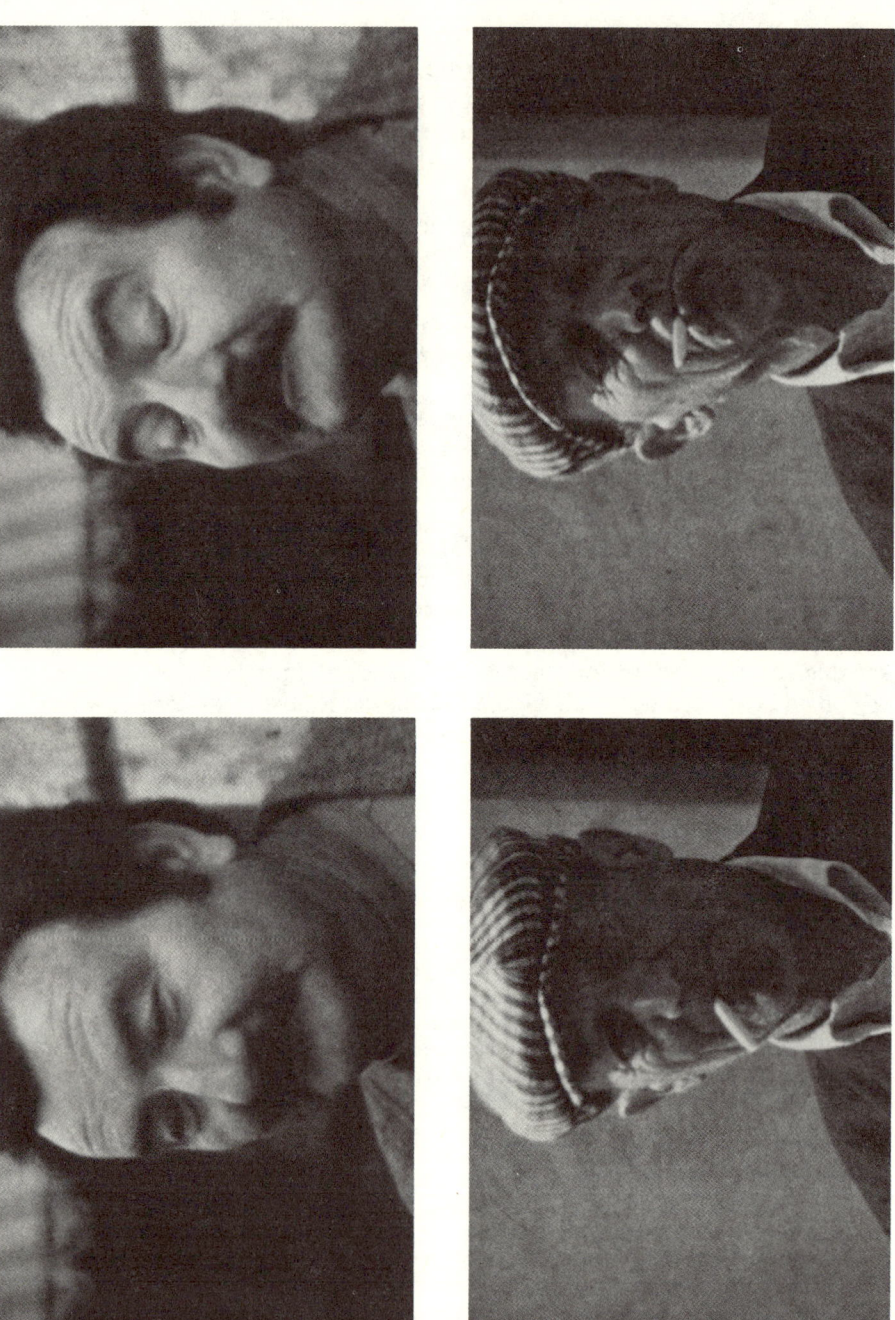

FIG. 18.2 The Headtoss performed by a Greek (above) and a southern Italian (below).

THE TESTIMONY OF THE WRITTEN WORD

Since the invention of writing, it has been possible for people to communicate directly with others who are removed from them in both space and time. Descriptions of events which were set down in earlier ages are therefore available to us without interruption, and, except where they have been translated or copied, we can be reasonably assured that such descriptions have not been contaminated by intervening readers. Written documents can serve the student of expressive behavior just as they do the historian, but like the historian the psychologist needs to evaluate the written testimony of the past. First, there is the possibility that a document may be fraudulent, or that it may be misguided, inaccurate or simply designed to convey a favorable image of the events which it describes. We know, for example, that not all the letters which bear Marie Antoinette's signature were written by her, that the authors of the Protocols of the Elders of Zion were not Zionists, and that Baron Munchausen, the famous German explorer who regaled Europe with fantastic tales of foreign lands, was not a Baron and probably never set foot outside Germany.

Without doubt the most fantastic accounts of other peoples that have come down to us are from the classical Greek writers, Ctesias and Megasthenes, from a lengthy document which Alexander is purported to have sent to his old tutor, Aristotle, and from Pliny's descriptions of the races of Aethiopia, India, and beyond. These documents conjured up a fabulous picture of the world outside Europe, a world populated by monstrous beings such as the Blemmyae, who had faces on their chests, the Hippopodes who had horses' hooves instead of feet, the Cynocephali, who had the head of a dog, and the Sciopods who lay on their back under the shadow of an enormous foot that shielded them from the sun. These and other fabulous creatures were an integral part of the classical world-view, and they persisted, with very little modification, through medieval times and well into the seventeenth century. They appeared in Montaigne's (1580) *Essais* and in Bulwer's (1650) *Anthropometamorphosis,* and continued to exercise the imagination of Europeans until they had been properly dispatched by the Ages of Discovery (Friedman, 1981; Hodgen, 1964). But if we look back to the originators of these marvelous creatures we find that Ctesias never visited the countries he described, and that his works and those of Megasthenes were more in the nature of fantastic travelogues than geographic documentaries. Alexander's letter to Aristotle was probably a fictional exercise required as part of a training in Rhetoric, and it is known that Pliny drew some of his observations from rather dubious sources.

If fraudulent and fictionalised documents confound the task of the historian, then they are also a potential problem for the psychologist who wishes to consult the textual evidence of the past[3]. But for the psychologist it is more a matter of having to deal with authors who have either nudged the truth, committed an error of observation, or simply borrowed the unreliable testimony of others. To check his or her sources the psychologist must therefore endeavor to consult what other documents there are. If several chroniclers have described the same practice then their descriptions should be compared. Failing this, one may need to rely on internal evidence or on commonsense. The only trouble with commonsense is that it is time-bound, and what seems unlikely to us may be completely plausible to people in some future age. Herodotus relates that when contemporary voyagers sailed past the Horn of Africa they noticed that the sun traversed the sky to the north rather than the south. Herodotus dismissed this observation as being contrary to what was known about the motion of the sun. But from our privileged position, we can see that the story was totally plausible.

When the psychologist consults textual evidence of the past, there are, as we have just seen, problems of its veracity. But the psychologist who uses textual evidence may also encounter another serious problem, namely the fact that certain textual records of events and practices are enigmatic, so that there is an indeterminate relationship between the written description of an event or practice and its actual realisation. This arises out of the incapacity of language to do complete justice to events, coupled with the fact that a single description can cover a multitude of events, just as a single event can be captured by a multitude of descriptions. These problems are nicely illustrated by the historical investigation of gesture, to which we now turn.

In the first act of *Romeo and Juliet,* Sampson and Gregory, who are servants of the Capulets, are strolling together through the city. As they spy two servants of the Montagues, Sampson says to Gregory, "I will bite my thumb at them; which is a disgrace to them, if they bear it." It is patently clear from his remark that Sampson intends a provocation, and this interpretation is soon borne out by the response he gets. Abram, at whom the gesture was directed, asks, "Do you bit your thumb at us, sir?" Sampson replies with deliberate ambiguity, "I do bite my thumb, sir," so Abram is forced to pose the question again, "Do you bite your thumb at us, sir?" Sampson now turns to his colleague and asks, "Is the law on our side, if I say -ay?", to which Gregory replies "No." So Sampson turns back to his interrogator and says, "No, sir, I do not bite my thumb at you, sir; but I bite my thumb, sir." As we read this episode it is evident to us that Sampson plans to insult the Montague servants and to provoke them into some ill-considered action. We can see what Sampson intends by the act of "biting

---

[3]For an interesting analysis of news distortion, see Knightley's (1975) discussion of the war correspondent.

his thumb," and we can reasonably assume that Shakespeare's early audiences knew the gesture and understood its significance. But we cannot actually say how the gesture was performed or what its significance might have been, other than as some kind of insult, threat, or provocation.

The case of Shakespeare's thumb-biting gesture offers a neat example of the kind of problem that the psychologist may encounter when attempting to reconstruct the expressive actions of the past. Here the psychologist is offered a rough descriptive gloss, but no precise details, and this leaves open two possibilities—either that the gesture is still being used and can therefore be identified by examining those gestures which now involve the thumb, or that it is no longer in existence and therefore needs to be identified using other procedures.

In considering the first possibility we find that there are several candidates for Shakespeare's thumb-biting gesture. One is the act of sucking the thumb, either as a phallic gesture or as a way of suggesting that someone is childish. The problem here is that thumb-sucking does not fit the description of biting, so we need to look elsewhere. This leaves two other gestures which are worth considering, both of which are used today in various parts of Europe. The first occurs where someone bites the knuckle of the thumb to show that he or she is containing his or her rage, and the second is the gesture of flicking one's thumbnail from behind the front teeth in order to suggest that someone or something is worthless. Although either could be the thumb-biting gesture, there are good reasons for rejecting both. First, the act of flicking one's teeth involves the thumbnail rather than the thumb, and second, the act of biting the knuckle connotes containment of rage, which is difficult to connect with provocation. This suggests that the thumb-biting gesture is no longer in currency, and that its actual morphology needs to be determined by considering how the act of biting one's thumb could have served as a provocation *in Shakespeare's time.*

The clue, it seems, is to be found in the fact that during the latter half of the sixteenth century men were in the habit of wearing gloves, and these were usually removed prior to any confrontation—not unlike the present-day Irish habit of taking off one's jacket to show that one means business (Fox, 1976). In fact, the practice of removing and throwing down one's glove had become ritualised as a challenge long before Shakespeare's time, and it is common knowledge that medieval knights used this device to invite each other into the lists. It seems likely that the medieval convention, or some version of it, was still around in a stylized form during Shakespeare's time, but it had become abbreviated to the point where an intention movement of removing one's gloves would suffice. There are basically two ways of removing one's gloves—either by using one hand to take the glove off the other, or by biting the tip of the glove with one's teeth. When the latter method is used, it is not uncommon to begin with the thumb, and thus the simple gesture of biting one's thumb could have come to stand as a signal for the confrontation that was to follow. Of course, until corroborative evidence comes to light we shall have no way of supporting the suggestion that removal of gloves formed the basis of the thumb-biting gesture, but it does at least have the virtue of explaining why the gesture fell into disuse with the decline of dueling.

The case of the thumb-biting gesture shows how extraneous historical evidence can be brought to bear in an attempt to recover the morphology of a gesture from its verbal description. But there are also less fortunate cases where no amount of extraneous information will reveal the actual shape of a gesture, just as there are cases where extraneous information is completely unnecessary for understanding what is being described. To illustrate these two cases, we turn to Rabelais' (1535) fictional account of a confrontation between Panurge, a Frenchman, and Thaumast, an Englishman, which was conducted in the form of a gestural duel, that is, solely through the use of hands, face and body. As the combatants face up,

> Panurge suddenly lifted up in the aire his right hand, and put the thumb thereof into the nostril of the same side, holding his foure fingers streight out, and closed orderly in a parallel line to the point of his nose, shutting the left eye wholly, and making the other wink with a profound depression of the eye-brows and eye-lids.

It is evident from this description that Panurge is thumbing his nose at the Englishman, and there are several reasons for supposing that he is using this gesture rather than another. First, there is no other candidate for this description—that is, we can think of no other gesture which would fit the description. Second, we know that the gesture of thumbing one's nose is used widely throughout Europe today (Morris et al, 1979; Taylor, 1956), and third the nose-thumb gesture was depicted in an engraving by Brueghel a few years after the publication of Rabelais' book, which suggests that the gesture was being used in Europe at that time. Finally, nose-thumbing is used as a gesture of mockery, which is totally in keeping with the nature of the encounter between Panurge and Thaumast. None of these reasons offers definite proof of the identity of Panurge's gesture, but when taken together they provide a convincing case in favor of its being the nose-thumb gesture. Of course, insofar as it contains certain facial embellishments, the gesture described by Rabelais does not conform to the standard way of thumbing one's nose. But this may simply be regarded as a literary conceit, as a way of dramatizing Panurge's performance and the occasion as a whole.

After Panurge has thumbed his nose at Thaumast, the Englishman responds with his own manual retort. The gestures fly back and forth, becoming more elaborate and vulgar, until it is Panurge's turn again. Now . . .

> stretched he out the forefinger, and middle or medical of his right hand, holding them asunder as much as he could and thrusting them towards Thaumast.

Unlike Panurge's earlier gesture, the description offered here is open to several readings. It is sufficiently clear that in this case Panurge extends and splays his index and middle fingers, but it is not immediately apparent which gesture he is using. There are at least three quite separate gestures that he could have performed with his fingers in this position. He could have executed the gesture with the palm of his hand facing back in the manner of the British insult, or with his palm facing forwards as in the Italian imputation of cuckoldry, or with the tips of the fingers pointing directly at his victim as a way of threatening his eyes. The task of choosing between these three gestures is complicated by the fact that we still do not know whether they were around in sixteenth century France, or whether Rabelais simply meant to describe a gesture that was employed elsewhere in Europe. Although the eye-poking gesture seems the most likely candidate, all three gestures we have mentioned fit the description. In this case Panurge's gesture remains something of a mystery.

We see that a number of problems arise when one attempts to identify a gesture on the basis of its verbal description. In the case of the thumb-biting gesture, we demonstrated how additional historical evidence can be brought to bear in order to determine the likely morphology of a gesture and its probable origins. In the case of the nose-thumbing gesture we saw how it is possible to recover a gesture because no other gestures fall under the same description. Here we also showed how a gesture can be identified by considering its present geographical distribution, its representation in another medium at the time the gesture was described, and its meaning or purpose in relation to what individuals are trying to achieve in that context. Finally we have demonstrated that there are cases where the indeterminacy of a written description cannot be resolved.

FROM ETIQUETTE TO CUSTOM

Most of our examples so far have been taken from authors like Homer, Shakespeare and Rabelais—in short from literary sagas and products of fiction. But there is also another literary genre on which the psychologist can draw, namely etiquette manuals. Of all the literary forms, etiquette books speak most directly about expressive action and gesture[4]. They also have the advantage that they have been produced for many centuries and by writers in several countries. They go back to the *Instructions of Ptahhotep*, which were set down in Egypt during the third millenium B.C., and extend all the way up to Emily Post (1940) and the latest edition of *Debrett* (1981). In between there are literally hundreds of volumes by various didactics who set out to improve the manners and conduct of their contemporaries.

If any single country could claim the etiquette book as its own it would almost certainly be Italy (see Aresty, 1970; Rossetti, 1869). The etiquette book really came into its own in thirteenth-century Italy with the appearance of books like Brunetto Latini's *Tesoretto* (1260) and Bonvicino da Riva's *Fifty Courtesies of the Table* (1290). Latini was Dante's tutor, but his influence on his student's manners was rather meagre because in later years Dante repaid his old tutor by consigning him to one of the inner circles of Hell. Etiquette books were slow to appear in England. Although Caxton printed several books of polite instruction in the fifteenth century, it was only with the resurgence of courtly manners in Italy that books on the subject began to appear in England. Renaissance Italy saw a whole spate of books on social graces, deportment, and chivalry. These included Castiglione's *The Courtier* (1528), Machiavelli's *The Prince* (1532), and Della Casa's *The Galateo* (1564). These and other books provided the impetus for a proper emergence of the etiquette manual in England. In the years that followed the English public were treated to books which ranged from table manners to behavior in the bedroom. Henry Fielding instructed his readers on how to hold a conversation and Jonathan Swift offered directions to servants, while notables such as Henry Percy, Sir Walter Raleigh and Lord Chesterfield created the genre of letters of advice to their sons.[5]

Etiquette books offer a rich vein of information that can readily be mined to advantage by the student of human behavior. This has already been done with some success by authors like Wildeblood (1973) and Elias (1978, 1982,

---

[4] Our reference to etiquette books is also meant to cover courtesy books. Although courtesy books appeared much earlier and were more concerned with sentiments and proper values, they often contained the kind of detailed treatment of behavior that was later to be found in etiquette books.

[5] Chesterfield, for example, tried to dissuade his son from the lowly habit of smiling. Raleigh, on the other hand, seems to have been more in need of advice than his son. Aubrey (1898) tells a wonderful story how Raleigh found himself sitting beside his son at a circular table, around which several other men were seated. Raleigh sarcastically asked his son what he had been doing, and his son replied that he had come from a whore who told him that only that morning she had given her favours to his father. Raleigh was incensed by the remark and slapped his son in the face. The son, knowing that he could not reciprocate, turned to the gentleman sitting beside him and slapped his face, saying "Box about, 'twill come to my Father anon".

1983), but the material in etiquette books still awaits the historically minded social psychologist. Wildeblood has traced the development of various conventions associated with greetings, facial expression, and deportment from medieval times to the present, while Elias has drawn on etiquette books in order to show how Europeans have become more civilized. For Elias the yardstick of civilization is the way people behave toward each other. He reveals how, as Europeans became more considerate, their table manners became more refined, and how practices like spitting and blowing one's nose were gradually hedged about by restrictions which stemmed from a concern for the feelings of others. Whatever one may feel about Elias' theory of mannerly progress, there is no doubt that etiquette manuals offer useful information about social practices through the ages.

Recently we conducted a study of introductions in which etiquette books proved to be an essential key to understanding how polite conventions have changed (Collett & Lamb, 1981). Our material consisted of videotape recordings that had been made at various social gatherings. These were later analyzed in detail to find out what is said and done when people introduce strangers to each other. One of the features that interested us was the principle on which an introducer assigns strangers to their respective roles within an introduction. For example, when the host at a party wishes to introduce two people to each other, it is necessary for him to cast one of them in the role of "introducee," and to present him or her to the person whom he casts in the role of "receiver." When we examined the characteristics of people who had been cast in these two roles we discovered that they could not be distinguished in terms of sex, relative age, or how well they were known to the introducer. Instead we found that introducers invariably assigned people to the roles of introducee and receiver on the basis of whether they were stationary or on the move prior to the introduction. If, for example, an introducer was talking to someone and they were joined by another person then the introducer would introduce that person to the person to whom he had been talking. If, on the other hand, the introducer took one person over to meet another, he would then present the person whom he had taken over to the person whom they had approached. That is, the introducer always assigned the newcomer to the role of introducee and the other person to the role of receiver. Although this practice has its own inner logic, it is completely different from what we can reasonably assume was the Victorian technique for assigning people to their roles in an introduction. Victorian etiquette books agreed that men should be introduced to women, that subordinates should be introduced to superiors, and that youth should be introduced to age—in other words, that introductions should always be performed upwards. It was suggested, furthermore, that before performing an introduction the introducer should always obtain the consent of the prospective receiver.

The introductions that we recorded did not conform to these prescriptions. In only one of the cases that we observed did an introducer enquire whether someone wished to take part in an introduction, and generally introducers did not assign people to their roles on the basis of sex, age, or seniority. There are good reasons for supposing that Victorian introductions followed the stipulations contained in etiquette books. Not only were Victorians obsessional about correct form, but there are several literary accounts which describe introductions as following the etiquette format. If we assume that Victorian introductions were organised on the basis of sex, age, and seniority, then it is clear that introductions have changed since then. It seems that they have changed because they no longer serve the same function that they did in Victorian times.

Victorian England witnessed great social upheavals, which were largely a consequence of the Industrial Revolution. The middle classes quickly became prosperous and threatened to enter the upper classes. But as the upper classes never regarded wealth as a sufficient qualification for entry into their circles, they set about elaborating a whole host of conventions that would keep the nouveau riche at bay. One of these was the introduction. The introduction was perfectly suited to their purposes because it required the consent of the nominal superior and because it marked social identities in terms of who was introduced to whom. Through the introduction and other polite practices the upper classes were therefore able to choose their company and decide who would enter their drawing rooms. But things have changed since those times. Despite the fact that England still retains a fairly rigid class structure, its barriers are much more permeable than they were during the Victorian era. Consequently, the need for the introduction to perform a selective function has diminished, and this has allowed the introduction to be organised on the basis of where people are standing physically rather than socially. The historical transformation of the introduction illustrates how societal requirements can impress themselves on social conventions. For our immediate purposes it also shows how the material contained in etiquette books can be used to chart historical changes in social practices, and how, by charting changes in social practices we can begin to explain changes in society.

There are, however, two important problems that arise in any attempt to reconstruct the behavior of an epoch from its etiquette books. One concerns the extent to which a description of behavior is representative, the other the distinction between descriptions and prescriptions of behavior. If we accept that etiquette books summarize the behavior of an age, then the question arises as to whether they reflect society as a whole or just the literate, and possibly etiquette minded, sectors of that society. There are good reasons to suppose that the latter was more frequently the case. For one thing, manuals of etiquette tend to be didactic. They usually contain instructions on how the reader ought to behave rather than descriptions of how he or she does behave. Then again, etiquette books have tended to proliferate during times of increased upward mobility in society. For example, during the Victorian era the upper classes excluded the undeserving from their circles by inventing ever more baroque conventions of polite behavior. These in turn were codified in manuals which offered the socially aspiring a way of passing themselves off as members of polite society (Davidoff, 1973). For the most part, people who consulted etiquette books used them as teach-yourself manuals. They had not hitherto behaved in the manner identified by such books, and to that extent these books could not be said to describe their behavior. The degree to which etiquette books reflect actual practices as opposed to recipes for correct behavior is an enduring problem. Sometimes this problem can be resolved by obtaining independent evidence which shows that a convention was actually being practiced at the time. But there are numerous instances where such evidence is not available, and where it is therefore difficult to ascertain whether a practice is being decribed or simply prescribed. However, there are a few rough and ready ways of finding out whether the prescriptions in etiquette books were actually observed. One is by determining whether such books were actually purchased and read. The other is by obtaining independent evidence on whether people at the time felt it necessary to conform to the canons of correct behavior.

In discussing textual evidence provided by the past we have dealt with the problem of textual veracity, and shown how enigmatic descriptions can be clarified by alternative types of historical evidence. We have also shown that while certain textual descriptions may present no problem, others may be totally resistant to interpretation. We have demonstrated how historical evidence can be enlisted to explain the present-day distribution of gestures like the headtoss, and we have shown how the material contained in etiquette books can be used to compare the practices of the past with those of the present. The time has now come to consider other types of historical evidence available to the social psychologist.

VISUAL IMAGES AS WINDOWS ON THE PAST

We have seen that textual descriptions can present certain problems for the psychologist who is interested in reconstructing the expressive behavior of the past, and that this is due to the limited capacity of language to depict things which are essentially visual. Things which are visual are usually best depicted by a visual medium.

A classic instance of the use of visual media in historical analysis may be found in the work of Di Jorio (1832). Di Jorio was a canon of the Cathedral in Naples and also a serious archeologist. He was involved in the excavations at nearby Herculaneum and Pompeii, and held the post of Curator of Greek vases at the Bourbon Museum. As he was guiding local Neapolitan dignitaries round the museum, Di Jorio noticed how they inadvertently accompanied their comments about the vases with gestures that were depicted on the vases. This led him to undertake an encyclopedic catalogue of the everyday gestures of Naples and to consider the influence that the ancient Greeks might have had on his fellow Neapolitans. When Di Jorio compared the gestures that he had catalogued with those depicted on the vases, he found that a large number of the gestures used by Neapolitans appeared on the vases. On this basis he concluded that the Greeks were largely responsible for the expressive repertoire of Naples.

Apart from undertaking what was in effect an investigation of historical and cultural diffusion, Di Jorio also left an extremely detailed account of the gestures used by Neapolitans at the beginning of the nineteenth century. Using the catalogue and the illustrations he provided, it has been possible to take this story one stage further by comparing the gestures that were reported by Di Jorio with those that are used by Neapolitans today. Recently we found that about 90% of the two hundred or so gestures described by Di Jorio are still being employed by Neapolitans (Collett, O'Shaughnessy & Contarello, in preparation). Some of the gestures that were around in Di

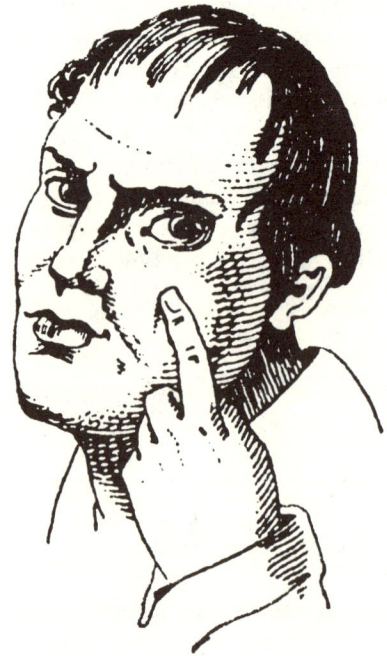

FIG. 18.3 The Eyelid Pull gesture was used as a sign of vigilance or warning in 19th century Naples (from Di Jorio).

FIG. 18.4 The Eyelid Pull gesture being used as a mock warning in present-day Naples.

FIG. 18.5 The Mouth-flap gesture was used as a sign of hunger in the 19th century Naples (from Di Jorio).

Jorio's time seem to have disappeared because their symbolism relied on objects like muskets and pipes that are no longer in use, or because there is no longer any reason for conveying certain meanings which were important then. Ignoring the fact that there may be explanations for the disappearance or persistence of particular gestures, what strikes us here is the remarkable durability of the Neapolitan repertoire as a whole. A large portion of the gestures that are used in Naples today can be traced back to the beginning of the last century, and, through the work of Di Jorio, to the expressive habits of the ancient Greeks.

Even before Di Jorio, some attention had already been paid to the gestures of the ancient Greeks. Bonifacio (1616) in Italy and Bulwer (1644) in England both referred to classical gestures, but the bulk of their evidence was taken from written descriptions rather than visual depictions left by the Greeks. Since Di Jorio, there have been several attempts to document the expressive habits of the ancient Greeks. Sittl (1890), for example, produced

18. HISTORY AND THE STUDY OF EXPRESSIVE ACTION 389

an extremely detailed account of their gestures using the evidence provided by vases, frescoes, and written descriptions. This had been amended by Kapsalis' (1946) research in the same area. These two works are very little known, even by students of gesture. Much the same is true of Brilliant's (1963) analysis of the representation of rank and status in Roman sculpture, and Barash's (1976) recent study of expressions of despair in Renaissance art.

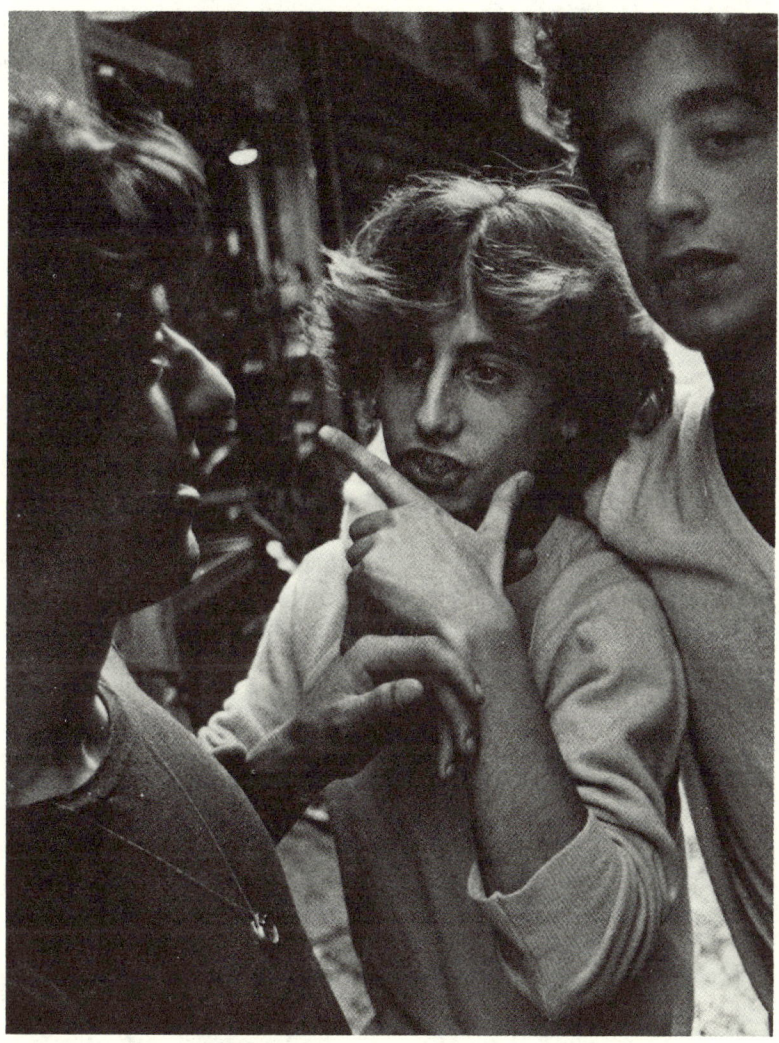

18.6   A Neapolitian employing the Mouth-flap gesture to indicate hunger.

When painting tries to imitate nature, it faces the challenge of how to organize color and form so that they convey a sense of three dimensions in two. But when it includes human subjects, it also needs to satisfy certain requirements of composition, human anatomy, and expression. Several schools of painting have been concerned with the problem of verisimilitude, and none more so than those which flourished in Italy during the fifteenth century. The painters of the Renaissance were highly self-conscious. They talked and wrote about painting at great length, and in the process they developed several criteria which could be applied in the appraisal of their craft. One of these was the extent to which a painting imitated nature, especially the natural aspects of human form and expression. Painters like Leonardo, Michelangelo, and Botticelli took great pains to capture those postures, gestures, and facial expressions that were consistent with the scene and characters they were depicting. Leonardo was quite explicit about the need for careful observation and faithful representation of human behavior. He offered the following advice to the novice:

> Therefore you must know that you cannot be a good painter unless you are a universal master to represent by your art every kind of form produced by nature . . . When you have well learnt perspective and have fixed in your memory all the parts and form of objects, you should go about and often as you go for walks observe and consider the circumstances and behaviour of men as they talk and quarrel, or laugh or come to blows with one another; the actions of the men themselves and of the bystanders, who intervene or look on. (1980, p. 218-20)

Leonardo certainly took his own advice to heart. When we look at a painting like the *Last Supper* we gain a strong impression that he incorporated his observations into the figures of Christ and the disciples. The painting depicts the scene after Christ has announced that someone present would betray him. Christ is seated in the center of the picture with the disciples on either side. As convention and circumstance would dictate, he appears beatific and resigned. But each of the disciples is caught in a different posture. Some are standing, others are seated. Andrew, for example, has his hands raised in astonishment and Philip denies the accusation by placing his hands against his chest, while a group at the end of the table are caught in heated discussion. Leonardo may have seen some of these gestures on the streets, and set them into the painting so as to capture the animated horror of the occasion as well as the unique character of each disciple.

For us this painting has a special fascination because it contains a range of manual gestures and facial expressions that may very well have been employed in Renaissance Italy. However, there are reasons to believe that not all the gestures in the *Last Supper* were colloquial in nature, and that some of them were probably stylized, if not theatrical. In considering this and other paintings, it is always necessary to distinguish gestures that occurred in everyday conversation from those which were part of a conventional language of the visual arts. Of course, in order to know whether a gesture is colloquial or conventional it is necessary to decode the gesture in the context of the scene being depicted (cf. Gombrich, 1982). Unfortunately, as Baxandall (1972) has pointed out, there are no dictionaries to Renaissance gestures, although there are various procedures and sources which may assist in the interpretation of a gesture. One of these is to compare painterly gestures with those used in everyday encounters. This in effect was the method employed by Goethe (1817) when he analyzed the gestures contained in the *Last Supper* (see Gage, 1980). Several problems are posed by this historical method. For example, if we discover that a gesture in a painting is part of everyday life, we can confidently assume that the former has drawn on the latter, but if we find that a gesture in art is not part of everyday life, then we have the problem of deciding whether it is conventional or whether everyday gestures have changed since the painting was composed. However, other methods of detection are available. The provenance of a gesture can also be ascertained by considering other paintings which contain that gesture, by examining contemporary references to gesture in literature, or by consulting the manual argots of the deaf and those ecclesiastical orders which have forsworn the use of speech. The amount of confidence we place in an inference drawn from painting should always be in proportion to the number of alternative methods that have been used to support that inference. But even when paintings are considered without the assistance of other methods they can reveal a great deal about the expressive behavior of the past. As Baxandall (1972) points out, this is

FIG. 18.7 The Last Supper.

never a mechanical affair. "An old painting is a record of visual activity. One has to learn to read it, just as one has to learn to read a text from a different culture, even when one knows, in a limited sense, the language: both language and pictorial representation are conventional activities." If they are approached in the proper way, "pictures become documents as valid as any charter or parish roll" (p. 152).

The analysis of expression in painting illustrates the uses to which visual materials can be put in an historical social psychology. More generally, however, visual materials may conveniently be divided into those which are static, such as painting, drawing, sculpture, and photography, and those which are mobile, notably film, and more recently videotape. Mobile media have the advantage of being able to capture movement, whereas static media can only freeze events in a moment of time. On the other side of the coin, static media have the advantage of maturity. With the exception of photography, they can all claim pedigrees which extend back thousands of years. This means that while they can inform us about ancient practices, their technological offspring can only tell us about fairly recent events—in fact only those of the last hundred years or so. Painting, drawing and sculpture are sometimes contrasted with photography and film, along with the suggestion that while the former are artistic and subjective, the latter are somehow scientific and objective; in short, that paintings, drawings and sculptures are distinctively human achievements whereas photographs and films are simply the disinterested products of technology. In recent years this argument has come under attack, largely through a growing appreciation of the selective element in photography and film (Sonntag, 1979). But although it is no longer possible to claim that photography and film are unmotivated, it still remains the case that painting, drawing and sculpture are open to error in a way that photography and film are not. In other words, leaving aside the fact that cameras have high-speed shutters, a photograph is always less likely to contain a mistaken image of an event than, say, a painting or a drawing[6].

Although photography came into existence round about the middle of the last century, it was not until the beginning of this century that students of human behavior began to use the new medium. This was partly due to certain technical problems, and partly because photography was initially linked to the established art of painting. Early photographers tended to be interested in either architecture or portraiture (Jeffrey, 1981). Their cameras were often cumbersome and some required exposure times of up to half a minute, which, although it presented no problem for the photographer of buildings, certainly tested the endurance of those who sat

---

[6]There is evidence to suggest that ethnographic drawings sometimes provide faulty depictions of expressive behaviors like greeting practices (see Collett, 1983).

for the portrait photographer. In due course, cameras became lighter and their exposure times shorter, and the emphasis began to shift to subjects that were more fleeting and further from home. Muybridge and Marey managed to freeze the motion of animals and humans in a fraction of a second, and Doolittle and Thompson brought back photographic images of the Chinese. In 1898 cameras were taken on the Torres Straits Expedition, and in the years which followed they became a standard part of the anthropoligist's equipment. This process reached its fullest expression some decades later when Bateson and Mead (1942) published their photographic study of Balinese character.

But photography did not develop alone. No sooner had the movie camera been developed by Marey and the Lumieres than it was being taken abroad to document the behavior of the natives. Regnault, a physician who specialised in anatomy, filmed various African peoples, Haddon and his colleagues made motion pictures of the inhabitants of the Torres Straits, and before the century was out the foundations had been laid for ethnographic film. Among human scientists anthropologists are the only group to have made extensive use of film and still photography. They have collected film as a means of illustration, as a way of salvaging and documenting behaviour for posterity, and occasionally for the purposes of analysis. When the social psychologist turns his or her attention to photography and film there is, therefore, a wealth of material which remains lodged in various archives, and which could be used to illumine certain aspects of behavior in the past (see De Brigard, 1975). There are also archives which house documentary and news film which could serve the same purpose (see Barnouw, 1974)[7].

In recent years social psychologists have been turning increasingly to the use of film and videotape, but this has largely been as a means of recording contemporary behavior. Although this material has usually been collected for the express purpose of analysis—and therefore been shaped by this purpose—there is in principle no reason why the social psychologist cannot analyze ethnographic and documentary film that has been collected with other ends in mind (cf. Webb, Campbell, Schwartz, & Sechrest, 1966). Of course, in embarking on this kind of venture, we should remember that not all ethnographic and documentary film is unprejudiced, and that certain shots have been selected and juxtaposed for effect. But this, in itself, should not present unsurmountable problems. With the proper exercise of judgment, patience and imagination, we may yet see the day when social psychologists perform historical studies by applying their methods to film that was collected many years ago.

---

[7]It is worth noting that there have already been several attempts to enlist film, especially feature films, as a source of historical evidence. See Grenville (1971), Smith (1976), Sorlin (1980) and Short (1981).

SUMMARY

In this essay we have explored the various ways in which the social psychologist can draw on historical materials as a means of studying expressive action. We have examined the kinds of evidence available to the psychologist and considered the problems that need to be addressed if textual and visual materials are to offer a reliable basis for comparing previous actions with those of the present. Our standpoint throughout has of course been that of the psychologist looking at history. But there are also historians who have been looking over the fence and scrutinizing psychology. Like most disciplines, history has been subject to debates about self-definition, and one of its concerns has been with what it should take as its model. In this regard it is worth noting that there are certain historians, such as Thomas (1963), Carr (1964), and Marwick (1981), who have placed history firmly on the side of what, rather loosely, may be called the social sciences. Ironically, Marwick has even gone so far as to suggest that "Social psychology may in some cases be a *sine qua non* of the intelligent analysis of certain historical problems." (p. 113).

In social psychology today there is an unfortunate tendency to regard all findings as pertinent to a condition which, although it is defined culturally, is nevertheless seen as timeless. We are quite prepared to qualify and locate our studies in relation to particular groups of people, but for some inexplicable reason we insist on overlooking the fact that they also inhabit a particular slot in history. Our view presupposes that all people occupy a kind of psychological present. But this fallacy of the psychological present ignores the fact that actions are conditioned as much by the epoch as by the society in which they are performed. However, when we insist that behavior is located in an epoch, we must take care that we do not commit ourselves to a notion of history as essentially whimsical. Too often there is the temptation to demonstrate that behavior is a function of history and to leave the matter there, without attempting to understand why and in what ways actions are related to historical facts.

REFERENCES

Aresty, E. *The best behavior.* New York: Simon and Schuster, 1970.
Aubrey, J. *Brief lives.* (A. Clark, Ed.). Oxford: Clarendon Press, 1898.
Barash, M. *Gestures of despair in medieval and early renaissance art.* New York: New York University Press, 1976.
Barnouw, E. *Documentary: A history of the non-fiction film.* London: Oxford University Press, 1974.
Bateson, G. and Mead, M. *Balinese character: A photographic analysis.* New York: New York Academy of Sciences, 1942.

Baxandall, M. *Painting and experience in fifteenth century Italy.* Oxford: Clarendon Press, 1972.
Boardman, J. *The Greeks overseas.* Harmondsworth: Penguin, 1964.
Bonifacio, G. *L'Arte dei Cenni* . . . Vicenza: Grossi, 1616.
Brilliant, R. Gesture and rank in Roman art. *Connecticut Academy of Arts and Sciences, Memoirs.* 1963, *14.*
Bulwer, J. *Chirologia . . . Chironomia.* London: Thomas Harper, 1644.
Bulwer, J. *Anthropometamorphosis: Man transformed; or the artificial changeling.* London: J. Hardesty, 1650.
Carr, E. H. *What is history?* Harmondsworth: Penguin, 1964.
Collett, P. Mossi salutations. *Semiotica* (1983, in press).
Collett, P. and Lamb, R. *The introduction: ceremony in everyday life.* Unpublished manuscript, 1981.
Collett, P., O'Shaughnessy, M. & Contarello, A. Neapolitan gestures. (in preparation).
Davidoff, L. *The best circles.* London: Croom Helm, 1973.
De Brigard, E. The history of ethnographic film. In P. Hockings (Ed.), *Principles of visual anthropology.* The Hague: Mouton, 1975.
Debrett. *Debrett's etiquette and modern manners.* (E. B. Donald, Ed.), London: Debrett's Peerage Ltd., 1981.
Di Jorio, A. *La Mimica Degli Antichi Investigata nel Gestire Napoletano.* Naples: Fibreno, 1832.
Elias, N. *The civilizing process: The history of manners.* Oxford: Blackwell, 1978.
Elias, N. *The civilizing process: State formation and civilization.* Oxford: Blackwell, 1982.
Elias. N. *The court society.* Oxford: Blackwell, 1983.
Evans-Pritchard, E. E. *Anthropology and history.* Manchester: Manchester University Press, 1961.
Fox, R. The inherent rules of violence. In P. Collett (Ed.), *Social rules and social behaviour.* Oxford: Blackwell, 1976.
Friedman, J. B. *The Monstrous Races in Medieval Art and Thought.* Cambridge, Mass.: Harvard University Press, 1981.
Gage, J. *Goethe on art.* London: Scolar Press, 1980.
Goethe, J. W. Joseph Bossi über Leonardo da Vincis Abendmahl. *Uber Kunst und Alterthum,* 1817, I(3), 113-88.
Gombrich, E. H. *The image and the eye.* Oxford: Phaidon, 1982.
Grenville, J. A. S. *Film as history: The nature of film evidence.* Birmingham: Birmingham University Press, 1971.
Harris, M. *The rise of anthropological theory.* London: Routledge & Kegan Paul, 1968.
Henige, D. P. *The chronology of oral tradition.* Oxford: Clarendon Press, 1974.
Hodgen, M. *Early anthropology in the sixteenth and seventeenth centuries.* Philadelphia: University of Pennsylvania Press, 1964.
Jeffrey, I. *Photography: A concise history.* London: Thames & Hudson, 1981.
Kapsalis, P. T. *Gestures in Greek art and literature.* D. Phil thesis, Johns Hopkins University, 1946.
Knightley, P. *The first casualty: The war correspondent as hero, propagandist and myth maker from the Crimea to Vietnam.* London: Andre Deutsch, 1975.
Le Bon, G. *Psychologie des Foules.* Paris: Bib. de Phil. Contemp., 1895.
Leonardo. *The notebooks of Leonardo da Vinci.* (I. A. Richter, Ed.) Oxford: Oxford University Press, 1980.
Lewis, I. M. (Ed.) *History and social anthropology.* London: Tavistock (A.S.A. no. 7), 1968.
Marwick, A. *The nature of history.* London: Macmillan, 1981.
Montaigne, M. de *Essais.* Bordeaux: Millanges, 1580.

Morris, D., Collett, P., Marsh, P. & O'Shaughnessy, M. *Gestures: Their origins and distribution.* London: Jonothan Cape/New York: Stein & Day, 1979.

Post, E. *Etiquette: The blue book of social usage.* New York: Funk & Wagnall, 1940.

Rabelais, F. *Pantegruel.* Lyons: Pierre de Saincte Lucie, 1535 (For English version: *The works of Mr. Francis Rabelais.* London: Navarre Society, 1933).

Rossetti, W. M. *Queene Elizabethes Achademy . . . with essays on early Italian and German books of courtesy.* London: Early English Text Society, 1869.

Short, K. (Ed.) *Feature films as history.* London: Croom Helm, 1981.

Sittl, K. *Die Gebarden der Griechen und Romer.* Leipzig: Teubner, 1890.

Smith, P. (Ed.) *The historian and film.* Cambridge: Cambridge University Press, 1976.

Sonntag, S. *On photography.* Harmondsworth: Penguin, 1979.

Sorlin, P. *The film in history.* Oxford: Blackwell, 1980.

Stephanus, H. *Thesaurus Graecae Linguae.* Paris: Didot, 1831.

Taylor, A. The Shanghai gesture. *Folklore Fellows Communications,* 1956, *166,* 1–76.

Thomas, K. History and anthropology. *Past and Present,* 1963, *24,* 3–24.

Vansina, J. *Oral tradition.* (H. M. Wright, Trans.). London: Routledge & Kegan Paul, 1965.

Webb, E., Campbell, D., Schwartz, R. & Sechrest, L. *Unobtrusive measures: Non-reactive research in the social sciences.* Chicago: Rand McNally, 1966.

Wildeblood, J. *The polite world: A guide to English manners and deportment.* London: Davis-Poynter, 1973.

Wundt, W. *Volkerpsychologie.* Leipzig: Wilhelm Engelmann, 1911.

Author Index

A

Abelson, R. P., 19, *29*
Adams, G. R., 17, *29,* 83, *98*
Adams, H., 338, 339, *342*
Adelson, M., 148, *153*
Adorno, T. W., 84, 88, 91, 94, 95, *98,* 132, *137*
Agassi, J., 49, *55*
Ajzen, I., 204, *208*
Albert, R. S., 140, *152*
Albert, S., 160, 161, 162, 165, 170, *172,* 305, *322*
Allison, P. D., 146, *152*
Alpers, M. P., 217, *234*
Altman, I., 17, 20, *29,* 83, *98,* 211, 213, 214, 215, 216, 232, 233, *234,* 319, *322, 324*
Amery, J., 114, *123*
Anderson, J. W., 19, *29*
Angrist, S., 39, *55*
Antaki, C., 94, *98*
Apfelbaum, E., 17, *29,* 108, *123*
Appleyard, D., 310, *322*
Ardener, E., 277, *279*
Ardener, S., 277, *279*
Aresty, E., 382, *394*
Argyle, M., 18, *29*
Argyris, C., 91, 95, *98*
Ariès, P., 27, *29*
Armistead, N., 38, *55*

Aschenbrenner, J., 289, *301*
Asplund, J., 95, *98*
Atkinson, J. W., 241, *255*
Atkinson, R. F., 43, 45, 46, 52, *56*
Atkinson, S. W., 63, *80*
Aubrey, J., 382, *394*

B

Babad, E. Y., 341, *342*
Bachman, J. G., 20, *30*
Badinter, E., 27, *30*
Bahr, H. M., 282, *302*
Bain, B., 337, *342*
Bakeman, R., 18, *30*
Bales, R. R., 288, 292, *302,* 306, 318, *323*
Baltes, P. B., 23, *30,* 19,*34,* 125,*138,* 192,*208,* 245, *253*
Bandura, A., 90, *98*
Bane, M. J., 282, *301*
Barash, M., 386, *394*
Barker, R. G., 212, *234*
Barnes, H. E., 37, 38, *56*
Barnouw, E., 393, *394*
Bartholomew. D. J., 20, *30*
Basseches, M., 17, *30,* 83, 89,*98*
Bateson, G., 393, *394*
Bauer, J., 116, *123*
Bauer, R. A., 238, *255*
Baum, A., 316, *323*

397

AUTHOR INDEX

Baumgardner, R. S., 95, *98*
Baumgardner, S. E., 108, *123*
Baxandall, M., 391, *395*
Beane, W. E., 20, *32*
Beard, G. M., 140, *153*
Becker, E., 340, *342*
Becker, G. S., 273, *279*
Belous, R., 282, *302*
Bem, S. L., 39, *56*
Benjamin, E. C., 142, 144, 146, 150, *153*
Benne, K. D., 341, *342*
Bentley, A. F., 213, *234*
Benton, J. F., 328, *342*
Berelson, B., 15, *30*
Beresford, J. C., 261, *279*
Berger, D., 303, 305, *324*
Berger, T. W., 349, *370*
Berkeley, G. A., 332, *342*
Berkowitz, L., 306, *323*
Berlin, I., 25, *30*
Berlyne, D. E., 349, 352, 362, *368*
Berman, J. S., 134, *138*
Bernard, J., 39, *56*
Berry, S. D., 349, *370*
Bettelheim, B., 119, *123*, 174, *188*
Betz, F., 83, *100*
Bickman, L., 303, *323*
Birnbaum, D., 355, *368*
Birnbaum, M., 341, *342*
Birren, J. E., 23, *30*
Blalock, H. M., Jr., 20, *30*, 197, *208*
Blank, T. O., 6, 18, 19, *30*
Blau, P. M., 195, 202, *208*, 273, *279*
Bledstein, B. J., 49, 50, *56*
Block, J. H., 39, *56*, 191, *208*
Blumenthal, A., 37, *56*
Boardman, J., 374, *395*
Bochner, S., 48, *56*
Bock, K. E., 334, *342*
Boehnert, G. C., 113, *123*
Bohrnstedt, G. W., 134, *137*
Bonifacio, G., 386, *395*
Borgatta, E. F., 306, *323*
Borges, J. L., 330, *342*
Borgida, E., 207, *209*
Boring, E. G., 47, *56*
Borowski, T., 113, *123*
Bottomore, T. B., 336, *342*
Boulding, K. E., 348, 368
Bourne, E., 28, *35*
Bowers, K., 90, *98*

Branca, P., 54, *56*
Brandon, S. G. F., 330, 340, *342*
Braudel, F., 48, *56*, 64, *80*, 326, 327, 336, 338, *342*
Brehm, J. W., 12, *30*
Brehm, S., 19, *30*
Brenner, M., 18, *30*, 40, *56*, 94, *98*
Brilliant, R., 386, *395*
Bringmann, W. G., 37, *56*
Brittan, A., 336, *342*
Broadbent, G., 310, *323*
Bronfenbrenner, U., 63, *80*
Brown, B. B., 213, 214, *234*, 319, *324*
Brumbaugh, R. S., 330, *342*
Bryant, F. B., 243, *255*
Bucher, C., 261, 267, 268, *279*
Buckley, J. H., 325, *342*
Buck-Morss, S., 94, *98*
Bulwer, J., 377, 386, *395*
Bunt, R., 310, *323*
Burby, K., 319, *323*
Burckhardt, J., 328, *342*
Burgess, E. W., 289, *302*
Bury, J. B., 48, *56*
Bush, D., 19, *31*
Buss, A. R., 17, 18, 23, *30*, 68, *80*, 83, 94, *98*, 105, *123*, 149, *153*
Butterfield, H., 46, *56*

C

Campbell, A., 238, *255*
Campbell, D. T., 13, *30*, 77, *80*, 127, 130, 134, 135, *137*, *138*, 148, 149, *153*, 197, *208*, 310, *323*, 348, *368*, 393, *396*
Campbell, J., 305, 306, *324*
Caplan, R., 321, *323*
Caplow, T., 282, *302*
Caponigri, A. R., 50, *56*
Carlson, R., 39, *56*
Carr, E. H., 52, *56*, 394, *395*
Carroll, B. A., 53, *56*
Carter, H., 278, *279*, 294, *302*
Carter, P. A., 340, *342*
Cattell, R. B., 148, *153*
Cavalli-Sforza, L. L., 348, *368*
Chadwick, B. A., 282, *302*
Chandler, M. J., 17, *30*
Chapin, F. S., 7, *30*
Chemers, M. M., 211, 214, *234*
Cherlin, A., 383, *302*

Chiriboga, D., 191, *209*
Chomsky, N., 76, *80*
Cioran, E. M., 330, *342*
Clarke, D., 18, *29, 30*
Clausen, J., 192, *208*
Clayton, K. N., 127, *137*
Cohen, H. R., 95, *98*
Cohen, J., 350, *368*
Cohen, S., 303, 306, *323*
Cohen, S. H., 130, *138*
Cohler, B. J., 174, *188*
Colby, B. N., 147, *155*
Coleman, R. P., 291, *302*
Collett, P., 18, *29, 30,* 372, 380, 383, 386, 392, *395, 396*
Collingwood, R. G., 25, *30,* 43, *56,* 182, *189*
Colson, E., 285, *302*
Comeau, H., 358, *368*
Comte, A., 6, *30*
Contarello, A., 386, *395*
Converse, P., 238, 239, 240, *255, 256*
Cook, T. D., 197, *208,* 310, *323*
Cooley, C. H., 335, *342*
Cornelius, S. W., 245, *255*
Cornforth, M., 84, 86, 87, *99*
Cott, N. F., 54, 55, *56*
Coulter, J., 19, *30*
Cox, C., 140, *153*
Cox, D. R., 20, *30*
Cozby, P., 303, *324*
Crandall, R., 306, *324*
Cronbach, L. J., 63, 64, 66, *80,* 203, *208*
Cronen, V. E., 19, *34*
Crosby, F., 22, *30*
Csikszentmihalyi, M., 315, 321, *323*
Cullen, I. G., 305, *323*
Cunningham, M. R., 13, *30*
Cvetkovich, G., 83, 94, *99*

D

Dadrian, V. N., 116, *123*
Danto, A. C., 26, *31,* 45, *56*
Darrow, C., 191, 194, *209*
Darwin, C., 348, *368*
Datan, N., 192, *209*
Dauer, D. W., 337, *342*
Davidoff, L., 385, *395*
Davies, J. C., 22, *31*
Davis, J. M., 206, *209*
Dawidowicz, L. S., 115, *123*

de Boer, T. L., 63, 65, 66, *80*
Debrett, 382, *395*
De Brigard, E., 393, *395*
De Charms, R., 149, *153*
Di Jorio, A., 385, *395*
de Mey, M., 78, *80*
Dennis, W., 140, 141, *153*
Depner, C., 241, *256*
Descartes, R., 330, 331, *342*
de Solla Prize, D., 330, *342*
Deutsch, M., 91, *99*
De Waele, J. P., 174, *189*
Dewey, J., 213, *234*
Dicks, H., 113, *123*
Dilthey, W., 25, *31*
Dodgson, C. L., 326, *342*
Donogan, A., 42, *56*
Douglas, M., 328, 338, *342*
Douvan, E., 20, *36,* 241, 242, 244, 248, *256,* 283, 284, *302*
Dovey, K., 232, *234*
Dray, W., 26, *31,* 42, 43, 45, *56, 57*
Dryden, J., 330, *343*
Dujiker, H. C., 79, *81*
Dumont, L., 330, *343*
Duncan, B., 240, *255*
Duncan, O. D., 134, *138,* 195, 202, *208,* 238, 240, 241, *255*
Dunford, C., 348, *369*
Dunphy, D., 354, *370*
Durant, A., 151, *153*
Durant, W., 151, *153*

E

Eagly, A. H., 23, *31*
Easterlin, R. A., 241, *255*
Ehrenreich, B., 54, *57*
Ehrenzweig, A., 354, *368*
Eisdorfer, C., 340, *343*
Eisenga, L. K. A., 77, *81*
Ekehammar, B., 213, *234*
Elder, G. H., 19, 23, *31,* 191, 192, 201, *208,* 245, *255*
Eliade, M., 330, *343*
Elias, N., 28, *31,* 61, *81,* 382, *395*
Elms, A. C., 303, *323*
Emmerich, W., 39, *57*
Endler, N. S., 90, *100*
Engels, F., 67, *81,* 84, 86, *99*
English, D., 54, *57*

AUTHOR INDEX

Erikson, E. H., 191, *208*
Errington, S., 214, *234*
Evans, G. W., 303, 306, *323*
Evans, S., 293, *302*
Evans Pritchard, E. E., 328, 330, *343*, 371, *395*
Ewen, S., 286, *302*

F

Faegre, T., 215, 216, *234*
Fahim, H., 219, 222, *234*
Farr, R. M., 15, *31*
Farthing, G. W., 358, *368*
Favreau, O. E., 39, *57*
Feddema, R., 327, *343*
Fee, E., 54, *57*
Feffer, M., 337, *343*
Feld, S. C., 241, *255*
Feldman, M. W., 348, *368*
Feldman, S., 19, *31*
Ferguson, W. K., 327, *343*
Fernea, R. A., 218, 219, 220, 221, 225, 226, *234*
Festinger, L., 10, *31*
Feuer, L. S., 336, *343*
Feyerabend, P., 110, 120, *123*
Fierabend, I. K., 21, *31*
Fierabend, R. L., 21, *31*
Finison, L. J., 19, *31*
Firey, W., 318, *323*
Fischer, R., 358, *369*
Fiske, D. W., 130, 134, *137*
Flacks, R., 293, *302*
Flanagan, O. J., Jr., 53, *57*
Flavell, J. H., 19, *31*
Fohl, F. K., 142, 144, 146, 150, *153*
Foner, A., 192, *209*
Foss, C., 319, *324*
Foucault, M., 48, *57*, 71, 74, 75, *81*
Fowlkes, M., 202, *302*
Fox, R., 13, *31*, 379, *395*
Fraser, J. T., 328, *343*
Frenkel-Brunswik, E., 132, *137*
Fried, M. J., 142, 144, 146, 150, *153*
Friedan, B., 293, *302*
Friedlander, H., 118, *123*
Friedman, J. B., 377, *395*
Fromm, E., 15, *31*, 93, *99*, 351, *368*

G

Gadamer, H. G., 28, *31*, 183, *189*
Gadlin, H., 17, 18, 23, *31*, 83, *99*

Gage, J., 391, *395*
Gallie, W. B., 26, *31*, 45, *57*
Gardiner, P., 47, *57*
Gardner, G. T., 303, *324*
Garelick, H. M., 119, *123*
Garfinkel, H., 19, *31*
Gauld, A., 19, *31*, 183, *189*
Gauvain, M., 17, *29*, 83, *98*, 211, 213, 214, 215, 216, 232, *234* 319, *322*
Georgoudi, M., 86, *100*
Gerard, R. N., 77, *81*
Gergen, K. J., 11, 16, 21, 23, 24, *31*, *32*, 38, 40, *57*, 63, *81*, 88, 94, 95, *99*, 110, *123*, 173, 175, 182, *189*, 192, 203, *208*, *209*, 303, 304, 305, *323*, 338, *343*
Gergen, M. M., 173, 175, *189*
Gibbons, F. X., 19, *30*
Gibson, J. J., 312, *323*
Giddens, A., 183, *189*
Gilliam, H., 52, *57*
Gilligan, C., 17, *32*
Ginsburg, G. P., 18, *30*, *32*
Glass, D. C., 305, 306, *323*, *324*
Glick, P. C., 261, 278, *279*, 294, *302*
Glock, C. Y., 127, *138*
Goethe, J. W., 391, *395*
Goldberger, A. S., 134, *138*
Goldenweiser, A., 37, *57*
Göller, A., 350, *368*
Gombrich, E. H., 391, *395*
Goodheart, E., 328, *343*
Gordon, C., 338, *343*
Gordon, L., 54, *57*
Gossman, L., 46, *57*
Gottman, J. M., 20, *32*, 361, *368*
Gouldner, A. W., 120, *123*
Gove, W. R., 250, *255*
Graham, J. Q., 27, *35*
Graumann, C. F., 18, *32*
Gray, C. E., 141, 142, 144, 145, 147, *153*
Greenberg, D., 125, *138*
Grenville, J. A. S., 393, *395*
Griaule, M., 330, *343*
Grunberg, N. E., 316, *323*
Gurin, G., 241, *255*
Gusdorf, G., 328, *343*
Guttentag, M., 259, 260, 262, 272, *279*

H

Haber, F. C., 330, *343*
Habermas, J., 16, *32*, 38, *57*
Hacker, A., 246, *255*

Halbwachs, M., 328, 338, *343*
Hale, J. R., 327, 328, *343*
Halwes, T., 333, *344*
Hampden-Turner, C., 17, *32*
Handel, G., 291, *302*
Harackiewicz, J. M., 130, *138*
Hare, A. P., 306, *323*
Hareven, T. K., 50, *57*
Harré, R., 6, 18, *32, 33,* 38, 40, *57,* 94, 95, *99,* 174, *189*
Harris, A. E., 17, *32,* 83, *99*
Harris, M., 326, 327, *343,* 371, *395*
Harris, R. M., 18, *33*
Hartup, W. W., 19, *32*
Harward, J., 263, *279*
Hasenfus, N., 355, *368, 369*
Haugh, L. D., 365, *368*
Hay, R. A., Jr., 20, *33*
Hays, W. L., 128, *138*
Heelas, P., 28, *32*
Heer, D. M., 261, *279*
Hefner, R., 40, *59*
Heilbroner, R. L., 104, 107, *123*
Heise, D. R., 134, 136, *138,* 151, *153*
Helmreich, R. L., 20, *32,* 39, *60*
Helson, R., 39, *57*
Hempel, C. G., 26, *32,* 42, *57*
Henige, D. P., 375, *395*
Henretta, J. A., 52, 55, *57*
Herlihy, D., 267, *279*
Hermans, H. J. M., 65, *81*
Hettema, P. J., 62, *81*
Hexter, J. H., 41, 52, *57,* 259, *279*
Higgins, E. T., 19, *32*
Hildreth, R. E., 142, 144, 146, 150, *153*
Hill, R., 282, *302*
Himmelweit, H., 20, *32*
Hines, D., 358, *370*
Hirsch, E. D., Jr., 28, *32*
Hodgen, M., 377, *395*
Hoffman, L. W., 39, *57*
Hofstadter, R., 28, *33*
Hogan, D. P., 205, *209*
Hogan, R. T., 17, *32,* 83, *99*
Holsti, O. R., 144, *153*
Holzkamp, K., 18, *32,* 68, *81*
Homans, G. C., 62, *81*
Hook, S., 83, 88, *99*
Horkheimer, M., 16, *32*
Horowitz, I. L., 116, *124*
Hovland, C. I., 15, *32*
Howard, D., 84, 86, 93, *99*
Hrdy, S. B., 273, *279*

Huesmann, L. R., 20, *33*
Hughes, H. S., 41, *58*
Huizinga, J., 327, *343*
Hull, D. C., 46, *58*
Hume, D., 333, 334, *343*
Humphreys, P., 20, *32*
Humphreys, R. S., 51, 52, *58*

I

Iggers, G. G., 25, *32*
Illich, I., 111, 120, *124*
Ingle, G., 18, *31*
Israel, J., 7, 17, 18, *32,* 38, *58,* 83, 84, 85, 87, 91, 92, 94, *99*
Itelson, W. H., 322, *323*

J

Jacobi, M., 304, 310, 313, *323*
Jaeger, M., 20, *32*
James, W., 6, *32,* 51, 52, *58,* 338, *343*
Janik, A., 120, *124*
Janousek, J., 17, *33,* 93, *99*
Jay, M., 16, *33,* 84, *99*
Jaynes, J., 18, *33*
Jeffrey, I., 392, *395*
Jenkins, G. M., 365, *368*
Jessor, R., 304, *323*
Johnson, M. E., 192, *209*
Jones, E. E., 86, *99*
Jones, W., 160, 161, 162, *172*
Judd, C. M., 129, *138*

K

Kagan, J., 205, *209*
Kahler, E., 332, *343,* 354, *368*
Kahneman, D., 207, *210*
Kail, R. V., 306, *324*
Kammen, M., 41, 54, *58*
Kaplan, A. G., 40, *58*
Kaplan, S., 322, *323*
Kapsalis, P. T., 386, *395*
Kassin, S. M., 19, *30*
Katona, G., 239, *255*
Katz, M., 20, *32*
Kaufman, W., 337, *343*
Kelley, H. H., 86, *100,* 273, *279,* 280, 306, *324*
Kellner, H. D., 51, *58*
Kellog, R., 46, *59*
Kelly-Gadol, J., 53, *58*

Kendon, A., 18, *33*
Kennedy, J. G., 219, 220, 226, *234*
Kennedy, S. E., 54, *58*
Kenny, D. A., 129, 130, 131, 133, 134, 135, *138*, 149, 151, *153*
Kenworthy, J. A., 40, *58*
Kessler, R., 125, *138*
Kessler, S. J., 19, *33*, 165, *172*
Kessler,-Harris, A., 54, *58*
Key, M. R., 18, *33*
Kidd, R. F., 303, *323*
Kierkegaard, S., 337, *343*
Kitchener, R. F., 194, *209*
Klein, D. F., 206, *209*
Klein, E., 191, 194, *209*
Klinnert, M., 19, *35*
Kluckhorn, F., 77, *81*
Knightley, P., 378, *395*
Kobasa, S., 321, *323*
Koch, S., 16, *33*
Kohlberg, L., 194, *209*
Kohli, M., 174, *189*
Kolakowski, L., 71, *81*
Komarovsky, M., 291, *302*
Konrad, V., 305, *324*
Korać, V., 93, *100*
Krakow, M., 162, *172*
Krantz, D. S., 303, 306, *323, 324*
Kreckel, M., 19, *33*
Kren, G. M., 107, 111, 114, 117, 120, 122, *124*
Kress, P. F., 173, *189*
Kris, E., 351, *368*
Kristeller, P. O., 331, *343*
Kroeber, A. L., 21, *34*, 141, 142, 147, 148, *153*
Kroger, R. O., 18, *33*
Kubler, G., 350, *368*
Kuhn, T., 49, *58*
Kuklick, H., 53, *58*
Kulka, R., 20, *36*, 241, 242, 244, 248, 250, *255, 256*, 283, 284, *302*
Kuttner, B., 300, *302*
Kvale, S., 17, *33*, 83, 84, *100*

L

Labouvie, G., 23, *31*
Lagemann, E. C., 54, *58*
Lamb, R., 18, *30*, 383, *395*
Lana, R. E., 25, *33*, 86, *100*

Lane, H., 334, *343*
Lasch, C., 111, 120, *124*, 253, *255*, 290, *302*
Latané, B., 10, *33*, 319, *324*
Laver, J., 350, *368*
Lazarsfeld, P. F., 15, *30*
LeBon, G., 372, *395*
LeGoff, J., 328, 331, *343*
Lehman, H. C., 141, *153*
Lennenberg, E., 76, *81*
Le Roy Ladurie, E., 50, *58*
Leonardo, 387, *395*
Lévi-Strauss, 73, *81*
Levinger, G., 20, *33*
Levinson, D. J., 132, *137*, 191, 194, *209*
Levinson, M., 191, 194, *209*
Levitan, S., 282, *302*
Lewin, K., 212, *234*, 319, *324*
Lewin, M., 54, *58*
Lewis, B., 331, *343*
Lewis, I. M., 371, *395*
Lieberman, M. A., 249, *255*
Lingoes, J. C., 356, *368, 369*
Lipset, S. M., 28, *33*
Litwak, E., 288, *302*
Llorens, T., 310, *323*
Lobkowicz, N., 94, *100*
Locke, A., 28, *32*
Locke, H. J., 289, *302*
Loevinger, J., 191, *209*
Loftus-Senders, V., 110, *124*
Lonner, W. J., 13, *33*
Loosley, E. W., 293, *302*
Lopez, R. S., 327, *343*
Lott, B., 50, *58*
Lotze, H., 14, *33*
Louch, A. R., 45, *58*
Lourenço, S. V., 83, 94, *100*
Lovejoy, A. O., 325, 330, 331, 332, 333, 334, 338, 340, *343*
Lowenthal, M., 191, *209*
Lubek, I., 17, 19, *29, 33*, 108, *123*
Lucker, G. W., 20, *32*
Luchmann, N., 80, *81*
Luria, A. R., 69, *81*
Lym, G. R., 310, *324*
Lyman, S., 276, *279*
Lyons, J. O., 328, *343*

M

MacIntyre, A., 120, *124*
Mack, S., 161, *172*

Magdoff, H., 294, *302*
Magnusson, D., 90, *100*
Mancuso, J. C., 83, 90, *100*
Mandelbaum, M., 28, *33,* 42, 52, *58*
Manicas, P. T., 260, *279*
Mannheim, K., 139, 142, *153,* 326, 327, *343*
Manuel, F. E., 48, 49, 50, *58*
Manz, R., 268, *279*
Maracek, J., 39, *58*
Marias, J., 139, *153*
Maritain, J., 354, *369*
Marsh, P., 18, *33,* 40, *56,* 372, 380, *396*
Martindale, C., 348, 350, 351, 353, 354, 355, 356, 357, 358, 361, 362, 363, 367, *368, 369,* 370
Martinez, J., 305, 306, 311, *324*
Marwick, A., 394, *395*
Marx, K., 16, *33,* 84, 92, 93, *100*
Marx-Engels, Werke, 70, *81*
Maslow, A., 118, *124*
Matthews, K. A., 20, *32*
Maurice, K., 333, 334, *344*
Mauser, G., 50, *58*
Mayr, O., 333, 334, *344*
McCleary, R., 20, *33*
McClelland, D. C., 15, 21, *33,* 139, 140, 146, 149, 150, 151, *153,* 248, *255*
McConnell, E. W., 268, *279*
McCord, J., 205, *209*
McGuire, W. J., 17, *33,* 144, *153*
McKee, B., 191, 194, *209*
McKenna, W., 19, *33*
McNeil, D., 76, *81*
McPhee, W. N., 15, *30*
McQuarie, D., 93, *100*
Meacham, J. A., 17, *34,* 83, *100*
Mead, M., 393, *394*
Medawar, P. W., 77, *81*
Meehl, P. E., 192, *209*
Menaghan, E. G., 249, *255*
Merton, R. K., 145, *155*
Meyerhoff, H., 325, *344*
Michaelis, J. D., 335, *344*
Michelson, W., 306, *324*
Miller, H. D., 20, *30*
Miller, I., 357, 362, *369*
Miller, R. C., 10, *35*
Mills, C. W., 287, *302*
Mindick, B., 303, 305, *324*
Mink, L. O., 26, *34,* 43, 45, 46, *58*
Mischel, W., 90, *100*

Mitroff, I., 108, *124*
Mitroff, J. J., 83, *100*
Moeller, G. H., 149, *153*
Moller, H., 261, 265, 266, 267, *279*
Montaigne, M., 377, *395*
Morawski, J. G., 17, 18, 19, 24, *32, 34,* 40, 57, 94, *99*
Morley, J., 326, *344*
Morris, C., 328, *344*
Morris, D., 372, 380, *396*
Moscovici, S., 18, *34,* 75, 76, 79, *81,* 91, 94, *100*
Moss, H. A., 205, *209*
Motta, E., 303, 305, *324*
Mukarovsky, J., 350, *369*
Mullar, J. T., 249, *255*
Mullen, B., 19, *35*
Mumford, L., 327, 333, *344*
Murchison, C., 15, *34,* 37, *59*
Murray, H. A., 191, *209,* 358, *369*

N

Nagel, E., 26, *34*
Naroll, R., 142, 144, 146, 150, *153*
Nauta, L. W., 62, *81*
Nelson, E. E., 6, *34*
Nesselroade, J. R., 19, *34,* 125, *138,* 192, 208, 245, *255*
Neugarten, B. L., 192, *209*
Nisbet, R. A., 48, 51, *59,* 326, 327, *344*
Nisbett, R. E., 86, *99,* 207, *209*
Norling, B., 151, *153*
Novaco, R., 305, 306, *324*
Nydegger, C., 214, *234*
Nydegger, W. F., 214, *234*

O

Oakeshott, M., 43, *59*
O'Connell, E. J., 130, *138*
O'Donnell, J. M., 47, *59*
Ogburn, W. F., 339, *344*
Ogilvie, D., 354, 358, *369, 370*
Ollman, B., 103, 104, 107, *124*
O'Mally, P. M., 20, *30*
Oppenheimer, V. K., 291, *302*
Ortega y Gasset, J., 139, 140, 142, *153,* 328, 330, 337, *344,* 354, *369*
O'Shaughnessy, M., 372, 380, 386 *395, 396*
Oskamp, S., 303, 305, *324*

Ossorio, P. G., 19, *34*
Otto, M., 340, *344*
Overton, W. R., 4, 6, *34*

P

Parsons, T., 80, *81,* 288, 292, *302*
Passmore, J., 44, 48, 53, *59*
Pavlov, J. P., 11, *34*
Pearce, W. B., 19, *34*
Pearlin, L. J., 249, *255*
Peckham, M., 350, *369*
Peeters, H. F. M., 19, 27, *34,* 326, *344*
Pepitone, A., 303, 304, *324*
Pepper, S., 44, *59*
Perkins, J. A., 328, *344*
Perlman, D., 303, *324*
Pettit, P., 94, *100*
Pierce, D. A., 365, *369*
Pieterson, M., 4, *34*
Piotrowski, C. S., 281, *302*
Pleck, E. H., 54, *56*
Polanyi, K., 327, *344*
Pomeroy, S. B., 263, 264, *280*
Pomper, P., 47, *59*
Popper, K., 62, 65, 69, 77, 79, *81*
Porschnev, B., 20, *34*
Post, E., 382, *396*
Poulet, G., 328, 331, 334, 336, 338, *344*
Praz, M., 54, *59*
Price, D., 147, *154*
Proffitt, D. R., 333, *344*
Psathas, G., 19, *34*
Pulliam, H. R., 348, *369*

Q

Quinn, R. P., 240, *256*
Quinones, R. J., 328, 333, 337, 338, *344*

R

Rabelais, F., 380, *396*
Rabinow, P., 53, *59,* 183, *189*
Rainwater, L., 217, *234,* 291, *302*
Rapoport, A., 77, *81,* 211, *234*
Rapoport, R., 295, *302*
Rappaport, E. A., 124, *199*
Rappoport, L., 18, *34,* 107, 111, 114, 117, 120, 122, *124*
Rappard, J. F. H., 77, *81*
Rebecca, M., 40, *59*

Reese, H. W., 4, 6, *34,* 192, *208*
Reichardt, C. S., 129, *138*
Reid, T., 335, 336, *344*
Reis, H. T., 20, *34*
Rekers, G. A., 40, *59*
Rholes, W. B., 19, *35*
Richards, R. J., 49, *59*
Richardson, J., 21, *34*
Richardson, J. T., 299, *302*
Ricoeur, P., 28, *34,* 46, *59*
Riegel, K. F., 17, 18, *34,* 68, 70, *81,* 83, 89, *100*, 106, *124,* 191, *209*
Rifkin, J., 105, *124*
Riley, M. W., 6, *34,* 192, *209*
Rinaldi, P. C., 349, *370*
Ring, K., 303, *324*
Robinson, J., 240, *256*
Rochberg-Halton, E., 315, 321, *323*
Rogosa, D., 134, 136, 137, *138*
Rokeach, M., 65, *81*
Rommetveit, R., 19, *34*
Rosen, A. C., 40, *59*
Rosenberg, M., 39, *59,* 341, *344*
Rosenberg, R. L., 54, *59*
Rosnow, R. L., 6, 7, 18, *35,* 38, 40, 50, *59,* 95, *100*
Ross, L., 19, *31,* 207, *209*
Ross, M., 357, 362, *369*
Rosser, E., 18, *33*
Rossetti, W. M., 382, *396*
Roth, W., 358, *370*
Rowles, G. D., 321, *324*
Rowney, D. K., 27, *35*
Royce, J. R., 105, 122, *124*
Rozelle, R. M., 135, *138*
Rubin, L., 291, *302*
Rubin, S. H., 17, *31*
Ruble, D. N., 19, *32, 35*
Runyan, W. M., 19, *35,* 191, 192, 197, 204, 205, 208, *209*
Rychlak, J. F., 17, *35,* 83, 88, 91, 94, *101*
Ryder, N. B., 139, *154*
Ryff, C. D., 19, *35,* 204, *209*
Ryle, G., 61, *81*

S

Sabini, J., 18, *35*
Sachs, C., 352, *369*
Sahakian, W. S., 338, *344*
Saks, M. J., 303, *323*

Samelson, F., 19, *35*, 95, *101*, 109, *124*
Sampson, E. E., 17, *35*, 40, *59*, 95, *101*, 107, 110, 120, *124*
Sanders, C., 77, *81*
Sanford, R. N., 132, *137*
Sarason, S. B., 38, 40, *59*
Scanzoni, J. H., 289, *302*
Schaefer, J. M., 142, 144, 146, 150, *153*
Schafer, R., 46, *59*
Schaie, K. W., 23, *30*, 192, *208*
Schapp, W., 186, *189*
Schlenker, B. R., 18, *35*, 62, *81*
Schmookler, J., 149, *154*
Schneider, D. J., 204, *210*
Scholes, R., 46, *59*
Schuman, H., 240, *255*
Schwartz, R., 393, *396*
Scriven, M., 42, 44, *59*
Scudder, T., 217, *234*
Sebba, G., 328, *344*
Sechrest, L., 393, *396*
Secord, P. F., 18, *32*, 38, 40, *57*, 259, 260, 262, 272, *279, 280,*
Seeley, J. R., 293, *302*
Segev, T., 113, *124*
Seigel, J., 107, *124*
Serafica, F. C., 19, *35*
Sereny, G., 113, *124*
Sève, L., 68, *82*
Shaver, P., 19, *35*
Sherif, C., 306, *324*
Sherif, M., 306, *324*
Shields, S. A., 54, *59*
Shklovsky, V., 350, *369*
Short, K., 393, *396*
Shotter, J., 19, 25, *31, 35,* 40, *59,* 94, *101,* 183, *189*
Showalter, E., 54, *59*
Shumaker, S. A., 212, *235,* 304, 305, 306, 311, *324*
Shuster, R. G., 188, *189*
Shweder, R. A., 28, *35*
Silver, M., 18, *35*
Sim, R. A., 293, *302*
Simonton, D. K., 21, *35*, 128, *138*, 140, 141, 142, 143, 144, 145, 146, 147, 148, 149, 150, 151, 152, *154, 155,* 363, 369
Singer, J. E., 316, *323*
Sittl, K., 374, 386, *396*
Skinner, B. F., 191, *210*
Smith, A., 335, *344*

Smith, B. M., 83, 90, *101*
Smith, M., 354, *370*
Smith, M. B., 17, 18, *35*, 303, *324*
Smith, P., 393, *396*
Smith-Rosenberg, C., 54, 55, *60*
Snoek, J. D., 20, *33*
Snyder, M. L., 306, *324*
Sommer, R., 334, *344*
Sontag, S., 392, *396*
Sorlin, P., 393, *396*
Sorokin, P. A., 139, 144, 145, *155*, 352, 353, *370*
Spence, J. T., 20, *32*, 39, *60*
Spencer, H., 7, *35*
Spencer, W. A., 349, *370*
Spengler, O., 7, *35*
Stack, C., 288, *302*
Staines, G. L., 240, *256*
Stalin, 67, *82*
Stam, J. H., 335, *344*
Stanley, J. C., 148, 149, *153,* 197, *208*
Stanley, N. F., 217, *234*
Stapp, J., 39, *60*
Starn, R., 49, 50, 51, *60*
Steiner, I. D., 91, *101,* 305, *324*
Stent, G. S., 50, *60*
Stephenus, H., 375, *396*
Stern, F., 49, *60*
Stern, P. C., 303, *324*
Stokols, D., 212, *234, 235,* 303, 304, 305, 306, 307, 310, 311, 313, 321, *323, 324*
Stokols, J., 305, 306, *324*
Stone, L., 27, *35*
Stone, P., 354, *370*
Stroebe, W., 91, *101*
Sullivan, H. S., 6, *35*
Sullivan, W. M., 53, *59*, 183, *189*
Suls, J. M., 10, 19, *35*
Sumner, W. G., 7, *36*
Sutton, K., 218, *235*
Sutton-Smith, B., 358, *370*
Swap, W., 306, *324*
Sweezy, P., 294, *302*
Swierenga, r. P., 27, *36*
Sydnor, C. W., 113, *124*

T

Taagepera, R., 147, *155*
Tajfel, H., 91, *99*
Tarrant, J., 268, *280*

Taylor, A., 380, *396*
Taylor, C., 25, *36*
Taylor, D. A., 20, *29*
Taylor, S. M., 305, *324*
Teich, M., 49, *60*
Terkel, S., 238, 239, *256*
Tesser, A., 22, *36*
Thernstrom, S., 27, *36*
Thibaut, J. W., 273, *279,* 280, 306, *324*
Thomas, K., 394, *396*
Thompson, R. F., 349, *370*
Thorlby, A., 335, *344*
Thurnher, M., 191, *209*
Tebbitt, J. E., 198, *210*
Tichelman, F., 327, *343*
Tinbergen, N., 77, *82*
Toulmin, S., 120, *124*
Toynbee, A. J., 150, *155*
Triandis, H. C., 232, *235,* 304, *324*
Trotsky, L, 355 *370*
Tudor, J., 250, *255*
Tversky, A., 207, *210*
Tweney, R. D., 37, *56*
Tyler, L. E., 192, *210*
Tynjanov, J., 350, *370*

U

Uemura, A., 357, 362, 363, *369*
Ullmann, W., 328, *344*
U.S. Forest Service, 321, *324*

V

Vallacher, R. R., 337, 341, *345*
van den Berg, J. H., 27, *36,* 326, *344*
van Hoorn, W., 4, 19, *34, 36,* 77, *82,* 326, 337, *344, 345*
Vann, R., 55, *60*
Vansina, J., 375, *396*
Verhave, T., 77, *82,* 326, *345*
Vernant, J. P., 70, *82*
Veroff, J., 20, *36,* 241, 242, 243, 244, 248, *255, 256,* 283, 284, *302*
Vico, G., 7, 14, 25, *36*
Vinsel, A., 213, 214, *234,* 319, *324*

Vossen, J. M. H., 79, *82*
Vygotsky, L. S., 15, *36*

W

Warmington, W. A., 277, *279*
Waters, F., 330, *345*
Watt, I., 333, 338, *345*
Watts, D. G., 365, *368*
Webb, E., 393, *396*
Wegner, D. M., 337, 341, *345*
Weingartner, J., 113, *124*
Weiss, S., 319, *323*
Weiss, W., 15, *32*
Weldon, J. E. C., 263, *280*
West, A., 358, *370*
Wexler, P., 7, 17, 18, *36*
White, H., 46, 47, 51, *60*
White, M., 26, *36*
White, M. S., 39, 40, *60*
Wicklund, R. A., 12, *36*
Wildeblood, J., 382, *396*
Williams, R., 335, 336, *345*
Williams, R. M., 65, *82*
Williamson, M. H., 282, *302*
Willmott, P., 287, *302*
Wilson, E. O., 13, *36*
Winch, P., 25, *36*
Winter, D. B., 248, *256*
Winthrop, H., 50, 51, *60*
Wise, G., 44, *60*
Womack, J., 116, *124*
Woodruff, D. S., 23, *30*
Woodward, W. R., 14, *36*
Worell, J., 40, *60*
Work in America, 240, *256*
Worringer, W., 352, *370*
Wundt, W., 6, 11, 14, *36,* 371, *396*

XYZ

Yancey, W. L., 217, *235*
Young, M., 287, *302*
Young, R. M., 49, *60*
Zajonc, R. B., 306, *324*
Ziller, R. C., 83, *101*
Zurcher, L. A., Jr., 337, 338, 339, 341, *345*

Subject Index

Aesthetic evolution, 347, 366
Aesthetic preference, 349, 350, 354
   selection criteria, 348
Aleatory orientation, 23, 24, 193
Alienation, 106, 107
Annales school, Les, 27, 48, 52
Anthropology, 371, 372
Anti-Semitism, 115, 117
Applied social psychology, 303
Arousal potential, 349, 350, 353, 354, 361, 362, 364, 366
Attitudes, 20, 239, 240
Autocorrelation analysis, 361, 364
Beguines, 268
Behavior settings, 310-319
Closure, 159, 160, 169, 171
Cognitive processes, 15, 17, 89, 90
Cognitive psychology, 107
Cohort analysis, 23, 139, 244-247, 261
Collative variables, 350
Concept of self, 62, 253, 254, 327-335, 339-341
Consciousness, 336
Contextualism, *see* Historical explanations
Correlational analyses, 147
Correlations, 126-149
   cross-lagged panel, 126, 129, 130, 149
Courtly love, 265, 266
"Crisis in social psychology," 16, 303
Crowd phenomena, 91

Data analyses, 37, 125-130
   archival, 37, 128
   longitudinal, 125, 126, 130
   temporal, 130
   time-series, 125
Dialectics, 17, 18, 40, 66-71, 83-101, 103-109, 121-123, 178, 211-214, 233
Disattenuation, 132
Divorce, 272, 283, 295
Empiricism, 16, 17, 29, 84, 90
Environmental psychology, 212-233, 305-321
   symbolic aspects of, 305, 310-321
Ethnomethodology, 19
Etiquette, 381-385
Evolutionary theory, 18, 77-80, 326, 342, 348-350, 355, 367, 368
Experimental design, 21
Explanation, forms of, *see also* Dialectics, Evolutionary theory, Models of change, Narrative forms, Structuralism
   conflict theories, 7
   cyclical theories, 7
   law like, 42
   mechanistic, 4-8, 13, 15
   narrative, 44-47
   organismic, 6
   rational, 43
   teleological, 6

SUBJECT INDEX

Factor analysis, 146, 148
Gender differences, 244, 250, 251
    issues of, 53-55
Generative theory, 110, 122
Generational analysis, 139, 141
    generational unit, 141
Genius, 145, 147, 152
Gestures, 372-376, 378-381, 386-392
Habituation, 349, 150
Happiness, 241-243, 253
Historical explanations, 41-55, 177, *see also* Evolutionary theories, Explanation
    contextualism, 44, 122
    cyclicity, 50
    degeneration, decline, 50
    narrative explanations, 44, 45, 47
    rational explanations, 43, 46
    societal evolution, 177
Historical materialism, 93, *see also* Dialectics
Historical records, 375, 377, 387, 392, 393, *see also* Data analysis
    film, 392, 393
    oral records, 375
    painting, 387
    photography, 392-393
    writing, 377
Historiography, 18, 19, 26-28, 37-41, 47, 51-55, 326
Holocaust, 105, 111, 114, 116, 118-122
Homeostasis, 48
Interactionism, 89, 205
Interpersonal attraction, 168, 169
Jewish heritage, 115, 116, 118, 313-316
Labor, 70, 71
Lesbianism, 264
Life accounts, 180, 182, *see also* Narratives
Life course, 191-197, 206-208
Life span development, 23, 106, 122, 192, 252
Linguistics, 371-372
Logical positivism, 38, 41, 51, 87, 109
Marriage, 253, 261-264, 270, 282
Metaphors, 347, 352
Metatheory, 40, 94, 111
Misogyny, 267
Models of social behavior, 37-49
    evolutionary, 37, 47, 49
    lifespan, 37
    revolution, 49
Modernization, 300
Multidimensional scaling, 356
Multiple regression time-series designs, 150
Multitrait-multimethod matrix, 130

Music, 363, 365, 367
Narrative action, 26, 162
Narrative forms, 44-47, 174-182
    progressive, 176
    regressive, 176, 179
    stability, 176
Narratives, 173-189
    construction of, 182-189
    self-narratives, 173, 180, 181, 182, 184, 185, 187, 188
National character analysis, 247-249
Need for achievement, *see* Social motives
Need for power, *see* Social motives
Painting, 364, 365, 367
Path analysis, 151, 201, 202
Personality, 62, 63, 204
    implicit theories of, 204
Planned communities, 319-322
Pluralism, 41-47
Poetry, 354-357, 365-367
Primary process, 351-367
Privacy, 219-223, 230-232
Psychoanalysis, 120, 170
Psychohistory, 19, 111
Psychosocial epistemology, 108-111, 120-123
Quasi-experimental designs, 148
Reciprocity, 185, 186, 187
Reductionism, 11, 29, 304
Regression, 351, 352, 358
Regressive Imagery Dictionary, 357, 362
Renaissance, 386-391
Resettlement, 216-218, 226
Role theory, 253
Self, *see* Concept of self
Self-definitions, *see* Narratives, Self-narratives
Sequence composite analysis, 160-163
Serial dependency, 125
Sex-ratios, 259-279
Sex roles, *see* Social roles, Gender roles
Similes, *see* Metaphors
Social cognition, 207
Social construction, 18, 19, 40, 107
Social exchange theory, 273, 274, 278
Social history, 37, 47
Social indicators, 242, 243, 244
Social motives, 140, 150, 241-252
    achievement motive, 140, 150, 241, 247, 251, 252
    affiliation motive, 241, 248, 251, 252
    power motive, 140, 241, 248

Social power, 273-277
  dyadic power, 273, 276, 277
  structural power, 275
Social roles, 38-41, 53-55, 185, 186, 187, 250-254
  gender roles, 38-41, 53-55, 250, 251
  work role, 253, 254
Social support, 249
Social theory, 3-29
  diachronic, 3, 12, 3, 14, 16, 20, 21, 22, 29
  synchronic, 3, 21, 22, 29
Sociorationalism, 110, 122
Soul, 62, 331-335, 340, 341
Stability, 40, 131
  transhistorical, 40
Standard error of measurement, 132
Statistical reliability, 131, 145
Stimulus generalization, 349
Stress, 226, 231, 321
Structuralism, 71-76

Survey research, 237, 238, 241, 245
  cross-sectional survey, 246
  hypothesis surveys, 243
  political surveys, 243
  replications, 249, 253, 254
Technological change, 322
Teleology, 86, 87
Temporal definition, 142
Temporal invariance, 129
Temporalization, 325, 327, 330
Time, 64, 126-129, 305, 306
  psychological perspectives on, 305, 306
  time-reversed analysis, 126-129
Transactional perspective, 212, 233
Trend analysis, 148
Victorians, 384-385
Völkerpsychologie, 15
Women's movement, 261, 268, 269, 278, *see also* Beguines